The Letters of Lytton Strachey

THE LETTERS OF
LYTTON STRACHEY

EDITED BY PAUL LEVY

ASSISTED BY PENELOPE MARCUS

FARRAR, STRAUS AND GIROUX   NEW YORK

In memoriam
F.P.
T.J.B.

Farrar, Straus and Giroux
19 Union Square West, New York 10003

Library of Congress Control Number: 2005934533
ISBN-13: 978-0-374-25854-2
ISBN-10: 0-374-25854-6

www.fsgbooks.com

1 3 5 7 9 10 8 6 4 2

Contents

Introduction

Lytton Strachey was a great letter writer. He believed that you only really get to know a writer when you read his correspondence, and though his own life is the subject of a classic of biography by Michael Holroyd (which altered the writing of biography as much as did Strachey himself), this is certainly true in his case. His letters are still full of surprises, though they have been mined extensively by Holroyd and quoted in several other books – and they can still shock. The more obvious revelations concern his sex life, and some of them will startle even those who regard themselves as unshockable, and who thought, moreover, that they knew all there was to know about Strachey. But there are other new things to be learned from his letters: about him, about his Bloomsbury friends, and about the culture and even the politics of Britain before the Second World War.

As the historian of *Eminent Victorians* Strachey gave English-speaking people our image of the Victorian age as one of prudery and priggishness rather than an era of great and unbroken progress; as biographer he introduced Freud's ideas of subconscious motivation into the accounts of his subjects' lives. (In *Elizabeth and Essex*, he used the then new Freudian theories to link, as Freud himself said in a letter to Strachey, Elizabeth's 'character to the impressions of her childhood'.)

He was a political radical who was born into the ruling class, a member of the intellectual aristocracy who cherished his contacts with the aristocracy of blood, a democrat who did not always trust the people, and one of the original champagne socialists.

He was a cynic capable of sentimentality, a sceptic who believed in love. He thought war was the greatest evil, closely followed by religion. He was an open homosexual whose affair with a woman painter was one of the most poignant love stories of the twentieth century.

Despite his unrelenting care for his own comfort, he played the victim in a sado-masochistic relationship with his last male lover. His sex life appeared to his friends largely to be fantasy, but he bore scars that proved otherwise. Though physically unprepossessing, etiolated and always too thin, he was a dominating figure, capable of manipulating strong and fit men and women to get his way. But he got his deepest joy from being the passive recipient of pain.

He was a bon vivant who cared seriously about the quality of food and drink, but could scarcely make a piece of toast for himself, and was forced by lack of money (until almost the end of his life) to live austerely.

He was an authority on French literature who was often too timid to speak the language. He was a shy man and a flirt. His friends and family regarded him as a hypochondriac, but he had been genuinely ill all his life, and died aged only fifty-one of an undiagnosed cancer from which he had obviously long suffered.

He was in the vanguard of the Modernist movement, but his tastes led him more naturally to the writers of the eighteenth century. He recognized the genius of his friends Virginia Woolf and T. S. Eliot, but hated the works of James Joyce. He was more moved by music than by any of the other arts, but he never wanted or tried to make music himself. As the intimate of Clive Bell and Roger Fry he was one of the first to recognize the importance of Post-Impressionism in the visual arts but, though he could have bought work by Picasso (whom he knew), he mostly confined his patronage to Bloomsbury artists such as Duncan Grant, Vanessa Bell and Henry Lamb. I doubt that he ever so much as waltzed at a ball; but he went as often as possible to the Russian Ballet, and knew Diaghilev, Nijinsky and Lifar as well as Lydia Lopokhova. He worked – successfully – as a theatre critic, and knew his Chekhov and Ibsen as well as his Shaw, Shakespeare and Racine; but his own efforts as a playwright were as poor as were most of the pages of verse he wrote.

He was in close contact with – and was often influenced by – the greatest analytic thinkers of his century, Freud, Keynes, G. E. Moore, Bertrand Russell, Wittgenstein and Frank Ramsey. But, despite the fact that his work as a biographer and historian depended on argument, his own gifts were fundamentally creative. His three great books, *Eminent Victorians, Queen Victoria* and *Elizabeth and Essex*, are intended as works of fact, not fiction; yet, beyond the quality of the research upon which they are based, their success owes everything to their author's imagination. Still, this creative writer left no novel, and really no plays or poems that will last. His whole life was organized around his work, although he thought his real genius was for friendship.

He scoffed at the posthumous cult of Rupert Brooke, and was wryly amused by T. S. Eliot's and Virginia Woolf's growing fame, but rejoiced in his own celebrity when it finally came. He was the ultimate elitist, but revelled in being a household name.

In short he was very like the rest of us, a bundle of contradictions – only more interesting; and he was the beneficiary (and fortunate not to be the casualty) of the famous Chinese curse, for he lived in interesting times.

Born in the last quarter of the long Victorian century, Strachey grew up in uncomfortable houses, in an upper-middle-class family that depended on servants to keep them warm, clean and fed. In his short life he saw transport change from literal horsepower and railways, to the internal combustion engine car and eventually to aeroplanes. Communications developed from the penny post and the telegram to the wireless radio and the telephone. It was our good luck that progress was slow with respect to the last. Of course houses had only a single telephone, but Strachey never liked the gadget – perhaps because of his peculiar voice, which was that of a permanently adolescent boy with a breaking voice that went from profound bass notes to a shrieking treble. Strachey disliked the telephone, so he wrote letters, thousands of them.

His first are to his parents, General Sir Richard and Lady Strachey, and to some of his nine siblings. It was more like an extended family group, for the oldest, Elinor (Rendel) was born in 1859 (the year Darwin published *On the Origin of Species*) and the youngest, James, in 1887 (by which time Darwin's theories were so universally known and accepted that the publishing event of the year was Darwin's *Life and Letters*). The children of James Strachey's elder siblings called him 'Uncle Baby'. Socially, the Stracheys were an old land-owning West Country family with yeoman origins in sixteenth-century Saffron Walden. Lady Strachey was of slightly grander, Scottish stock, a Grant of Rothiemurchus. Ten or eleven generations of Stracheys before Lytton had shown military, administrative and literary talents. His generation, though, was the final flowering of the plant from which they stemmed – there are few if any descendants of Lytton's siblings. On the other hand, that generation saw an explosion of talent – not merely Lytton, but James, who, himself psychoanalysed by Freud, went on to edit the standard edition of Freud's works. Dorothy (Bussy) is still familiar to us as the translator of Gide (and the pseudonymous author of the classic *Olivia* by Olivia); Pippa was a leader of the movement for women's suffrage; Pernel was head of Newnham College, Cambridge; and Oliver a celebrated codebreaker in both wars.

Good though these juvenile letters are, this volume has its limits, and my selection really begins when the nineteen-year-old Strachey discovered Cambridge, and Cambridge discovered *him*. Neither party ever recovered from the encounter. Lytton's intellect was marked for ever by his exposure to the philosopher G. E. Moore; and generations of Cambridge undergraduates contrived to sound and behave like (their usually exaggeratedly camp idea of) Lytton Strachey. Apostles such as G. M. Trevelyan and Bertrand Russell have complained that Strachey subverted that ancient (founded in 1820) secret society from high-minded debate to the Higher Sodomy. His letters tell another tale, making it evident that he found these traditions of (at least latent) homosexuality in the Society that had nourished Hallam and Tennyson, and did not himself create them.

At Cambridge his closest friend was Leonard Woolf, and he is the correspondent most heavily represented in this selection of Lytton's letters; for when Woolf left to be a colonial administrator in what was then Ceylon in 1904, he and Lytton wrote to each other several times a week for some years. Lytton's letters to Leonard are a virtual journal (sometimes an explicit one) of his doings and thoughts. It is as important as it is difficult to come to grips with this relationship, for Woolf was heterosexual, yet Lytton confided his homosexual feelings to him without disguise or reservation. And Leonard was Jewish, but Lytton seems capable, even in his letters to him, of casual, and sometimes bitingly cruel, anti-Semitism. Shortly before she died in 2004, Frances Partridge discussed this with me. She reminded me that we are incapable of reading these letters with eyes innocent of Hitler and the Holocaust – though that was the state of their author. Frances also thought that Lytton felt that his intimacy with Leonard gave him licence – street cred – to talk and write in language that is today simply unacceptable. Virginia, Frances pointed out, sometimes did the same – and with the same justification, as she was even more intimate with the same Jew.[1] Their anti-Semitism is always of the stereotyping rather than the name-calling variety, and was common until the Second World War more or less put an end to it. I'm afraid I am not convinced that this excuses it, though, and probably you aren't either. There is also some racism – virtually always anti-black. The fact that in his life Strachey saw few black people, knew almost none, and that his remarks were commonplace and almost conventional does not excuse them either.

There are those who find other reasons for disliking Strachey. Post-Cambridge, having failed to get a Prize Fellowship at Trinity College, he turned to his pen to make a living. He had to rely on nepotism for his first work, which he got from his cousin, St Loe Strachey, editor of the

1. This is perhaps the place to record that the late Sir Isaiah Berlin once told me that when, as a young man, he met Virginia Woolf (first in 1933), 'She always began the conversation by saying, "You know, Isaiah, we Jews . . ."' The implication is that she at least felt she had earned the privilege to tease – the right Jews enjoy to tell jokes about themselves, a right denied by history to non-Jews.

Spectator. Because St Loe regularly interfered with his copy, Lytton cordially disdained his patron from the start, though their differences of political opinion did not much matter until the drums of war started to bang and conscription became Lytton's big issue. There is, however, little sense of gratitude to be found in the letters he wrote while working as a theatre critic and journalist.

These years are marked by his infatuation with his first cousin, Duncan Grant, and his love-hate relationship and rivalry with Maynard Keynes for the affection or favours of Duncan, Arthur Hobhouse and Bernard Swithinbank. There were probably others, and Keynes invariably triumphed. Two non-Apostles were important to him, Thoby Stephen and Clive Bell, and through them Strachey became part of the Thursday night at-homes in Gordon Square that evolved into a self-conscious Bloomsbury Group. At nearby Fitzroy Square, in 1909, Lytton played out a drawing-room comedy with a twist when he proposed to Virginia and – for a brief and terrible moment – was accepted. All his letters to Virginia Woolf are published here, complete and uncut, for the first time.

Strachey's correspondence to – and about – his patron and near-permanent hostess, Lady Ottoline Morrell, is not always attractive. Virginia was often bitchy about this exotic, generous aristocrat, but she was not dependent upon Ottoline for hospitality – indeed for food and shelter – for weeks at a time. But Lytton was. Ottoline's Christianity was anathema to Lytton, her sexual adventures (of which he approved) were at odds with her piety, she was guilty of a double standard when it came to her husband, Philip's, affairs, and there often wasn't enough food. But Strachey's lack of appreciation isn't pretty.

Some readers will feel that, though Strachey came from a proto-feminist family, when it came to household matters he was, despite being gay, what used to be called a male chauvinist pig. In the middle period the bulk of his letters are to Carrington, the talented ex-Slade painter with whom he shared his domestic life. Here the correspondence comes to the rescue of his reputation. He did not, as many feminist writers on Bloomsbury claim, discourage Carrington from practising her art. Far from it, he took every opportunity to urge her to paint – and especially to exhibit. The reader of this part of the correspondence who sets aside his prejudice will recognize that here we have the record of one of the strangest, and most touching, love stories ever. For it was a love affair. In the late summer of 1916, Lytton and Carrington went together to Wales and the West of England, where they both at last lost their virginity – to each other. Lytton was at first alarmed, for he was 'officially' gay, and though homosexuality was illegal, he did not want the world – his world – to know about his bisexual tendencies. However, as these letters show, when he and Carrington were first looking for a house to share they were intending to live together in the full (hetero)sexual sense.

Lytton lapsed rapidly, and so did Carrington. Her letters aren't included here, but if they were, it would become apparent that she, too, was robustly bisexual.

Writers have got into the habit of referring to Bloomsbury 'pacifism'. This is an understandable error, for Frances Partridge, who outlived everyone else and therefore had the last word, really was a pacifist – viz. she believed all war was wrong, under any and all circumstances. In fact, this was a relatively rare position in Bloomsbury. Most of the group, living dangerously, shared Lytton's non-absolutist opposition to World War I on moral and political grounds. Even though it could have meant him going to prison, he refused to say that he could not conceive of a just war, or that there were no circumstances in which he would fight. He insisted that he was a non-pacifist Conscientious Objector, at a time when Conscientious Objection on non-pacifist or non-religious grounds was simply not recognized as a reason for exemption from conscription. Neither Lytton nor James would have escaped conscription (and a prison sentence resulting from their refusal) had they not been found medically unfit – by medical examiners who were none too sympathetic to them. And Frances and her husband, Ralph Partridge, though they met little hostility for it, had even less support or sympathy in Bloomsbury for their objection to World War II.

In what no one could have imagined would be his last years, Lytton made new and younger friends, such as the painter and future Communist peer Wogan Philipps, and his wife, the novelist Rosamond Lehmann; Bryan Guinness and his wife, Diana Mitford (later Lady Mosley); and new boyfriends, Dadie Rylands, the Cambridge don who was well-connected in theatre circles, Sebastian Sprott, an academic psychologist, and the last love of his life, the publisher and translator Roger Senhouse. Senhouse was Lytton's sado-masochistic partner. It should be noted that Senhouse himself preserved the letters that tell us about their activities. He annotated many of Lytton's letters to him; and it was Senhouse who sold them to the Berg Collection of the New York Public Library. My wife, Penelope Marcus, who has helped me throughout the long labour of preparing these letters for publication, and has formed her own idea of Strachey's character, shares my view that Lytton's masochism was probably less important and pronounced than Senhouse's taste for inflicting pain. We both incline to think that Lytton, who had been achingly lonely, wistful and unhappy through much of his adolescence and early manhood, was almost astonished to find that Senhouse returned his affection, and was so smitten with love that he would agree to almost anything to keep his young man. While Lytton's earlier correspondence reveals some interest in schoolboys being caned, this is more on the level of smutty stories than sexual fantasies.

When I at last completed editing these letters, most of the people who had observed my travails asked the same question: did I like Lytton Strachey as much as when I began the book? My own view has changed, certainly. The man was more complicated even than I had imagined. I cannot share all his tastes. But this does not indicate a lack of sympathy— I doubt if the person closest to him, Carrington, could have coped with the details of his relationship with Roger Senhouse. Carrington, of course, chose not to live to be haunted by Lytton's ghost, and we cannot know what she knew.

We can, however, be fairly confident that some people did know this secret (if it was a secret). Sebastian Sprott handled and filed all Lytton's correspondence during his life and again after his death. He never mentioned the S/M relationship to me; but then, I didn't know what questions to ask, and I was, at the time, in any case writing about G. E. Moore. The same is true for my interviews and correspondence with Leonard Woolf, Duncan Grant, Bunny Garnett, Dadie Rylands and E. M. Forster. At any rate, Lytton had grown a little less close to all these in the relevant last two years of his life. What about James and Alix Strachey and Frances Partridge? James read and re-read and annotated Lytton's correspondence. I don't know if Roger showed him Lytton's letters, but I shouldn't be surprised, and he certainly had read Roger's replies to Lytton. I never met James, but his widow Alix entrusted me with all her papers, and I carried them off to my Oxford college and catalogued them. I spoke to her often about them and she made it clear, especially in connection with the correspondence between her husband and Rupert Brooke, that her policy (and James's) was publish and be blessed. She *insisted* that the truth be told. I, of course, thought this referred to homosexuality; but as a good Freudian analyst herself (another alumna of Freud's own couch), Alix believed in maximum tolerance. However, if James and Alix knew this aspect of Lytton, surely they would have told Michael Holroyd, not me. On the other hand, I benefited greatly from the new, easier atmosphere Michael Holroyd's book had done so much to bring about. Frances was a different case. As readers of her published diaries know, she was not squeamish about the feelings of the living or the reputations of the dead; her truth-telling was fierce. Had she known that Lytton and Senhouse's relations involved punishment, she would only have been shocked if someone else had hinted at intolerance. There is, of course, the possibility that some or all these people read the passages of these 1930 letters, but did not realize their significance. Perhaps I should say *probability*, for despite the remarkable exhaustiveness of his biography, neither Michael Holroyd nor my wife and I at first thought these paragraphs amounted to anything more than the usual moaning about his health.

To answer the question, then, I *do* like Strachey more for having read his letters. On balance I find more to admire than to deprecate. His stance over conscription, for example, was unnecessarily risky. He could have said he was opposed to all war, on whatever grounds he chose to adduce, and given himself a fair chance of eluding both conscription and jail: the only casualty of this strategy would have been truth. I agree whole-heartedly with his mocking view that religion is a set of false beliefs and practices appropriate to mankind only in its infancy and childhood. I also agree with him that we must not scorn the art and artefacts these infantile beliefs have produced, though; we should understand their origins, and be *pious* militant atheists. As for his tedious whinging about his health, I have concluded that the stomach cancer, or the condition that led up to it, must have begun to show itself early on, and that he was, on balance, as brave about that as he was about the war, censorship and homosexuality.

It must be stressed that this is a selection of letters. If Strachey's letters were to be collected, they would run to nearly the six volumes needed for Virginia Woolf's, though she lived almost a decade longer than he. In the present publishing climate, this is an obvious impossibility; so huge cuts have had to be made – and many excellent letters have had to be sacrificed. The choices have been painful. Two criteria governed them. The first was literary merit. It will be evident on even a casual glance that that is not the sole reason for inclusion – I have also selected letters because they contribute to a narrative, either telling of an incident that is familiar from Holroyd's life, or from the film *Carrington*, or from one of the many other books dealing with Bloomsbury, or shedding a new light on the now old, old story.

We had the immense good fortune that this project began soon after Michael Holroyd had done his root and branch revision of his biography of Strachey. One day he appeared with a box that contained photocopies of most of the letters from which those that appear here are selected. In a sense he is a partner in this enterprise (as well as having been the senior partner in our thirty-year-long joint literary executorship of the Strachey Trust's copyright holdings); for he in effect did all the preliminary research. Thanks to him we have been spared the expense of journeys to the Berg Collection, and to check our earlier copies of letters with the originals now at the Humanities Research Center of the University of Texas, Austin, and to many libraries closer to home. The donkey work my wife and I have had to do has been mostly in the British Library, among the papers I had myself originally handled and sold to the BL on behalf of the Strachey Trust. There are some additional collections of Strachey's letters there, and I am very grateful to my Strachey Trust colleague Dr Sally Brown for calling my attention, and facilitating my access, to his letters to Henry Lamb and Saxon Sydney-Turner. We have microfilms of most of the Strachey Trust material, and my wife spent many tedious hours at the microfilm readers of the Bodleian double-checking these. I have tried to make clear the present location of all the letters included in this volume. Strachey's sometimes unorthodox beginning and ending of his letters has been retained – he often omits the salutation. While his eccentric constructions and spellings have usually been retained too, obvious spelling errors in English and French have been silently corrected. Editorial interference has been indicated by square brackets *and* italics; omissions are indicated by an ellipsis inside italic square brackets. All cuts have been made for reasons of space, not in order to be tactful or to spare anyone's blushes. With the death of Frances Partridge there are now no survivors of that Bloomsbury generation, and all their relations, like the living people named in Lytton's letters published here, are veterans of the Bloomsbury battles to tell the truth.

Acknowledgements

Without Michael Holroyd's material help and encouragement this edition of Lytton Strachey's letters would not have been possible. My wife Penelope Marcus has shared much of the burden: she did all the preliminary arranging of the letters, and much invaluable, meticulous research. Her advice has been heeded at every stage of the editing. My daughters Tatyana and Georgia Levy were pressed into service as the deadline loomed, and typed the texts of the remaining letters with astonishing accuracy and speed. The late Dr T. J. Binyon went well beyond the bounds of our long friendship by reading the vast pile of print-outs from which this selection has been made, and helping me to reduce this book to readable proportions.

Dr Sally Brown, my colleague on the Strachey Trust, gave me some essential assistance. My thanks to her and the staff of the British Library, and to the other members of the Strachey Trust, its chairman, Mark LeFanu, and especially Olivier Bell, who has spent many a pleasant (for me) half hour on the telephone answering my queries. The scholarly apparatus to her edition of Virginia Woolf's diaries was always my first resort for factual questions, and almost always yielded the answer. I owe her extra thanks for sending me Clive Bell's angry letter. My old friends Robert Skidelsky, Keynes's biographer, and Hugh and Mirabel Cecil, the biographers of Desmond and Molly MacCarthy, have answered all the questions I put to them, as has Victoria Glendinning, Leonard Woolf's biographer. My wife and I often discussed the project with the late Frances Partridge, whose frequent stays with us in her last years gave us so much pleasure. I hope this book has benefited from the historical perspective I gained from our many long talks. Richard Morphet helped us with a particularly arcane query, as did Vivienne Guinness. Because of her and Kieran Guinness's hospitality at Knockmaroon, Rosalind and Leonard Ingrams's at Garsington and Mary and Richard Gray's at Ham Spray, I've been able not just to imagine the places where Lytton Strachey lived and stayed, but to see them for myself. Kenneth O. Morgan and Darryl Pinckney gave me some vital historical information. Rowan Boyson helped me with the research at King's College, Cambridge and the Cambridge University Library; her transcriptions were rapid and accurate.

For answering other queries I am indebted to Angelica Garnett, Henrietta Partridge and Richard Garnett. Unfortunately we failed to solve the mystery of the whereabouts of Lytton's letters to David Garnett, and I'd be grateful for any information that would enable me to include some of them in a later edition.

I want to thank Karen Kukil, Librarian Rare Books, Smith College, for her help with the letters to Virginia Woolf and for her kindness to me when I visited Smith, also her colleague (and my childhood friend) Marjorie Wikler Senechal; also Elizabeth Pridmore, Archivist, King's College Library; the staff of the Bodleian; and Leslie A. Morris, Curator of Manuscripts, for Strachey's letters to T. S. Eliot, *MS Am 1432* by permission of the Houghton Library, Harvard University. I am grateful to Nick Atkins, who gave me technical help when years of work were nearly sabotaged by a sloppy program emanating from Seattle. Thanks to Tom Wallace, who was the agent for this book, Eleo Gordon, my editor at Viking Penguin, Jonathan Galassi at Farrar, Straus and Giroux, and Annie Lee.

Additional Acknowledgements to the U.S. and Paperback Editions

I am indebted to those reviewers and readers of the first British edition of this large book who took the time and trouble to write to me pointing out, and often correcting, errors. Chief among these is Professor S. P. Rosenbaum, who not only alerted me to the unsuspected existence of a letter to Virginia Woolf, published here for the first time, but provided a transcription and went to the heroic bother of suggesting many more corrections and additions. Peter Parker also gave me the benefit of the notes he had made for his *TLS* review. Anne Chisholm, who is writing the life of Frances Partridge, has shown me many kindnesses, and Olivier Bell has doubled hers. Francis Golding and Howard Hodgkin have my gratitude for their corrections, as well.

Professor Rosenbaum has solved the mystery of the long-missing letters to David Garnett but, sadly, too late for inclusion in this volume. They are in the Robert H. Taylor collection of Princeton University, whose Meg Rich, Don Skemer and Mark R. Farrell have been prompt and generous with their help. Lorin Stein and Kevin Doughten at Farrar, Straus and Giroux have supervised this revised edition.

Michael Holroyd and Margaret Drabble have put up with graciously, and pretended to enjoy, an almost daily flow of telephone calls and emails since the publication of the first edition. In my earlier acknowledgements

I neglected to thank the Society of Authors, whose Authors' Contingency Fund came to my rescue early in the life of this project. I want to make good this omission now, and also to record my debt to my close friends Caroline, Lady Conran and Michael Seifert, for their unfailing generosity and affection.

Select Bibliography and Sources

Bell, Anne Olivier (ed.), and McNeillie, Andrew, *The Diary of Virginia Woolf*, 5 vols., London, 1977–84.

Bell, Quentin, *Virginia Woolf*, 2 vols., London, 1972.

Cecil, Hugh and Mirabel, *Clever Hearts: Desmond and Molly MacCarthy – A Biography*, London, 1990.

Edmonds, Michael, *Lytton Strachey, a bibliography*, New York, 1981.

Furbank, P. N., *E. M. Forster: A Life*, 2 vols., London, 1997–8.

Garnett, David (ed.), *Carrington: Letters and Extracts from Her Diaries*, London, 1970.

Garnett, Henrietta, *Anny: A Life of Anne Thackeray Ritchie*, London, 2004.

Gerzina, Gretchen, *Carrington: A Life of Dora Carrington*, Oxford, 1990.

Hale, Keith (ed.), *Friends & Apostles: The Correspondence of Rupert Brooke and James Strachey (1905–1914)*, New Haven and London, 1998.

Holroyd, Michael, *Augustus John*, 2 vols., London, 1974–5.

Holroyd, Michael, *Lytton Strachey: The New Biography*, London, 1994.

Holroyd, Michael (ed.), *Lytton Strachey by Himself*, London, 1994.

Holroyd, Michael, and Levy, Paul (eds.), *The Shorter Strachey*, London, 1989.

Lee, Hermione, *Virginia Woolf*, London, 1996.

Levy, Paul (ed.), *Lytton Strachey: The Really Interesting Question*, London, 1972.

Levy, Paul, *Moore: G. E. Moore and the Cambridge Apostles*, London, 1979.

Levy, Paul, Introduction, Lytton Strachey: *Eminent Victorians, The Definitive Edition*, London, 2002.

Marler, Regina (ed.), *Selected Letters of Vanessa Bell*, London, 1993.

Meisel, Perry, and Kendrick, Walter (eds.), *Bloomsbury/Freud: The Letters of James and Alix Strachey (1924–1925)*, New York, 1985.

Monk, Ray, *Ludwig Wittgenstein: The Duty of Genius*, London, 1990.

Nicholson, Virginia, *Among the Bohemians: Experiments in Living 1900–1939*, London, 2002.

Nicolson, Nigel, and Trautmann, Joanne (eds.), *The Letters of Virginia Woolf*, 6 vols., London, 1975–80.

Partridge, Frances, *Memories*, London, 1981.

Rosenbaum, S. P., *Aspects of Bloomsbury*, New York, 1998.

Rosenbaum, S. P. (ed.), *The Bloomsbury Group: A Collection of Memoirs, Commentary and Criticism*, rev. ed., Toronto, 1995.

Rosenbaum, S. P., *Georgian Bloomsbury: The Early Literary History of the Bloomsbury Group, 1910–1914*, London, 2003.

Rosenbaum, S. P., *Victorian Bloomsbury: The Early Literary History of the Bloomsbury Group*, London, 1987.

Schilpp, P. A. (ed.), *The Philosophy of G. E. Moore*, Evanston and Chicago, 1942.

Seymour, Miranda, *Ottoline Morrell: Life on a Grand Scale*, London, 1992.

Shone, Richard, *Bloomsbury Portraits*, Oxford, 1976.

Skidelsky, Robert, *John Maynard Keynes*, London, 2004.

Spalding, Frances, *Duncan Grant*, London, 1997.

Spalding, Frances, *Vanessa Bell*, London, 1983.

Spotts, Frederic (ed.), *Letters of Leonard Woolf*, London, 1990.

Wilson, Duncan, *Leonard Woolf: A Political Biography*, New York, 1978.

Woolf, Leonard, *Autobiography*, 2 vols., Oxford, 1980.

Manuscript Sources

The British Library, London: Has the major holdings formerly owned by the Strachey Trust. Correspondence between Lytton and James Strachey, Duncan Grant and Carrington. Also Lytton Strachey to Clive Bell, 'Topsy' Lucas, Saxon Sydney-Turner, Henry Lamb and several other correspondents.

The Oriental and India Office Collections, The British Library, London: Letters from Lytton Strachey to his grandmother, brother Ralph, and his mother.

House of Lords Records Office, London: Correspondence between Lytton and St Loe Strachey.

Victoria and Albert Museum National Art Library, London: Lytton Strachey letters to Boris Anrep.

King's College Library, Cambridge: Correspondence between Lytton Strachey and John Maynard Keynes, E. M. Forster, George 'Dadie' Rylands, J. T. Sheppard, W. J. H. 'Sebastian' Sprott, Bernard Swithinbank, et al.

University of Cambridge Library: Letters to G. E. Moore, Edmund Gosse and Philip Gosse.

University of Sussex Library, Brighton: Copies of letters between Lytton Strachey and Leonard and Virginia Woolf; also photocopies of the original 'Charleston Papers', which were held by King's College, Cambridge, until their sale at Sotheby's in 1980.

National Library of Wales, Aberystwyth: Letters to Dorelia John and a single letter to Augustus John.

Humanities Research Center, University of Texas at Austin: Lytton Strachey to J. R. Ackerley, James H. Doggart, Mary Hutchinson, Ottoline Morrell, Ralph Partridge, Lady Strachey, Sir Richard Strachey and other family members.

Berg Collection, New York Public Library: Letters to Barbara Bagenal, Rupert Brooke, John Maynard Keynes, Katherine Mansfield, John Middleton Murry, Roger Senhouse and Leonard Woolf.

Robert H. Taylor Collection, Princeton University: Letters to Vanessa Bell, Dorothy Bussy, Leonard and Virginia Woolf.

Houghton Library, Harvard University: Letters to T. S. Eliot.

Mortimer Rare Book Room, Smith College: Correspondence between Lytton Strachey and Virginia Woolf.

To Sir Richard Strachey

Written from Leamington College, the minor public school where Lytton went in the summer term of 1894.

Wednesday, June 6th 1894

My dearest Papa,

As you say – 'a certain amount of the unpleasant everyone sooner or later has to put up with' and as I think mine is a case of 'petty bullying' I will to the best of my ability grin and bear it, which I think is the only thing to be done. As to the other matter all I know is that conversations frequently take place without any regard to decency, but whether it is carried on further than this I do not know as I have only been here such a short time.

But I hope that eventually matters will clear up and that I'll have a happy issue out of my difficulties.

The best day for coming to see me is either Wednesday or Saturday – both are equally good – I stop work at half past twelve and am free till a quarter to seven. Tell Mama that I have arranged for my music, but have not had a lesson yet.

Your letters cheered me greatly for you see I am not *very* happy and it's so nice to feel that there *is* a place from where I can be sure of help, in time of need.

Give my love to everyone.

Good-bye

Ever your loving son
Lytton

‡

To Leonard Woolf

Lytton went up to Cambridge in 1899. He was so ill in the summer that he was not allowed to return to Cambridge for the autumn term. Lady Strachey took him to the coast near Biarritz for his health, which was improving (by November he had gained two stone and weighed eleven stone). She left him in the care of her first cousin, Annie King, and her family, who accompanied him on his weekly excursion to the casino.

Hotel d'Angleterre
St Jean de Luz
Basse Pyrénées
France
December 21st 1900

Dear Woolf,

I got your kind letter with much joy. The sunny south is at present not quite so sunny as it ought to be, but it has been charming – blue sea, and hills and fresh air and heat enough for anyone. The country is Basque and rather strange, with bullock-carts and things at every turn – flooded with English of course, which makes it more or less unpleasant. The only man of any amusement (barring a decayed millionaire and a gouty Baron) is an Oxford person, who teaches little boys, and in the intervals writes poems for the Spectator. You can imagine the sort of Oxford Schoolmaster poetical absurd sort of person. I go and listen to him and laugh for evenings at a time. He gives me his poems to read (bad enough) and good advice (rather worse) and his views on Shakespeare (quite ridiculous). We talked the other day of people we should like to meet. I mentioned Cleopatra. He said: 'I should rather see Our Lord than anyone else.' I had to reply 'Oh, I put him on one side as inhuman.' And so we were embarked on the Grand Controversy. He was silly enough but not so silly (I should think) as the Junior Dean, and allowed me to laugh as much as I liked, even going so far as to admit that the divinity has its ludicrous side. I said that purely as a matter of taste four in one pleased me rather more than three in one, and seven in one most of all – but he wouldn't follow up this line of argument. *[. . .]*

your loving
GLS

[. . .]

‡

To Leonard Woolf

This was the first of the two letters Lytton wrote to Leonard this day.

  This year Sarah Bernhardt repeated the title role she'd played in 1899 in the French production of Hamlet *in London; in 1901 she was also seen as the Duc de Reichstadt, the son of Napoleon I, in Rostand's* L'Aiglon, *written for her that year.*

  Saxon Sydney-Turner (1880–1962) was one of the five Trinity undergraduates who, in Lytton's second term, formed a reading club they called the Midnight Society. Others who became lifelong friends were Woolf and Clive Bell. Sydney-Turner took a double first in classics, worked in the Treasury, solved crossword puzzles, was devoted to Wagner and in love with Barbara Hiles. Sir Leslie Stephen and his young family were spending the summer at a school he had rented five miles away; 'the Goth' is Thoby Stephen, and this summer Lytton met his sisters Vanessa and Virginia, as well as the younger brother Adrian.

Cuffnells
Lyndhurst
August 23rd *[1901]*

Dear Leon

I admit I have been shameful. Your letter reached me a million years ago. It was chiefly (as you probably forget) about the divine Sarah in Phèdre. What you said annoyed and pleased me. Annoyed because I wanted to have been there, pleased because at last (I think) you really agreed with me. My sister saw it too and raved – but not I think the same day as you. Did she laugh when she mentioned the Gods in the scene with Hippolyte? Oh! I wish I'd seen her again! In the fourth act I'm sure she was supremest.

> Minos juge aux enfers tous les pâles humaines!
> Je crois voir de ta main tomber l'urne fatale![1]

Oh! Ah! Um!

Turner I have had here for a week, which was pleasant. I fear he is now hard at it in Brighton. Here it is delicious – the New Forest – beautiful trees and weather. The Goth within five miles with his family. It is a school they live in, and the Goth at night retreats to the dormitory, where he magnificently sleeps among the small surrounding beds! *[. . .]*

> your loving
> GLS

1. Lytton (mis)quotes from memory: it is 'l'urne terrible'.

‡

To Leonard Woolf

The X Society was another play-reading group based at Trinity College. Aeneas's isle: Endymion, book III, line 414. St Agnes's Eve: verse XXIV. 'When with flame . . .' from Swinburne's 'Dolores'. Quotation from Phèdre, I,3.

> *[Cuffnells, near Lyndhurst, Hants]*
> August 23rd 1901, 11.30 p.m.

[. . .] I have been reading Keats in raptures. Doesn't he come out with them just! That perfect thing –'Aeneas's isle was wondering at the moon' – and the marvellous stained-glass verse in St Agnes's Eve! They are like mosaics on the roof of heaven – patterns of bright gold – one thinks of the Albert Memorial! Which leads me to ask what you imagine will happen to us all when we have got rid of every vestige of early Victoria? Shall we be cold and shiver or shall we be feverish and fret? (That is one half a line by Swinburne and one half not.) Shall we be modern French, shall we be Ancient Roman, or shall we be American? Shall we be – we shall if his Majesty insists – fringilly *[sic]* Celtic? Oh! If the climate was

respectable *I* should vote for Paganism and no Clothes which would be delightful! Have you ever met an Ancient Roman? I have, and it was most instructive. He was a Nero sort of a man – enormous and absolutely selfish and rather vulgar – I meant Nero-like in appearance, for who would risk the assertion as to *him*?

> 'When, with flame all around him aspirant
>   Stood flushed, as a harp-player stands,
> The implacable beautiful tyrant
>   Rose-crowned, having death in his hand;
> And a sound as the sound of loud water
>   Smote far through the flight of the fires,
> And mixed with the lightning of slaughter
>   A thunder of lyres.'

– Well, mine was not an artist, but he would – and this is the crucial point – have constantly ripped up slaves in cold weather in order that he might plunge his feet into their warm entrails. This I believe I have read ces gens-là magnificently used to do. He would have done it and thought nothing of it. I have – or have I always had? – an obsession for Paganism – but I prefer it (thank you) Greek.

I hope you have written a play for the X Society as you said you would – otherwise I shall certainly resign. I shall do the same if you are neither at Land's End or John of Groats, and attempt to read this letter – it is exclusively meant for the moors. If you forgive me – write!

GLS

Ariane ma soeur de quel amour blessée
Vous mourûtes aux bords où vous fûtes laissée !

Racine – Phèdre – Perfection

‡

To Leonard Woolf

The omitted first paragraph queries Woolf's whereabouts – Putney or Tintagel, Cornwall – and suggests that he visit Lytton in the New Forest.

Sir Leslie was almost seventy at the time of writing, Vanessa twenty-two, Thoby two days short of twenty-one, Virginia nineteen and Adrian nearly eighteen.

Cuffnells
Lyndhurst
September 10th 1901

Dear Leon,

[. . .] As for London in August the thought is blistering. I am not allured
by your description. The bare brutality of ugliness is to me sheer death –
the opposite of fascination. The aesthetic titillation of a slum strikes me
as something painfully modern, which I am altogether too pagan to
understand. Zola I believe has it. Ugliness for its own sake is to me
anathema maranatha *[a terrible curse]*. As a view of life – all right, but in
itself – conspiracy. Measure for Measure is ugly in both ways. With
what a lurid splendour the ugliness is heightened in the main story, with
what grovelling blatancy it is shot out at one in the comic scenes. Vive
la beauté! say I. *[. . .]*

I have been up since four this morning! (Excuse this disgraceful
paper.) We started out to visit the Goth and cub hunt. Of course when
we laboriously got there the hunt was off, and we all tramped about till
breakfast. It is a nice though wild family – two sisters very pretty – a
younger brother Adrian, and Leslie with his ear-trumpet and tam-o-
shanter. What is rather strange is the old man – older than he really is –
among so young a family. He is well kept in check by them, and they
are well bustled by him. They know each other very well I think. *[. . .]*

your aff.
GLS

‡

To Leonard Woolf

*The occasion for this letter was an Apostles' Easter reading party; these were
organized by G. E. Moore.*

  '*Dans une pension miteuse de la rue Neuve-Sainte-Geneviève, la maison
Vauquer (du nom de sa tenancière), se côtoient des pensionnaires et des
habitués . . .*' Balzac, *Père* Goriot.

  '*The tragedy*' *is a play Lytton was writing for the X Society.*

  *The artist Turner didn't think Carisbrook 'a poor sort of castle', and his 1828
watercolour of the majestic medieval ruin features horses, rather than a donkey.*

Blackgang Chine Hotel
Ventnor
Isle of Wight
Good Friday
[March 28th 1902]

[. . .] There are at present five of us here. Two (Sanger and Robin
Mayor) arrived yesterday; the rest – Moore, Ainsworth and myself –
have been here since Monday. The place is I find a little *[illegible]* owing
to the violence of the wind which never ceases. We are supposed to
work in the morning, walk in the afternoon, and amuse ourselves in the
evening. Can you imagine the scene? We have a sitting-room to
ourselves – a table in the middle, very uncomfortable red plush chairs,
pictures of whores on the walls, a piano (at/on which Moore plays and
sings), a marble mantelpiece, and 43 red and yellow glass ornaments.
Not so bad quite as La Maison Vaquer *[sic]*. We are all very nice and
happy I presume – though sometimes your humble servant sinks into a
demi-depression. The tragedy does not, and I fear will not, proceed,
amid such an entourage –! Today has been spent in walking to
Carisbrook – a poor sort of castle with a donkey. *[. . .]*

your aff.
GLS

‡

To Leonard Woolf

*Despite his second in Part I of the History Tripos, Lytton was awarded a
Scholarship at Trinity. This prompted the letter from George Trevelyan that so
annoyed him, in which Trevelyan said he must get a first in Part II: 'To do that
you will have to work reasonably hard . . . Your answers are . . . clever essays to
cover a good deal of ignorance.'*[1]

In Balzac's best-known novel, as in King Lear, *a father gives everything to
his daughters, only to die a miserable death abandoned by them.*

Blackgang Chine Hotel
Ventnor
I of W
[Easter 1902, c. March 30]

Dear Leon

It is no longer cold – we are sitting out in the sun on a quasi-lawn overlooking a blue-grey sea. (We = Ainsworth and I.) *He* is reading Anna Karénine in French; I have Montaigne, Swinburne, Webster and Hamlet on the table in front of me, and have just found your letter indoors. Don't be any more depressed. God's on his thorn – the snail's in his heaven . . .

> For the soul that is wisdom and freedom, the spirit of England redeemed
>   from her past,
> Speaks life through the lips of the master and lord of her children, the first
>   and the last.
> Thought, touched by his hand, and redeemed by his breath, sees, hears, and
>   accepts from above
> The limitless lightnings of vision and passion, the measureless music of love!

We take immense walks most days – which is rather pleasant. Two others called Sanger and Robin Mayor have been with us – but have now gone. We laugh a good deal. I nearly quarrelled with Ainsworth t'other night but not quite. I don't like the personification of irrelevance – but that's all. The 'scholarship question' perhaps is hardly that. But when you see the GREAT LETTER you'll understand altogether.

I never heard of anything quite so mad as your and the Goth's proceedings. Dear, dear! Did he see his buds? In Suffolk, I mean. Mania! Mania!

I have not finished Père Goriot and so I shall not yet say what I think about it. Maxim Gorki sounds death indeed. *Yes*, the great absurdity of most writers is that they *will* write about *[illegible, perhaps Greek characters]* and fools – or mere fantastic cranks. Down with them! Shakespeare's chief point, I think, is that he deals so much with geniuses. Meanwhile I have three Maupassant stories that I long to write – only for the most private of all circulation, of course. Can't write any more poetry, can you? If one only had indefinite empty years –! *[. . .]*

your
G.L.S.

A word as to Père Goriot, which I have just finished. Yes! It reaches heights! But sometimes too – don't you think? – rather descends to depths? As far as *he* is concerned it's *all* magnificent – the last scene overwhelming – but *I* got rather bored with the *[illegible]* in the middle and the high society dame *[Madame Beausant]*. Of course what's most against it is the extraordinary parallel it must *[illegible]* with Lear. One feels the instrument: weaker for one thing; and perhaps because of that, it strikes one as less universal. I notice they both say nearly the same thing, which perhaps gives the essence of the problem. 'Elles ont toutes les deux des coeurs de roche.' 'Then let them anatomize Regan; see what breeds about her heart. Is there any cause in nature that makes these hard hearts?' *[Lear, III, vi.]* Voilà la question!

GLS

1. Quoted in Michael Holroyd, *Lytton Strachey*, p. 71.

‡

To Leonard Woolf

With some Strachey family members, Lytton had gone to stay with the Homeres, 'my Greek lady friends', who had once lived next door in London, at 70 Lancaster Gate. They now lived in Oxfordshire, on what remained of the fortune their father had lost on the stock market. Holroyd writes of 'the three daughters – the severely practical and embittered Ianthe, the nondescript Ina, and Angelica, a nymphomaniac, of great beauty apparently infatuated with Lytton'. They took paying guests at their modest house at Kingham.[1]

'State Express "Quo Vadis" turkish leaf cigarettes' tins are occasionally offered for sale to collectors.

Care of Miss Homere
Kingham
Chipping Norton
Oxon, July 1st *[19]*02

[. . .] For me I *[illegible, perhaps* scribble*]* on among ladies, whom I *cannot* fall in love with. One of them is beautiful, young, charming – oughtn't I to be in love with her? We go for walks together, read each other sonnets, sit out together o' nights, among moons, stars, and

the whole romantic paraphernalia – oughtn't I to be in love? Oughtn't I –?

It's *my* disease, I'm afraid, not to be!

Meanwhile, how is one to write tragedies? I saw Sarah in Phèdre – thought all was lost in Act I – Act II hardly better – but Act III very fine, and Act IV absolute. Yes! I looked out for you – but didn't spot you – perhaps you went the second time. My tragedy I want to write – a new one – but I don't think I ever shall. If I did – as I want to – it would be more utterly horrible and more supremely *[rude?]* than anything ever before heard of. But I shan't of course.

It just seems to me that there are some women whom I feel I *am* attracted to – and those – are precisely the ones that aren't women at all – girls, you know, of fourteen.

Isn't it ouff?

> your
> GLS

Non, non, mon amour, je n'ai pas de 'Quo Vadis'! Ah, mon dieu, c'est du tabac, n'est-ce pas? Des Cigarettes?

1. Michael Holroyd, *Lytton Strachey*, p. 84.

‡

To Leonard Woolf

The brother was probably Ralph (1868–1923), who married Margaret Severs in 1901, and the birth that of their eldest child, Richard, who became a novelist and writer of children's books.

'G.M.T.' was the older Apostle George Macaulay Trevelyan, the historian. He and Lytton fought a continuous skirmish on the question of homosexuality. As Russell said in his autobiography, 'There was a long, drawn out battle between George Trevelyan and Lytton Strachey . . . in which Strachey was on the whole victorious. Since his time homosexual relations among the members were for a time common, but in my day they were unknown.'[1] This was perhaps strictly true, but the Apostles had celebrated homosexuality, if not actually practised it, since the 1830s.

Lytton was distantly related to Sir Walter Raleigh, a much older Apostle, who was very kind to him when he first went up to Cambridge.

'Forth' was the Strachey family idiom for defecation.

Verdley Place
Fernhurst
Sussex
July 20th *[1902]*

Private

[. . .] A propos to Byron, I have one or two remarks. (1) Perhaps I have
said so already: Shelley was obviously in love with him. But not he, of
course, with Shelley. Though I daresay B. was a sodomite (as G.M.T.
would roar) and if he was, and Lady B. discovered it – perhaps that was
the mysterious reason of the separation. (2) Don Juan is without doubt a
lineal descendant of La Pucelle (Voltaire). I don't know whether anyone
has mentioned this before, but I'm convinced of it – after a cursory dip
into the latter. (3) John Morley (rather an old Early Victorian Liberal
fool) has written something on Byron – probably not worth reading –
but you might like to look – if you're still going on with the affair.

A crisis in this house occurs in a week or two which forces everyone
to leave it – viz. a birth. My brother has unwisely married – with the
inevitable result – a new nephew (or niece) for me. I go to spend a
week with the Raleighs, which rather alarms me.

I must forth.

your
GLS

1. Quoted in Michael Holroyd, *Lytton Strachey*, p. 103.

‡

To Leonard Woolf

Leonard suffered from hand tremor all his life. 'Forth' = lavatory.

Stanford in the Vale
Berks.
August 6th 1902

[. . .] I hope your doctor knows more about Delirium Tremens than
Plato, and I hope you assured him that the dear good man was rather

against all that than otherwise. A little outspoken perhaps, but at heart –
oh! I must think it – one of the earliest of the Puritans. I shall forever
fail to see what difference (medicine apart) a particular act can make.
Personally I feel far from inclined to commit it, but if anyone else does
– let 'em by all means crowd in among the other country copulatives.
Medically, I tell you in confidence, that I don't believe your medical
man. To be as healthy as the Greeks would be quite sufficient for my
small desires. Today we have discovered how dismally and bitterly
virtue is its own reward. Devoured by every disease from the
grandmother's to Bright's, from syphilis to constipation générale (which
indeed is now upon me), paralysed, blind, and delirium trementic, we
totter to our graves at twenty-nine, or seek dreary distractions amid the
embraces of hospital nurses or whores, yet proudly conscious of one
supreme truth – one undying Reality – we are not buggers, or even
Catamites! Should we not, after such lives, deserve the eternal
consolations of the Kingdom of Heaven, if we were not too noble
even for them, too proud in our intellectual twiddle, our spiritual
ouf? Behold us, oh Alcibiades, oh Benvenuto! Behold and admire!
Bow down to us, oh Sophocles, oh Shakespeare! Oh Frederick, oh
Caesar! As boys we denied, as youths we understood, but did we, like
too many of you, alas, let slip the zones of our virginity? As men we
have felt those mutinies, as dotards we have dreamed those dreams, but
have we, for a single moment, given way? No! A thousand times, no!
Triumphant answer! Let posterity and the All-knowing judge betwixt us
and you.

I am staying with the Raleighs in a sort of farm-house. It is somewhat
fetid – for one thing physical discomfort assumes such terrible
proportions. Not enough water, not enough wine, three male children,
and a most uninviting forth – not the kind of things I like when staying
with quasi-strangers. *He* is very eminent, but frantically taken up with a
book on Wordsworth, and at other time paralysing conversationally.
She jabbers sans cesse – rather amusingly – altogether unconceitedly – of
persons more than things. *[. . .]*

I find this country singularly stale and unromantic. My five minutes
in London on the way here was the Arabian nights. This is utter
prose. *[. . .]*

I spent a desperate day lately in trying to write an utterly shattering
poem. Not at all erotic, curiously enough – but not a success, either.

I feel now that I shall not be able to finish it, or anything, for two years.

Are our letters disgraceful? I put 'private' on my last in case of accidents, but I don't think it's worth it. You see, people might look all the more. But would it, if they did, at all matter? Heavens, this is a wretched, disembodied world, but it has not yet been deprived of its genitalia, though I admit those parts are in rather a parlous state. They need excitation. Shall we deny it them? Heaven forbid! What Christian would refuse so charitable an office?

> Besundered are all things and broken.
> My body is beaten with lust,
> The stars in their silence have spoken.
> Oh, terror, and ruin, and dust!
>
> I have heard the inaudible warning,
> I have seen the invisible goal,
> But a glory has fled from the morning,
> And the light and the height from my soul.

‡

To Leonard Woolf

The coronation of Edward VII was originally scheduled for 26 June but was postponed until 9 August, as the king had to undergo an emergency appendectomy operation. The 'event' was the birth of Lytton's nephew, Richard Strachey.

Verdley Place
Fernhurst
Sussex
Monday evening, (11.45 p.m.) August 11th 1902

I wrote you a postcard on Sunday, but left it to roost in my pocket. As it was raining, and as I had to be at Waterloo at 5.30, and as I had no umbrella, and as I was exhausted by coronations, and as it was generally Sunday, and as my estomac dilaté★ made me feel rather more lazy than usual [. . .]

The event is over – occurred on Sunday morning – so that's all right. It's a he. I've not yet braced up courage to go and look at it – but I suppose I shall have to. Why? Why? Why? Why?

? ? ?

[. . .] Their Majesties** had the honour to be cheered by me on Saturday. A purely mechanical stimulus. Kitchener looked almost absurdly proud and Roberts of course absolute. To have been in the Abbey would have repaid. My mother reports sumptuosities of dresses and trains unspeakable – also other things. *[. . .]*

*this is one of quite the latest diseases – very fashionable and aristocratic, but a little wearing too
**of England

‡

To Leonard Woolf

Saxon-Turner had written some 'dialogues', which were circulating to Woolf and Strachey. There is also a reference to a work in '24 stanzas', which Lytton says he hopes is not too much like In Memoriam, *'which I have just been reading for the first time with some interest' and also to a 'Prose Idyll (of a somewhat peculiar sort)'. As the text makes clear, though, Lytton is here defending his own verses.*

Verdley Place
Fernhurst
Sussex
August 31st 1902

[. . .] If I were a lawyer with the case for the defence in my hands I think I could make out rather a good one. Perhaps one might say, if I were Turner: Where, my lord, is the proof that there *is* an obsession? Nay, if there is any obsession at all, is it not rather in the mind of my learned friend, the counsel for the prosecution? You have cast your eyes, my lord, over the afore-mentioned poems? Good, and what do you find there? You find, it is true, genitals, buttocks, stomachs, but do you not also find, to an equal, or even a greater extent, eyes, shoulders, hair,

suns and heavens? In every one of these poems, my lord, you will find mention, either explicit or implicit of youth and love, but does my learned friend accuse the writer of being obsessed by youth and love? Not at all, my lord, only with genitals and buttocks. [. . .] This then, is my case, my lord; the prosecution, obsessed by buttocks and genitals, have, on reading the words of the defendant, in which these objects, among others, are referred to, become convinced that the obsession, which they clearly feel to exist somewhere, lies with the writer, and not with themselves. For it is in the nature of an obsession that its possessor should be unaware that *he* possesses it. If, however, the prosecution reply that they take buttocks and genitals merely as typical of the naked fleshliness of the writer, I beg leave to note (1) that the ground of the prosecution is thereby considerably changed, and (2) that, in these altered circumstances, the defendant has no compunction in admitting the charge. Does, for instance, my learned friend declare the defendant to be obsessed by paiderastia? I cannot be certain that he would use the term of 'obsession' in connection with such a condition of mind, but in no circumstances, my lord, can I conceive that he would go the length (in this 20th century) of basing a criminal prosecution on a display of affection for beautiful youths. At any rate, the defendant is willing to admit (noticing as he does, my lord) that the general public have been very properly excluded from the court, that he *has* an obsession for the aforementioned beautiful youths, and further that he prefers 'em without their clothes. Such an attitude of mind he admits to be fairly easily discernible in those of his works, my lord, which you have under your hand; but he does *not* admit that the attitude arraigned by the prosecution – viz. that of obsession by genitals and buttocks is, to any unobsessed vision, discernible in any way whatever.

[. . .] My point is that we are *all*, as compared with the Greek, reader and writer equally, obsessed by the fig-leaf, or, if you like to call it so, the genital question. (They're of course the same thing.) This being granted, I make the further remark that this obsession is, to me at any rate, probably one it's worth while being obsessed by. It's *not* merely buttocks and genitals – it's, if you like, flesh. Of course buttocks and genitals are the head and front of flesh, so they naturally occupy culminating positions in my poems. But it's the extraordinary question of the naked body which really fascinates and absorbs. Heavens! It's mysterious and splendid! Terrible, melancholy, and divine. Those strange, inevitable, silent, operations of nature! The lust and strength of youth! Death –!

[. . .]
Till then, let us smile, not frown, on these $\begin{Bmatrix} \text{happy} \\ \text{melancholy} \end{Bmatrix}$, too $\begin{Bmatrix} \text{few} \\ \text{frequent} \end{Bmatrix}$ occasions, when, at night, thinking of the boy we laughed with in the morning, we feel a peculiar movement among the sheets.

Your

GLS

‡

To Saxon Sydney-Turner

This letter records Moore's Easter reading party. Lytton often calls Saxon 'king' or 'tsar'.

Penmenner House

The Lizard

April 11th *[1903]*

Dear Turner,

[. . .] Woolf has now gone, and I remain with Moore, MacCarthy, Ainsworth, Sanger, and Bob Trevy. Can you imagine the collection? I am mainly depressed and lonely – unable, you see, to speak. *[. . .]*

    Moore sang magnificently last night. *Really*, when he laughs! But it's quite impossible to describe anything about him in a letter – and probably out of it. My writing seems to be falling away. Venus is exhausted, poor lady. Ah! mon roi, savez-vous, savez-vous, mon désespoir et mon bonheur?

Your

GLS

‡

To G. E. Moore

Moore's Principia Ethica *had been published the week before this letter was written. The part of the Dedication to* Principia Ethica *in which Lytton figured was 'Fratribus'.*

69, Lancaster Gate, W.
October 11th 1903

Dear Moore

I have read your book, and want to say how much I am excited and impressed. I'm afraid I must be mainly classed among 'writers of Dictionaries, and other persons interested in Literature', so that I feel a sort of essential vanity hovering about all my 'judgements of fact'. But on this occasion I am carried away. I think your book has not only wrecked and shattered all writers on Ethics from Aristotle and Christ to Herbert Spencer and Mr Bradley, it has not only laid the true foundations of Ethics, it has not only left all modern Philosophy bafouée – these seem to me small achievements compared to the establishment of that method which shines like a sword between the lines. It is the scientific method deliberately applied, for the first time, to Reasoning. Is that true? You perhaps shake your head, but henceforward who will be able to tell lies one thousandth time as easily as before? The truth; there can be no doubt, is really now upon the march. I date from October 1903 the beginning of the Age of Reason.

The last two Chapters interested me most, as they were newer to me than the rest. Your grand conclusion made me gasp – it was so violently definite. Lord! I can't yet altogether agree – I think with some horror of a Universe deprived for ever of real slaughters and tortures and lusts. Isn't it possible that the real Ideal may be an organic unity so large and of such a nature that it is, precisely, the Universe itself? In which case Dr Pangloss was right after all.

I long to talk to you about a great many things. I come up probably on Tuesday, and as I don't know where you are I send this there. Dear Moore, I hope and pray that you realise how much you mean to us. It was very pleasant to be able to feel that one came into the Dedication. But expression is so difficult, so very difficult, and there are so many cold material obstructions, that the best of Life seems to be an act of faith.

This is a confession of faith, from your brother.

Lytton Strachey.

‡

To Leonard Woolf

The nickname 'the Yen' for G. E. Moore in full was 'Yen How', the Mandarin in San Toy, or The Emperor's Own, *composed by Sidney Jones, with book by Edward A. Morton, lyrics by Harry Greenbank and Adrian Ross and additional music by Lionel Monckton. The show opened at Daly's Theatre in London on 21 October 1899 and ran for 768 nights. Yen How was something of a philosopher, who knew how to exploit the power of contradiction – and the plot is sympathetic to adherents of the Higher Sodomy. Married to the 'six little wives' (of the fifth song in the show), he has got around the conscription law (allowing the Emperor to have any woman he chooses) for his favourite daughter, San Toy, by having her brought up as a boy. Unfortunately, the student Fo Hop has discovered the secret, and his price for silence is San Toy's hand in marriage. Yen How allows this on the condition that no one must ever know that San Toy is a girl – thus preventing the marriage taking place. In Act II, however, San Toy has come to the Emperor's attention despite her father's ploy, but Yen How, seeing in what favour San Toy is held by the Emperor, plans for the day when he is made Viceroy and introduces the benefits of British life into his country (song 24 – 'I mean to introduce it into China'). This fits well with the Apostles' tongue-in-cheek project to make Moore Minister of Education.*

Leonard's family lived in Putney. 'Old Dora' Sanger was the wife of C.P. Sanger. Robin Mayor was elected to the Apostles three years before Russell and Sanger. The book on Turkey was Mark Sykes, Dar-ul-Islam. A Record of a Journey through Ten of the Asiatic Provinces of Turkey. *J. M. Barrie's* Little Mary *was playing at Wyndham's Theatre in October 1903. Ralph Hawtrey became an Apostle two years before Strachey and Woolf. MacLaren figures in volume 1 of Woolf's autobiography, where the author seems unable to remember his given name.*

69, Lancaster Gate, W.
Sunday, October 11th 1903

Christ! I have just written off a letter to the Yen. It *had* to be done and
the knot is now cut, the Rubicon crossed and the alia jacta. Nominally,
of course, about his book. I hope I have managed all right, the difficulty
of course supreme. If it doesn't come off the doom is too frightful. But
after all I've only said the truth.

Have you read it? The last two chapters – glory alleluiah! And the
wreckage! That indeterminate heap of shattered rubbish among which
one spies the utterly mangled remains of Aristotle, Jesus, Mr Bradley, Kant,
Herbert Spencer, Sidgwick and McTaggart. Plato seems to be the only person
who comes out even tolerably well. Poor Mill has simply gone. I have got
a grand scheme in my head which with luck I may bring off – it will be
something altogether new and very startling, but can't yet be revealed.

Are you still in P? I'm afraid so. I go up prob. on Tuesday next.
Dined with Old Dora on Friday. Bertie was there. The talk was
practically all fiscal, wh. was rather a bore as I wanted to talk about the
P.E. But Bertie shone as usual. Robin M. came in afterwards, and there
was a pretty Miss Verrall. I had expected Helen, and was surprised – her
cousin, whom I suppose ought to have excited my amatory emotions.
Angus I'm sure would have been properly in love. Mais je n'aime pas
les femmes, moi. Elles ne sont que les objets d'art. Oh! I unfortunately
met Hugh Smith yesterday at a matinée of Little Mary. He was his old
intolerable self. Rather reddish and more German-looking, I thought,
but the identical utter fool. He's bringing out a book with Mark Sykes
on Turkey. Thank God, doesn't mean to be a Fellow. I haven't yet seen
these which the Goth, whom I met in Oxford Street on Friday, told me
came out yesterday. The G. goes to Loren's – can you imagine it? but I
think he's certain to chuck it soon. He seemed fairly cheerful – had
been staying with Hawtrey in Surrey – came out 115th in the exam. He
told me an *awful* story about McLaren. He's vanished! Isn't it too utterly
appalling? Without, apparently, sending in a dissertation. The Goth
thinks he's raped Miss Hinkman, but it's clear something shocking has
occurred, and I'm afraid we may never see him again. The only hope is
that the whole story, which rests on Macgregor, may not be true. *[. . .]*

I don't know whether I shan't burn my letter to the Yen.

Yours
GLS

☩

To Leonard Woolf

Leonard was temporarily away from Cambridge, and this is a rare letter from Lytton to him written during termtime. The 1903 Greek play was Aristophanes' The Birds. At Apostles' meetings held on Saturdays in term, the speaker was obliged to stand on the hearthrug. 'Whales' were sardines on toast, the regular fare served after the discussion.

Trinity College
Cambridge
[November 24th 1903]

I am *completely* drunk – having absorbed the greater part of a bottle of Chablis. I cannot walk, speak, or think. Turner and I have sat down to absorb. We are *drunk [underlined several times]*!

I have been to the dress rehearsal of the Gk Play. Quel horreur! A scene of desolation and dirges, crucifixions, moans and general Cornfordisms. Notre vie est comme ça. Turner thinks I'd better stop: why be drunk? Il y a toujours quelque chose. I hope you're better and that you'll return before the week is out. If Turner and I are left nose to nose on Saturday Evening I shall piss into the fire from the hearthrug, and the whales will be uneatable.

[. . .] Turner thinks I'll never stop. Can he still think I'm not drunk? My point is that it's so curious that people who are drunk should pretend to be drunker. *He* thinks it's only natural – because they want to show that they're not drunk at all. But *I* don't want to show anything – except my bare arse *[the writing here slides off the page]*.

Your loving,
Lytton

☩

To Leonard Woolf

Auguste Rodin's (1840–1917) first exhibition of a large-scale plaster of The Thinker took place at the International Society of Painters, Sculptors and Engravers in London, before he showed a bronze version at the Salon in Paris.

The Racine quotation is from Phèdre, IV,6. *Goldsworthy Lowes Dickinson (1862–1932), an older Apostle, later an advocate of the League of Nations. Lytton seems to have disliked the poetic diction of the poems in the* Spectator *referring to the Lisbon earthquake of 1755 and the great Chicago fire of 1871. Middleton and Rowley's 1622 drama* The Changeling *is one of the most celebrated Jacobean plays. The 'great scene' is where the disfigured De Flores, having conspired with Beatrice to murder her fiancé, demands her virginity as his price. Strachey was frequenting the British Museum to research Warren Hastings for his Cambridge fellowship dissertation. The person whose movements Lytton wants to know is probably Sheppard, with whom he was now infatuated.*

69, Lancaster Gate, W.
January 13th 1904

I only just got a glimpse of the red-grey beard of Rodin. But his Penseur thundered above the ladies and gentlemen in evening dress, and one could look at it as much as one could. Very violent. My theory is that the French imagination is nearly always *material*. Rodin is *grossly* so. Imagine, if Shelley had been a sculptor, how he would have done Le Baiser – a winged Eros just touching the earth; Rodin has a thick man cuddling a thick woman. Le Penseur is rigid banks and heaps of muscle. The imagination of Michael Angelo was 'spiritual' in some way that R's isn't. What it means I don't know – but the spiritual imagination suggests things which are not material. Racine is the only Frenchman I can think of who is what I call properly imaginative –

'Ils suivaient sans remords leur penchant amoureux;
Tous les jours se levaient clairs et sereins pour eux.' [Strachey's emphasis]

That's the grand triumph! But how different to the rest of French writing.

There was a young Persian Prince (I suppose) at the New Gallery. Almost perfectly beautiful. *Never* saw such a sight! He was pursued by a mob – as my sister tastefully put it – of ladies and artists! The mouth was wonderfully subtle; but everything! –

Met Dickinson at the B[ritish] M[useum] and went to tea with him in his faded house. Wouldn't speak. He said your article amused him – it was so mature – it *had an air* of such maturity. Talked of the Cosmos as usual. By God! Have you seen the poem in this week's Spectator? After the Disaster of Lisbon the Catastrophe of Chicago. I have read the Changeling. It certainly carries it off. The great scene is very good indeed. The situation all along splendid. The characters thoroughly thought out, and put in with that curious Elizabethan calm. Add to this an underplot of complete folly.

My dear, *could* you find out this – without letting it be found out that you're finding it out? – Whether he's going down on Saturday? It seems to me just possible, and I'd stupidly rather like to know. – If you could let me know by Friday . . . It's mere absurdity really, not asking him and wanting to know at all. *[. . .]*

‡

To Leonard Woolf

Lytton is here matchmaking between his elder sister, Pippa, and Moore, at thirty-one a year younger than she. For his part, as the scatological parenthesis shows, Lytton was tiring of Sheppard. 'On a stool': e.g. in the Civil Service.

Trinity College
Cambridge
February 18th 1904

Would you have stayed up if I'd asked you – as I wanted to – to come to dinner tonight with Moore and my sister Philippa? As it was it was a four – the inevitable Sh*[eppard]* making the fourth (or forth). Went off, all things considered, fairly well; and he conducted her back to the Hosp. D'you think his affections have been already engaged? I have hopes for the supremest of all marriages.

I hope you'll be already much better when you get this, and will return soon. I feel absolutely seul. I am to all intents and purposes out of love. Bored to death with dreary conversations. Only two things I find amuse me (and perhaps everyone) – wit and the flesh – booff! he gives me neither. . .

There is nothing to say, you see. I am sleepy, not drunk, this time. I shall go to the Party at the Lodge tomorrow with a clear conscience; in a week I shall forget that I was ever a sodomite. In a year I shall be in Morocco, very likely, or in gaol, or on a stool, or under the earth. In a few minutes I shall be in bed.

your
GLS

‡

To Leonard Woolf

The wedding is that between George Macaulay Trevelyan (1876–1962) and Janet Penrose Ward (b. 1879), the daughter of the novelist and anti-women's suffrage campaigner, Mrs Humphry Ward (1851–1920). Mrs Ward had insisted that the couple be married in church, which was against the bridegroom's Apostolic principles. A compromise was struck about the wording of the service, but only a few weeks after the wedding Trevelyan had a nervous breakdown that he attributed to the conflict. Theodore and Crompton Llewellyn Davies were Apostles a little older than Trevelyan. A char-à-banc in 1904 was a horse-drawn carriage with benches across instead of seats. Marie Souvestre (1830–1905) taught the Strachey children, as she did Eleanor Roosevelt. She was a great friend of Lady Strachey, and famously agnostic. The quotation from Mazzini was a sop to Trevelyan's academic interests. 'Let copulation thrive', King Lear, IV,6. Hunter's Inn, near Lynton on the north coast of Devon, was the location for Moore's Easter reading party.

69, Lancaster Gate, W.
March 20th 1904

This is to give you news of the wedding. I'm not sure that you missed much, except the general 'atmosphere', which certainly was distinctly high. Coming back the train stopped at somewhere for some reason or other, and just as it was moving off again, a young man – clearly third class – dashed across the platform and managed to get into our compartment, in spite of the cries of guards. But it needed no compulsion to make him leap out again. The atmosphere – that was quite enough. My mother said we were a 'cultured crowd', and we certainly were. Mostly matrons, in grey silk and hair – Henry James, Sheppard, Hawtrey, Theodore, C.D., etc. filled up the gaps. The lunch was *free*, and at separate tables, but the whole train was interconnected, so that there was a good deal of moving about. A high char-à-banc, with a horn, drove us off from the station; flags were waved of course, and there was some cheering. Can you imagine the scene? It's a good deal of it only imaginary, I feel. The service was fairly dull, in a chapel with Burne-Jones windows. Mr Eiothen Carpenter[1] officiated. He began with an address composed of quotations and platitudes, during which, as Miss Souvestre said, the bride and bridegroom looked at the windows as much as they could. The quotations were from St Th*[omas]* à K*[empis]*, Mazzini and St Paul (Revised Version). There was then a very churchy hymn. Then a prayer, beginning 'Almighty Power', – it was the thin edge of the wedge. The prayer ended with 'Our Heavenly Father'. Dear me! I thought. And then followed a simply blatant benediction, with the Father, 'Our Lord Jesus Christ', and the Holy Spirit. Wasn't it monstrous? Or perhaps only Christian.

On the platform going away, as Sheppard and I were talking, I turned round – and there was Cornford. He was in the most antique of toppers, and was travelling third. I suppose I looked at his hat too much, for at last he said – 'I thought it would do my top hat good to have an airing. I haven't worn it for seven years.' Then he looked at Sheppard's, and added – 'Yours looks comparatively new.' 'Yes,' I just remarked, 'but then you see Sheppard isn't quite as old as you are.' He positively blushed, and stepped into his non-special train.

The bride and bridegroom were almost completely hideous. But I suppose one must let copulation thrive. The service was practically all balls in both senses.

I've settled to go to France, after a week at the Hunter's; and hope to see you on Tuesday.

your
G.L.S.

1. Michael Holroyd reads this as 'Edward Carpenter' (*Lytton Strachey*, p. 95), but Edward Carpenter had left the Church in 1874, and in any case, was not really respectable enough for this company.

‡

To Leonard Woolf

Moore's postcard was about arrangements for meeting on Paddington Station to travel to the Devon reading party. The Chinese labour question was about South Africa's importation of 50,000 indentured Chinese workers to remedy labour shortages in Transvaal's diamond mines, which Lord Milner, the British High Commissioner, welcomed to help in his aim of reconstruction. Douglas William Freshfield (1845–1934), English explorer and mountaineer, and his wife Augusta were Strachey family friends, and they conducted a sort of salon at their London house. It was Lytton's older brother, Oliver, who saw Moore, now living in Edinburgh with Ainsworth.

69, Lancaster Gate, W.
Sunday, March 27th 1904

I should like to come and walk tomorrow, but I fear I can't. I have the beastly Walpole thing to do – and whether I ever shall do it I don't know. Is there anything to say do you think but cursing of Macaulay, and vague 'appreciation' of the 18th Cent? I got a postcard from Moore. I suppose you did too – telling me to be there at 10.50 on Thursday. I went to Sanger on Friday, and found him alone. We talked religion and politics. He was wonderful on Chinese labour – violently anti-Milner – and really half converted me. He was very voluble with 'D'you see what I mean?' at the end of every furious sentence. I felt at home with him a good deal more than I could have with MacCarthy.

Went to dinner with the Freshfields on Thursday, and was (to their minds) properly brilliant. Mr Freshfield is a curious rich sensible and half-conventional man – by no means a Christian, but a respectable gent. He said he didn't think it was worth going to all the bother of the Humphry Ward wedding in order to change the Holy Ghost into the Holy Spirit. I didn't tell you Henry James's *mot* on the occasion. – 'The ordinary service binds, and makes an impression – it's like a seal; this was nothing more than a wafer.' Theodore was at the dinner. We talked, when the ladies had gone, of Chinese labour. Old Freshfield said he had heard the Chinese had been accused of all sorts of crimes. Theodore fairly tittered when he mentioned the unmentionable one. It was a curious scene – Theodore giggling, and old Freshfield swinging his eyeglasses. Later on he said he thought these tactics of snap divisions and trying to turn the government out by trickery was a miserable policy, and quite unworthy of 'the nation'. Don't you think it's odd such people should exist? Only he's not pompous – he's only curiously moulded.

I get madly excited in the British Museum. Really, Hastings –! The only man! All that interests me is dead things – like Turner. I am in terror that I shall have to give up half my dissertation. I am altogether blockaded. Are you expiring? I suppose that we shan't meet till the platform at Paddington. Sanger said he was coming then. My brother had dinner in York with Moore the other day, so I suppose he's left Edinburgh.

your
GLS

☨

To Leonard Woolf

*The Théâtre Antoine was a company founded in Paris in 1887 by André
Antoine, an advocate of the naturalist drama of Zola, Becque, Brieux, and of
contemporary German, Scandinavian and Russian playwrights. Lytton's almost
comic reluctance to speak French, a language he knew extremely well, was
lifelong.*

Chez Mme Bussy
La Souco
Cabbé Roquebroune
A.M.
France
April 13th 1904

Can you imagine June? I'm out of doors, no clothes, roses, oranges, and
flies that copulate all over you. The weather is inclined to be showery,
and the tops of the mountains are covered by clouds. Everything else
high perfection. I turn my head and see the sublime promontory of
Monaco displayed before me, the whole town of Monte Carlo,
mountains and rocks in all the intervals, and a purple sea straight
under my nose. A few hundred feet above us is the antique town of
Roquebroune – antique to rotting. Motor cars whizz past, electric trams
and trains never stop. It is a most extraordinary place. The house is three
inches square – and a dream of beauty. The floors are tiled with smooth
red hexagonal tiles, and partially covered with matting; the walls are
white, the furniture replete with every beauty. A few impressionist
pictures are on the walls. If the whole place were taken up and plunged
400 miles away from everywhere and everything but the flowers and the
frogs, I could live in it forever; as it is there are too many Germans
whirling past it through the air – too many terrific English driving
tandems from Mentone to Monte Carlo and from Monte Carlo to
Mentone just below us and just above us – can you imagine the
amazing scene? Well, I can bear it for three weeks.

I stopped in Paris for a night, and actually went to the Mecca of all
Meccas – the Théâtre Antoine. It was nothing, after all, very
remarkable. The play was a French bourgeois family suddenly plunged
into Russian nihilists – but it didn't really come off. There was a good

deal of Ibsen, and of highly moral and noble tirading – also some jokes, and a rather exciting attempt at a rape – no, not really – only one imagined it might have been. The acting was good, but very studied. The audience were hopelessly stupid and convinced of their brilliant powers of criticism. They said 'C'est très bien, ça' as if it really was.

This household is queer, and I find it difficult enough to talk to my brother-in-law. How can I – in French? And about what? My sister has been reading Moore's last chapter; she thinks it omits all the difficulties, is untrue, and doesn't believe in 'good in itself'. She seems to be in favour of self-determination – or whatever it's called – as being the real good. This is rather discouraging for posterity. The complete conversion of my brother was a great thing – but if intelligent females can't manage it, who can?

I got a long witty letter from Lamb – also a mad biblical one from Turner about his grandmother – I don't pretend to understand it. *[. . .]*

GLS

‡

To Leonard Woolf

La Souco
April 18th 1904

I have been writing to Sheppard and to Turner. Difficult jobs both. To the first I could only tell a quantity of lies, to the second I could say nothing, but nothing, when I should like to say so much. Mon dieu! how much more my imagination likes the second than the first. *There* is someone who at least has prescience, also really supremely understands. But what a terrible occurrence! What a strange phenomenal incrustation! Turner, I think, was still-born into the Society; it was only as an embryo that he really lived.

Cambridge terrifies me with its nearness. In four days it all begins again – are you at all prepared? Have you taken tonics, to brace you up for your wonderful succession of Saturdays? And what on earth are you going to do with the Yen? You'll be nose to nose with him now, and after these confidences – lord! it'll be a business. Wouldn't you like to take over my rooms? Or will everything be a general mist of error and a hideous dream of terror! I feel rather cruel on my terrace, among my

Alps, my roses, and my Mediterranean, so infinitely out of it all. But I'm not, you know, in actuality. I even think of writing to Keynes.

This is a wonderful and fascinating country, but as for living in it −! I don't think I could live anywhere out of England − I should always be moving on. My brother-in-law I cannot talk to, because I cannot talk French − simply not a *word*. He is very 'spirituel' − has a great deal of 'esprit' − paints I suppose well − and − bouffe! − nothing more, that I can see, or anyone perhaps, except my astounding sister. I must say that I am sometimes a little annoyed at their affectionateness. Wouldn't you be? Two people loving each other so much − there's something devilishly selfish in it. Couples in the road with their silly arms round their stupid waists irritate me in the same way. I want to shake them.

I have written to the Goth about Paris and Bell. The meeting will be indeed wonderful if it takes place. I suppose we'll all be arrested and lodged in the Bastille if it does. The noise −!

Dear, dear! Only a quarter past one. Déjeuner over. No tea till four. Too hot to go out. Can only write a hundred letters in this cool green and white room.

> your
> G.L.S.

‡

To Leonard Woolf

Clarissa *is the very long epistolary novel (1745) by Samuel Richardson, whose* Sir Charles Grandison, *published in 1754, was meant to balance it (and his* Pamela), *by portraying a supremely good male character.*

> La Souco
> Cabbé-Roquebroune
> Alpes Maritime
> Friday, 29th April 1904

Your letter was gloomy, but I expected gloom. *[. . .]* I have heard from the Goth, but I'm afraid it will be impossible to bring off the grand meeting in Paris, though I shall perhaps try to see Bell. *[. . .]*

This morning is perfection, and I think of walking up with luncheon into the mountains, where I shall probably be arrested as a spy. I have finished Clarissa. Have you Sir Charles? C. became so dull at the end that I thought I should die – but managed to pull through by inter-mittent doses of the New Testament. My theory of Christ is that he *merely* preached a doctrine of ends, and I now think that the secret of the Xtian religion is that it entirely disregards means of every sort, and gives itself up to the cultivation of ends which are hopelessly inadequate even if they were possible, without telling one how they are to be got. The result of course is complete anarchy; but the theory must have been comparatively sensible when one thought that the world would be abolished the year after next.

I am trying hard to do my damned Spectator article on Shakespeare, but it seems very hopeless. *[. . .]*

I am so out of love that I hardly wish to be in it again. Adieu.

‡

To Leonard Woolf

Russell's 'brood' included his wife, Alys, and her brother, Logan Pearsall Smith, a disappointed, self-styled man of letters, who had bouts of bipolar disease. The family were American, and the women 'plain-speaking' Quakers, who used 'thou' and 'thee'. It must have been difficult to take R. C. Trevelyan seriously as a poet, but Moore managed to do so.

69, Lancaster Gate, W.
June 18th 1904

[. . .] It was going to see the divine Wharton that I passed you – they were giving a garden party. He was fairly divine, but there was a young sister – 15? – with short skirts and long hair, whom I really was more in love with. I believe it's the most degraded form of womanising – but one must begin somewhere. She had a wonderful squashy red mouth all on one side, and as she tipped back in her chair, I really did want just to lift up her short petticoats and see what I should see. When I do love a woman, she'll be immense, and a whore. Isn't that precisely your position? But you, I believe, already do.

Oh dear! Bertie and his brood nearly killed me. I had to fly at the first possible second. He, of course, was the best; he was amusing, he was nice, he read the Athanasian Creed out loud; but good God! his method! I fancy that at heart he is nothing more than George Trevy

with a sense of humour. J'enrage! No – perhaps it's only infinitely
boring. Though at one moment I really thought . . . however, I suppose
it's only invention. But still. . .

As for Pearsall Smith he's only Bob Trevy + America. But how
terribly we're stamped. We can't take Bob Trevy seriously, and no one
else ever thinks of doing otherwise. Are we mad? Is the Yen mad? Or is
the whole world sensible and sane? *[. . .]*

✠

To Leonard Woolf

*Lytton rented Morhanger Park near Cambridge, and away from London, in
order to force himself to work harder on his dissertation. While here he invited
some of his Apostle friends, including Moore, to stay. Leonard was about to
sit his Civil Service examination, a task made worse by the unusual summer
heat. The great mathematician G. H. Hardy had 'taken wings' (formally
resigned) from the Apostles in 1901, and was therefore not obliged to attend
Saturday night meetings even though he was in residence. Lytton has
misunderstood the Scottish sense of 'tenement' – it does not imply a
'slum' but a block of flats. Another resident in their tenement was Dame
Rebecca West, then a child, who once told the editor that she thought the two
men 'remarkably ugly', though contemporary photographs show that Moore at
least was ethereally handsome.*

Morhanger Park
Sandy, Beds.
July 31st 1904

I believe you begin your dreadful affair on Tuesday. I hope you're really
not too depressed. Turner I imagine is in London. So Sheppard reports,
who is here. Oh dear! I'm *fairly bored by him, and as frigid as if he
were a lovely young lady. He talks mostly tosh, of course; does he know
or think of what I think? I am in a *fairly hellish state, which makes me
seem rather magnificent to myself. Horrible illnesses attack me, and I
sometimes think all's lost. But really perhaps the only supremacy is the
supremacy of effort. I feel occasionally like an unchained tiger. Do you?
Perhaps always? But by God! one does have hours of hideous collapse!
Also, I find, of a sort of wonderful, sublimated sentimentality. D'you
know? I have it often at breakfast, when my stomach is all wobbly with

being up so early. I don't know. I seem to have a physical feeling in my abdomen of spiritual affection. But perhaps it's merely lust.

I went to Cambridge the other day, and found Turner in spectacles, with an ear-trumpet, reading the Faerie Queen. Keynes seemed rather important, and Ainsworth was up. As I wasn't there on a Saturday, I missed Hardy at the (quasi) Society, for apparently he really did come one night [. . .] The Ainsworth interlude was *fairly amusing and rather worrying as might be imagined. He came to Moore's quite late at night while I was there and began at once talking the most utter balls to me very hard and without stopping for about an hour and a half. Moore was seen to be simply black with rage on the sofa. I was dead asleep, and found it impossible to relieve matters, so at last departed. Next day, of course, it all came out. Ainsworth complained of the Yen's harsh treatment of him – said that after I'd gone he was simply abused by the Yen for several hours. *I* was all right apparently.

Poor people! They've got a flat in a large slum in Edinburgh. It has two bedrooms, each with two beds in them, so that, as Ainsworth said, if one doesn't mind sleeping two in a room they can put up two guests. He didn't calculate how many if one didn't mind sleeping two in a bed. This joke took rather a long time coming. I suppose you saw it early.

Ah! I'm sleepy. It's past 12. Everyone's in bed; I'm in tears. Quelle vie! To have loved, to have been loved. Oh dear! – so horribly much! To have been forever at such astounding sixes and appalling sevens! Is any of it credible? We begin life in a very odd manner – like ship-wrecked sailors. The world is our desert island.

your
GLS

*3rd time of using in this letter

‡

To Leonard Woolf

This manic letter was preceded by several to Woolf, either urging him to join Lytton at his rented house (Lytton refused to accept Leonard's refusal to come because of lack of funds, saying he had £10, which was surely enough for both of them), or detailing Lytton's occasional forays to nearby Cambridge, mostly to see Moore and Ainsworth. The philosopher Henry Sidgwick (1838–1900) was an

earlier Apostle (elected 1856). Moore was conscious of his debt in Principia
Ethica *to Sidgwick's 1874* Methods of Ethics, *especially to the earlier thinker's
ethical hedonism. The Wright brothers' flight was January 1904.*

Morhanger Park
Sandy, Beds.
September 9th 1904

[. . .] Yes: our supremacy is very great, and you've raised my spirits
vastly by saying so. I sometimes feel as if it were not only ourselves who
are concerned but that the destinies of the whole world are somehow
involved in ours. WE are – oh! in more ways than one – like the
Athenians of the Periclean Age. We are the mysterious priests of a new
and amazing civilisation. We are greater than our fathers; we are greater
than Shelley; we are greater than the Eighteenth Century; we are
greater than the Renaissance; we are greater than the Romans and the
Greeks. What is hidden from us? We have mastered all. We have
abolished religion, we have founded ethics, we have established
philosophy, we have sown our strange illuminations in every province
of thought, we have conquered art, we have liberated love. It would be
pleasant to spend one's days in a perpetual proclamation of our
magnificence; shouldn't all our works be inscribed with the signs of our
grandeur; our splendours, our affirmations, and our desires?

Your letter was wonderful, and I was particularly impressed by the
curious masculinity of it. Why are you a man? We are females, nous
autres, but your mind is singularly male. The 'one word' in mine you
were afraid of I have of course attempted to guess at, but I have no
certainty I'm right, nor can I see, if I am, precisely in what way you're
afraid of it. My unfairness – though at first I naturally believed in it –
now appears to me at least doubtful; and I can only imagine that if
you're not a brute you're utterly absurd. My misery was added to by
Moore's departure – the thought of it, I mean. I really half cried when I
had to see him for the last time in those rooms. Ainsworth I found even
more charming than ever, his comprehension superb, and I loved and
love him more than before. Do you laugh? Well! I admit a stupidity
quite as great as the rest, of course – whether as infinite as Keynes's
seems open to question; but his body at any rate, if not absolutely his
face, is, what Keynes's isn't, and what the Yen himself wonderfully
declared it to be – 'very nice'.

I have read the first two books of Sidgwick, and am much impressed.

He seems to make hardly any false propositions, and the whole thing seems to be extraordinarily weighty and interesting. But Lord! What a hopeless confused jumble of inarticulate matter. It is a vast vegetable mass of inert ponderosity, out of which the Yen has beaten, and welded, and fused his peerless flying-machine. Don't you think Sidgwick contains the embryonic Moore? *[. . .]*

GLS

‡

To Leonard Woolf

The correspondence previous to this shows Lytton's almost despairing reaction to the prospect of Woolf going to work abroad – Hong Kong then seemed the most likely destination. This letter illustrates the workings of the Apostles' old boy network. Sir Edward (Eddie) Marsh (1872–1953), an Apostle of Moore's generation, was then a junior clerk in the Colonial Office, working under Alfred Lyttelton (elected an Apostle in 1878). The next year he became private secretary to the Parliamentary Undersecretary for the Colonies, Winston Churchill, at whose side Marsh remained for the next twenty-three years. Sir Charles Strachey was not an Apostle, but his boss, Bernard Henry Holland (elected a month later than Lyttelton), was. The Greek scholar Sir Richard Jebb OM (1841–1905) had been elected in 1859 and the Master, Henry Montagu Butler (1833–1918), in 1853. In Apostles' argot, only they and Lytton were 'real', as all non-Apostles were merely 'phenomenal'. Networking did not work for Lytton: his fellowship dissertation was rejected. A week later he wrote to Woolf that his supervisor had not encouraged him to resubmit it. So 'I'm almost sure I'll absolutely chuck it' and he would try to live on journalism.

Kingham
Chipping Norton
Oxon
October 4th 1904

Your letter encouraged me a good deal. I hope you really are going to Marsh. Isn't it advisable? I've constantly heard of people quite low down being put in to places because their Uncles happened to be dining with the Under Secretary. If you can get Marsh to put things in train I think it would be worth while my writing to my cousin Charles, who's in the Colonial Office, and could probably induce Holland to do things. These are sordid affairs to fill one's letters with! But I shudder to think of the awful sea of horrors, interviews, crises, jabberations you must be going through. I am here in a sort of nunnery – a happy forgetful sort of place after the gloomy ruin of Cambridge. No, I was never brilliant – generally silly – and of course I ought to have been particularly sane. The whole thing ended up with a dinner at the Lodge. Which really was terrific. *[. . .]* There had been a corresponding party the night before with the rest of the candidates. Good God! It was a shocking business. *[. . .]* I felt it funny to be, with Jebb and the Master, the only reality there!

‡

To Leonard Woolf

This is not so much a letter as an epistolary diary kept by Lytton from 20 November to 1 December 1904, when he was staying at Trinity and attempting to aid the Society in recruiting new Apostles. There was a crisis, as no new members had been elected since Keynes in February the year before. As the document is so detailed, it is difficult to identify some of the people named in it. Hubback, for example, was a failed candidate, as there was no Apostle with that surname.

In a previous letter Lytton had expressed his worries about the safety of their collected correspondence – he wasn't keen on sending it in the post, lest it get lost or be seen by prying eyes. Lytton's 'own experiences' refers to the winter of 1893, when Lady Strachey sent her twelve-year-old son to stay in Gibraltar with his Uncle Charles for five months, in the hope that escaping the English winter would improve his health. The reference to 'I' is to the staircase where the closest lavatories were located. 'Bumf' is toilet paper.

Sir Arthur Lee Hobhouse (1886–1965), disguised as 'Edgar Duckworth' in Holroyd's first edition, was a Trinity undergraduate whose curly yellow hair seemed to some of his contemporaries the brightest thing about him. Lytton and Maynard alike fell in love with him, bamboozled Moore into supporting him, and Hobhouse was elected at the next possible opportunity, in February 1905. He took an undistinguished degree in 1907, and became a respectable Somerset squire and JP; it was to avoid embarrassing him that Holroyd hid his identity. His mother, Margaret, was Beatrice Webb's favourite sister, and his father, Henry, was a Liberal MP and privy councillor. Several Apostles, especially George Trevelyan, felt that the Society had been compromised by the election of Hobhouse on the basis of his looks and the fact that Maynard and Lytton were sexually attracted to him. But, in fact, Trevelyan wrote to Keynes in February 1905, 'I am immensely glad about Hobhouse. I remember him very well and thought he had a distinction of mind which raised him above the other candidates.'[1] *Walter Lamb was never elected an Apostle.*

James Duff Duff (d.1940) had been Lytton's tutor. He was an Apostle of the generation of Whitehead and Lowes Dickinson. George Gilbert Aimé Murphy Murray (1866–1957) was an Australian-born classical scholar. His lecture was on the Euripides play now usually called The Trojan Women. *Jane Harrison, Margaret Verrall and Francis Cornford were all part of the Cambridge classics establishment. 'The Nose' was William Spens, who became a fellow of King's in 1907 and subsequently master of Corpus Christi College. Robert Skidelsky says 'he was religious and musical'.*[2]

On the night of 21 October Rozhdestvensky's Russian Baltic Fleet, on its way to the Far East to fight the Japanese, fired on a Hull fishing fleet at Dogger Bank. 'Moriarty's report' to Cunningham was on the subject of Lytton's rejected dissertation on Warren Hastings. In it, wrote Lytton in an earlier letter to Leonard, Moriarty had used the phrase 'the ethics of composition', but Lytton did not amplify on this. The quotation is from Swinburne's 'Dolores'.

The Decemviri was an undergraduate debating society.

[Cambridge]
November 20th 1904

I suppose the letters will be quite safe – though it would be awful if the ship sank and they were drowned. You wouldn't be, of course. I thought of you starting off yesterday. My own experiences of it I remember distinctly, and wonder if it was the same. Did you find yourself rolling and heaving in the Channel at about nine or ten at night? I wonder if you'll go to bed for two or three days as I did, and wake up on the coast of Spain in high summer. When you get this you will have forgotten all that in the endless succession of new perceptions. Will you see Gibraltar like an island in the distance? Will you be tossed in the Mediterranean, will you sail into Alexandria in a wonderful sapphire sea? I don't know whether to write in the past or the future and I can hardly believe that you'll read this letter. Oh, I don't know, but as I watched your ship in the Channel last night, I thought that all was lost. You have vanished and the kisses that I never gave you, and your embraces that I have never felt – they are all that remains – non-existent and disconsolate entities – the eternal ghosts of our desires and dreams.

Did you pack up the old Anatomy? Have you Sir Thomas in your tin-lined trunk? Does Voltaire accompany you? Is Catullus with you? What news of Shakespeare and Plato? Alas! Beethoven thunders in vain for you, and the ocean has swallowed up Mozart!

I am unhappy because I am speechless and solitary, and happy because I feel so curiously at home. It is charming, I find, to sport in the Society, to go through in pumps to Kings, and to forth in that appalling region in I, with the Cambridge Review for bumf. Do I feel this more now because you don't feel it at all? You're occupied with hideous ladies, I imagine, whom you've never seen before, and never will see again. The freshmen are hideous enough to be ladies as far as I'm concerned, but they're very far from fresh. D. S. Robertson – Hubback's embryo – I talked to for several hours the other evening. He's a trifle Hubbackie – capable, that is to say, de rien – and damned respectful. My favourite Hobhouse still looms unheard, and meanwhile don't be surprised if at any moment you receive a telegram announcing the election of Lamb.

The Society yesterday was graced with the presence of Forster – also the hearthrug. I read – Does absence make the heart grow fonder? – a silly paper on the disadvantages of marriage.[3] They were as silly as the paper, and Sheppard lingered and lingered on the hearthrug in the manner which seems to be fashionable now, with nothing to say. The taupe is up till past next Saturday – when he reads. Meanwhile, for some unknown reason he lives in my room, writing a novel. I feed him with bread and milk, and he never hears anything I say until I've repeated it.

[. . .] It's one in the morning, and I only write to say good night. The Rump was hell. Sheppard was really I believe at his absolutely worst. He raved and ranted and smoked cigarettes without any sort of restraint. Everyone else except Keynes was quite degraded. Nous sommes tous condamnés. Good night!

November 21st–22nd. It's again one. I have just come from Duff who talks a great deal or there wouldn't be much said. Is this method of quasi-diary not too boring? It gives me a good deal of pleasure to write to you once a day, but Cambridge events are horribly monotonous. I'm afraid you may even find them parochial – they twist and turn in so drivelling a circle. And I'm afraid you may feel more unhappy when you read my letters than you ought. Will you write to me? Whatever you do write remember that I shall like it. But I suppose it will make me unhappy too.

This afternoon I went with Lamb to a lecture by Gilbert Murray on the Troiades. Have you ever seen the man? He was really astonishing.

With a bald head and altogether absurdly refined. But he certainly managed to carry affairs through, intoning his own translations in such as way as to make them sound respectable. He's very handsome, slow, deliberate, solemn and refined. The lecture was in the archaeological theatre, and was crowded by Jane, Mrs Verrall, Cornford, The Nose, and all the riff-raff of Cambridge. I wish you could have seen.

Besides that, and Duff, who lectured on Catullus and how to pronounce Admiral Rozhdestvensky, the only other thing I've done today has been to write to Cunningham, expressing my opinion of Moriarty's report. I rather dread the results, but I suppose they'll be really nil. Oh! Duff tells me that Hobhouse is a nephew of Mrs Sidney Webb – i.e. that his mother was one of the seven Miss Potters. Good Lord! But I haven't spoken to him yet. I perceive that this system of letter writing has some of the advantages of a conversation and of a romance. Things will gradually develop as time goes on, but it's a poor substitute for conversation!

> are they, Cotytto or Venus,
> Astarte or Ashtaroth, where?

I said that only a few days ago, and you could hear me. You were sitting where I am sitting now – in the shell *[chair]* directly in front of the fire. Isn't it absurd that now I should be alone? *[. . .]*

November 25th. I've got the devil of a cold, and the whole place has been below freezing point for the last two days. Oh dear, the discomfort! The Decemviri dinner was not so bad as it might have been, as I sat between Hom and Adrian, and there was George Lyttelton to look at. But after it we played blind man's buff, which was most unpleasant. I was in terror of being caught, but fortunately escaped. On the whole I don't think it's worth a pound to sit very close together eating course after course of King's kitchen food and to rag after it until one's digestion has got into one's brains, and one's brains into one's digestion. Bye the bye, have you had a fancy dress ball yet? Or is that reserved for the Red Sea? Your brother had tea with me yesterday and gave me instructions about sending this. But I have few hopes of its reaching you. I must stop, but though for you it's for a week, it's not for me – so there's really no stopping.

I am a mere mass of sniffles and snuffles, but the*[y're]* your

GLS

1. Quoted in Robert Skidelsky, *John Maynard Keynes*, vol.1, p.127.

2. ibid., vol.1, p. 179*n*.

3. Published in Paul Levy (ed.), *Lytton Strachey: The Really Interesting Question*.

‡

To Leonard Woolf

A. J. Robertson was the historian of Anglo-Saxon Charters, the common law and other medieval subjects. In the first volume of his autobiography, Woolf wrote that it was only possible for him to write it because he was able to consult the letters he wrote in reply to Lytton.

   G. M. Trevelyan's book published in 1904 was England Under the Stuarts.

December 2nd 1904

I am an unhappy, cursed creature. My desolation is absolute! Keynes and Sh*[eppard]* are blocks of stone, Lamb a loathsome putty. I only speak to say what I don't think, and they go on eternally in their rounds of dim stupidity. I can get advice from no one, but I feel half sure that it would be best not to come up next term. Hobhouse I think could be easily elected, and to do what I should like to do – to get him, if only in some small way for myself – would I'm afraid need a desperate struggle. The whole place is after him hot foot, and the mere presence of Lamb, like an albatross around my neck, is enough in itself to handicap me vilely. I am like Wolfe on the heights of Abraham – shattered in the hour of victory. For victory I'm sure it is. He's clever –really! – and remarkably charming, though God know it's not in *that* way that I'm likely to be taken. J'ai perdu ma force et ma vie. And perhaps after all even *he* has no feelings. . . I murmur and rave. Oh! It's a poor consolation to get an answer from you – in a month's time.

   Meanwhile I remember the old obliterated scenes – they're all so near me, you see. Going up to Duff, I think I might be going up to you. I pass Turner's old room, and wish I was back again in its cool dark quietness. Do you remember Mafeking night in your room, when Turner smoked five cigarettes all at once? Do you remember the early morning in Angus's New Court room, when Angus made disgusting coffee? Ah! The chaunts of the Urn Burial! And the feeling – new, strange, delightful – of lying in bed at half past two in the afternoon, and getting up to have tea with A.J. Robertson! The sense of these things afflicts me like a physical pain, and I seek relief in sleep. Do you feel them? I fear you may much more horribly than I.

Keynes is the best person to talk to, for he at any rate has brains, and I now believe is as kind as his curious construction allows him to be. Sh. is a wretched spectacle, whom I alternately despise and pity. His bad parts have swelled terribly, but sometimes – I don't know how often – perhaps most when he's alone – he's utterly aware of his abasement. He's genuinely anxious to show his feeling for me – and does so by asking me to be his guest at the Union Presidential Dinner. Isn't this rather pitiful? He knows I hardly like him. And I have cause.

[. . .] On Wednesday morning I trudged off to Trevy, to tell him that I could not do my Voltaire article in time for the January number. He didn't seem to mind, and at once launched into lecture after lecture. It was truly awful. Everything he said was stupid and rude to such a painful degree! I came out grey with rage, and my knees quivered like aspen leaves. In addition to all the old ordinary horrors, he has now become curiously dumb and numb – I don't know what – for he talks as much as usual. But the mechanicity of it all is perhaps what's really so depressing. He's written an article in this week's Independent – is anyone sending you this periodical? or will you be able to get it? – on 'Religious Conformity', full of the rubbish which he's scraped together from all the lieux communs du voisinage for the last hundred years. I believe he's disappointed, almost embittered, and perhaps he doesn't like Janet anymore. His book has come out. Does he think he's immortal? Does he consider that in 200 years' time this passage will be his only memorial? Mort aux vaches! *[. . .]*

‡

To Leonard Woolf

It was the custom following the Trinity College Commemoration feast for college residents and the visitors to gather in a fellow's rooms ('Laurence's') to smoke and talk. The 'tabloids' used to make soup were not newspapers but stock cubes. Henry Jackson O.M. (1839–1921) was an Apostle and eminent classicist; as was Nathaniel Wedd (1864–1940), a younger Apostle of Roger Fry's generation and a self-proclaimed radical.

The Hon. George Lyttelton (1883–1962) was the second son of the 8th Viscount Cobham, who had himself been an Apostle, as had George's uncle, the Hon. Alfred Lyttelton. Educated at Eton and Trinity, he married Pamela

Adeane in 1919 (the jazz musician and wit Humphrey Lyttelton is their son)
and became a master at Eton. In October of 1955, having retired from Eton,
Lyttelton and a former pupil, the middle-aged London publisher Rupert Hart-
Davis, began exchanging weekly letters and the correspondence lasted for seven
years. It was published in six volumes in the 1970s and 1980, and Lyttelton
achieved posthumous fame through The Lyttelton/Hart-Davis Letters. *The*
Way of All Flesh *by Samuel Butler (1835–1902).*

[Cambridge]
December 13th 1904

12 p.m. I haven't written for a long time. I've been overpowered by
sloth. And now I am in the depths of depression. A good many things
have happened – principally Commem – which was exactly as it has
always been – minus anyone to talk to. The speeches – Warre and
Mr Justice Warrington (whoever he may be) were completely dull;
Jackson's was crowded and stupid. There was no Laurence's afterwards,
and a few persons, including MacCarthy and McT[aggart] came and had
soup here, which I made out of tabloids. The MacCarthy revival has
been rather remarkable, but I doubt if it will last. We talked hard for
hours at Jackson's – but the lack of prescience was already beginning to
make itself felt. I expect I shall fade away from him in London – him
and his mother. The zid[1] against Trevy is spreading, and Wedd is
affected. Trevy had engaged to write 'paragraphs' on politics etc. for the
Independent, but now thinks that this is 'not the best use he can make
of his life'. He says he must 'market garden', and then corrects himself
and says he means 'landscape garden' – which means that he is to cut
human minds like Dutch trees into the shapes of balls and peacocks. But
he's so muddled that he's constantly saying 'market gardening' instead,
so that the whole thing is in horrible confusion. *[. . .]*
      December 18th 11 p.m. I forgot to mention my visit to Jackson last
Sunday afternoon – to consult him about Hobhouse in form. You know
his dictum against electing freshmen. I went to inform him that we
thought of doing this. He agreed that it was advisable, admitted that his
rule had exceptions, and said that he thought two years at a Scotch
University was really equivalent to one year here. Wasn't that very
Jacksonian? *[. . .]* On Monday I had lunch with Lamb – to meet – who
do you think? George Lyttelton. The poor creature has sunk into a sort
of demi-semi-intellectual condition, has become an admirer of
Cornford, and takes a deep interest in the question of compulsory

chapel. But he still looks very nice; he is Gothic – but more beautiful and less supreme.

Oh! I forgot to tell you that Turner the other Sunday appeared at breakfast in a peacock-blue silk scarf tied in a bow round a collarless shirt à la a French student. The affair was pronounced a winding-sheet trying to pass off as a domino – a memorial tablet disguised as a triumphal arch – a mortuary chapel fitted out as a temperance lecture hall – an obituary notice printed among the births. I have no more paper, so these similes must cease. Good night!

December 16th. There can be no doubt that the chief boon of the term has been in Keynes. He has become quite merged in the Society – the old phenomenal flair has left him, and he's really interested in the election question – not the Union one. I don't believe he has any very good feelings – but perhaps one's inclined to think that more than one ought because he's so open. Perhaps experience of the world at large may improve him. He has been ill, and I have been twice to see him in Harvey Road. Really the entourage is shocking. Old ladies call, and gossip with Mrs. Keynes. He joins in, and it flashed upon me that the real horror of his conversation is precisely that it's moulded on maiden aunts. After two years in London I believe he'd be much better – but is that saying much?

[. . .] I have been reading La Fontaine's Fables, which I find very soothing, and trying to read the Way of All Flesh. Dead failure. Its dullness seemed to me portentous and its satire very very poor. Nor did I think the interejaculatory remarks profound, and the whole thing is written in MacCarthy's worst style. But perhaps I'm diseased. So all I can say is that Russell admires it. [. . .]

1. This seems to be period Cambridge or Apostle's argot. Though its meaning is clear from the context, I cannot trace its origins.

‡

To Leonard Woolf

As the reference to 'this ghastly cupola' shows, Lytton is writing from the Round Reading Room of the British Museum. Sir Leslie Stephen had died on 22 February this year, and the Stephen family had moved in October from 22 Hyde Park Gate to 46 Gordon Square, where Lytton had tea with them. In the next cabin to Leonard on the ship going out were an Army captain, his wife and

*small daughter, whom the father beat for bedwetting, until Leonard could stand it
no longer and dissuaded him from it, to the fury of the mother. The Italian comic
poet Francesco Berni (1497/8–1535) is often cited as one of the sources for Don
Juan. Sir Sydney Lee (né Solomon Lazarus Levi, 1859–1926), editor of the
DNB from 1891, wrote a celebrated life of Shakespeare, as well as works on the
Elizabethan sonnet. Sonnet 129 begins 'Th'expense of spirit in a waste of
shame/Is lust in action' and concludes 'All this the world well knows, yet none
knows well/To shun the heaven that leads men to this hell'. Lytton was toying
with reviewing Henry Charles Beeching (1859–1919),* The Character of
Shakespeare. *Marie Souvestre was the headmistress and proprietor of
Allenswood school at Southfields, Wimbledon, where Dorothy Strachey (who
had a passionate crush on her) taught courses on Shakespeare, and the school's
pupils included Joan, Pernel and Marjorie Strachey, and Eleanor Roosevelt. She
did indeed die three months after Lytton wrote this letter.*

British Museum
December 21st 1904

I got your Aden letter today, and heard on Saturday that you had
arrived at C[olombo] the day before. It's awful to think how perpetually
you've been moving during the last month, and how I've sat still,
walked a few steps out and in, journeyed a few miles in a train, and sat
down again, while you've been ceaselessly vanishing, away, away, away,
every hour and every second of the day and night. But when you get
this I suppose you'll be settled down, and will hardly remember that
you've ever moved. I am told to write to a hotel. I hope they'll send
things on. It would be pleasant to sweat at 8 a.m. Fogs reign here, and
this ghastly cupola is a vague phantasm of fog and stinking humanity. I
spend the time writing my Spectator sonnet review, which I have not
yet done.[1] When it's printed I'll send it to you – though I'm afraid it
may be boring, pedantic, pompous, involved and sentimental.

　　The Hobhouse crisis took another turn before I left C[ambridge] on
Saturday. He and I generally lunched together during that week at the
Union, so we became rather better acquainted. On Friday I asked him
to tea. He said he couldn't come, as Darwin was coming to him, but he
did come after all, and apparently threw off Darwin. Keynes was there
and we argued and discussed for about two hours. Oh yes! he was really
interested and really nice. Keynes at last went – because, he afterwards
said, he felt that if he had remained a moment longer, he would have
kissed him. Keynes professes himself altogether in love. I don't. I take

what I feel is a sort of Dickinsonian-Sheppard interest in him. I lie
awake and think of him at night. But what else is there to think of?
And I believe he has more feelings than anyone else that's left.

On Sunday I called at the Gothic mansion, and had tea with Vanessa
and Virginia. The latter is rather wonderful – quite witty, full of things
to say, and absolutely out of rapport with reality. The poor Vanessa has
to keep her three mad brothers and sister in control. She looks wan and
sad. I don't wonder.

I have not yet seen Turner – and have taken no steps to do so. It's
wicked; but my mind recoils from the vision of him at our deaf dinner
table – or from talking to him about wills and Aristotle at number 37.
I might, too, go by accident into the working men's college, which I'm
told is in the same street. Could anything be more fearful? Dr Furnivall
– the old Shakespearean donkey – made a speech there the other day, in
which he proposed that 'girls' should be allowed to join. He wanted, he
said, to see the young men with their arms round the young women's
waists; – and their penises, I suppose down the young women's cunts.
Good heavens!

Dickinson sits doing 'politics' out of American authorities, and today
he, Sheppard and I had tea together at the Vienna Café. He doesn't
believe, poor man, that we'll elect Hobhouse – because we didn't elect
Hubback – and they both begin with an H. Did I tell you that Trevy
wrote Keynes a letter saying – I say nothing , but *why* don't you elect
Hubback? He had been for a 'walk' with him, and had discovered that
he 'liked all the right things and the right people'. Keynes replied that
the creature was a reptile. The answer came pat – 'Ah! But if you'd only
elected him a year ago!' All this from one walk. Well, we told Trevy
about Hobhouse – and they went out for a walk together. Keynes
walked with them, and for 15 miles Trevy lectured without any
cessation. There was no possible hope for even the strongest speaker
getting in a word edgeways. Hobhouse was completely dumb. Ecce
Trevy!

Sheppard went for a night to Edinburgh to speak at their Union, and
stayed at that ménage. Moore, in Ainsworth's absence, declared that he
always agreed with Trevy, and that the only thing that could be really
brought up against him was his boringness. Did you ever hear such
perversity? Poor Ainsworth seems to be sinking, and I got a letter this
morning saying that Moore had gone.

December 23rd. Your adventures in Port Said sounded too shocking.
I suppose you will never hear of or see any of the ship's occupants

again, which ought to be rather a relief. I long to hear what Col*[ombo]* is
like, and what you do.

I have been reading Byron's letters, and I find them enthralling. He
was the most beastly brute who ever lived, and perhaps the most
magnificent. I've discovered that Don Juan and La Pucelle have a
common origin – in Italian – perhaps Berni – not as I had thought, that
D.J. was modelled on La P. I find that Lord B. often describes turkish
baths as 'marble temples of sherbet and sodomy'. Isn't that rather
supreme? Why they allowed it to be printed I can't conceive. A propos,
I have had rather a wonderful conversation with my mother on the
subject of the Sonnets. She sent my younger sister out of the room, and
then began – Saying that Sydney Lee presented the dilemma of (1) their
being addressed to a patron or (2) to a catamite – or words to that effect.
I think that this is true, and of course absurd. It's quite clear to my mind
that one *can* be in love with a man without having sexual feelings about
him. I gather that my mother is certain that this was the case. But do
you altogether believe that? There are lines in Sonnet 20 which look
suspicious –

> And for a woman wert thou first created
> Till Nature, as she wrought thee fell a-doting,
> And by addition me of thee defeated,
> By adding one thing to my purpose nothing.

My mother admits that this passage has to be 'got over', but urges a
good many reasons in favour of Shakespeare's 'purity' – no! she didn't
use the word – especially the great no. 129 on lust in action. I think that
only shows he was perfectly aware of the degradations and horrors. But
that he didn't feel them with W.H.? . . . I can't see it. And, good lord,
what does it matter? It really does seem the apex of idiocy to make
everything turn on the wretched physical movements of our unhappy
bodies – but this is the only point of the anti-sodomy movement, *I* was
too discreet to *say* this. But my rage is so great that I want to smash that
fiend Sydney Lee, who – whatever Shakespeare may have been – is
certainly a bugger. I think of reviewing Beeching in the Independent.
And I believe I can do it without hurting susceptibilities – other
people's or my own. This I believe can be done by refraining from use
of the word 'unnatural', which is the root of all evil, muddling and
tomfoolery.

There is a quasi-crisis dragging its slow length along in this
household. Do you remember our infinitely fat Italian Butler? The

other day the Irish 'boy', Timothy, came to my sister, and announced that Bastiani was a drunkard. And it's pretty certain that he is. But he manages to conceal it by staying in bed all day, and only lumbering out to wait at table. So I have already inspected the cellar, and obtained the key. He's to be dismissed after Xmas. There is no other particular news that I can think of. Except that Mademoiselle Souvestre – the eminent woman is ill with nobody knows what. She refuses to let any doctor examine her – no one knows why – but they guess it may be because she's afraid she's got cancer – and writhes in agony. They *think* she hasn't got cancer – but can't tell. It would be a sad loss of so eminent a person if it were.

I shall send you the poems of Alfred de Vigny, when I've a chance. I read some the other day – they're supreme. Oh! They've discovered a Keats MS of Hyperion. It's very interesting – with incredibly marvellous improvements – e.g. Saturn's eyes are described as '*ancient* eyes'. 'Ancient' is scratched out and 'White-browed' put instead; that is scratched out and – oh! triumph – 'realmless' – which is the printed epithet, inserted. But there are many more. I hope an edition, with facsimiles etc., is soon to come out.

This is mainly a phenomenal letter – but I live in a phenomenal world. I say good-bye for the present, and send my love.

your

GLS

1. 'Shakespeare's Sonnets', published 4 February 1905, reprinted in James Strachey (ed.), *Spectatorial Essays*, London, 1964.

‡

To Leonard Woolf

Lytton is comparing the trial of Oscar Wilde to the Calas case in seventeenth-century France. A Treatise on Toleration: In Connection with the Death of Jean Calas, published by Voltaire in 1763, was a tale of a horrible judicial wrong done to a Protestant family. Voltaire's intervention resulted in the king overturning the conviction and pensioning the remaining family.

69, Lancaster Gate
January 6th 1905

I seem to have done a great deal during the last week, but I suppose not
so much as you. The multitude of our actions surprises me; our energy
is really marvellous, and no wonder we sometimes sink into weeks of
sloth. I have been to two plays, a concert, have written a review, and
had two long interviews with Turner – all since last Friday. Isn't that
prodigious? Tomorrow I fly to York, where I suppose I shall subside.

The plays were *[. . .]* Lady Windermere's Fan, which amused me
much more than I'd expected. The wit is really supreme, though the
story balls of the first water. Poor Oscar I believe would have written
something good if they'd allowed him – they made him work the
treadmill instead. Do you think that someday people will wonder at that
story, as they wonder now at the story of Calas? Are we the Voltaires of
the future – freers of the emotions, as he freed the intellect? Dear me!
We hardly take ourselves so seriously. And the case is rather different;
for what do the affections matter, so far as the world is concerned? They
are only good in themselves. *[. . .]*

I visited Turner – for tea – in his Ormond Street lodging house.
[. . .] He came to dinner yesterday, and only just seemed to breathe.
My sister, coming down late, sat down, and began to eat soup, without
having noticed that he was at the table. She jumped when a ghost
nodded. But it was his general tone of apology which seemed to me
so very melancholy; there was hardly any obstinacy to be seen. It was
pitiful – and – good god! – it was dull. At a quarter past eleven he
said that he must go. I summoned up every feeling of antiquity – of
midnight Swinburne, of old jokes – old everything! – and asked him
not to go so early. But it was a difficult job. He lectured on Book
Lamda[1] for half an hour more, and went. But you know, I like him
better than almost anyone. Don't you? We've never said that before.
But isn't it, after all, what *is* the thing? *[. . .]*

1. Book Lambda of Aristotle's *Metaphysics*, sometimes even referred to as
Metaphysics Lambda, where Aristotle argues for the existence of a substance
whose actuality consists in pure contemplation, the prime mover that moves
the entire cosmos without being moved itself.

‡

To Leonard Woolf

Howe Hill was near Harrogate. Strachey's family had removed Oliver from Balliol and sent him on a trip around the world under the wing of the poet Robert Bridges (1844–1930). Oliver then persuaded Lady Strachey to allow him to go to Vienna to study the piano with Leschetizky. Oliver, says Holroyd, was consequently one of the two Englishmen at Brahms's funeral. He was not up to concert standard, returned to England 'in disgrace', and was sent to join the East India Railway. He came back from India with a Swiss wife, Ruby Mayer, and set up house at Howe Hill with (Sir) Ralph Lewis Wedgwood (1st Bt, 1874– 1956), who became, as head of the LNER, the most important railway administrator in the country. He was, in fact, strikingly handsome. He was Moore's contemporary in the Apostles.

Howe Hill, York
January 8th 1905

Your letter came here this morning, with the account of your arrival in Columbo. [. . .] What do you do? Are you a judge, or still a secretary? I am eager to know – I have no idea of anything but what you tell me, which gives me very clear visions. I wonder if you will be able to see across to India, and whether your food is very queer.

This household consists of Oliver and Ruby and Julia (his wife and child), and Wedgwood. Moore has been here since Saturday, and I expect goes to Edinburgh tomorrow. Wedgwood is a quasi Goth – large, strong, ugly and inordinately good-natured. He is rather stupid, but argumentative and jocose; and much better than it's possible to convey in a description. His face is often positively wreathed in kindness of a strange fatherly sort. He likes music and has no perceptions. Moore has been much the same as usual, and of course rather wearing – especially with his damned Turnerismus. He has sung a good deal and played very violent duets with Oliver. I find it rather difficult to talk to him, and he has said nothing of much interest to me. Tonight he came out in a grand discussion with W. and O. with all the usual forms and ceremonies – the groans, the heaves, the tearing of hair, the starting up, the clutching of fists, the frowns, the apoplectic gaspings and splutterings. His point was interesting, but the others seemed to me a little too obtuse and persistent, and I rather wondered how the Yen managed to get so excited. He said that he thought that perhaps scientists had no more reason for saying that ether exists than Christians have for saying that God exists – the point being that neither ether nor God have ever been perceived. He said that ordinary proof demanded that *both* things should be known to exist – or at any rate something like them – I mean by 'both' things like cause and effect. Thus it is possible to argue that sound is carried by waves of air, because it is observed that a tuning-fork vibrates when a sound is made, and it is known in general vibrations are caused by waves. In this case both the vibrations of the tuning-fork, and waves have been observed. But in the case of light, no effect is produced which can be compared to the vibrations of the tuning-fork, and the wave theory is simply assumed. But why should it be assumed? Why should it not be simply stated that light does this, that, and the other because those are the properties of light? Do you understand? The whole interest of this question lies in the meaning of proof, which he is trying to pin down. But of course he admits that he doesn't know how scientists argue in favour of ether, and until he finds that out, it's all a little dim.

I had hoped that he would come to Cambridge next term to give a cachet to Hobhouse's election. But he seemed to dislike the idea so that I hadn't the heart to press him. He said he had to come in the May Term because he's examining.

I feel much less interested in everything that I did two years ago. At least so I think in moments of depression. I have no one to say anything to – except here, in this distant, frigid way. I see no face, no expression; I hardly can imagine that you will ever hear. It is late, and I am exhausted with Schubert and Wedgwood's cheap sherry. [. . .]

‡

To Leonard Woolf

The Durand-Ruel exhibition at the Grafton Galleries, Pictures by Boudin, Cézanne, Degas, Manet, Monet, Morisot, Pissarro, Renoir, Sisley, *was gargantuan, with fifty-five works by Monet, for example, and fifty-nine by Renoir. In his championing of Impressionism Lytton has singled out Titian's* Bacchus and Ariadne *for his (ludicrously) unfavourable comparison probably because of the familiarity of the picture in the National Gallery. Among the 'sordid and terrible' pictures by Degas was the 1876–7* Woman Ironing.

Lancaster Gate
January 16th 1905

[. . .] Oh, I was really excited in York for a few minutes. Over what do
you think? The Kreutzer Sonata. I suppose you must have read it,
though I can't remember your having said anything definite about it.
But don't you agree that the description of the murder is tremendously
exciting? I simply tore over the pages in a way unknown to me for so
many million years. I also thought the description at the beginning of
the railway carriage, etc. quite superb. Of course all the sermon padding
is maddening, although I must say it's at any rate outspoken and not
ashamed to expose its fundamental indecency. Talking of fundaments,
my present opinion is that one's best feelings occur at the age of
fourteen – at the time of one's first passion. It isn't because one's not
indecent. I'm sure one completely is – but because one's feelings are so
marvellously simple, and yet so violent. I'm sometimes overcome with
desperate wishes for those immaculate states of mind, which will never
return. *[. . .]*

January 20th. I forgot to mention the wonderful exhibition of French
Impressionists now going on in London. It is the collection of a person
called Durand Ruel, who bought all these pictures for 2½d when they
were first painted. There are millions of them, and all worth looking at.
The general effect is one of dazzling beauty – sheer physical pleasure to
the eye. It's quite clear, after looking at them, that no one knew how to
do colour before. The idea of other pictures revolts me. Imagine the
utter horror of the colouring of Bacchus and Ariadne! Red and blue
simply laid on thick, as a child lays them on in the nursery. The worst
of it for you is that you *must* see the real things, because it's part of their
very essence that they can't be photographed. Perhaps the most
supreme, and certainly the most amazing are the Degas. They're utterly
sordid and terrible – materially tragic. I grovelled and fled. *[. . .]*

‡

To Leonard Woolf

*This over-excited letter was written over a period of at least five days. Several
repetitive pages of analysis and reporting of Lytton's relations with Hobhouse,
Keynes and Lamb are omitted from the middle of this epic-length letter. Lamb
seems at one point to be getting close to learning the secret of the existence of the*

Apostles; at any rate, he senses that Lytton and Maynard have a secret they are keeping from him and, thinks Lytton, is offended.

'The curse' was a recitation of the anathema pronounced on Henry John Roby (d.1915), who had been Senior Classic in 1853. He was elected the 134th Apostle in February 1855, but decided he didn't care for the already venerable Society's ethos, and quit – the only member ever to have done so. The 'Book' containing the signature of every member notes beside his name, 'Resigned and cursed 1855'. It became the custom to read the curse aloud when initiating a new member. The explanation of Wedd's choice of paper at the Saturday night Apostles' meeting is that occasionally when no one had prepared a paper, one previously given would be retrieved from the archive, the 'Ark'. Wedd, instead of reading one of his own previous papers, asked to be allowed to deliver one from the Ark, and the choice fell upon a paper first read by Russell on 3 March 1894. Its Ibsenite title ('Loöberg' = Lövborg) concealed an argument that women should be admitted to membership of the Society. Robin Mayor (1869–1947) was an Apostle elected in 1889, and O.B. was the preposterous Oscar Browning (1837–1923), elected in 1857, and the subject of hundreds of stories.

'Mrs. Gov't Agent' was the wife of John Perry Lewis, 'the kind of wife', wrote Woolf in the first volume of his autobiography, 'which so many slow, silent, shy men marry. Large, plump, floridly good-looking, she never stopped talking at the top of her voice. She exploited what, I think, must have been a thick streak of congenital vulgarity and went out of her way to say the most outrageous things at the most awkward moments.'

Trinity
February 15th 1905

I must tell you at once that all has passed off well – no refusal, or crisis of any sort. He declares he has not heard of the Society before, and he seems correspondingly vague. I don't think he yet grasps the essentials, but regards it as an inflated and ornamental debating society. Sanger was up, and came to lunch etc., which gave a glow to the proceedings. He (S) talked wonderfully and almost continuously, arguing a great deal with Hawtrey, and slandering the members of the Cabinet without any restraint. The meeting was gloomy, though Keynes's paper wasn't so bad. It was impossible to say anything, except what was irrelevant, and this Hawtrey accomplished with some skill. Hawtrey says he's discovered a new disease – irrelephantiasis. It's true he himself suffers from it a good deal less than other people. But doesn't one wish he had it a little more? *[. . .]*

The grave crisis is with Keynes. I saw him alone this afternoon, and told him nothing. I fear he may have guessed, and it would be wretched if he thought I was deceiving him. But why should I have told him? It was in the nature of a confidential communication – what passed between Hobby and me. And Hobby is just as much in the Society as Keynes is. But here am I, who eagerly sucked in Keynes's own revelations, remaining mum when my turn arrives. I feel uncomfortable, and what's worse despair of avoiding some terrible éclaircissement. Also I can't help thinking that a great deal of it has only arisen from my own folly. My blithering must have encouraged Keynes to fall in love. He's in, and what am I? Heaven knows (and you, I hope); and is it my business to put obstacles in the way of so legitimate a passion? *[. . .]*

There is nothing to tell but that he likes me enough to say that he'll come and see me every day. There can be no doubt that we are friends. His conversation is extraordinarily alert and very amusing: He sees at least as many things as I do – possibly more. He's interested in people to a remarkable degree. N.B. He doesn't seem to be in anything aesthetic, though his taste is good. His prescience in character is really complete. He analyses with amazing persistence and brilliance. I've never met so active a brain. (I believe it's more *active* than either Moore's or Russell's.) His feelings are charming, and, as is only natural, in perfect taste. His youth is extreme; this makes you wonder whether I'm not sentimental about him. But I'm not – and I can prove it: he perpetually frightens me. One can't be sentimental about a person whose good opinion one's constantly afraid to lose. *[. . .]*

Saturday – the meeting, curse, etc. Wedd was to have read an old paper – it was supposed of his own; but when the moment came he asked for one. We could only produce good old Loöberg and Hedda – the worst possible paper for the occasion. Theodore was there, and Mayor, who had nobly come up at the last moment on hearing of the birth. Hobby was very much embarrassed on the hearthrug, said merely twaddle, and hurriedly fled to his seat. I discovered afterwards that he actually had thought that the curse was the minutes of the last meeting – did you ever dream of such a thing? Isn't it a little too much – even for a babe? *[. . .]*

Dear, dear, I find I have forgotten a singular interlude. On Sunday I lunched with the O.B. He caught me a few days before, going down Keynes's staircase, and at once asked me why I never went to see him. I didn't know what to say, and was forced to accept Sunday lunch. 'Do you know, Strachey,' he wound up, 'I don't believe you know how much respect I've always had for you, and, if you'll allow me to say so, how much affection.' The old reprobate! His smutty stories, as reported by Keynes, would I expect startle Mrs. Gov[ernmen]t Agent. He declares that when he was at Eton it was the universal fashion for two persons, whenever they were alone in a room, to abuse each other with their hands as they sat. So much was this the case that it was not good form to come into the room without giving a little cough as one did so. He got so much into the habit of giving these little coughs that when he came up to Kings no one could imagine why he always did it. His railway journey story is a good deal worse. He was in a corridor train – there were a lot of Winchester boys – and a lavatory at the end. At the beginning of the journey one of the boys went into the lavatory and stayed there. One by one all the other boys went in and came out again, having buggered him in the interval. The result was that towards the end of the journey the floor was inches thick in semen, and the boys slipped about, one on the top of the other. Eventually the O.B. himself swam through the ocean to the appointed spot. *[. . .]*

‡

To Leonard Woolf

Edgar was one of Leonard Woolf's brothers.

At Eton Maynard Keynes had an intense and probably sexual relationship with Alfred Dilwyn ('Dilly') Knox (1885–1943), with whom he took his meals for four years. Knox became a classics don and ace cryptographer – along with Oliver Strachey he played an important role in the Bletchley Park team that cracked the German 'Enigma' code in World War II. Lytton originally thought that Maynard's confession about a second romantic liaison at Eton was about Bernard Winthrop Swithinbank (1884–1958), a Balliol man who became a career civil servant in Burma. But, as Lytton indicates with his asterisk, Maynard was actually talking about the boy who later became his publisher, Daniel De Mendi Macmillan (1886–1965), who was also at Balliol with Swithinbank. The boy who interrupted the tryst between Knox and Keynes was Gerard Mackworth Young (1884–1963).

Moore was coming to Cambridge to take part in the vote to retain or abolish the University's compulsory Greek entrance requirement. The play by GBS was How He Lied to Her Husband, *which had opened at the Berkeley Lyceum Theatre on 26 September 1904.*

Trinity
February 28th (Tuesday) *[1905]*

On Friday I walked with Edgar, who told me that all your books had
been destroyed by bad packing. How appalling, if true! E. seemed
somewhat sterilised – perhaps it is old age. He said you said you were
depressed in your last letter. I asked him whether he hadn't known that
before. Apparently he hadn't thought of it, which seems queer. *[. . .]*

Well, I hadn't done with confidences. Can you bear another one? At
any rate it's a contrast. On Sunday evening, in that awful state one gets
into then, I went to my pigeon holes, and took down the letters from
Sheppard. As I read them, I nearly expired with horror – they were
echoes of such a remote and agonising past. Do you know that there's
no doubt that he was in love with me quite as he ought to have been at
the beginning of the incident? His letters show this plainly, though I
hadn't realised it before. However, that's a side issue. Keynes came in,
and found me reading; I couldn't avoid retailing some of the memories;
and then *he* began to retail his. Very odd, and really rather pathetic – his
Eton story. He had – well, very curious relations with two of his
younger companions – Knox and (I presume, for he didn't say so)
Swithinbank★ (★No. Macmillan *[added later]*). His goings on with Knox
were the most amazing. Their intercourse was quite unrestrained, but
limited altogether to the physical. Knox never spoke; he just submitted
himself; and no one ever knew. I said 'quite unrestrained' – that is
essentially. In practice there was one pitch that was never reached. The
incident was singular. One evening as he passed Knox on the stairs he
said 'Come to me tonight at ten.' Knox gave no answer, but came, lay
on the sofa, and, when lights were put out, stayed on. Keynes undressed
and got into bed. Knox was just hesitating, when another boy, Young,
knocked at the door, and asked for matches. He came in before he
could be stopped – there are no locks to Eton bedrooms – and Keynes
had to get out of bed and get him a match, which Young immediately
struck. He saw queer things – Keynes stark naked, and Knox still lying
silent on the sofa. He fled without a word, and so did Knox – his nerve
had left him. Both he and Young are now at King's. But still Keynes has
never spoken to him on the subject, and still he doesn't know how
much Young gathered in that astonishing second. Do you smile?

The Knox affair paled off because of Swithinbank, which was a very
different business, almost devoid of lust. In the night, as Swithinbank lay
in bed, Keynes sat with him. On the bed, talking, long after lights were

out. How often this happened! Perhaps, for all I know, every night. And then, when their talk was ending, Keynes would lie down on the bed, and embrace him and kiss him, and kiss him, and kiss him, again and again; and so they would part at last. I don't know – the image of our ugly Keynes makes all this rather ridiculous – and rather pathetic too. The vision of the dark room and the white bed and the curious ecstasy there I find attractive – soothing in a strange way. These last three pages are I suppose unparalleled in the annals of known correspondence. How many persons do they put under criminal imputations? What scandals! What disclosures! And yet Heaven knows there's nothing abnormal in the whole account. It's only that I happen, for the first time, very likely, in the world's history to give the account. And, aren't you touched by it? Poor little Swithinbank could never quite believe that he wasn't doing something wrong when he let himself be kissed. The brutes! The devils! To such a length have they carried their abominable★ (★I really must put it in for the swing of the sentence *[inserted at the top of the page]*) perversions of things! They were the best moments of his life.

Do you wonder where I am? – In London! I came up on Wednesday – it's now Friday – to go to the Gothic housewarming party. It wasn't very amusing, but amusing enough. Yesterday I went again, for the Goth is 'at home' on Thursday evenings, and, of course, found simply Turner. Nothing was said of any interest, but the vision of the Goth among his books is a pleasant one. I return to C. today; and expect to see Moore there. He is coming up to vote for Greek, but whether he'll stay over Saturday I don't know, but rather suspect not. I got a letter from Ainsworth the other day about the 'Reading Party'. Apparently there is to be one – in Yorkshire. It sounds cold, but I think I shall go for the whole time. Is it true that you are going to the Pearl Fisheries – wherever they may be? Edgar said something about it. Will you discover a pearl worth half a million, and come home and found hospitals? Oh, by the bye, I went to the theatre yesterday – a curious hole and corner matinée, with a new one-act play by Bernard Shaw in it. I suppose Bernard Shaw is dimmer even than other things to you – he is so typically temporary and local. But I was amused. Marsh I saw in the stalls (I was in the Pit) with one of his lovely ladies. He irritated and charmed as usual.

Love to Mrs Gov't Agent!

✝

To Leonard Woolf

The third paragraph refers to the 'Zanzibar Hoax', when Adrian Stephen and a group of his Cambridge friends impersonated the suite of the uncle of the Sultan of Zanzibar, who was visiting England at the time. Lytton got it slightly wrong, as they decided not to pretend to be the Sultan himself, he was too recognizable. They hired costumes in London and sent a telegram to the Mayor of Cambridge, alerting him to the grandee's arrival. The costumed hoaxers were welcomed by the mayor and taken on a tour of the town and colleges. The Daily Mail *later exposed the hoax.*

Elizabeth von Arnim (1866–1941) was a popular novelist whose best-known work was Elizabeth and Her German Garden, *published anonymously in 1898, and describing her life in Pomerania (and the garden she made there) as the wife of a German count. Like Forster, Hugh Walpole tutored her children. She had been a lover of H.G. Wells and, following her husband's death, married Bertrand Russell's brother, the 2nd Earl Russell, in 1916. A cousin of Katherine Mansfield, she had been born Mary Annette Beauchamp in Sydney, Australia. She was respected in Lytton's circle for her wit, and for her interesting feminist slant on marriage. Dean Swift became intimate with his 'Stella', Esther Johnson, and it is even possible that some form of marriage took place. Though it seems astonishing that Forster did not know about the affair, English literature was not yet taught at Cambridge and Swift was a less familiar writer to that generation than he is now.*

Trinity
Wednesday, March 8th *[1905]*

Oh dear! Something has happened of such a nature –

But I *can't* go into it yet, I must give some account of other things. – I feel I must. *[. . .]* Look here, I'm writing the merest balls – I want to tell you –

Well, shall I tell you about the Sultan of Zanzibar and the Mayor of Cambridge and who the Sultan was and why the Trinity Porters didn't recognise Adrian? I can't.

Oh my God! I'm almost at the end of my tether. I'm in a state of intolerable collapse. Do you bear with me? Do you think of me? Will you understand? I feel so shattered, so abjectly shattered, that I don't know how to say anything, or what I have to say. Ciel! Que lui vais-je dire? Et par où commencer?[1] Hold my hand, be kind, love me; for I need all your love.

I walked out with Hobby on Monday. We got as far as the Observatory, when it began to rain; we turned back, and, when we parted at the Kitchen Office, I felt a hideous void. It came upon me suddenly that I was bored with everything, with every look, with every thought – everything, you know, except him. [. . .] I went round to Keynes, seething and wild. I half let him know that I was almost as much in love with Hobby as he. [. . .] On Tuesday [. . .] Keynes burst in, radiant. I wondered vaguely what was up; he beamed and talked at me from the fireplace in a wild confused way – for Keynes, and then I realised it. He'd, as he said, 'proposed'. And been accepted. [. . .]

[. . .] In the meantime try to realise the reason of my excitement, my desperation, my tears. Perhaps you'll do this better than I. You won't think I've been describing a merely sordid little drama; you'll see what at least I *think* is involved. I mean Hobby's goodness – his best parts, his affection, whatever you like. Oh! and there's something else. My own unutterable silence – my dead, shattered, desolated hope of some companionship, some love. The door of Paradise has been cruelly sported in my face.

Meanwhile my daily fare of martyrdom are the confidences of Keynes. Exactly what happened, what each said, how he looked, how restrained it's going to be, etc. etc. I try hard to keep myself in some sort of control, and am dreadfully afraid that I may receive Keynes's pity or ridicule. I'm in half a mind to go down at once, and sometimes I have wild thoughts of putting out all my strength and snatching the prey from under his nose. Isn't the whole thing too loathsome? Today it's been crescendoed by the Taupe – who has lingered out several hours here quite indeterminately, while I lay and grunted and asked him what he thought of Keynes. He liked him. I said he was mechanical. He said 'I beg your pardon?' And then, when I had remained silent for some moments, added 'Yes, I heard.' He's going to teach English to the infant daughter of Elizabeth and her German Garden. I asked him whether he wouldn't feel like Swift with Stella. But he hadn't heard of them.

Friday. I am comparatively calm and happy. Yesterday my horrors seemed to fall from me, and I suddenly wrote a poem, which was surprising. I believe I'm in the state it describes. I'll copy it out.

Keynes is vague and doesn't really care. Hobby is vague and doesn't really take an interest. I am vague and don't really mind. I seem to have written very frantically, and to have spelt 'way' 'weigh'. Well, I felt it all, and I daresay I'll feel it all again this evening or tomorrow or next year. Have I really a strain of madness in me, which occasionally bursts out into as fizz? Yes! Don't I wish that I was floating with you over golden seas to golden suns. Les choses les plus souhaitées n'arrivent point: ou, si elles arrivent, ce n'est ni dans le temps ni dans les circonstances où elles auraient fait un extrême plaisir.[2] I consulted the sortes Falstaffianae upon Keynes, and found 'Hang the mechanical salt-butter rogue!'[3] Rather good? Dear, dear! When one goes into Hobby's now, one has to be careful to knock very loudly and wait a few moments before going into the room. It's like the OB's story of his days at Eton. One doesn't know what one mayn't be interrupting. My poem suggests that all *that* should be given up.

> Well, let us make the best; and that shall be
> That, to the end of things, we shall be free.
> Let us wipe up for ever all our tears,
> And you forget your youth, and I my years.
> Oh! let us smile, not laugh; and never miss
> The daily circumcision of a kiss.
> Let us be patient, virginal, and proud;
> And let one garment wrap us, and one shroud.
> Are you not I? I you? Both, if you will,
> One healing soul that stands divided still?
> Or one wide river branched about an isle?
> Or one glance from two eyes? Or two lips' smile?
> One benediction from two hands that bless?
> No name can bound or part us, limitless!
>   Then, if these things be so, why to the smart
> Apply fresh salt, and break the broken heart?
> No, no! With bitterness our days too full
> Must hold that fruit which all the world may pull;
>
> Our house, our book, when all is built and said,
> One secret room, one sentence never read
> Must keep; and then at last we'll mount above
> Our little less than lust and more than love
> Into that region where our strange belief
> Shall find the long dim triumph of our grief.

Farewell! I think of you all day.

GLS

1. Racine, *Phèdre*, I.
2. Jean de la Bruyère, *Les Caractères*.
3. Shakespeare, *The Merry Wives of Windsor*, II,2: 'Hang him, mechanical salt–
butter rogue!'

‡

To Leonard Woolf

This letter contains hundreds of lines of verse, of which these are the most
interesting.

Trinity
Saturday, March 11th [1905]

[. . .] I have become a poet. I sit up till three a.m. writing in the style of
Dr. Donne. Isn't this very remarkable? And what is more so is that
everything I write is strictly fit for Publication. Shan't I achieve fame,
accept a deanery, and live happily ever after?

[. . .] I have been ill with a suppressed cold all the week, and with
never going to bed, and never stopping poem writing. I send you what
I've done, though I feel it's a wretched way to make up for a letter. I
don't know whether my poems will cheer you, but I expect they'll
chiefly puzzle you. Remember that 'You' in them = Hobby, and
'He' = Keynes. I notice that since Saturday some of them have become
a little unfitted for print. *[. . .]*

Je suis épuisé.

VI.   To Him

What do I think of when I think of you?
I think of a type-written billet-doux;
A coloured photograph of Cupid's balls;
A safety bicycle with genitals;
A rocking-horse endeavouring to fuck;
A weather-cock that happens to be stuck;
A paper rose; a manufactured egg;
A highly self-complacent wooden leg;
A eunuch with his fly-buttons undone;

A puzzle that is plain to everyone;
A tedious poem that one learns by heart
For an examination; a faint fart
Made by a bishop reading family prayers;
A gramophone that plays Corelli's airs;
A useful cypher; an abortive womb;
A box of biscuits by an empty tomb.

March 16th

The Category

I am not of them, though I see
Their long line stretched in front of me,
Where each awaits in turn your phantom kiss,
Like ticket-takers at a box-office.

Who would be of them? Who would seek,
In herds, your indiscriminate cheek?
Or strive in competition to hold tight,
With firmer fist than theirs, your shaft of light?

Yet he is of them; though his dreams
Have even, Danae-like, subdued your beams,
His very triumph puts him in his place:
He's most a runner who has won the race.

March 16th

✝

To Leonard Woolf

'The C Minor' symphony is Beethoven's Fifth, op. 67.

The 'Anthology' became Euphrosyne, A Collection of Verse, *published privately in the summer of 1905, with contributions by Turner, Lytton, Leonard, Clive Bell and Walter Lamb, and some others. Virginia Stephen thought it pretentious and conceited, and wrote an unfinished but scathing essay about the poor use to which these University men (whom she so envied) had put their education. In later life most of the 'poets' wished to forget the book had ever been produced; but, said Quentin Bell, Virginia did what she could to keep the memory of it green.*[1]

69, Lancaster Gate
Monday, April 3rd *[1905]*

Wonderful to say I have finished the essay. The work was appalling and
degrading, as you may imagine, and how it was carried through I can't
conceive. Yesterday my prowess reached its height. I still had a chapter
on Elizabethan letter-writers to write. I wrote one page in the morning.
In the afternoon the C. Minor was being performed; I couldn't resist it,
and went, finishing the chapter somehow or other in what remained of
the day. The Symphony wrecked me just as usual, and in the same place
– the sudden plunge into infinite glory at the beginning of the fourth
movement. On the whole I hardly think it's worth it – I don't believe
you miss very much – only the opportunity of getting spiritually drunk.

Today – imagine! – I went to Cambridge. I had to – to deliver the
essay before the end of Term into the hands of the Vice Chancellor. I
was there exactly an hour, having tea with Erasmus Darwin. I believe
I forgot to tell you that one of the events of last term was a rapprochement with Erasmus. Oh! we like each other so much. He's a dim dim
Goth to me; – Lord knows what I am to him – a loud loud Lamb,
perhaps. However, there it is – the rapprochement; and you may expect
to hear that I've seen him once a fortnight next term.

I'm tired to death – both my legs are broken, my heart sunken, my
purse emptied, and all my body breaking into boils. If I get £50 it'll be
worth it; but supposing I don't?

On Friday I join Moore and Ainsworth at Harrogate, whence we
proceed together to Pateley Bridge, or somewhere – on a moor in
Yorkshire, MacCarthy to follow. *[. . .]* I'm rather nervous at not having
had a letter from you this week – only because I conceive that my
letters may not have arrived. Supposing one of them went astray, how
should we know? Could you tell from the rest?

[. . .] Wednesday 12.30 p.m. Yesterday I went to Somerset House to
discover Turner and have lunch with him. It's an appalling place – a
vast rabbit-warren of rooms, all pullulating with human beings. I found
Turner by chance, after whirling up a thousand staircases and down a
thousand passages. Someone came out of a room – No. 284 – and left
the door open. I thought I'ld look in, without showing myself. I did
and there was Turner. There were three other people in the room,
which made it rather awkward. However, we went out and had lunch
in a Slater's Restaurant. The dullness was rather heavy, though slightly
enlivened by Turner's revived project of an 'Anthology'. He seems to

think that he'll be able to induce Bell to finance it, in which case I, at
any rate, don't mind contributing, under the strictest veils of anonymity.
Will you? Mightn't it be rather fun? But quite, quite mad.

Tonight I went to pay the Goth a visit. He seemed rather low
spirited – I suppose we both did. But we didn't say so. He works hard
preparing for the bar, and talks mainly about dreary cases. But, when I
consider, wasn't his conversation always dull? *[. . .]*

1. See Quentin Bell, *Virginia Woolf*, vol. 1, p. 98; her commentary is reprinted
as Appendix C.

‡

To Leonard Woolf

*At Moore's annual Easter reading party this year, Lytton was alone with Moore
and Ainsworth for most of the three weeks. Moore was either engaged upon a
late review of Russell's 1903* Principles of Mathematics *or he was working on
Russell's 1905 article in* Mind, *'On Denoting'. Lysias, the fifth-century BC
rhetorician, was one of the protagonists of Plato's 'Phaedrus'. Lysias's speeches
were edited by Walter Lamb.*

The eponymous protagonist of Sir Charles Grandison *is both heroic and a
great fixer, a paragon of virtue. Jane Austen admired the book so much that she
dramatized parts of it. In Racine's* Phèdre, *Théramène is the 'governor' of
Hippolyte, the queen of the Amazons.*

Moore played Beethoven's Waldstein Sonata, *Op. 53.*

*'Bob' is Robert Trevelyan; Walter Dodgson (b.1866) was elected in
November, 1890; he was 'lapsed' in the sense that he never bothered to resign
formally from the Society.*

The Crown Hotel
Middlesmoor
Pateley Bridge
Yorks.
Sunday, April 16th *[1905]*

We still drone on here – a somewhat blighted trinity. No MacCarthy as
yet, so that I still have to support as I can the burden of amusement.
You may guess that I more often subside than not. Moore seems to
have relapsed almost altogether. He himself admits that he's 'always

comatose' – i.e., I suppose, takes no interest in anything. He's at present engaged on an elaborate review of Russell's book. This I expect will be supreme – his intellect certainly hasn't stopped soaring; the question is whether the rest of him isn't simply drying Turnerianly up. The only stimulation he can possibly get now is from his work – Ainsworth may stimulate his irritation, but that's all. Ainsworth has sunk into a state of incredible imbecility. That is to say, he's managed to retain all his old familiar folly, and to lose the one thing which, my present theory is, kept it within bounds – his discontentedness. He's now quite happy. He reads the speeches of Lysias, and gives muddled accounts of them in his conversation; he occasionally says – 'Strachey – you look unhappy'; and that's all. He seems to live in a sort of futile complacent dream made up of incorrect Greek derivations, with an undercurrent of frenzied disconnected babble about aesthetics and Plato's philosophy. He remembers Cambridge merely as a place where the O.B. once lived, and Jackson used to lecture. Hobby he has mentioned precisely once – in a bracket, in a sentence about compulsory Greek. Perhaps I'm laying it on rather thick and black – it's just conceivable that the presence of Moore may keep him in an artificial state of repression; and of course it may be *my* fault that he doesn't speak – but really if you'd heard him at tea just now on the state of mathematics in the Age of Pericles – Well, I believe my irritation is founded on good stolid fact. But isn't it rather a poor outlook for the Yen if this is true? *He's* not contented, there's no doubt; if anything he's peevish and snappy – almost spoilt. It is preposterous how easily one's attitude towards a genius becomes purely human, after one's lived in the same room with him for a week. We would have found Shakespeare quite intolerable, Beethoven would have driven us mad – in a fortnight we would have fled – leaving them in the arms of Ainsworth. Oh, Christ! my loneliness here, with these friends of so many years, who have shared so much, who have known so much, who are so intimately bound – I believe it almost equals yours. I feel desperately homesick – but for what home? My mind is sick with imagining heavens and havens of wedded happiness. Contrived and triumphal dreams nauseate me; I have a surfeit of unexperienced splendours. I long for real kisses which will come in ways I have never guessed of, and unexpected hands which I can touch.

The country here is on the whole loathsome – also the weather. Of this 'Hotel' the best that can be said is that it has a fascinating forthing arrangement – a sort of close-stool (oh, by the bye, when I used the

word, Ainsworth asked what I meant), which somehow swivels down
when you sit on it, and, when you get up, flies up again, bringing a
suitable quantity of earth onto your turds. I really can't exactly explain
it, but I'm sure it's far the healthiest method, and then it's so
entertaining. Pray introduce it into Ceylon.

Tuesday 18th. It's perfectly absurd, but I'm simply longing to depart.
Last night it came upon me violently that I should be so much happier
anywhere else. Is it altogether my fault? Am I impossible? I believe
perhaps I am – one of those 'eccentric English' who can only live in a
splendid isolation. I shall buy a hut on a hill in Heligoland, and live and
die there. Isn't it ridiculous that after a week one should find one's
dearest friends quite insupportable? I suppose the disease is really
mutual. Moore's got into a state of almost cynical depression, from
which only a delicate feminine cajolery could get him out; *that* I can't
supply. Ainsworth – oh, lord! I suppose some wonderful Grandison
could manage even him. As it is – I don't know, of course, whether it's
not simply the result of my own self-centeredness – but both of them
constantly strike me as being brutal. On the whole it would be folly, I
think, to blame anyone, even myself, and all that can be reasonably said
is that *this* ménage à trois, at any rate, is incompatible. Je pars, cher
Théramène! But without any assurance of being happier in London. I
am restless, intolerably restless, and Cambridge is the only place I never
want to leave, though I suffer there more than anywhere else. And
Cambridge I shall have to leave, in two months, for ever. I talk blither,
and what is worse egotistical blither. I can only believe it may amuse
you, for I can think of nothing else to say. I might regale you with a
few select specimens of Ainsworth's conversation, but the horror of
transcribing them –! Moore cannot be transcribed because he never
speaks. He limits himself to 'Ohs' which are sufficient to blockade any
remark of yours, and then everything lapses. MacCarthy, I forgot to say,
hasn't yet come – he says he will tomorrow. I haven't yet announced
that I intend to go on Friday – I originally said I'ld stop three weeks.
The only amusement I now have to look forward to is their remarks
when I do make the announcement.

Wednesday. Well, I've made it, and – did you expect it? – had to
give way. I'm to stay for heaven knows how much longer. Yesterday
evening we had the Waldstein. It seemed to stimulate the Yen, who
became, after it, almost excited. I saw the old Moore again – yes! It's
come to that. He talked without being made to, and was almost
affectionate. So you see, when I said I should have to go, I was already

beginning to be melted; and when they both at once declared it was out of the question, I simply lapsed. It is true that I shall have to borrow from the Yen, but that's a detail. *You* certainly gain, as there may be something amusing to report. Angels are expected at the end of the week.

Thursday. At present there's damned little in the reporting line. No MacCarthy; but Sanger expected today, Crompton tomorrow. Bob on Monday, and possibly Wedd. Also a mysterious lapsed brother called Dodgson, who lives at Leeds, may be brought by Crompton, who apparently elected him. Quel mélange! I hope for Wedd – it would add so much to the madness, but on the whole I feel bored. There is nothing to do but to eat, and have stomach aches – it's impossible to face the perpetual blizzard out of doors. Don't you feel that I'm very remote? Oh! I half want to stay here – by myself – forever. It would be so charming if everything were to become altogether a dream. If one could infinitely lapse! At present I'm in one of those dreams when one knows one's dreaming. I remember that Cambridge exists. I'm haunted by a dread – by an uneasy remorseful feeling – about Hobby. I don't know – it's a doubt, a damned doubt, which is too real to fit in with any fantasia. – Ought he to have been elected?

your

GLS

To Leonard Woolf

A 'grind' is late nineteenth-century Cambridge slang for a ferry. 'Cole' is probably William Horace de Vere Cole (1881–1936), the greatest practical joker of modern times.

The 'Trevy-Pollock' gossip concerned the situation a year earlier, when Jack Pollock had wanted to marry Gladys Holman Hunt. The couple refused on principle to be married in church, which outraged his mother, Lady Pollock. George Trevelyan, who had suffered a nervous breakdown shortly after his own marriage, owing, some thought, to similar pressure from his own mother-in-law, Mrs Humphry Ward, was incensed by what he called Lady Pollock's persecution of Jack and Gladys. Sir Charles Philips Trevelyan, 3rd Baronet (1870–1958) was the elder brother of George and Robert Trevelyan; he had entered Parliament in 1899 as a Liberal; resigned in 1914 as he disapproved of the war; and in 1922 joined the Labour Party. His expectation of £40,000 a year in 1905 was worth more than £2.5 million in 2002.

John Beazley (1885–1970) became a celebrated classical archaeologist.

Trinity
Tuesday, June 13th 1905.

I am ill and tired, deserted too; and, after your letter of this morning
(given to me, as I lay in bed, by MacCarthy) I haven't even the
certainty that you're at present in existence, and that you're not already
engulfed in the expanding pit of death. I hope you have boats to take to
if necessary, and that, in the hurly-burly, you'll manage to leave behind
the Govt. Agent's wife. As it is, I don't see how I'm ever to find out if
the grand bouleversement really takes place, because what newspaper
would think of mentioning the disappearance of Jaffna? If you have to
float off in an ark, will you let your owl out after some days, to bring
news of an abatement of the waters? And, if there's no abatement, may I
expect to discover it one morning perched upon the statue of Urania
over the Library? If so, will it talk Tamil to me, or have you taught it a
little Henry James English? Pray observe the admirable rhythm of this
paragraph; it has been composed entirely for the sake of our future
Editor, who will doubtless be more charmed with it than you.. [. . .]

Since I last wrote, I've been positively gadding about. On Saturday I
was asked by Sheppard to go with him, his young brother, and his
sisters, to the Races. I said I would – on one condition – that I should
not have to row. He agreed, and of course I discovered when it came to
the point that I was expected to. You can imagine my rage and torture.
The spectacle was much the same as usual, as far as I could see, though
on the whole I thought everyone looked a shade uglier. In the whole
crowd I only recognised two persons – A. R. Brown and Mrs Sidgwick.
I spoke to neither, though if I'd been polite I would have congratulated
Brown on his first – for he'd got one, and so, I presume, will stay up
another year, and so, I foresee, will be elected. The return row was
distinctly alarming (I'd never experienced it before), but somehow or
another none of *us* was drowned. Other people were, however. A grind
turned completely over, packed with persons, and three females were
submerged. Cole is reported to have saved someone else. He saw some
hair apparently floating on the river, pulled it up, and found a female
attached to it. Cole, hearing this story told by Adrian, denied that he'd
pulled the lady up by the hair, and said he'd done it by taking hold of
her under the arms; on which Bell (yes, our Bell), who was there, said
'Surely that isn't incompatible.' [. . .]

On Sunday I lunched with the George Darwins, where was the
Goth. He and Bell have come up for various balls, and are really

marvellous. They tell exactly the same stories in exactly the same words, and it's impossible to say which they really belong to. They mainly talk about Pollack and Trevy, who have now finally quarrelled – why I don't know. The other day the Goth went to County Court, and found Trevy on the jury. He rushed to the Goth, and asked him whether he thought he ought to take the oath. The Goth said 'You must certainly affirm.' But of course Trevy was only too anxious to relax his principles and kissed the book with as much gusto as a nonconformist butcher. After the case was over Trevy asked the Goth to lunch; the Goth went, and found macaroni, rice, and stewed prunes upon the table. Voilà tout. Servants at meals are against the principles of the simple life, so that one has to eat one's macaroni very quickly in order to get one's rice and prunes before they're absolutely cold. The Goth was starved and furious. When the meal was nearly over, Trevy remembered that he might want something to drink, and left the room to get something. The Goth's hopes rose. Alas! Trevy returned with a syphon of soda water, which is the highest point of luxury allowed to the simple life.

Charles Trevelyan and *his* wife live in the country. They rise at six. While Charles is shaving his wife reads Ibsen aloud to him, and while she's doing her hair he reads Bernard Shaw aloud to her. They work till 12, when they have a light vegetarian lunch; they then walk over ploughed fields till six, when they have a light vegetarian dinner. After dinner Charles Trevelyan reads aloud for an hour and a half, and at eight they go to bed. This is supposed to be the simple life, but my private view is that Charles Trevelyan's one object in doing it is to save money, as he's the heir to £40,000 a year.

Thursday. In the train – Cambridge to London (en route for Oxford).[1] I must just tell you a story of Bell's about Turner before anything else. The Goth and he were discussing art. Bell said 'No satisfactory book has ever been written on aesthetics.' The Goth answered 'I suppose not, except perhaps Longinus on the Sublime.' Bell said 'Probably no one has ever read Longinus on the Sublime.' The Goth said 'No; except possibly Turner.' At that moment, of course, Turner entered. They both asked him whether he *had* read it. He replied – but I need hardly tell you – 'Why? It's rather good.' But d'you think he had?

God! God! God! Je suis abîmé – overcome, almost lost. [. . .] All is over; I am but the vision of a vision, the agonised spectre of an intolerable ghost.

No, no, I'm afraid you won't follow all these gyrations. But imagine me (for this at any rate is true) squatting on a bed in an upper room in a corner of Balliol, trying to write to you so that you shall understand, while I still have the tremor of my experiences upon me. I'm drifting off again towards the borderland of frenzy – but how can I describe what's certainly happened? After all it comes merely to this – that I have found Swithinbank charming, and that I've hardly dared, for the three hours I've been with him, to open my mouth. I like him so much, I'm attracted so unmistakably – oh, not in the manner of the flesh. *[. . .]* I believe that my soul is diseased in a curious and distressing way – it has no skin, it's raw, and every touch upon it agonises a nerve. I should have learnt by this time to avoid promiscuous embraces. *[. . .]* I wish I could at least describe the wonderful Beazley (did you perhaps once see him at Keynes's?) with his red unthinkable hair, sitting so quietly and mysteriously on Swithinbank's sofa, impenetrable, almost perturbed, obviously in love, tightly swathed in dark grey flannel, gliding out of the room at last very slowly and without a word. If you could then see 'Dan' Macmillan grinning and twinkling, and remember, as you looked at him, of *[sic]* the marvellous prolonged affair with the Etonian Keynes – if you could sweep in a few insignificant stop-gaps – if you could gather the whole of Swithinbank's delightful, delicate, untainted charm, his surprising quickness, his humour, his kindness – it's no good, it's simply ridiculous, and I resign. *[. . .]*

Friday. I have only time to say that I still live and that I've learnt strange stories, which I hope I may survive to tell you. Adieu!

GLS

1. The writing of this paragraph is shaky from the motion of the train.

‡

To Leonard Woolf

Lytton had returned from Oxford, where he lunched with Bertrand and Alys Russell at the house they built in 1905 at Bagley Wood, Lower Copse, on the southern outskirts of Oxford.

The Jewish playwright Israel Zangwill's father-in-law was Professor William Edward Ayrton (1847–1908), an eminent electrical engineer and physicist and supporter of women's rights. Alfred Sutro (1863–1933) came from a grand Sephardic family and was the brother-in-law of Rufus Daniel Isaacs, later the 1st

Marquess of Reading. He was a distinguished translator. Following a string of failures, the 1904 Wall of Jericho was his first successful play and established him as one of the leading playwrights of the age. Though I don't know how to explain Lytton's apparently anti-Semitic remark about him, it is inconceivable that he intended to insult or wound Woolf. The actress Lottie Venne was a good age when this letter was written, and her mots were famous.

Harley Granville-Barker (1877–1946), actor, playwright, producer, director and Shakespearean scholar, had become actor-manager of the Court Theatre in 1904.

Arthur Christopher Benson (1862–1925) became fellow of Magdalene in 1904 and was Master from 1915 to 1925; his literary output was voluminous, but it was his brother E. W. Benson, author of the 'Lucia' series, whose work has lasted longer.

The artist Neville Lytton (1879–1951) was the son of the 1st Earl of Lytton and grandson of the novelist Bulwer-Lytton. He succeeded as the 3rd Earl in 1947.

Lancaster Gate
June 20th 1905

[. . .] Yesterday, I went to another dinner – rather queer – with the parents-in-law of Zangwill. Mrs Russell took me instead of Bertie, and though I went in the spirit of rag, it was more painful than anything else. The stupidity reached heights. I was between the daughter of the house, aged 18, an utterly ordinary and brainless and rather sulky jeune fille, and a disgusting married woman, who thought she knew everything, and made hideous faces, and simply adored Bernard Shaw. Would this have pleased you? The married woman was too conceited to let me get my knife in her properly, so I turned to the girl and led her as much of a dance as I could. What finally broke me down was that I had for precisely one minute, a distant feeling of physical attraction towards this hideous stupid creature. Supposing that minute were to prolong itself into an hour, a day, a year! I shudder – one's so absurdly helpless. Even women overpower one in the end.

I don't know whether you've heard of the Walls of Jericho – it's a rotten play that's had a vast success. Its author is Sutro, who was there, and utterly vulgar with the sort of placid, easy-going vulgarity of *your* race. When the ladies went, the depression deepened. There were seven men all, except myself, quite half idiotic, some more than half asleep. Sutro told stories of actors etc. of which the following is the highest example. 'Lewis' (whoever he may be) is a man of very retired habits, and was giving an account of his solitary ways to Lottie Venne (or some such person). Lottie Venne, who is 'a little bit of a malaprop,' said 'Ah. Mr Lewis, but then you're such a pisseur.' He replied 'Po, not pee.' – 'And she never forgave him, you know, she never forgave him.' Everyone guffawed, and I wondered how many thousands roll into Sutro's circumcised pocket per year. I reeled home, stuffed with filthy food and reeking with every sort of intoxicant. Quelle horreur! The expense, the elaboration, the dullness, the ugliness, the pomposity, the unreality – one's almost converted to the simple life.

[. . .] Tomorrow I'm going to dinner with MacCarthy to meet (at least so he says, but I haven't much trust in him) a new actor called Granville Barker. Have you heard of him? He now acts Bernard Shaw with great persistence at the Court Theatre, and he and all his company do it extraordinarily well. I expect, though, he's foolish – mustn't anyone be that who persistently acts Bernard Shaw? I went to see Man and Superman the other day, and suffered a good deal from irritation. It's just as maddening to be preached at from the stage as from the pulpit. (Did you ever read such a pompous conclusion to a sentence? – My sense of humour's giving day by day.) I was amused by his boldness; he actually talks about having children without being married. How many centuries will it be before one can allow a man to be in love with a man on the stage? Imagine how shocked Bernard Shaw would be at the suggestion!

Oh dear, oh dear! Arthur Benson has now retired to Magdalen [sic] (Cambridge), and spends his time in a diarrhoea of writing. His last, or almost last book is called the Upton Letters, and Upton = Eton. They are supposed to be by an Eton master, and discuss most questions, including the education of boys. The whole subject of what he calls 'impurity' I find very odd.

Friday. Reflections on that subject were about to follow, but lapsed. I did dine with MacCarthy last night, and Granville Barker was there – he was not particularly interesting. Nor were Neville Lytton and his wife (except for their appearances), who were also there. Later on MacCarthy and I went to the Gothic at home, which is now unfortunately ruined by the presence of Vanessa and Virginia. Besides them and the Goth there were Gerald Duckworth, Turner and Bell. Very queer. The Goth and Turner have tea regularly in Bell's rooms in the Temple. The other day I went and it was purely Cambridge, so, as I'm now at the British Museum, I shall go again today. [. . .]

‡

To Bernard Swithinbank

Raleigh was now Professor of English at Oxford, where he was founding the English school – until his time it was not possible to take a degree in English literature at Oxford. Granville Proby (1883–1947) became Clerk to the House of Lords and Lord-Lieutenant of Huntingdonshire. Lytton met him at Oxford, where he was, according to Holroyd, 'a fat, aristocratic, old Etonian friend of Maynard's'.[1]

69, Lancaster Gate
July 1st 1905

My dear Swithinbank

[. . .] I'm not surprised that you find Raleigh a relief. It's difficult to think of anyone less capable of that sort of scholastic brutality which is not unknown even in Cambridge. But what do you think of Mrs. Raleigh? Don't you like her brimstone and vitriol? Have you talked to her about Russell? They hate each other like poison; he's a moralist and she's an anarchist. And, secretly, I'm on her side.

Last week I stayed for a 'week-end' with the Freshfields (parents of Elinor Clough) in Sussex. Their house is incredibly vast and new, and packed with priceless cabinets, rugs, china vases, and pictures. I was horribly depressed by the magnificence, and by the conversation, which was always on the highest levels. We discussed Henry James and Cymbeline and the essence of architecture from morning till night. Fortunately Elinor Clough, who's far the best of the family, was there. She told me that she'd met you in a wonderful reading-party in the New Forest. I was very amused by her descriptions, and saw, what you said in your letter, that I'd been absurd about Granville Proby. I think I have him in my mind now completely; and he's most pleasant to have.

You ask about my life in the West-End – but I'm afraid it's not very interesting, and it's certainly not typical. I live in the bosom of a large and vivacious family; I spend my days in the British Museum; my nights are diversified by an occasional tedious dinner-party, or by conversations with the relics of my Cambridge friends. The latter might amuse you, and I'll try to give an account of the three of them whom I talk to most.

1. Sydney-Turner. When I first knew him he was a wild and most unrestrained freshman, who wrote poems, never went to bed, and declaimed Swinburne and Sir Thomas Browne till four o'clock in the morning in the great court at Trinity. He is now a civil servant at Somerset House, quite pale and inanimate, hardly more than an incompletely galvanised dead body. He is capable of sitting silent in a room-full of people for hours at a stretch, or of talking tête-à-tête for hours at a stretch on the most uninteresting of subjects – cricket shop, Aulus Gellius, or the technique of Wagner. I feel that he'll be a tragic figure, if only he was only aware of his tragedy. But then, how can one be sure that he isn't? In appearance he's small, bloodless, and éffacé; he looks like some puzzled night-animal blinking in the unaccustomed daylight. Sometimes, even now, for a few moments, one realises as one watches him that he still possesses a mystical supremacy and a sort of sibylline power.

2. Thoby Stephen. He is the son of Leslie Stephen, and a heroic figure. He has a vast and massive frame, and a face hewn out of the living rock. His character is as splendid as his appearance, and as wonderfully complete. In fact, he's monolithic. But, if it were not for his extraordinary vein of humour, he would hardly be of this world. We call him the Goth; and when you see him I'm sure you'll agree that he's a survival of barbaric grandeur. He'll be a judge of great eminence, and, in his old age, a sombre family potentate. One day we composed each other's epitaphs. He said that mine should be 'The Universal Exception' and mine for him was 'The Forlorn Hope'.

3. Bell. His character has several layers, but it's difficult to say which is the fond. There is a country gentleman layer, which makes him retire into the depths of Wiltshire to shoot partridges. There is the Paris decadent layer, which takes him to the quartier latin where he discusses painting and vice with American artists and French models. There is the 18th Century layer, which adores Thoby Stephen. There is the layer of innocence, which adores Thoby's sister. There is the layer of prostitution, which shows itself in an amazing head of crimped straw-coloured hair. And there is the layer of stupidity, which runs transversely through all the other layers. He happens to be more or less rich, and has college-like rooms in the Temple, where the Goth and Sydney Turner regularly have tea. I sometimes join them, and it's very dull, as you may imagine.

July 3rd. Not less dull, I'm afraid, than this letter, which I now seem to be finishing after a procession of interruptions. It's one o'clock and

I'm partly drunk, having been to Sarah Bernhardt in Phèdre. Do you know the play and the lady? Lord! But one can't expatiate. C'est Vénus toute entière à sa proie attachée.

I shall look out for the succession of triumphs which I hope will crown your contributions to the Westminster Gazette. Oh, by-the-bye, why destroy papers? Surely it's very wrong. Doesn't one's dull old age deserve a thought? [. . .]

your

G. L. Strachey

[King's College, Cambridge]

1. Michael Holroyd, *Lytton Strachey*, p.167.

✝

To Leonard Woolf

In 1905 Sarah Bernhardt (1844–1923) began the first of the three 'farewell' tours that continued until 1912. It was in this year (in Rio de Janeiro) that she sustained the injury that eventually led to the amputation of a leg in 1915.

Lancaster Gate

July 4th 1905

[. . .] Yesterday what do you think I did? – Went, with Bell, if you please, to see Sarah in Phèdre. She was splendid as ever – twice I was almost killed – and the Connais donc Phèdre et toute sa fureur in Act II, and the Que fais-je? in Act IV. Max as Hipolyte (I don't know *[how to spell Hippolyte]*) was absurdly modern, but otherwise talented. The Goth and Adrian were there, and the Goth was enthusiastic. He really sees the point – but Bell? He's really rather a mystery – what can be his raison d'être? He takes himself in deadly earnest, I've discovered, as art critic and littérateur. Very queer – and he likes, or says he likes, such odd things – Glück, Racine, Pope and Gibbon. If it's mere imitation of me, the question remains – why the dickens should he imitate me? For he's not under our control, like Lamb. He's even independent of the Goth. His stupidity is of course gross, yet he can be occasionally almost witty. His verse, as Turner says, isn't nearly as bad as one naturally expected. He's modest and retiring; he's also quite unrestrained in general conversation. What'll become of him? He declares that he's depressed, that he's 'poitrinaire' *[a tuberculosis sufferer]*, and that he's in love with Vanessa. I suppose he'll end as a country magnate prodding up his turnips in Wiltshire, at the age of 84, with an ugly old wife who certainly won't be the Goth's sister.

[. . .] Thursday evening. I lapsed, and, in the present domestic turmoil, think it highly probable that I shall lapse again. Family life is horribly trying, when there's no room for it; thank God we go into the country on the 11th. I've begun my dissertation, but can't write, and don't want to. Since Tuesday, my chief occupation has been Bell. The engine of his situation titillated my curiosity, and I felt that I couldn't rest till I discovered the whole thing. Et bien, last night I discovered it. It was really more exciting than might have been expected – and he was curiously, almost incredibly, conscious. I stayed there till two o'clock with him in the Cambridge-like remote chambers in King's Bench Walk. We were intimate, yes, strangely so; but I think his method did deserve what I gave it – a little affection. The whole circumstance simply is that he's wildly in love – and with Vanessa. I couldn't doubt that he's fallen into a sort of distraction – it seems at times to be almost a mania. When he's alone I'm convinced that he's haunted, desperately haunted, by visions of Vanessa; his frightened pathetic face shows it, and his small lascivious body oozes with disappointed lust. What's so superb is that he completely recognises how ridiculous he is. He's impelled towards a declaration; he itches to know the worst, but he's terrified at the absurd figure he'll have to cut if he does try to say what he feels. Supposing she simply laughed! He's made up his mind to the worst, and is prepared to fly the country the moment it occurs. Of course it's inconceivable that she'ld say anything but no; and yet, – he was so unpompous and sincere and frantic – he laughed so much, just as he ought to have laughed – that I can't help wishing that she might be so utterly absurd – However, we shall know before the summer's out. He's going to stay with them in Cornwall, and has made up his mind to take the plunge then. He walked back with me as far as St James's Street through the empty early London, and the whole thing did seem what he said it was – playing at Cambridge. But, good lord, what a depressing game! As far as he's concerned, of course, the most depressing part is the extent of his limitations. If he could soar only a little higher, how high he'd soar! But there's a dead weight of vague inertia that keeps him down. He's so far from heroic! But he's human – much more human than I'd ever guessed. *[. . .]*

‡

To Maynard Keynes

In reply to a letter from Strachey of 27 July, Keynes had sent Strachey a draft of a piece in which 'I meant to include an analysis of "good" on the analogy of "yellow" and some fuss about organic unities, but was too lazy to continue'. The paper was about Aristotle. Also staying at what Lytton called 'our Elizabethan mansion' was his first cousin, Duncan Grant (1885–1978), the son of Lady Strachey's younger brother, Major Bartle Grant, and Ethel McNeil.

Great Oakley Hall
Kettering
August 3rd 1905

Dear Keynes,

Your Aristotelian dissertation I found most absorbing. I should like to discuss several of the points by word of mouth.

As for Hobby – well, I was amazed! Though I suppose really one might almost have expected something of the sort. On the whole I can't help feeling rather irritated with the little bugger. I'm pretty clearly convinced that at the basis of *some* of his feelings on the occasion were considerations of an altogether wrong sort – such as hatred of the idea of not being liked (this perhaps brought to a pitch of jealousy of me – he may have felt, I mean, rather left out in the cold, and this would have rankled), and also terror of your departure to Switzerland bringing the whole thing to an end. Of course I don't mean to say that he hadn't *other* very different feelings as well – but lord, lord! who can be certain about their depth or permanence? I quite recognise that *you* are lost – how can you refuse his overtures, however much you may guess that the consequences will be fatal? You're regularly caught. Why didn't you – it would have been the only thing – rape him before you left? And then abandon him altogether? Well, well, perhaps you did. But in any case my prayers, you may be sure, are with you. And, if you see enough of Dan, who knows how things mayn't end?

As for me – I don't quite know what I'm doing – writing a dissertation, presumably. But I've managed, since I saw you last, to catch a glimpse of Heaven. Incredible, quite – yet so it's happened. I want to go into the wilderness, or the world, and preach an infinitude of sermons on one text – Embrace one another! It seems to me the grand solution. Oh dear, dear, dear, how wild, how violent, and how supreme are the things of this earth! – I am cloudy, I fear almost sentimental. But I'll write again. Oh yes, it's Duncan. He's no longer here, though, and he went yesterday to France. Fortunate, perhaps, for my dissertation.

your

G.L. Strachey

‡

To Leonard Woolf

Theodore Llewellyn Davies (b.1870) was the youngest of six brothers (and the uncle of the 'lost boys' who were the originals of J. M. Barrie's Peter Pan*). He was the best-loved Apostle of his generation, and when he drowned, aged thirty-four, in a swimming accident near his home at Kirkby Lonsdale, his elder brother Crompton was almost crazed with grief. Theodore had been in love with Margaret, the daughter of Charles Booth, who had refused his proposal. Following his brother's death, Crompton tried to carry out his intentions by proposing to her himself in the autumn of 1905; but she rejected him as well.*

Great Oakley Hall
Kettering
Thursday, August 3rd 1905

I'm exhausted – for various reasons, and have put off writing till the eleventh hour. The serious news is that Theodore was drowned last week, bathing by himself in Westmoreland (where apparently his family lives). It's supposed that he was attacked with sudden cramp, or that his heart failed: but I haven't heard any really detailed account. There was an obituary notice, with a letter from the Master, in the Times of last Monday. Pretty stiff, isn't it? I feel that I ought to write to Crompton, but what to say? There seems to *[be]* a fate against the phenomenal stars of the Society's heart.

    [. . .] I've just had, with Duncan, a glimpse of Heaven. Ah! Quelle vie! That people should really have such exquisite, such supernal feelings – it's that that amazes me, and leaves me in a lascivious trance. If I could give you the same vision that I reached of his peculiar timbre! The strong strange splendour! The submission . . . am I a volage adorateur de mille

objets *divers*[1]? Am I too promiscuous? I'm willing to give up Lamb, to admit – didn't I always? – that that was only a case of extended self-abuse. But, oh! in this wonderful instance, I'm just as certain that

Le ciel n'est pas plus pur que le fond de mon coeur.[2]

I'm in something of a state – a little afraid of being sentimental. He's gone to France. I wondered why I wasn't in love with him. Folly! – But that *he* should be in love with me!

your
GLS

1. Racine, *Phèdre*, II,5.
2. 'Le ciel n'est pas plus pur que mon bonheur de te voir.' (A common borrowing playing on Racine: 'Le jour n'est pas plus pur que le fond de mon coeur.')

‡

To Duncan Grant

'The Begums' were characters in Lytton's dissertation on Warren Hastings. The Plowdens were related to the Stracheys. Alfred Plowden, who was famous for the legal witticisms he made in court, and which were reported assiduously in the popular press, was Lady Strachey's first cousin. His daughter, Pamela, was married to the 2nd Earl of Lytton, Lytton's godfather, and formerly acting-viceroy of India. Dick and Grace were Lytton's eldest brother by twenty years, Richard (1861–1935), and his wife, Grace Norman.

Great Oakley Hall
Kettering
August 30th 1905

My dearest Duncan

Your letter came this morning, as I expected it would, after I had written and despatched a somewhat querulous note to you, care of your father at Woolwich. I don't know if it has reached you, but if it has, I hope you weren't annoyed, I was feeling depressed and edgy, the Begums were weighing upon my spirit, and I began to wonder whether there was any hope, whether life was worth living, and whether I should ever hear from you or see you again. However, please ignore all that. The Begums have at last been vanquished, and today they were despatched to Cambridge, where they may rot at ease till the judgement day. Your letter came just in time to see the tail ends of them. Whisking out of Great Oakley like so many witches on broomsticks. The result is that I am now considerably reanimated. I am looking forward to seeing you very much indeed at the earliest possible moment after the 12th. I assure you my razor is crying out for you, and, as I passed the Georgian summer-house the other day, it inquired very kindly after your health. The roses and elms are much the same as usual, thank you, except that the old ghostly stump – do you remember it? It was a model of our friend Mr Macwhirter – has been knocked down, and cut into firewood by two ancient and obscene women who appeared with hatchets one afternoon and fairly did for it, poor thing. Mary Plowden is here, but she goes tomorrow. Pernel returned convalescent a few days ago. Before the week is out the following people will I believe enter the house – Ruby and Julia, Dick and Grace, Cousin Minnie and Rupert Brooke. The last is the only one who interests me, but I suppose he'll be disappointing. Is he purely Oxford? Is it worth persuading him to go to King's? I'll write and tell you about him when he comes.

I'm going to bed, worn out by my various labours, and I shall finish this tomorrow. So good-night, my dearest Duncan. Do you say good-night to me? *[. . .]*

‡

To Duncan Grant

Camille Mauclair's monograph on Antoine Watteau was published in London in 1905.

Great Oakley Hall
Kettering
September 5th 1905

My dearest Duncan,

I hope this may reach you before you leave the golden groves of Wales, or that, if it doesn't, it'll be sent on to you. I've nothing to say – except the unsayable, and you must imagine that.

The house is occupied with Minnie, Ruby, Julia, etc. also Rupert Brooke, who seems pleasant. He has rather nice – but you know – yellow-ochre-ish hair, and a healthy young complexion. I took him out for a walk round the Park this morning, and he talked about Poetry and Public Schools as decently as could be expected. The Oxford–Cambridge question is still hanging in the balance. I shall try to give a push to the Cambridge scale, but I'm not *very* anxious about the matter.

Dorothy is translating a book by Camille Mauclair on Watteau. I've read the manuscript – it's entertaining and rather charming, but the poor man had a sad mania – viz. that the reason why Watteau painted as he did is that he was consumptive. He tried to prove this by showing that all other consumptive artists resembled Watteau. Among others he cites Edgar Allan Poe – whom for some reason he says wrote à la Watteau – but he had to admit that Poe was not consumptive; but, he adds, his wife was! Peculiar?

I have discovered some charming walks here, down the long elm avenues. Yesterday I came upon a veritable Watteau avenue, and wished you'd been with me.

your loving
Lytton

[. . .]

‡

To Duncan Grant

Lytton's twenty-nine-year-old elder sister Pernel was beginning her career as Tutor and eventually Principal of Newnham.

Trinity
October 9th 1905

My dearest Duncan

The wicked dons of Trinity have refused to make me a fellow. I'm sorry, but resigned. I had imagined so many splendid things for us, if it had come off. Poverty, drudgery, etc. must now be faced. But I feel, my beloved, that there is nothing that really matters, so long as we're each other's. Don't you agree? Let's both be great artists and great friends. Je t'embrasse de tout mon coeur.

[. . .] Pernel is settling into her room at Newnham, though most of her things haven't arrived yet. She has two pictures – the beautiful Bussy, of Monte Carlo – blue sea, red toy houses, and no sky – do you know it? – and your charming patrician trees, which I love so much. I am going to tea there today, so I shall see them again before I return. James's room is now finished – a symphony in white and apple-green, perhaps too violent, but rather amusing. The bedmaker thinks it's very tasty.

I am longing to see you again.

your loving
Lytton

‡

To Duncan Grant

69, Lancaster Gate, W.
Wednesday night
October 11th 1905

[. . .] My great difficulty is in understanding exactly what it is you feel; but whatever you feel, I *know*, and could never for a moment doubt, that you are not, as you call yourself 'a brute'. I think that you may think your affection for me on a lower level than it really is. I don't believe it's really more selfish than mine for you. You don't know what it is to be twenty-five, dejected, uncouth, unsuccessful – you don't know how humble and wretched and lonely *I* sometimes feel – how glad – how selfishly glad – I was to find you cared for me, in spite of 'tout l'age et le malheur que je traine avec moi'. My dearest Duncan, you *do* care for me – I wonder if you think that there's some miraculous way of caring – of 'flying into limitless space forever' – which you haven't reached to, and I have. That may be so; but I can't help doubting. Isn't your passion precisely that? Passion may end; but that doesn't mean that it's not to count. I know there's a sort of passion – an animal feeling, a passion without affection – which is merely a bodily pleasure and doesn't count. But you have affection towards me – of that I'm convinced. When you embrace me, you really do love me –

oh God – these are wretched things to be writing. Perhaps I'm beating against a brick wall.

For heaven's sake come tomorrow to lunch. I shall be in my room all the morning. I'm not blind. After what you've written I see that your affection for me may be utterly different from mine for you. But I honestly honestly think you may be mistaken. You think you may be yourself. Oh no, no! How could I ask for anything more than what you've given me? You're still to me exactly what you were. I am your loving

Lytton

I think you may think my feelings wonderful and dazzling and beyond you, because I can express them better perhaps than you can yours. It's only because I'm older.

I kiss you. Goodnight.

☩

To Leonard Woolf

Woolf lost his virginity in 1905, aged twenty-five, to a Burgher girl who fancied him and arranged a tryst with him in his Jaffna bungalow. (The Burghers were descendants of Dutch or Portuguese colonials.) She turned out to be the niece of one of his own clerks, and she had some notoriety in Jaffna.

'Rosy' (sometimes he spells her as 'Rosie') was Lytton's gyp, his college servant. The two Trinity prize fellowships went to Harry Bateman (1882–1946), who became an eminent mathematician and emigrated to the US in 1910, and James Clerk Maxwell Garnett (1880–1958), who became secretary of the League of Nations. Bateman was a grammar-school boy from Manchester, where his father was a pharmaceutical chemist and commercial traveller.

I had not read this letter when, in 1970, I discussed Bloomsbury sexual relations with Duncan Grant. I asked him whether the Apostles' lexicon of 'buggery', 'proposals' and so on was merely verbal, or whether actual sexual relations took place. He replied, 'I can't speak for anyone else, but I had relations with anyone who would have me.'

James had taken over his elder brother's room at Trinity.

Henry Tertius James Norton (1887–1936) was elected to the Apostles the next year. James Strachey later said that he was 'one of the only three or four people I have ever known in the same intellectual category as Russell – with

*whom he was perfectly able to argue on equal terms'. Harry Norton suffered from
hypomania, which later became severe depression. He did pioneering work on the
mathematical theory of genetics, but his work on the Cantorian theory of
numbers remained unfinished on his death. He became an important figure in
Bloomsbury, and loaned Lytton the money that allowed him to write* Eminent
Victorians.

*This letter marks Lytton's first sight of the painter Henry Taylor Lamb
(1883–1960).*

Lancaster Gate
October 23rd 1905

I haven't written for Lord knows how long. I've had at least three letters
from you since I wrote last; but I now sit down for pages – finally urged
on by your last magnificent half-caste whore account, which made me
laugh for my own reasons, as well as for yours.

The refusal of the persons at Trinity to give me a fellowship has left
me here, nominally a journalist, really, as far as I can see, a complete
drifter, without any definite hopes, and the New Age as far off as ever.
If I were energetic – but it's so absurd – how can one be energetic over
reviews? I pray to God, though, that I may miraculously take a turn
towards the practical – for a year or two – which I believe would be
enough. But it's all very dull and vague and quasi-infinite. I was at
Trinity when the fellowship result was read out. I could see everything,
and Rosy's enraged disappointed red face told me all at once that all was
over. She was very angry – apparently because Bateman is so poor –
'They never elect anyone who spends any money in the College' – my
prestige must have been pretty great for her to think of giving *that* as a
recommendation for me. [. . .]

The fellowship question hasn't been my only agitation. While it was
going on, I couldn't help occasionally murmuring to myself – 'qu'un
soin bien différent me trouble et me dévore'.[1] I gave you a slight sketch
of the Duncan incident, but lord! I'd no idea what sort of a thing it was
coming to. I began it merely vaguely. He was nice and young and on
the spot, and there was nobody I was in love with. One morning it
occurred to me that it would be pleasant to stroke his hair; I stroked
it, and all was lost. But it took me a long time to realise what had
happened. What surprised and charmed me so much was his wonderful
reciprocation. He caressed me as much as I caressed him. He seemed to
feel that it was all the most natural thing in the world, and he felt it

more beautifully than I'd imagined possible. I wonder if you remember his appearance, His face is outspoken, bold, and just not rough. It's the full aquiline type, with frank grey-blue eyes, and incomparably lascivious lips. Ah! but in spite of everything the expression changes wonderfully sometimes into a melancholy tenderness which seems to be the real essence, the true touch of the divine. All through August and September while I was at Great Oakley, and he was God knows where, I perpetually arranged the lines of our relation. Affection was to predominate. I was determined to have no repetition of the weary Sheppard round. I made up my mind to keep my lust well under control, to desire only his affection, and to give him nothing that he couldn't give me. Oh! We were to be eminently *friends*. But do observe the ingenious malignity of Fate. When we came back here, I went to see him in his house at Hampstead. We went out together, had lunch at an Inn at the top of the hill – a large intoxicating lunch, with beer – and then we strolled down the Heath, among the bowers. It came on to rain, and we had to take shelter in one of the bowers. The ground was rather damp, so we were obliged to crouch on my umbrella. You can imagine the discomfort and the absurdity; but can you imagine the exquisite splendour of our embraces? It was the grand triumph of innocence, goodness and love. I had hardly believed so much was possible; to be embraced so passionately, to be kissed so often, and not to know whether one was buggering, or being buggered! Inimitable delight! When I got your last letter I observed from the date that your half-caste debauch must have taken place within a few days of my incredible rapture. What could one do but laugh? Only you haven't heard the sequel.

'Les choses les plus souhaitées n'arrivent point ou, si elles arrivent, ce n'est ni dans le temps ni les circonstances où elles auraient fait une extrême plaisir.'[2] I thought I was going to find an exception to the rule, but I was mistaken. Within a few days arrived a letter, a superb, torrential letter – pathetic and adorable to the height of making this re-markable pronouncement: 'I only love your body. I cannot have the deep affection for your mind that you have for mine. I can give you admiration, worship, lust – everything you like but the love that you give me.' This has been translated into our language for the sake of precision – but did you ever hear such a thing? I went pretty mad, tried hard to deny what is yet obviously the case, and find myself at last simply tired out and hopeless. He was of course charming, and believed at once that he was wrong and that everything was absolutely right, but it won't work. Il ne m'aime pas. And the point of disagreement is not that I like his body better than he likes mine, but that he likes my mind less than I like his. Such is the reward of virtue!

However there are sorts of compensations – a little half-caste, perhaps, but there. Last Saturday we went together to Cambridge, and in the afternoon visited James. The room is grotesquely changed – an art nouveau symphony in green and white, with James, very prim and small, sitting in the extreme corner of the sofa, which is covered with green sack-cloth. He's got a pianola, too, with which he played us the 5th Symphony. When he left us – well, the sofa has seen many things, but it never saw anything to equal what occurred on it in its mask of green. Have you kissed with inward lip? Have you embraced with tongues? Have you wanted to stop before the other? I had a violent cold, and the two things together so reduced me that next morning – oh! I forgot to mention the Society, which doubtless also acted – I was too faint to get up to breakfast. I've now crawled back here, more unhappy than happy, less desperate than resigned. Is it exhaustion? Is it nobility? Is it old age? I look back upon the days of Sheppard as upon a nightmare a little too much like reality.

Friday 27th October. *[. . .]* Another freshman is called Norton. He's an Etonian, and created some sensation there by being observed to read Russell's book. He's very cultured and quotes poetry by the year *[of publication?]*. Keynes, however, swears that he has 'a good logical foundation'. I hope he has, but admit that it's a little damning to be (as he is) a profound admirer of Arthur Benson.

I was to have met him at breakfast, but was too ill, but I'll send you ocular descriptions of both later on. The other day I got a somewhat elevated letter from Keynes, describing a superb Austrian freshman, aged seventeen and a half, with all knowledge and complete savoir faire. It seemed to me of course absurd, but Keynes distinctly sniffed at the embryonic. However today he writes to say that 'Ernst Goldschmidt' is – imagine what! – head prostitute of Vienna, and has fled to Cambridge to avoid the ceaseless course of buggery to which he finds himself exposed. Isn't it a little comic to choose Cambridge as a refuge? But it sounds amusing and mad, and I'm longing to hear the story, which Keynes declares to be incredible.

I am established in a room here, with a folding bed, and all my books ranged in two bookshelves. It's pretty dreary, and when I'm to do any work heaven alone knows. I went to see Turner the other day and found him in a chair which has embroidery with a pattern of crowns;

and when he leans back a faded crown is to be seen on his head – it's a ghostly vision of defunct supremacy. Yesterday we went to the Gothic at home, and found Barwell in full swing – absolutely blatant, and unceasing as ever. Lamb's brother was also there. He's run away from Manchester, become an artist, and grown side-whiskers. I didn't speak to him, but wanted to, because he really looked amazing, though of course very very bad. Oh but the Goth! Don't you see that if God had to justify the existence of the World it would be done if he were to produce the Goth? If the Devil still demurred – which I don't think he could decently do – I see very clearly whom God would have to fall back upon as his final argument – Swithinbank.

I'm going to Oxford on Wednesday next, and shall stay a night with the Raleighs. I shall then, I hope, move on to Balliol, so my next letter will probably come from there. Poor divine Swithin! The fiends of Balliol perpetually threaten to take away his scholarship because he cuts their blasted lectures. Damn them all! He was at Cambridge a week or two ago, and quite perfect. I love him as one might love a spirit.

your
GLS

Sorry – missed the mail. Couldn't be avoided. I wonder how you keep my letters. Isn't it dangerous?

Oh heaven! If I could speak to you.

1. Racine, *Phèdre*, Act II, Scene 5.
2. Jean de La Bruyère, *Caractères*.

‡

To Leonard Woolf

It's interesting that Strachey should have been so enamoured of the operas of Gluck. Though there was a celebrated revival of Orfeo ed Eurydice *at Covent Garden in 1890 (it had first been heard in London in 1770), Gluck's operas were not much performed after that until Beecham revived* Orfeo *in 1920 with Clara Butt.*

Oxford
November 2nd 1905

I'm at the Raleighs, and go today to Balliol to stay with
Swithinbank. *[. . .]*

I'm too sick to write any more. I can't believe you know the operas
of Glück; if I sent you some I wonder if you could play them with one
finger. They're now with me more almost than Racine. Pure beauty
and grandeur – elysian airs, exquisite crescendos, inimitable heights.
There is a ballet in the third act of Orfeo – but what's the good of
talking?

The other day I saw the Wild Duck acted. It's terrific. Most of the
audience giggled at the tragic parts, which made me begin to despair of
the human race. You've always done that, of course. Might not Lamb
have written the last sentence? – Enfin! One's come pretty low when
one's afraid of being the Corporal. My self-confidence has really sunk to
the lowest ebb. What a come down! To have begun so proudly, with
such flying colours and trumpet calls! And then to find oneself in a
muddy ditch, copulating with Keynes. Don't be too alarmed. By good
luck I haven't yet done it physically, but I promise you only by good
luck; and mentally I do it all day long. Quel dégoût! For heaven's sake
write. It's still something that you exist.

your
GLS

Don't you think you might send me back to look at, in a wonderful
parcel, my letters during the last year? I should return them, and it
would amuse me. Only perhaps it wouldn't be proper. I don't know.

‡

To Leonard Woolf

*Roger Cuthbert Quilter (1877–1953), whose work consisted chiefly of songs, was
part of a circle of composers that included Percy Grainger.*

    Lytton's Apostles paper discussed whether love required a physical expression.

Lancaster Gate
Thursday, December 7th 1905

I really think it's rather splendid to 'run' even Ceylon. I'm expecting to
see your photograph in an Illustrated Paper, as a distinguished civil
servant. You might be 'at home' – in your large plaster-dropping home,
with a glimpse of the lady in the background. I wish you could see the
drawings of Augustus John, which are now beginning to boom. He is a
confirmed drunkard with three wives, and his pictures are mere violent
beauty and degradation. They'ld be very suitable on your walls – visions
of awful women in theatric and deathly landscapes, moving idyllically
through a quite mad and filthy world. The beauty of line and shape is
incomparable. They're very cheap – but I've no money and can't make
what I'm sure would be a supreme speculation.

    I went to the 'Friday Club' with Pippa last Friday, as guests of the
Stephen family. It was in a flat belonging to Walter Creighton, son of
the late Bishop. The proceedings were curious and unpleasant. Nearly
everyone – male and female – sat on the floor back to back, while
Walter Creighton sang Brahms or posed with a cigarette, and his friend
Mr Roger Quilter – a pale young man with a pale bottle nose – played
his own compositions on the piano. Henry Lamb was also there – rather
stupid and very slimy, I thought – and his quasi-mistress, a very young
female dressed in the regulation harlot clothes. The whole place
depressed me by its air of third-rate incompetence blindly aiming at
it knew not what. The Gothic family seemed strangely out of place.
Poor people! They so hate propriety that they're driven out into this
wretched sort of groove. The Goth came here to dinner last night, and
was of course as superb as ever, though a little weighed down, I
thought, by existence in general. He's certainly ageing – his upper lip is
getting longer, and the ruggedness grows. – Duncan has just come in –
Oh damn! Damn! Damn! Que je suis tormenté. Quelle soufferance
horrible! I know quite well that it will pass, that in a few moments I
shall be as placid as I was a few moments ago, and that the time will
come when I shall be as indifferent when he appears as when Sheppard
does; but in the meantime the half-hearted wound shoots and stabs –
one feels too much.–

    I went to Cambridge last Saturday and read a paper on Temperance
in Love,[1] which I had scrawled off in five minutes. Only Sheppard,
Keynes and Hobby were there, and the discussion was fairly dismal, but
not so dismal as it might have been, I thought. The situation is dreadful

– though I believe I'm the only person who thinks it so, except Pippa who doesn't of course know the real horror. Lamb has made up his foetid mind that the proper thing is to be in love with James. Accordingly one day last week he proposed – in form. Doesn't it revolt you? James put him off with vagueness, but on the next night began to think that 'perhaps he'd been rather unkind'. Apparently – though it seems impossible – he does really like Lamb. He went to his door, found it sported, came away, and walked up and down meditating for half an hour in the Great Court. Then he went up again, knocked at the sported door, and was admitted. He told Lamb that he thought that perhaps he'd been rather unkind, and then – according to James's account given to Norton – 'Lamb lost his head.' This means, I find, that he tried to kiss; but James preserved his virginity. Did you ever hear anything quite so foul? The sterility of Lamb is what shocks me. And that I should be in such a state! – But one can only pray that the passage of Time may come to the rescue. What adds to my distress is that I feel that I'm somehow almost responsible for the whole affair. That's what comes of propagating one's doctrines among corporals. Enfin! *[. . .]*
[Berg]

1. 'Shall We Take the Pledge', in Paul Levy (ed.), *Lytton Strachey: The Really Interesting Question.*

‡

To Duncan Grant

69, Lancaster Gate, W.
December 21st 1905

My dearest angel,

I'm really quite cheerful – only I'm afraid that you may be pained when you think of me. Oughtn't we both to keep our spirits up, and to have faith in one another and ourselves? I feel that we ought to believe that we do really love each other, that we *both* ought to believe that you do really love me – and to believe that the other believes it. I don't mean that we ought to fudge – I mean that we oughtn't to be distracted by twists and turns – distracted away from the real goodness of the whole thing. I think you said last night, and I only say it now to make sure. My dear, when I think of our feelings as a whole, including *all*, the total effect carries me away – the goodness is almost unbelievably great. A sort of divinity seems to clothe my senses. We are among heavenly things.

You are my angel, my dearest, my best, my own.

your loving
Lytton

‡

To Leonard Woolf

By 'secondary qualities' philosophers mean things such as colour, smell or taste, which are apparent only to an observer, as opposed to the 'primary qualities' of size, motion, number and shape, which may be thought of as belonging to objects independent of any observer. Moore's reflection, that the preposterous Kantian position (attributed to Hawtrey) that hens-laying-eggs was a 'necessary condition' of someone's mental state could only be held by someone muddled by philosophy, seems to anticipate the attitude of the later Wittgenstein.

January 4th 1906

I'm at Ledbury – a village in Herefordshire – in a cottage lent by my aunt – with Duncan. We came yesterday, and stay till next Tuesday. It's a sort of honeymoon à la mode de chez nous. We are fairly happy and idyllic. We have blue skies, comfortable chairs, lots of books, and a sprinkling of copulation. I wonder how you are, and whether you've gone to the hills, as I guess is probable, to convalesce. I had dimly gathered via your family that your fever might be enteric. I do hope you're not too horribly pulled down. [. . .]

Moore came to lunch on Tuesday, and stayed to tea. We talked busily, and he was very fine, especially on Hawtrey, Russell, and philosophy. His paper on secondary qualities is I'm sure superb. He thinks they exist, and argued by an analogy, which I didn't quite grasp, with the inferences made by scientists as to the existence of light waves. He said that you could not infer the existence of a thing unless you or *somebody* had seen it. Thus you could not infer that hens laid eggs unless you or *somebody* had seen both a hen and an egg. Hawtrey denied this, and said the argument was 'much too simple'. The real fact was that the laying of eggs by hens was a necessary condition of your mental state, and that therefore you could infer it from your mental state. Moore said that he never could have said such a thing unless he muddled himself up with philosophy. The worst feature of the case is that Russell remains purely wobbly, and this really seemed to depress Moore, who said that unless his paper was right he'd have nothing to say in his book – which he hasn't yet begun. The poor Yen! I thought his face had changed. It looked thinner and old – more obviously intellectual, and sad. I wish he'd come to London. I'm to go and see them in February. Oh dear!

[. . .] Can you conceive of us in this inconceivable habitation? – It's a dowager's 'cottage' – rather like the little house that the grand lady retired to in the Spoils of Poynton. Peerless pieces of furniture line the walls. We eat our pressed beef off Crown Derby, and the very piss-pots are Worcester. One feels, whenever one sinks into the cushions of the vast armchairs, that one ought to be dressed in silk skirts, and be a widow. Isn't it scandalous that if one wants to be one, one shouldn't be able? I pray God to make me a rich widow! – With all his omnipotence what can God do? It's scandalous – but perhaps there are compensations.

your

GLS

I do want very much to hear that you're getting on.

✝

To Clive Bell

Lytton was following the general election of 1906, spread over many days from 12 January to 8 February 1906, as the various constituencies reported their totals. The Liberals, led by Henry Campbell-Bannerman, gained an overall majority in Parliament. The Conservatives under Arthur Balfour lost more than half their seats, while the newly formed Labour Party were far more successful than the Labour Representation Committee had been in the 1900 general election. Billy Ritchie was 'Aunt Anny' Ritchie's son.

Richard Buhlig (1880–1951), born in Chicago but trained in Europe, was well established as a concert pianist before his return to the US in 1916. A champion of Schoenberg and Korngold, he was also one of the first to perform Bach and earlier masters.

69, Lancaster Gate, W.
January 17th 1906

My dear Bell

[. . .] Last Thursday I went to Gordon Square. The family were all
there, precisely as usual. Turner wasn't – and they thought he was
probably dead. I haven't heard whether he is. The Goth told me a little
about Paris, which amused me a good deal. His inimitable style! No I'm
not in love with Vanessa, though I rather gather that Adrian is with
Henry Lamb. They've been to the New Forest together for a week or
so – nominally to 'hunt'. H.L. gave me an account of their daily life –
their riding, hunting, etc. I couldn't help asking at the end – 'And how
did you spend your evenings?' He was discreet.

My dear Bell, I too am pretty depressed. I constantly find life simply
épouvantable. I shudder, and almost resign. One's affections are so
utterly blasting, so cruel and remorseless, that one sometimes almost
wishes to be one of those stony women one sees in omnibuses. And
one's lusts are just as bad. Que faire? Retire to St Symphorien? I
wonder; and I remain here, in this mad prosy filth-packet, pretending
to be a journalist. The rest of the world is apparently occupied with
'elections'. Even I find myself drawn in to the extent of sticking
coloured pieces of paper onto a map every morning after breakfast. Can
you imagine it? At the Goth's on Thursday, Hilton Young of course
talked politics with Billy Ritchie, but I'm glad to say that no one else
noticed them. One of my sisters was there. She studied H. Lamb's face,
and declared afterwards that he was abominably wicked, and looked like
a Chinese devil. I suppose it's true; but I couldn't help wanting to
stroke him.

Oh! I went to several Buhlig concerts, and at the last went into the
Artist's room (at Mrs Wedgwood's invitation) and shook hands with the
poor exhausted man. It was very amusing, but must have happened
about fifty years ago.

Cambridge has begun again, and is a good deal more putrid than
ever. Walter Lamb adores my brother James, who adores Walter Lamb.
They sit in each other's rooms and on each other's knees the whole
time without intermission, but whether things have got any further I
don't know. And don't very much want to know. Keynes sits like a
decayed and amorous spider in King's, weaving purely imaginary webs,
noticing everything that happens and doesn't happen, and writing to me

by every other post. There's a poor young freshman called Norton, who is very innocent indeed, so innocent that he has been an atheist from birth, and a sodomite from puberty. Keynes perpetually talks to him, but is now getting a little nervous, because he's beginning to think that Norton thinks that Keynes is in love with him. And he doesn't know whether he is. Eh bien! I suppose I shall find myself trundling down there in a Saturday or two to take the cover off the pullulating pot and have a sniff. Whenever I step into that train at King's Cross I feel à la Baudelaire –

> Je m'avance à l'attaque et je grimpe aux assauts
> Comme après un cadavre un choeur de vermisseaux.[1]

But I suppose you've given up Baudelaire.

Do please, if you ever feel in the mood to return good for evil, write. I'm almost as solitary as you. I can never get to see anyone and hardly want to. I have fallen in love, hopelessly and ultimately. I have experienced too much ecstasy. I want to thank God, and to weep, and to go to sleep. As it is, I can only totter to a concert or a picture gallery, and write blither. Adieu!

your
Lytton Strachey

1. Charles Baudelaire, *Les Fleurs du Mal*. I advance at the attack and join in the onslaught/ Like a band of worms on a corpse.

‡

To Leonard Woolf

In the 1906 general election, the apolitical MacCarthy was electioneering on behalf of a friend. Ainsworth is 'the only possible subject' for conversation because MacCarthy and Moore were extremely close friends, and Strachey was curious to know what MacCarthy thought about Moore's strange liaison.

Lancaster Gate
January 19th 1906

[. . .] About the letters – I think certainly it's best that they should be sent to me – though the thought rather terrifies me. I expect them by

next mail, and shall be on tenter-hooks till they arrive. What a parcel of dynamite! I shall keep them in a special coffer, and look forward to reading them a good deal – past history is entertaining.

[. . .] I had dinner with MacCarthy the other night – nose to nose. He had been making electioneering speeches in Yorkshire – can you conceive it? – and he was going to return and make more in a few days. I found him as usual pretty stupid and very nice – but conversation did flag once or twice. What is one to say to him. He won't talk about Ainsworth, which is the only really possible subject of conversation, and it ends in his reading aloud passages from Walter Savage Landor, which he has read aloud every time I've been there. [. . .]

I gleaned one rather amusing thing from MacCarthy – a book privately printed by Lord Lovelace on the subject of Byron's separation. It proves beyond a doubt that he *had* committed incest with Augusta Leigh, and that Lady B. knew it. The book is written in the most disgusting semi-Byronic manner – Lord L. is his grandson – what ought to have been a mere statement of facts and proofs has been hashed up into a muddle of invective and expatiation. But several letters are printed which are the height of interest I think, though very sordid. One's opinion of Byron couldn't be very much lower, but it adds to the disgust to see him in these circumstances – thinking purely of himself, and of what people will think about himself, without a grain of decent affection, and every sort of stupid snobbish muddled feeling wreathing through his mind. Augusta was a miserable weak-kneed creature who, in spite of an uncontrolled passion, didn't care. They neither of them cared – she because she was too silly, he because he was too selfish; otherwise they would have gone together and faced out the world. As it was, she stayed, and he hardly wanted her not to, though he perpetually pretended that he did. He wrote Manfred in order to half-exhibit in his beastly ogling manner the depth and darkness of his sentiments. Astarte equals Augusta, and Manfred's anguish was the effect not of indigestion but of incest. The idiot! To think it *grand* to have copulated with one's sister! And to begin saying so, and to break off, and to look round over one's shoulder to see what effect one has had. Filth! The most interesting figure is Lady Byron – horribly unsympathetic and horribly good – in love with Byron, and hating him like Hell, furiously jealous of Augusta, and trying hard to save her soul. One thing she did which every feeling she had forced her to do – she prevented Augusta (who was weak and havering, and open to persuasion and almost domination) from leaving England. This satisfied Lady Byron's hatred of Byron, jealousy of Augusta, and love of morality. But Augusta was able to get in some digs at Lady Byron, which must have pleased her a good deal. Byron wrote to Augusta from Venice, swearing eternal devotion etc. The letter's extraordinarily Byronic, and contains one parenthesis in the best Don Juan manner – 'It is heartbreaking to think of our long separation – and I am sure more than punishment enough for all our sins. Dante is more humane in his "Hell", for he places his unfortunate lovers (Francesca of Rimini and Paolo whose case fell a good deal short of *ours* – though sufficiently naughty) in company – and though they suffer, it is at least together.' Then follows the usual blither – 'Circumstances may have ruffled my manner – and hardened my spirit – you have seen me harsh and exasperated with all things round me . . . but remember that even then *you* were the sole object that cost me a tear, and *what tears!*' *What tears*, indeed! But Augusta was decidedly up to snuff. She enclosed the letter, with a deeply affectionate rigmarole – a sort of mirage of vague ejaculations – 'damned crinkum crankum' as Byron called it – to Lady Byron. Imagine the feelings of the outraged puritan wife – feelings made all the more furious by her not daring, in her terror of driving Augusta into Byron's arms, to express them. The affectionate correspondence between the two women is a study in feline amenities. Byron's death, though, put an end to everything. Augusta went to the bad and the bankruptcy court, Lady Byron retired from the world and lived for years and years in silent virtue. After her death, everyone said that she had been an excellent woman, but, in one particular, a little mad. She seemed somehow to have got an obsession into her head which never left her – the poor woman believed that Byron had committed incest with Mrs Leigh.

[. . .] I went to see Mr Tree in the Enemy of the People last night, and had to come away in the middle, as I felt uncomfortably faint. Today I'm considerably better, but rather worn out. There's some damned crinkum crankum about my constitution.

your

GLS

‡

To Duncan Grant

69, Lancaster Gate, W.
January 25th 1906

Oh Duncan, Duncan, what a mad drivelling world! This is all I have to say, but I can't help sitting down at this most absurd and unletterish of hours – a quarter past ten, just after eggs and bacon – to tell you how mad and drivelling the world is. I suppose I am too, and all of us, the only difference is that *we* know it. Oh! let's keep the secret very close, let's tell no one – let's laugh and laugh and never say why. I want to run out into the garden without my hat, and pick some of those nice sunshiny flowers, and throw them in the faces of the world and all its fools. Won't you come too? In a few minutes we shall be middle-aged, married, respectable, and quite oblivious of how ridiculous we are. Oh, do hurry out, and let's gather rosebuds while we may. Vive! Vive! Vive la vie!

I'm pretty ill, and in very high spirits. I suppose in a few hours I shall be dismally depressed, Heaven knows why. I was last night, and thought of writing to you to say so, as a sort of relief, you know, – only I didn't see why I should annoy, and now here I am saying just the opposite. If you get this when you're tired and down in the mouth, I can imagine the lightning flashes of fury darting from your eyes. Well, do smile a little at your mad drivelling and loving Lytton

†

To Leonard Woolf

E. M. Forster published his first novel, Where Angels Fear to Tread, *in 1905. He had been in Germany the summer before this letter was written.*

69, Lancaster Gate, W.
January 26th 1906

I had hoped to have amused myself with my letters to you in the semi-collapsed state of cold which I've been in for the last week – but they haven't yet arrived. I'm beginning to get a little nervous. I got your letter saying you had sent them last Monday; it's now Friday, and there's no sign. I can only suppose that the parcels post starts several days later than the ordinary mail – but it seems queer.

[. . .] I went yesterday to the London Library, and saw something that I thought seemed familiar burrowing in a corner. I looked again, and yes! it was the Taupe. We talked for some time – almost for too long. He's a little changed – very bronzed and healthy-looking, and with very nearly the air of a settled establishment. His book has gone into a second edition, and he sits in Weybridge writing another, and will go on doing so all his life. He admits he's 'successful', and recognises, in that awful taupish way of his, the degradation that that implies. But he's of course perfectly contented. The thought of him sickens me. I think if one really does want a sign of our lapse, the Taupe's triumph is the most obvious. If we ever do boom, shan't we be horribly ashamed?

I went to the Gothic at home last night. Jack Pollock and Henry Lamb were the only other guests. I talked the whole time to Vanessa, who's exquisite in the real Gothic way, and whom I should fall in love with if I could. Tonight Duncan, Pippa and I go off to the 'Friday Club' in Chelsea to hear MacCarthy read a paper on 'Art'. I'm prepared for a frost – there generally is one when MacCarthy's concerned – but something fairly amusing will probably happen. Duncan hasn't been there before, and hardly knows any of the people, so it will be rather nice to watch him. We go to Cambridge tomorrow – I to Keynes and Kings, he to James and Trinity. I dread the hearthrug, and the terrible necessity for coming to some sort of a decision about elections. Keynes is in favour of Norton at once, and I suppose that will have to be. As to James – heaven knows – I turn pale when I think of our Morning Star plunged in the embraces of the corporal. D'you remember our hopes? – Ugh! – Is it all our fault? Or only God's? *[. . .]*

‡

To James Strachey

69, Lancaster Gate, W.
January 26th 1906

I'm coming tomorrow morning to stay at Kings. D*[uncan]* will travel with me, he says, but, he says 'we must part at the station, and never meet again'. Very well. I asked if we mightn't go from the station in the same motor bus. 'No.' Very well. I asked if I might go and see you.

'Only when I'm seeing Keynes.' Very well. I'm discretion itself, as you observe. But perhaps, after all, King's has its compensations.

your

Lytton

This letter might have been so much more indecent – it cuts me to the heart. But there's no time, and the envelopes are so damned transparent.

‡

To Leonard Woolf

In his December 1900 Apostles paper 'Is this an awkward age?' MacCarthy said it was evident that 'this is a self-conscious analytical age. Intellectual speculation is commoner . . . between friends than it was.' He remarked on the 'barrenness of the Society' and went on to say 'it seems that we take everything much more personally *than our predecessors. It is much more difficult for* us *to feel things in various capacities, from citizenship or membership of the University to membership of the Society, and the fact that they did so naturally gave them a superior versatility and definiteness of interest.'*[1]

Lancaster Gate

February 2nd 1906

My letters have come – in their wonderful tin box – and I have spent an entire day reading them. I read yours to me too, and I felt like a drowning man, who sees the whole of his past life flash before his inward eye. I quite agree with you about the different places and the gathering gloom – though it struck me, and I don't know with what truth, that your letters were more depressed than mine – though the depression itself seemed to be mine, and not yours so much. But perhaps this only applies to 1903–4. I wonder if future readers – if there ever are any – will think our gloom justifiable. It made me feel horribly low – the mere repetition of it. I wanted to weep and wring my hands as if I still felt those old agonies and agitations, as if my centre of the world was still at King's.

I went to Cambridge on Saturday to stay with Keynes. Sheppard read – the merest wash – a sort of resurrection of everything that anyone had ever maundered about for the last five hundred years – ever since

MacCarthy gave the society a premonitory shock with 'The Awkward Age'. Of all dim things a meeting of the Society is now the dimmest – to me no less than to you. Sheppard is like a fluffy doll, Keynes is like a Dutch doll. Hobby is like a wax doll that opens its eyes when you put up its head, and I'm like a doll that squeaks when you pinch it. The present theory is to elect Norton and James in a fortnight; the whole thing rests absolutely with me; and as far as I can see it's the best thing that can be done. James I'm sure is apostolic, though damned young; Norton is much more doubtful, but much more apparently right, for he talks 'philosophy' and 'sodomy' with great ease, in spite of his perpetual lapse into mere silliness. I think if only as a companion for James, who'd otherwise be so utterly left – that his election is advisable; and I don't think he'll do discredit. The question of V.P. I haven't yet decided, but I think it'll have to be Norton. Have you any idea what he's like? Fair, with rather a baby face, and rather ugly and honest looking. I expect you'd hate him a good deal for his affected silliness and his lack of thick feelings. But he's a mathematician, and Hawtrey and Keynes are perhaps sufficient precedent. *[. . .]*

I'm rather sick too – in a sort of prophetic manner. I have scarcely any doubt that James will fall in love with, or is in love with, my own seraph – Duncan. I've already noticed an irritating tendency in him to shoot over those preserves. And, if he declares himself, I see plainly enough that Duncan may, as likely as not, surrender. If it happens, I only know one thing more – that I shall crumple up; though how, and after what contortions and disgraces, passes my imagination. I've never been so completely bound. He has given me more joy than I ever dreamt of. He has satisfied my body, and my mind, and my heart. *[. . .]*

1. This paper is quoted more fully and discussed in Paul Levy, *Moore*, p.222ff.

‡

To Leonard Woolf

This is a second letter written this day, begun 'a little before going to bed'. MacCarthy was celebrated for failing to write his papers, and for his extemporaneous delivery of their matter. 'Art stopped short' (W. S. Gilbert, Patience). (Sir) William Rothenstein (1872–1945), best known as a portrait painter, studied at the Slade School and in Paris.

Desmond's marriage to Mary Warre-Cornish (1882–1953) is 'somewhat

incestuous' because her father, Francis (1839–1916) was an Apostle, and thus a
'brother' of Desmond. 'Buccleuch Place' refers to the flat in Edinburgh where
Moore was living with Ainsworth at the time this letter was written.

  The older Apostles Gerald Balfour, Harry Cust, Alfred Lyttleton and James
Parker Smith all lost their seats in Parliament in the Liberal landslide of the
general election of January 1906.

Lancaster Gate
Friday, February 2nd 1906

[. . .] I forgot to give an account in my last letter (posted I hope today)
of MacCarthy's paper last Friday at the Friday Club. It was in Henry
Lamb's studio in Chelsea – a large square room, with a great north
sloping window. There was a vast collection of persons – nearly all
artists, or quasi artists, male and female. The whole Gothic family was
of course there, and I came with Pippa and Duncan. MacCarthy had
naturally not written a paper, so he 'spoke' it as best he might. It was
the vaguest maunder about 'art' and 'technique' and 'surface' and
'the beauty of what was represented', but it served its purpose of
rousing a fiery discussion. Neville Lytton was there – a sort of Arab
faced, thick and thin adherent of Roger in his frenzy against Impressionism – a religious dogmatist who would have been a Roman
Catholic if he hadn't been an artist – who believes that Art stopped
short in the cultivated Court of the Empress Josephine just as a monk
believes in the infallibility of the Pope, and whose only test of the
beauty of a picture is whether it feels nice. He managed to rouse the
anger of the impressionists, male and female, who simply harangued
and gibbered at him by turns. I must say that I thought they came off
precious badly, though they were so obviously right. He, at any rate,
had, via Roger and the Society, a fairly definite and consistent set
of ideas; *they* were quite content with reiterating all the silly old
catchwords they had been content with reiterating from puberty. The
Artist 'interprets life', you may be glad to learn is the opinion of Mr
Rothenstein. How discriminating! My heart rather sank to hear them
blither. The occupation of arranging different coloured pigments is, I
can't help thinking, very lowering to the intellect. The thought of
Duncan allowing his mind to stagnate in Paris, while he thinks of
nothing but canvases and paint, sickens me rather. I want him in the
Society, on the hearthrug, in our own wonderful, exciting, intimate,
eminent world. I hate the thought of him as a furious genius – tout

entier à sa proie attaché;[1] though the result, one must suppose, will be magnificent. Baudelaire's account of Delacroix simply terrifies me. There seems to me something essentially odious and cruel in a universe which demands such awful sacrifices, which gluts itself with works of art, without caring two straws for the artist. Art is a sort of Moloch to which all the best feelings of man are offered up hideously and recklessly. No! Let us forego our Venuses and our Crucifixions, we shall be content with a few more hours of quiet laughter and happy affection, of kisses, and remembrances, and human warmth. I believe this is true, I believe Delacroix became at last a mere animal at work, sans thought, sans feeling, sans everything, and my belief becomes a terror because of Duncan's having – oh, so rightly for his art – made up his mind to go, almost immediately, to Paris. The phenomenal world stands there. Gaping to swallow him up. Heu, miserande puer![2]

Saturday 3rd. I received this evening the following from MacCarthy – 'Dear Strachey, I send you a piece of news! I am going to marry Molly Cornish. Now think of anything to say if you can! Your affect. D.M.' I really can think of nothing to say – even to you. I presume the lady is a daughter of the Vice P*[rovost]* of Eton, so the marriage'll be somewhat incestuous. But marriage! Lord! What squalid visions – the little ménage, and the dirty servant, and the bad cooking, and the respectable cops *[copulations]*! Ugh! I shudder at the thought. Is it marriage in itself or only marriage with females that's so execrably sordid? I don't know, but somehow I can't believe that if I were to marry Duncan it would be quite so bad. Buccleuch Place is flat, but it's not disgusting – and that's what I'm convinced the Desmond–Molly establishment will inevitably be. Perhaps I'm rather piling it on – only can you conceive of anything more dismal than the 'salon' which everyone must foresee they'll have? Is it only, after all, because they're so dismal themselves?

I wonder if it's because you look at him as a brother, and I as a human being, that you at any rate *talk* as if you put D.M. higher than I do. I admit that as brothers go he's certainly not to be sniffed at. Consider, pray consider, our wonderful 'successful' brothers, who have now been spewed out so delightfully by the phenomenal world! It really pleases me – Gerald Balfour, Cust, Lyttelton and Parker Smith – all sent about their business, all dismissed, buzzing, from their vacuum! I believe there's hardly an Apostle in the House of Commons. What a triumph for the whales! *[. . .]*

I find everything very maudlin and insipid and out of date, except the

question of when Duncan will have his next erection, and whether it's
pleasanter to feel his buttocks or look into his eyes.

your

GLS

1. 'C'est Vénus toute entière à sa proie attachée.' Racine, *Phèdre*, I,3.
2. *Aeneid*, Book 6, line 851, 'Alas, pitiable boy!'

‡

To Leonard Woolf

*The French poet Jean Moréas (1856–1910), born at Athens, was the grandson of
Papadiomontopoulos, one of the heroes of Missolonghi. A leader of the symbolist
movement, he advocated a loosening of the rigid rules governing French verse.*
    *Henry Sidgwick had died in 1900. The biography published in 1906 was by
his brother, the Greek scholar Arthur (1840–1920), and his widow, Eleanor
(1845–1936). She was the sister of A. J. Balfour, and herself Principal of
Newnham College from 1892 to 1910. Bishop (Joseph) Butler's (1692–1752)
ethical theory of objective intuitionism was important for Moore. Lytton's
exasperation is with respect to Butler's view that any objection to revealed
religion can also be levelled at the way nature is constituted.*
    *Van Dyck was in Italy from 1621 to 1627. In Genoa he received several
major commissions from the new rich and made several important portraits.*

Hôtel Helvetia
Piazza Nunziata
Genova
March 21st 1906

I cannot, cannot write. I only send this to show you where I am. It's
queer. I don't quite know why I've come – perhaps to enlarge my
mental horizon. Keynes is with me – en route for Florence. The day
after tomorrow I go back to Menton, and he proceeds on his way.
We came here yesterday – I in a steamer, which coasted along rather
charmingly, but as the boat was a second sardine box, and as all the
sardines were German (except me, and an old American who lectured
to me on Jesus Christ and Voltaire) it had its drawbacks. This town
is not very inspiring. There are streets of 'Palaces' – infinitely high,

broad, and solid, which écrasent; and that's about all. Travelling is a fraud, and all the fuss about it merely a relic of the Romantic Movement.

Talking of the R.M., I've seen a very sad specimen of its last oozed-out dregs – a magazine brought out by the very modern French – 'Symbolistes', etc. which they want me to subscribe to. I had expected something pretty bad, but really the reality surprised me. The flatness, the contortion, and the propriety of the whole thing pass belief. I wish I had it with me here to give you a specimen. Their prose is inconceivably vile – utterly formless and ugly and clumsy, and intolerably dull. Poor esprit français! There was an article on Rome by Maeterlinck, who said that Rome was a very beautiful place and full of objects of interest. There was an article on Napoleon by their greatest idol – Jean Moréas, whom I can only imagine is an imbecile. The article is entirely composed of two extracts about Napoleon from a life of him that everyone can read, and an anecdote that everyone knows. The only original statement of J.M. is that his copy of the life from which the anecdotes are taken had a blue paper cover, but that the sides had been torn off, and only the back remained. Their verse is on a par – it's all 'vers libre', which means verse without bones in it – a mere misshapen blob. Every word is written for effect, so that the whole thing is not only bad, but consciously bad, which really I think makes them worse than the worst 18th century grinders. It's all very depressing, and I can only hope that the triumph of Yennism may eventually make such things impossible for ever more.

I have begun to read the life of Sidgwick, which has just come out. It's chiefly letters – very heavy, but interesting as showing the deplorable states of mind of that generation. The wretched Sidgwick spent his whole life regretting Christianity. What an occupation! How could intelligent persons have fallen back so very far behind the encyclopedists? What would Voltaire have said to Sidgwick pompously setting out to learn Hebrew and Arabic, in order to sift the 'gospel story' to its foundations? As if l'infâme hadn't been écrasé a hundred years before Sidgwick was born! On people, of course he's too heartrending. 'I never heard of any man' he writes at the age of 21, 'even the most wholesale scoffer, saying a word against Butler.' Mon dieu!

Thursday. It's raining, and has been ever since we've been here. I fear we shall have to go the round of some more palaces and churches this afternoon, to inspect Guido Renis and dusty Vandykes. I want to stay

here forever. I want to eat nothing but omelettes and café au lait, I want
never to go out, I want to dream about copulations in the night, and
write about them in the day, or vice versa, or both at the same time. I
want to remember everything, and hope for nothing, and I want to die
a hundred years hence, with a volume of Voltaire under my pillow, and
the ghost of an erection still lingering between the sheets.

your
GLS

⁑

To G. E. Moore

*Henry Sidgwick's (1838–1900) resignation of his fellowship in 1869, because he
had become an agnostic, influenced Gladstone's decision to abolish religious tests
for college fellowships – which was thought to have been a great victory for the
Apostles. However, Sidgwick later became President of the Society for Psychical
Research and exposed himself to ridicule for his interest in what were certainly
fraudulent experiments. The philosopher who had, in his time, been the 'pope'
of the Apostles was seeking to smuggle the God whom he had banished by the
use of reason in through the back door of parapsychology.*

Villa Henriette
Menton-Garavan
(A.M.)
March 28th 1906

Dear Moore

I wrote to Ainsworth some time ago to say that I should probably
appear at the Reading Party, but I have now decided to stay on here
till the beginning of May, so that I'm afraid it's impossible. The sun
and the Dowagers of Menton have proved overpoweringly attractive;
also, I am here, and the strength of inertia contributes to hold me
rooted. How could I make up my mind to face the snows and whirl-
winds of the Peak, with the peacock-blue Mediterranean spread out
under my nose? The die is cast; I have 'extended' my return ticket; so
that I am no longer a free agent – a mere pawn in the vast and weaving
strategy of Messrs Cook. I hope other people will be less faithless. Will

you write and tell me what happens – where you go, who goes, etc.? I long to hear all about it.

I spend the days here pretty lazily, though I have breakfast at a quarter to eight. I write a few reviews, and spend the rest of the day having tea with ladies of sixty. My last great intellectual effort was the perusal of Sidgwick's Life. I wonder if you've read it. I found it extra-ordinarily fascinating – though I can't think why, as *every* detail was inexpressibly tedious. I never realised before what a shocking wobbler the poor man was; but my private opinion is that his wobble was not completely honest – I believe he did it because he wanted to, and not because he thought it reasonable. Really his ethical reason for postulating an Almighty is a little too flimsy, and I don't see how an intelligent and *truly* unbiased person could have swallowed it. His letters irritated me a good deal in other ways – but perhaps you wouldn't find them so. The conscientiousness and the lack of artistic feeling combined occasionally drove me wild. Also the tinge of donnishness – however, I suppose one must forgive a good deal quia multum amavit.

I made an expedition the other day to Genoa which isn't far off, and met Keynes there en route for Florence. He is going to whirl through Italy in a motorcar with the Berensons, which sounds highly unpleasant – they asked me, but I judiciously declined. He had read your Aristotelian papers in proof (via McT*[aggart]*), and gave me a sketch of it, but it seemed to me very different from *your* account. And I inferred that his was nearer reality.

I'm now reading Lockhart's Life of Scott, Blake's poems, & the Correspondence of Voltaire. It's a frightful mixture – but if one's a JOURNALIST what can one do? I read the first because I want to have read it, the second because they do me good, and the third because I like it – or because I think I might. How charming it would be to 'tear the heart out' of books, like Dr. Johnson! That's to say, if one liked hearts. I think I prefer the spinal marrow.

If you wrote to me, it would be charming. But I don't expect you will, and I'm not sure that I deserve it. However I'm only faithless in deed, and shall always be your

G. L. Strachey

[. . .]

‡

To Leonard Woolf

As Richard Monckton Milnes (1809–95), Lord Houghton, elected in 1829, was an Apostle of Tennyson's generation.

Villa Henriette
Menton-Garavan
France
April 3rd 1906

[. . .] I have now plunged into Lockhart's life of Scott, in order to be able to read Andrew Lang, who has brought out a boiled-down version of it. Scott was I suppose tolerable in the flesh – possibly Johnsonian or slightly Gothic – no! I don't think so – but in print one sees his defects a little too obviously. His lack of subtlety and of artistic sense is very shocking, and, after Voltaire, his lack of irony is overwhelming. What I wonder is whether we would have tolerated him if he had been at Trinity.

[. . .] My charming aunt remembers that she met, at the country house of our brother Lord Houghton, a young and unknown poet, called Mr. Swinburne. He had red hair and a green complexion; and he sat down with his hands between his knees, and recited one of his own poems, which had 'the most extraordinary rhymes'. This was before the publication of Atalanta. What a remote past! Shall we ever have such memories? Well, well, perhaps ours will be more exciting. Goodnight!

Friday *[. . .]* I'm going off in the train to see my sister and Simon Bussy and their new daughter, at Roquebrune, between this and Monte Carlo. They lead an 'ideal existence' there, living on painting and love and twopence a year. But why have babies?

your
GLS

✝

To Leonard Woolf

*Norton Senior really was seriously rich: £20,000 was worth the equivalent of
£1,220,439.84 in 2002. The younger daughter, present that weekend, was Lucy
Norton, the celebrated translator of the* Memoirs *of the Duc de Saint-Simon,
who became a founder of the Strachey Trust. Some time in the spring of this
year, the nickname 'Hobby' changed to 'Hobber', and some of his friends began
referring to Keynes as 'Maynard'. George Tomlinson (d.1863) founded the
Apostles in 1820.*

Oxford
June 14th 1906

I'm here, in this comfortable union, in rather a hurried moment, and
rather an unsettled state of mind. I came here, with Keynes, the day
before yesterday, and we have been staying with Swithin in Balliol. I
have floated and watched and smoked too many cigarettes and lunched
up the river on salmon and cold duck. *[. . .]*

There has been one adventure – odd, at any rate, and possibly
thrilling – since I last wrote. Norton – did you know? – was the eldest
son of a rich – a vastly rich father, at the head of a solicitor's business,
which brings in about £20,000 a year. So, at least, we seemed to gather.
The father, sixty, disagreeable, 'worldly', appeared to be the one block
in the way of a curious realisation of dreams – a millionaire in the
Society. We all plotted his death, naturally enough, wondering, when
we weren't arranging to have him stabbed or garrotted, how long he
would manage to last. The other day he, and his wife, and his two
daughters came up to lodgings for the 'May Week', and on Friday they
all had dinner with Norton and the Society. Harry, who was as ready as
anyone to do what he could, thought of putting a little arsenic in one of
the glasses of liqueur. Apparently he didn't, and it got into the wrong
one, for the only result was that Keynes got abominably drunk, and
when I came up the next day (Saturday) I found him lying on his sofa,
preparing to be sick. I dragged him off to tea with Hobber; we sat there
for a short time, when Norton rushed in. 'I shan't come to the Society.
My father has had an accident. He's fallen down the stairs.' We couldn't
help reflecting how singular it would be if this *was* what we had waited
for. Would we be murderers in the eye of Tomlinson and God? – Well!
Perhaps we are. The wretched man did actually die within six hours of

the accident. He had tripped on a dark staircase, he was heavy and old, and he fell down, bashing his head from side to side as he went. There was nothing to be done; the brain was shattered; and he was hardly conscious again. Remarkable? Poor Harry, at any rate, must have found it so, if he has had time in the horrible confusion and general upset. His mother he thought was going mad; but she was immediately comforted when it occurred to her that he was now happy in Heaven. I think she is the heir; but what can she do now, if Harry insists upon getting what he wants.

While this tragedy was going on, Verrall was reading on Tragedy to the Society. We all went there to dinner, with Dickinson, McTaggart, Sanger, and champagne. The paper was Verallian and very vague. The discussion was a full-bottomed wig one – i.e. all pomp and speeches, and no conversation. McTaggart seemed to me a little phenomenal, but perhaps it was only his endless 'wit' that made me think him so. The present Society (including me) were insufficiently serious and rather shy. What else could we be? In such a galère? What would they have thought of us, if they had heard our laughter when we knew – so soon and so incredibly – that ce bonhomme-là was dead?

your

GLS

‡

To Leonard Woolf

Lytton was correct in thinking that Russell was unhappy in his marriage. In the autumn of 1901, Russell recorded in his autobiography, he was riding his bicycle and suddenly realized that he no longer loved his wife, Alys.[1]

Trinity College
Cambridge
July 11th 1906

I am here, in the room which was once mine and is now James's. The change has not improved it. [. . .] I have fled here from Duncan, I saw him in London about a week ago, and was much more wrecked than I'd in the least expected. [. . .]

On Saturday I went to Oxford to the Russells, and returned on

Monday. It was as usual – very brilliant and appreciative and polite.
Poor Bertie struck me as being somehow pathetic – I daresay he wishes
he hadn't married his wife – but dear, dear, one's too far off to do or say
anything, or even quite to realise. He belongs to another world, don't
you think? It was absurd to get a letter from Duncan there, and written
with a wittering which none of *them* will ever understand.

I'm not well, or I could say a good deal. But perhaps it would only
be dreary. I think love makes one selfish – at least unfortunate love.
One can do nothing but nurse one's wounds. *[. . .]*

I saw Edgar the other day – rather gloomy and savage, I thought, and
very amusing. He says he doesn't care what he does in the damned
examination, and that all he knows is that in three months he'll be on
the streets. I suppose he really doesn't very much care, so that it doesn't
very much matter. I have been seeing a good deal of Norton; he's very
comforting to be with, and rather interesting. The comfort is merely
the result of his good spirits; the interest is in the character. He has a
sort of hardness, which sometimes is mere hubris, but is generally
latent in a curious kind of way. Perhaps it's really only youth – he
seems unbroken. Also combined with a good deal of intelligence about
people, he is almost Hawtreyan in density upon the most important
points. He has no real prescience, but sees things when they're shown.
I wonder very much what he'll be like a few years hence, and whether
you'll quarrel with him when you meet. He can be so abominably
rude! But I think on the whole you're so dangerous that he wouldn't
dare to be to you. Even I almost entirely quell him. It's chiefly to
phenomena that he's intolerable. They hardly any of them speak to him,
have blackballed him at the Sunday Essay, etc. etc. Hubback and Brown
hate him like poison, and he is consistently insulting to them in return.
[. . .]

1. Bertrand Russell, *Autobiography*, vol. 1, London, 1967–9, p. 222.

✝

To Leonard Woolf

Loch Merkland is twenty-five miles northwest of Lairg. Sir Charles Oman's
History of the Peninsular Wars *had recently been published in seven fat
volumes. Lytton's fellow guest was George Denholm Armour (1864–1949), who
contributed to* Punch *for thirty-five years. He was hunting-mad, and his editor,*

Owen Seaman, complained that Armour's cartoons were always about either
hunting or sport.

Loch Merkland Lodge
Lairg
Wednesday September 19th 1906

I am here, have been for more than a week. *[. . .]* One is incredibly
distant here from the entire world. I stayed for two nights with the Yen.
It was a nose-to-nose affair, as Ainsworth was absent, and accordingly
far from pénible. He was identical – except that his spectacles seemed to
have grown – they were complete circles, through which his eyes shot
hither and thither. I gather that he writes hardly anything, and spends
his time reading Peacock and the History of the Peninsular War. It was
mere Cambridge to be with him – the identical furniture, and pictures,
and piano, and food. What was absent was the excitement – there was
none. There was not even cynicism. It was all charming, smooth, and
urbane.

This is twenty miles from an infinitely remote Highland Station. It
is a shooting-box such as one imagines, completely composed of
pitch pine, if you know what that is, and close to a long lake, with
mountains, moors and stags in every direction. The beauty is often
great – the colours on the hills are soft, and the water is sometimes so
superb and blue – and the general sensation of health is exhilarating.
Needless to say though I am already bored, and am glad to be off
tomorrow, to join Keynes, James, and Norton in a lodging-house near
Rothiemurchus. Oh! I shall be bored there too, after the first few days;
and then I shall fly again – God knows where to – I suppose eventually
to the Yen once more, and then back to an eternity of London.

The ménage I found here was a queer one – Bell's squalid family –
abominably rich and devoid of any shred of gentility – Welsh and
good-natured and dull. They eventually vanished, leaving me with
Bell and a curious Scotch camel of the name of Armour. This has been
my company for the last week, Lord help me! Armour I think might
do well in Ceylon. He has a mind somewhat resembling that of a
respectable cook, he draws for Punch, and talks hunting without
intermission. Bell has at last appeared in his true colours. He's a perfectly
healthy and normal English sportsman with a tic for intellect. His fading
decadence in London is affectation, and gross affectation. His nature is
to shoot stags, and jump ditches; you should hear him exchange

sporting reminiscences! He moves among them with an ease −! The paraphernalia of cultivation sits upon him most clumsily. He's a Monsieur Jourdain up to date. In spite, though, of one's natural irritation, his good nature (which, of course, is blind enough) does reconcile one − or at any rate me − to not any more than a week of his society. He thinks that Vanessa will eventually marry him. It's impossible to say what may or may not happen in this monstrous universe, so that I can't help feeling a trifle nervous. If it should by any mad chance occur it would be a complete amalgamation of the disgusting and the grotesque. Imagine, please, the family!

Imagine, also, me (it'll be more truthful, though hardly less incredible) fly-fishing on the wet and windy loch, bouncing on ponies over cataracts and precipices, shooting in motors through endless vistas of desolation, tearing grouse with my fingers on impossible moors, and reading Baudelaire to an evening accompaniment of whisky and steeple-chasing. [. . .] But here is Bell. 'Don't you think, Strache, that Velazquez is simply − simply excriable?' Adieu!

your
GLS

‡

To Leonard Woolf

Feshiebridge is in Inverness-shire. Near the beginning of this letter Lytton laments that he is still 'desperately in love' with Duncan. Marie-Thérèse Rodet Geoffrin (1699–1777) became a power in Paris society only at the age of fifty; she held two salons a week, on Monday for artists, and on Wednesday for her friends the Encyclopedists and other literary people, who included Horace Walpole and David Hume. 'The poor old Doctor' was Keynes's father, the logician John Neville Keynes (1853–1949).

Woodside Cottage
Feshiebridge
Friday, September 28th 1906

I am quite alone in a dim Highland Cottage beside a roaring Highland stream, wondering what I am doing here, and weeping over the web of life. [. . .]

The blue calm of Highland life was ruffled this morning for a moment. A telegraph boy appeared with a telegram for Keynes. It announced that he was second in the Civil Service Examination. Don't you think it's almost incredibly appropriate? To be second! – Poor Maynard! He has hurried off to London to consult Hawtrey as to what it is worthwhile for him to take. As I watched him go off into the darkness, it seemed to me that I'd seen the last of him. Do you know the remark of Madame Geoffrin? She used to say 'Voilà qui est bien' whenever the conversation in her salon was getting a little dragging or a little out of hand, and then everything relapsed immediately into quiescence. Really the telegram this morning with the poor old Doctor's 'very hearty congratulations' was simply, after all the fuss and worry of whatever, in Keynes's life, there has been of tragi-comical, God's 'Voilà qui est bien.' Don't you see him, dead and galvanised, at the Treasury? *[. . .]*

Poor old Keynes! (For there can be little doubt that now he's in the category.) Don't you think one's final observation on him must be one of grateful recognition? A testimonial for services seems to me the only thing. MacCarthy's spiteful remark that his chief object in life was to impress men of forty has an air of truth, and, when I was angrier with him than I ought to have been, I did think it true. But now it seems to me that his object really is to be impressed by boys of nineteen; and such a pursuit can only raise one's pity. Oh no! it's not because I'm bitter that I've come to that conclusion, but simply because I'm conscientious (as I always was) and can't help seeing what a bad taste he's got, and what a good heart. *[. . .]*

‡

To Leonard Woolf

Lancaster Gate
Sunday, November 4th 1906

[. . .] If you were here, I should try to give you a description of the meeting in Trafalgar Square the other day, in favour of Women's Suffrage. I couldn't drag myself to it, but my mother and Pippa and Marjorie went, and stood among the lions and looked at the crowd. Their accounts were amusing *[. . .]* One incident you may be able to smile at. The resolution in favour of Women's Suffrage was 'Passed

unanimously, except for some boys'. This was wit, and pleased the mob. But an old gentleman was furious. He pointed to two appalling hags standing beside him, and said 'What do you call these ladies, sir? Are they boys?' Before the chairman could think of a repartee, some boys from the background shouted out, 'No! Thank goodness they're not!' Rather delightful! [. . .]

Tuesday midnight. *[Duncan]* has been here again this evening, and Keynes too. I have suffered dreadfully. I have felt more utterly discouraged than I ever have before. My health has gone, I spend hours in miserable trances, I feel almost as if I were really dying. It's pretty bad to have Keynes as one's solitary comforter. He asks me why I'm so particularly shattered today, and he asked the same question yesterday, and will ask the same tomorrow. [. . .]

Thursday. I went the other day to the Temple, and heard sad news of the Gothic ménage. Vanessa has returned to England, and is recovering though still very weak; but a week ago Thoby was seized with pneumonia and was, I gather, very ill indeed. He's now also recovering. Adrian and Virginia nurse the patients as well as they can. Bell hovers around a good deal. I haven't been there yet, but they said they'ld let me know when visitors could be allowed.

[. . .] My sister-in-law is a character in Jane Austen – the silliest in the world. The other night someone said something of the Christians hating the Jews. – 'What! D'you mean to say that Jews aren't Christians?' Pippa whispered nervously that they killed Christ, and were glad they had done so. 'Ho! But don't they go to church?' [. . .]

‡

To Leonard Woolf

The picture dealer Agnew's has been at the same Old Bond Street address since 1876. William Henry Salter (1880–1969), lawyer and 'psychical researcher', went up to Trinity in 1897. President of the Society for Psychical Research 1947–8, Salter was the son-in-law of Prof. A. W. Verrall and his wife, Margaret, who thought she was a 'medium'. There were many Haldanes associated with Cambridge. George Morland (1763–1804) was an English painter of animals and rustic scenes. This painting was made into a famous engraving by Edmund Scott, first published in 1790. The scene is wholly decorous.

Lytton's animus against Sir Sydney Lee springs from Lee's insistence that Shakespeare's private life has nothing to do with the greatness of his work.

Frances M. Brookfield published her book on the early Apostles in 1906. It
had a few good stories about 'Jackie' Kemble and others, but, as Lytton archly
implies, Mrs Brookfield was misled about her father-in-law's membership of the
Apostles, and got a good many things wrong.

Lancaster Gate
Saturday, November 10th *[1906]*

I went to Agnew's this afternoon, to look at some pictures. I'd hardly
got into the room, when I heard 'Hullo, Strachey!' in familiar tones.
I looked round, and there was Salter. He looked perhaps a little less
infirm, but his mind was certainly identical. – 'Have you seen the
picture of the old lady? It's absurdly like Haldane. He must be her
reincarnation.' It was a wonderful Franz Hals, and while I was gazing,
Salter vanished. I've never known him so tactful before. The exhibition
was charming. There were several Gainsboroughs, with faces of Turkish
delight, and a very eminent Vandyke. There was also a Morland, called
'Boys Bathing'. I saw the name in the catalogue and hurried to it. My
expectations were not disappointed – there was a most mischievous-
looking boy coming out of a pool, with a large Newfoundland
dog. *[. . .]*
    I am reviewing a book for the Spectator by Sidney Lee, and it's on
Shakespeare. I shriek at every page, but I'm afraid the poor dear
Spectator won't allow anything but a very veiled frenzy. He actually
comes out with all that ghastly garbage of Churton Collins, about
Shakespeare's 'moral sense' and 'optimism'. However, it's not
worthwhile getting angry about, though really it's a little too dreary to
laugh at. It would be charming to write a dunciad on them all, don't
you think? But I suppose if it was really true and virulent no one would
publish it – not even the Times Book Club.
    I have finished Keynes's epitaph, and here it is, such as it is –

In Memoriam J.M.K. Ob. Sept. 1906

Here lie the last remains of one
Who always did what should be done,
Who never misbehaved at table,
And loved as much as he was able;
Who couldn't fail to make a joke,
And, though he stammered, always spoke;
Both penetrating and polite,

A liberal and a sodomite,
An atheist and a statistician,
A man of sense, without ambition,
A man of business, without bustle,
A follower of Moore and Russell;
One who in fact, in every way,
Combined the features of the day.
By cursing blest, by blessings cursed,
He didn't merely get a first.
A first he got; on that he'd reckoned;
But then he also got a second.
He got a first with modest pride;
He got a second, and he died.

[. . .] The 'Cambridge Apostles,' which you ask about, is to come out in a few days. It is by Mrs. Brookfield, whose father-in-law was an old Mr. Brookfield who went about with old Apostles. She thinks he was one himself, I gather, and the book is to be about him and his Cambridge friends. She wrote to McTaggart for information; he passed the letter on to Sheppard, who replied that he had none to give. No more was heard, but heaven knows what she may be saying. I suppose there'll be fine reviews in all the papers. There was an extract from the preface in the Daily Mail, in which it spoke of the Apostles being a Cambridge society, which, 'it is understood', is still in existence. Rather a good phrase! How splendid it'll be if there's an appendix on the present Society! *[. . .]*

‡

To Leonard Woolf

69, Lancaster Gate, W.
November 21st 1906

I can only hope that you may know the dreadful thing that has happened, from other letters or papers, for I feel that to break it to you is almost beyond my force. You must be prepared for something terrible. You will never see the Goth again. He died yesterday. I know no more, except that his pneumonia turned out to be typhoid; Lamb told me this in Cambridge, I thought it sounded grave, but thought no more; this morning a letter came from MacCarthy, supposing that I knew it, I guessed, and found it in the Times. One can say nothing. Indeed I feel that I hardly realise now what it means; I say it to myself – but how can one grasp it? Only I know that as time goes on, we shall feel it more and more. This is the contrary way of grief; but then, in this, nature herself has grown unnatural. Oh my dear, if you were here now! Turner is in Denmark. Bell I dread to see, and Adrian – poor thing! – how shall I meet him? I don't understand what crowning pleasure there can be for us without him, and our lives seem deadly blank. There is nothing left remarkable beneath the visiting moon. It is idle to talk; but it is only to you that I can say anything, that he was the best, the noblest, the best – oh God! I am tired out with too much anguish. Oh God!

The funeral is tomorrow. It will be right for me to go, though I can't bear the thought. I hope to hear then that Vanessa is going on all right. You are with me, I know; and I with you.

Thursday. The funeral was at Golder's Green Crematorium – beyond Hampstead. My mother and I drove there. There were between 20 and 30 people there, I think – most of them relations. Adrian and Virginia were there, and the two Duckworths, and poor old Mrs. Fisher, his mother's sister. Neither MacCarthy nor Bell was there. George Trevy read the service – it was the part of the burial service which Leslie Stephen had chosen to be read in his own funeral. I think it was chiefly from Ecclesiasticus. He read quite well, and there was only the very slightest trace of affectation – I shouldn't have noticed if I hadn't feared it'ld be there. I think the verses must have been chosen by Leslie when he was an old man – at least they seemed to apply strangely to that – there was a constant reference to the repose of death, and the weariness of life – just as there was in Leslie's own face. It was curious and terrible to be reminded that the life of man was four score years and ten. The coffin was covered with flowers, and slid down into an opening in the wall till it was out of sight.

Nox est perpetua una dormienda.

your

GLS

I have looked at the prayer-book, and find that the verses were taken from Psalms 39 and 90 and two from the Book of Job.

✝

To Leonard Woolf

The lines Lytton quotes are from Songs from Death's Jest-Book III.
Athulf's Death Song *by Thomas Lovell Beddoes (1803–49) is very apposite to
Vanessa's situation, and continues 'Death and Hymen both are here'. Virginia
asked several of Thoby's Cambridge friends to write a commemorative piece about
him, to help her come to grips with her brother's death, and to get to know those
aspects of his life of which she felt she did not know enough. After a year had
passed, however, Lytton had to admit that he still could not bring himself to
write about Thoby.*

Lancaster Gate
Monday, November 26th 1906

I feel as if after my last letter there could be nothing more to say; and
yet there is more. The horror of my last I'm afraid I may have given too
abruptly, almost callously, – but what words are there, and how is one
to utter any at all? I am a bringer of bad news, and feel the disgrace of
this almost reflected upon myself. Oh! Please be ready for something,
which, after all, perhaps you have already guessed. Vanessa and Bell are
engaged. I had feared the possibility of it, and here it is! It's easy to
imagine how it happened, not so easy to see how she can be happy,
radiantly happy, in such strange company. What comment is there?
Only, I suppose, that one must hope for the best, and remember the
fundamental goodness of Bell, and say nothing of what remains. Poor
Virginia! And Adrian! They must set up house together now. The mind
recoils. Time may do something; but how little! Oh, tears! tears! I saw
them yesterday, and you can imagine that it was awful. Virginia in the
drawing-room; Vanessa in bed, with Bell flitting round. I could only
think of Beddoes' poem –

> A wedding-robe and a winding-sheet,
> A bridal bed and a bier.

Your letter came two days ago, in which you say that the Goth is the
one person to fall back upon, and end with 'He stands, doesn't he?' One
wants to cling on to one's chair. I saw your brother Cecil when I was
last in Cambridge, and he said that you thought you might be able to
come home in the spring. How I hope so! But what a bitterness in that

cup. The miserable Turner struggles home today from Copenhagen; I haven't seen him; but Pippa says he was quite lost. Don't you feel like Job? Terrors are turned upon me: they pursue my soul as the wind: and my welfare passeth away as a cloud.[1] I am a brother to dragons, and a companion to owls.[2]

Friday. I am too unhappy to write more. They have asked me to write something about him, to be privately printed. But how? I went to lunch with George Trevy yesterday. He thought me sick and crazy; and you, from your last letter, I suppose think so too.

1. Job 30:15.
2. Job 30:29.

‡

To Leonard Woolf

69, Lancaster Gate
Wednesday, December 5th 1906

I want to attack you about your wickedness in tearing up my letter. I really did feel inclined to be bitter about it, and I should still be irritable if I were to speak. Was it so dangerous as all that? And if so, couldn't you have put it into an envelope and sent it straight back to me? I don't make it out. Surely it was worth keeping, if only as a document; or ought it, even as a document, to have been destroyed? It's that I really can't – if I do take your meaning – quite get over. You mention the Yen as a certain objector. – 'But at last I would fall back upon the certain condemnation of Moore.' – His condemnation of what? Of finding out the truth and telling it? Doubtless the truth may make one 'feel a little sick', but heavens! is that relevant? Two things add fuel to my fury. – Your talking about 'healthy' vice. Really! Really! – And also the conviction that the letter was a chef-d'oeuvre. I can't be quite sure which it was, but I think it must have contained the description of the wonderful scene in Hobber's bedroom, and his astounding – 'How would you like me? – Au naturel?' With his equally astounding excuse to Duncan – 'I thought it would be so amusing to see Keynes contort.' Well, it's quite true that when I wrote it, it did strike me as a trifle high, but it never occurred to me that you'ld do what you did with it. I suppose this letter will follow it, you demon! Eh bien! I'm resigned to most things; only, if it really is only fright, why not just post them back?

I went to Cambridge on Saturday, and saw the Greek play. It was grotesque. The chorus consisted of the twelve ugliest undergraduates in Cambridge, dressed in mauve gauze; they looked exactly like a melancholy band of harlots who had grown too old for work and were lamenting their situation. [. . .] There was only one moment of relief – the appearance of Rupert Brooke as a herald, dressed in gold armour, and with red-gold hair, and looking (if you didn't see his ridiculous profile) the image of an exquisite youth from an early Italian picture. But the total effect was so gloomy that I hardly remembered that I had ever seen a Greek play before [. . .]

As for Keynes – [. . .] I can't help recognising that, in the obvious and proper sense, he is my friend. Yet sometimes, when he says something, the whole thing seems to vanish into air, and I see him across an infinite gulf of indifference. That there should be anyone in the world so utterly devoid of poetry is sufficiently distracting; and, when I reflect that somebody is Maynard, I can't be surprised at my cracking jokes on him with the Corporal about empty biscuit-boxes, and yet. How well I know that he'ld do most things one could think of for me, and his eyes – – !

[. . .] I went to Gordon Square on Tuesday. They are all well, Vanessa recovering quickly. The marriage they think will be in March. Virginia and Adrian are going to set up house – they don't quite know where. They're all of course very splendid! Oh! Oh! –

Are you coming home in the spring? It seems a good way off still, but I suppose we shall get to it, and find ourselves in pretty much the same state as we're in now. As for my own particular future, I admit I feel a little wobbly. I wish I could talk to you about it. There are some complications, but on the whole it seems to me clear that I *ought* to stop journalism and begin some sort of a real chef-d'oeuvre. But the necessary effort! God! Can I? I shudder on the brink. It would mean not only comparative poverty, which I think I might stand, but the dreadful weight of the responsibility attaching to meandering idleness. How am I to know that I can write a comedy? And, even if I can, have I the energy? I see myself in an eternal trance. [. . .]

‡

To Leonard Woolf

Sir Richard Strachey's expectations of a pension stemmed from the fact that,
during his career in India, he was largely responsible for the country's vast
network of railways and canals. John, 1st Viscount Morley (1838–1923), was
Secretary for India from 1905 to 1910. Lytton's expectation of £200 a year had
the purchasing power of £12,000 on 2002 values; so it was not a very great deal
of money; but, of course, his current allowance was worth only £3,000. Lady
Strachey's will sounds particularly odd because James was younger than Lytton
and, presumably, equally dependent on his parents. This letter marks Lytton's
return to signing his name rather than his initials – a Bloomsbury practice
gaining currency. Incidentally the envelope containing this letter was preserved; it
is addressed simply to 'L.S. Woolf Esqre., Jaffna, Ceylon.'

69, Lancaster Gate, W.
January 24th 1907

I seem to live in a whirl of money affairs, which is a new thing to me.
My father wishes to retire – he's in his 90th year, and beginning to get a
little bored. We have saved enough to live on comfortably, but not in
this ocean of a house. However, it was reasonably thought that he'd
receive some sort of a pension, which might enable us to stay on here,
and so escape the horrors of moving, and then (as would have to
happen) moving again. The Railway belongs in part to the Government
of India, so that it can't spend money without the consent of the India
Office. Application was made to the India Office by the Directors, who
hadn't any doubt that his incredible services would be recognised. This
morning, however, a letter has arrived to say that Morley *in person* has
refused to allow a single penny to be spent. This is pretty sickening, but
apparently other things can be done – the most probable being that the
shareholders will *themselves* give a large bonus – apparently they have the
power – but the complication's frightful; and meanwhile everything's in
the balance. My own particular affairs are queer. All our money now
belongs to my mother (to avoid death duties) and she has made a will,
by which I am left £200 a year. The peculiar thing is that, as far as I can
make out, I am the *only* one of the sons left anything – the daughters are
each to have corresponding sums, and then whatever's left over is to be
divided among the other sons. But it doesn't seem at all probable that
anything will be left over – especially after today's news. But everything

that's saved now will go into this fund, to be divided among my brothers eventually. It's therefore my plain duty to cost as little as possible, so that the fund may be increased. If this were the only consideration, it would be clear enough that I ought simply to devote myself to journalism, by which I could at once earn enough to support myself, and give up the allowance of £50 a year I get at present. *But –* here's the rub. I think it's equally my duty to write plays if I possibly can. And, as I shall eventually have enough to live on, it seems to me madness to embark on a career of journalism, which I don't mean to follow up, and which is beastly. I've therefore pretty well made up my mind what to do. Thank heaven MacCarthy's projected Quarterly seems to be really coming off. By this – which will only involve slight and pleasant work – I shall get with luck £100 a year. I shall then be able to drop all other journalism, and give up the rest of my time to plays. I should then, I think, be able to reduce my allowance to £25. Don't you think this is the best thing? I have been thinking about it for months, and I feel more and more that a stand *must* be made, and that to go on pottering over reviews (unless absolutely necessary for life, which it fortunately isn't) is an utter waste. Say a word on this financial letter!

your
Lytton

✝

To Leonard Woolf

Cecil Francis Taylor was in fact elected to the Apostles in November 1910. His grandfather, the English mathematician George Boole (1815–64),was a pioneer of symbolic logic. Ethel Lillian Voynich (1864–1960), née Boole, wrote best-selling period novels as 'E. L. Voynich', such as The Gadfly *(1897, set against the background of the Young Italy movement),* Jack Raymond *(1901),* Olive Latham *(1904) and* An Interrupted Friendship *(1910).*

69, Lancaster Gate, W.
February 1st 1907

[. . .] There is a dim embryo whom nobody ever speaks to, called Taylor. He is a grandson of Boole, the mathematician, and a nephew of that dreadful Mrs Voynich, who wrote Jack Raymond and other ghastly works. I suppose I shall never meet him, and they'll never elect him, so it doesn't much matter. *[. . .]*

It is now settled that we leave this house as soon as possible – probably by the end of March. I daresay Hampstead will shelter us – it sounds dreary, but I shouldn't think it'll turn out much worse than this. The move will be écrasant, won't it? Mon dieu, the books! But one must draw a veil – since one can't draw a pension. What do you think of Mr. Morley, who has been getting a thousand a year for heaven knows how long because he was once a cabinet minister for a few months? But I suppose it's to be expected that politicians should think that talking politics is the only thing that deserves reward. The thought of the House of Commons fills me with nausea – doesn't it you? When I pass it – you fortunately can't – I curse it, so loudly that the policemen stare. When one reflects upon the utter fatuity of everything that is said and done in public, one prays for the government of Venice, where at any rate people were fools in secret. The newspapers! – do you read them? They're simply incredibly orgies of bosh. I think of bringing out one printed in sympathetic ink, which one'll only be able to read by holding it over the fire. With these precautions, I shall venture to say that Mr Gladstone was a fraud, that God does not exist, and that Plato was quite right to want to kiss Alcibiades. How many people would subscribe? Do you think six?

I went to see the Doctor's Dilemma the other day, and was amused. The stage is I believe the one hope. The acting was magnificent, the dialogue adequate, the play absurd. If only Bernard Shaw had been screwed up a peg higher, it would be worthwhile living. As it is, I can only hope that I'm screwed up high enough myself. But isn't that dreadfully doubtful? Oh, lord! I'm simply in *terror* at the thought of making the plunge. I really doubt if I've got the guts. It sometimes strikes me that I haven't the very dimmest notion of how to do the business, and that all my efforts will be simply grotesque. Well, well! I must put my trust in the Almighty. *[. . .]*

‡

To Leonard Woolf

69, Lancaster Gate, London
Wednesday, February 6th 1907

Bell and Vanessa are to be married tomorrow at 10.30 in a registry office. They have invited no one – not even their nearest relations – and some distress has been caused. Her aunts weep and wail, and George Duckworth does the same, Very silly, but perhaps natural. They go to Wales for two months, and then to Paris; and in the meantime Virginia and Adrian will have to find themselves a house. Bell now does his hair in the most outré manner conceivable, and really looks absurd. It's brushed right back off his forehead, so that it forms a sort of yellow aureole. His moustache is off, and the result is queer, though perhaps on the whole more pathetic than anything else. I dined with them on Monday, and we seemed to talk a great deal. She's very intelligent: how long will it be before she sees he isn't? Perhaps she never will, or perhaps she'll think (and perhaps rightly) that it doesn't much matter whether he is or not. *[. . .]*

Everyone in this household is a 'Suffragette', or at least a Suffragist. Pippa is organising a vast procession, which is to march to Exeter Hall next Saturday, in order to impress the public with the necessity of giving women votes. As for me, je ne vois pas la nécessité, but I do think it would be an excellent thing. Whether I shall join the procession or not is another question. As a matter of fact, I shan't, as only women are allowed. But I suppose I shall find myself in Exeter Hall, waving a banner, inscribed with the words 'File the Fetters!' or something of the sort. *[. . .]*

‡

To Clive Bell

The pastels shown at Leighton House were the work of Simon Bussy.
Eugene Brieux's (1858–1932) plays were didactic, aimed at some weakness or
iniquity of the social system. Les Hannetons, *a comedy in three acts, was first*
staged in 1906.

69, Lancaster Gate, W.
March 25th 1907

Dear Clive,

I have been wicked not to write before now – but I have been engulfed
in Cambridge, and what can you expect from Cambridge besides
laziness and talk? *[. . .]* If you have the time and strength, take Vanessa
to Leighton House before you go, to look at my brother-in-law's
pictures, which I think you'll both like. They are all pastels, and most
of them dreams of beauty.

Cambridge was delicious. Lamb's rooms were ideal, with books and
every comfort imaginable, and I simply lapsed through a fortnight of
vague delights. Would you have hated it? Very probably, but then – In
the interval, I've been to the MacCarthys' rural residence, in Suffolk I
believe, which was amusing, but damned cold. We talked about
Bernard Shaw, of course, and modern poetry, and whether the Nation
is better than the Speaker, and not much else. But what a dreadful
business is conversation! So many remarkable contingencies are
necessary to make it anything but intolerable that it's surprising that it
ever *does* come off. The worst of it is that with advancing years it
doesn't seem (to me at any rate) to grow more easy or more amusing.
But perhaps I should be 'thankful' that it doesn't grow less.

I went the other day to Hedda Gabler. Mrs Patrick Campbell was fat,
old, and lumpish, and the play was very very dull. When I came out, I
couldn't make up my mind whether I was more like Hedda's husband
or Hedda, but it really doesn't matter. Today I went to an even more
depressing performance – a translation of 'Les Hannetons' by Brieux –
which is not only sordid and tedious but highly moral into the bargain.
Ought this to be allowed? But I daresay Brieux is one of your favourite
authors (I know he's Jack Pollock's), and perhaps Les Hannetons is your
favourite play. Great, oh great, are the glories of modern French.

Poor Turner's volcanic energy has deserted him. His lava flows no
more. It is all dust and ashes now, and decrepitude and sciatica. I
suppose nothing can be done, but it's melancholy to see him, pale and
épuisé, hardly able to sit in a chair, or to get out of one when he has
once got in. He showed me the MS of his opera this evening. Will its
final resting-place be the British Museum, beside the notebooks of
Beethoven? Well! At any rate *we* shall never know, because we shall
never survive him!

Tell Lamb that I was delighted to get his letter this morning, and that I'll answer it when I have anything (or nothing) to say. My dear Vanessa, will you look up my little cousin, when you're in Paris? He would like it very much, and this is his address –

Duncan Grant, 22 Rue Delambre, Boulevard Raspail

yours ever
Lytton Strachey

✝

To Leonard Woolf

Woolf's thoughts on democracy at this time seem to have been that there were some advantages in not having democratic rule in countries such as the one he was helping to administer.

Lancaster Gate
Tuesday, March 26th 1907

I hope you will really continue the subject of your last letter in your next. I don't think I agree with you, though I quite see that your view of 'Democracy' is calculated to make you hate it. I believe in it – purely as a gamble. It seems to me that we've put all our money on the one possible thing there was to put money on, and that if we win it'll be glorious, and if we lose it'll only be very much what it's always been. The old system was essentially unreasonable, and now there's at least the chance that reason may come out top. I admit that the spectacle of the East conducting itself on 'liberal principles' is sufficiently sickening; but in the meantime the West has produced Moore – and isn't that a counterpoise? And, if we're going in for the gamble, let's do it thoroughly – that's I'm sure our only chance now. Votes for Women!

[. . .] It distresses me to see my father getting very old. The other day he fainted suddenly, and for some time we were very anxious. However, he seems to have got over it now. But how horrible! how horrible! I go away from here with a sinking of the heart. I hardly dare to think of what my mother feels. The great comfort is that it has been a great life.

'No weakness, no contempt,
Dispraise, or blame; nothing but well and fair.'[1]

Can you hear the Goth saying these lines? Alas!

[. . .] We really are going to leave this house, and Hampstead looms in the foreground. I daresay in some ways we shall be more comfortable – no butler, and hardly any stairs, and the fresh breezes of the heath. On the other hand, how we shall ever manage to see anyone again beats me. Mais il faut vivre. *[. . .]*

1. Milton, *Samson Agonistes.*

✝

To James Strachey

Court Barton

North Molton

Devon

April 15th 1907

[. . .] We play Jacoby now, instead of bridge, and Moore wants to know what is *meant* when somebody has 15, and somebody else six. How can you *have* a number? And what *is* it that you have? He asked Russell what he thought about it, and Russell at once replied 'It's a conventional system by which the progress of each player in the game is indicated.' But that didn't at all suit the Yen. 'It's a very queer relation, and I want to find out exactly what it is.' But of course he never will, poor fellow! *[. . .]*

✝

To Leonard Woolf

Court Barton

North Molton

Devon

Wednesday, April 17th 1907

[. . .] I'm very much tempted to give you a surprise when you come – so that you'ld start back and wonder who on earth *that* could be, so tall, and thin, and spectacled, *and* – with a beard! – No! I'm afraid I shall have to shave it; but now, at the end of three weeks' unimpeded

growth. It seems very sad to have to do away with it – so fine and red as it is, and almost half an inch long. However, the world would revolt, or at any rate mention it, which would be sufficiently tedious, so I shall have to wait until I'm an established literary man, and can carry the whole thing off with a corduroy coat and a peacock blue tie à la Turner. *[. . .]*

†

To Leonard Woolf

H.O. Meredith is sometimes cited as one of the models for Ansell in Forster's 1907 novel The Longest Journey. *Oddly, Lytton did not seem to recognize Ainsworth as the chief model for the character of Ansell.*

Russell's successful Conservative opponent for the Wimbledon constituency was Henry (later Viscount) Chaplin (1841–1923). The 'sweepstakes' refers to an earlier letter in which Leonard said he thought he'd won £100, enough to allow him to visit England.

69, Lancaster Gate
May 2nd 1907

Here we are in May, and in another week or two it'll be winter again. Dieu! My laziness! I lapse and lapse, I read Voltaire, I walk in Kensington Gardens, I talk to MacCarthy, I flutter round the British Museum. I dream of masterpieces, and I go into a trance. Isn't it scandalous? I'm in a backwash of time, where one swings from side to side and never advances; but some day shan't I come out into the open? The Lord knows. En attendant, I must tell you the latest piece of gossip I've discovered about poor dear Voltaire. In an edition of Gray's commonplace books, I found a mysterious omission – 'quite impossible to print' – on the subject of V. I went to the B.M. to see what it was, and was rewarded with this. – When he was in England, one day he was dining with Pope, and cursed and blasphemed very violently because of his bad health. They asked him what he supposed was the reason. He answered – 'When I was boy, those damned Jesuits buggered me to such an extent that that I shall never get over it as long as I live.' This in English in front of the servants and ladies. Rather supreme? He must have been the most amusing person in the world.

Forster's novel has come out. I wonder if he's sent it you. I shall eventually get it second hand, and send it you if you haven't got it by then. I think it's a good deal worse than the last, and it certainly contains things infinitely more foul. There's a great deal about Cambridge and the Society, and Hom is one of the principal figures. The morals, the sentimentality, and the melodrama are incredible, but there are even further depths of fatuity and filth – but you'll see. I believe that in time he'll become a popular author, and rake in cash. How horrible!

The latest news in the political world is that Bertie Russell is standing for Parliament as a Woman Suffrage candidate. Queer? He only does it on the express understanding that he won't get in, and as he's against Chaplin in Wimbledon, there's no chance. You can imagine me supporting him on Putney platforms – will you be back in time to join? You say nothing of your sweepstakes. Was it a mirage after all? Though really I shouldn't be surprised if you suddenly walked in one day, and found me copulating with – whom?

I've been once or twice to see Mr and Mrs Bell – d'you know whom I mean? – Is it conceivable? They are obviously in love with each other, though last time I was there, coming into the rooms unannounced, there was a most violent scrimmage heard, and they appeared very red and tousled. It was like those charming days in Cambridge, when one had to cough before coming into a room, for fear of disturbing Keynes and Hobby. Good lord! did that ever really happen? Don't you think of all fates, Hobby's has been the most amazing? He's now very fat and pompous and discusses amicably whether one ought to copulate or not. He's working hard for his Science Tripos, but he's far too stupid to do anything but just get through. Even to do this, he'll have to sweat his podgy eyes out, and he's promised his father to give up all his clubs and societies, including the Apostles Club. James and Norton are blue with terror, because if he doesn't pass he'll be up for another year; so they do everything they can to encourage him, and agree that he'd better go to bed on Saturdays at 10.30, in case he should get tired. *[. . .]*

‡

To James Strachey

69, Lancaster Gate, W.
May 19th 1907

[. . .] I am feeling pretty wild here. If one were sarcastic what an account one could give of one's dinner table! Really family life does carry away the palm with a vengeance! However, it's no good dwelling on such things. In addition the move fever has just begun to bubble and simmer. This morning I spent an hour with her Ladyship and a tape-measure, noting down the dimensions of the chairs, tables, etc. so that we could know whether they'ld fit. I felt rather as if I were a Laputan. Isn't it the sort of thing that would have happened there?

[. . .] I've joined the men's league for the promotion of female suffrage. And now I really doubt whether the whole thing isn't a *[illegible]* whatever that may mean – at any rate very alarming. I believe the ladies will try to forbid prostitution; and will they stop there?

‡

To Leonard Woolf

Sir Thomas Browne's The Garden of Cyrus *was published in 1658. It ends: 'Though* Somnus *in* Homer *be sent to rowse up* Agamemnon, *I finde no such effects in these drowsy approaches of sleep. To keep our eyes open longer were but to act our* Antipodes. *The Huntsmen are up in* America, *and they are already past their first sleep in* Persia. *But who can be drowsie at that howr which freed us from everlasting sleep? Or have slumbring thoughts at that time, when sleep it self must end, as some conjecture all shall awake again?' The 'usual' essay on Death by Sir Francis Bacon is the one that begins, 'Men fear death, as children fear to go in the dark; and as that natural fear in children, is increased with tales, so is the other.'*

In 1886 a group of English Impressionists founded the New English Art Club – a stronghold of French influence, as can be seen in the work not only of Augustus John, but also of Wilson Steer and John Singer Sargent. Augustus John's first wife, Ida, had died of puerperal fever in March, after giving birth to their son Henry. Dorelia, his second wife, was also pregnant at the time, and John had taken a fancy to Henry Lamb's mistress, Nina Forrest (whom Lamb called Euphemia), while Lamb was in turn infatuated by Dorelia.

Henrietta Grant (d. 1915) was dropped on her head when she was two.

Lancaster Gate
Wednesday, May 29th 1907

[. . .] Thursday. *[. . .]* I'm preparing an 'article' on Lady Mary Wortley
Montagu; I shall make it as indecent as I can, but I haven't much hope
of pulling anything particular off. She was a superb woman, I believe –
an amazing combination of intellect and lust. She saw that love was
the only thing worth having, but she never hit it off – hence a sort of
bitter and eminent pessimism which gives a fine flavour to her remarks.
She ought to have dominated London, instead of which she spent
most of her life trailing about in France and Italy with disreputable
young Counts, who copulated with her, robbed her, and ran away.
A deplorable fate! But really redeemed by the fact of her knowing
absolutely how deplorable it was. By-the-bye, do you read Bacon's
essays? I find them astonishingly magnificent. There is one on Death
(not the usual one) which ends à la the Garden of Cyrus, but, in its
way, I think perhaps more stupendously. Sir Thomas must of course
have studied him, and his style (though so different) owes something
to Verulam – look and see.

    I went to that depressing spectacle, yesterday – the New English Art
Club. Most of the pictures were as incompetent as the Academy ones,
and rather more unpleasant – in general futility of idea. That convention
has become quite worn out; every dull dog now paints in spots and
dashes, and dirt, as they used to paint in wax and sentimentality. But I
wonder if you've ever heard of John? He is a reality, though a terrific
one. His drawings are triumphant – both in execution and filth. (The
filth is generally only latent. But it's always there, and makes one give
up hope.) He's an abominable man, lives as if he were a gypsy, had
two wives until the other day he took a third, on which the first two
quarrelled with him, and one of them died as she was producing a child
– and is in fact a typical 'artist'. Henry Lamb and his prostitute-wife
have clung onto his ménage, and a few weeks ago they all went over to
Paris, where they were to be seen rolling down the boulevards, drunk,
in a long line across the street. The complications of their copulations
became intense, and at last they all quarrelled, all threatened to kill each
other and commit suicide, and eventually all went off in different
directions. 'Nina', as she is called (Henry's lady) was left behind in Paris,
without a penny, and with nothing to do but to prey upon Duncan.
This she certainly did, though to what extent, and in what way, still
remains a mystery. I shouldn't be at all surprised to hear that he was

keeping her – oh! in every meaning of the word. But what does it matter? Only aren't 'artists' horrid sordid creatures? And don't you think it would be almost worthwhile to become a 'philistine' once and for all? But of course poor dear Duncan is by no means one of them – yet! These were my thoughts yesterday, as I gazed at John's ghastly drawings of ghostly women (his wives I suppose), and for the moment did really give up hope. But after all, Aunt Henny's verdict on hope is the only wise one; let's give it up, and take refuge, if not in despair, in memory.

your
GLS

✝

To Leonard Woolf

69, Lancaster Gate
Monday, June 10th 1907

I came back from Cambridge today. *[. . .]*

Cambridge was in the May week – hot and coloured, as usual, and very fatiguing. At the Society we wandered round about love and copulation, and when MacCarthy said that he thought the latter was unimportant in the former, I wish I'd been able to quote from your letter – 'After all 99/100ths of love is always the desire to copulate; otherwise it is only the shadow of itself.' How wretched these people are who take no account of passion! As if it wasn't the climax and crown of love! But, if they don't know it, who will teach it them. Turner was there too and of course among the eunuchs. I really believe, you know, that in a queer way he *is* the billiard marker – the billiard marker of Death. It's blood-curdling to hear him talk of the wills he's been registering – one can see him at the board of fate, moving along the pegs with an impassive finger. I suppose at last he'll register *our* wills; and then his own. *[. . .]*

Friday. I have been overcome by bile, and am only now struggling out of it. Such is mortality! Do you realise that the Dinner is next Thursday (20th June)? Perhaps you had a card. It seems highly doubtful whether the Society will survive. Hobhouse goes down – he has just got a third in 'Natural Science' – I daresay he would have got a first in Unnatural. His last phase is very fine – fat, jocular, perfectly self-confident, almost forty. On the hearthrug he was positively pronounced. I roared with laughter. Yes! He's neither Hobby nor Hobber now – simply Hobhouse. And that's the end of him.

[. . .] James is infinitely exclusive and infinitely bashful. He'ld like Rupert, and so I suppose it must turn out – but Rupert is a dangerous unknown entity. He'ld probably flood the Society with his penumbral aesthetic adorers, and if that happened I don't see how we could ever go near it again. *[. . .]*

George Lyttelton has been to Germany, and has returned (according to the Corporal) a free man. He raves against Christians, swears that nothing will induce him to be an Eton schoolmaster, and intends to live at Cambridge and coach – how or whom I can't conceive, but it all sounds very glorious. *[. . .]*

‡

To Leonard Woolf

Charles Herbert Workman's (1873–1923) roles included the Lord Chancellor in the production of Iolanthe, *which began on 14 June, 1907.*

69, Lancaster Gate

Thursday, June 20th 1907

I am in the midst of one of my short whirls of dissipation. Yesterday, a Joachim concert (without Joachim), dinner at the Trocadero (with Keynes), and Iolanthe; today the Dinner. *[. . .]* Have you ever been to the Trocadero? It's filled with little messenger boys, who do their best to play the catamite, but it hardly comes off. The nearest one of them got was to put his arm round Keynes's neck as he was helping him on with his coat! Remarkable? The truth is sodomy is becoming generally recognised in England – but of such a degraded sort! Little boys of 13 are what the British Public love. There are choruses of them at most Comic Operas, and they flood all but the most distinguished of the Restaurants. In Florence people have better taste. Duncan (who's there) writes to say that large crowds collect every day to see the young aristocrats bathe in the Arno – and *they* are eighteen or so. As each one steps out of the water a murmur of approbation or the reverse rises from the crowd. They criticise details – that young man's legs are too fat – oh! the beautiful torso! etc. I long to go and live there – or at any rate to stay there a week.

The astounding thing about Iolanthe is the acting of Mr Workman, who really does reach the most magnificent tragic heights. It's impossible to believe that a Lord Chancellor in love with a fairy can be anything but ridiculous, but one goes, and when the moment comes, it's simply great. The audience was completely mastered, and I believe many of them were in tears. When he says 'Iolanthe, livest thou?' the climax is reached, and one has forgotten everything but the triumph of love. The subtlety, restraint, and exquisite emotion of his acting is amazing – and altogether unnoted by any critic – only by the public itself, who applaud him with the greatest enthusiasm. I should like to go every night, for the comedy and wit is as enthralling as the tragedy. In a few weeks the Savoy is sold to Bernard Shaw's troupe, and Gilbert and Sullivan gone forever. [. . .]

Friday. The dinner was disappointing. There was no Moore, and whether because of that, or because of the disgusting food, or because I was feeling diseased, the whole thing seemed to me painfully hollow. [. . .]

I am rather sickened, by having just received an offer from St Loe of a place on the staff of the Spectator – a review a week, and £150 a year. I fear I shan't be able to refuse it – but I can give it up if I can't stand it – i.e. if I find that I have no time for anything else. Oh! this is a damned world. And now it's begun to be hot, after being too cold; oh, curse! I sit and gibber. When are you coming back?   your   GLS

‡

To Leonard Woolf

Lytton's Lear *citation is to the pre-1914* Oxford Shakespeare.

69, Lancaster Gate
Friday, July 19th 1907

Since my last letter I have been at Versailles. For a week, with Duncan. We returned yesterday. I have been lazy, and also partly stupefied, and so haven't written before. In many ways it was a delightful week: the weather was excellent, and the Château and the Gardens were even more superb than I had imagined them. We had rooms close by, and spent most of our days lying in wonderful bosquets by bassins of quiet water under the shade of enormous trees. It was charming and very strange – like a pleasant dream – so infinitely unreal! The beauties of the place are so intense that it seems extraordinary that they should be so visionary: they hang mysteriously between life and death; and, as one looks out from the great terrace in front of the vast and magnificent palace down the long perspective of water and trees and statuary, one feels – oh! not that the past has come to life again – but simply that the present is no more. The good bourgeois from Paris are curiously inoffensive in the general scheme – they are irrelevant – or hardly even that. They are certainly far more in place than the ghosts of Kings and Duchesses would be, if they were to come back in their ancient splendour and one were to meet them, round the corner of a grove of yews. One can see no ghosts, one can only be a ghost oneself.

I'm no longer in love – I can't imagine why I ever was; and as I say so I wonder whether I'm lying. I was nose-to-nose with him for a solid week; he was charming, amusing, even beautiful – but – he was cold, and his coldness left me calm. My desires are usually active, and you've never dreamt of a place more obviously constructed for the convenience of copulation; he would be chaste, and, as we wandered side by side, in the full romance of dying twilight down gloomy avenues among statues of Ganymede and Silenus – I could feel nothing but the ridiculousness of the situation. The place was so wonderfully appropriate – so thick with melancholy memories of vanished splendours, with every fountain dead, and a fig-leaf on every statue – oh! oh! – it was the summary of our adventure, our indifference, and our love. To suffer, and to forget – that is the business of mortality, – the cruel task whipped out of us by Fate and Time. One evening, in the darkness, we sat our chairs close together between two clipped yews on the great terrace, and looked down over the beautiful dim landscape, sitting there, in utter silence, for more than half an hour. Some bourgeois – a family of three – were going home, winding along, with a paper lantern tied to a stick, among the pools and statues, and the light was all one could see – a large firefly tumbling through the dark. *[. . .]* At last I said something, and his answer was 'far wide'; and we walked back in silence; and it seemed to me, looking up at that infinite dead palace, that Louis must have known what I knew – the incurable solitude of the human heart. (King Lear. Act IV, Scene VII, line 50.) *[. . .]*

‡

To James Strachey

Burley Hill
Ringwood
Hants.
August 1st 1907

[. . .] I can never decide whether I'm an utter fool, a genius, or an ordinary person. Today two years ago, I kissed Duncan for the first time – oh! It was hardly a kiss – and plunged into a sea of passion – my god! – Yesterday morning I sprang out of bed, happy, and found myself free as air, and felt that at last I was beginning to taste the calm, delicious, gradual, *unpassionate* things of life! Dieu! When I saw his name in your letter at breakfast today, I had the old shock – yes, the old jealousy almost! – and, though I can't care – how can I? – I'm still wondering what it was he did at Florence, and why he never told me, and how long I shall go on being such a fool. Is it mere automatism? – the chicken running when the head is off? Or is it the last remaining flicker of my old wild magnificent self? Well! One can do nothing. One must submit, and wait, and transact one's businesses. Also, one must never forget what's happened; one must remember that one was or is a genius or a fool. *[. . .]*

‡

To Clive Bell

The London Library, then as now, sent books by post to its country members. The splendid Joseph McCabe (1867–1955) was an aggressive atheist who had joined the Franciscan order at nineteen and left it ten years later, denouncing the Vatican along with every other aspect of religion in over 250 books.

Burley Hill
Ringwood
Hants.
N.B. not Castletop
August 9th 1907

Dear Clive,

I hope your sister is now well enough for the doctor to have left the house, so that you no longer have to discuss life, art, etc. with medical men. They are certainly a dreadfully tiresome species – they seem, somehow, always so moral, more desperately so I often think, than even clergymen. Have you found this? And then they really do believe that health is the summum bonum; but really, can anyone be good and healthy at the same time?

I think I'm less good than usual, for I believe I'm rather less accablé by disease. I lead a life of extraordinary regularity. And am more often than not in a benevolent trance. I took the first volume of a vast edition of St Simon out of the London Library – you never saw such a monument of erudition; I thought I'd read the text, and skip the notes, appendices, and excurses; but, lord! I read it every word, and have sent for the next two volumes. If I stay here much longer I shall become a scholar, and when we meet you'll think I'm Turner.

I've just got a book in which some notes by Baudelaire on the Liaisons Dangereuses are printed – do you know them? They're really splendid – all this wonderful sanity and precision, and grasp of the situation are finely displayed. He says, comparing modern life to the 18th century – 'En réalité, le satanisme a gagné. Satan s'est fait ingénu. Le mal se connaissant était moins affreux et plus près de la guérison que le mal s'ignorant. G. Sand inférieure à de Sade.'¹ Isn't he divine?

Does Vanessa really walk? I hardly believe it. Croquet and conversation, I expect. If you find family life growing too much for you, my prescription is – a letter of Les Liaisons before going to bed, and a Fleur du Mal first thing in the morning. Ask your doctor if he doesn't agree. Am I as prurient as this wonderful Joseph McCabe?

yours ever
Lytton Strachey

1. In reality wickedness has won. Satan has become innocent. Evil knowing itself so is less ghastly and nearer being cured than unconscious evil. George Sand is inferior to Sade.

‡

To Leonard Woolf

In 1907 many Liberals sanctioned extreme measures to deal with outbreaks of sedition in India.

67, Belsize Park Gardens
Hampstead, N.W.
October 10th 1907

[. . .] I have been here for about ten days now, and find it quite pleasant – far more pleasant than Lancaster Gate, though the house is much smaller, and in a provincial ménage. Air and light, and no butler! Comfort reigns. *[. . .]*

Keynes is beginning to drive me mad on the subject of 'Indiar', as he calls it. These fucking liberals! The filthy garbage of cant that they give utterance to – je tremble, je frisonne! Is there *any* hope? I believe *none*. But does it matter?

‡

To Leonard Woolf

Woolf said in his memoirs that in Kandy he had 'to see six or seven men hanged'. Executions 'took place in the Bogambra Prison in the early morning before breakfast. To be present at them was a horrifying experience, and the more I had to witness, the more horrible I found them.'[1]

67, Belsize Park Gardens
Hampstead, N.W.
Saturday, October 19th 1907

I have this minute read your hanging letter. It's Society time *[i.e. Saturday night]*, and here I am alone over the fire – with your letter. Shall we discuss it? But I hardly feel as if I could tonight. I happen to be rather ill, and you've frightened me. I feel horribly alone. I have read the Bovary paragraph, and I'd rather discuss that. It's funny, but I hardly care for any of that any more. I suppose it's really a question of taste, and now I find it very difficult to taste real life in fiction — I mean what you call 'the futility and sordidness of actual existence'. I can just bear it in real life, but in fiction I don't care about it, and can hardly realise that I ever did. Your letter is superb; but if what you describe came into a novel — oh no! do let's create things that are only dimly real! *[. . .]* My chefs d'oeuvre shall all be in the style of Racine, Watteau, and Mozart; and if I must be real, I shall be so à la *le Misanthrope. [. . .]* My health has on the whole been better lately. At any rate I am far less depressed. Isn't it madness your staying out in your ghastly wild? I'm sure it's madness, and that the only thing to do is simply to take the English train, and damn the consequences. I do think that; though I know it's not much good just thinking it. And very easy to say. But after all it must, it *must* be, impossible to starve in England, and if that's so — oh, for heaven's sake take the train. England is a nice, good, quiet, sensible place — yes, even more than you imagine! One can be happy in England, one really can.

Duncan lives a few streets away, and is constantly here. I am in love with him as much as ever, perhaps more; and he is completely out of love with me. The odd thing is that this isn't a tragedy. He's delightful, he's amazing, he's divine, he understands all — can you believe it? I worship him, and I believe I almost find that that is enough. *[. . .]*

1. Leonard Woolf, *Autobiography*, pp. 240–1.

‡

To Leonard Woolf

Sheppard was teaching classics at Emmanuel, and had hoped to become a don there, but was refused a fellowship worth £500 a year, says Strachey, on the grounds of his 'atheism'. Keynes's 'stool' is his civil service job.

67, Belsize Park Gardens
Hampstead
November 14th 1907

[. . .] I went to Cambridge about a fortnight ago, and I don't believe I ever told you about it. There are two embryos — Rupert Brooke and

Mr Taylor of Emmanuel. Rupert you've often heard about – at
James's private school, poetical and pseudo-beautiful, with red hair
and complexion complete. James is in love with him, in that sort
of desperate dazed way in which James *is* in love, and longs for
his election, and swears that he's all right, though he can't say why.
The worst feature of the case is poor Rupert's dimness – almost a
second Corporal I often think; and that, too, is the worst feature of
Mr Taylor's. He's an Emmanuel pupil of Sheppard's, and Sheppard has
suddenly discovered that he's absolutely apostolic, and that he must be
elected at once. *[. . .]*

Poor Mr Taylor! The last news is that in his rage against the dons of
Emmanuel *[for refusing to give a job to Sheppard]* he's torn off the mask,
and written off to tell his mother (a quiet ritualist) that he doesn't
believe in God, and hasn't for the last three years. The only result has
been that all the blame's been put onto the innocent Sheppard, and they
seem to think that Mr Taylor's outraged mother may take him away
from Cambridge.

The only other agitation – and it really is disagreeable – is connected,
oddly enough, with Hobby. He went to America in the summer – to
learn 'business methods', and came back the other day. On his return his
mother awaited him with an opened letter. – 'Explain this!' – He
looked, and it was from Greenwood, rank with sodomy, implied or
expressed – the woman had simply opened and read all his letters in his
absence, and this was one of them. He tried to get out of it by saying
that the poor fellow was very 'morbid', etc. etc. whereupon she stormed
and raved, declared that sodomy was fatal for success in life, – 'I'd rather
a man had five mistresses than one catamite' – (she's a dreadful female),
and wound up by accusing the Society, if you please, of being a hotbed
of unnatural vice. I can only suppose that she allowed her tongue to run
away with her, for it's a little too absurd to say such things, even if one
thinks them, but she can have no reason for that. Nothing more has
happened – that we know – though no doubt she'll be careful to spread
slanders at every opportunity; and poor Hobby is having new locks put
into his drawers, and sealing all his letters. Whether anything serious will
follow heaven alone knows. But it's difficult to see how it can go
beyond mere talk, unless there's some particularly odious accident. Mais
quelle vie! Mon dieu, quelle vie!

Keynes is beginning to get sick of his stool, which strikes me as
singular. He went to Cambridge for a fortnight's holiday, and found it
so infinitely heavenly that he's beginning to think of chucking India

Office and prospects, if he gets a fellowship. His dissertation's on Probability, as I must have told you. I expect the matter will be excellent (mere Moore, of course), and the manner vile. He showed me some of it once, and it seemed a mass of muddled facetiousness – but I daresay that will please the electors. *[. . .]*

‡

To Leonard Woolf

The play-reading group was the first organized manifestation of the Bloomsbury Group. Vanburgh's The Relapse *(1696) was his successful first play;* Every Man in His Humour *is Ben Jonson's 1598 comedy; Milton's masque* Comus *was presented in 1634, whereas his 1671 'closet drama', the tragedy* Samson Agonistes, *was not intended to be performed; Dryden's* Aurang-Zebe *was first produced in 1675.*

Lytton's invitation to Knebworth is easy to explain: Lord Lytton was his godfather, and he was presumably named for him. Eddie Marsh was being disingenuous in his comments about Moore. As undergraduates they had been firm friends, and Moore's diaries show that he was still seeing Marsh socially as late as 1911.

February 6th 1908

There have been things to tell you, but I have been extraordinarily unable to write, and I suppose now you've heard the most important. Rupert Brooke has been elected, and so far it seems to be satisfactory. They all got into a panic when they'd done it, but now they've calmed down. I went to Cambridge the Saturday before last to assist at the curse. Sanger, Dickinson, and also Ainsworth were there. The reason for Ainsworth is the other piece of news – the break-up of the Edinburgh ménage, which occurred suddenly about three weeks ago. Ainsworth's father died, and I gather it was thought desirable that he should live with his people if he could for the sake of economy. He applied for a post in the Education Office and was at once given one, and he's now established at Tooting with his family. The Yen appeared for a few minutes and was undecided what to do, but he thinks that he'll probably live with his sisters in the country near London. They won't live *in* it, and he can't bear to be alone. Someone suggested that he should set up house with Keynes! Imagine the ménage! There was also some talk of his going to St Andrews as professor of philosophy, but I think that has been quashed. Ainsworth has taken a new lease of life, and is almost charming once more. At the Society he seemed to me to be far the best person on the hearthrug – as sympathetic as he used to be, and much less tiresome. But I daresay it'll wear off when the weariness of the stool begins to make itself felt. Whether he's relieved at escaping from the Yen heaven knows – and vice versa – but it's certainly possible.

Rupert is a pseudo-beauty with yellow hair and a good complexion, but without any features of body to boast of. His mind from all I can see is merely washy and cultured, but James (who's madly in love with him) swears that when he's at ease he soars into the highest brilliancy. On the hearthrug I found him rather nice in a queer way – so young and poetical! He quoted poetry with a prophetic manner which somehow reminded me of us in our earliest days; but I think he must have been a good deal sillier. He was very much overcome, and by all accounts feels the prestige of the Society ad infinitum. Only I daresay he's more bored than anything else. [. . .]

Has Turner told you of our readings? Rather charming, I find, and the only jar (which of course *is* there) from Clive. Adrian is astonishingly good – I really think better than the Goth as far as the mere reading goes, which is odd. Virginia of course too is very fine, and Turner sometimes positively rises. We have read The Relapse – Vanessa said that we'd better begin with the most indecent thing we could, so as to get it settled – and Every Man of [sic] His Humour, and Comus and Samson. Next time we are to do Aurang-Zebe. If only Clive were a little less Clivy, it would be perfect, and as it is there is great pleasure in it – they're so beautiful and intellectually reckless, and the intimacy is so very nearly complete.

Last Saturday to Monday I spent at Knebworth chez Lady Lytton (widow of the Viceroy). It was interesting and rather unpleasant, as I was so absolutely out of everything. Marsh of course was there, and the conversation rolled unendingly on the highest spheres – gossip about Countesses and Cabinet Ministers, at which I could only look as complacent as was fit. They all talked so easily – so horribly easily! Their only intelligence was in that. Nothing that was said was of the slightest interest – how could it be? I thought of Moore's groanings and contortions, and longed for them. That devil Marsh! I mentioned the Yen. – 'Moore? Which Moore do you mean? – Little George Moore? Oh yes, what does he do now?' – 'He writes philosophy.' – 'Oh really.

– does he write good philosophy?' Of course I could think of no
repartee. But I don't believe after all he meant anything offensive. He'd
simply inconceivably lapsed.

your
GLS

‡

To Virginia Stephen

*Virginia had written to Lytton that when she was commissioned by George
Smith, editor of the* Cornhill Magazine, *to review the life of Delane, editor of*
The Times, *the covering note from Smith instructed her to praise 'the human
side' of Delane.*

67, Belsize Park Gardens
Hampstead, N.W.
April 23rd 1908

Dear Virgina,

Your letter came to console me in a solitude – caused by a return of
my cold in a more violently nasal form than ever. I am trying the
desperate remedy of staying in one room. I have been here the whole
of yesterday, and shall be the whole of today, and I suppose tomorrow,
and so on for ever and ever, crouching over a gas fire and snivelling and
cursing and drinking quinine. *This* sounds like the end of a novel by a
decadent Frenchman. I prefer Galsworthy – as you write him, and I'm
really jealous of you and your Cornwall, with its Nature that I have
very little feeling for. You should see the dreadful state of rainy fog
going on here now, and you should feel the cold wind on your
backbone, but I daresay you really do, for your descriptions sounded to
me a little too literary, what with the gorse – is gorse really yellow? –
and the white May which ought to have been pink, and the Atlantic.
And, dear Miss Stephen, I don't believe a word you say about poor Mr
Smith. It's all a gross libel and invention, and I won't believe it till I see
it in his own hand.

   I went away last Friday, partly to get rid of my cold, to the Green
Dragon on Salisbury Plain, where James and Keynes and others were for

Easter. Of course it finally destroyed me – the coldest winds you can imagine sweeping over the plain, and inferior food, and not enough comfortable chairs. But on the whole I was amused. The others were Bob Trevy, Sanger, Moore, Hawtrey, and a young undergraduate called Rupert Brooke – isn't it a romantic name? – with pink cheeks and bright yellow hair – it sounds horrible, but it wasn't. Moore is a colossal being, and he also sings and plays in a wonderful way, so that the evenings passed pleasantly. I wish you could have been there, disguised, perhaps as another undergraduate. Would you have been bored to death? The conversation was less political than you would think, but I daresay you would have found the jokes a little heavy – as for me, I laughed enormously, and whenever I began to feel dull I could look at the yellow hair and pink cheeks of Rupert. James, too, is an interesting character – very mysterious and reserved, and either incredibly young or inconceivably old. I constantly looked out of windows, in the hopes of seeing Adrian come stalking over the plain in his lavender stockings, but he never appeared. Have you heard from him? I wonder what adventures he's been having at his inns.

Oh, adventures! Does one have them nowadays! Your letter was one for me, but I can think of no other, though I think I do occasionally have them. Do you? Is the antlantic [*Atlantic*] enough for you? I am a wild man of the woods, I often think, and perhaps inexplicable to civilised people who live in Cornwall and write on Delane as a man.

I have been out into the cold for dinner, and I'm back again very unhappy and chilly, wishing I hadn't moved, with snow dropping down the chimney and spitting in the fire. I should like to speak to someone. If you'd walk in it would be delightful, especially as I might then explain exactly what I meant by saying I was a wild man of the woods – but of course I never would explain it really; but there would be a chair for you to sit in, and some warmth, and some conversation. As it is I imagine you in your dining-room listening to your landlady's children, and inventing scandalous letters from Mr Smith. Or are you perhaps starting the Description of Cornwall? That would be exciting.

I have been reading Racine once more, with almost complete pleasure. There was never a greater artist. And he writes about the only thing worth writing about, in my opinion – the human heart! 'J'aimais jusqu'à ses pleurs que je faisais couler' – very, very divine!

It's getting late, and I must go to bed. This will start off to you tomorrow morning. I'm afraid it's rather an invalid's letter. I actually sat down to write the minute I'd read yours. So you must answer.

Do you really live in Trevose house? Rhyming to nose? Your writing's a little doubtful. It seems a queer name.

yours ever
G.L.S.

‡

To James Strachey

> 67, Belsize Park Gardens
> Hampstead, N.W.
> May 1st 1908

Keynes has just left me – it's past 12 – after boring me almost to death by probability and the 'Congress'. Dreadful! He says he's probably going to C. tomorrow, and Duncan too, I gather. I'm in a deplorable state – working all day at Racine and the Spectator alternately, and there's no hope of my moving from here for at least a fortnight, I'm afraid. I wish you were here. My solitude's pretty intense. I see Maynard only occasionally, and then I'm bored, and Duncan I see in that dreadful fragmentary way of his that sometimes drives me mad, and even with him there seems nothing much to talk about. I understand that he doesn't understand me, but I hardly realise it yet, and I daresay he doesn't like me besides. Why should I care? And yet I do, in one way or another, and want him to come and see me in the evenings – and how rarely he does! It's partly the solitude, I suppose, that makes me want impossibilities; perhaps when he's safely out of London I shall subside comfortably into domestic life. *[. . .]*

‡

To James Strachey

> 67, Belsize Park Gardens
> Hampstead, N.W.
> May 26th 1908

[. . .] This spot is at present wormwood to me. I am having an acute fit of family fever, and the world is black. Certes, plus que je médite, the

less it appears tolerable to lead the sort of hole and corner, one-place-at-a-table-laid-for-six life I do at present. It's impossible to think, and hardly possible to breathe. Oh! Oh! I have serious thoughts of flight. But where? Where? Could I ever face poverty, journalism, and solitude? The whole thing's sickening. It's bad luck that Duncan should be so singularly hopeless as a companion – what a great difference a little difference would have made! And now too, just now, when I seem to see clearly that I ought to go, Keynes makes up his mind to go too, so that avenue of retreat – the ménage à Maynard – is cut off from me. [. . .]

I went today to Mr Shaw. Very odd indeed – so good and so bad – and eventually incredibly ridiculous. But what to say as Ignotus I really cannot tell. Tomorrow I go to Mr Pinero, and the day after to Maurice Baring's 'Grey Stocking', and on Saturday afternoon to Bérénice. So my time is cut out, which is something.

The Dowager Countess of L[ytton] came to lunch yesterday, and Mabel Maclery (?) and her daughter to tea. It was a veritable study in contrasts, and by god the triumph of the aristocracy! The bourgeoise woman simply stank in one's nostrils after the equally silly grande dame with her refinements and ingrafted subtleties. But to have to put up with meeting such filth-packets! J'enrage!

your

Lytton

‡

To James Strachey

July 15th 1908

I am suffering now too much. I have been through too much. Things are spectral to me now, or is it I – ? Oh! There are cruelties in the world – but how can one speak or think or even feel at last?

I do feel, though, and write to you, though I told Maynard that I wouldn't until he did, tomorrow, in a wretched agony. It's utterly stupid and absurd, besides being incomprehensible. Ils s'aiment. There can be no comment that I can think of. It's been going on for 'the last five or five and a half weeks' as that imbecile said. They've kept it horribly secret. He has come to me reeking with that semen, he has never thought that I should know. Ah! But there's only one thing I think – that the nature of Love has been hidden from him, that he is playing, that they are all playing, and taking themselves in. Is it a mercy or a hell that we at any rate should know what Love is? I am ill and tired. I have been with that person, from whom I surprised this, up to the last tube, you can imagine in what a state. But they had determined, after what happened yesterday, that I should be told. J'ai des visions affreuses.

Lytton.

They're in terror that it should get about and especially, of course, of Norton's hearing. I said I wouldn't write till he had, to beg you not to speak. Could he have thought I wasn't lying? I shall write again I suppose tomorrow. I wish I could see you. I'll forward the letter to Moore.

$$\ddagger$$

To Maynard Keynes

Lytton had spent a month in Cambridge, and Maynard and Duncan had started their affair almost immediately upon his departure from London. In his letters to Maynard in 1907, Lytton frequently asks if he'll be at Simpson's 'at the usual time', which appears to be 1.30; so it appears that Keynes regularly lunched at Simpson's in the Strand. The 'Court' refers to Maynard's flat in St James's Court.

　　Maynard replied the next day, saying Lytton's letter had made him cry, but that he was glad to have received it, and invited Lytton to see Isadora Duncan dance 'and forget that real Duncan, with whom no one in the world could help but fall in love'.

67, Belsize Park Gardens
Hampstead, N.W.
July 21st 1908

My dear Maynard

I found your letter here this morning, on coming back from C. I thought you might possibly be in the hall at Simpson's – but that was foolish. I looked in at the Court at about 4 (is it a new and rather charming lift-boy?) but you were out, and I didn't leave a message, as, if you're really going tomorrow, I suppose you'll be occupied tonight.

My confusion has not died away, and I'm afraid it never will, because, as far as I can see, it was born with me. Such a dreadful and gibbering creature as I am! However, you seem to have put up with that hitherto, and I daresay you will in the future. Dear Maynard, I only know that we've been friends for too long to stop being friends now. There are some things that I shall try not to think of, and you must do your best to help me in that; and you must believe that I do sympathise and don't hate you and that if you were here now I should probably kiss you, except that Duncan would be jealous, which would never do!

your affectionate
Lytton

‡

To James Strachey

'Daddy D' was Edward Hugh John Neale Dalton (1887–1962), the future Labour politician and Chancellor, an old Etonian reading economics at King's. He was initially Rupert Brooke's closest friend, then he was thrown together with James in the Fabian Society, and both Rupert and James flirted with him – but he was not elected to the Apostles.

67, Belsize Park Gardens
Hampstead, N.W.
July 23rd 1908

There was an interview last night with Maynard – it went off on the whole as well as might have been expected. He wept, and I had an erection, and that was all. But I'm now quite sure that I've taken the only possible course. *[. . .]* And how is Daddy D?

> One little word I beg of you,
> One little word to me –
> Ah tell me, tell me, tell me true –
> How is my Daddy D?

> I've wandered far through dry and wet,
> And far o'er land and sea,

But never, never, have I met
   The like of Daddy D!

His dim and excremental grace,
   His drear and drooping ee
Who ever could forget the face
   Of darling Daddy D?

But oh! My heart misgives me quite,
   Lest he should faithless be:
For how should I behold the light
   Without my Daddy D?

So tell me he is true, I pray,
   Or in the W.C.
One morning I shall pass away
   For love of Daddy D!

   your
      Lytton.

‡

To James Strachey

67, Belsize Park Gardens
Hampstead, N.W.
July 27th 1908

[. . .] I've seen Duncan off to the Orkneys, and altogether I'm about
ready to hang myself. Dieu! What a life one leads! I feel like a half-eaten
gorgonzola. I've been more wept over and kissed during the last few
days than most persons would easily imagine.

[. . .] Oh, thank the lord, there *are* other things in the world – though
it's difficult enough to believe it, there are books and Moore and visions
and the supremacies of art. Oh, above all, there seems to be you. If
there wasn't, where should I be pray? *[. . .]*

‡

To Maynard Keynes

*In early August Lytton and James went to Scotland, staying first for a week
at Sligachan Inn, near Portree, on the Isle of Skye. Lytton was hoping to
recuperate, and James to recover from his lovesickness for Rupert Brooke. It
was not a success, so they moved south, near to their mother's childhood home.*

Rothiemurchus
August 15th 1908

This is not our address but we don't know what it is, so this has been
adopted – it's where Pippa and Pernel are staying with Trevor about a
mile along the road. The road is the road to Loch an Eilan, and we are
almost touching it – a divine situation but a damned small cottage, with
only a room and a cave at our disposal. But so long as it's as fine as it's
been up to now all will be well. The beauties of the place (I mean the
beauties of Nature) are resplendent, and one feels it's worth living to be
among them once more. The beauties of humanity are rarer, though
we're in rather a good position for observing them – the whole world
goes past our windows in carriages, breaks and motors all day. As the
road divides just in front of the house, they usually stop and ask our
good landlady the way to Loch an Eilan, so that we can press our noses
against the windows and stare our fill. Today there really *was* rather a
beauty, and – what's more singular – an aristocratic one. Pale and
melancholy with astounding eye-lashes, and sitting beside the most
preposterous dowager in purple satin and lumbering lace that you can
imagine. I forgot to say that they were in a motor and as they trundled
past James swears he saw a coronet on the door. Why, why am I not a
preposterous dowager? Alas. *[. . .]*

‡

To Maynard Keynes

*Bishop Tomlinson is a 'deity' because he was the founder of the Apostles. 'Dill'
is Alfred Dilwyn Knox (1885–1943).*

Milton Cottage
Rothiemurchus
Aviemore N.B.
August 16th 1908

Whether I'm mad or merely silly I can't conceive, but it's at any rate
certain that I'm astounded. I'd thought that adventures were over and
now – oh dear, how can I help thinking that I've had one, except that
it's so impossible – but will you listen and try to believe, and then
perhaps I'll find it easier myself. Lord! – But listen.

This afternoon – yes, it was this afternoon – I went out alone, as
James would sit over his translation of Tacitus in the Everyman's
Library, and began walking towards the lairig *[a hill or mountain pass]*.
I was vague, but then, directed by heaven knows what deity – by
Tomlinson – I at last decided to go as far as I could, and abandon tea,
and only be back for dinner. I had got up pretty high on the verge of
the tree-line, by about five, and was thinking of nothing in the world
but mountains and Beethoven, when I observed a human form against
the sky. It was male so of course I had the usual expectations and the
usual hopelessness. I was mainly bored to think of a tiresome tourist
who'd certainly ask me the way to Balmoral. I advanced, and suddenly
found myself face to face with – but it won't convey much to you – but
to me it was electrical – the beautiful melancholy youth who passed the
other day in the motor with the Dowager Duchess! There was no
mistaking it. He was perched on the highest point of the road, looking
over the forest. The eyelashes flashed before me, and I thought I should
go down on my knees and gibber. I didn't of course; I merely passed
by; but then – then comes what makes this adventure different from all
others, what makes it, in fact, an adventure, and something impossible
and incredible which is still whirling me, and driving Venus forward
in a fury to make you share my swirl. He turned round with amazing
affability and began to talk. I didn't run away, as you, I suppose,
would have, I stopped and tried to be affable too. We conversed, but
good heavens, it wasn't an ordinary conversation. Imagine the most
refined and exquisite beauty, the most charming manners, the most
overwhelming verve, and then imagine all this literally thrown at your
head, showered at you and crowding over you, so that you have
nothing left to do but pick up what you can hurriedly and gasp for
breath. I really thought after the first five minutes that I should be
copulating with him before the next five were past. I'm still not quite

sure why I didn't – perhaps I've been an utter fool – or perhaps – oh
Christ! – try, try to imagine my feelings and his looks – it's hopeless to
attempt to describe. He gave me his sandwiches, he got water for me in
his cup, and, as we walked back together through the forest, we were
intimate friends. Can you believe this? I don't think I can – but then
I've seen him, which makes it more incredible. He's tall and dark, with
grey eyes, and when he talks the melancholy vanishes completely and
his expression becomes wonderfully animated and fascinating and gay.
There's a touch of Dill about him – the faintest – but without the full-
blooded lasciviousness – and if you could imagine an infinitely
etherialised Dill with a dash perhaps of Duncan – but it won't do, this
is all rubbish – how many pages can describe an eyelash? How many
volumes the arch of a nose? You may believe in his beauty, but of
course you won't believe in his intelligence. We talked almost at once
of God, with fits of laughter. Where do you think he's staying? – this is
the triumph – at least with luck it *will* be – in Kinvara, on the other side
of the river, under Tor Alvey, you know – the mountain with (very
appropriately) the penis on the top. I gathered that his family was
Roman Catholic, that he'd been educated partly by Jesuits at Narbonne,
that lately he's been with a tutor, and that he's to go to a University –
perhaps to the new Irish one, but now won't it be Cambridge?, in
October year. He's between 18 and 19 – I should have said between 19
and 20. He laughs the whole time and talks the rest. He's as wild as
anyone can imagine – wilder, I believe, even than I was when I first
went up – and what can be more heavenly than that? I'm pretty sure
he's *not* a womaniser, but I can't be sure of more – I hardly dare to
speculate about it – it seems so probable and yet so impossible that he
should have reached – even with the aid of Jesuits – our point of view.
I say 'probable' because of his general unrestrained habit of mind.
What's amusing in his conversation is that, though it's all au fond
curiously unconventional, it's filled up with the most absurd public
school phrases – old chap, and ripping and so on – that he must have
picked up from stray boys in the street. – 'I say, old fellow, you know'
(of course I was very soon that) 'I feel as if I'd always known I should
meet you, and of course now I have, and it's really awfully ripping, and
you must come and see us, and, I say, what's your name?' – I really
can't reproduce it. But what would *you* do if somebody with eyelashes a
foot long and a dream of a face, whom you'd spoken to for the first
time half an hour before, talked to you like that? *I* didn't even blither, I
was exhilarated, and became highly flirtatious. I told him my name was

Lytton, and he said his was Horace; and we giggled – oh, dear, dear! – 'What do you think of me?' he said at one point, and I had the courage to reply 'I think you're a perfect scandal.' His answer was something like this – 'As for you, old fellow, I'm sure you're the Holy Ghost, or the Holy pigeon – I don't know – half angel and half bird, and if you're not careful you'll jolly well find yourself fucking the Virgin Mary.' At this point, I admit there was a slight rag, but it went off without much loss of semen, and then we parted, and he walked away past Loch an Eilan – I can't think why, if he was going to Kinvara – and I returned to James and Tacitus, in a condition of trembles. I'd told him at last my complete name (and he his, Townsend) and now I'm merely one vast expectation for the letter to invite me to go and see him, which he swore he'd send. If it never comes I shall hardly be surprised; if it does, and I go, I suppose I shall simply see that I've been as cracked as usual. In the meantime, I gibber. I have confessed a little – a very little – to James – I'm already fiendishly jealous – and I think I've prevented suspicions so far. This is a *[illegible]* letter, and perhaps you'll dislike Horace – but please, please, remember the high spirits and the laughter and the eyelashes too! Townsend is mysterious – I gathered that they are *not* aristocrats in the sense of being lords, but perhaps James did see a crest on the motor, and they must be rich. If I go there I shall be able to give an account. I've been able as yet to glean nothing from my relations. I can write no more of anything. Horace! Horace! – I shall write odes, sonnets, elegies – I shall dream, I shall eternally weep! Am I quite mad? Or is it, at last, Fate.

your

GLS

‡

To Maynard Keynes

James was leaving Lytton to go to the Fabian Summer School.

Milton Cottage
Rothiemurchus
Aviemore N.B.
August 19th 1908

Yes, I think I am now definitely plunged. In fact I believe I am so
thoroughly that I'm hardly surprised any more. I take things as a matter
of course which, five days ago, would have sent me gibbering. I've been
acclimatised. But I suppose you haven't, so perhaps you'll be startled by
this. And it's true that *I* was too at the beginning of today's occurrences.
But I haven't told you that yesterday Horace's letter came inviting me
to lunch at Kinvara House today. You can imagine the agitation of its
arrival. I tore out into the woods to open it, pretending I was going to
forth. I was rather disappointed for there was nothing more than the
invitation in rather a sprawling Andrewish handwriting and 'yours ever
H. Townshend'. – the 'H' in the Townshend I hadn't realised before. I
told James as little as I could, and he was discreet as usual, and at two I
was being ushered into the Kinvara drawing room by a pompous
footman. (Did you ever see the house? – on the other side of the Spey,
about a mile further down from Mr Black's – but wait! wait!) I was
ushered in and saw straight in front of me – but it was too amazing, and
I felt myself diving finally into the Arabian Nights. Imagine if you can!
– A pair of divine pink knees which I realised immediately were not
Horace's, for I looked up, and saw, in a kilt, charming, yellow-haired,
rose-complexioned and embarrassed – a divinity of eighteen! It was
the very last thing I had been expecting – I had been looking forward
to so different a vision; I was visibly shattered, I suppose, for he became
pinker than ever and didn't know what to do. At last I managed to
speak and he answered and I sat, staring as much as I dared, in an
ecstatic trance, until the ladies entered, and then everyone else, and
we were introduced and he turned out to be Gilbert Maclehose
(pronounced Mackly-hose) – son of the Scotch publisher who's taken
Mr Black's house. My mind of course at once leapt to a romance, but I
was too agitated to take in anything definite. Horry – that's what I now
must call him forever more – was charming, and, so long as the family
was there, comparatively subdued. The family seemed to be a father of
60, very dull and rigid, and gentlemanlike, two daughters (older than
Horry) – I thought mainly devotional with crosses, a chaplain (RC) and
the dowager – the most amusing of the party – Lady Louisa Murcheson
talked most of the time in the approved dowager style, of the decadence

of the present age, the German invasion, and the laziness of the lower classes. Oh! I was extraordinarily happy, discussing my cousin the Treasurer of the Household with Mr T and observing out of the corner of my eye the exquisite cheeks of Gilbert and Horry's suppressed grins. And I drank claret and wondered why the whole of life wasn't thus. But can you conceive of me walking in the garden between these two inconceivables? They're *not* hideous and stupid, whatever you may think. You should have heard Horry reproducing Lady Louisa (I forgot to say that she's the aunt, apparently of the deceased Mrs T), and you should have seen Gilbert's demureness and extraordinary youth! Lord! We went and ate gooseberries and threw the skins at one another. Oh no, these things *are* the Arabian Nights. And then the ultimate – no, the penultimate – adventure, when Gilbert insisted on walking back over the Spey by the ford, carrying his shoes and stockings. It seemed to me most alarming, but they swore it could be done, and so it could – by means of holding his kilt up so high – oh well, I saw that his cheeks were not the only pink things about him. It was scandalous and deliberately scandalous, and we died of laughter. As for the ultimate – but I've written so much and perhaps you're sick of the whole circumstance, but heavens! [. . .] – Oh! Oh! we sat on a seat, I and Horry, and he poured out the affaire – the meeting last month with Gilbert, and – which I was *not* surprised at – the violent intimacy, the curious affection, and the passion, it seemed to me, of a wonderfully intense and yet ethereal kind. Am I inventing? He's an astounding character, and to hear him talk sends me off into a region which, with anyone else, would be the sheerest invention, and with him seems absolutely true. – 'I say, old chap, what do you think of Gilbert? I'm in love with him.' – a pleasant beginning for a conversation but I've become acclimatised. I said that I was too. If I'd added that I also was with him, it might have been more to the point [. . .] – I found myself thinking that if this was fraudulent he was the most incredible flirt. But he's certainly not a second Hobber – there's no suspicion of that. I don't know how near I got to kissing him, nor why I didn't. [. . .]

your
GLS

I forgot to say that Gilbert's at Marlborough. James goes off on Saturday to stay with his young friends in a farmhouse near the Webbs (Sidney) and then on to the Summer School. I haven't any idea of how long I'll stay. I don't know what you mayn't hear of me next.

‡

To Maynard Keynes

Milton Cottage
Rothiemurchus
Aviemore N.B.
August 21st 1908

Dear Maynard,

One seems to lead a very healthy and exhausting life here. Unceasing walks and sittings out in the sun and brushings away of flies – to say nothing of speculations literary and copulatory. Well, well! I expect I shall return to the groves of Hampstead as bronzed as Andrew and as muscular as George in his finest days, but in the meantime it's damned fatiguing. My romance seems rather to have petered out – at any rate for the present. Perhaps I've had a surfeit, and then there's the cruelty of James, which would dash anyone's enthusiasm. I've had to give him a sketch of the affair, and of course he wouldn't hear of it – they were both of them certainly very ugly and stupid, and Horry was mentally disordered and Gilbert was simply Scotch. Today Horry came to lunch, and I admit I was rather bored. No doubt it was partly James's funeste influence at work. The poor thing did his best to be high-spirited, and even James had to confess afterwards that some of the jokes amused him; but the party was certainly a failure on the whole. I walked a little way with him afterwards, and felt what I'd never felt before with him – almost nervous – and then everything seemed quite hopeless, and I left him rather abruptly. Was I a fool or a brute? – I don't know, people are so desperately unsatisfactory. Even Horrys seem to ring a little flat.

James goes back tomorrow to the South, and I shall stay on here for the present. *[. . .]*

‡

To Maynard Keynes

Maynard replied to Lytton's letter of the 16th that he was still not sure if he believed a word of it. Duncan, to whom he showed it, was certain 'it is simply an essay composed for my amusement'. But Maynard made it obvious that he was eager to hear more.

Milton Cottage
Rothiemurchus
Aviemore N.B.
August 22nd 1908

Dear Maynard,

Your letter with the address came this morning, and we just had time to clap it on to ours – by a barbarous system the post goes and comes at the same time. I'm not altogether surprised that you find Horry a little difficult to swallow – I do myself – who wouldn't? – but it's something that you manage to combine incredulity or half-incredulity with sympathy and even kisses. As for Duncan, I don't know what he'll say to a letter that ought to have reached you by now, though perhaps in the course of its various forwardings it's fallen into the hands of the police and the Sheriff of Inverness – a letter which really might have been 'an essay composed for your amusement'. Lord, Lord! And this letter too may surprise you. – But I'm too excited. I can't discuss an actuality that I'm in now up to the eyes; and Duncan must be punished for his wickedness by not being allowed to hear a word more of any of my adventures. I forbid you to show him this letter or any future letter until he apologises. Perhaps after all, though, it's only sub-conscious jealousy; but if he's secretly in love with Horry, let him wait till he sees Gilbert. Oh no, the one thing in the world that Horry *hasn't* a dash of is precisely Andrew, but I'm afraid I must have made a dreadful hash of my description if that wasn't clear. It's too tantalising – to have the vision and to be so unable to hand it on – and a vision so wonderfully complete – but listen, for I can beat about the bush no longer – I have seen things – oh God Almighty, I hug myself and shriek.

After lunch today, James trying to begin to pack, a knock on the door, and enter Gilbert. I had somehow half expected it, but when it came I was sufficiently excited. 'Oh Strachey, I came to ask if you'd come to tea? – and bring your brother,' nervously added, with blushes such as Cherubs might envy. James wouldn't budge, either from tact or malignity, bringing out a paltry excuse about going away, as if a hundred trains mightn't be missed with joy for such an occasion. We eventually left him throwing his boots into that extraordinary bag of his, and Gilbert timidly admitted terror. He's too charming, and we got on very well, and at last he talked of Horry – and me! – 'I'm awfully glad you like Horry.' – 'Horry says you're the most amusing person in the world.' – 'I think Horry will be a very great man some day.' – 'Horry says that you think we ought both to go to Cambridge – do you really? Horry thinks we shall like it, and I do too,' etc. etc. I was never so happy – marching along with this cooing creature, with the pink cheeks and the green kilt in the corner of my eye. I ached to say something to show a little of what I felt, but I was shy. I only ventured at last, after one of his repeated 'I *am* glad you like Horry' ejaculations, to blurt out with 'And I like you, Gilbert, too.' If James had seen those blushes even his stony heart would have melted. 'Horry said he thought you might.' Dieu!

Mr Maclehose père is a tall vague individual with a large head, very unlike his offspring, who takes after Madam – fair and forty. What they thought of me I can't conceive – 'a friend of young Townshend's' I gathered. Before tea, Gilbert led me away mysteriously 'to wash my hands' in an upper bedroom, where he collected flannels and tennis shoes, and then insisted on our going down to the river, across two rather large fields. I couldn't make any of it out, until he observed 'Horry's going to swim across, and these are for him to wear' – and in another minute, lo and behold! Horry appeared running out without a stitch from some trees on the opposite bank. He plunged in and swam, while we waited – you can imagine the state *I*, at any rate, was in – almost as breathless as Horry. What would you have given – your ears? Your head? – if you could have seen him panting on the bank, and seizing the towel from Gilbert and drying himself, and then dancing and springing and prancing in the sun like a Faun in a Greek bas-relief? But by God he was no bas-relief, he was solid and flesh and blood. We were lying on the grass, Gilbert and I, and at last he flung himself down between us, lying out at full length in the heat in all his unimaginable splendour. I plunged through infinite abysses. I had expected beauty, but I'd had no idea of that – of the astonishing form, the moulded sinuosity, the divine strength and colour and firmness and flow! I was a fool not to have realised before how much the clothes had hidden. I had only thought of gracefulness, and there was power! The shoulders, the stomach, – but what can one say? I was within an inch of it all, if I'd moved a muscle I should have raped him under Gilbert's nose. I didn't move a muscle – and nor did Gilbert. But Horry did. He leapt up suddenly, and before I knew what had happened he had flung his arms round Gilbert's neck and kissed him, and then, before I'd realised that, before I'd had time to gasp or breathe, the exquisite and inconceivable creature had done the same to me. I shake as I write. It was far quicker than you can imagine – it was like a butterfly, but it was tremendously there. He's Shelley, he's more superb than Shelley, he's Shelley and Byron and Keats. I can say no more. Eventually I tore myself away, I don't know how, to see James as he passed Kincraig Station. The train of course was half an hour late. I paced the platform in a frenzy. – Arcadia! The Elysian Fields! – Ah! Ah! That such heavens, that such divinities, should be revealed to me.

your

GLS

Sunday. There's no post, so this can't go till tomorrow. I've spent all day over the Spectator and lunch with the Sheriff and the inscrutable Ian and the darling little boys. Tomorrow they come to take me for a walk, I live in a whirl of madness. I am one vast note of exclamation. I have amazing visions. Do you remember the bush of Michael Angelo's David? But that, after all, is nothing to the rest.
Monday morning, 10.30. If you don't believe this, who shall I write to? We go out together in half an hour.

GLS

‡

To Virginia Stephen

The publisher Sidgwick was offering the equivalent of about £312 in today's money for the introduction.

Milton Cottage
Rothiemurchus
Aviemore, N.B.
August 24th 1908

Dear Virginia

I suggested some time ago Boswell's letters to Frank Sidgwick as a
book to publish. He agreed and asked me to write an 'Introduction',
offering five guineas and saying it must be done by September 15th, on
which I refused. He then asked if I knew anyone who would do the job
– I've just written suggesting that you possibly might care to, so if you
hear from him be prepared. It seems to me damned little pay, but what
finally put me off was the necessity of doing it so soon. I can't bear
this hideous worry and hurry, I must breathe. At present I'm hardly
breathing, but when I do it's good clear Scotch air, which is something.
I've been here I think about a fortnight, after a wild wet week in Skye.
This place, qua place, is perfection – one begins to realise in it that
nature may be romantic and beautiful. I linger by lakes and tear up
mountains, all day long. The nights are spent over a peat fire writing
endless letters which – it seems to me – are never answered. Are you
in Wales? Perhaps if you are you will meet brother James with a
company of Fabians – but I hardly think so. A letter came from Clive
in Wiltshire to tell me (among other things) that after Catullus, 'and
perhaps some others' my poems appealed to him most of all. This is
very encouraging. I suppose he and Vanessa are at this moment playing
bridge in a shooting lodge. What curious things we all seem to do. I
have been reading Voltaire, Vathek, and Mlle. de Lespinasse; and I
think I shall soon go on to Darwin (Emma). Do you really start for Italy
the day after tomorrow? Quelle joie! When you are among your olives,
think occasionally of a panic-stricken and scribbling ghost, through
whose phantasmal brain a million frenzies are forever pouring – in
vain! in vain!

To my somewhat dilapidated imagination you seem to me, at this
particular moment, to be a woman of sound and solid sense. I rave, and
you order a pill for the liver. Is this true? My whole being is so faint and
frail that I haven't any idea. My only consolation is that my health, as a
matter of fact, is almost tolerable. I am sunburnt, and I digest. Do write
to me if you can. Pippa and Pernel are in a cottage half a mile away, and
hundreds of dread relations lurk behind every bush. They are of all

varieties – Countesses, country cousins, faded civil servants, and young heirs to landed property – and all eminently repellent. I think I shall make an Encyclopaedia of them. It would be enormously large.

your
Lytton Strachey

‡

To Maynard Keynes

August 24th 1908

Only one word to say that I *have* achieved. High Mass, as you call it, has been said – in a nest of heather in the lairig today where we wandered. I am tired and can hardly write. I'm happy – too happy? – What is Love? Tis not hereafter. – He is all one can possibly desire, and he is mine. Beyond words, beyond words, are those kisses and those ecstasies. It's strange – he's in love with *him* – with Gilbert – and he has said so, and that he is still in love with me – and I believe it, and I am even glad. *[. . .]*

I've just come back in the motor – having dined there – swaying among the rainy branches – why not forever? I was alone with wonders, and they are with me still, won't they be always with me? He looked in at the last minute as I went off, and then 'Lytton! Goodbye!' *[. . .]*

‡

To Maynard Keynes

On the 24th Maynard replied to 'your second Horatian epistle', saying that in Lytton's hands Horry ('not a very nice name – does his character absolutely require it?') is 'purely a dramatic figure'. Though his letter allows the possibility that it's all true, he still finds it had to believe 'and am divided between admiration of Horry for his conversation and of you for inventing it'. Keynes encloses a letter headed King's College, addressed to 'Dear Mr Townshend, old chap', inviting him to stay next term with Lytton, 'who's in love with you, you know'. Also in the correspondence is a sheet of drawings of boys' heads numbered 1–4, and ranging from one of exquisite beauty (number 3) to a faun with pointed ears (number 4). They are almost certainly drawn by Duncan.

August 25th 1908

Tuesday evening. I'm in no state to write, but I must tell you. You may have seen it in the papers. I've lost all. I feel almost stony now. There's an incredibility in things – a hideous incredibility – that it should have happened so. Oh God! God! But at least it's true that I've known Horry. Isn't that true? Maynard, *you'll* never know him. This is all horror. He was drowned in the Spey last night, crossing back from Little Kinvara, he had swum over after I'd gone, to him, and then returning – no one knows. He was found early this morning near the Aviemore bridge. I learnt most of this in a dreadful note which awoke me to this despair, from Gilbert – the wretched, wretched Gilbert. I found him at Kinvara House. We looked together on the end. No word of that. It is over. Write to me if you can.

your
Lytton

Wednesday. I have not said all, I could not. Only this more. *[. . .]* What could I do but lose myself in that profundity, and kiss those lips which had come so close to mine?

GLS

✝

To Maynard Keynes

Maynard, writing on 26 August, says he's had two letters from Lytton since he last wrote. He was annoyed by the first, in which Lytton seemed to be bored with Horry, but thrilled by the second letter; and says that Duncan 'is painting a large oil of the naked Horry embracing you and Gilbert for next year's Academy'. Keynes points out that it is awkward for Lytton to be in love with both Horry and Gilbert, and says that Lytton will have to 'eliminate' Gilbert eventually, and wonders how he will manage that. He also says that whatever Lytton writes, he will believe that he kissed Horry as 'it would have been very bad manners if you haven't'. Finally, Maynard wrote from Orkney on 13 September, when he had received the final letter of the series, and berated Lytton for his 'wicked deceit' and the 'waste of good emotion to which it might have led – as well as for your bad taste in misbehaving with Gilbert over a corpse'.

Milton Cottage
August 27th 1908

Dear Maynard

I hope poor Horry's death wasn't too great a shock for you. His life and adventures were elaborated by us over our evening fire, and we thought they might amuse you in the intervals of other romances [. . .] Duncan's presence made the game almost hopeless – it's impossible to deceive two people combined. But I wonder how much of it you really *did* believe. I never saw anything so amazingly hedging as your letters. I rather wish I hadn't disillusioned you about Horry's death, because even you couldn't have hedged over that. The effort to keep up the realismus was terrific, and many exquisite scenes had to be given up because they would have been out of tone. Did you know, by the bye, that Horry wrote poetry? On the morning of the High Mass I received some verses from him, which I didn't send, as I thought they hardly did him justice [. . .] and as to that wretched Gilbert, he now insists upon going to Oxford, so that I've declined to have anything more to say to him [. . .] I have had a letter from James with a somewhat sketchy account of his intermediate party near the Sidney Webbs. He says they're all horribly unromantic, and I can believe it. I only hope that he won't try to convert them – it would be exceedingly dangerous.

your affectionate
Lytton

‡

To Leonard Woolf

In his brief autobiography Moore wrote: 'At Richmond, I was again invited to give two courses of ten lectures each, this time at the Morley College in Waterloo Road. These lectures, which were called lectures on Metaphysics, I wrote out in a completely finished form and merely read them to my audience, just as I had done earlier with my lectures on ethics.'[1] *Morley College started in the 1880s, when the social reformer Emma Cons took the lease of the Old Vic, and staged, in addition to un-typically non-smutty variety performances, public lectures by scientists. By 1885 regular evening classes were being held in the theatre's dressing-rooms, and in 1889 this aspect of the activities had its own part of the*

Old Vic building dedicated to it, and was renamed Morley College to mark the
benefaction of Samuel Morley MP, textile magnate and temperance worker.

6, Pembroke Villas
Richmond
Thursday, September 24th 1908

[. . .] I'm at Moore's. He's sitting within an inch of me writing a review
of a German book on Values. Can you conceive it? He appears to me
exceeding thin and perhaps on the whole unhappy. At any rate uneasy –
he does so infinitely little, and hasn't as yet written a single word of his
book on Metaphysics. It's really rather shocking, but I don't see what
else can happen. His slowness is absolute. Do you think we'll all simply
fizzle out? Well! If he does too, we'll perish in good company. But I
suppose, in any case, there's the correspondence.

Have I told you about James's romance? He's desperately – 'madly' is
the right word – in love with Rupert Brooke, who doesn't return his
passion. Rupert is a queer personage – an odd mixture of acridity and
flabbiness – and on the whole he rather annoys me. He's behaved to me
with the utmost negligence. When I was in Cambridge in June I lived
for three weeks on his staircase, and I hoped that I'd make friends with
him then, but he refused, I can't think why. He seems to have a sort of
pride which makes him afraid of going outside his own dunghill. Where
he enjoys immensely being cock. He writes rather futile poetry, and
proposes a philosophy of quietude and general mist. I don't understand
these philosophies. James I imagine is in love with him because of his
complexion, his hair, and his eyes; but it's certainly conceivable that
there's something underneath. If he took a sudden turn I shouldn't be
much surprised – James declares there have been signs of wobbling –
and in that case he might branch out into something magnificent. But
do people take sudden turns? I daresay they do. They're so very
singular.

Friday. I return today to Hampstead and family life. This morning
was spent discussing the love of God. Moore defended it, but at last was
obliged to admit that a person's love of God was indistinguishable from
the love of a catamite for a bugger, though he didn't put it in those
words, and I hadn't the courage to.

I never mentioned how delightful the Ouse looked near Huntingdon
as I passed it coming from Scotland. I seemed to remember every part
of it I saw. I felt so infinitely reminiscent, looking out at it from my

window, among the commercial travellers and the American tourists. Extraordinarily long ago, was it? Just how many years?

your

GLS

I've missed the post – as usual – but send this in the desperate hope that it may catch a tramp steamer in some miraculous way.

1. P. A. Schilpp (ed.), *The Philosophy of G. E. Moore*, p. 27.

‡

To Virginia Stephen

Virginia was staying at the Hotel Voltaire.

67, Belsize Park Gardens
Hampstead, N.W.
September 27th 1908

Dear Virginia

I've no idea whether this will reach you. Turner murmured something about Voltaire, so I'm trying a random shot. There's no reason for it, other than mere conversation, and as I gather you've to return very soon there's not much chance of a reply.

I returned about a week ago to the London Life, and am already up to the eyes in it. – Very dim and misty I find it. I've been of course to two plays and to Simpson's, not to mention the London Library and the Spectator office. I've spent several shillings in taxicabs, and at the present moment I'm writing a review of Mr Swinburne on the Elizabethans. Did you ever hear such a hideous record? You I imagine exhilarated in the Place de la Concorde – is it fine or horrible? Several weeks ago in Scotland I thought for a moment that I should like to be in Paris, but the feeling hasn't returned, and now I think I should burst into tears if I woke up and found myself on the Pont Neuf. If you appeared it might comfort me – dashing the three of you to the Louvre in a cab. But I daresay out of sheer inanition I should let you go by.

There are moments – on the Heath, of course, – when I seem to myself to see life steadily and see it whole, but they're only moments; as a rule I can make nothing out. You don't find much difficulty, I think. Is it because you *are* a virgin? Or because, from some elevation or another, it's possible to manage it, and you happen to be there? Ah! There are so many difficulties! So many difficulties! I want to write a novel about a Lord Chancellor and his naughty son, but I can't for the life of me think of anything like the shadow of a plot, and then – the British public! Oh dear, let's all go off to the Faroe Islands, and forget the existence of Robin Mayor and Mrs Humphry Ward, and drink rum punch of an evening, and live happily ever after! It's really monstrous that we shouldn't be able to. Vanessa would cook for us. Why not? – But you must come back to London first.

Yours ever
Lytton Strachey.

I can't write to this address without sending my respects to the ghost of the dear old skeleton. Will you give them him? Have you seen him yet?

‡

To Leonard Woolf

Clive, Vanessa, Virginia, Adrian and Lytton stayed for a few days in November at Penmenner House, on the Lizard peninsula in Cornwall.

67, Belsize Park Gardens
October 29th 1908

My Cambridge adventures were more unpleasant than I'd expected. *[. . .]* I stayed with Maynard in his palatial half-furnished King's rooms in the New Buildings, *[. . .]* – where he'd returned from Orkney the day before. It was horrible. His futility, his utter lack of delicacy amounting to cruelty, his strange physical attractions *[. . .]*

November 19th. I stopped, you see how long ago, in a sort of despair of uneasiness which has been going on ever since. I write now partly because it'll amuse you to hear where I'm writing from – I wonder if you could guess – Penmenner! I dashed down here a week ago with Clive Bell and Vanessa and Virginia and Adrian. They went last Tuesday, and since then I've been alone. Tomorrow I return to

Hampstead. I shall still be uneasy. Your letter came to me here. Your letters are always exciting, and this time your outburst on Keynes and our not electing the Goth was quite a tonic to me. I don't believe though, that we behaved so badly about the Goth as you say. The whole thing seems to me to have been a purely phenomenal question, and I believe we thought so at the time. As for Keynes, I saw him again the other day, in Duncan's arms, to all intents and purposes – and it was quite sickening. The affair leaves me pale with horror. It's extraordinary that you should find some sort of peace in your Asiatic pilgrimage, that you should positively be almost happy, while I'm horribly tossed. What is it, do you think? Do you understand my condition? *[. . .]* Perhaps some day I shall make up my mind – or not make it up. At any rate don't be surprised whatever may happen, or if you hear one day – I don't know that you ever will – that I've married Virginia.

Your
GLS

‡

To Virginia Stephen

Penmenner House
[The Lizard]
November 17th 1908

Dear Virginia

Ten o'clock. I wonder where you are at this minute – perhaps at Gordon Square. It seems preposterous that you shouldn't all be sitting round the fire here as usual. As it is, imagine me in extraordinary solitude, willing to sell my soul for a little conversation. How long I shall bear it I haven't the faintest idea. There have already been moments in the long evening when I've shuddered, but Saint Simon supports me, wonderful as ever. Oh, Madame de Chaulnes! Oh, le Président Harlay (for the second time too)! Oh, Mademoiselle Choin! Oh les Parvuls de Meudon *[Paroles de Meudon]*! Don't you wish you'd got to them all? I don't know what I shall do when I come to the end – but that's still 15½ volumes off. And I suppose one can always begin again.

I had two charming walks today. I don't think I could ever grow tired of this country. One looks down over precipices into such astounding surges, and there are so many changes, and then, when one's tired of the sea, one can begin to attend to the coast, which is divine. The chief excitement of the afternoon was an auction, which occurred a little way down the road, outside a cottage, a variegated crowd of village ladies and gentlemen attending. The auctioneer was red, fat, and raucous, and amazingly (I thought) unsuccessful. – 'These two nice little vaises – how much now? Sixpence – did I hear someone say sixpence? – fivepence, then, *going*' – but I didn't dare to stay very long, for fear of having part of a dinner service and five eggcups knocked down to me for eightpence. I'm sure it would have happened if I'd looked at him at a critical moment – in fact it *did* happen to one poor lady who got a glass lampshade for 3d quite by accident, and it couldn't be helped.

Did you find a nice fog waiting for you at Paddington? And how many letters at Fitzroy Square? When you get this letter it'll be Thursday, which seems very far off. By that time I daresay I'll be fuming and packing my bag, especially if it rains, and I believe it will, confound it. But it doesn't matter – it will have been worth it – those two wonderful sunny mornings were alone worth the voyage. Tell Adrian that he's a perfect pig to have taken away the decent map and left nothing but a little wretch of an object, 600 miles to an inch. Tomorrow perhaps I shall go to Mullion in a motor bus.

your   G.L.S.

‡

To Virginia Stephen

The historian, later Warden of New College, Oxford, H.A.L. Fisher (1865–1940) was related to Virginia's mother. Lettres à une Inconnue is by Prosper Mérimée, a collection of letters from Mérimée to Jenny Dacquin, published posthumously in 1874.

Mermaid Club
Rye
Sussex
January 3rd 1909

Dear Virginia

Perhaps you have heard rumours of my flight here? I arrived on
Thursday and have been spending the time since in a semi-stupor,
among mists and golfers, so that by this time I'm feeling so much à la
hashisch that I can hardly imagine that I shall ever be anywhere else, in
fact that anywhere else exists. However, by an effort of will I can just
bring to my mind a dim vision of Bond Street, the Heath, and a Square
or two. Have you really been there all this time, and are you there still?
I shall come and see on Thursday. I wonder if I shall find the Fishers,
but if I do I shall be able to speak of nothing but cleeks and greens –
though no doubt Herbert would be very well able to cope with that.
Besides the golfers there are some of the higher clergy – bishops and
wardens – and two lawyers at the chancery bar. Of course these are all
golfers as well, so it all comes to very much the same thing. Their
conversation is quite amazing, and when I consider that there *must* be
numbers of persons more stupid still, I begin to see the human race en
noir. Oh God! Oh God! The slowness of them, the pomp, and the
fatuity! They're certainly at their best when they argue, which they did
last night on the subject of cruelty and sport. – 'I console myself with
the thought that animals themselves are very cruel – of course not stags,
no – but look at a weasel!' I shrieked with laughter, and it was quite
unnecessary to control myself, because they can notice nothing. Good
heavens, how happy they must be!

　　In the intervals of sleep I read those Lettres à une Inconnue, which
have troubled us so. They're an odd mixture of disillusionment and
flatness – I don't know what – very 'brilliant' and well written, and yet
somehow staggeringly grey. The French seem to me a melancholy race
– is it because they have no imagination, so they have no outlets when
they find themselves (as all intelligent people must) vis-à-vis with the
horrors of the world? There's a sort of dry desperation about some of
them which I don't believe exists with the English – even with Swift.
Talking of Great Authors, I've seen Henry James twice since I came,
and was immensely impressed. I mean only seen with the eye – I wish I
knew him! He appeared at his window as I passed the other day – most

remarkable! So conscientious and worried and important – he was like an admirable tradesman trying his best to give satisfaction, infinitely solemn and polite. Is there any truth in this? It has since occurred to me that his novels are really remarkable for their lack of humour. But I think it's very odd that he should have written precisely them and look precisely so. Perhaps if one talked to him one would understand.

Write to me if you can an enormous letter full of exciting narrative and profound reflexions upon human life. Of course you can – but will you? Even a quarter of a sheet would be an oasis in my desolation. I've been rather ill, but I'm better – I've also been rather upset – I wish I were a golfer. Has Gordon Square returned yet? What happened at Rumpelmayer's? Has Adrian had another brief? R.S.V.P.

your

G.L.S.

‡

To James Strachey

Ye Olde Mermaid Inn

Rye

Sussex

January 4th 1909

[. . .] I've also seen Henry James – twice. Both times exceedingly remarkable, but almost impossible to describe. He came in here to show the antique fireplace to a young French poet – you never saw such a scene – the poor man absolutely bouche béante *[gaping]*, and all the golfers and bishops sitting round quite stolidly munching buttered buns. He has a colossal physiognomy, and it's almost impossible to believe that such an appearance could have produced the Sacred Fount. I long to know him. He seemed infinitely conscientious and immensely serious, and this was especially so the second time I saw him – at a window in his house; he had just come there to look more closely at a manuscript – and then the polite worry of it all! I think he must be quite extraordinarily slow. *[. . .]*

‡

To Virginia Stephen

'The Correspondence': a few of the proto-Bloomsberries had decided to start a cod-correspondence, in which each wrote as an imaginary character. Lytton wrote the first such letter on 31 January (as 'Vane Hatherley') and Virginia replied as 'Eleanor Hadyng' on 1 February, after which the scheme collapsed.

67, Belsize Park Gardens
Hampstead, N.W.
January 27th 1909

So shocking! Your glove appeared the minute you'd left the house. I'm afraid you must have shivered without it. I've just finished my solitary dinner (the whole of my family are at Brighton, I believe, for suffragism), and now I've settled down for the evening before my gas fire, surrounded by my Maintenon and the Dictionary of National Biography. I envy you, talking at Gordon Square. If I could have my way, I should go out to dinner every night, and then to a party or an opera, and then I should have a champagne supper, and then I should go to bed in some wonderful person's arms. Wouldn't you? When one reflects on one's pallid actual existence one shudders. But I suppose there are always the triumphs of Art.

I forgot to tell you how extraordinary my novel about the Lord Chancellor is becoming, as I lie in bed creating it after breakfast. You never heard such conversations, or imagined such scenes! But they're most of them a little too scabreux, and they're none of them written. What's so remarkable is the way in which I penetrate into every sphere of life. My footmen are amazing, and so are my prostitutes. There's a Prime Minister who should be fine, and a don's wife à faire mourir de rire. But it's impossible to get any of it together.

By the bye, will you send me all the particulars as to the Correspondence? I'm dying to hear from Adrian. I wonder how old I am. Thirty-five? Are you going to write to Lady Eastnor?

your
G.L.S.

I wish you'ld come to tea with me every day.

‡

To Virginia Stephen

Virginia replied by return, posing as a muffin-making 'Yorkshire woman'. The correspondence was promising – note that one of Virginia's characters was called Clarissa, and that her contribution ended by asking Hatherley to come to tea early, as she had a ticket 'for the Wagner opera – what d'you call it – and I don't want to miss the overture'.

67, Belsize Park Gardens
Hampstead, N.W.
January 31st 1909

My dear Miss Hadyng

I am visiting my editor on Tuesday, and before I return to my suburb I shall appear in Coram Street, if there's a chance of my finding you and some tea there. I was at the Philips's this afternoon, and found the poor lady in bed, as beautiful as ever. She was very interesting on Lady Eastnor, and on everything else, but was she a little uneasy? I've been immersed for so long that I'm out of date – or think I am, and even that's exasperating. To my unaccustomed eye she seemed to be watching dear James more carefully than usual. Perhaps you will be able to tell me how absurd I am, at tea on Tuesday. If you don't, I warn you that I shall jump to the most extraordinary conclusions; and on the whole I rather hope you won't, because as I advance in life I grow more and more convinced that extraordinary conclusions are the only things I care for.

Yours very sincerely
Vane Hatherley

‡

To Leonard Woolf

In his previous letter to Leonard, dated 5 January, from Ye Olde Mermaid Inn, Rye, Sussex, where he'd gone 'for a little rest', Lytton had wailed about Duncan, 'can you imagine the torture of imagining, of knowing for a fact that someone for whom one would be disembowelled is prostituted to Keynes?' Gerald

Shove (1887–1947), economist at King's. John Edwin Nixon (d.1916) was dean of King's in the 1870s and 1880s. According to E.F. Benson in As We Were, *Nixon was composed almost entirely of prosthetic devices – with false limbs, teeth and hair.*

'That worm' Stephen Gaselee was an Old Etonian friend of Maynard's, who played bridge with him, and once wrote to Swithinbank that 'Gaselee wears starched pyjamas in bed'.[1]

67, Belsize Park Gardens
February 5th 1909

My last letter was rather 'from the depths', I'm afraid, but fortunately I vary, and at the present moment I find myself extraordinarily happy. Perhaps it's all a matter of health, for otherwise I can see no reason for the variations. But it's terrifying as well as consoling – never to know from minute to minute whether one's going to be in the inferno, or a first class compartment, with fur rugs and foot-warmers and a beautiful young man on the opposite seat. Alas, it's on the whole, I think, rather pointless; but of this I can never be quite sure; I have dreams and imaginations, but so far they've ended as they began.

I was in Cambridge at the beginning of the term, and was unable to prevent their electing Gerald Shove. Heaven knows what he's like, but I expect rather dull and heavy, but at any rate not disgusting in the Greenwood or Hobber style. He's honest, but with damned few sparks, as far as I could see, and ugly. I gathered that James elected him because Rupert wanted it, and Rupert wanted it because he's an owl. Mon dieu! there was actually a scene at breakfast on the Sunday, in which I completely lost my temper and burst out into a violent personal attack on Rupert, who of course didn't care in the least. His condition is infinitely putrescent – all dim and soft and pseudo-aesthetic; even James I believe has glimpses of the horror of it, and Norton and Sheppard gnash their teeth. Sheppard is far more charming than he ever was before. Norton is very brilliant and wise and important, but with that curious lack of decision of character which mathematicians seem to have. As for poor old Keynes, he's quite absolutely sunk – it's really remarkable, the unveiled collapse. If ever a human soul were doomed, it's he. And by God I think he deserves his fate. Looking back I see him, hideous and meaningless, at every turn and every crisis, a malignant goblin gibbering over destinies that are not his own. The moral is – never put your penis into a french letter that's cracked. Those

sorts of compromises always end in abortions. But when one's utterly
lonely and stranded, and utterly disappointed too, how can one avoid
seizing on the only piece of india-rubber handy, and using that? What's
curious is that he, at this moment, must be imagining – if he imagines
anything – that he's reached the apex of human happiness – Cambridge,
statistics, triumphant love and inexhaustible copulations – what more
could anyone desire? His existence is the thinnest shell, and he believes
it's solid, and will go on believing so, until one day it shivers into
splinters, and even then he'll believe it can be patched. He'll end a
spiritual Nixon, with a whole internal economy of metal makeshifts for
lungs and lights and heart and genitory organs; but he'll never know;
he'll never hear the clank.

I managed to see your brother Philip and his surroundings. – Full of
interest, and just what you say. He seems to move in a queer circle of
decadents – but decadents who are at any rate very young. There is
Mr. Towsey, of Trinity, vulgar and oozing with lust, and an immense
admirer of the corporal and me. He talks – they all talk – with the
Strachey accentuation absurdly exaggerated, but even that doesn't make
them very witty. For a wild moment last summer, I trembled on the
brink of copulation with the Towsey, only fortunately he was too ugly
and coarse. If I'd done it, he would have borrowed two pounds of me,
and I should have had to give them, and I couldn't have afforded it, and
altogether it wouldn't have been nice. The other principal figure is a
freshman called, I think, Davis, perhaps at Sidney, subservient to the
Towsey, and more degraded, very Jewish and very stupid, but I imagine
more intimate with Philip. Philip himself is certainly the most interesting
and perhaps the most unpleasant of the group. I had a look at his rooms –
decorated completely with Aubrey Beardsley drawings. He seems to have
a character, but it struck me as oddly bitter, and I couldn't be sure of the
intelligence. James has seen more of him, and thinks as I do, only more
favourably. He's a curious contrast to Cecil – so charming and vague
and soft. I suppose there is just the hope that he may come out of the
rubbish he's in, and then I don't see why he shouldn't soar.

The Brookfield book I've only just looked at. It seemed purely
fatuous. She's a book-making woman of a low type – tried to get
information from McTaggart and Sheppard, but didn't succeed. It's
rather surprising though, isn't it? that she should have been so discreet.
As far as I remember, you could hardly gather that the Society still
exists. One only wonders whether it *did* exist then. They were devils –
or was it simply that they didn't know how to write?

If only you would come home and live with me in a small and commodious flat I should be perfectly happy. Can't you bear to part from your blacks and your executions? Is everything quite impossible? The world is too intolerably confused. I understand nothing. I see too many points and too few. I wander eternally between Duncan and Virginia and Sicilian prostitutes and chastity and resignation and the wildest hopes and despair. I'm dreadfully afraid that I may do something mad for one minute and ruin my life, but it's just as likely that I shall never do anything at all. The only consolation – and the true one – is that whatever may happen or not happen in this frantic universe we shall always have been ourselves.

your

GLS

The Nose is going to marry – a sister of that worm Gaselee; and Duncan's painting his portrait in honour of the event.

1. Robert Skidelsky, *John Maynard Keynes*, vol. 1, p.121.

‡

To Virginia Stephen

This is the letter Lytton wrote the day he proposed to Virginia and either was refused or managed to withdraw the proposal. The 18th Lord Dunsany, Edward John Moreton Drax Plunkett (1878–1957), was a writer of fantasy tales. One of his Fifty-one Tales *published in 1915 was 'The Trouble in Leafy Green Street'.*

67, Belsize Park Gardens
Hampstead, N.W.
February 17th 1909

I'm still rather agitated and exhausted. I try to imagine you at your Green Street dinner, between Lord Dunsany and Thomas Hardy, but it's difficult. I do hope you're cheerful! As for me, I'm all of a heap and the future seems a blank to me. But whatever happens, as you said, the important thing is that we should like each other; and we can neither of us have any doubt that we do.

I hope to see Vanessa tomorrow morning. This world is so difficult to manage.

Your
Lytton

‡

To Leonard Woolf

Leonard had sent Lytton a poem of his own, beginning 'When I am dead and you forget' and ending 'I . . . know that our bodies never die'. In the same letter he wondered whether Virginia might marry Saxon. Leonard does not seem to have responded immediately to the suggestion that he should himself marry Virginia, and Lytton continued to press him about it.

> 67, Belsize Park Gardens
> Hampstead, N.W.
> February 19th 1909

Your letter has this minute come – with your proposal to Virginia, and I must write a word or two of answer, though the post is all wrong. You are perfectly wonderful, and I want to throw my arms around your neck. Everything you say is so tremendously to the point! Isn't it odd that I've never really been in love with you? And I suppose I never shall. You make me smile and shudder – oh! And long for you to be here. It's curious – are you after all happier than I am? In spite of the silence of four years? – This is all rubbish, but I'm rather ill and rather excited – by your letter.

The day before yesterday I proposed to Virginia. As I did it, I saw that it would be death if she accepted me, and I managed, of course, to get out of it before the end of the conversation. The worst of it was that as the conversation went on, it became more and more obvious that the whole thing was impossible. The lack of understanding was so terrific! And how can a virgin be expected to understand? You see she *is* her name. If I were either greater or less I could have done it and could either have dominated and soared and at last made her completely mine, or I could have been contented to go without everything that makes life important. Voila! It was, as you may imagine, an amazing conversation. Her sense was absolute, and at times her supremacy was so great that I quavered. I think there's no doubt whatever that you ought to marry her. You *would* be great enough, and you'ld have too the immense advantage of physical desire. I was in terror lest she should kiss me. If you came and proposed she'ld accept. She really really would. As it is, she's almost certainly in love with me, though she thinks she's not. I've made a dreadful hash, as you see, but it was the only way to make sure of anything. I was brought to it by the horror of my present wobble and the imagination of the paradise of married peace. It just needed the *fact* of the prospect of it to show me that there simply isn't any alternative to the horror, that I must face it, and somehow get through or die.

Is this sheer raving? The curious thing is that it's all true, and that it's only by imagining how it may strike you among your buffaloes that I can get a glimmering of it being unnatural. I confide in Vanessa, who's quite unparalleled, but she doesn't see the real jar of the whole thing – doesn't take in the agony of Duncan, and the confusion of my states. I copulated with him again this afternoon, and at the present moment he's in Cambridge copulating with Keynes. I don't know whether I'm happy or unhappy. What do you think?

Your poem disproves your theory. Imaginations are nothing; facts are all. A penis *actually* erected – on becoming erect – is cataclysmal. In imagination, it's a mere shade. That, in my view, is the point of art, which converts imaginations into actualities. But I'm sleepy and ill, and I've got to write on Swift, Stella & Vanessa for the Spectator.

your
Lytton

Friday 20th.
I've had an éclaircissement with Virginia.
She declared she was not in love with me, and I observed finally that I would not marry her. So things have simply reverted.
Perhaps you'd better not mention these matters to Turner, who certainly is *not* upon the tapis. I told Vanessa to hand on your proposal, so perhaps *you* are.

your
GLS

To James Strachey

Lytton was hoping 'to escape' from his feelings of bitterness about Duncan and Maynard. James has annotated an extract from this letter, saying that Lytton's giving the date of his proposal to Virginia as 19 February is 'evidently a mistake for 17th'. Curiously, there is no mention of the proposal in his earlier letter (19 February) to James.

> 67, Belsize Park Gardens
> Hampstead N.W.
> March 9th 1909

[. . .] In my efforts to escape, I had a decided reverse the other day. I haven't mentioned the incident before for various reasons. On February 19th I proposed to Virginia, and was accepted. It was an awkward moment, as you may imagine, especially as I realised, the very minute it was happening, that the whole thing was repulsive to me. Her sense was amazing, and luckily it turned out that she's not in love. The result was that I was able to manage a fairly honourable retreat. The story is really rather amusing and singular, but its effect has been to drive me on to these shoals more furiously than ever. I need hardly mention the immense secrecy of the affair *[. . .]*

[British Library and Smith]

‡

To Maynard Keynes

Strife was by John Galsworthy (1867–1933), who won the 1932 Nobel Prize for Literature. 'Ignotus' was the pseudonym assigned to Lytton when he made his debut as drama critic of the Spectator *on 30 November 1907. In* Strife *Galsworthy shows the conflict of the extremes of capital and labour, the lock-out and the strike, resolved by accepting the compromise that had been available at the beginning of the terrible events and dismissing the stubborn leaders of both sides.*

George Leigh Mallory (1886–1924), the mountaineer who was lost on Everest in the expedition of 1924, was educated at Winchester and Magdalene College,

Cambridge. He became a schoolmaster. Strikingly good-looking, Mallory had flirtations with several of Lytton's circle as well as with Lytton himself.

67, Belsize Park Gardens
Hampstead, N.W.
March 17th 1909

Dear Maynard

I was very glad to hear of the fellowship. One couldn't feel absolutely sure with those devils! I suppose you're now established for the rest of your days, and it seems very clear that you've acted wisely. I'm sure you'll be as useful at Cambridge as on the Office Stool, and you certainly enjoy it more.

I've been wanting to write to you for some time, though really I think it's hardly necessary – only to say that you must always think of me as your friend. I shall think of you in the same way. But I've been rather afraid that lately you may have felt that things had become different. I don't think it's the case. The only thing is that I'm some-times uneasy and awkward perhaps, partly I suppose because of my nervous organisation, which isn't particularly good – but I don't see how it can be helped. I can only beg that you'll attend to it as little as you can, and believe me to be a sensible decent person who remembers and knows.

Were you at Strife yesterday? I went there at the last moment as Ignotus, and looked for you everywhere, but you were the only people there I couldn't see – everyone else in the world was congregated. Perhaps you went to the Master Builder. That fiend James, after keeping me in inconceivable suspense for 36 hours, tells me that the Paris scheme is off. I'm on the whole rather glad – at least I realise that it's *best*, but by God the thought of George arm in arm with me on the Boulevards makes me weep and gibber. Now I shall never never get to know the divine creature. Oh! Oh! [. . .]

yours ever,
Lytton

No answer required to this in the very least!

‡

To James Strachey

Lytton adored clubs, and joined many in his lifetime. Most of the rest of this long letter laments Lytton's failure to persuade Duncan to live with Maynard in Cambridge.

Lytton nicknamed Keynes Pozzo di Borgo simply because he and James found the name funny. Carlo Andrea, count Pozzo di Borgo (1764–1832), was a devious Corsican politician who became a Russian diplomat.

Savile Club
107, Piccadilly, W.
April 6th 1909

I really am here at last – in the bow window, perfectly happy, with the Green Park in front of me, Piccadilly streaming below me, and the Smoking Room, Cousin Alfred, Mr Newbolt, and Lord knows who else, behind my back. I've just had tea, which (with toast) you can get for the modest sum of sixpence. My adventures on Friday, when I arrived here for the first time, were extremely painful. After having been certified as a member by a purple-bottle-nosed servitor in a guichet in the hall, I didn't in the least know what to do. There was a door, a staircase, and a notice-board; I was in my hat and coat, carrying an umbrella; the servitor merely stared from his guichet. In a moment of weakness, I began to read the notices on the notice-board, and while I was doing so the servitor became involved in an endless conversation with an imbecile Major. I was therefore lost. I couldn't ask him where I was to put my hat, coat and umbrella, I had read every notice six times, and there seemed no hope. At last I made a wild plunge at the door – opened it, entered and found myself in the dining-room, nose to nose with a somewhat surprised and indignant waiter. I then fled upstairs, and so managed to get in here safely. But there are further mysteries to be explored – the second floor? – dare I penetrate there? – Dieu! – I find that among these elected last January are George Lyttelton (hurrah! hurrah!), Erasmus Darwin (my dear old friend) and – Geoffrey Scott! As for lunching or any such thing I haven't ventured on it yet. In my desperate entry into the dining-room, I *think* I saw one long white table, but I was too agitated to be at all sure.

[. . .] I spent this morning deliciously on the Heath, dreaming of idylls and fantasies and naked beauties with golden hair, until I went off

into a Haschish swoon, and awoke to find that an elderly tramp had taken his seat beside me, and that there was an unpleasant smell. Is Moore really a mere veneer, and is Gerald really more incompetent than Pozzo? *[. . .]*

‡

To Clive and Vanessa Bell

This house in the New Forest belonged to Thena Clough, who often lent it to members of the Strachey family. Lytton was reading Voltaire.
   Russell Kerr Gaye was a tutor in classics at Trinity. The don who dealt with his suicide was Reginald St John Parry, who was Gaye's senior at Trinity by twenty years. Sir Arthur Stretton Gaye (1881–1960) was a civil servant.

Burley Hill
Ringwood
Hants.
May 21st 1909

My dear { Vanessa / Clive

I'm rather late, I'm afraid in answering your letters, and perhaps by this time you've moved off somewhere else, or are even en route for Gordon Square. I've been rather ill and rather lazy, though I'm now on the mend – in Thena's charming establishment, which she's kindly lent me for the month. Did I tell you of this before you went? However, neither illness nor laziness has been the real basis of my condition. Your letters, I may tell you, fell extraordinarily flat. All your Florentine glories, your warmths, bedrooms, roses, even the young men on the balcony – oh I simply laughed when I read of them – and your kind regrets at my not being with you to share those joys! I spent the last week of April in Cambridge, and need I say that I there found myself plunged into a throbbing world of romance? That's obvious, but what's not was the extraordinary and wonderful quality of my adventures – the intensity and exquisiteness of what I felt. Mon dieu! – George Mallory! When that's been written, what more need be said? My hand trembles, my heart palpitates, my whole being swoons away at the words – oh heavens! heavens! I found of course that he'd been absurdly maligned –

he's six foot high, with the body of an athlete by Praxiteles, and a face –
ah, incredible – the mystery of Botticelli, the refinement and delicacy of
a Chinese print, the youth and piquancy of an unimaginable English
boy. I rave, but when you see him, as you must, you will admit all –
all! The amazing thing, though, was that besides his beauty, other
things were visible more enchanting still. His passion for James was
known, but it so happened that during my visit he declared it – and
was rejected. James alone in Europe is capable of doing such a thing
as that. Poor George! I met him for the first time immediately after
this occurrence, and saw in my first glance to the very bottom of his
astounding soul. I was écrasé. What followed was remarkable – though
infinitely pure. Yes! Virginia alone will sympathise with me now – I'm
a convert to the divinity of virginity, and spend hours every day lost in
a trance of adoration, innocence and bliss. It was a complete revelation,
as you may conceive. By God! the sheer beauty of it all is what
transports me. I'm wafted over seas of amaranth, plunged up to the
eyes in all the spices of Arabia, and lulled in the bosom of eternal spring.
To have sat with him in the firelight through the evening, to have
wandered with him in the King's Garden among violets and cherry
blossom, to have no, no! for desire was lost in wonder, and there was
profanation even in a kiss. Have I said enough? We correspond, I've
asked him to stay here, but there's little hope of that. For the rest, he's
going to be a schoolmaster, and his intelligence is not remarkable.
What's the need?

I wonder if you're still enjoying yourselves. Places are horribly liable
to get worn out in ten days. But I really don't believe the beauties of
Florence can be greater than those of England, without counting
George. It's astonishing to sit out here in the sun, flowers covering the
ground, birds packed upon the trees, and the Faerie Queene (unopened)
within reach. If my health was less uneasy, it would be perfect, for then
I could explore the Forest and perhaps write a century of sonnets, every
one of which would breathe the purest spirit of ethereal love.

I heard vaguely of Adrian from Saxon, who appeared in Cambridge
to attend the post mortem of Gaye – or something of that sort. The
younger Gaye was also visible – as black as thunder, and altogether
terrifying. Barnes slinks through the Great Court with the haunted
look of a murderer. Hardy is slightly hysterical. Ernest Harrison alone
preserved his accustomed calm. Altogether I found Cambridge quite
delightful. Apart from George, the place was thick with stupendous
crises, and I rolled from one to the other in fits of laughter and floods

of tears. I hope to go back there soon, but it's damned difficult to get
a satisfactory pied-à-terre. Perhaps you will write to me again before
you return, with what news there may be. Pippa is here, which is
agreeable. I've read Jeanne d'Arc with much more pleasure than I'd
expected – it's probably the most masterly piece of history since l'Esprit
des Moeurs.

yours ever,
Lytton

Yes, he had Chinese eyes – incredible!

‡

To Leonard Woolf

*Swinburne had died on the morning of Saturday, 10 April – it was announced
on Monday the 12th, so Lytton must have spotted a fugitive newspaper poster
that hadn't been taken down.*

Burley Hill
Ringwood
Hants.
May 27th 1909

[. . .] *You* haven't written for months and months. I wonder what
you're up to. Perhaps you're packing up to come home – that would
be the most satisfactory thing. If you came, as I think I've mentioned,
you could marry Virginia, which would settle nearly every difficulty in
the best possible way. Do try it. She's an astounding woman, and I'm
the only man in the universe who would have refused her; even I
sometimes have my doubts. You might, of course, propose by telegram,
and she'ld probably accept. That would be very fine; but in any case
you'll have to come back.

Gaye's extinction was altogether expected – by three people – Hardy,
Turner and myself. The whole affair was so singularly futile as might
have been supposed. Six weeks before it happened I had a mystic letter
from Turner demanding a long and strictly private interview. I went to
his indescribably sordid lodgings and found him seated among docketed
manuscripts – a veritable dossier, by means of which he got through a

strange narration. But it all remained highly mysterious. Gaye had arrived in Brighton one afternoon to inform Turner that he was going to commit suicide. Turner thought that a rest-cure would meet the case more suitably. He corresponded with Hardy, and Hardy came to see him, and he corresponded with Gaye. The letters were read out to me, but I couldn't discover definitely what it was all about. Perhaps Gaye had come to the conclusion (the correct one I imagine) that Hardy no longer cared for him as much as he cared for Hardy, or perhaps he was merely fantastic and depressed.

It's difficult to be certain about anything, because these people carry on their affairs under a cloud of ambiguity, and one never knows whether it's love or friendship or passion or money that's at stake. However, everything lapsed, until on Easter Sunday Gaye did it in those rooms in the Great Court, with which we're acquainted. The bedmaker found him stiff in the morning, and Parry then arrived. Occurrences of this kind are really cheering to people who live in London and not in Hambantota; they give a sense of life. The funeral service must have been a remarkable spectacle. The Master came from Scotland to attend it, it was 'conducted' by those two limping clergymen, and the 'chief mourner' was Arthur Stretton. So you see my imagination of four years ago was far surpassed by the reality. In fact, how could you believe any of this, if you hadn't seen the press-cutting that proves it? Among other complications, there was an intrigue (or a supposed one) between Barnes and Laurence to keep Gaye off the staff. At any rate he *was* kept off, and his place given to that dull Stuart – d'you remember him? – It may have pulled the trigger, but I don't see how it could have loaded the pistol. A. S. Gaye, however, is rampant. He appeared, black as thunder, while I was there the other day, swearing eternal vengeance, and breathing smoke and fire over Trinity. I saw him – literally black all over, and incredibly vast – outside the Great Gate, and just had time to shrink into Matthews before he saw me. Hardy is flushed, disordered, and hysterical. I can't take much interest in his fate. In spite of his fascination, or perhaps because of it, he annoys me. There's a barrenness about him which is exasperating; and then – to have left Moore for Gaye!

This, though, is all very unimportant – simply decorative, and the things I really want to describe are too difficult and obscure. In that Easter of Gaye's there was a combination of crises, as so often happens after a long pause – like the sudden shift of a kaleidoscope. My own history was violently disturbed. Ever since the Virginia business, I'd been sinking more and more hopelessly into the mud of my passion for

Duncan. Everything combined to torture me – my ill-health, my lust, my doubts, his compliance and his frigidity, and Maynard forever grinning in the background – a triumphal death's head. The thought of it is quite horrible, the experience was nearer Hell than I've yet been. At last the pair went off to spend their Easter at Versailles, among those wonders and glories, and I was left at Hampstead in complete desolation. Suddenly, for no apparent reason, there was a physical breakdown. I was attacked by vertigo in Piccadilly, and found it difficult to get home. As I went along I saw Swinburne's death written up on the posters, and nearly burst into tears. The following day I did altogether, and doctors were sent for, and complete rest and no work commanded, and I subsided into a state of nothingness. When James came back from the Lizard – he'd been there with the reading party – he insisted on taking me off to Cambridge for a little change. Good gracious heavens! I began to feel almost happy again in those extraordinary surroundings. One afternoon, while I was sitting in the sun on the seat by the scholars' bowling-green looking onto the river, the news arrived that, at Versailles, Duncan had broken off his liaison with Maynard, and was fancy-free once more. As I was reading this, Sheppard and his beloved Mr. Taylor came floating past in a canoe. We went, James and I, down the sunny green bank to talk to them, and made our jokes, and laughed and laughed again, as if there were no more troubles in the world.

Shall I tell you any more? Do you remember Cambridge? [. . .] If you do, it's James that you must see, waxing and waning through infinite trances of love and laziness in his lodgings in King's Parade, with the window wide open onto the King's Gate, where the whole world endlessly passes under his eyes. He too had his crisis at Easter – had proposed desperately to Rupert Brooke at Penmenner, with Moore snoring in the next room, and had been brutally refused. Had proposed merely for 'affection', and had not got even that. Eh bien! At Cambridge he at once found himself in Rupert's situation. George Mallory proposed to *him*. – The sequel I shall for the present leave unwritten – partly because I don't know it, and partly because – but who *is* George Mallory?

Oh my dear, my dear, good-bye for a little. This is an impertinent, grotesque, but not altogether indefensible world.

your
Lytton

‡

To Lady Strachey

Saltsjöbaden is a seaside resort on the Stockholm peninsula.

Saltsjöbadens Sanatorium och Badenstalt
Stockholm
Sweden
August 3rd 1909

My dearest Mama,

The news from here is not exciting, as you may imagine, but it is
satisfactory. The treatment seems to be beginning to have effects. After
the first week of it, my weight has gone up by nearly 1¾ lbs, which
isn't so bad. My general health is also better, I think, and the internal
functions are greatly improved. Today I started on some of the
mechanical exercises – most singular arrangements, by means of which
the various muscles are worked without being tired. The hall where one
does them looks exactly like a torture-chamber – terrific instruments of
every kind line the walls, and elderly gentlemen attached upon them go
through their evolutions with the utmost gravity. The baths are less
exciting; I have not had any massage yet. The weather was disgusting
last week, but now it seems to be improving. When the sun shines it is
most charming, the atmosphere becomes wonderfully light and clean,
and I sit on my deck chair under the pines doing nothing with the
greatest contentment – especially as I feel that my health is really going
up. The ladies in my suite are most agreeable. What I should have done
without Daisy I can't imagine; I don't think I should even have got
here. Her knowledge of the language alone saved an immensity of
trouble, and at Stockholm she was of the greatest assistance with the
doctor. I hope you will mention my high appreciation to Ethel if you
have the opportunity.

On Sunday I lunched with the Spring Rices, who are in a small
country residence not very far off. They were on the whole rather too
diplomatic and Oxfordish for my taste, but they were at any rate
civilised, which was a relief after the incredibly middle-class collection
of Scandinavians in this establishment. I'm afraid, however, I shan't be
able to see much of them, as the steamers (which are the only means of

communication) are very inconvenient, and my various cures occupy nearly the whole of the day. I don't know what the truth is as to the 'General Strike'. The Spring Rices have laid in a vast store of provisions, but I gather that there's not much reason to suppose that it will come to anything. The food-supply here, at any rate, has at present shown no signs of stopping. If there's a revolution, I shall do my best to put myself at the head of the mob.

I've just finished the Peninsular War. My reading consists of Tolstoy, Saint Simon, Voltaire, and Swinburne. I only regret that I forgot to bring a copy of the Holy Bible. The Daily Mail supplies me with news two days late. There's so much going on that it's unexpectedly exciting reading. Among other things, I saw that Asquith had consented to see a deputation of Suffragettes. Does this mean anything? *[. . .]*

‡

To Leonard Woolf

The 'X' was an undergraduate society; among Leonard's papers is 'Rules and standing orders of the "X" Society of Trinity College March 1902'.

Henry Yates Thompson (1838–1928), an Apostle of the 1860s, had been the Liberal proprietor of the Pall Mall Gazette *and made one of the age's greatest collections of manuscripts, by limiting the collection to 100; whenever a better one became available, he sold off a less good one.*

Badanstalten
Saltsjöbaden
Stockholm
August 21st 1909

You frighten me with your expectations of the 'great work'. If it ever does come, you'll certainly be well warned beforehand, but will it? The difficulties are écrasant, and the most obvious of all is bad health. That's the reason for this filthy address. Did you get a fragmentary letter some months ago from the New Forest? If it had been continued – I think it broke off with George – it would have explained the present state of affairs. It's true that for the present I have 'Stopped writing' – viz. for the Spectator, to which I've been in the habit of contributing two columns of balderdash every week. At Easter I became so ill that this was forbidden and I had to rest – I've been resting ever since. About a month ago I arrived here, and I shall stay I suppose another fortnight; probably it won't have done much good. I have medicinal baths and other horrors, I sit out in the cold sunshine, and I bore myself to extinction. When I return I shall try to go and live somewhere away from my family, which has got on my nerves, and there I shall either die or conquer.

Your destiny is clearly marked out for you, but will you allow it to work? You must marry Virginia. She's sitting waiting for you, is there any objection? She's the only woman in the world with sufficient brains; it's a miracle that she should exist; but if you're not careful you'll lose the opportunity. At any moment she might go off with heaven knows who – Duncan? Quite possible. She's young, wild, imaginative, discontented and longing to be in love. If I were you, I should telegraph. But at any rate come and see her before the end of 1910.

I wish I could give you a notion of George Mallory. My pen trembles as I write the name. He appeared at the psychological moment – so exquisitely, so incredibly! – I'd really thought that such a thing was an impossibility, and there was I in five seconds absolutely overwhelmed. The whole affair can only be compared, for intensity of sudden emotion, to the moment when Swithin first swam into my ken. Oh, there are wonders! But will you ever believe? Do come and see – not Swithin – alas! that's too late – he goes to Burma in October, in pursuit of his mad visions – but George. The sheer beauty of it is what you'ld *have* to admit! A refinement, a delicacy, a sort of Chinese grace, – and mingled with all the strength and health and flush of two and twenty. His body – vast, pink, unbelievable – is a thing to melt into and die. I *have* melted, but, so far, I haven't died. Perhaps I hardly want to – kisses seem almost to be enough. Gracious heavens! That's something to have lived for, to have known. Need I say that I'm not in love? No more than I was in love with Swithin – it's been all joy. He's a child – innocent and in love with James and charming and affectionate – oh, come and see!

August 24th. Something rather funny has just happened. I was sitting out among the mangy pine trees at the back of the house when a young clergyman passed. The dog-collar was what I first observed; then I looked at the face, and seemed to remember something. It was very young and sheepish and might have been attractive if it hadn't been overlaid with niaiserie *[silliness]* – I racked my brains – someone at Trinity, I was sure – someone we'd had some odd dealings with – at last it flashed on me – Brandy and Soda Smith! His existence had completely gone out of my mind – do you remember the creature? He was in the X, figured in the crisis of 'The Only Way', in short his father was a clergyman. And now *he* is! I find that he's chaplain to the British Embassy at Stockholm, and was only here for dinner. I went up to him, and, as I thought, he'd recognised me. I didn't find much to say, and he was infinitely putrescent. All self-satisfied and sickeningly stupid and very stand-offish, too. I suppose we must have behaved shockingly to him, I certainly hope so. He positively asked after you, and you were the only person he asked after. He thought he'd heard you were dead. No doubt you must have been more brutal than any of us. But let's forget him again, and return for a second to George.

He finally has put me out of love with Duncan, and made me more or less content. It's a great pleasure to think of him. They pretend, of course, that I'm sentimental, but I'm not. No doubt *you* think he's a second Hobber; but I don't want to elect him, and you're quite wrong.

There has been a Dinner since I wrote last. It was chiefly remarkable for the extraordinary competence of the Vice President. Everyone feared the worst, but dear Gerald made a speech such as a middle-aged Angel would like to make but can't, with the result that he went off in a furore. I came in very late – 'alone and palely loitering', Bob Trevy said – with the result that I had to sit between Macnaughton (in whose house it was) and Parker Smith. It was pretty intolerable, and I was very hubristic, but not quite so much so as Norton, who was just opposite, pretended to be drunk, and insisted on telling Yates Thompson that he was going to pump *[piss]* under the table. The President was Whitehead, in place of Wedd who's ill with consumption – did I tell you? – he's thought to be on the mend. Sheppard spoke disgracefully, and all the usual people in the usual way. What a fatuous business it is! And yet the amusement manages to be dominating. It's still worthwhile to see the Yen laughing, and MacCarthy telling stories, and Bob Trevy arguing with Sanger, and there's even some entertainment to be got out of watching Eddie Marsh ogling Rupert Brooke. James and I came away from it in a taxicab with Hobber, and – was it the champagne? – I certainly should have attempted a rape, after all these years and circumstances, if James hadn't been there.

[. . .]

your loving
Lytton

Saxon (as he's now called) is I believe at this moment at Bayreuth with Virginia and Adrian. But you're safe so far as *he's* concerned; only I don't know what charming German Barons may not be there. Telegraph.

‡

To Maynard Keynes

Lytton had written to Maynard from Sweden asking if he could come to Burford in late September, and Keynes had replied that he would be alone there with Duncan at that time, and would rather Lytton did not come, as he thought he would not feel at ease with Lytton and Duncan − 'all the feelings would be too uncertain'.

> 67, Belsize Park Gardens
> Hampstead, N.W.
> October 1st 1909

Dear Maynard,

I quite understand about not coming. But I wonder when I shall see Swithin. I have a scheme for living at Grantchester, next door to Rupert, so perhaps we shall next meet there.

> your
> GLS

‡

To Virginia Stephen

'Mahomet's coffin' = 'up in the air'.

> Belvedere Mansion Hotel
> 61, King's Road
> Brighton
> October 13th 1909

I hope to come tomorrow evening, or at any rate to tea on Friday. On Saturday I go to my moated grange. If I can, I shall stay there forever, but I suppose I can't. My health seems still to be something of a Mahomet's coffin. However, vogue la galère [*come what may*]!

Your
Lytton

☨

To Vanessa Bell

Pythagoras House was George Mallory's former lodgings, and it was he who arranged for Lytton to be installed in them for ten weeks.
    Lytton's 'competition tragedy' was for Stratford-upon-Avon. He finished his blank verse 'Essex: A Tragedy' and submitted it just before Christmas. It did not win the prize – a performance there during Festival week.

Pythagoras House
Cambridge
October 21st 1909

This address will perhaps hardly surprise you – Fate does these little things. My Grantchester house was incredibly disgusting, and I had prepared to beat a quick retreat to Hampstead, when I discovered from George (who's up here, staying with Arthur Benson) that his old rooms were empty, as the person who had taken them was ill. I tore round at once, and after some agitating negotiations secured the place for rather a cheap sum. It's really very comfortable. And then how delightful to live among such memories! Unfortunately I shall only be able to stay for this term, as the owner will then return, and I suppose Hampstead *will* be inevitable. Perhaps by that time I shan't be sorry. But at present I find myself in a wonderfully contented state. Such leisure! Such repose! And then, too, the weather is still warm enough for an occasional morning in the garden, and I find the beauty of the trees and the country quite divine. The view from the King's bridge this morning – you should have seen it! Certainly this is the most beautiful time of year for Cambridge. Won't you come for a weekend?

    I imagine that the stream of London life has once more closed over you. How nice it would be to be a young married lady, to be sure! What a pity one can't now and then change sexes! I should love to be a dowager Countess, and you I think wouldn't mind (for a minute or two) being George. But what do you think? It was just as I'd feared. The first meeting was a sad shock – his beauty had vanished, and he was seen to be absolutely complexionless and far too fat. I turned away in despair from his washy and bulbous face . . . but oh! I soon forgot all that in the contemplation of his exquisite soul; and now, as you may suppose, I haven't the faintest idea of what he looks like. Such things are really too unimportant. Eh! What?

I am preparing for my competition tragedy. When it's finished we might read it at Gordon Square; but it would be a miracle if it ever was. In the intervals of my labours, I write a line or two of poetry, and visit Walter Lamb. It's a charming life.

yours
GLS

‡

To James Strachey

Pythagoras House
November 6th 1909

I'm most miserable. George has departed, and I find it very difficult to be consoled. The sunshine has gone out of my life. What made it doubly melancholy was that we parted in something of a mist. I suppose this was chiefly my fault, but that doesn't make it any more cheering, and I'm oppressed by the agony of human relationships. It's not only the love affairs that are bound to fail! – And now I shall never see him again, or if I do it'll be an unrecognisable middle-aged mediocrity, fluttering between wind and water, probably wearing glasses and a timber toe. And you will only say that he's always been like that. *[. . .]*

‡

To James Strachey

The letter begins with news that Norton thinks he's found a new embryo called Alfred or Albert. The Equinox *was a periodical run by Aleister Crowley.*

Pythagoras House
November 14th 1909

[. . .] The latest vice is rather more interesting – but perhaps you've
heard of it – eating turds con amore – especially one's lovee's. Mr Towsey
confessed with blushes that it was done, and it transpires that a Neapolitan
boy begged as a last favour from Leigh that he might be allowed to eat his
turds – and was (very cruelly, I thought) forbidden! Isn't it perfectly
darling? It's gathered that it adds immensely to one's joys (if one's lucky
enough to be constructed so) and that, at the critical moment, one
'kneels up' in bed and has a motion, to prepare the way for the final
frenzy. Won't you write a letter about it to the Equinox? *[. . .]*

‡

To Virginia Stephen

*In the published version of this letter, James and Leonard replace Walter Lamb's
name with '[Arthur]', the square brackets indicating that the editors had altered
the text. The point of this small deception was that Lamb became one of
Virginia's more pressing and least happy suitors; also that Clive later stage-
managed Lamb's wooing of his sister-in-law. Clive's own flirtation with
Virginia was something even the valiant-for-truth James would not have liked to
make public.*

Pythagoras House
Cambridge
November 26th *[1909]*

I learn that you are to be at the George Darwins'. Dear Walter has been
asked there to supper to meet you: I have not. Couldn't you have lunch
here on Monday? You might perhaps apparently go away in the
morning. It seems melancholy not to meet. I shall call there at the tea
hour, and try to intrigue, but it will be difficult.

The so-called Greek Play has begun. I imagine you will go on
Saturday. How dreadfully bored you'll be, to be sure! I hear, too, that
there's to be no one beautiful.

your
G.L.S.

‡

To Maynard Keynes

This letter is the first not written on black-bordered writing paper – the year of
mourning his father's death was over. Sir Richard born 1817 and died 12
February 1908. Keynes had written earlier in the month to say he had found
rooms for Lytton in Downing Street, Cambridge, for £10 for the term, including
cooking but not the cost of the food.
   Sir Austen Chamberlain (1863–1937), one of the sons of Joseph Chamberlain,
the Mayor of Birmingham, was the leader of the protectionist wing of the
Conservative Party. The general election of January 1910 was held from
15 January to 10 February, and resulted in a hung parliament, so another
election was held from 3 to 19 December, the last to be held over several days.

67, Belsize Park Gardens
Hampstead, N.W.
January 17th 1910

Dear Maynard,

I've just heard from your mother to say that the Downing rooms have
failed. I don't mind, as I've decided not to go up this term. I've been
attacked by what I'm convinced is the same thing as your disease – gastric
influenza isn't it called? I'm pretty sure I caught it from you at Fitzroy
Square. The symptoms are exactly the same. But my doctor won't
admit it. What's particularly enraging is that I'd apparently recovered,
when it all began again, and here I am still living on slops and altogether
disgusted. I don't know how long it mayn't go on for now. It would be
shocking to have to face such a thing in a Cambridge lodging.
   What an abominably bad state of mind you must have got into at
Birmingham! Or was it merely negative? I suppose there's no chance of
dear Austen being booted out.
   James and Gerald – did you hear? – went on Saturday night to the
Palace Music Hall to hear the results. The whole audience was violently
Tory. When Liberal victories appeared on the screen, they yelled 'Take
them away! We don't want it!' etc. Eventually they began singing Rule
Britannia, standing up. James and Gerald remained seated. The mob
howled at them to stand, and such was their terror that they did. The
rest of the day they spent getting voters to sign petitions for Women's

Suffrage. 'I don't approve of it,' said a rich and respectable voter. 'Why?' said James. 'Because it's unnatural,' was the reply. 'Do you think everything that's unnatural bad?' James asked. 'Well,' answered the voter, 'in love affairs I do,' and left James pulverised amid a crowd of highly amused and exquisite boys, who'd gathered around him during the conversation.

your
Lytton

‡

To Rupert Brooke

67, Belsize Park Gardens
Hampstead, N.W.
March 31st 1910

Dear Rupert,

Is there any chance of your being able or inclined to go away with me only, for a week or so? James thinks there may be, and says that you know of a cottage on Dartmoor . . . My health seems to be giving way, and I want to go off somewhere; but I fear it's hardly probable that you're still free. If you were I could go as soon as you liked, with songs of Thanksgiving. Otherwise, perhaps if the cottage does exist you would give me the information about it, as I suppose I might go there in some shape or other possibly.

Do you really admire Henry?

yours ever,
Lytton Strachey

‡

To Rupert Brooke

67, Belsize Park Gardens
Hampstead, N.W.
April 1st 1910

Your letter is very consoling. As you don't seem to have any particular wishes, I'm telegraphing against Dartmoor, as my medical man was in favour of a place near the sea and warm, and I imagine Mrs Hern is neither. I should have adored Holland, but I daren't risk it with my health. I hope yours is improving. A change of air I suppose will do it good. My medical man declares that I should like Exmouth. I know nothing about it, do you? It sounds as if it *might* be attractive – with brigs coming in and beautiful sailor-boys. (He didn't mention these.) But of course it's impossible to say.

The ABC says that it's four hours from Waterloo, and there are hotels. On the map it seems to be at the end of an estuary. Do you think it would be suitable? I should think James could easily come for the week-end. I observe that Falmouth looks a good deal more amazing, but it's much further off.

The earlier you can come the better, but it doesn't matter for me. Would you stay the night here en route for wherever it may be? Have you any suggestions?

In any case, of course, I shall bring my football clothes, but I doubt if I shall be able to talk about anything but Henry.

your
GLS

I felt that Moore, if he would come, would be too difficult en tierce. Don't you think so?

To my mind, the worst of Exmouth is that it *may* be a mere town. Do you know of other places in Devon – possibly on the North Coast?

‡

To Clive Bell

Virginia had been ill in bed in mid-March. On 26 March she and the Bells were in lodgings at Harbour View, Studland, for three weeks' rest.

67, Belsize Park Gardens
Hampstead, N.W.
April 4th 1910

Dear Clive,

I can hardly write, and this is only to state a few facts. My health has given way as usual, and I'm probably going to Lulworth for a 'change' with Rupert on Thursday or Friday. The prospect does not attract me. I don't know where Lulworth is, except that it's in Dorsetshire, but I imagine it's far enough from you. If we can't go there, I imagine we'll go somewhere else.

I'm particularly embittered because a letter has come from George urging me to go to Paris. This is now impossible, as I'm obliged to spend all my cash in having a 'change' – which at the best will only set me up for a month or so, and at the worst will finish me off. Damnation!

I'm glad to hear that Virginia is winning onwards. But your party sounds a little pénible. I wonder why on earth you went there in such quantities. Or is it really agreeable?

I saw Russell yesterday who said he'd seen you. Everything here wobbles along in the old way. There were a few interesting passages with Henry after you left. But I haven't seen him since he went to Ottoline's – or heard from him. *She* has sent me an invitation for Tuesdays in April. Dust and ashes! Dust and ashes!

your
GLS

‡

To Lady Strachey

Lytton's request for £10 to be paid into his account was not trivial. In terms of 2002 purchasing power it amounts to £623.94. Friday, 20 May 1910 was the funeral of Edward VII.

Rupert Brooke would later blame Strachey for some of his own psychosexual difficulties. He was no doubt thinking of Lytton and James the conscientious objectors when he wrote the lines in the first of his war sonnets:

> *'Leave the sick hearts that honour could not move,*
> *And half-men, and their dirty songs and dreary,*
> *And all the little emptiness of love!'*

But at this point in 1910 Lytton and Rupert were firm friends.

Longmans had just published The Letters of John Stuart Mill, *edited by Hugh Eliot.*

14, St. John Street
May 22nd 1910

My dearest Mama,

I suppose James has given you some account of my establishment. The rooms are small but comfortable, and as the weather has been so good I've been able to spend most of my time out of doors. My health is satisfactory, and I'm able to do some writing every day, so that, as I also see a certain number of people pretty often, I'm enjoying myself very much. My plan at the present is to stay here till the end of the term – June 15th and then to consider what I shall do next. My money is running rather low; I am hoping to get a little out of MacCarthy for the article in the New Quarterly, but I feel that he's not to be depended on. Will you tell Joslings to put £10 in my account? If MacCarthy pays I shall not want it all. I wish I could earn some money, but I think that really the best thing I can do at present is to try for something on a large scale.

Is there any news of Dorothy? I suppose the rest of the family are going on as usual. I wonder if anyone went to the show on Friday? I fled from Cambridge to Rupert at Grantchester for that day, as all the Colleges were draped in black, and all the fellows walking to and fro in funeral processions. The lodging-house keepers are ruined, as the May Week balls have been abolished, and no ladies are expected in consequence. But this has its advantages for literary persons.

Have you seen Mill's letters? They're singularly impersonal and doctrinaire, but full of interest – and one feels all the time an odd kind of eminence in the background.

your loving,
Lytton

‡

To Maynard Keynes

James worked on the Spectator *for six years as private secretary to the editor,
their cousin St Loe Strachey. The magazine's offices were at 1 Wellington
Street, Strand (which is why Simpson's was Lytton's normal lunchtime resort).*

67, Belsize Park Gardens
Hampstead, N.W.
July 7th 1910

[. . .] James is temporary sub-editor, and I expect the shutters will soon
be put up at 1 Wellington Street. The Ladies are engulfed in Suffrage.
What will happen? In the meantime demonstrations and petitions in
every direction. I hope to get a seat in the House for Tuesday and if
I do of course I shall have to shriek and be torn to pieces. An uncomfortable but no doubt a noble death.

By the bye, do you want a copy of Public Works and Finances? I can
lend you one before I go. I looked into it again, and it seemed
entrancing. I have also been examining some antique family letters –
temp. *[in the time of]* Warren Hastings. During one of the risings letters
were carried in quills, rolled up very small. This was known – I've now
discovered that the quills were put up the blacks' arses who carried
them. The letters were called 'fundamental chits' and they usually
arrived, my grandfather observes, 'safe, but not sweet'. Do I dare to put
this enthralling piece of information into my great work? Would it
shock the ladies? *[. . .]*

‡

To James Strachey

*The stomach-pump was after all used, to provide specimens – presumably to see
how well Lytton's stomach was managing the process of digestion.*

*Shortly before Easter 1905 Major Sir (Frederick) Carne Rasch, a Unionist
Member of Parliament representing the Chelmsford Division of Mid-Essex since
1900, had become ill with influenza. Three MPs reported seeing Sir Carne's
'grim double' in the Commons, though he was neither dead nor dying.
Naturally the newspapers were enchanted, and Sir Carne became a celebrity.*

Saltsjöbadens Sanatorium och Badenstalt
Saltsjöbadens
July 20th 1910

Well! It's singular how soon one settles down into the old routine! I already feel as if I'd been here for twenty years, and should be quite put out if dinner was later than six or the porridge was made of porridge. *[. . .]* I saw Dr Zander this morning, and it has been decided that I should come under the aegis of Dr Sandberg (kknife) *[sic]* who turns out to be what they call a 'specialist' for the digestion. It seems to me immaterial, and it saves the bother of trundling to Stockholm for Johnson. I also hoped it would save other things – that that old man's methods were no doubt out of date and that the stomach-pump would not this time come into requisition. *[. . .]*

[. . .] It's quite true – literally the first person I saw on the platform at Liverpool Street was Sir Carne. He was in splendid form – shrieking for porters. 'Porter! Porter! Send another porter I say! Where's the man gone to? Would you believe it, he's left my bag?' – And on the Saga he was the life of the party. You should have heard his account of the foreign policy of Germany. – 'The Socialists are growing stronger every day. The government's bound to divert the attention of the country sooner or later by going to war – it doesn't matter where; otherwise they'll be ruled by Socialists.' The British occupation of India, too, he summed up as 'inevitable'. – 'Couldn't help ourselves – forced into it. And then in Egypt – no one else would take the responsibility.' It all seemed as clear as day. *[. . .]*

The reptile Davis and his mother are here. He is a dreadful cretin. We had an argument about conscription this morning in which I tore him limb from limb – ugh! the fangs of these people's minds! It's really harrowing. And then to read the Daily Express, which is now taken in here – oh, it makes one sick. I really believe we've lost. God almighty! *[. . .]*

‡

To James Strachey

A Royal Commission to examine the workings of the Poor Law was set up in 1905, with Beatrice Webb as one of the commissioners. She dissented from the majority, and she and Sidney Webb published their Minority Report calling for

(1) revoking the Poor Law; (2) establishing local employment bureaux to make efficient use of the nation's labour resources; (3) improving education and health. Asquith's Liberal government accepted the report of the majority.

Terence Rattigan's play The Winslow Boy *was taken from the case of George Archer-Shee, a thirteen-year-old naval cadet accused of stealing a postal order from another cadet. He was expelled, many felt, only because he was a Catholic. When his Liverpool bank manager father tried to take legal action to restore his son's honour, he discovered that he could not, as the Naval Training College on the Isle of Wight belonged to the Crown, and the King could not be sued. In the end there was a trial, with Edward Carson acting for Archer-Shee, but on 26 July Sir Rufus Isaacs announced on behalf of the Admiralty that he accepted the boy's innocence. But there was scandal later when the boy received no formal apology. He was killed in action in 1914 at Ypres.*

Dr Hawley Harvey Crippen was accused of murdering his wife. He disappeared with his mistress Ethel Le Neve. On 20 July, as his ship was beginning a voyage to Canada, Captain Henry Kendall spotted that one of his passengers, though accompanied by a boy, resembled a newspaper photograph of Crippen.

Saltsjöbadens Sanatorium och Badenstalt
Saltsjöbadens
August 6th 1910

[. . .] I have just finished the Minority Report. I was immensely interested – it's really wonderfully done. The amount of information supplied is quite amazing, and the state of affairs disclosed incredibly disgraceful. Do I gather from indications in the papers that the Webbs have quarrelled with the Cabinet? If the Tories came in and introduced their schemes en bloc I think it *might* be worth Tariff Reform – but Heaven knows really what their scheme may mean. There certainly is an air of horror about it – the sterile itch for organisation – but perhaps that doesn't matter much. I should like to know a good deal more about the facts.

The Law Report is the part of the Times that's best worth reading. Did you follow dear little Georgie Archer-Shee's case? Perhaps you went and looked at him. Such a happy ending! And then Mrs Tugwell! – But it was very badly reported. Did you see, too, the admirable observation of the Magistrate when a girl of 15 was brought up for appearing in boy's clothes and asked if there was a law against it – 'No! But that sort of thing can't be allowed – it's thoroughly bad form.' Apropos, did you see the absurd statement of that dreadful sea-captain in the Crippens case? – 'He squeezed the boy's hand immoderately, and this seemed to me unnatural in two males, so my suspicions were aroused; they were confirmed when I noticed that the boy's knickerbockers were split behind and done up with safety-pins.' Very suspicious indeed!

> I really think it's rather comic
> That God should be so economic
> In taking such a deal of trouble
> For making all our functions double.
> We've eyes for looking and for winking,
> And heads for shaking and for thinking,
> And legs for walking and for kicking,
> And tongues for talking and for licking,
> And mouths for eating and for kissing,
> And Johns for fucking and for pissing,
> And bottoms — why pretend it's not so?
> For shitting and for — well, ask Pozzo.

>   your
>   Lytton

‡

To Clive Bell

The announcement in The Times *was of the birth of Quentin Bell on 19 August at 46 Gordon Square. On the 16th, Virginia, who had spent the earlier summer in a Twickenham nursing home, went on a walking tour of Cornwall with Miss Jean Thomas.*

> Saltsjöbadens Sanatorium och Badansalt
> August 22nd 1910

Dear Clive,

I've just seen the announcement in Saturday's Times. I hope both are well? Will you let me know? I am as usual recovering my health here at the cost of the higher emotions. However, Pernel and Jane Harrison are with me, so I've not quite lost touch with civilisation. I shall probably be here for about another month.

Is there any news of Virginia? The last rumour I heard was that
she had retired into the country, where she was dominating her
surroundings. Do you think she is now well enough for letters. It
would be so charming to hear from her that I should like very much
to write if you thought it permissible.

ever your
Lytton

╪

To Maynard Keynes

*Maynard had again taken the house at Burford, and Lytton was once again in
Sweden for a cure. The 'George' at Charterhouse was George Mallory.
Piccadilly was notorious as a haunt of rent boys.*

*'Jim' was Lytton's brother-in-law, James Meadows Rendel (1845–1937),
chairman of the Assam Bengal Railway, but then working as an expert on
administration of the poor law. Moore did not return to Cambridge until the
next year. Lloyd George was then Chancellor and Sydney Buxton (1853–1934)
was President of the Board of Trade.*

Saltsjöbadens Sanatorium och Badanstalt
b. Stockholm
September 26th 1910

Dear Maynard,

I've been hoping to the last that I should be able to retrieve my promise
of paying you a visit in your country mansion. Now alas! it is
impossible. I've stayed on here week after week, lured by the hope of
attaining eternal health: on Friday I shall drag myself away, arriving in
London on Monday – and by that time I fear you will have returned to
Cambridge – for the Church Congress and other functions. I wish I
could have come. I feel that this has been a wasted summer for me,
except that I've put on a few kilograms of flesh, which I suppose is
something. But no English country life, no conversation, and – ah! –
no Eric! It's very sad. *[. . .]*

I've had some letters from the ever-faithful George. The poor dear
fellow is now established at Charterhouse, getting ready, I gather, to

instruct the youth of England in History, French, the Higher
Mathematics and the Lower Sodomy – also any other subject that may
come to hand. I wonder how long it'll last. I deeply fear that he'll be
found to be too incompetent even for a Public School, and then
Piccadilly really will be the only thing left for him. After a year's
training he's now almost fit for it, but by the time he is quite it'll
probably be too late, and he'll be so fat and heavily bearded that I
shall be the only person in England capable of erecting over him.
Such is the way of fate.

There's a divine bath-attendant here, who precisely suits me. Most
Michael-Angellically developed, and with an extraordinarily lascivious
kalmic *[Kalmyk, i.e. Mongolian]* face. I have erections now regularly
when he washes me, but he doesn't seem to notice. The other day the
climax was reached when he was so hot that he tore off his vest, and
became inconceivably naked to the waist. The worst very nearly
happened – I pulled his hair – he looked up smiling – and at that
moment somebody came in. It was my last chance, for I now find to
my horror that he has vanished – I can only suppose dismissed for
buggery, but not, alas, with me!

Pernel, Pippa, and Jim have been here at various periods, but I am
now alone and bored to fits. I heard from James that he had been
staying with you, and found Gerald there. *[. . .]* Any further Moore
developments? Is it true that the young Clarke discovered the
Chancellor of the Exchequer buggering the President of the Board
of Trade? That he then asked for the Viceroyalty, and that, after some
negotiations, he agreed to take a seat on the Council? – It seems the
most probable explanation. *[. . .]*

‡

To James Strachey

La Souco
Cabbé-Roquebrune
Alpes Maritimes
February 4th 1911

[. . .] The Lloyd Georges have been staying in the neighbourhood. You
can imagine the comments of the upper classes. At the table d'hôte *he*
drank with his mouth full and *she* pointed with her fork. *[. . .]*

‡

To G. E. Moore

Beckey House
Manaton
Devon
July 5th [1911]

Dear Moore

This is my address. I hope you're coming – on the 11th? – Woolf
comes then. The place seems good and not expensive – but so far I have
only been in a temporary dog-hole, as the proper rooms are occupied
till tomorrow by the headmaster of Exeter school and his beautiful son.
I glimpsed in at the window today, and observed a piano – so you'd
better bring some music, in case it's playable. The country is very fine,
with moors and hills, to say nothing of rocks & waterfalls, and the
weather is at present supreme.

The station is in Bovey (pro. Buvvy or Bovvy) – 4 miles off. [. . .] Will
you also bring some poetry – if possible in small volumes? – I find I
have only the heaviest of histories. Have you read Whitehead on
mathematics? I enjoyed it very much, though my brain reeled. I wonder
whether we shall be as bright!

yours
G.L.S.

Oh! I must mention that in a moment of épanchement [expansiveness] I
asked Henry Lamb to come here for a day or two en route for Brittany.
I don't expect he really will. But I'm afraid if he did you might expire;
– if you thought you would, measures might be taken. Only really he's
very nice, and I think you *might* like him, and it would only be (if at all)
for a couple of days, and – he's even more beautiful than the son of the
Headmaster of Exeter.

‡

To James Strachey

Vanessa returned Roger Fry's feelings, though Lytton does not seem to have been aware of this. Julian Bell was three years old.

Studland
September 24th 1911

[. . .] The group here is grim, and would be ghastly, if it were not for the sand, sun, sea, etc. and the general unconsciousness. Clive presents a painful study in decomposing psychology. The fellow is much worse – fallen into fatness and a fermenting self-assurance – burgeoning out into inconceivable theories on art and life – a corpse puffed up with worms and gases. It all seems to be the result of Roger, who is also here, in love with Vanessa. She is stark blind and dead. And Virginia (in dreadful lodgings) rattles her accustomed nut. Julian is half-witted. *[. . .]*

‡

Clive Bell to Lytton Strachey

This is a draft of a letter from Clive Bell to Lytton Strachey. Olivier Bell thinks it was probably written in autumn, 1911. From the absence of any reply, I doubt if it was actually sent. Another oddity is that it exists only in typescript, apparently typed by Virginia Woolf (based on a comparison with her typescript of Leslie Stephen's Mausoleum Book*), and corrected in pencil and pen by Leonard Woolf. It is included because so little correspondence from this time has survived, and this is the only indication we have of this serious breach – and also because of the light it sheds on relations in Bloomsbury. It is reproduced by the kind permission of Olivier Bell, who called it to my attention.*

Dear Lytton,

For the last week or two I have been thinking a good deal about our relations with each other and now that I have arrived at a conclusion it is necessary that you should know it. As I imagine you would attach but little importance to the results of my independent thought I had better tell you that both conclusion and argument have the approval of

Vanessa. I should be even more obtuse than you suppose had I not perceived long ago that you despised me. Your arrogant manners, your condescending attitude, the things that you are in the habit of saying to our common acquaintances, leave no doubt as to your feelings. You are painfully alive to the fact that I was trained outside the mystic circle of metropolitan culture wherein alone a young man may hope to acquire the distinguished manner. My manners you find florid and vulgar, over emphatic and underbred, whence you infer – wrongly as I think – that my appreciations are more or less blunt and that I am deficient in sensitiveness to the finer shades of thought and feeling. Your consciousness of my faults – my lack of refinement in particular – is a cause of constant irritation in you, in me a cause of sporadic bitterness. Such feelings are incompatible with anything approaching confident friendship. As you are never at the least pains to conceal your opinion of me, though diligent enough in making it manifest, I shall not hesitate for once, to speak frankly of you, though I should not care to publish my thoughts abroad. You are clever, you have wit and a nice taste in books – within limits a subtle appreciation of literature – your intellect is not powerful but well trained. You have the charm of an artist; you have temper and, stupid as you think me, I can avoid the common error of mistaking temper for hypochondria. You see part of life clearly but it is a very small part. I would not have believed that an intelligent person could be so limited. You walk in an alley sheltered and comely, from which you see nothing of what goes on outside, only you hear the noise and take it for reality; your hedges are grown so tall that you know nothing of the sun, save that he falls some times perpendicular on your vanity and warms your self-complacency at noon. In that alley you move an incomplete shadow, dimly aware of, flattered and fretted by, those other shadows your satellites. That vanity of yours more than balances your acuteness: it blinds you cruelly to others' feelings and mercifully to your own absurdity. When you sit gloomily asserting your own individuality, like some small Chateaubriand or lesser Byron, or waiting for a chance to astonish the simple with a squeaky whim, or an esoteric paradox, you are not impressive; as romanesque au désespoir you cut a silly figure. You can make nothing of people unlike yourself; were you to undertake a realistic novel which I am sure you are too clever to do, your characters would be for the most part ludicrous. You are so selfish that you have lost the power of seeing what people feel; you are interested in them insofar as they affect you and no further. You are an egoist, and what is worse a decrepit one. How have you dealt with your friends? Petted and patronised them so long as they flattered you, abused them as soon as they began to use their critical faculties. Have you so much to give that one should for ever tolerate your arrogance and selfishness? I think not. You are clever, brilliant even, charming; but you are far from being that genius to whom one could pardon anything. You are not tall enough to look down on your fellows, and I can see in you nothing that would entitle you to be treated as one apart. With all your faults you are loveable, and I could care for you still had you not lost the power of caring, the art of friendship at all events. Do you suppose that Thoby was or Vanessa is blind to my florid ways? When one cares, such superficial things become a joke, an attraction almost, not a source of constant irritation and an excuse for studied contempt.

Intimacy, you know, and have known for some time, is impossible between us. Is it not then a little innocent, incongruous a little with that refinement and sensibility of yours that you should continue to use my house as an hotel? I write brutally because I do not mean this to be patched up by one of those scenes of facile emotion that cost you so little but may cost your dupes much. Be assured that I have taken my stand deliberately. At Gordon Square the coin in which you pay is no longer current, and I fear you have no other.

Yours sincerely,
Clive Bell

‡

To Henry Lamb

Lytton and Henry had gone on holiday to Scotland and Ireland. Lamb was in prolonged sulk, the rain never stopped, and they were sharing a bedroom in an isolated hotel, which meant they could not avoid each other's company.

The letterhead boasts: 'New Daily Express Twin Screw Steamers between Belfast and Liverpool, Open Sea Passage 5½ Hours'. These were the S.S. Patriotic, Heroic, Graphic, Magic, Comic, and Logic.

Belfast Steam Ship Company Ltd.
S.S. *Patriotic*
Monday evening, August 20th 1912

I want to write you a few words from this penitential steamboat before going to bed. I've been in such a complete haze – and such a wretched one – but now, coming here, it occurred to me what the matter was. I ought to have gone away before – wasn't it that was enraging you? I see now that I must have bored and irritated you horribly to make you treat me so. I saw that you were enraged, but somehow like a fool I never realised that you wanted me to go – some hints you dropped now appear clear to me. – I suppose I was partly blinded by wanting to stay so very much. I had been looking forward to so many things! – To being taught to dive, and writing poems on the sand, and going to see the Islands with you – and now I've come away without even having been to the port! I'm painfully aware that when it comes to human intercourse I'm a great fool, and frightfully irritating; but ever since those first crises you have borne with me so wonderfully. What a wretch I must have been to make you treat me with such extraordinary bitterness! It was only when I felt that the horrors of those perpetually recurring estrangements and grim inabordabilités would only be stopped by my going that I brought myself to it at last.

Well, now I do hope you will enjoy yourself. Shall I hear from you? – At any rate, try to think soon with charity of

your diminished
and
disappointed
Lytton

‡

To Lady Strachey

There is still evidence of the soldiers billeted in the capacious attics of Broughton Castle during the Civil War.

Broughton Grange
Banbury
August 24th 1912

My dearest Mama,

I haven't written before, as I have been waiting to be really settled
down; but so far various catastrophes have intervened. My excursion
with Henry Lamb was not a great success – we went first to Scotland,
then to Ireland, whence I returned here last Tuesday. In Scotland we
found it impossible to discover a good place to fix ourselves in. We tried
Rothiemurchus – the Glasses at Loch-an-Eilan took us in; but we
regretfully had to depart after a few days, as the vagueness and discomfort
of the ménage was too great to be borne. Willie Glass would play the
violin outside our bedroom from 4 to 5 a.m. in the morning, and Annie
never by any chance had a meal ready within 2 hours of the appointed
time. They were both of course full of inquiries and messages about you
and everyone else. Willie told endless stories dated usually 1450, and was
otherwise very cultured and agreeable – but the horrors were too great
in the long run – especially as the weather was disgusting also.
    I am here chez Lady Ottoline, and I expect I shall stay another week.
After that my plans are chaotic; but I hope to meet James somewhere. It
has of course done nothing but rain since I've been here, so it's been
difficult to enjoy the country. We have had one motor drive – to
Compton Wyngate – a most lovely early Tudor house belonging to
Lord Northhampton, in greyish red brick, with an inner court, and
trees rising up behind it most exquisitely. We have also been to see
Broughton Castle, which is quite near here, and also very fine. It
belongs to Lord Saye and Sele, and was held for the Parliament at the
time of Edge Hill, which is not far off. A regiment of soldiers was
lodged in the attic – not the cellars, as at Syston.
    My principal occupation in the intervals if the rain flood [*stops*] is to
be taught tennis by Phillip Morrell, who is a champion, so I don't score
many points – but the exercise is good. [. . .]

‡

To Henry Lamb

Lytton had written to Ottoline on the 14th that 'I am not (no, I really am not) in love with him' and four days later sent a telegram to her announcing his flight to and imminent arrival at Broughton Grange.

Broughton *[Grange, Oxon]*
August 26th 1912

I am very glad to have had your letter.

I wasn't surprised to learn that I'd got it all wrong as usual. Dear me!
. . . When shall I be able to keep my head clear? I get very hysterical. I
am ashamed of myself.

You say that I perpetually raised the question of our relationship, and
that that seriously enraged you. Oh, couldn't you have told me so, if it
was as grave as that? It still seems very difficult to me to understand
what I was doing wrong. Was it my manner and gloomy face? I think it
must have been that. How shall I make you believe that I *do* agree about
the digging up of the roots? I suppose I don't practise it, though. I can
only try to be better in the future.

I was overcome by the horror of your rage and animosity – so it
appeared to me. I was miserable, those first two or three days, and said
to myself that perhaps it would pass off, but that if it came on again the
only thing to do would be for me to go. I wrote to Ottoline saying this,
and asking whether, if I wanted to come suddenly, she could have me.
The telegram here came in reply. That very night the terror began again
(so I thought). Next morning I was écrasé. Oh mon cher! How could
you think I was judging then? If anyone ever had mort dans l'âme it was
I, as I went away from you.

Now from your letter I see that you thought it was much less serious
than I felt it. I have been thinking since that I exaggerated the seriousness
of it; but at the time I did feel it extremely. I think I see how we each
failed to see what the other was up to. But you must have been very
irritated too, I think; and I'm sure with cause.

This is very confused, I'm afraid. The surroundings are not conducive
to clarity. – Pouring rain out of doors, and Philip and Julian playing
cricket in the passage. I wonder how your coast has been, and Errigal
and Thomas John and the rest of them. It's all fixated in my mind's eye
with the most vivid accuracy. I should like so much to come back

again. Do you think we could manage that? Perhaps if we could have separate bedrooms, the nervous tension would be less, and it would be possible . . . It seems a disgrace to have made such a mess. Do please consider it. I don't know where I can go when I leave here, which will have to be in another week. The thought of going back, and lying (the weather will be fine by then, won't it?) on the sands in those surroundings, is heavenly . . . and after this beau monde . . . Also my hair wants cutting very badly, and there's only one person in the world who can cut it – a certain general in Donegal. If I engage to sit very still, and stiff, in any position required, with my hands beside me, making no speeches, and occupying my mind with the most industrious virtue, couldn't I trust the general not to snip off the ears of his secrétaire?

‡

To G. E. Moore

Moore's gift was his little book Ethics, *in the Home University Library series, about which he said, 'This book I myself like better than* Principia Ethica, *because it seems to be much clearer and far less full of confused and invalid arguments.'[1] Nonetheless, at the end of the smaller book, the reader who requires to see the argument set out and developed fully is referred to* Principia Ethica.

Van Bridge
September 18th 1912

Dear Moore,

I ought to have written before to thank you for the kind gift. I had already read the book – so you see my enthusiasm. It is of course wonderfully interesting: but I felt it would be more interesting to someone who didn't know the theory, though knowing something in general about the questions. I think for the uninstructed working man it would be difficult. Perhaps there might have been some more *general* expositions of the main outlines – and the last chapter seemed scrappy. I suppose you are écrasé by want of room, towards the end. Some parts at the beginning had I thought too many repetitions – e.g. those five meanings of excess of pleasure over pain etc. – which, if omitted, would have given more room for brighter things. The chapter on Free Will I found very exciting and superb – but there were very difficult bits in it. I don't know how stupid I am about these affairs, but p.201 baffled me. 'Very often an action which we *could* have done' etc. – I have puzzled for long, but haven't been able to decide in the least what kind of actions you have in mind – James too seemed to find that passage confusing. If only (here and in some other places) you had given an illustration! They do help the poor lay mind so! The illustration of the cat and the dog – about the only one in the book isn't it? – cheered me up enormously.

Enclosed is a horrid bill. Did you ever do anything about those accounts? If so, this seems a necessary document. I must owe you a lot. If you can't be bored to figure it out, and would guess at an approximate sum, it would do, wouldn't it?

Are you in Cambridge, chatting with the King? I am shivering with James in this cottage, but I leave tomorrow, so if you ever write, address to Hampstead?

yours ever
Lytton Strachey

1. Quoted in Paul Levy, *Moore*, p. 264.

‡

To Virginia Woolf

Virginia and Leonard had married on 10 August. Calprenède and Scudéry were French novelists of the seventeenth century. Lytton was working on his article for the Edinburgh Review *on Madame du Deffand.*

The Chestnuts
East Ilsley
Berks.
Friday, November 8th 1912

I saw you for such a short time the other day: it was tantalizing. I should like to see you every day for hours. I have always wanted to. Why is it impossible? Why is everything that is satisfactory in this life impregnated with unsatisfactoriness? Alack! (As Mrs Humphry Ward's

characters all say – have you noticed it?) Why is London the only
place to live in, and why must one have the strength of a cart-horse,
or you, to be able to manage it? You are not to suppose from this that
I am unhappy here. No, my hours pass in such a floating stream of
purely self-regarding comfort that that's impossible, only one does
have regrets. . . . Will you at any rate write to me? I hardly think so.
You always say you love writing letters, but you never do it. – The
inconsistency of your sex, I suppose. Yours would be more soothing to
read than George Meredith's. What do you think? I opened that
volume just before I left Belsize yesterday, and was so nauseated by the
few sentences that met my eye, that I shut it up, put it down, and
deliberately left it behind, so if you want it you must ask them to send it
to you. Nothing will induce me to read another word the man wrote. Is
it prejudice, do you think, that makes us hate the Victorians, or is it the
truth of the case? They seem to me to be a set of mouthing bungling
hypocrites; but perhaps really there is a baroque charm about them
which will be discovered by our great-great-grandchildren, as we have
discovered the charm of Donne, who seemed intolerable to the 18th
century. Only I don't believe it. Thackeray and G. Meredith will go
the way of Calprenède and Scudéry; they will be curious relics in 50
years. I should like to live for another 200 years (to be moderate). The
literature of the future will, I clearly see, be amazing. *At last* it'll tell
the truth, and be indecent, and amusing, and romantic, and even
(after about 100 years) be written well. Quelle joie! – To live in those
days, when books will pour out from the press reeking with all the
filth of Petronius, all the frenzy of Dostoievsky, all the romance of the
Arabian Nights, and all the exquisiteness of Voltaire! But it won't be
only the books that will be charming then. – The people! – The young
men! . . . even the young women! . . . – But the vistas are too
exacerbating. –

I've spent today trying to write in an unemphatic and yet forceful
manner for the Edinburgh. It's very difficult. How, oh how, do you
avoid periods? My paragraphs *will* all wind themselves up to a crisis, and
come down with a thump – it's most disturbing. I believe there's some
trick for getting round it, which I should be glad if you'd tell me.
Horace Walpole seems to avoid it. It's some sort of whisk of the tail that
one has to give. But if one hasn't a tail to whisk? . . .

Tell Leonard that I wrote a wild letter to his two brothers the other
day, and have had no answer. Are they enraged?

Also, talking of Victorians, did I enrage *you*, by my rather curt remarks on ton père? I meant to imply the necessary reservations, but I'm afraid I didn't. Of course I think qua man he was divine.

your

Lytton

☩

To Maynard Keynes

The Society was having some difficulties. In January 1912 they elected Gordon Hannington Luce (1889–1979). 'Lucy' was Maynard's lover for a short time before he went to Burma and married a Burmese woman. He dedicated his Poems (1920) to Keynes, who paid for their publication by Macmillan. At the same time they elected an aristocratic Hungarian poet, Ferenc István Dénes Gyula Békássy (1893–1915). However, shortly before this letter was written, they had also elected Ludwig Josef Johann Wittgenstein (1889–1951). Wittgenstein's sophisticated Viennese Jewish background disposed him to loathe his fellow Austro-Hungarian, especially as Békássy's father was a landowner. Worse, elected at the same time as Wittgenstein was Francis Kennard Bliss, with whom he had nothing at all in common.

Thus on 13 November Keynes wrote to Lytton, summoning him to Cambridge, because of 'what a beast Bertie has been making of himself'. Wittgenstein had come to Cambridge to study with Russell, but Russell had made a miscalculation in introducing him to the Apostles. Keynes went on to say that Wittgenstein's 'only objection to the Society is that it doesn't happen to be Apostolic'. He calls Wittgenstein 'an amazing character', who says 'he vastly prefers angels', for, 'to see active brothers is to see those who have not yet made their toilets. And the process though necessary is indecent. At any rate, he couldn't say that you've *not made your toilet, could he.'*

Lytton telegraphed: 'Can you guarantee warm room fairly warm reception and modicum of cold food if so would come tomorrow reply Hampstead Lytton.'

The Chestnuts
East Ilsley
Berks.
November 20th 1912

Dearest Maynard,

I must write one word to say how much I enjoyed my visit. It was
really a great pleasure to see the Old Place again. The hopeful aspect of
affairs for the future was particularly exhilarating. Our brothers Bliss and
Wittgenstein are so nasty and our brother Békássy is so nice that the
Society ought to rush forward now into the most progressive waters. I
looked in on Bliss on Sunday night, and he seemed quite as odious as
Rupert ever was. It was indeed cheering! I am also told that he plays
the clarinet.

I had only just time to swallow down my breakfast on Monday
morning, and dash off, or I should have come to say goodbye to you in
your chambre à coucher. I felt there were a great many more things to
say to you – among others that if you ever want a scamper on the
downs you'd better come here, where you'll find horses,
accommodation, and the smutty talk of

your
Lytton

‡

To Saxon Sydney-Turner

*Békássy was killed in the war, fighting for the Hungarian army in Bukovina on
the Eastern Front in June 1915. Bliss, a Kingsman from Rugby, got a first in
Classics Part I in 1914. He did not share the Apostolic view of the war; he
joined up as a private in the Artists' Rifles and was killed at Thiepval in
September 1916. In a letter to Michael Holroyd of 14 September 1966, Russell
denied what Strachey said about him and Wittgenstein in the letter to Turner.
Russell said that he hadn't had any strong interest in the question of
Wittgenstein's election and, indeed, would have welcomed anything that
distracted Wittgenstein from the all-night monologues in which his Austrian
protégé examined his own character and motives. This wasn't entirely true, for
Russell had written to Ottoline that he had attended the meeting of 9 November*

in order to warn the Society 'of the dangers of Wittgenstein'. For the record, Wittgenstein rejoined the Society on 19 January 1929, attended subsequent meetings, and on 20 April was 'Declared to have been absolved from his excommunication at the appropriate time'. He also went to the trouble of formally resigning from the Apostles in the year of his death, 1951.[1] It was only then that he became an 'angel', pace his most recent biographer, Ray Monk's, assertion that he became an honorary member in 1929.[2]

The Chestnuts
East Ilsley
Berks.
November 20th 1912

I don't know whether you gathered from my mumblings the other day that a twin birth had taken place – or whether you had already gathered it. It was impossible to be more definite, and I was obliged to rush off, I fear abruptly. They are Wittgenstein and Bliss (both in their 2nd year and both very disagreeable). I was at the Curse on Saturday. Everything went off quite well, except for a few antics on the part of Bertie. The poor man is in a sad state. He looks about 96 – with long snow-white hair and an infinitely haggard countenance. The election of Wittgenstein has been a great blow to him. He clearly hoped to keep him all to himself, and indeed succeeded wonderfully, until Keynes at last insisted on meeting him, and saw at once that he was a genius, and that it was essential to elect him. The other people (after a slight wobble from Békássy) also became violently in favour. Their decision was suddenly announced to Bertie, who nearly swooned. Of course he could produce no reason against the election – except the remarkable one that the Society was so degraded that his Austrian would certainly refuse to belong to it. He worked himself up into such a frenzy over this that no doubt he got himself into the state of believing it – but it wasn't any good. Wittgenstein shows no sign of objecting to the Society, though he detests Bliss, who in turn loathes him. I think on the whole prospects are of the brightest. Békássy is such a pleasant fellow that, while he is in love with Bliss, he yet manages to love Wittgenstein. The three of them ought to manage very well, I think. Bertie is really a tragic figure, and I am very sorry for him; but he is most deluded too. Moore is an amazing contrast – fat, rubicund, youthful, and optimistic. He read an old paper – on conversion – very good and characteristic. Hardy was there – pp [*pianissimo*] and quite dumb. Sheppard was of course complaining that nobody likes him, Keynes produced the statistics on the relative sizes of cock-stands in Brazil and Bavaria, Gerald divulged a plan for murdering his younger brother (who is now editor of the Review!). Me you can imagine.

I returned to this incredibly solitary spot on Monday. I am enmeshed in an article for the Edinburgh on Madame du Deffand. I hope to be in London again about December 10th. Shall I see you then? I thought you were looking very well. Is that true? – I went to see the Woolfs about a fortnight ago at Clifford's Inn. They seemed very cosy.

your

Lytton

1. The Wittgenstein episode is dealt with more fully in Paul Levy, *Moore*, pp. 260*ff*.
2. Ray Monk, *Ludwig Wittgenstein*, p. 256.

‡

To Virginia Woolf

Leonard's novel was The Village in the Jungle.
   In Tennyson's poem 'Mariana', line 63, 'The blue fly sung in the pane'. Combe was Ottoline's Swiss doctor. The Morrells had just given up their house in Bedford Square.
   Samuel Butler (1835–1902) was the author of Erewhon, *published in 1871; his namesake wrote* Hudibras *between 1660 and 1680. Both were satirists. The later Butler sought to prove that the* Odyssey *was written by a young Sicilian woman, and that, if the order of the sonnets were changed, it became clear that they recorded a homosexual affair. He was actually sympathetic to Darwinian evolution, but cavilled because he felt Charles Darwin had not given sufficient credit to his grandfather, Erasmus Darwin. Butler's life was written by his friend Festing Jones.*
   James and Leonard omitted Lytton's plea to Virginia to 'refrain' from reopening the quarrel with Henry Lamb.
   Lytton had misread Virginia's last letter, in which she had said the nineteenth century was 'a great deal hotter in the head than the 18th'.

The Chestnuts
East Ilsley
Berks.
December 1st 1912

Ah! Quelle vie! Quelle vie! Breakfast at 8 (and in this weather too),
forthing 9–10 (frozen entrails), 10–11 prayers, 11–1 gallopading on a
grey pony over the downs, mad with terror and ecstasy. 1–2 lunch,
2–3 assoupissement *[drowsiness]* général, 3–4. brisk walk, 4. tea (Sir A.
Clark's blend), 4.30–7.30 desperate efforts with Madame du Deffand . . .
how after such a day am I to keep alive the art of letter-writing, and
vitiate John Bailey? I leave it to you. I am dying to hear from you again.
My silence has been scandalous, I feel, after your four large pages of
bumpf (oh! I see I've put in a supernumerary p. never mind): but I have
constantly written you brilliant letters in the spirit. How are you? Is
Clifford's Inn as cosy as ever? What books do you review? It was superb
to hear that Leonard's novel had been accepted. I hope the negotiations
have been successful, and that he has insisted on a royalty. When is it
coming out? – And yours? –

The account of Ottoline you gave me 'passing through on her way
South again', was mysterious, and the style hardly seemed to be
Leonard's. However, she is established six miles off – the South? –
across the downs, rather like Mariana with a blue fly buzzing in the
pane, or words to that effect. I went over to see her, and spent the night
unexpectedly in Philip's nightgown (pale blue cambric) – otherwise all
went well. Her health seems to be getting on as well as can be expected
after the terrors of Combe and Lausanne; but she is to return there. I am
écrasé by the loss of Bedford Square, but I suppose you hardly feel it. I
think you've never taken to that caviare. As for Desmond, I had an
immense tête-à-tête with him at the Savile when I was last in London,
and found him singularly soothing. The thing is to keep him off
literature, and insist on his doing Music Hall turns: if he'd only make
that his profession he'd make thousands. Can't you see him coming on
in a mackintosh?

I'm reading among other things (a) Un Adolescent by Dostoievsky –
more frantic than any, I think – 12 new characters on every page, and
the mind quite dazed by the conversations; and (b) the Note Books of
Samuel Butler – have you read them? They are full of amusement. And
the man was certainly very intelligent, and writes very well; but he's
oddly limited. The Victorian taint, perhaps, was on him too, though to

be sure he wore it with a difference. Such an anaesthetic view of life! No swaggering at all – only paradoxes – intellectual acrobatics. One longs for a panache. However, I gather from a remark in *[Henry] F[esting]* Jones's preface that there are lots of indecent things left out. It's odd how he resembles the author of Hudibras. But I imagine he was ruined by a perverse character. He ought to have written nothing but satire, and he *would* devote himself to the Odyssey and Shakespeare's sonnets and his rubbishy science and philosophy – which of course nobody could put up with, and so he became a disappointed man and said he was writing for posterity. Can you conceive anyone writing for posterity? or indeed for anyone? or indeed writing at all? –

I expect to hear any day that Henry has returned to Hampstead. How long he intends to stay there I don't know. A smoothing-over of the late crisis has taken place by means of long and amicable letters, so if the dear fellow should go and see you, I hope you'll be discreet and refrain from pouring salt on the wounds by injudicious repetitions of long-since-cancelled abuse. I'm longing to see him again, but I have the greatest fears that he's cut his hair short, which would be a severe blow. Have you seen John's pictures at the New English? Are they as colossal as the Times says? It's all I can do to prevent myself tearing up to the Metropolis to see them – but Madame du Deffand holds me – just holds me – by the leg.

It's the Victorians I hate – not the Nineteenth Century. Had Tennyson a better head than Pope?

your
Lytton

‡

To G. E. Moore

The Chestnuts
East Ilsley
Berks.
December 4th 1912

Dear Moore

I have had rather a perturbing letter from Turner, who was in
Cambridge last week. He says that Wittgenstein is still talking of
'resigning'. It would, I think, be rather a pity if he did. Turner is of
course vague, so I don't know whether there is any imminent crisis. If
there is, would it be of any use for me to come next Saturday? I might
possibly be able to give the fellow a more correct and sensible notion of
the Society than, so far as I can see, he at present has. On the other
hand it might be only an added disturbance. Turner wrote as if you
were au fait with the situation – but if you're not perhaps you could ask
Keynes or somebody what they thought. Other things being equal, I
don't particularly want to move from here at present, but of course if it
was thought desirable I'ld come. And in that case, would you get me a
room?

yours
Lytton

‡

To Maynard Keynes

Maynard had written the day before to say that the Cambridge Magazine *was
about to appear with a portrait of Lytton, captioned 'G.L.Strachey, King's
College', and urging Lytton to write to the editor 'repudiating the connection'
before someone from King's wrote in to do so.*

The Chestnuts
East Ilsley
Berks.
December 4th 1912

Many thanks for your information. The Magazine has not arrived yet. I suppose it will tomorrow morning, and I'll try to deal with it. I'm rather mystified – what portrait could there possibly be in existence? And altogether it seems an odd proceeding on their part. Who am *I*, pray?

I had rather an agitating letter from Turner this morning – vaguely announcing that Wittgenstein (so I make out) is going off the books – I mean saying he'll 'resign'. I wrote to Moore suggesting that if it would be any good I'd come up and try and ameliorate him. I thought I *might* be able to effect something – but I'd much rather not come, unless it was considered useful. I'm blissfully happy here, drowned in health, riding and unconsciousness.

My only connection with the world at large is via the Times, which arrives just after lunch and soothes me into slumber. I notice today that the report of the Departmental Committee on the night employment of male young persons is issued. But it doesn't seem to touch the most important facts of the subject.

The other day I had a strange postcard from Swithin, from 'Saigon Cochinchine' – with the photograph of a barrack. Where is Cochinchine? And does it mean that he's in love with a black bugler?

your
Lytton

I send this to Cambridge, probably wrongly – but it'll reach you in time, I suppose.

‡

To Lady Strachey

Lady Strachey was correcting Lytton's 8,000-word article on Mme du Deffand for the January number of the Edinburgh Review. *All Stracheys, male and female, were in favour of women's suffrage; they differed, however, on tactics, with Lady Strachey being firmly against violence.*

The Chestnuts
East Ilsley
Berks.
December 23rd 1912

Dearest Mama,

Many thanks for the corrections and observations. I shall try to deal
with the nightmare of Louis XIV's court – which is indeed a nightmare
– as you suggest. I am very glad you liked the article. I'm afraid I
haven't brought out properly the intensity of the psychological interest
– but it would have needed more space. The pathos of it can I think
only be realised by reading the letters in all their detail – then one *has* to
be sorry for her. As for the winding up of the article, it was not properly
led up to. I meant to suggest the kind of nasty turn that the easy-going
optimism of every day life gets, when it comes face to face with her sort
of disillusionment.

If this letter escapes the hand of God and the acids of the suffragettes
as successfully as yours, it ought to arrive on Xmas day, with the
comp[liment]s of the season.

your loving
Lytton.

Don't you think there ought to be a new clause in the litany? – 'From
the Terrors of the Suffragettes, good Lord deliver us.'

‡

To Henry Lamb

*Karin Costelloe (1889–1953) was the daughter of Mary Berenson by her first
marriage, thus the stepdaughter of Bernard Berenson and the niece by marriage of
both Bertrand Russell and Oliver Strachey. Her subject was Bergson, whom
Russell demolished in* The Philosophy of Bergson *(1914). Two years later
she married Adrian Stephen. She was socially acquainted with Moore, as well as
having attended his lectures. Ethel Sands (1873–1962) was a painter who lived
with Nan Hudson at Newington in a handsome square stone house (inaccurately
attributed to Inigo Jones) and at 15 The Vale, in Chelsea. (There is a gallery at
the Ashmolean, Oxford, named for her and her brother Morton.)*

Savile Club
107, Piccadilly W.
February 4th 1913, 5:30 p.m.

[. . .] I went at the last moment to the Asiatic *[Aristotelian]* Society to hear Karin *[Costelloe]*'s paper. The boredom was infinite – also the interest. There was the strangest collection of people – sitting round a long table, with Bertie in the middle, presiding, like some Inquisitor, and Moore opposite him, bursting with fat and heat, and me next to Moore, and Waterlow next to me, and Woolf and Virginia crouching, and a strange crew of old cranky metaphysicians ranged along like half-melted wax dolls in a shop-window, and – suddenly observed in the extreme distance, dressed in white satin and pearls and thickly powdered and completely haggard . . . Miss Sands! – que diable allait-elle faire dans cette galère? – buggering Karin, I suppose, – the incorrigible old Sapphist – and Karin herself, next to Bertie, exaggeratedly the woman, with a mouth forty feet long and lascivious in proportion. All the interstices were filled with antique faded spinsters, taking notes. Everyone had a printed copy of the paper, which for some absurd reason Karin then proceeded to read through very quickly – and it was horribly dull. – 'Inter-penetration', 'durée', 'simultaneity', etc. etc. Things improved with the discussion. Bertie, no longer the Grand Inquisitor, but the Joconde, with eyelids a little weary, delivered some pungent criticisms, but the excitement came with Moore. I wish you'd been there. I think even you would have been converted. As for me I became (for the first time for ages) his captive slave. The excitement was extraordinary, and the intellectual display terrific. But display isn't the right word. Of course it was the very opposite of brilliant – appallingly sensible, and so easy to understand that you wondered why on earth no one else had thought of it. The simplicity of genius! But the way it came out – like some half-stifled geyser, throbbing and convulsed, and then bursting into a towering gush – the poor fellow purple in the face, and beating his podgy hands on the table in desperation. The old spinsters in the background tittered and gaped at the imprévu spectacle. He is really really a grand maître – 'Cela vaut le Rembrandt.' – Karin didn't seem particularly good. There's too much of the woman in her, I fancy.
[. . .] Adieu, mon cher. This letter is probably as dull as Karin's paper.

your own loving oiseau
Gilles

✦

To Saxon Sydney-Turner

Lytton's 'Chinese play', A Son of Heaven, was finally staged in 1925.
    Strachey had read Woolf's The Village in the Jungle *in typescript and knew perfectly well that the characters were Sinhalese and not black; he had disliked it on first reading, and the conventionally racist remark in this letter was probably meant to be taken ironically. His experience of black people (though soon to change with the coming of American troops near the end of the war) was at this time almost entirely confined to the journey he had made when he was thirteen, to Egypt, Mauritius and South Africa.*

Pension Hayden
Piazza Poli
Rome
Monday, April 11th 1913

I was very glad to get your letter yesterday, forwarded from Ravello.
I've been here for a week now, and find it a charming place – except
for the weather, which is getting colder and colder, and rainier and
rainier – however there are many brilliant intervals when one can
float about in the Forum, and listen to the band on the Pincio –
and there is always the hope that at any moment it may become
serene. I don't think you've ever been here, have you? I'm sure
you'ld like it. But perhaps your holidays always come at the wrong
time.
    You hadn't written before about the Chinese Play. I'm glad you
think it would work on the stage. If only I could persuade some
manager to think so too! At present it's in the hands of G. Barker,
I sent it to him on the advice of Barrie, who was encouraging – but
I shall be much surprised if anything comes of it.
    I hope you are proceeding satisfactorily. You say nothing of your
health, so I imagine it is good. Woolf sounds rather acerb – but I'm not
surprised as far as I'm concerned. He sent me his novel when it came
out, and I paid no attention, and have not since. Really I've had good
excuses. It came when I was ill in bed with a raging cold and fever, then
it was removed by my sisters, and now my journeys seem to make it
very difficult to read anything. But I shall shortly deal with the matter.

I was disappointed to see that it was about nothing but blacks – whom really I don't much care for. However . . .

As for *my* novel, it is very much in the air. I drift and dream in the most horrid way. I wish I knew how people managed to have a regular output. The only thing I've produced lately was a Conte or Facetie entitled 'Ermyntrude and Esmerelda' – which is either in the hands of H. Lamb or Norton. If you would like to look at it, do try and get it from one or other of these. I think it might be rather in your genre.

My experience of Pension life is most painful, and I find that Forster has quite misrepresented it – whitewashed it absurdly. For sheer stark ignorance, imbecility, and folly the conversations here can't be beaten. I'm rapidly becoming a second Flaubert under these influences. I can think of nothing but la Bêtise Humaine.

your
Lytton

‡

To Augustus John

67, Belsize Park Gardens
N.W.
July 16th 1913

My dear John,

I too have been rather ill, or I should have answered your letter sooner. So far as I am concerned, I should not be sorry to relinquish the business of the book. I am pleased by your thinking that I might do it satisfactorily; but on consideration I suspect that my brain is too arid and my knowledge too incomplete to enable me to make a really good job of it. Of course I never supposed that you wanted anything from me but such honest criticism as I could give – tempered by an occasional flight of the purest imagination. I hope I may say, though, in the privacy of a letter, how immensely I admire your work and with what enthusiastic hopes I am filled by the thought of your genius. I'm afraid that a certain dumbness that descends upon me when I find myself face to face with pictures may have given you a false impression of indifference.

Perhaps Jack Squire may still succeed in persuading you to undertake your part of the book – I hope so.

Yours Sincerely,
Lytton Strachey

‡

To Clive Bell

Lytton is writing from the inn where, the year before, the newly-wed Leonard and Virginia had stayed before going to France on their honeymoon, and where they returned on 23 August 1913. The summer camp that summer was in Norfolk. Most of Bloomsbury was there, under canvas – the Bells, Adrian Stephen, Duncan, Molly MacCarthy, Saxon, Roger Fry (with his children), Maynard and the Olivier sisters representing the Neo-Pagans. After writing this letter, Lytton joined Henry Lamb for a regimen of daily fifteen-mile walks at Brampton, Westmorland, in the Lake District.

Lytton and Wyndham Lewis (1882–1957) loathed one another, with Lewis finding Lytton physically repellent, while Lytton pronounced his painting 'execrable' and his writing 'affreux'. Spencer's paintings are mentioned in other letters; I think Lytton was asking Clive to look out for a work by Stanley, rather than his brother, Gilbert.

Hilton Young's cottage was The Lacket, at Lockeridge, near Marlborough.

Plough Hotel
Holford
Bridgwater
Friday, August 8th 1913

Dear Clive,

It was charming to get your letter, which I've rather neglected answering. I'm afraid – owing to the lap of idle pleasures in which I've been sprawling during the last fortnight. I suppose that by this time London has pretty well broken up, and the old familiar faces have drifted away to their various summer hiding-holes. What is this mysterious camp, of which you tell me, and of which I've heard other doubtful rumours? Virginibus puerisque? Are there such things left nowadays? But I suppose that was only a façon de parler. I should think you will be fortunate if you escape it. If only on the score of comfort – as I suppose the physical agonies of those otherwise admirable reunions must be too horrible to contemplate.

I am leaving this spot tomorrow – probably to join Henry for a week or so in some remote region – but as when I last heard of him he was hopelessly involved in his father's portrait at Manchester, it's all rather dubious. He was up to his ears in the effort of trying to combine filial feelings, municipal expectations, and high art on one small canvas – rather a hopeless job, and if he comes out of it alive I shall be surprised. Your account of dear Wyndham was most enthralling. I long to hear further details. Shall I never see him again? Have you, by the bye, taken any further steps about Spencer? I saw a photograph of that picture of his – numerous persons among numerous objects – and was amazed.

How happy you sound – 'writing daily and diligently' at a book! I wish I was doing the same; but I find inspiration too maddeningly difficult to seize upon. Oh for some magic salt to drop upon their tails. When your book comes out – how can I avoid reading it? It certainly won't make me dislike you. I should only utter some pshaws – which would probably make *you* dislike *me*! – The Edinburgh article you ask about was on Madame du Deffand, and came out last January. But you'll never be able to get a copy, and if you like I'll bring mine when I come to Asheham. The 29th would suit me very well for that, so far as I can judge. Will you write to me again? – with news of Virginia – also of Molly. As I don't at all know what my address will be, Hampstead alone would reach me. Did you hear that I've got Hilton's cottage for a year beginning in October? My hope is that I shall be able to catch some inspirations in that solitude. At the present moment I am lying embosomed in heather and flies – incredibly hot – but it's really rather nicer than it sounds.

yr

Lytton

‡

To Henry Lamb

Katherine ('Ka') Laird Cox (1887–1938) left Newnham College in 1910 and befriended Virginia the next year. She had a difficult affair with Rupert Brooke before she married Will Arnold-Foster in 1918.

Michaelhouse
West Dyke
Redcar
September 13th 1913

[. . .] There has been a horrible occurrence. Virginia tried to kill herself last Tuesday, and was only saved by a series of accidents. She took 100 grains of veronal and also an immense quantity of an even more dangerous drug – medinal. The doctors at one time thought there was very little hope. But she recovered, and is apparently not seriously the worse for it. Woolf has been having a most dreadful time for the last month or so, culminating in this. Fortunately Ka has been upon the scene, and has been of great assistance. I saw her and Woolf on Thursday on my way here. The doctors all agree that the only thing required is feeding up and rest, so really now the prospect seems to be pretty hopeful. George Duckworth has lent them his country house in Sussex, and they intend to go there in about a week. *[. . .]*

Giles

I should think it's better not to say anything about Virginia to people in general.

✝

To Henry Lamb

Lytton had visited the Bloomsbury 'camp' at Brandon, Norfolk, from his base at Wiveton. Vanessa became the leader, but did not sleep under canvas, preferring the comforts of a farmhouse. Virginia was in a nursing home and could not come. Molly MacCarthy fell ill and decamped to London. But Lytton had for company Adrian Stephen, Saxon, Maynard, Roger Fry and Duncan, Ka Cox, and the other younger people. James was in love with Noel Olivier (1892–1969), with whom he went to Rothiemurchus. Her sister Bryn (1887–1935) had just married 'Hugh' (Arthur Ewart) Popham C.B. (1889–1970), a distinguished art historian whose career culminated in the post of Keeper of Prints and Drawings at the British Museum. Their daughter, Anne Olivier Bell, edited the great edition of Virginia Woolf's diaries. Noel had broken with Rupert (who was now in love with Cathleen Nesbitt and out of the country) but wrote to Rupert that the mutual affection of her and James was 'distressing'.[1]

The Contemporary Art Society was founded in 1910. The practice was to appoint one annual buyer, who chose the CAS's acquisitions for the year – these were then given to institutions, most often the Tate. Wyndham Lewis and Frederick Etchells (1886–1973) were in revolt against the ideas and taste of Roger Fry. The 'English Reviews' were of the show at the New English Art Club.

Milton Cottage
Wednesday, September 24th 1913

[. . .] I liked the Popham couple. Noel is of course more interesting, but difficult to make out: very youthful, incredibly firm of flesh, agreeably bouncing and cheerful – and with some sort of prestige. I don't quite know what. I suppose somehow of character: as for the intellects, I couldn't see much trace of *them*. A great fish-wife's mouth, which it might be nice to ram one's prick into . . . mais enfin – I could hardly be interested. *[. . .]*

Asheham was on the whole an amusing interlude, though I was so non-compos most of the time with a cold in the head that existence was difficult. I can't remember whether I told you any details – I think I must have – Roger and famille were encamped in a field. Duncan, Keynes, Turner (horribly écrasé with rheumatism) were the guests, and Adrian appeared from Dieppe, where he'd been with Lewis and Etchells who had spent their time pursuing bonnes with amorous advances – in vain, ever in vain. Lewis (from some of Clive's accounts) sounds more of an ass than I'd thought possible. I'm sorry to say Clive has *not* bought that or any picture by Spenser for the Cont*[emporary]* A*[rt]* S*[ociety]* – It might have been expected. All his money has gone on Lewis and Duncan. I sat to Roger & Duncan through several mornings. Roger's production was infinitely foul – the principal feature of it being a pair of extraordinarily short legs. Duncan était niais *[silly, simple]*. The publicity of it all shocked me considerably. I could see hardly any sign of effort. But enough of that. In the intervals I played badminton with great vigour, and found that it was far more agreeable than tennis – which is merely a matter of brute agility – no place for the intellect, which I brought to bear in badminton with considerable success and excitement. I also won 30/– from them all at poker, by means of which I was just able to reach here without bankruptcy. It was a gift from Heaven. My debt to you will have to wait till October 1st. I hope you can bear it. (I've always forgotten to mention this before.)

Mary B. has sent me the English Reviews all right – also a note in which she says that you've done some particularly nice paysages – is that true? I'm afraid I shan't like your painted heads very much. Shall I? Perhaps if they're male . . . Of course I've done not a stroke of work in these peregrinations and angoisses. It's very annoying. I shall make for Lockeridge as soon as possible and sit down steadily there. If I could only get some perfumed youth with well-oiled curls and rosy shoulders and a handsome and serviceable bauble, to come in unto me there from time to time the prospect would be more flattering. Mais où le trouver?

I didn't tell you that D[orelia] in her letter sent some charming photographs of those babies – naked – some of them wonderfully like those groups of Donatello cupids. I wonder if you've seen them. Is there any news of that lady? Duncan had some good stories of the lady of B[edford] S[quare, viz. Ottoline] – and her goings-on with Nijinsky. On one occasion they were in the minute inner room together, when Duncan came in. As he advanced from the drawing room, he heard her ladyship saying with infinitely modulated intonations – 'Quand vous dansez, vous n'êtes pas un homme – vous êtes une idée. C'est ça, n'est-ce pas, qui est l'Art? . . . Vous avez la Platon, sans doute?' – The reply was a grunt.

It's very late. Poor James has gone to bed, and I must follow. Many more things could be written, I expect. Details of the Virginia crisis, though, are too difficult to write about.

So now good night.
Giles

1. Michael Holroyd, *Lytton Strachey*, p. 293.

‡

To Dorelia John

Boris von Anrep (1883–1969) first met Lytton in 1910–1911 when he was at Edinburgh College of Art.

[No Address]
October 6th 1913

[. . .] Your postcard of the smallest house in England found me in what I
rather think was the smallest in Scotland. At any rate, if it had been any
smaller I should certainly have expired, for there I was, crammed in
with two young ladies, two young gentlemen and – a dog! I really
believe the terrible animal must have come straight from that Institution
we passed on that Sunday walk of ours, as it was identical in size,
colour, and shape with those monsters. Imagine my horror. As the two
young ladies and two young gentlemen very naturally paired off
together, I was left to solace myself with it as best I might. –

I came here a few days ago, and so far I'm enjoying the desolation.
There are downs, woods, skies, etc. There is an old woman who looks
after me, and there is the Times by the second post, and that is all. I
thought of ordering the New Age too, but now it has gone up to
sixpence, and it seems too great an extravagance. Or do you think it
would be worth it? Surely there are very few things worth sixpence, and
it would be strange if the New Age were one of them. When you visit
you will see various remarkable sights, including a drawing of a lovely
lady by . . . and another of a lovely youth by xxxx. But when will that
be? I've heard very little of Henry lately, and I imagine he's enmeshed
in Ireland for some time to come. But with that fellow one never
knows.

The other day in London I found Anrep engaged in arranging his
show in Chelsea, and we spent most of the day together. I found the
strain rather heavy of hardly even knowing whether he heard or
understood what I said – do you have that experience with him? But
otherwise I enjoyed being with him. His mixture of solidity and
neurasthenia is particularly pleasing. He gave me an inscribed copy of
his poem which he has had printed with some affectation in that dismal
periodical 'Poetry and Drama'. Do you know it? His pictures are
preferable.

[. . .] I hope you'll forgive this very *un*exciting letter, and kindly
believe that any reply to it of whatever shape, size, or colour, will be
hailed with delight by
                THE SOLITARY GILES [. . .]

‡

To Clive Bell

Clive Bell's book was his Art. *John Leicester Warren, Lord de Tabley (1835–95), was also a scientific botanist, an authority in numismatics. He published no verse until he was nearly thirty, then a dozen volumes in as many years, including a novel or two, and nothing for another twenty years. Then, on succeeding to the title, two volumes of selected poems were published just before his death. These reminded the critics of his slender talent – the point of Lytton's joke.*

The 'lovely cubist' was probably Mark Gertler, whose work the Bells had first noticed in 1910.

Katherine (Kitty) Maxse, née Lushington (1867–1922) 'served as a foster mother in the ways of the world' to Virginia Woolf,[1] who used her, at least in part, as a model for Clarissa Dalloway. She had married (in 1980) Leopold Maxse, the owner and editor of The National Review.

The Lacket
Lockeridge
Marlborough
November 9th 1913

My dear Clive

Your letter arrived at a most suitable moment, as I was down with the squitters (I hardly dare mention them to you!) and badly wanted cheering up. I don't at all agree about l'espèce humaine – especially in its physical attributes which I invariably adore, and as for corruption of course I can't resist it in any form – in that of a turd least of all. Whether this is because I came to the age of puberty in that fatal epoch of the 90s, I don't know – I feel it must make some subtle difference to one. But you seem to have escaped – or have you? – Ah! We shall see when your book comes out. – I wonder what 25% on all sales means. Does it mean that you get a quarter of the profits or of the gross takings? If it's the former they'll probably swindle you in one way or another. And how very strange to be published by Chatto and Windus! I thought they did nothing but bring out superannuated editions of Swinburne variegated with the Children's Theological Library and the Posthumous Essays of Lord de Tabley.

I shouldn't take 'my' Henry's tantrums very much to heart. The dear fellow can't help seizing every opportunity for kicking up his heels – but generally it doesn't mean very much, so don't worry, and especially don't put poor Spencer into your black books, for I'm sure he'd be willing to sell his pictures for whatever he could get for them. It seems a pity there isn't some comfortable arrangement à la journalism by which painters could be sure of getting a decent minimum per square foot. I think it might almost be worth starting a middleman's shop on that principle.

Your account of this lovely cubist is extremely tantalising. Is one really 'expelled' from the Slade for . . . cubism? Most singular! Well, at any rate, if he's joined Omega, he'll no doubt find Duncan very ready to give him further instruction in that branch of art. I almost feel inclined to run up to town and join in the lesson. Dear, dear! The worst of living in this unimaginable chastity is that when one does come back to civilisation one quite forgets oneself, and as likely as not falls on Hester Ritchie in her blotches and ulster outside the London Library.

I spent last week-end with the St Loe Stracheys in Sussex. There was a large and distinguished party there, including the Maxses. Do you know Kitty? She seemed to me a most sweet woman but her brain *[illegible]* a little too much like an underdone egg. I don't understand how the inhabitants of that world manage to get along in such a perfect flux of ignorance – and so bright about it all too! 'Oh yes, Post Impressionism! I don't care for it myself, but I'm always in favour of new experiments. A short time ago there was a rage for painting nothing but skulls and skeletons, and I didn't like that either.' Do write again.

yours

Lytton

1. Quoted in Anne Olivier Bell and Andrew McNeillie (eds.), *The Diary of Virginia Woolf*, vol.1, p. 87, n.16.

‡

To Lady Strachey

Lord Ripon (1827–1909) was appointed Viceroy by Gladstone, serving from 1880 to 1884, and being better liked by his subjects than any of his predecessors. Lytton's point is that the author of the life of Florence Nightingale has been careless. She could not have urged reforms upon Lord Salisbury that were carried out during the viceroyalty of Lord Ripon. Salisbury did not become Prime Minister until the year after Lord Ripon returned home; the Viceroy when Salisbury took office was Lord Dufferin.

The Lacket
Lockeridge
Marlborough
January 15th 1914

Dearest Mama,

[. . .]

I have been reading Florence Nightingale's life – I wonder if you've seen it. It's extremely interesting. She was a capable woman, but rather disagreeable in various ways – a complete egoist, and also full of a very tiresome religiosity; and I don't think really intelligent. In spite of spending all her life in medical concerns, she never seems to have got a scientific grasp of things. For instance, she steadily disbelieved in inoculation! Some of her Indian doings were peculiar. She apparently thought that she'd invented irrigation, and kindly advised Lord Salisbury to take it up, and worried the Indian Office about it for years. The writer of the book gives one to understand that the whole development of Indian irrigation is owing to her, and says that these great reforms were at last carried out under the Viceroyalty of . . . Lord Ripon! However, perhaps she wouldn't have been so good in her real business if she'd been less self-sufficient. English political life comes out of it pretty badly. If she'd died in the Crimea, it's appalling to think of the things that would probably never have got done. *[. . .]*

your loving,
Lytton

‡

To Virginia Woolf

This letter, apparently never before published, is in the Robert H. Taylor Collection, Princeton University Library, and was called to my attention by Prof. S. P. Rosenbaum. The fact that Leonard and James did not include it in their 1956 edition argues that it was already lost, or at least fugitive, by then. Arthur Schnitzler's 1908 The Road to the Open (Der Weg ins Freie) *does not seem to have been translated before 1922, so Lytton was reading in German this novel about Viennese intellectuals and musicians, most of whom (in fact as in fiction) were Jewish. The novel details the arguments among Jews themselves about Zionism, assimilationism and self-hatred, and Lytton's reading it shows that he was more sympathetic and sophisticated about these questions than I had previously imagined.*

The Lacket
Lockeridge
Marlborough
January 17th 1914

I have requested various people in London to send you those things, so I hope you'll get them before long. As they belong to the terrible Maynard, perhaps you'd better not give them the treatment they deserve, in the E*[arth]*. C*[loset]*.

I'm sorry to say the Lord Lytton I wrote about was not Bulwer but his son – a person of a very different complexion – about whom I shouldn't think you could have any curiosity but if you have it won't be satisfied by my article. I've just finished the life of F. Nightingale, which I think you've been reading. What a vision of the Victorian Age! And what a fearful woman! Don't you think she's an example of the queer paths the frenzies of egotism may lead people into? Napoleon conquered Europe. Miss N. went through Scutari [sp?] and her War Office struggles. The same selfishness impelled both, but she, poor woman, fancied she was doing good and the will of God – as no doubt she was, but as accidentally as a steam-engine. Mr. Jowett, too, coming to give her the sacrament! Oh, Lord, Lord! They were a crew!

I'm now hard at work over *The Road to the Open* by Schnitzler, which is certainly the dullest book ever written; but I recommend it to Leonard for further studies of the Jew Question.

I hope you continue to p[1] . . . *[large blot of ink]* and absorb ovaltine. I try to do the same, but this seasonable weather is rather disheartening. One's blood gets congealed in one's veins, and then, I find, all is lost. I wonder if there's anything else in the world – from a sapphire ring to a Siamese cat – you'd like me to procure for you. If there is, let me know, and it shall be yours.

Your
Lytton

1. Prof. Rosenbaum reads this as *prosper.*

‡

To Henry Lamb

As is clear from the ending of this letter, Henry is the 'acrobat'.
   Lytton was starting to write the Cardinal Manning chapter of Eminent
Victorians.

The Lacket
Lockeridge
Marlborough
February 20th 1914

[. . .] After I left you I went into the Tube, and saw a very nice red-
cheeked black-haired youth of the lower classes – nothing remarkable in
that – *but* he was wearing a heavenly shirt, which transported me. It was
dark blue with a yellow edge at the top, and it was done up with laces
(straw coloured) which tied at the neck. I thought it so exactly in your
goût that I longed to get one for you. At last on the platform I made it an
épreuve to go up to him and ask him where he got it. Pretty courageous
wasn't it? You see he wasn't alone, but accompanied by rather higher class
youths in billycock hats, whom I had to brush aside in order to reach him.
I adopted the well known John style – with great success. It turned out (as
I might have guessed) that it was simply a football jersey – he belonged to
the Express Dairy team. I was so surprised by that that I couldn't think
what other enquiries I could make, and then he vanished. I reflected that
perhaps at that point the man of action would have shown his qualities –
that it's easy enough to begin, but the great thing is to be able to go on
and pousser les affaires jusqu'au bout. I think I can sometimes manage it
in writing, but when it comes to a platform in the Tube, a black-haired
youth, and a football jersey, I'm as hopeless as I am with those bloody
clippers. But that there cove with the shaved 'ead, bless yer, 'e's a
different sort o' cuss. Why 'e'd do any bloody fuckin' thing yer arst 'im,
'e would. I'll tell yer wot 'e is, I'll tell yer strite. God rot my bloody
balls if 'e's not a bloomin' Hakkerebat, and no mistake.
   The poker party was rather fun. The other players were Clive, Adrian,
Turner, and Shove. Besides the amusement of the gambling, I had the
pleasure of feeling a hardly-in-the-least faked-up tendresse for Gerald,
whom I haven't seen for ages, and whose black hair is quite as nice still as
any youth's in the Tube. I found, too, in a moment of slight ivresse, getting
drinks together in the other rooms, that my advances were very agreeably

treated. Of course between 2 and 3 a.m., with the inevitable slackening of the moral fibres, Clive and Adrian began to misbehave themselves – with quarrels and self-consciousness. Turner maintained his inevitably perfect demeanour throughout, and gained vast sums. He says that the only effect sitting-up late has is to make his eyes feel rather sore the morning after. The effect on me was that I longed for a Haydn quartet the morning after. Instead of which I had the pleasure of hearing Philip on the pianola. That lunch was a wretched affair. She still keeps up the pretence (to herself included) that she's deeply interested in me, but in fact her disregard is almost complete – the interruptions were incessant, and ended with the arrival of that loathsome Turk with his rugs – upon which I fled. *[. . .]*

I hope to begin the Manning affair very soon, but I must first dispatch that odious Spectator Dost*[oevsky]* Review, which I ingenuously hoped to do in London, where of course there wasn't a second of time. I'll keep you informed of any progress, mon cher.

A letter from James came this morning, he seems more cheerful, and occupied with various Moscow people – including the director of the 'Artistic Theatre' who seems to be very accueillant. His hostess is a widow with blonde hair who talks to him about her past life in broken French – 'il y avait mon beau-frère, qui est folle et alcoolique, et autre beau-frère, qui aussi est folle, et voulait me tuer' etc. It sounds extremely 'Russian'. He says the difficulty of the language is appalling.

Dear acrobat, adieu for the present. I said I'd send you short letters, and this is the result *[four pages]*. Pense un peu de cette vieille machine disloquée, grinçante, idiosyncratique, et péripatétique,

qui se nomme,
Gilles

‡

To Henry Lamb

The Lacket
Lockeridge
Marlborough
Saturday morning, March 14th 1914

Here is a good morning, mon cher, which must change into a good evening as it flits along to you. I wonder how those cocky naked lugs are, and whether they're beginning to get fatter and pinker at last.

It's very early. Woolf has just driven off in pouring rain and a howling wind – what Mrs Templeman calls 'old-fashioned weather'. The poor fellow has been in rather a bad way, with acute headaches and general debility, but he says being here has done him good. Anyone more angelically good tempered I've never known. Not a word of complaint and not the dimmest sign of snottishness from start to finish. Is it the result of Jewish training do you think? Perhaps it's in the blood – after 1900 years of persecution I daresay the last shreds of peevishness have been worn away, and they've simply resigned themselves to being infinitely nice whatever happens. – Or perhaps after all it's just the result of being happily married.

Norton's appearance last week-end was very bright and brilliant. He seems to float most oddly through life – no raison d'être that I can see – but I daresay it doesn't matter. He's going to Sicily for two months to finish at his mathematical calculations in Mendelism, as he says he can't work in London. It's distressing to think of a person going to a place like that and thinking of nothing but little black marks on pieces of paper. Even the boys at Taormina he declares he'll have nothing to do with. But perhaps he's wise there. His remarks on Ottoline may be summed up as follows – 'She will lie so – on every possible occasion. And it's such a pity, because she's such a nice creature, really.'

I'm enjoying my Manning a good deal so far: the chief drawback seems to be that it's such a slow business. And of course I'm quite prepared to find when it's done that it's all a fantasia, but the only way of knowing that is to go through with it to the bitter end, and hope for the best.

I wonder if you've read any Bacon. I sent him because it occurred to me that he at any rate was an Elizabethan writer in prose who's not babyish. But perhaps you'll think he is. The essay on Dissimulation I love. There's a sentence in it containing the whole duty of man in that respect. I once quoted it with approval in a review for the Spectator, and the editor was so shocked that he cut out the approval and put in something of his own to the effect that 'we' entirely disassociated ourselves from all such sentiments. Then the garden one has some lovely things.

By-the-bye, I also had the thought that if you were ever in want of something to read, it might turn out to be repaying to take a look at . . . Antony and Cleopatra! If you did, *I* would promise to read that old Plutarch right through, and with honest bienveillance.

Such a divine walk I had yesterday evening, between two immense bombardments of storm! Some nice plough-boys, too, floating about in the middle distance. But what is one to say to them? Very difficult, very difficult. And they're not accustomed to the manners of Taormina.

your

Giles

‡

To Henry Lamb

Eddie Marsh edited five anthologies called Georgian Poetry, *starting in 1912. He included in them work by Gordon Bottomley (1874–1948), Lascelles Abercrombie (1881–1938), John Drinkwater (1882–1937), and Walter de la Mare (1873–1953) as well as by Rupert Brooke, with whom he was hopelessly infatuated.*

The Lacket
Lockeridge
Marlborough
March 16th 1914

[. . .] No news, not an atom, from this quarter of the globe – except that a solitary primrose has appeared in the back region of the garden – visible from the path as one stands pumping. – Which reminds me of a nice line I found the other day, by Dryden – describing the fate of misers –

> 'And once possessed of what with care you save,
> The wanton boys shall piss upon your grave.'

Well, well! I only hope the dear creatures will come and do it on mine. If Rupert could ever write a single line as good as that I'ld . . . forgive him. I see that he and three others and Lascelles, some Mr Drinkwater, and someone else – are bringing out a quarterly magazine entitled 'New Numbers' to contain nothing but their inspirations. It seems appropriate that they should all have such watery names, these young fellows. There's Brooke and Drinkwater and De la Mare – what can one hope from such an assemblage? – Except that they'll be patronised by a Marsh! – And if they don't suggest pumpship they suggest farts – vide the great Bottomley.

Oh, away with them! – Yesterday's leisure moments I spent reading – what do you think? – A Midsummer Night's Dream! It was a good corrective to these March hurricanes –

> 'Fair Helena, who more engilds the night
> Than all you firey oes and eye of light.' –

Tiens! – Nothing watery about *his* name, you observe.

your
Giles

‡

To Clive Bell

Leonard was the wandering Jew who stayed with Lytton at The Lacket, once in January and again in March. By late March Virginia was recovering fairly well from her September suicide attempt.

The Lacket
Lockeridge
Marlborough
March 27th 1914

Gracious me! Ce juif errant seems to be getting me into hot water all round! I gather, though, from your P.S. that in your direction it's not quite boiling. What happened was that he begged me to let him read the contents of a large box of letters, while I went into a trance after lunch. Yours were among them. I didn't think they were too confidential. Well, it's all very painful. I suppose it's no good saying that I shouldn't in the least mind your showing him mine. That doesn't go down, I suppose. But one thing at any rate I'm sure – I do certainly distinguish your letters from those of Our Lady of Bedford Square.

I hope eventually to appear once more – but I expect not till after Easter. And then the water will perhaps have simmered down to about 102.

yours ever,
Lytton

‡

To Henry Lamb

The Lacket
Lockeridge
Marlborough
April 3rd 1914

Mon vieux, [. . .]

On Sunday I had the most gruesome experience at B*[edford]* Square.
That wretched little Nijinsky was there – utterly thick-headed and
abject – only fit to be very swiftly buggered and then immediately
thrown on the dustbin – ouff! – MacCarthy, too, quite comatose, her
Ladyship all over the shop, and Philip alone shining brilliantly – it was
terrible, and went on forever, as I'd unfortunately promised to stay to
dinner & so couldn't go. At last they set him down at the pianola – he'd
never seen one before. – 'Ah, mais c'est très commode – mais oui. On
peut jouer très bien. Aimez-vous Back? J'aime beaucoup Back, moi. Je
trouve qu'il a l'ésprit grecque, n'est-ce-pas? Mozart, non. Mozart
romain etc. etc.'

[. . .] That Anatole France, which I began with the greatest
enthusiasm, I've had to drop, owing to sheer boredom. I've relapsed
into Voltaire, whom I adore more than ever. I picked up a charming
book by him in London on Newton – explaining the theory of
attraction and the solar system and the rest of it – all decorated with
18th Century cupids at the beginnings & ends of the chapters – and
occasionally one had strayed into the mathematical diagrams. He was a
nice, gay, inquisitive, ingenious, fellow. I've also got another book with
some English letters in it. The style has a tinge of Anrep's.

The other day an account arrived from the publishers of my French
lit. book, with a list of the sales for every six months. The number of
copies sold seems enormous – about 11,800 altogether! I think there's a
chance of my being able to make a little more money out of it, as the
sales, after steadily going down, began to recover slightly during the last
six months. It would be fun to get another £5 or so out of the damned
thing.

What do you think I did in a moment of frenzy on Monday? –
finding myself outside the Royal Academy, I went in and asked for Mr.
Lamb! – as luck would have it, it was the day of the hanging committee,

and so Mr. Lamb was too busy to see me. The politesse of the attendants (generally the rudest people on earth) was most remarkable. I can only suppose that they thought I was John, arrived at last to sue for admittance. *[. . .]*

>   your
>   Gilles

‡

To Clive Bell

Mudies was a commercial lending library. Leonard's novel The Wise Virgins *upset not only his family, but also Virginia's, especially Adrian. Duncan had been having an affair with Adrian, and was a little annoyed when he married Karin Costelloe.*

>   The Lacket
>   Lockeridge
>   Marlborough
>   October 22nd 1914

Dear Clive,

I wonder how you are – I've been struggling in vain for some time to take up the pen to write to you. I learn from James that you have decided never to write to me again! It is heartrending and a cloud has come over my life. I was much annoyed at not being able to come to Asheham at the right time; and afterwards things seemed to lapse. I did not feel sure whether there would be room for me, and so I did not write more definitely to suggest coming. I wonder whether it would be possible or suitable for me to come and stay with you for a little in Gordon Square? Perhaps you are full up, or perhaps other crises interfere; but will you let me know? If it can't be managed, perhaps you would be able to come here for a week-end? But I think the other would be nicer at this time of year. Winter seems to have set in.

I am feeling slightly melancholic, as I am recovering from some sort of chill or other which reduces me to ashes for some days. I spend most of my time knitting mufflers for our soldier and sailor lads; but I expect that by the time I've finished them the war will be over, and they'll have to be given to Henry and Duncan. I also read innumerable books from Mudies – oh lord! Lord! they are a dreary lot. Henry James's Notes on Novelists – have you seen it? It measures 6ft x 12ft, is printed in black-letter, and has to be lifted by a crane. Also, it is not inspiriting. Then I have purchased 'The Wise Virgins' – have you seen *that*? I cannot say that I like the book – which, I assure you, does not mean that I dislike the author. Is there any news of that couple? I heard a rumour that they were going to settle in Hampstead. Will you be allowed to go and call?

Duncan is coming here for the week-end, so I hope to glean a little dislocated information. The Karin-Adrian affair seemed to me very tedious, but on the whole a relief. By-the-bye, I hope they *have* been married – I've seen no announcement of it, so perhaps after all neither party could brook it when it came to the point. I must say I should see nothing unnatural in that. James said he enjoyed himself greatly at Asheham – I hope you'll try and poke him up a little. Give my love to Vanessa (if you don't mind).

ever your
Lytton

‡

To Maynard Keynes

On 27 November Keynes had written from Kings: 'For myself I am absolutely and completely desolated. It is utterly unbearable to see day by day the youths going away first to boredom and discomfort and then to slaughter. Five of this College, who are undergraduates or who have just gone down, are already killed, including, to my great grief, Freddie Hardman.' Hardman, a student of Keynes's who had become a friend, was killed leading his men in hand-to-hand combat.

6, Belsize Park Gardens
Hampstead, N.W.
December 1st 1914

Dear Maynard,

I'm very sorry that you should be so personally hit by this horror. From
every point of view it seems to me the very Devil. I think being in
Cambridge must intensify the distress. I hope you're coming to London
soon, and that I shall be able to see you. I don't know your London
address. I find it won't be possible for me to come to Cambridge.

I saw that Hardman had been killed. The last time I saw him was at
that party at Ottoline's, and I liked him much more than even before. I
think what the Greeks meant by that remark of theirs about those who
die young was that they escape the deterioration of growing old; and
perhaps if Freddie had gone on living he could hardly have gone on
being so nice. But I'm afraid this reflection won't be much of a
consolation to you.

yours ever affectionately
Lytton

‡

To Leonard Woolf

*The French Yellow Book was the equivalent of the British Blue Book,
containing official state documents pertinent to the war, setting out the
Government's arguments and justifications for belligerence.*

Leonard's January 16 New Statesman *article was "The Diplomatic
Service."*

The Lacket
January 21st 1915

Have you read the French Yellow Book on the War? There is some
rather good material in re effects or armament preparations in some of
the earlier dispatches of Chap I — which it might be worthwhile looking
at. I am now in the middle of the Diplomatic Blue Book — some of the
evidence is amusing. I thought your article in the N.S. very bright. But

what pernicious pig's wash that was about 'Compulsory Training'! Why, oh why, are they so reactionary? Surely they must see that if compulsory 'service' would be a menace to Europe, compulsory 'training' would be so too. Je ne comprends pas ces gens-là.

Saxon is here – rather ghostly even for him, with a perpetual head-ache. He synchronises with cold rain. I should like to fly to London, but it seems impossible. What news of Virginia's novel? Do let me know as soon as it comes out.

your
Lytton

‡

To Virginia Woolf

Strachey had sent Virginia Woolf his chapter on Cardinal Manning, the first of the essays in Eminent Victorians, *which she had praised highly in a letter to him, and he was now at work on the second, on Florence Nightingale. The remarks on Ottoline were deleted when the correspondence was originally published. Probably Lytton here refers to nothing more than Ottoline's dental problems and physical appearance. Vanessa Bell had recently resumed her friendship with Ottoline and delighted in hearing descriptions of Ottoline's bizarre dress sense and taste.*

The Lacket
Lockeridge
Marlborough
February 28th 1915

My dearest Creature,

I was very glad to get your letter this morning. Won't you and Leonard come down here for the next week-end? Couldn't you come on Friday? It would be very nice if you could.

As for gossip – no doubt there's a lot going about, but . . . but . . . One lives on such volcanoes nowadays. However, I think I may safely say that the hiatus in Ottoline's jaw has been satisfactorily filled. But have you heard Vanessa's account of the rest of her appas *[French, charms]*? Oh, mon dieu! I spent a few days at Gordon Square the week before last, and enjoyed myself greatly. But I lived in almost too extreme a whirl of gaiety, and tottered back here at last quite worn out – it took me days to recover.

I think your idea of the Parrot is an excellent one, though I doubt whether we should be able to find a really adequate one at the docks. The best plan would be for you to go out to the Amazons and catch one there, which you could afterwards train. The presentation ceremony, too, would be pretty.

I am in rather a state just now with Miss Nightingale, who is proving distinctly indigestible. It's a fearful business – putting pen to paper – almost inconceivable. What happens? And how on earth does one ever manage to pull through in the end?

Well, I hope I shall see you before long. What do you think occurs tomorrow? I shall be 35! –

Ever your dévoué
Lytton

‡

To E. M. Forster

This is Lytton's most discussed letter; it was quoted by Prof. Gardener in E. M. Forster: The Critical Heritage; *and since the advent of the internet it has figured in discussions of both Forster's novel and the Merchant/Ivory film. In September 1960, Forster wrote a 'Terminal Note' to* Maurice *(which was only published in 1971, the year after his death), his only book explicitly about homosexual love. In the Note, he refers to this letter:*

> *Clive's earlier life is easily recalled, but Alec's, when I tried to evoke it, turned into a survey and had to be scrapped. He certainly objected to nothing – one knows that much. No more, once they met, did Maurice, and Lytton Strachey, an early reader, thought this would prove their undoing. He wrote me a delightful and disquieting letter and said that the relationship of the two rested upon curiosity and lust and would only last six weeks. Shades of Edward Carpenter! – whose name Lytton always greeted with a series of little squeaks. Carpenter believed that Uranians remained loyal to each other for ever. And in my experience though loyalty cannot be counted on it can always be hoped for and be worked towards and may flourish in the most unlikely soil. Both the suburban youth and the countrified one are capable of loyalty. Risley, the clever Trinity undergraduate, wasn't, and Risley, as Lytton gleefully detected, was based upon Lytton.*

Forster's portrait of Lytton/Risley is deft. Maurice hears 'the symphony of Tchaikovsky Clive had taught him to like'. The effect of it is spoiled when he meets Risley after the concert:

> 'Symphonie Pathique,' said Risley gaily.
> 'Symphony Pathetic,' corrected the Philistine.
> 'Symphonie Incestueuse et Pathique.' And he informed his young friend that Tchaikovsky had fallen in love with his own nephew, and dedicated his masterpiece to him, 'I come to see all respectable London flock. Isn't it supreme!'

('Pathic' is an obsolete English word for homosexual.) Maurice immediately gets a biography of the composer from the library and regards it 'as the one literary work that had ever helped him'. Mr Ducie was a master at Maurice's prep school, who recognizes Maurice during the scene in the British Museum when Alec is attempting to blackmail him, but gives up because Maurice shows such 'pluck'. The expression Lytton queried in Alec Scudder's letter was 'share', used intransitively to refer to a sex act: 'Dear Sir, let me share with you once before leaving Old England . . .' At the end of the book Maurice tells Clive: ' "I have shared with Alec," he said after deep thought. "Shared what?" "All I have. Which includes my body." '

The Lacket
Lockeridge
Marlborough
March 12th 1915[1]

Dear Forster,

I should have written before, but I have been laid up with some horror or other – the Dr says influenza – I think a chill – but anyhow it's been very unpleasant, and I'm only just beginning to feel that I exist again, after about a week in bed. Your novel was an agreeable surprise in the middle of it. I enjoyed it very much indeed – I think really more than the others. The absence of the suburb-culture question was a relief. I wish I could talk to you about it – the difficulty and boredom of epistolary explanations is rather great.

Qua story, first. I thought it seemed to go off at the end to some extent. The beginning – especially up to the successful combination of Maurice and Clive – I liked very much: it appeared solid and advanced properly from point to point. The psychology of both excellent. The

Maurice-Alec affair didn't strike me as so successful. For one thing, the Class question is rather a red herring, I think. One suddenly learns that Maurice is exaggeratedly upper-classish – one wouldn't at all have expected it on the face of things – and then when the change comes, it seems to need more explanation. No doubt his falling in love with Alec was possible, but it's certainly queer as it happens – perhaps because the ground isn't enough prepared: and Alec's feelings I don't quite seize. As you describe it, I should be inclined to diagnose Maurice's state as simply lust and sentiment – a very wobbly affair; I should have prophesied a rupture after six months – chiefly as a result of lack of common interests owing to class differences – I believe even such a simple-minded fellow as Maurice would have felt this – and so your Sherwood Forest ending appears to me slightly mythical. Perhaps it simply is that the position isn't elaborated enough. The writing gets staccato (for the first time) at the end of Ch. XLIV – just at the crisis. 'Adamantine', too, can't be right.

This is my main criticism of the story – I wonder if you'll see anything in it. A minor point is that I find it very difficult to believe that Maurice would have remained chaste during those two years with Clive. He was a strong healthy youth, and you say that, unless Clive had restrained him 'he would have surfeited passion' (Ch. XV). But how the dickens could Clive restrain him? How would he have failed to have erections? Et après ça –? – Well! I suppose it's just conceivable, but I must say I think you seem to take it rather too much as a matter of course.

I admire the cleverness very much. The opening scene with Mr Ducie is very good, and his reappearance 10 years later. The upper class conversations and that awful household in the country – how can you do it? Then the ingenuity of the machinery – e.g. the piano-moving incident – seems to me . . . '*supreme*'! I liked enormously Alec's letter. Is it true that the lower classes use 'share' in that sense? – I must find out.

There remains the general conception – about which I don't feel at all certain. I don't understand why the copulation question should be given such importance. It's difficult to distinguish clearly your views from Maurice's sometimes, but so far as I can see, you go much too far in your disapproval of it. For instance, you apparently regard the Dickie incident with grave disapproval. Why? Then, à propos of Maurice tossing himself off (you call it a 'malpractice') (Ch. XXXII), you say – 'He knew what the price would be – a creeping apathy towards all things.' How did Maurice know that? And how do you? Surely the truth is that as often as not the effects are simply nil. Also (Ch. XXXI) you describe Maurice's thoughts in the railway carriage as 'ill-conditioned' – which appears to me to be the sort of word Mr. Herbert Pembroke would have used.

It almost seems that you mean to indicate that Maurice's copulating with Alec is somehow *justified* by his falling in love with him. This alarms me considerably. I find the fatal sentence inserted (Ch. XLIII – British Museum) – 'He loved Alec, loved him not as a second Dickie Barry, but deeply, tenderly, for his own sake, etc.' More distressing still, there is never a hint afterwards that Maurice's self-reproaches during that period were exaggerated. I think he had still a great deal to learn and that the très-très-noble Alec could never teach it him. What was wanted was a brief honeymoon with that charming young Frenchman who would have shown Mr Eel that it was possible to take the divagations of a prick too seriously.

Another thing is – perhaps even more important – that you really do make a difference between affairs between men and men and those between men and women. The chastity between Maurice and Clive for the two years during which they were in effect married you consider (a) as a very good thing and (b) as nothing *very* remarkable. You then make Clive marry (without any change in his high-falutin' views) and promptly, quite as a matter of course, have his wife.★ I really think the whole conception of male copulation in the book rather diseased – in fact morbid and unnatural. The speechification by which Maurice refuses to lie with Alec on the last night – no! – That is a sort of self-consciousness which would only arise when people were *not* being natural. It is surely beastly to think of copulation on such an occasion – shall we copulate? shall we not? ought we to? etc. – all one can think of is that one must embrace.

I could write a great deal more – especially about 'the triviality of contact for contact's sake' – but it's too difficult – and I feel half the time you have satisfactory answers. I wish we could talk. I hope to be in London before very long. I also hope this critique isn't too much of a good thing, and will fit in nicely along with those of Bob Trevy, Waterlow and Hilton Young.

★ So that when he said to Maurice 'I love you as if you were a woman,' he was telling a lie.
[King's College, Cambridge]

1. The transcription made for this edition by Rowan Boyson in 2004 of the original letter at King's College Cambridge differs slightly from that made by Prof. P.G. Gardener in 1972. The letter appears in P.N. Furbank's *E.M. Forster*, vol.2, pp. 15–17.

‡

To Dorelia John

Elizabeth Ann John (always known as Poppet, b.1912) was Dorelia's daughter.

The Lacket
Lockeridge
Marlborough
March 18th 1915

I had a feeling that my letter might arrive at an inopportune moment! – it was very good of you to write, and I am delighted to learn that the creature has arrived in safety. I hope you are going on all right: so long as you are, I will forgive the creature for being . . . what it is; besides, my education is progressing so rapidly that . . .

But isn't the Poppet furious? I imagine profound disapproval depicted on her features.

I am still in rather a shattered condition – but I hope to be able to get to London soon and be revived. I suppose there's nothing I could send you – in the way of books or anything? The worst of it is there doesn't seem to be any book worth reading that I can think of, can you? But perhaps you don't particularly want to read.

I doubt if my hair will ever grow long again – though of course it might make a special effort if monsieur would really immortalize it. I rather fancy, though, that that scheme of his may be one of his little jokes. As for my beard, it seems to be getting steadily shorter and shorter, and will soon I expect vanish altogether into my chin.

Give Rom's full moon a kiss from me.

yours
Giles

‡

To Lady Ottoline Morrell

The Morrells had been living in Oxford and in a succession of country houses including nearby Broughton Grange, waiting for the lease to be up on Garsington Manor. Though they had bought it in 1913, they had to wait to move in until May 1915. Ottoline went the next day to a spa in Buxton, Derbyshire, to cure her rheumatism. Lytton obviously did not know about her affair with the lover she was going to meet there – Bertrand Russell. Victor Beigel was a singer, one of Lauritz Melchior's singing teachers in 1923, when he was developing his Heldentenor voice. Lytton conceived '"a violent, short, quite fruitless passion" for the twenty-one-year-old painter Geoffrey Nelson'.[1] John began his portrait of Ottoline in 1908, but finished it only in 1920.

6, Belsize Park Gardens
Hampstead, N.W.
Sunday night, April 18th 1915

It was very sad going away today – so much seems to have come to an end. But I hope there may be new and happy beginnings – at Garsington, perhaps! – I only wish I could feel a little surer that such affection as there is going about in this world was not quite powerless . . . that it was not impossible for anyone to be of any use to anyone else.

It's difficult to refrain from melancholy reflections – but you won't thank me for them in your solitude, which I'm afraid will be a dreary one. However, it will be a great thing if it sets you up in health. And then at Garsington occupations and amusements are sure to come. *[. . .]*

I wanted to tell you how much I enjoyed the party – that Beigel was a revelation – how could such a fat little fellow with waxed moustaches bring forth such sounds? I liked Nelson, and would like to see more of him – and many other things. Do you know if John is in London? Or what he is doing? Do you think he'd like to paint me? He's often said he would – and there seems to be an opportunity for me to sit to him now – but I should hardly dare to suggest it. What has happened to the portrait of you?

Well, good-bye. I thought perhaps you might be cheered by finding a note from a familiar hand waiting for you in your hydro – though the contents can't help being a little elegiac. Good-bye,

your
Lytton

1. Michael Holroyd, *Lytton Strachey*, p. 314.

‡

To Lady Ottoline Morrell

Bertrand Russell foresaw that the move to Garsington was going to cause difficulties in his affair with Ottoline, as she couldn't really have him to stay there except when her husband was away. So he saw Buxton as their last chance to have some days together, and planned a surprise visit for them to Bolsover Castle, the home of one of Ottoline's ancestors, which had been inherited by her half-brother Arthur, 6th Duke of Portland. Following the sinking of the passenger ship Lusitania *on 7 May, there were anti-German riots in Birkenhead and Liverpool, reported in* The Times *the next day. The quotation is from Racine's* Phèdre.*

Josiah Wedgwood (1872–1943), 1st Baron Wedgwood and the fourth to bear that name, was wounded at Gallipoli. He wrote a five-page letter to Winston Churchill, begun on 24 April, vividly describing the landings (University of Keele Library). Rupert Brooke died of blood-poisoning aboard a French hospital ship anchored off Skyros on 23 April. Ironically, in view of the dramatic breach with his Cambridge Apostle and Bloomsbury friends caused by his enlistment and strong pro-war views, he never saw action, and was thought to have contracted his ailment from being stung by a fly. The myth-making began almost immediately with the valedictory obituary published in The Times *on 26 April, over the initials 'W.S.C.' – Churchill himself.*

The Lacket
Lockeridge
Marlborough
May 19th 1915

I've been trying to write to you for several weeks, my dear Ottoline, but the agitations of London, and its depressions, alternately made it impossible. I'm now back here again – arrived last Saturday –

immediately caught a violent cold, which is only just passing off –
cursed cold weather, too – such is my bulletin. I suppose you are now
at Garsington, beginning to settle down. How do you find it? Are you
overwhelmed with things to do? Or are you reasonably idle? I hope
Buxton did you good: it must have been fearfully gloomy there.
Bolsover looks amazing in the photographs – almost *too* romantic, one
might guess. But the detail – that doorway – totally divine. Why, oh
why, is Portland permitted to own such a thing? Why? And echo
answers 'Why?'

    [. . .]

As for public events, they seem to be going from bad to worse. I feel
utterly depressed about them. If (as I gather from the Times) there's
really going to be a 'Coalition Government', what hope will there be
left of *anything* decent in this wretched country? It seems to me it will
simply be a betrayal – conscription, protection, and all the rest of it will
become inevitable – and of course we will be no nearer beating the
Germans. The anti-German riots were disgraceful, but they were not as
disgraceful as the conduct of the authorities, who, in effect, encouraged
them, and then used them as an excuse for further maltreatment of those
miserable people. Oh! Doesn't it all make one want to go and bury
oneself somewhere far, far, away – somewhere so far away that even the
Times will never get to one.

'Où me cacher? Fuyons dans la nuit infernale!' But even in Hell, no
doubt, the Times appears on the breakfast table.

The news of Jos, so far as I've heard, is that his wound was in the
leg, and, though very painful, not dangerous – which sounds pretty
satisfactory. Wasn't Rupert's death a grim business? I felt so much of
my past raked up by it. Poor, poor Rupert! What a pointless thing this
life can be.

I hope you'll let me know how you're getting on. I fancy I shall
remain here for about a month, and then have a last look at London
before it closes.

ever your
Lytton

‡

To Leonard Woolf

Parts I and III of his forthcoming book were published as special supplements in the New Statesman *on 10 and 17 July.*[1] *Clive Bell's pamphlet,* Peace at Once, *was later burnt by the order of the Lord Mayor.*

    'Going from room to room' at Garsington can hardly be avoided, as all the ground-floor rooms open on to the large central hall.

Garsington Manor

Oxford

July 10th 1915

I found your Supplement very interesting. Will you bring it out as a book? I hope so. I'm sure it would have a beneficial effect. When is your next one coming out? Do go on providing them, I beg.

    Have you seen Clive's Pamphlet? It's curiously unlike your Supplement; yet I do find merit in it – much to my surprise. He seems to express himself, in rather an odd way; and it's difficult to see what can be said on the other side.

    I'm here momentarily among the usual retinue of embroidered parrots – and a few china ones. Her Ladyship has made a most suitable roost for herself in an Elizabethan mansion, with the aid of gold paint and the rest of it: there is a great deal of going from room to room, pianola-playing, peppermint-sucking, dressing, and undressing – but more of the latter than anything else. In the evening one dances, and in the afternoon one bathes. As it is at present the afternoon, I shall have to get ready for a plunge in the fishpond, together with Vanessa, Duncan, Barbara Hiles, Barbara Hiles's young man, the Swiss governess, and the French maid, to say nothing of the Queen of Sheba herself . . . I fear you are shocked. Why? Will you ever be able to come and see me in Hampstead? I should be there for the next fortnight or so, and, if you could get away, it would be agreeable to meet.

    Oh! The intellect! The intellect! Where shall we find it, I should like to know? – At the very end of the chapter?

yours ever

GLS

1. Duncan Wilson, *Leonard Woolf*, p. 258, n. 16.

‡

To Lady Ottoline Morrell

Augustine Birrell (1850–1933), writer, politician and father of Francis, who ran the famous bookshop with David Garnett, was in the Cabinet as Irish Secretary until he resigned following the Sinn Fein uprising the next year. Ottoline had known him even before her marriage. Lytton's relationship with Harold Cox, editor of the Edinburgh Review, *always followed a pattern like the one that had resulted in Cox rejecting Lytton's offer to do a piece on Tolstoy (whom Cox considered 'out of date'), but suggesting he instead write about Voltaire and Frederick the Great. In 9,000 words he argued that though Frederick saw events close to him with great clarity, his perspective as a military man meant that he was only seeing with one eye, whereas Voltaire, the most celebrated thinker of his day, could see things with both eyes, and so outwitted the great man of action. The translator Constance Garnett was David's (Bunny's) mother. Lytton had been reading Aylmer Maude's biography of Tolstoy at the same time, and wrote to Bunny on 23 August: 'I have no patience with a man who decides to commit suicide because he can't see the object of existence, and then decides not to because everything becomes clear to him after reading the Gospel according to St Mark.' The author of the silly letter was the Irish writer George Moore (1852–1933). The actress Lady Tree (1863 or '4–1937) was Helen Maud, wife of Sir Herbert Beerbohm Tree, a famous Mrs Quickly, Mrs Malaprop and Lady Teazle, who made her last appearance in the 1936 film* The Private Life of Henry VIII.

The Lacket
Lockeridge
Marlborough
August 21st 1915

Dear Lady,

I wonder how you are, and if anything amusing has been happening to you lately. Have you been keeping up your series of week-end parties, or are you taking a rest? I never heard anything about the Birrell week-end – did it go off successfully, and did the Rt. Hon. Gentleman plunge into the pond? I long to have news of these details – and of any others that may be going about. My seclusion here has been profound, my health rather vile, and my temper not all that could be wished – chiefly,

I think, owing to the abominable weather, which I began to think would never end, though it now seems to be changing – probably into something worse. My Voltaire-Frederick article occupies me to the exclusion of everything else; it is a fearful task, and must be finished by the end of the month. I feel like a negro slave: whenever I look up from my writing-table, I seem to see Mr Harold Cox over my shoulder whirling a cat o' nine-tails. Lord have mercy upon us.

In the intervals of literary composition, meals, and sleep, I've managed to re-read War and Peace – in Mrs Garnett's translation. It is an amazing work, and I really think the best chance of putting a stop to War would be to make it obligatory for everyone in Europe to read it at least once a year. In the meantime I think it ought to be circulated broadcast – though to be sure it would make rather a bulky pamphlet! But oh dear me! In between whiles, what an ass the poor dear man makes of himself. 'Matter and impertinency mixed!' but luckily there's a good deal more matter than impertinency.

By-the-bye, did you see a little letter from me in the New Statesman on the subject of Mr George Moore and his theory that Shakespeare's women are all 'soulless shadows'? What is it that leads people to say that sort of thing – and not only to say it, but to clamour loudly for credit being given them for saying it? Nobody would have known that George Moore was quite so silly as to think Cleopatra a soulless shadow, if he hadn't himself taken the trouble to write to the papers to say so. Rather like Lady Tree who insisted on appearing on the stage as a Roman boy with nothing on but a short toga; and no one need ever have known that her legs were . . . as they appeared on that occasion!

[. . .]

‡

To Lady Ottoline Morrell

In a letter dated 31 July, Lytton wrote teasingly but fulsomely to Ottoline about her efforts in the vegetable garden. Faith Bagenal was Nicholas Bagenal's sister; she married (Sir) Hubert Henderson, and they were the parents of (Sir) Nicholas Henderson (Nicko). Following Rupert's death the year before, James and Noel Olivier began an affair, resumed in 1932 after his marriage to Alix Sargant-Florence and hers to Arthur Richards (in 1919, by when she had become a doctor). Clive Bell's mistress was Lytton's cousin Mary Barnes (Mrs St John Hutchinson). T. B. Strong was Bishop of Oxford.

Helen Dudley was a well-off lady from Chicago who was also having an affair with Russell. He treated her brutally, inducing her to come from America to marry him, then changing his mind. She had a breakdown before dying insane and with multiple sclerosis. She had returned to London in 1915 and called on Ottoline immediately.

The Lacket
Lockeridge
Marlborough
September 4th 1915

Your really superb letter, dear Lady, arrived at a most psychological moment – just as I was on the point of dropping to pieces under the stress of my wretched Voltaire article – and brought me back to life. The sight of that fat envelope sitting by my bedside in the morning, and more still the leisurely perusal of its contents, had a wonderfully cheering effect. I wound up the article in fine style and, after weeks of torment, breathed again. At one moment I positively thought I was going to have a nervous breakdown! I seem to be growing more and more of a sensitive plant as old age approaches, instead, as I had hoped and expected, of turning gradually into a solid and heartless rock. There's nothing I should like so much as to do as you suggest and 'write more and more and more', but how is that to be managed if one's bones turn into shaking jelly after six hours' work? How I wish I were like you – an agricultural labourer! That would really be a satisfactory existence: and probably a more useful one. However, for the moment, I am flourishing once more. I've been having a great many visitors, and more still to come – so of course I am feeling very brisk. I had a great crowd last Sunday – Faith and her young man, Barbara, Nick, and (suddenly arriving at 11 o'clock at night on Saturday in a motor) James and a young lady (*not* Noel! But Alix Sargant-Florence, whom I don't think you know). So counting me there were seven of us, and as there were only six beds . . . well, all I can say is that I assure you *I* slept alone. It poured with rain continuously of course, but we crouched round a large fire in the small sitting room, and I think the young people enjoyed themselves, and I gave them champagne at dinner, and off they went next morning by their various vehicles towards the four quarters of the earth.

It was a very different affair from Tuesday till yesterday, with Clive and his Mary – much more intime and sympathetic, and also (be it said in passing) considerably more intelligent. Clive was in a very good 'so-happy-that-I don't-care-whether-I-impress-you-or-not' sort of mood – which suits him better than some others; and the lady was extremely agreeable, and really most taking, I thought. So young too! – which is such a comfort as one hobbles around on crutches. They arrived bursting over with accounts of your week-end party and it certainly did sound a brilliant success, and they all evidently enjoyed it enormously. They went off yesterday, and today my sister Pippa, Roger, and Forster arrive – so you see I am going it! I see that if I stayed here much longer I should become a dangerous rival to Garsington. But I'm going away for good and all on Tuesday next. The opportunity turned up of letting this place for the last three weeks in September, and as my finances are on their last legs I thought I'd better take it. On Tuesday I go to the Bosham establishment – I think for about a week: after that shall I come and see you? It would be very delightful to catch perhaps the last deliciousness of summer in your garden.

I am dying, also, to see and hear Queen Alexandra. Were you a great success in royal circles? Will you be made a Lady of the Bedchamber? And when you're Mistress of the Robes will you forget me altogether? I am inquisitive, too, about the young man 'lying perdu in the village'. But you don't mention the colour of his eyes, or whether his hair curls. However, I feel that it's incumbent upon me to draw the line somewhere – and so I draw it at the Bishop of Oxford. I cannot believe that the fellow is anything but a ninny. You see, I happen to have read a volume of his sermons.

Birrell does sound an engaging old creature, though, I suspect, slightly irritating as well. It pleases me to think of a Cabinet Minister taking the war so casually. When he said 'after all, the men out there will be returning some day', didn't you feel inclined to answer 'But there are rather too many who *won't*'? But no doubt it is better to be casual than hypocritical; only it's a pity that, in the matter of our governors we should be faced with such a choice.

Miss Dudley's American plan for me is tempting. I have long felt that I was cut out for a succès fou in the States. I can imagine myself delivering perfectly shameless lectures to crowds of ecstatic ladies – but on the whole I don't think the Atlantic's quite safe enough just now – and besides I must wait for a little more celebrity to bring it off with the proper éclat.

Is Norton with you? If so, please give him my love. I was very glad to hear from Moore (who was also here for a few days) that his health was better and that he had been working. Well, good-bye. Perhaps I shall hear from you at Bosham.

ever yours
Lytton

‡

To Mary Hutchinson

This is a Collins for Lytton's 'long comfortable visit' at Eleanor House, West Wittering, Sussex, which Mary's broad-minded barrister husband, St John ('Jack') Hutchinson, had rented the year before. Mary's grandfather, Sir John Strachey, was a younger brother of Lytton's father. Her mother, Winifred Strachey, married Sir Hugh Barnes. Mary had begun a life-long affair with Clive Bell. It was said that Bloomsbury found her too 'chic', but she and Lytton were intimate. Lytton's letters to his cousin are often bawdy.

6, Belsize Park Gardens
October 22nd 1915

Ma chère

[. . .] I was nearly killed on the way back, as my taxi did its best to collide with a coster's cart in Park Lane; but I got off with nothing worse than a stupendous swerve and a few 'fucking buggers' from the coster.
   Goodnight

Your
   Lytton

‡

To Clive Bell

Henry Lamb, who had returned to medicine, enrolling as an assistant at Guy's Hospital in September 1914, fundamentally disagreed with Lytton about the war, and their relations were cooling.
   D. H. Lawrence's novel had been subjected to police censorship, and J. C.

Squire, as 'Solomon Eagle', literary editor of the New Statesman, *defended their action.*

6, Belsize Park Gardens
November 17th 1915

Dear Clive,

Unless you're in a hurry, I hope you won't have that prospectus printed until I've seen it again. (Mary showed it me yesterday.) A criticism has occurred to me – I'm not quite sure whether I'm right – but I should like to make sure. I thought it on the whole excellent.

The lunch and tea yesterday I enjoyed immensely. It is too delightful and wonderful that she *[Mary]* exists. No more for the present – I am tired out and rather shattered, as I've been spending the whole day with Henry. It is a most distressing case; there is nothing to be done; but I think it can't last long. O Jesu!

your
Lytton

I wrote an ironical letter to the New Statesman in favour of the suppression of the Rainbow; but the joke was too heavy, and has also been suppressed.

✝

To Lady Ottoline Morrell

Lytton had invited himself to Garsington several times this autumn. He wrote to Ottoline on the 12th, saying that Clive had mentioned an invitation for Christmas. Lytton's political comments all concern the Registration Act introducing conscription, which actually became law in February of the next year. In October Lord Derby began his infamous recruiting campaign, designed to induce men who had not enlisted to do so on the condition that they would not be forced to serve before other men whose claim to exemption was weaker. This was meant to be a voluntary plan: men were to 'attest', to agree to enlist whenever called upon to do so, but the obligation was to be moral, not legal. As James Strachey's own experience with St Loe Strachey, his relative and employer on the Spectator, *showed, the Derby Scheme led to coercion and blackmail. By Christmas the Derby Scheme had failed and the government made the 'terrible announcement' that it proposed to conscript all unmarried men under forty-five who were physically fit and not exempt on grounds that they did work of national importance or had exceptional domestic responsibilities. Oliver is Lytton's brother. Reginald McKenna, Chancellor of the Exchequer, and Walter Runciman, President of the Board of Trade, did not resign in protest at the implementation of the Act. Nor did Maynard, to the fury of Lytton and Russell, who felt he had ratted on his agreement and his friends.*

6, Belsize Park Gardens
December 31st 1915

My Dear Lady,

How can I thank you for that delightful time? You know, I think, how much I enjoyed it – and how sad I was at having to bring it to an end. And besides the pleasure of it, there was such an accretion of health! Really, I feel a different being after that rest, comfort and pure feeding, and all the amusements of the mind, and the satisfactions to the eyes . . . but you spoil me, I'm afraid you spoil me . . . you must be careful, as one day I shall get above myself.

The news here is distinctly less abysmally depressing than when I left you. There does seem now just a chance that things may come out right. People seem to be recovering from the knock-down blow of that terrible announcement. The papers are improving. You will have noticed the changed tone in the Daily News today. The Manchester Guardian has been quite staunch throughout; and today it is really splendid – very impressive, serious, and firm; I recommend you to take it in – it is a wonderful tonic for depression and pessimism. Then Labour too is distinctly beginning to show its claws. Of course in the long run everything depends on that; but it looks as if it might be possible to play for time successfully – and time is very important. I have seen James, Bertie, Maynard and Oliver. It is the greatest comfort to find oneself in such complete agreement with one's friends. Bertie was most sympathetic; I went to see him this morning, and we then had lunch with Maynard in an extraordinary underground tunnel, with city gents sitting on high stools like parrots on perches, somewhere near Trafalgar Square. Maynard is certainly a wonder. He has not attested, and says he has no intention of doing so. He couldn't tell us much – except that McKenna is still wobbling; but he seemed to think it not unlikely that he and Runciman would resign – in which case he would resign too, and help them to fight it. Well, we shall see! I am to meet him again tonight, and shall perhaps hear some more news.

It's all very agitating, or rather exhausting – especially as in a moment of distraction this morning I walked straight into a lamp-post coming against it as hard as I possibly could with my forehead; but I still exist. I should like to write reams more, but it's late and I shall have to sally forth again. Let me hear from you soon, I beg. Give my love to all the Denizens of Garsington – especially the Backgammon board and its master. When shall I see you again? Oh! Ce monde, as the poet says, est une étrange chose! Farewell.

your affectionate
Lytton

‡

To James Strachey

The first reading of the Military Service Bill on 6 January passed with Sir John Simon alone resigning from Asquith's Cabinet. The week before, four others – McKenna, Runciman, Grey and Birrell – had threatened to join him. It is their change of mind that occasioned Lytton calling them 'Reptiles'. Gerald Shove was almost the sole male member of Bloomsbury who was a genuine absolutist pacifist. He was running the magazine War and Peace *for Norman Angell while waiting to be called up. Lytton was fond of Shove, but felt that his pacifism confused the argument against conscription by giving those whose job it was to enforce conscription, especially the tribunals, an easy way out, in that they could appear to be sticking to principle by granting exemption only to those who espoused pacifist beliefs, thus dodging the question of conscientious objection altogether.*

Henry William Massingham (1860–1924) resigned the editorship of the Daily Chronicle *in 1899 because of his opposition to the Boer War. As editor of the* Nation *from 1907 to 1923, he transformed this liberal weekly into a powerful organ of advanced but independent opinion; at the end of this period he joined the Labour Party and transferred his 'Wayfarer's Diary' to the* New Statesman. *Massingham wavered in his feelings about the war, and had even supported it in its early stages.*

John Atkinson Hobson (1858–1924) was an economist, and a frequent contributor to the Nation *when Massingham was editor. His original approach to economics, though later praised as pioneering work by Keynes and Tawney, earned him the wrath of his colleagues to such an extent that he never held a university post. He was a founder of the Union of Democratic Control. Niall Fergusson in* The Pity of War *(1999) refers to 'influential theories such as J. A. Hobson's about the malign relationship between financial interests, imperialism and war, or H. W. Massingham's on the perils of secret diplomacy and the disingenuous doctrine of the balance of power'.*

 Lord Henry Cavendish-Bentinck was Ottoline's half-brother. 'Harold' was evidently the subject of one of Strachey's amorous intrigues. There are references to him in other letters this year, one in connection with a visit from the police.

Garsington Manor
Oxford
January 14th 1916

I had a most depressing conversation with Pippa before coming down here, in which she sketched the proper course of action for opposing the Bill; it seemed clearer than ever that the Reptiles in charge of the business were inconceivably incompetent. I departed in despair. But Philip now seems to think that it may take a fortnight or even three weeks getting through the Committee stage; and in that case isn't it still possible that something should be done? Surely there ought to be a continual stream of leaflets and pamphlets. Also if possible meetings all over the country, and signatures collected against the Bill. Don't you think it might be worth while seeing Gerald, and if necessary supplanting him? He is clearly a mere blockade. But if you do anything, go and talk to Pippa first. Probably it's all pretty hopeless by this time, for *us* to try and intervene effectively; but the abomination of those Massingham-Hobson creatures makes one itch to. I am beginning to believe in Napoleon and Mr Lloyd George.

 It's pretty dreary here – they're so stupid, so painfully stupid; but I suppose it's healthy. Huxley is just what you described. I really don't know what to say to him. The Lord Henry Cavendish-Bentinck arrives today. Did he see me last Saturday walking past his window with Harold?

yours
Lytton

I return Monday or Tuesday

‡

To Lady Ottoline Morrell

On 18 January at Caxton Hall, Westminster (which remained the fashionable venue for Register Office weddings until the late 1970s), Bertrand Russell delivered his first lecture in his 'Principles of Social Reconstruction' series. The substitution of 'disgusting' by 'repulsive' refers to Russell's remark that 'most men and women were repulsive' to Carlyle. Evidently Russell had showed the lecture script to Ottoline, and she had discussed it with Lytton. At the end of 1915 it became obvious that there was an urgent need to organize those who were against conscription, and Lytton and James Strachey, along with most of their Bloomsbury friends and fellow travellers, joined the No Conscription Fellowship (NCF) as well as the National Council against Conscription (NCC). Both were founded to resist the act introducing general conscription, and the activities of both groups consisted chiefly of distributing propaganda. Members of Bloomsbury were among the volunteers who stuffed, addressed and stamped huge numbers of envelopes, and Lytton even wrote one of the pamphlets they contained:

CONSCRIPTION

WHY they want it, and why they **SAY** they want it.

They say they want it to punish the slackers
They want it to punish the strikers
They say they want it to crush Germany
They want it to crush labour
They say they want it to free Europe
They want it to enslave England.

Don't let them get what they want because they keep saying they want something different.

The Cat kept saying to the Mouse that she was a highminded person, and if the Mouse would only come a little nearer they could both get the cheese.

The Mouse said 'Thank you, Pussy, it's not the cheese you want; it's my skin!'

NATIONAL COUNCIL AGAINST CONSCRIPTION, 18, Bride Lane, London E.C. LEAFLET No. 3.

Lytton's antipathy to H.W. Massingham, the editor of the Nation, *had its origins in the publication of this leaflet. Massingham got the point of the allegory, but decided it was seditious, and raced to the headquarters of the NCC to get it withdrawn from circulation. Sir John Simon, who had resigned from his cabinet post to lead the opposition to the Act, supported him in this. They prevailed, and it was decided to halt distribution of Lytton's tract. Lytton thought this cowardly, but as half a million copies had already gone out, he did not feel the need to protest too vigorously. In 1910 Adrian Stephen and Horace Cole were the chief perpetrators of the great* Dreadnought *hoax. He studied law at first, but later became a psychoanalyst, as did his wife Karin Costelloe. The syndicalist Clyde Workers' Committee was established to resist the provisions of the Munitions Act that made strikes illegal and obstruction of munitions production a crime. By January 1916 the CWC directed workers in twenty-nine Clydeside engineering works, and as the CWC no longer trusted moderate trade union leaders to represent their radical interests, CWC leaders attempted to negotiate directly with the responsible Government commission. In March workers went on strike in one firm in Parkhead, and the strike spread within four days to other Glasgow factories. On 24 March the Government clamped down severely on the strikers, leading to almost permanent labour unrest on the Clyde.*

6, Belsize Park Gardens
January 21st 1916

I've been very busy with various absurdities, or I should have written before. Not that there's much news. The chief Public Event has been Bertie's lecture, which was a great success. The room was crowded with ladies of fashion and intellectual young men, who hung on his words. I thought it very interesting – full of good things and originality; and I enjoyed it very much. N.B. I observed that he said 'repulsive' instead of 'disgusting'.

The anti-Conscription movement has been rather fading out as far as I'm concerned. After one more Committee, I'd decided I'd had enough of them – especially as there was nothing more that one was wanted to do. I enclose one of my leaflets, which has caused some stir. Old Massingham suddenly took it into his head that it was seditious, and came tearing down to the little office in the City to get it withdrawn. It was agreed to send out no more copies of it, but as half-a-million had already been distributed, it was rather late in the day! The Morning Post got hold of it and others, and has had an angry article about them.

After quoting some of mine, it says 'Would it be possible to imagine a more wanton and malicious indulgence in false witness?' Queer fellows they are!

According to Adrian, whom I saw last night, the Clyde men have decided to strike for a day – just to show the Government that they are in earnest. But I suppose if they do we shall never hear of it. Half England might be up in arms and the papers would never mention it.

I am feeling infinitely better since Garsington, and a good deal more cheerful. I did enjoy being with you so very much. It is a great pleasure that one can occasionally dip into fresh air and sympathetic quietude at your Manor House – the thought consoles me as I pace these murky streets. Though it's true the murky streets are extraordinarily attractive too. How I adore the romance and agitation of them! Almost too much I fear!

I dined with Maynard yesterday – he had met Sir J. Simon at Montague's [sic][1] the night before. He found him rather a poor creature, and uneasy at finding himself in disagreement with everyone else he knew. Poor man! I shouldn't be much surprised if *he* ratted before long.

Did a letter from Mary Hutchinson come for me? She apparently wrote to me. I spent the week-end with Roger – tête-à-tête, most surprising! But I make it a rule never to refuse an invitation.

With love,
your
Lytton

1. Because of Lytton's persistence in spelling the name incorrectly, the editor has been guilty in the past of thinking Lytton was here referring to Charles Edward Montague (1867–1928), a writer, poet and liberal *Manchester Guardian* journalist who had crusaded against the Boer War and for free trade and home rule, but in 1914 dyed his grey hair and enlisted as a private soldier; at the time of this letter he was serving in the intelligence service. Bernard Shaw was among those who noticed that Montague had a yearning for combat. In fact Strachey meant, more prosaically, the Liberal politician Edwin Samuel Montagu (1879–1924), the Minister for Munitions. I am indebted to Robert Skidelsky for correcting me.

‡

To Maynard Keynes

6, Belsize Park Gardens
February 1st 1916

Oh dear! I had a narrow shave coming back last night – and by no fault
of my own. I'd successfully passed through the temptations of the
Corner (including a romantic looming figure with a cigarette); but on
the tube platform there appeared a languishing beauty in khaki, who
pushed into the train with me, and planted himself opposite me, and
made languorous drooping eyes at me in the most marked manner. I
got more and more agitated as we sped along, and station after station
passed, and he didn't get out. At last, at Chalk Farm (the station before
Belsize) he did get out – very slowly: but I didn't follow. In a kind of
trance of obstinate virtue (partly the result of your admonishments) I
remained rooted (in more senses than one) in my seat. And so I shall see
him no more. Of course I am almost in tears, as I now feel sure that that
languishingness would have been all that the prick of man could have
desired.

yours
Lytton

☦

To Lady Ottoline Morrell

*Keir Hardie and others founded the Independent Labour Party (ILP) in 1893
with the objective of establishing a socialist commonwealth in Britain. It was
internationalist in outlook, and pacifist in both world wars. It was one of the
bodies that coalesced in the formation of the modern Labour Party, and still
exists today as a publishing enterprise with the same initials, Independent
Labour Publications.*

6, Belsize Park Gardens
February 5th 1916

Our letters have crossed. It was good of you to write – it is very
encouraging to hear of other people's sympathy. I have applied for

absolute exemption on the grounds of health and conscience: but have heard nothing from the authorities so far. I expect that after a medical examination and an interview with the tribunal they will put me into what they call Class IVb – viz. They will tell me that I am liable to be called up for clerical work. I shall then appeal, and if my appeal fails, they may call me up to sit in an office. I shall refuse to do this, and what they will then do remains to be seen. The worst of it is that I have very little confidence in my physical capacity for resisting indefinite pressure. However, let's hope it won't come to this: and of course there's the off chance that they may grant an absolute exemption without too much fuss.

James is in pretty well the same position, though as his health is better I should say the chance of absolute exemption was less. I'm told that there is an I.L.P. man on the St. Pancras tribunal, before which Duncan and Bunny will have to come – which sounds encouraging. I have heard nothing of what's happening to Norton.

This is all very sordid and farcical. Let's read Madame de Sévigné, and think no more about it.

With love,
Lytton

‡

To James Strachey

James already had a copy of Constance Garnett's new translation of Dostoevsky's A Raw Youth, *so Lytton was pleased that the bookseller had misinformed him. James had written to Lytton (who had already read it in French) on 2 February: 'I note that Mrs Garnett has invented a new exclamation. Not only Ach! And Ech! but now Och!' 'Foma Formitch' is presumably a reference to Dostoevsky's short novel* A Friend of the Family *(1859).*

It was at 46 Gordon Square that Lytton put the letter on Maynard's plate. Edwin Montagu had been helpful to Keynes early on in his career.

This letter was written just over four months before Lord Kitchener's death by drowning. Keynes's gossip about his distance from real authority was correct and widely known. William Robertson (later made a baronet) had accepted the appointment as Chief of the Imperial General Staff in December 1915, on condition that a small War Council to coordinate strategy in all war theatres was formed with himself as its military adviser in direct touch with his commanders without intervention of the Army Council; he also demanded a reorganization of the General Staff in the War Office. The reason for Lytton's class-conscious joke was that Robertson was the first British general in history to have begun his career as a private soldier and come up through the ranks. While his non-Standard English (Lincolnshire) accent was an unusual one for a CIGS, it was hardly accurate to call him 'our Cockney General'.

> 6, Belsize Park Gardens
> Hampstead N.W.
> February 22nd 1916

It's all terribly bleak in every direction. I'm glad you're going to Burley, perhaps by then things will improve.

The man at Bicken assured me with such complete conviction that the *Raw Youth* was not yet out that I believed him, luckily. I'm looking forward to it. I'm now half way through Foma Formitch.

Do you really want the *M. Guardian* a day late? I suppose you realise it will be that, and so – I'll order it.

I cut out the *Observer* report of Montagu's speech (it had *every* horror, not only protection but the necessity for smashing Germany etc.) and wrote on a piece of notepaper the following – 'Dear Maynard, why are you still in the Treasury? Yours, Lytton.' I was going to post it to him, but he happened to be dining at Gordon Square, where I also was. So I put the letter on his plate. He really *was* rather put out when he read the extract. He said that two days before he had had a long conversation with Montagu in which that personage had talked violently in exactly the opposite way. He said the explanation was cowardice. I said that if their cowardice went as far as that there was no hope. And what was the use of his going on imagining he was doing any good with such people? I went on for a long time with considerable virulence, Nessa, Duncan and Bunny sitting around in approving silence. (Luckily Clive wasn't there.) The poor fellow seemed very decent about it, and admitted that *part* of his reason for staying was the pleasure he got from his being able to do the work so well. He also seemed to think he was doing a great service to the country by saving some millions per week. I maintained that sort of thing was mere fiddle-faddle, and that the really important things were the main principles, such as Free Trade, over which he had no control whatever. He at last admitted that there *was* a point at which he *would* think it necessary to leave, but what that point might be he couldn't say.

He had a little gossip – (1) that the other day the French made a frantic effort to involve us at once in a grand Ally Protection scheme, and that this would probably have been done, if he hadn't written an unbridled minute. And (2) that K. is now a mere dummy, everything of importance being done, and signed, by Robertson (our Cockney General). He also told a story about him in France, when it became necessary to get rid of several French liaison officers, and nobody knew how to dismiss them tactfully. At last Robertson was asked to see to it, as he had such a reputation for diplomacy. So he said he would, and summoned the French officers to meet him. They all appeared, were put to sit round a table, and Robertson sat at the head. He then slowly pointed his finger at each of them one after the other, saying, with every point, '*You* go 'ome,' '*you* go 'ome.' – And 'ome they went!

My health is far from satisfactory. It is horribly cold here, and I feel chilled to the bone. I have fearful nights too. Well! The Lord save us. Ach! Ech! Och!

yours
Lytton

‡

To Virginia Woolf

Mary Berry (1763–1852) was Horace Walpole's literary executor. She lived at Little Strawberry Hill with her younger sister Agnes. The Berry Papers *were published in 1914. General Charles O'Hara (1740–1802) represented the British at the surrender at Yorktown. In 1795 he became engaged to Mary Berry, but the marriage never took place because when he was appointed Governor of Gibraltar later that year she refused to leave England. 'Maleboge' is the name of the eighth circle of Hell in Dante's* Inferno, *ten rocky concentric circular trenches – a place of filth. Strachey was concerned about the arguments for his total exemption from conscription that he was going to make before the Hampstead tribunal in early March. The* Voyage Out, *published 26 March 1915, contained an unflattering portrait of Lytton as the thin-skinned, physically awkward St John Hirst. Lytton knew that Virginia had had a breakdown in 1913, after having finished the book. Was his lavish praise and faint criticism (which Virginia seemed happy to accept) meant to spare her feelings? It seems strange, though, that he waited almost a year after its publication to write this letter.*

6, Belsize Park Gardens, N.W.
February 25th 1916

Dearest Lady

I wonder if you have got three stout volumes of Miss Berry's life and
letters, belonging to me? I have a dim memory of having lent them to
you some centuries ago. If by any chance you have got them, and
would send them to me – by special truck, I should think – I should be
very grateful. I have engaged to write one of those Edinburgh articles
on Horace W, and thought I might drag in something about the Berrys
too – and, perhaps, General O'Hara.

My conduct has been so shocking about writing to you that it's far
beyond excuses. There are moments when it seems clear to me that I
can never possibly be forgiven; and other moments when I realise that
you, if no one else, will be able to tout comprendre et tout pardonner.
I have been in such a sluggish, deathly state for the last – I don't know
how many months! Maleboge, I think it must be. And the worst of it is
that these torpors do not entirely overcome one – if they did one would
at any rate be unaware of one's horrid state; but they leave one
conscious – hideously conscious – of one's damnation.

Well! I seem to be rising a little out of them now. I don't know why
– perhaps because the horrors of the outer world are beginning to assert
themselves – local tribunals, and such things – and one really can't lie
still under *that*. At any rate, here I am with a pen in my hand, and
writing a letter – who could have believed such a thing? The nuisance is
that there's so much to write about that I don't see how I'm to write
anything at all. For instance, The Voyage Out –! You know how I
adore that book. I read it with breathless pleasure, the minute it came
out – a special messenger came running out with it from Bickers. I
don't think I ever enjoyed the reading of a book so much. And I was
surprised by it. I had naturally expected wit and exquisiteness – what
people call 'brilliance', but it's a wretched word – but what amazed me
was to find such a wonderful solidity as well! Something Tolstoyan, I
thought – especially that last account of the illness, which really – well!
– And then the people were *not* mere satirical silhouettes, but solid, too,
with other sides to them: Shakespeare wouldn't have been ashamed of
some of them, I thought. I love, too, the feeling reigning throughout –
perhaps the most important part of any book – the secular sense of it
all – 18th century in its absence of folly, but with the colour and

amusement of modern life as well. Oh, it's very, very unvictorian! The handling of the details always seemed to me divine. My one criticism is about the conception of it as a whole – which I am doubtful about. As I read I felt that it perhaps lacked the cohesion of a dominating idea – I don't mean in the spirit – but in the action. I wonder if you at all agree about this – but it is difficult to explain in writing. There seemed such an enormous quantity of things in it that I [one] couldn't help wanting still more. At the end I felt as if it was really only the beginning of an enormous novel, which had been – almost accidentally – cut short by the death of Rachel. But perhaps that really *was* your conception. – I won't say more now, we must meet soon, and talk about it. But oh! the chapel scene! – That I think is the best morceau of all. – And the Dalloways – oh! –

This is very helter-skelter stuff, I'm afraid. But what can you expect from an aged inhabitant of the Inferno? Write me a word or two, Santa Beatrice, and ask me to tea.

yours ever
Lytton

‡

To James Strachey

The conscription question was coming to a head this winter and early spring. Though his eyesight had always been poor, James was less likely than Lytton to be exempted on medical grounds, and was having to think through his position and the consequences. The final statement, which he sent to the Hampstead Tribunal on 22 February, said: 'I conscientiously hold it to be wrong to take any part in the war; and my objection applies not only to combatant service but to any action which is likely to assist its prosecution. (As evidence that this opinion is genuinely held by me, I may perhaps mention the fact that last November I gave up a position which I had held for many years on the staff of the "Spectator" newspaper, rather than attest under Lord Derby's scheme, as I was requested to do by my employer.)' He commented to Lytton: 'I now think that all is lost; I feel sure from studying the papers that at the most they'll put you in Class 4 and exempt me from combatant service. On the other hand I now envisage prison and even execution fairly calmly, chiefly because I've been reading The Times *for that last half hour.*

'I note another thing as to you. It looks to me as though the tribunals were

absolutely refusing (illegally?) to exempt anyone on medical grounds. That's to say they prefer to leave the decision to the military authorities. In that case you'ld be "called up" and be examined after you'd been "deemed". This complicates things extremely, especially in connection with "conscience". Are you preparing a short "statement" to read out to the Tribunal? It seems to me that might be wise.'

A further complication was that Pippa, who was 'violently anti-conscription', argued with James about the grounds for conscientious objection and seemed to be taking the position that only absolutist pacifists were entitled to claim it: 'I think she thinks you can only have a "conscientious" objection if it's to "war in general" or "taking human life" – in fact if it's an unreasonable objection. I fancy,' wrote James prophetically, 'the tribunal may take the same view.'

Charles à Court Repington (1858–1925) had to abandon his brilliant military career in 1902 owing to an indiscretion committed with the wife of a British official in Egypt. Forced to resign his commission, he was refused a divorce by his wife and was unable to make amends to the lady whose position he had compromised. He became the military correspondent of The Times *in 1904, and served on Recruiting and Exemption Tribunals from 1914 to 1918. The two books of reminiscences he published after the war (to revive his ailing financial position) revealed so much private information and caused such scandal that Repington once again lost his social position. He did, however, achieve reconciliation with his wife shortly before his death.*

C. P. Sanger was strongly against the war, and a great admirer of German culture; it was, however, legal advice about the interpretation of the new statute Lytton sought. Beatrice Chamberlain (1862–1918), the eldest daughter of Joseph Chamberlain, knew Lytton when he was a child. At the time of writing Lytton's cousin Mary Hutchinson was an art student at the Slade.

6, Belsize Park Gardens
February 28th 1916

I wish you could induce Pippa to realize the gravity of the situation. It also worries me to think she considers me either a humbug or a dunderhead. The conscience question is very difficult and complicated, and no doubt I have many feelings against joining the army which are not conscientious; but *one* of my feelings is that if I were to find myself doing clerical work in Class IVb – i.e. devoting all my working energy to helping in the war – I should be doing wrong; I should be convinced

I was doing wrong the whole time; and if that isn't having a conscientious objection I don't know what is. If she doesn't believe me when I say this I'm sorry, but I suppose she won't believe me any more if I add that I'm willing to go to prison rather than do that work. I'm afraid she may not have considered what that means. I have. I don't suppose I shall go to prison, but if they insist I am ready for it. Well! I must say it adds to the disagreeableness of things if one's to find that Pippa doesn't give one her support.

I'm glad to say I'm feeling much better – in fact almost normal. I only hope it'll last. I hope you've pretty well recovered by this time. The nervous strain of the tribunal hanging over one's head is getting rather intense, I find. Nothing has come from them. I'm told by Bunny that Colonel Repington is on the Hampstead tribunal (not as military representative) – it sounds quite likely. I think it quite possible that they may take up the same sort of view about conscience as Pippa – viz. That the act does not provide for conscientious objection against this war, but only for some flummery against war in general. I shall consult Sanger about this, as I gather he's up in it all. I am quite ready if necessary to tell any number of lies – *if necessary*. But I shall tell them with my eyes open. Footpads! Footpads at the street corner! Knock them down if you can, but if you can't cut and run!

Adrian has been watching the St Pancras tribunal (Duncan's and Bunny's) and reports darkly. He says it's entirely dominated by the military representative and one or two loud-voiced hooligans; that there are decent people on it, but that they're terrified and powerless. The amount of appalling and senseless misery caused by the act makes one's blood run cold to think of. I really think that that poor woman with her Jesus and her hysteria who was sent to gaol for six months on Saturday is nearer the Kingdom of Heaven than most of us. To have devoted her whole time since the beginning of the war to discouraging recruiting! It is wonderful that such people should exist.

I had rather an odd conversation yesterday with my old friend, Beatrice Chamberlain. She asked me to dinner by telephone. I felt, all things considered, that I couldn't stand it, so said I was engaged. She then asked me to come to tea on Sunday, and I said I would. We were tête-à-tête and, as a good opening offered, I thought it as well to explain the nature of my opinions: it seemed silly going on indefinitely with the poor woman in the dark. She was very calm, and we talked hard for an hour and a half. It was almost entirely about the justification of the war; the conscription business was just *effleuré*, but it gets me so

much on the raw that I thought it better to glissade away from that.
Rather a pity perhaps, as her *great* reason for wanting to smash Germany
(or so she said) was her love of freedom. She was very adroit, especially
in the *technique* of argument – viz. skimming over difficult places, and
the rest of it – but some of her arguments were curiously childish. Such
is my well-known fair-mindedness that I saw a good deal in her
position, but on the other hand nothing I said, I'm sure, had the
slightest effect on her – not the very slightest. She didn't budge by a
pin's point. I pressed her to give some account of how she thought we
should win. (She said she was *perfectly certain* that we should.) After a
little prevarication[1] she admitted that the West was jammed. I then said
'Well then how are we going to do it?' She replied 'There may be other
ways.' I said 'What?' And she answered 'Roumania may join us. I don't
say she will, but she may.' And that was all she had to offer. I said that it
seemed to me she was not using her reason on this matter, and she as
good as confessed that she wasn't. 'You underrate the power of
character in getting things done,' etc. I thought there was something
to be said for that; but time will show. I then elicited, bit by bit, the
terms that would satisfy her. They were as follows – a complete
indemnity for Belgium (also Serbia), Alsace Lorraine for France,
German Poland to join Russian Poland under Russia, and Galitia to join
too if it wants to (ahem!), Constantinople to Russia, and all German
colonies kept. (I forgot to ask about Italy.) This I gathered was a
minimum. It seems to me to throw a rather lurid light on the state of
mind of the moderate Tories. She sat there talking like that, with
Verdun (as she admitted) tottering . . . At last I went, and we parted on
friendly terms. But I don't think I shall be seen there again. Personally
she didn't come well out of the conversation. I do not care for her, no.
She has no feelings – she once had – for 'Papa', but they lie buried in
his grave, and now her heart is a piece of dried seaweed. One detail was
instructive. I said that I supposed she intended to keep Mesopotamia;
upon which she hummed and hawed, and at last said 'there are
difficulties about Mesopotamia'. Considering her family connections
with India, I think this must mean something – probably that the
Russians have signified that we must keep our hands off. But if so, is it
possible to imagine a more ghastly nightmare of folly than that
expedition?

I feel there must be many more things to say, but this letter is already
inordinate, and I have to go to lunch with Mary Hutchinson. Oh! I
finished off Miss Lowell t'other day – very nasty I was; so now I've only

H.W. to be done in 3 weeks — shall I live through it? I'll write again
soon. What a pity to miss H.G.!

yours

Lytton

Je meurs pour ne point faire un aveu si funeste.[2] — What would the
redoubtable Repington say to that?

1. An error; procrastination is meant.
2. Racine, *Phèdre*, I,3, Phèdre to Oenone.

‡

To Lady Ottoline Morrell

The police had suppressed D. H. Lawrence's The Rainbow *late the year
before, not so much because of its sexual content as because of its anti-war stance.
Lytton had written a letter to the* New Statesman *ironically in favour of its
censorship, but it was not printed. Lawrence's belligerent anti-homosexual
position (perhaps expressed in 'the other half' of the paper referred to below) was
not calculated to make Lytton sympathetic to Lawrence's utopian ideas.*

6, Belsize Park Gardens
N.W.
February 29th 1916

[. . .]
    Thanks for the Rainbow paper. I observe you tactfully removed
the other half! — It reached me, however, from other quarters, and —
no, that kind of thing is too much for me, and I'm afraid I shall never
be a passionate soul, nor rise up and form a nucleus of the living truth.
Hélas!
    I am rather excited as I've at last got into touch with Virginia again,
and am going to see her on Thursday. *[. . .]*

‡

To Lady Strachey

Lady Strachey was having trouble with her left eye. Dante, The Inferno, *Canto I, 1–3: 'Nel mezzo del cammin de nostra vita/mi ritrovai per una selva oscura/che la diritta via era smarrita.' (Midway upon the journey of our life, I found myself within a dark wood, for the straightforward path was lost.) It was Lytton's thirty-sixth birthday.*

6, Belsize Park Gardens
Hampstead
London NW3
March 1st 1916

Dearest Mama,

Hum quoth the bee! It was most noble of you to write – I was surprised to see your handwriting. It is a great relief to think that that horrible affair has not been even worse, and that reading will eventually be possible. I do hope that you'll soon find that in practice there's not much difference between the one-eyed and the two-eyed – and I don't think there can be, considering how many people with only one eye go on in quite the ordinary way. But I'm afraid the whole thing must have been dreadfully unpleasant, and that you must still be in great discomfort. It is something to be able to imagine you out-of-doors and warm – it has really been arctic; but now it's begun to thaw, with the result that the slosh and general filth are inconceivable.

I have now passed the mezzo del cammin di nostra vita, and am rather surprised to find that existence continues to be highly interesting in spite of that fact. I used to think in early youth that one's development would come to an end in one's thirties – but I don't find it so – on the contrary. Things if anything seem more interesting instead of less. Also, they grow more satisfactory. One seems, as one goes on, to acquire a more complete grasp of life – of what one wants and what one can get – and of the materials of one's work, which gives a greater sense of security and power. I think I can see now where my path lies, and I feel fairly confident that, with decent luck and if my health can go on keeping its head above water, I ought to be able to get somewhere worth getting to. Really I consider, apart from illness, and apart from the present disgusting state of the world, that I'm an extraordinarily happy person. One other reflection is this – that if I ever *do* anything worth doing I'm sure it will be owing to you much more than to anyone else.

[. . .]

your loving,
Lytton

‡

To Lady Ottoline Morrell

6, Belsize Park Gardens
N.W.
Saturday, [March 4th 1916]

[. . .]

I'm rather depressed at the moment, as I went yesterday as a member of the public to look at the Hampstead tribunal. It was horrible, and efficient in a deadly way. Very polite, too. But clearly they had decided beforehand to grant *no* exemptions, and all the proceedings were really a farce. It made one's flesh creep to see victim after victim led off to ruin or slaughter. – Worse than the Star Chamber, I think.

I had a very nice time with the Woolves. Virginia was charming.

Yours,
Lytton

‡

To Lady Ottoline Morrell

Michael Holroyd says of Anrep: 'In 1916 he joined the Imperial Guard and appeared, a terrific figure in full Russian Guard uniform, claiming that a battle at the Front wasn't nearly so alarming as one of Ottoline's parties.'[1] *His mosaic works include the floor, vestibule landing and pavement of the National Gallery, in which there are portraits of Virginia Woolf, Clive Bell, Mary Hutchinson, T. S. Eliot and Bertrand Russell.*

6, Belsize Park Gardens N.W.
March 15th 1916

Just a few hurried words – of thanks for your blessings and good wishes.
I had lunch with Philip yesterday, and he was most kind and
sympathetic. He is coming to speak for me tomorrow (if they allow
him). I feel most grateful. I think it's quite out of the question that they
should let me off altogether – almost certainly they'll simply exempt me
from combatant service; and then I shall have to appeal.

I am looking forward more than I can say to coming on Saturday –
unless any unforeseen horror turns up. My health is very vile: the most
unpleasant minor diseases crowd upon me! – I saw Dr. O. again
yesterday and he said that nothing serious was wrong, but that I needed
complete rest, and feeding up. Can you provide these for a little? The
only peculiarity in food is that I ought to have either rice or macaroni
with my meat or fish at both dinner and lunch.

[. . .] Anrep, even more than usually larger than life-size, in an
immense khaki overcoat, and covered with medals and crosses, *and*
accompanied by two equally vast, equally accoutred Russian officers –
entered the room this morning, while I was lying in my pre-prandial
trance. The little parlourmaid nearly fainted – especially when she
saw Anrep embracing me and kissing me on both cheeks. He seems
fundamentally unaltered, though decidedly more military on the surface.
He is only staying, I gather, for a few days, and is in a good deal of a
flurry. He's coming to dinner tonight.

[. . .]

P.S. The two officers couldn't speak a word of anything but Russian, so
they sat in silence side by side on the sofa, looking very nice, and
making me wish that they would follow Anrep's example in the kissing
department.

1. Michael Holroyd, *Lytton Strachey*, pp. 720–21, n.7.

‡

To James Strachey

*Lytton's preoccupation in March was his appearance before the Hampstead
Tribunal, where he intended to claim an absolute exemption from military service*

on grounds of conscientious objection. He had first to appear before the local
Advisory Committee, who summoned him on 7 March. Though nominally only
advisory, the recommendations of the committee were invariably followed. Lytton
read the following prepared statement:

> I have a conscientious objection to assisting, by any deliberate action of mine,
> in carrying on the war. This objection is not based on religious belief, but
> upon moral considerations, at which I arrived after long and careful thought. I
> do not wish to assert the extremely general proposition that I should never in
> any circumstances, be justified in taking part in any conceivable war; to
> dogmatize so absolutely upon a point so abstract would appear to me to be
> unreasonable. At the same time, my feeling is directed not simply against the
> present war: I am convinced that the whole system by which it is sought to
> settle international disputes by force is profoundly evil; and that, so far as I
> am concerned, I should be doing wrong to take any active part in it.
>
>   These conclusions have crystallized in my mind since the outbreak of war.
> Before that time, I was principally occupied with literary and speculative
> matters; but, with the war, the supreme importance of international questions
> was forced upon my attention. My opinions in general have been for many
> years critical of the whole structure of society; and, after a study of the
> diplomatic situation, and of the literature, both controversial and philosophical,
> arising out of the war, they developed naturally with those I now hold. My
> convictions as to my duty with regard to the war have not been formed either
> rashly or lightly; and I shall not act against these convictions, whatever the
> consequences may be.

The committee made no comment at all, and simply informed him that they
would recommend that the tribunal afford him 'no relief'.
   Lytton felt he would get no better hearing from the tribunal itself, but he was
prepared to create a stir anyway, and spent his time, as he wrote to James,
constructing 'imaginary cross-examinations of Military Representatives'.
   The tribunal finally heard the case at the Town Hall on 17 March, with an
audience including Philip Morrell, his chief character witness, and a host of
brothers and sisters, plus much of Bloomsbury. There followed the famous scene
with the pale-blue air cushion, solemnly handed by Morrell to Lytton, who
inflated it and, with a grave expression on his face, inserted it between himself
and the bench. He was suffering from piles. The audience laughed at this, and
was delighted by the celebrated repartee when he answered the tribunal's standard
question, 'What would you do if you saw a German soldier trying to rape your
sister?' Lytton: 'I should attempt to come – [significant pause] – between them.'
(Most accounts of this repartee are incorrect.) The double entendre was

intentional, but the members of the tribunal were not much impressed. They adjourned the proceedings to await the report of the physical examination by the military doctors. It took place a few days later at the White City and was a greater success, as he was pronounced unfit for any form of service. The appeal was therefore moot, and was never ruled upon. Had he not been declared, as he telegraphed James, 'Unfit for any class', and had this appeal failed, he would have been liable under the Act for a prison sentence.

[no date]

Will you look at this, and if you think it any good, and have the strength to reach the post-box, will you address it and post it? My brain spins round and round.

G.L.S.

I appeal against the decision of the Hampstead Local Tribunal to refuse my claim for a certificate of absolute exemption from combatant service only on the grounds

(1) That the Tribunal refused to give any reason for their decision.

(2) That their decision was unreasonable and not in accordance with the weight of evidence. I claimed exemption on the ground of an objection to the undertaking of combatant service and explained in my evidence that this objection was rested principally on an objection to taking any part whatever, direct or indirect, in the present war. The Tribunal stated repeatedly during the hearing that they accepted absolutely the veracity of my evidence and the honesty of my beliefs. The Military Representative stated in reply to a question that the ground upon which he resisted my claim was that my objection was not a 'conscientious' one within the meaning of the Act. It is clear from the fact that the Tribunal granted me an exemption that they did not accept this view. Since, therefore, the Tribunal accepted my objection as being a conscientious one, and also accepted the veracity of my evidence as to the grounds of my objection, I claim that it was unreasonable of them to withhold from me the only form of exemption which would appropriately meet my objection. If my objection to combatant service had rested upon such grounds as a feeling that human life was sacred, it might have been reasonable to grant me exemption from combatant service only. But since my objection

admittedly rested upon an objection to taking any part, direct or indirect, in the present war, the only exemption which could reasonably have been granted was an absolute one.

(3) That the Tribunal refused to me my right under the Act to put relevant questions to the Military Representative (Regulations, Part 1, Section 1, Sub-sections 9 and 16c). The Chairman after a discussion said he did not admit my right, but would let me put questions as a matter of courtesy. The Military Representative declined to answer my third question; whereupon the Chairman refused to let me press it, and again reminded me that I was putting the questions not as a matter of right but as a matter of courtesy. I was consequently obliged to abandon any attempt to put further questions, though they were of the greatest importance to the complete statement of my claim.

‡

To Lady Ottoline Morrell

White City became associated with greyhound racing following the Franco-British Exposition of 1908, when the centrepiece was a dazzling white 'Court of Honour' built, confusingly, in an Oriental style of architecture. The machine halls that were its main features had been demolished but the site was re-used during the War.

6, Belsize Park Gardens, N.W.
March 21st 1916

Well, I have been rejected – medically unfit. So that's over – except, I suppose, a few formalities. It's a great relief. I am just home, after spending from 11 to 3.30 at the 'White City' – a ghastly spot – where I sat reading Gardiner's History of England in the midst of a most promiscuous gathering of unmarried males – it *was* a change from Garsington! Everyone was very polite and even sympathetic – except one fellow – a subordinate doctor, who began by being grossly rude, but grew more polite under my treatment. It was queer finding oneself with four members of the lower classes – two of them simply roughs out of the streets – filthy dirty – crammed behind a screen in a corner of a room, and told to undress. For a few moments I realised what it was like to *be* one of the lower classes – the appalling indignity of it! To come out of it after it was all over, and find myself being called 'sir' by policemen and ticket collectors was a distinct satisfaction. I'll tell you the details when I see you.

I hope to come on Saturday, but I can't be quite sure yet – I'll let you know as soon as possible. James is to come up before the tribunal on Thursday: it will be rather an agitating business, I fear. We must hope for the best.

My party is to come off tonight; but I have a sinking feeling, and I daresay only three people will come. I wish *you* were coming! I've asked Philip, but I hardly supposed he will be able to.

[. . .]

Adieu, adieu!
ever your
Lytton

I hope your car is cured. Do let me know. It was a superb sight seeing you and Maynard drive off in the dog-cart!

‡

To James Strachey

On 29 March James wrote to Lytton that 'Norton got a letter this morning to announce that the Military Representative has appealed against his exemption! He's now plunged in gloom, and feels convinced we shall end all our days in the Tower.' Clifford Allen (1889–1939) was created Baron Allen of Hurtwood in the last year of his life. A courageous conscientious objector, he was imprisoned three times in the course of the war. James reported a conversation with him in which he said that the No Conscription Fellowship executive had decided 'to refuse any compromise'. The compromise being offered by the government, wrote James, was that 'an Order in Council should be made to the effect that the present occupation of all COs was of national importance, and that they were all exempted from the Act on condition they continued in it. There was to be a Black List of trades, fixed by a committee; and anyone in a Black List trade was to be draughted out into another. The Committee was to have representatives from the various conscientiously objecting bodies.' The Stracheys (and the NCF) opposed this fudge because it effectively denied the principled grounds on which their objection was based. A 1,000-delegate national conference of the NCF was scheduled for Saturday, 8 April, and it was to be followed by 'an afternoon demonstration to which the Press and Scotland Yard will be invited'. An Order in Council is a vehicle by which the cabinet assumes powers delegated to it by Parliament – though, as in this case, it is sometimes open to interpretation as to whether the legislature has, in fact, ceded the powers. Resorting to an Order in Council makes it possible for the government of the day to take action without returning to Parliament for authorization.

On 9 March Asquith spoke in Parliament about the forthcoming Paris conference. On the 28th the Inter-Allied Conference in Paris (26th to the 28th) made its Declaration of Unity between Belgium, France, Great Britain, Italy, Japan, Portugal, Russia and Serbia regarding military economic and diplomatic affairs. Edward Henry, Baron Carson (1854–1935), was the Ulster leader who was Attorney-General from May 1915 to October 1916. He was dissatisfied about the delay in applying conscription. Philip Morrell was using his position as an MP to ask questions about the war and conscription in Parliament, and depended on James and Lytton to supply him with questions to ask.[1]

Garsington Manor
Oxford
March 30th 1916

I was very glad to get your letter. It is too sickening about Norton. I hope he's not *abruti*.

The N.C.F. position sounds exciting. It seems to me that Clifford Allen's line is decidedly extremist, if the government has really offered what you say. But it's extremely difficult to say that he's not right. Probably the extremity of extremism is the best thing now. Bertie, I gather, is coming to London on purpose to help the N.C.F. It might be a good thing to get a sight of him.

Philip had heard nothing of the rumour that the Paris meeting was a Peace one. He said that the general impression before yesterday was that the government, or at any rate Asquith, was done for; but that after Carson's speech yesterday, which was a complete frost, everyone agreed that things would go on as before.

It seems to me that if the government has a grain of sense it will make peace as soon as it can, as that's the only way of getting out of all their difficulties.

I wonder how the domestic affairs are proceeding. I've heard from Pippa that her disease has broken out in a new form, which is very sickening. I am feeling very comfortable and cheerful, but still exceedingly exhausted. I hope before long this will stop.

Ott. Suggested that you should come down the Sat. after next. I told her I didn't know what your plans were.

yours
Lytton

Philip complains that in spite of his prayers he was only given one question by Mr Backhouse – said he would have liked to ask at least ½ a dozen. I suppose there must be material for endless questions, and it seems a mistake not to use it as much as possible.

1. As is made clear in James's letter to Lytton of 4 April: 'I made a speech at the Executive today about giving him questions to ask.'

‡

To James Strachey

Garsington
March 31st 1916

The more I think of it, the more certain I feel that the N.C.F. is right in refusing to compromise. If conscientious objectors once begin to allow themselves to be put into occupations by the government, they are done for. The duty of the government is quite clear – viz. to see that the Act is properly carried out, and that the 'out-and-out' C.O.s are given absolute exemption. There's really no reason on earth why they shouldn't be. And I expect it could be quite easily arranged by an Order in Council – if it's true that the government's compromise could be. No doubt an amendment to the Act is out of the question.

If you see Mr. Allen again, I beg you to encourage him.

God blast, confound, and fuck the Upper Classes.

yours
Lytton

‡

To James Strachey

The night before, wrote James, the bell rang at the Hampstead house. It was answered by the servant, Jessie; when James arrived he saw, 'standing in the hall by the front door, the stately figures of two police constables. I naturally jumped to the conclusion that I was going to spend the night in gaol, so you can imagine I was feeling rather agitated when I went up to them and asked if I could do anything for them. "Well, sir," said one of them, infinitely polite and kindly, "we've come to ask if Mr Giles Lytton Strachey lives here." "He usually lives here; — but I'm afraid he's away at present . . ." "I see, sir. The fact is, sir, the Military Authorities have been making some inquiries about him; so we just called round to see him." "I could give you his address, if that would be any good to you." "Thank you very much, sir." "Care of Lady Ottoline O double-T O LINE Morrell . . ." etcetera. "Thank you very much, sir. Stopping away for his health?" (Had they got this out of Jessie?) "Yes." "I see. (Making a note.) Stopping away indefinitely for the benefit of his health. — And you're his brother, sir?" "Yes. Mr James Strachey." "Thank you, sir. Then they'll be able to get in touch with him if necessary?" "Yes." "Goodnight, sir." "Goodnight."' James went on to speculate as to the reason for the visit, and wondered if 'it might be something quite different . . . Harold . . . but they mentioned the Military Authorities all right'.

Gilbert Cannan (1884–1937) was a minor novelist whose Mendel, *published in the year this letter was written, contained thinly disguised portraits of Carrington and Mark Gertler. He had replaced Harry Norton working with James in the offices of the NCF.*

Garsington Manor
Oxford
April 5th 1916

Very odd — the dear Bobbies. You don't say whether they were good looking; but I'm told the one here *is*, so perhaps if he does get 'in touch' with me . . . And then there's 'Harold' — but I suppose I can depend on the Military Authorities. Queer that one should positively fall back on *them* with relief. The worst of it is that when these things begin one never knows where they mayn't end; perhaps it's also the best of it.

I think probably it's the result of the Yellow Form, which I daresay called me up on Ap. 4th — and I paid no attention to it. Nor have I got any papers here of any sort; all those dealing with that question (including the Registration card) I left in that right-hand drawer. If you think it wise, will you send me whatever you think I ought to have? (Heavily registered!) – But perhaps really they won't take any more steps about it. And ought I to do anything with the Yellow Form? Rather late in the day, I should think.

Gilbert C. sounds a very dismal office companion. You'll never make him understand an Act of Parliament. I'm glad there's to be another debate, and I hope Pipsey will figure. He is so earnest.

I am getting on here quite satisfactorily – everything flows along in a comfortable way, though to be sure the week-end *was* rather a hurricane. But that only lasted for a day and a half, and otherwise I've done nothing but sleep, eat and read Prof. Gardner. I don't think there'll be anyone besides you next Saturday – it seemed on the whole best, so I didn't encourage other invitations. My health seems better, but the exhaustion is still rather great. I hope you're not absolutely dropping. And your Appeal?

I heard from Barbara about Duncan's affair. The prospect of the Suffolk Appeal Tribunal is I fear rather black. But Something, I presume, before then is bound to happen.

I think it would be madness to rush up on Saturday for the N.C.F. meeting, much as I should like it. I think I'll try and write them a few words of encouragement. But my invitation wasn't signed, so I hardly know who to address it to.

I've been spending the afternoon in Oxford, lingering among those mouse-eaten buildings, and trying to get up a few romantic memories. But really I couldn't; the streets were so full of soldiers that my attention was distracted; and I found that I was thinking of the Present and the Future, and not of the Past.

yours
Lytton

✝

To Virginia Woolf

Virginia had found Asheham, in the Sussex Downs, in late 1911, and spent a great deal of time there from 1912 to 1919.

Garsington
April 15th 1916

I am looking forward to coming to Asheham on Thursday – probably
hand in hand with Sanger. I hope you are getting over your flu all right.
I am still rather délabré [dilapidated], in spite of the infinite solicitudes
of her Ladyship. It's a great bore. I lie about in a limp state, reading the
Republic, which I find a surprisingly interesting work. I should like to
have a chat with the Author.

Do you think I might have either rice or macaroni with the meat
course at lunch and dinner? Dr Overy insists on it, so if it could be
managed without too much bother I should be much obliged.

Enclosed is a poem, written the other day. Her Ladyship *would* have
it written by Philip's Secretary at the Ministry of Munitions – a dozen
copies – so here is one.

With love
your
Lytton

Who has not, down the street, with a fond eye.
Gone vaguely voyaging, Love's secret spy?
Searching with subtle glance the moving crowd
For some new beauty – sweet, or quaint, or proud –
Some ravishing creature, whose delicious sight
Shall fill the soul with sudden long delight?
For me, how often all an idle day
Like a soft summer cloud has trailed away,
While my rapt steps have led me unaware
Lingering amid the thronging thoroughfares
Entranced, and my quick spirit, like a bee
At multitudinous flowers, sipped ecstasy!
For often – such has been my happiness –
Some gentle genii have conspired to bless
The hour, the place, the mood, and I have found
Myself a traveller o'er enchanted ground,
Where, at each turn, on my exploring eyes,
Shock after charming shock of rich surprise
– Visions delectable, and colours rare,
And sweet, strange looks, and smiles, and marvellous hair –

Came pressing, till I have felt as one who holds
A spell to cast o'er all things more than gold's
Glory in a glance, and like the Sun to blaze:
For loveliness was living in my gaze.
Yet oft it has befallen far otherwise;
Each barren minute has withheld its prize;
Beauty has sulked, and joy has hid his head;
And empty-eyed the grudging day has fled.
But then, sometimes, perhaps as the calm night
Came slowly on, and in ambiguous light,
Fleeting in veils before her, wrapped the world,
I have caught an eye that glowed, a lip that curled,
A form, a being, sudden, precious, blest;
My quivering heart has gasped within my breast,
My startled brain re-echoed with dim cries,
And all my senses rushed into my eyes,
And I have seen incomparable things
Heavenly and unknown imaginings,
Visible there before me in the mesh
And moving miracle of human flesh
Mysterious beauty! Whose far depths disclose,
Like the unfolding passion of the rose,
In beauty's heart still sweeter beauty wound,
And mysteries lost in mysteries more profound.
And I have known that all at once I'd come
Into my spirit's long-appointed home,
The gracious harbour in whose bosom deep
My ocean-wandering desires would sleep,
And all my doubts and all my pains be past,
All, all, I'd ever sought for found at last!

‡

To Vanessa Bell

Early this year Duncan Grant had acquired the small farm at Wissett Lodge,
Halesworth, Suffolk, on the death of an aunt; he moved there with his lover,
Bunny Garnett, so they could work as fruit farmers, attempting to avoid
conscription. Vanessa, who had been in love with Duncan for a couple of years,
began a physical relationship with him in 1915. She dealt with the triangular

relationship by trying hard to befriend Bunny. This was dangerous, for he was
mostly heterosexual. Bunny once told the editor that he'd been the lover of both
Duncan and Vanessa, and I suppose the liaison with Vanessa must have
occurred about this time. Vanessa spent the spring and summer of 1916 at
Wissett. In October the household moved to Charleston. In the spring of
1942 Bunny married Angelica, the daughter of Vanessa and Duncan, who
was born on Christmas Day 1918. Bunny had been present at the birth.

Lytton's obviously sincere praise of Ottoline is a response to Vanessa's
scepticism. 'Lytton's taste for Garsington and Lady Ottoline,' says Regina
Marler, 'was extremely suspect in the eyes of Bloomsberries.'[1]

Garsington Manor
Oxford
April 17th 1916

Dearest Nessa,

I wonder how you are all getting on. Are you beginning to settle into
your habitation, and your various businesses? Have all the rats been
killed yet? And how are the bees and the blackberries? I imagine it must
be pretty wet and grim in the Suffolk flats just now; but perhaps the
quietude and remoteness make up for all other drawbacks.

I gather from her Ladyship that nothing has happened so far about
Duncan and Bunny. There seems now, I should say, a fair chance of
fruit farming being accepted as a 'National Occupation' – if they can
only induce the Tribunal to grant them that. I am feeling very nervous
about James – in fact very nearly hopeless. I don't see why the appeal
Tribunal should allow him anything better than Non-Com; and that
is indistinguishable from the ordinary Army. The stories of the
maltreatment of COs when they get into camp are ghastly, and they are
being given now two years' hard labour as a matter of course. It is all
about as bad as it could be. Bertie has been here for the week-end. He
is working day and night with the N.C.F., and is at last perfectly happy
– gloating over all the horrors and moral lessons of the situation. The
tales he tells make one's blood run cold, but certainly the N.C.F. people
do sound a remarkable lot – Britannia's One Hope, I firmly believe – all
so bright and cheery, he says, with pink cheeks and blithe young voices
– oh mon dieu! mon dieu! The worst of it is that I don't see how they
can really make themselves effective unless a large number of them do
go through actual martyrdom: and even then what is there short of a

revolution which will make the governing classes climb down. It is all most dark in every direction.

As you may imagine, these mental agitations aren't doing much good to my health. I think I am a little better, but I'm feeling horribly wraith-like and incompetent. The only mercy is that my mind remains comparatively self-possessed. But it is a damned nuisance to be pestered with such a body. Tomorrow I go to London, and on Thursday on to Asheham – I hope I shall survive it. If I do then I shall probably return here, as Ott is so extremely pressing, and it seems on the whole a suitable place – though of course I can't help being afraid of some sudden tempest brewing up; but so far the skies have been of the bluest. Infinite solicitude showered upon me – so that really I do feel moved by the extraordinary kindness of the good woman, especially as the more distressing features of her outfit continue in abeyance.

[. . .]

1. Regina Marler (ed.), *Selected Letters of Vanessa Bell*, p.195, n.3.

‡

To Lady Ottoline Morrell

Asheham House
Rodmell
Lewes
April 23rd 1916

Dearest Lady-in-Chief,

[. . .] I found in London that I had laid up such a store of health at Garsington that I was able to face two days of constant bustle there with perfect equanimity, and now the rough and ready mode of existence here doesn't seem to be crushing me in the least. I am enjoying myself a good deal, in spite of the chilly wind and the general lack of romance in my companions. Virginia is most sympathetic, and even larger than usual, I think, she rolls along over the downs like some strange amphibious monster. Sanger trots beside her, in a very short pair of white flannel trousers with blue lines, rattling out his unending stream of brightness. Woolf and I bring up the rear, with a couple of curious dogs, whose attentions almost oblige me to regret the charms of

Socrates. I don't know how long it will last – certainly till Tuesday – perhaps a little longer – and if only the sun will occasionally come out (as it's doing at present) there'll be nothing much to complain of: the country is so splendiferous that so long as one's out in it one cannot repine . . .

I thought *[. . .]* I might try and collect some facts in London for a possible pamphlet. Everybody seems to think it would be a useful thing if it was written. Philip will have told you of my reconnoitring in the House of Commons. When I asked the policeman to tell Mr. Morrell that I was there, he said 'Do you mean Philip?' – which appeared rather familiar. The political outlook gets stranger and stranger, and the persons in control more and more imbecile and disgusting. Woolf is getting a good deal alarmed at the prospect of being forced either into the army or gaol, and obliged to leave Virginia to her fate. It is all horrible.

The Magic Flute was considerably slewed[1] over by Beecham's vulgarity, but the loveliness came through – like an exquisite youth in a ready-made suit of clothes. *[. . .]*

1. Others have read this as *slimed*.

‡

To Lady Ottoline Morrell

When the war actually began in 1914, St Loe Strachey fired James from the Spectator *because of his anti-war views, but the Stracheys thought he'd nonetheless act to keep James from going to prison. After appeal James was not arrested, but was granted conscientious objector status, and allowed to substitute working with Quaker Relief for military service. Oddly enough 'that old P.M.' Asquith was a regular visitor at Garsington, though he of course knew it was a hotbed of anti-war dissent – Lytton himself finally met the Prime Minister during the last week in May.*

6, Belsize Park Gardens
May 2nd 1916

Dearest Ottoline,

I'm afraid I shall only be able to come for the week-end on Thursday – so far as I can at present see. As things are going, James will probably become liable to arrest next Monday, and it will be important for me to be on the spot when that happens. His tribunal turns out to be the one bad one of the London Appeal group, so that it is extremely unlikely that they will alter the decision of the local people. In the meantime my mother, who has returned, will try and get St Loe to use influence, and failing him other people. I shall be very glad to hear from you in detail what that old P.M. said – everything seems to be hanging so horribly in the balance that one is anxious for any indication of the course things will take.

[. . .]

‡

To Maynard Keynes

James Strachey's appearance before the Hampstead Tribunal had the same result as Lytton's – his claim to exemption as a non-pacifist conscientious objector to the war was refused, and he was forced to appeal his case. The key was probably to Maynard's rooms at 3 Gower Street. Duncan's and Bunny's Suffolk (local) tribunal took place on 4 May at Blymouth. Maynard had given evidence for them, but Adrian Stephen's presentation of their case was poor. He confusingly offered as evidence for Bunny's non-absolutist CO status that his mother, Constance Garnett, was a lifelong pacifist who had visited Tolstoy. The chairman, says Robert Skidelsky, 'thinking Tolstoy was a town in Russia, was unimpressed'.[1] The appeal was heard later in the month at Ipswich, when they were granted non-combatant status. Harry Norton's appeal was successful. It had been complicated and unusually fraught because the exemption granted by his local tribunal in February had been appealed by the Military Representative. Arnold Rowntree (1872–1951) was Liberal MP for York. He was opposed to Britain's involvement in the war and was a founder in 1914 of the UDC, which he eventually left because of pressure from his party.

Garsington Manor
Oxford
May 10th 1916

Dearest Maynard

[. . .] The Suffolk result was very sickening; but the Appeal will be the important thing. It was surely going rather far even for a Tribunal to admit their genuineness and give them nothing. I met Ernst in the street in Hampstead just before coming here, and his account of Cambridge was appalling. Norton's appeal, I hear, comes off on Friday. I am horrified by seeing in the Daily News today that, according to Mr. Rowntree M.P., the C.O.s who have been shut up in underground cells in chains and fed on bread and water have now been removed to France. Is it possible?

Philip, as I daresay you've heard, is getting up a deputation to the P.M. (for tomorrow). His reports sound fairly hopeful.

I've been down here since Friday, and in spite of the incredibly loathsome weather, I've been enjoying myself. It's been unusually peaceful, and now it's positively got fine again, and I'm lying out under my quilt of many colours in the sun. I hope soon to have accumulated enough health to be able to face London again for a little. It is too horrid to sit helpless while those poor creatures are going through such things. But really one would have to be God Almighty to be of any effective use. *[. . .]*

your
Lytton

1. Skidelsky, *Keynes*, vol. 1, p. 327.

‡

To Clive Bell

This is the first mention in the correspondence of the talented East End Jewish painter Mark Gertler (1891–1939).

Lady Violet Bonham-Carter, Baroness Asquith of Yarnbury (1887–1969), was the daughter of Asquith by his first marriage to Helen Melland. The year before, she had married Sir Maurice Bonham-Carter (d.1960), a scientist and civil servant. She had invited herself to stay the weekend, along with Lytton, MacCarthy, Keynes and a young conscientious objector. Ottoline, who had not realized how much she hated the COs' cause, had welcomed the visit as giving her another chance to put their case before the prime minister. Violet squabbled with them all, and abused the COs for cowardice, saying they all ought to be deported. Far from discussing 'daylight saving', Lytton responded that there didn't appear to be much difference in the position of the government, for whom he presumed she was speaking, and that of the Prussians. Miranda Seymour writes: 'Violet snatched up her bag and rushed out of the room in tears. She did not leave the house, as Ottoline rather wished she might do, but contented herself with spoiling the weekend by ostentatiously refusing to speak to Lytton.'[1] *It took all Desmond's emollient charm to keep Violet from erupting again.*

Garsington Manor
Oxford
May 12th 1916

I've just heard from Gertler, who says he's on the brink of ruin – has taken his last £2 out of the bank, and will have nothing at all in another week. Do you think anything can be done? I'm sure £10 would make a great difference to him, and I thought perhaps you might be able to invest some such sum in a minor picture or some drawings. Or perhaps you could whip up somebody else. If you do anything, of course don't mention me, as his remarks about his finances were quite incidental, with no idea of begging.

Except for the weather, which is loathsome, it is very agreeable down here, and extraordinarily peaceful. I lead a very lazy life, eat largely (I have induced her ladyship to make an exception of my case), take a constitutional every afternoon, and read aloud to her ladyship and mademoiselle of an evening. Today, however, I fancy the week-end begins – and it's to be a pretty brisk one – with Violet and Bonham Carter as central figures, and Desmond and Pozzo as attendant coryphées. God grant me some small portion of speech and spirits. But what, oh what, can one say at this time of day to a Prime Minister's daughter?

I wish you would send me some of the London news. I am almost completely letterless, while her ladyship has sheafs every morning. She comes up with them after breakfast as I lie in bed, and we read them together. In a few moments she'll be here – and I shall doubtless learn how Pipsey's deputation went off yesterday. Public events seem to be getting more and more edgy. I have a feeling that at any moment the milk may boil over. *[. . .]*

The Suffolk tribunal sounded peculiarly shocking. But what can the Houynhms expect, when they come before the Yahoos for judgment? – Oh! the rustle of the skirts – ! –

– She has come and gone. The post brought letters from Goldie, Birrell, Peter Warren, Aldous Huxley and Margot. Also a note from Philip to say that the P.M. was apparently favourable, but gave no promise to do anything. But probably you've heard about this.

>Adieu
>>your
>>>Lytton

I've just thought of a subject of conversation with Violet – daylight saving.

Her ladyship asks me to ask you whether you can remember whether you paid the motor which brought you here from the station at Easter? She thinks she saw you doing it; but the man swears you didn't. Hinc illae lachrymae. She assures both you and me and the world in general that this inquiry over 3/6 is not owing to 'meanness', but . . . etc. She says she is going to write to you soon.

1. Miranda Seymour, *Ottoline Morrell*, p. 350.

‡

To Maynard Keynes

The letter begins with a paragraph asking advice on behalf of Lady Strachey about Duncan's finances in respect of his mother's estate. The deaf young lady was the Hon. Dorothy Brett, the daughter of Lord Esher, who told Michael Holroyd:[1] 'I really did not like Lytton Strachey. First of all he was so unpleasant to look at, to put it mildly, and he was secretively obscene. I did not know him intimately.' Maria Nys (later Mrs Aldous Huxley) was not French but the daughter of a Belgian industrialist. Lytton was coaching her in Latin for her entrance examination for Newnham, and was sexually attracted to her. (In an autobiographical essay written a month later, on 26 June, he asked himself: 'Why on earth had I been so chaste during those Latin lessons? I saw how easily I could have been otherwise – how I might have put my hand on her bare neck, and even up her legs, with considerable enjoyment; and probably she would have been on the whole rather pleased.') Nicholas Bagenal had been wounded in the hip, and was convalescing before his return to the Front. The maid rescued by Asquith couldn't have been in too much danger, as the pond at Garsington is neither very deep nor very wide, and the streams running through the grounds are narrow.

Garsington Manor
Oxford
May 22nd 1916

Dearest Maynard

[. . .]
   A rather noisy week-end is just drawing to a close. Various young ladies – either deaf or French, Clive, a wounded subaltern, and in the middle of it all the Prime Minister arriving to rescue a servant maid from drowning . . . altogether it's been more like a campaign in Flanders than anything else. The peacocks, too, have never once relinquished their shrieking.
   What a relief – that Tribunal result.

your
Lytton

1. 9 March 1966: Michael Holroyd, *Lytton Strachey*, p. 727, n.2.

‡

To James Strachey

Philip Snowden (later Viscount Snowden, 1864–1937) led the majority of the Labour movement who opposed the war. A champion of the COs, his unpopular opinions cost him his seat in Parliament in 1918. He was of working-class origin, and disabled. 'Massingberd' is a cruel joke on Massingham's name. Sir Archibald Armar Montgomery-Massingberd (1871–1947) was chief of staff to Lord Rawlinson in France from 1914 to 1918. The Irish Republic had been proclaimed by Patrick Pearse at the General Post Office, Dublin, on Easter Monday, 24 April 1916, signalling the start of the Easter Uprising.
   Sir John Grenfell Maxwell (1859–1929) the new British Commander-in-

Chief, arrived in Dublin on Thursday. Ireland was under martial law, so he had the ultimate authority. Maxwell had returned in March from Egypt, where he was Commander-in-Chief of the Anglo-Egyptian armies. Although related to the Countess Markiewicz, he was disastrously ignorant of the current political mood in Ireland and probably did more to undermine British rule in Ireland than all the rebels put together. Asquith's orders were that he should put down the rebellion as rapidly as possible, and Maxwell did just this, without any heed to the political consequences.

Lady Robert Cecil ('Nelly', 1868–1956), born Lady Eleanor Lambton, married Lord Robert Cecil, son of Queen Victoria's Prime Minister, the 3rd Marquess of Salisbury, in 1889. Lord Robert won the Nobel Peace Prize in 1937 for his work on the League of Nations, which was said to have originated in a document he wrote in September 1916. Nelly Cecil had been a friend of Virginia Woolf for at least ten years, so Lytton would have known of her, and might well have met her before.

Admiral Sir Hedworth Meux (1856–1929) was a former Commander-in-Chief at Portsmouth, and a Conservative MP at the time of writing. George V had supported him to become head of the Royal Navy over the objections of Churchill. Originally Sir Hedworth Lambton, he took the name Meux in 1910 when he inherited the estate of Theobolds (where Temple Bar was erected after its removal from London) from Lady Meux. Lytton's dislike for her reflects his general antipathy for some of the upper classes.

'Nathan' was Sir Matthew Nathan (1862–1939), Undersecretary for Ireland from 1914 until this year, when he and his superior, Augustine Birrell, were forced to resign a few days after the date of this letter, when the Royal Commission on the Irish Rebellion reported in June, and the two were accused of mishandling the British response. Sir Matthew had been a suitor of the Stracheys' elder sister, Dorothy, which accounts for the familiar tone. 'Uncle Trevor' Grant was Lady Strachey's favourite brother, about whom Lytton wrote in 1906 to Duncan (who was also his nephew), 'The truth is that he is a vagabond, not an ordinary civilized human being accustomed to living in houses, behave at table, and so on.'

In a memoir of Asquith written in 1918 (published in The Shorter Strachey*), Lytton revealed that Asquith had indeed courted Ottoline. The Falstaffian view of Asquith is there amplified by the revelation that about a year later, at Garsington, the statesman took the hand of Dorothy Brett's sister 'as she sat behind him on the sofa' and made 'her feel his erected instrument under his trousers'.*

Abingdon County Hall, built between 1678 and 1682, is, says Nikolaus Pevsner, 'the grandest town hall in England'.

Garsington
May 31st 1916

[. . .] The last week-end has been rather straining. Mr and Mrs
Snowden, Mr Massingham, Bertie, Pozzo, to say nothing of Carrington
and Brett. The Snowden couple were as provincial as one expected –
she, poor woman, dreadfully plain and stiff, in stiff, plain clothes, and he
with a strong northern accent, but also a certain tinge of eminence.
Quite too political and remote from any habit of civilized discussion to
make it possible to talk to him – one just had to listen to anecdotes and
observations (good or bad); but a nice good-natured cripple. Lost Mr
Massingberd came out much more than I'd foreshadowed – very much
in the French style, and oh! so bitter. Talked a great deal about Ireland,
where he's just been – says it's in the most fearful state – utter chaos and
horror – and furious with the government. Apparently they knew
Maxwell was a man of blood and iron, and must deliberately have
chosen him for that purpose. The stories of the misconduct of the
soldiery were very grim. As for Lloyd George's doing anything – quite
out of the question. There was a most powerful anti-Cabinet
atmosphere altogether; and then, as usual, in the middle of the Sunday
afternoon torpor, the Prime Minister 'and party' appeared. They *were* a
scratch lot: – Lady Robert Cecil, stone deaf and smiling at everything
she didn't hear, a degraded Lady Meux (wife of Admiral Hedworth)
with a paroqueet accent, and poor old Nathan, in Walrus moustaches
and an almost Uncle Trevor air of imbecile and louche benignity. I
studied the Old Man with extreme vigour; and really he's a corker. He
seemed much larger than he did when I last saw him (just two years
ago) – a fleshy, sanguine, wine-bibbing medieval-Abbot of a personage
– a gluttonous, lecherous, cynical old fellow – oogh! – You should have
seen him making towards Carrington – cutting her off at an angle as she
crossed the lawn. I've rarely seen anyone so obviously enjoying life; so
obviously, I thought, *out* to enjoy it; almost, really, as if he'd deliberately
decided that he *would*, and let all the rest go hang. Cynical, yes, it's
hardly possible to doubt it; or perhaps one should say just 'case-
hardened'. *Tiens!* One looks at him, and thinks of the war. . . . And all
the time, *perpetually*, a little, pointed, fat tongue comes poking out, and
licking the great chops, and then darting back again. That gives one a
sense of the Artful Dodger – the happy Artful Dodger – more even than
the rest. His private boudoir doings with Ottoline are curious – if one's
to believe what one hears; also his attitude towards Pozzo struck me –

he positively sheered away from him. ('Not much juice in *him*,' he said in private to her ladyship . . . so superficial, we all thought it!) Then why, oh why, does he go about with a creature like Lady Meux? On the whole, one wants to stick a dagger in his ribs . . . and then, as well, one can't help rather liking him – I suppose because he *does* enjoy himself so much. I felt most *sympathique* as I watched his conversation with Carrington.

Besides entertainments of this sort, I have been going through some other distractions. Rimbaud has been discovered, and (partly at any rate) read; which has led on to Verlaine, and re-reading and fresh reading of him – all very interesting; and their affair really absorbing. Then too I have been for some enormous walks – 'expeditions' – with, precisely, Carrington. One was to the town of Abingdon, a magical spot with a town hall by Wren perhaps – a land of lotus-eaters, where I longed to sink down for the rest of my life, in an incredible oblivion . . . until I remembered that that's what *has* been done by . . . Lady Norman. As for Carrington, she's a queer young thing. These modern young women. What *are* they up to? They seem most highly dubious? Why is it? Is it because there's so much 'in' them? Or so little? – They perplex me. When I consider Bunny, or Peter (he's close by, at Magdalen), or even Gertler, I find nothing particularly obscure there, but when it comes to a creature with a cunt one seems to be immediately *désorienté*. Perhaps it's because cunts don't particularly appeal to me. I suppose that may be *partly* the explanation. But . . . oh, they coil; and on the whole, they make me uneasy.

[. . .] The C.O. question seems to be hanging fire. Everyone declares that as soon as this bill is safely over, 'something' will be done. In the meantime, nothing absolutely nothing, is. The P.M. promised Pipsey, Bertie, Snowden, etc., with his own mouth that the detachment in France should be brought back; not only has this not been done, but more have been sent there. But what can you expect from a 20th century Silenus.

Do send a postcard or something in re coming here. And Noel? – Rimbaud, I assure you, is a good poet.

yours
Lytton

‡

To Carrington

This is Lytton's first letter to Carrington, following the incident in which she crept into his bedroom, armed with scissors, intending to crop his beard. He suddenly opened his eyes, and she experienced the coup de foudre *from which she never recovered. This letter makes it appear that he was struck by the same sensation.*

'Like quills upon the fretful porpentine', Hamlet, *I,5, line 19. 'Time's wingèd chariot' is found, aptly, in Andrew Marvell's 'To His Coy Mistress'.*

Garsington Manor
Oxford
June 2nd 1916

Will you write to me, I wonder? The last two days have been most distressing – passed under the thick cloud of the terrible old Paget woman (alias Vernon Lee), who is still here, and whose spoor insults my nostrils. How I detest people who won't listen to what one says! Grrrr! She luckily goes today, but then Philip returns, and tomorrow there is the week-end, and after that – oh, what a vista! – Whitsuntide . . . I should like to fly, but I feel helpless. My beard has got inextricably entangled in the apple jelly, and I struggle in vain.

Yesterday was physically dismal too, but this morning the distracting fine weather has begun again; everything is incredibly beautiful; the sky is full of exciting clouds, and it is hot, and one ought to be perfectly happy, I suppose, but is one? Perhaps one would be, if there were no pugs. But there always are – or very nearly always – except, perhaps, in Abingdon – and one can only get to Abingdon in a motor bus. If you go bthere as a drawing mistress at Miss Towser's school, we shall never meet again. If I tried to go and see you, I should cease to exist in the rattling of the glass, and if you tried to come and see me you would be raped and murdered by the Kangaroos. So probably you'd better not. Ah! God! If you had been for the last 36 hours in the clutches of the Paget nightmare you would sympathise with me more than you do . . . you wouldn't even want to imitate my high voice, but would sit holding my hand and weeping with me over the web of life. But it would require a Rimbaud to reproduce the effect of that Devastation: all *I* can do is to formulate appeals for mercy to the Virgin and the Holy Ghost.

As for Rimbaud, I've written out another of his poems (one of the most frantic) in that kind of Franco-English, but it's very long, and in pencil, therefore, illegible unless written out again, and I should doubt when, if ever, I shall have the strength for that. Perhaps, too, in your vertigo of ever-intensifying complications, you'ld hardly be in the vein for such stuff. Or would it fit in as a subsidiary whirl? . . . In the meantime, I enclose another work of my hands.

How *are* your complications? – Going on finely, I trust. Is Gertler working and therefore happy? And will you, in some tactful manner, give him my love? I wish – I wish – what do I wish? I don't know. But if one's overflowing of affection could be taken and done up in brown paper parcels, I think I should send him one – anonymously. Another thing I wish is that I'd talked a little to the deaf lady while I had the chance. Very stupid of me; but the days were so short and confusing; and no doubt I shall have more chances. Another thing I wish is that I could talk to you, now, instead of writing; and *then* perhaps I could make you understand (among other things) the Great Paget Horror – so that your hair would stand on end, like the fretful porpentine – and what a wonderful sight that would be!

Well, do you think we ever *shall* go for a walk on the Berkshire Downs? and Wiltshire? and Silbury Hill? – To say nothing of Dartmoor, Provence, and the Campagna.

> At my back I always hear
> Time's wingèd chariot hurrying near,

as the poet says. We shall have to make haste.
Adieu, ma chère bébé,

your

Lytton

✝

To Carrington

Early in June 1916, Carrington and Lytton had been discussing Rimbaud, and Lytton had offered her a translation of 'Le Bateau Ivre'. She wrote to him [dated only Sunday evening]: 'Send me the frantic Rimbaud poem even in pencil. I am even more excited now over him . . . Yesterday I spent the afternoon reading a life of Musset with Noel [her brother]. So that soon I shall be able to read

Rimbaud myself. I have a wonderful idea about it all. I will show you perhaps one day – a picture.'[1]

The exhibition was that of the New English Art Club. Kitchener had drowned on 5 June. Carrington's letter was illustrated with drawings of Ottoline's pugs.

On Tuesday morning, 13 June, Carrington thanked him 'for the amazing poem'. Later in that letter she asked: 'Are you still crouching over the fire reading life upon life of Rimbaud?' Lytton had made a rapid literal translation. It has a few obvious errors, and some infelicities caused by over-literalness. Probably he relied on his enormous vocabulary and did not resort to the French dictionary as often as he should have done. But the translation shows a fine grasp of the tricky syntax of the poem and sometimes strikes the exact right note.

In April, a CO and NCF member called Ernest F. Everett had been sentenced to two years' hard labour for defiance of military orders. On 19 April the NCF published a leaflet protesting the sentence, and six of its members were arrested and imprisoned for distributing it. In a letter to The Times Bertrand Russell said he was the author of the leaflet, and insisted that if anyone were to be prosecuted it ought to be himself. The authorities immediately complied with his wishes and instituted proceedings against him, and on 5 June he appeared at the Mansion House before the Lord Mayor, Sir Charles Wakefield, charged with publishing 'statements likely to prejudice the recruiting discipline of His Majesty's forces'. A. H. Bodkin (1862–1957), later Sir Archibald Bodkin, Director of Public Prosecutions between 1920 and 1930, appeared for the prosecution. Russell conducted his own defence, probably not much helped by the presence of Lytton, together with a strikingly apparelled Lady Ottoline.

Garsington
June 7th 1916

Chère Bébé,

Here is the Rimbaud affair. I hope you'll be able to read it – as far as comprehending it – that's another matter. I'm glad to hear you're pursuing your French studies. It's really a very easy language to read.

There is no news from this Abode of Bliss. The rain it raineth every day, and I crouch over the fire, reading English history. On Monday her Ladyship and I shot to London (as you may have heard) to see Bertie R*[ussell]* being tried at the Mansion House. In a spare moment we tottered over to the New English. I liked your flowers and their pot, and Brett's Widows, and Guevara's Whores . . . but the atmosphere is hardly exhilarating, what with all those yards of faded futilities, and Mr Winter's sad form forever in the background . . . and it was a relief to find oneself in the street again. The tubes and buses did *not* disappoint *me*. There was a soldier . . . but enough! – I had a wild notion of appearing suddenly and spectrally in Yeoman's Row, with a Ho! Heave! Ho! – but there seemed to be no time, and I was exhausted.

It was a pleasure to get your letter, which you may be glad to hear I perused in the privacy of my four-poster – and no further attack has been allowed upon its chastity. Write to me again, please, with further details upon every subject – discreet and indiscreet, Surely there must be a great deal of London gossip – or is it all sacrosanct? I feel strangely cut off from humanity, with Philip for ever at my elbow, and nothing before me but the prospect of an endless succession of indistinguishable week-ends. Oh! By-the-bye, the usual Asquith party turned up on Sunday. – Elizabeth this time – you can't think what a scrubby little kitchen-maid she looked, accompanied by Viola Tree, and a few of the choice gems of Society. Mon Dieu! Why aren't they at the bottom of the sea with Kitchener?

[. . .]

Forgive this scratch, which I realise is no fit reply for a single one of your PUGS – mais que veux-tu? I hope Rimbaud may make up for my exiguity.

your Grandfather in God –
Lytton

1. David Garnett, *Carrington*, p. 26.

‡

To Carrington

'Lulu' was the Rt Hon. Lewis Harcourt, whom Carrington called the 'arch-bugger'. She had had supper with him at Brett's studio, and said he had 'a night-mare of a face'. Carrington's 'Alaric' was the son of the Belgian Baron de Forest. She was teaching the boy to paint. The affectionate 'little boys' were Julian and Quentin Bell.

Wissett Lodge
Halesworth
Suffolk
June 16th 1916

Ma chère Bébé,

It was good of you to write, and I was very glad to hear that Bateau Ivre
had infected you. As you can see, and as you will already have heard
from her Ladyship, I am here, far far from Rimbaud and all such
orange-bound volumes, so that more translations are impossible for the
present. Some day, perhaps . . . Also you see that Newbury and Combe
are even more out of the question for me than you'd supposed, and
while you are racing over the Berkshire Downs, I shall be squatting
among these laurel bushes and rambler roses, chatting, probably, with
Norton, about the nature of Infinity or dreaming of the plot of Novel
no. 6. It has been horribly and incredibly cold, and yesterday I thought
several times that my last hour had come, but today the sun has reappeared so that it's possible, with more or less conviction, to sit out in
the garden. In spite of a certain sordidness in the surroundings (about as
much below par as Garsington is above) I find that I'm enjoying myself,
as I like the company, which is at present simply Vanessa, Duncan, and
Bunny. By the bye, why shouldn't you come down here for the week-
end after next? There'ld be plenty of room, and it would give me a
good excuse for staying on here, instead of going back to a rather
funeste party at Garsington. I should like to hear how you found those
Downs – also further details as to Lulu – also various other things.
    [. . .]
    Oh God in Heaven! Have you read 'David Blaize' by E. F. Benson?
It's what goes by the name of a 'school novel' – oh Christ! Christ! The
putrescence of it! I recommend it to you, as a vision into the abysses of
the English soul. It's symptomatic, too, I think, really, in a curious way
– of what, you'll see when you read it. It's queer how morality is
breaking up in every direction, while poor fellows like E. F. Benson are
trying their best to film it over with a nice smooth surface and explain
with uneasy smiles that it's really all quite solid and correct. If only your
Alaric were a year or two older you might make him read it with
advantage – for it's an undermining book – and the Baron couldn't have
any objection.
    Yes, I was very much taken by that Wittering country – very much

indeed. It's so unusual; and then I loved the distances – the Downs far off, and then, occasionally, the Cathedral pushing up across the flat country in between. The party sounded distressing, though I couldn't help being attracted by the male Jewett when I met him; but Jack Hutchinson is certainly not a pleasant object to contemplate. Either outside or in. Some day I'm convinced he'll go pop – and the mess will be horrid.

Please tell me – is it true that you and Brett are going to take up your residence at the Garsington pub for the month of July? I gathered it was projected, and I should like to know whether it's really likely, because my future is extremely vague, and if there was reason to think that that was to happen, it would be a considerable weight in the scale in favour of my returning to that Haunt about then. Let me know, do.

I would translate the whole of French literature for you, and give you lectures on the whole of English – Latin, Greek, Portuguese, and Low Dutch to follow. Without your support I doubt whether I should be able to face the place any more: the last few days there, with Philip back from Parliament, were pretty acute. I constantly longed to stab him, after he'd raced through that Beethoven Op. 111, coming in and saying, 'It's a thing by Beethoven. I don't like it.' Oh blood! –

The two little boys are here, and tend to cover one with hugs every five minutes, which is trying; but no doubt you would join them. Only just wait till *you're* 65 with a red beard.

ever your
Grand-père

‡

To Vanessa Bell

Lytton's question is about the appeal to Lord Salisbury's Central Tribunal. It was not until September that Duncan and Bunny learned that though the Central Tribunal had confirmed their right to non-combatant service, the Pelham Committee had refused to approve their work at Wissett, and they could no longer remain self-employed.

Mary Agnes Hamilton, née Adamson (1882–1966), had been at Newnham College, Cambridge, from 1901 to 1904. She was a writer and a socialist and would be one of the founders of the 1917 Club. Fredegond Maitland (1889– 1949) had also been up at Newnham, from 1910 to 1913. She was the daughter

*of Vanessa's cousin Florence Fisher and the historian (and Apostle) F. W.
Maitland, whose biography she wrote. In 1915 she married the economist Gerald
Shove, an Apostle and Fellow of King's College, Cambridge, now a CO
working as a farm labourer for Philip Morrell. Geoffrey Nelson (c. 1896–1941)
was a painter whom Virginia Woolf in her diary for 23 June 1919 called 'one of
the insignificant . . . who has attached himself firmly to the comforts of
Garsington'. Lytton had fancied him a few years earlier.*

   *Little Tich (Harry Relph, 1867–1928) was a tiny, four-foot six-inch music-
hall entertainer, whose career lasted forty years. He had six digits on each hand,
did a number called 'Big Boots', for which he wore boots thirty inches long, and
appeared in pantomime as Humpty Dumpty and Hop o' My Thumb. His stage
name was an ironic play on the Tichborne Claimant, who was a man of
enormous size.*

67, Belsize Park Gardens[1]
Hampstead N.W.
July 1st 1916

Dearest Nessa

I wonder if you have yet heard anything definite from that tribunal.
Philip seemed quite confident that all was well; but his vagueness as to
the actual decision drove me mad with fury; it never seemed to have
occurred to him to ask the man what it was . . . I longed to stick him in
the ribs. Do send me a postcard if you ever do hear.

   London is as absorbing as ever – like a sticky spider's web. My wings
are caught, and I flutter and flutter in vain. I have seen Clive, her
Ladyship, Mrs. Hamilton, Noel, Barbara, Fredegond, Carrington,
Gertler. But I've not yet succeeded in getting hold of Maynard, Oliver,
Saxon, Mary or Nelson. Luckily the sun occasionally shines, so that
with the added strength sucked in during those days at Wissett I walk
the streets in proud magnificence.

   Next week I propose to return to Garsington, where Brett will
already be installed – Carrington to follow. How long it'll last God
knows. I can't help sniffing squalls – but perhaps I'm visionary.

   I enjoyed Wissett enormously, and should like to live there forever.
May I, May I come again? Perhaps during the fruit-picking season? But
then, should I count as a female, or a male, or – ?

   The journey back with Norton was of a chastity – . He took care to
select a carriage with a boy in it who was so nauseatingly ugly that the

sight of him decided me on the spot never ever again to – hum! hum! –
until I saw, for a second, disappearing down the platform, a sailor with a
lock of hair bobbing on his forehead, and an incredible neck. But the
train rushed on, and we continued our conversation on prime numbers.

Today I'm doomed to go to tea with Gertler and choose a drawing,
which I've paid for but not yet got. I'm sure I shall hate everything he
shows me, and shan't know how to hide my despair. And then his
picture – I shall have to look at that, I expect, and make some comment
or other: and really what can one say, even if one likes a picture? But if
one dislikes it –

I went the other evening to view Little Tich, who is, I think the
most cheering feature in English life. There's ART, if you like! By-the-
bye, have you read Candide?

your
Lytton

[. . .]

1. Written on engraved writing paper left over from the earlier address.

✝

To Lady Ottoline Morrell

*Lytton had sent Gertler the considerable sum of £10 (more than £360 in
today's money) to buy a drawing, and went to the artist's studio in nearby
Rudall Crescent to choose it. There he saw for the first time Gertler's
masterpiece, the savagely ironic, anti-War* Merry-Go-Round. *Sir Roger
Casement (1864–1916), born in Ireland, had been a British consular official in
the Belgian Congo and the Peruvian plantations along the coast of the
Putumayo River, where he denounced atrocities committed upon natives involved
in the rubber trade. He was knighted in 1911 but degraded in 1916 when he was
charged with high treason. Arrested on landing in Ireland from a German
submarine, it was known that he'd returned in order to head the Sinn Fein
rebellion. He was convicted and hanged. Lytton evidently had not heard the
rumours of the 'Black Diaries', which were circulated, probably by Government
agencies, and recounted Casement's homosexual encounters. Many thought
they'd been forged to discredit Casement, but since their first full publication in
1960, most historians incline to believing them to be authentic.*

6, Belsize Park Gardens
July 3rd 1916

Dearest Lady

[. . .] Gertler! – I went to that little fellow's studio to choose a drawing, and he showed me his latest whirligig picture. Oh lord, oh lord, have mercy upon us! It is a devastating affair, isn't it? I felt that if I were to look at it for any length of time I should be carried away, suffering from shell-shock. I admired it, of course; but as for *liking* it – one might as well think of liking a machine-gun. But fortunately he does all that for himself – one needn't bother with one's appreciation. He said it reminded him of Bach. Well, well! These jewboys!

[. . .]

Casement I don't take much stock of, somehow or other, though I perceive the romantic bravery of the man. Yes, I do perceive it; but the absence of Wisdom refrigerates me – and something sentimental and cheap in his phraseology too. I could have imagined some much grander speech. Of course, I should be very glad if they didn't hang him; but I can't believe there's much chance of that – especially with Asquith Prime Minister. That odd buffer has certainly *not* been distinguishing himself lately. Is he a coward? Or a fraud? Or simply a dunderhead? I wonder.

[. . .]

‡

To Mary Hutchinson

Miles Malleson (1888–1969) and his wife, Lady Constance (1895–75), were actors. She had a passionate affair with Bertrand Russell. Eva Gore-Booth (1870–1926) was a social reformer and sister of Countess Markievicz (1868–1927), Irish revolutionary and first woman elected to Parliament – though as a member of Sinn Fein she never took her seat. Henry Nevinson (1856–1941) was a radical journalist and father of Christopher Nevinson, who was at the Slade with Gertler. Dorothy Brett's deafness might have accounted for her hiding herself away. But she also disliked Lytton. Evan Morgan (1899–1949), later Viscount Tredegar, was then an undergraduate at Christ Church.

Garsington Manor
Oxford
July 10th 1916

Dear Mary

[. . .]

Here I am – quite established and contented – in almost absolute
solitude. The week-end just over – the Mallesons, Clifford Allen, Eva
Gore-Booth, Nevinson, etc. So damned political and revolutionary that
I got quite sick of the name of the conscientious objector and the
thought of Ireland's wrongs. However, I had some amusing tête-à-têtes
with Lady C Malleson, who assured me that she set Life above Art, and
Eva G-B, who confessed to a belief in the transmigration of souls.

Brett is here – but very much en cachette. And now that the party's
over, I lie alone on a chair in the garden, gazing with Eternity. The
great excitement is that . . . who do you think? . . . is expected one of
these days? Who, oh who, but – Evan Morgan! Yes, positively! My
heart goes pit-a-pat, as you might imagine. *[. . .]*

The Catholic

I love the evening, and I love the noon;
I love the sunlight, and I love the moon;
I love the desert, and I love a throng;
I love a silence, and I love a song;
I love clear heavens, and a cloudy shower;
I love the green leaf, and the purple flower;
I love the sliding sand, and the firm rock;
I love a cunt, and oh! I love a cock.

‡

To Virginia Woolf

*Virginia was active in the Women's Co-operative Guild, the women's branch of
the Co-Operative Society. It organized working-class women into regional
branches – Virginia more or less ran the Richmond Branch, which attracted about
a dozen women to talks given by her friends, such as the poet Robert Trevelyan,*

E. M. Forster, Ray Strachey and her brother Adrian Stephen. Though the
Guild followed Owenite principles of consumer control and cooperation, Virginia
saw it more as a feminist movement. 'The dialogue' is 'Sennacherib and Rupert
Brooke', one of Lytton's highly polished Dialogues of the Dead.[1] Lytton refers
to Garsington as the House of Mystery in letters to other correspondents. The
witch Alcina changed her guests into beasts, stones or trees. 'Katherine
Mansfield' was the pseudonym of Kathleen Mansfield Beauchamp (1888–1923).
Virginia soon became jealous of her, and had far harsher things to say about the
New Zealand writer, describing her work as 'shallow' and 'hard'. She was one
of the founders of Signature, along with her future husband John Middleton
Murry and D. H. Lawrence. She and Murry had also spent a few weeks the
previous year living in Zennor, Cornwall, too close for comfort to Lawrence and
Frieda, whom some of the neighbours suspected of being a German spy. Despite
Lytton's description of her appearance, Michael Holroyd thinks she was one of
the few women to whom he was attracted.

Garsington Manor
Oxford
July 17th 1916

Dearest Virginia

I emerge from my wickedness once more, and long to know what is
happening to you. Are you well and at work? I heard a rumour the other
day of your appearance at a Co-Op. Congress, so I suppose you're the
former; as for the latter, your well known industry no doubt continues to
carry you along. But let me know about these matters and all others.

I finished (some months ago) that little dialogue, but thought it not
pompous enough to send you by post in a large envelope, so it lingers
in the discreet oblivion of my chest of drawers. Perhaps someday I
might come and read you the rest of it at Asheham. Are you going there
this summer? It would be delightful to tread those downs once more. So
ask me, if you can. I leave this House of Mystery or Palais d'Alcine at
the end of the week for Ray and Oliver who are now established in
Roger's house at Guildford. Perhaps I shall get a little Quiet there –
God knows I need it after the incredible Hurricane of this ménage.
There were 18 souls here for the week-end that's just over: from Friday
onwards the door seemed to open every two hours and new arrivals
appeared in batches of five or seven. I at last lost count and consciousness,
going into a cosmic trance, from which I was only awakened by the

frenzied strains of the pianola playing desperate rag-time, to which thirty
feet were executing a frantic concatenation of thuds.

Among the rout was 'Katherine Mansfield' – if that's her real name –
I could never quite make sure. Have you heard of her? Or read any of
her productions? She wrote some rather – in fact distinctly – storyettes
in a wretched little thing called the Signature, which you may have
seen, under the name of Matilda Berry. She was decidedly an interesting
creature, I thought – very amusing and sufficiently mysterious. She
spoke with great enthusiasm about The Voyage Out, and said she
wanted to make your acquaintance more than anyone else's. So I said I
thought it might be managed. Was I rash? I really believe you'd find her
entertaining. But just now she's in the recesses of Cornwall, so it must
be later on, if at all. I may add that she has an ugly impassive mask of a
face – cut in wood, with brown hair and brown eyes very far apart; and
a sharp and slightly vulgarly-fanciful intellect sitting behind it.

How is Leonard? Give him my love, and ask him if he remembers
the name of that Inn in the Quantocks where you stayed once – or
perhaps you do – and if either of you do, could it be sent me on a
postcard – as I had a notion of trying to drift there in September?

The week-end is over – true enough – but . . . the party still goes on.
Carrington and Brett are here (ever heard of *them*?) and now, a few
minutes ago, Gertler (ever heard of *him*?) turned up. The rag-time has
begun again. I have fled into the garden – but one might as well try to
fly from the Eye of the Lord. So if you find this letter syncopated, you'll
know the reason.

ever your
Lytton

1. In Paul Levy (ed.), *Lytton Strachey: The Really Interesting Question*, pp. 40ff.

✝

To Mary Hutchinson

*Lytton's brother Oliver and his wife Ray had rented Durbins from Roger Fry,
and Lady Strachey lived there for a total of eighteen months. 'Pumpship' is a
Strachey family scatological euphemism. In his imaginative pairing with Shelley,
Lytton means Carl Maria von Weber (1786–1826), the founder of German
romantic opera and forerunner of Wagner.*

Durbins, Guildford
July 23rd 1916

[. . .] the days whirled on and on, and the mass of material to tell you
about grew and grew to more and more preposterous heights, until at
last . . . well. I am here, in this suburban haven, on the same sofa with
Pippa, and Ray (very fat) on the chair opposite me, and Oliver at the
piano playing Bach *[. . .]*

I wish I could tell you *all* about the Garsington whirlpool, but who
can paint the tempest, or number the flowers of the forest, or render
account of the bushes thereof? My memory dips into the witch's
cauldron, and picks out a few choice tit-bits – e.g. Katherine Mansfield
– an odd satirical woman behind a regular mask of a face – but probably
you know her. She was very difficult to get at; one felt it would take
years of patient burrowing, but that it might be worth while. Then
there was Evan – considerably different from my imaginations. I had
envisioned a pale, slightly mysterious and small creature; and there
appeared a tall bright-coloured youth with a paroqueet nose, and an
assured manner, and the general appearance of a refined old woman of
high birth. I had also supposed a certain experience and some internal
cynicism – but nothing of the sort! He was a child of 17, writing
pumpship 'poetry', supposing himself the reincarnation of Shelley
and Weber, and falling in love with women for the ideal beauty of
their souls. It would have passed if he had been 17, but he's 23, and
not quite all there – no, I fear not. A pathetic creature, too – but there
seemed queer possibilities. There was a conversation with Bunny . . .
hum!

As for Carrington, it's all rather gloomy and complicated in that
region; but complicated only in a dull way. The poor thing seems
almost aux abois *[at bay]* with Gertler forever at her, day in, day out –
she talks of flying London, of burying herself in Cornwall, or becoming
a cinema actress. I of course suggested that she should live with me,
which she luckily immediately refused – for one thing I couldn't have
afforded it. And there she is for the present at Garsington, with Mark
gnashing his teeth in the background, and Brett quite ineffectual, and
her Ladyship worming and worming forever and ever, amen. The worst
of it is that she seems in some odd way to like and admire Mark, though
his behaviour to her (apart from the prick question) is disgusting. I
suppose he's a coarse taste that may grow on me – a kind of cheap gin –
but really fatal in large quantities. She's half hypnotised, and besides she's

a coward at heart. The poor little Jew *is* nice, too, and terribly pathetic
– but oh! Mon dieu! I prefer hock and soda as a daily drink.

Ott's condition has been becoming steadily more apoplectic – her
brain is for ever on the boil, and the results are not fortunate. Her
parting shows an inch of grey on each side (poor Evan could *not*
understand it), and her face is almost perpetually covered by peeling
flakes of white chalk. I doubt if she's long for this world. Her voice has
taken on a new register – the shrill wail of an aged dowager; and her
time is divided between writing letters to everyone she knows begging
them to get off Casement, declaring at every meal that the conscientious
objectors are being monstrously treated, counting the number of pieces
of macaroni eaten by Pipsey, and calculating the exact degree by which
Mark's finger-nails are dirtier than they were the day before, and the
day before that.

Of course my dream of doing work in that haunt *was* a mere dream; I
can only hope I may manage a little in this calmer retreat. Nick and
Barbara have come and gone, very sweet, both of them. They have
begged me to go and stay with them in Wales, and I fancy I shall –
though really I sometimes begin to wonder what the diable I am doing
in this galère of grandchildren. Eh bien! Eh bien! Heaven will make all
things plain in the end.

The weather is too frightful. I hover over a fire, but it is in vain. I
have caught a chill in every single one of my organs, external and
internal. Quelle misère!

Let me have a word from you.

Roger has just entered the house.

Work? . . .

Your

Lytton

‡

To Virginia Woolf

*The original of this letter is water-damaged, and a transcription in James
Strachey's hand is appended. But the words supplied in square brackets are
clearly omitted from the original – Lytton was in a hurry. Virginia had invited
Lytton to come to Asheham from the 15th to the 21st of August, adding a strong
inducement: 'Moore will be there then I think. Please bring the dialogues and*

any other pieces lately composed, and we will set you to read aloud after dinner.'
The inn Lytton had asked about was the Plough Inn, Holford. Virginia had
asked obliquely whether Lytton had found a cottage in the neighbourhood of a
woman '– what shall we call her? – but you know who I mean –' whom she
reported Duncan Grant to have described as 'raddled and putrid'. It was
Ottoline. Leonard's book was International Government. *It was published*
this month in the Webbs' New Statesman *magazine, and made his reputation*
as a political thinker. It had some influence on the formation of the League of
Nations. Virginia thought they had found 'the secret of life' at Wissett Lodge in
Suffolk, where Duncan and David Garnett had set up as fruit farmers, exempt
from conscription. Harry Norton was also a guest there with Lytton.

Savile Club
107, Piccadilly, W.
July 28th 1916

This is just to say that I'm afraid I shan't be able to come to Asheham in
August, as I have engaged myself to go *[to]* Wales then, with a small
juvenile party. I shall be at large in September, and will try to wend my
way towards Cornwall, and find you there – also K. Mansfield.

Many thanks for the Inn name. I might go *there* too.

No time for more. I am just up for a couple *[of]* nights, for Mozart
and Bach operas – very nice, but damned hot. Tomorrow I go to
Wittering.

Your
Lytton

No. I have not, and shall not (unless fate is completely against me) get
a cottage in the neighbourhood of the lady to whom you refer so
delicately. I see now that it would NOT DO. But I must find
somewhere else, or I shall be ruined.

How does one get Leonard's book, I wonder? My only bookseller
has mysteriously vanished – and I don't know its name.

Is the secret of life or of . . . something else . . . I don't quite know
what? . . . Oblivion? Stupor? Incurable looseness? – that they've
discovered at Wissett? I loved it, and never wanted to go away.

Give my love to Moore, if he goes to Asheham – It's sad that I can't
come too.

✝

To Carrington

Nick Bagenal was about to return to the Front, and Barbara invited Lytton as a chaperon on the fortnight's holiday they were to spend at her father's cottage near Llandudno in North Wales; he asked if he could bring Carrington. 'Nelson' was the twenty-one-year-old painter Geoffrey Nelson. At this time Carrington sometimes addressed her letters to Lytton 'cher Grandpapa'. Shandygaff Hall was their Laurence Sterne-ish joke about Garsington. 'The Jew', Mark Gertler, was madly in love with Carrington and bent on getting her to give up her virginity.

Savile Club
107, Piccadilly, W.
July 28th 1916

I hope you will have seen Barbara, and heard from her about Wales. Do you think you could come? It sounds as if it might be pleasant. From about Aug. 12th, I gather, for a fortnight or so. Rather a long way off, but does that signify?

I went this afternoon to your studio in the dim hope that you might have been there. Very distracted and hot. I came up for one night yesterday, and have been induced to stay another, merely to hear Bach. Fatal! fatal! Especially as I shall get no *fun* out of it – oh no! – not even Nelson.

In case you don't see Barbara, I'd better add that the place is a cottage belonging to her people in the region of Llandudno, and that the company will be she, Nick, and your grandpapa. Will you write and let me know what you think of it? Address – Durbins, Guildford, Surrey.

It seems to me so appallingly hot that a walking expedition would hardly be suitable. I think I should crumple away into tissue paper. What do you fancy? Perhaps we might walk back to England through Wales? It would then be September.

Tomorrow I go to Wittering for the week-end, then back again to Guildford, which is most reposeful. Really – to arrive there after Garsington! It was like plunging into a cool lake, far down. And on the first morning I ate three eggs (and their accompanying bacon) for breakfast. Quelle joie!

At Guildford I have positively been doing some work. What is

happening to *you*? Have you abandoned Shandygaff Hall yet? And the
Jew? I had from Maynard a dreadful account of his week-end, but he
said he thoroughly enjoyed it. That man enjoys everything. I wonder
why.

Write, write, write, for Jesu's sake! You must come to Wales. Your
utterly dissolved missionary. *[The 'y' trails off into a crude phallic
drawing.]*

‡

To Carrington

*Carrington had been staying with the Morrells at Garsington, where Ottoline
had done everything she could to assist Gertler 'to get my state of virginity
reduced'.[1] On July 30 she wrote: 'this attack on the virgins is like the worst
Verdun on-slaughter'. Carrington had referred to 'Rimbaud's "librarians"'.
David Garnett wonders whether she meant 'Illuminations', though he says
'librarians' is clear in the Ms. In the same letter of 30 July Carrington starts
another hare when she says: 'I read John Donne all day now. A lovely poem
about Fair ships in harbours.' Carrington's letter contains a jumble of French
and English: 'Il y en a qui m'enseignent à vivre – et d'autres qui m'enseignent à
mourir – Maintes and maintes fois I look at the hills.' She ends by saying that
she heard the nightingale sing last night. Barrister Montague (Monty) Shearman
was a loyal friend and collector of Gertler's. His collection was exhibited at the
Redfern Gallery in 1940. In her letter Carrington said she and Ottoline had
talked for an hour and a half 'in the asperagrass bed'. Ottoline had suggested
Carrington 'practically share a bedroom with' Harry Norton – more
matchmaking. In her letter Carrington playfully accuses Lytton: 'So you
betrayed me to Maynard! But he is much more truthful than you only rather
cryptic.'*

*In her life of Lady Ottoline, Miranda Seymour says that Carrington penned
'a spoof announcement of the forthcoming Garsington Chronicle, written in
a very passable imitation of Ottoline's most flowery style'.[2] In her letter of
30 July, Carrington writes as though the Garsington Chronicle is the work of
Ottoline who 'has already written a personal review of her visitors. But so dull.
Because she said nothing of them she has not told us all before.' Lytton is
responding to Carrington's question whether he will 'write outrageous verse' for
it. Lytton must have been taken in, for in her 5 August letter Carrington says:
'Of course I can hardly agree with you about the Garsington chronicle as I
invented the idea!' Garsington that summer was crowded with Ottoline's guests,*

*and also Conscientious Objectors, including Gerald Shove and Clive Bell, who
more or less pretended to do farm work.*

Durbins
August 1st 1916

[. . .]

What Devils they all are, with their proddings and preachings and
virginity-gibberings. Won't you write a poem on them in the style of
the Librarians? Have you looked at Donne's Satires? They're rather in
that style. I hope you like his poems. The ship and harbour one I don't
remember: and there isn't a copy of him in this damned house.

Did I tell you how divine the Seraglio was? I wished you had been
there. I believe it is to be done again – on Saturday perhaps – so do try
to get to it. *That* enseigners one à vivre, if you like! By the bye, how
idiomatic your French is becoming!

I am still sun-and-sea-drugged after Wittering. The salt has got into
my beard, too, and the result is that I can only write incoherences. It's a
pity, as I should like to discourse in long paragraphs upon many subjects
– viz. Dr Donne, Virginity, Jesus, the Relation between Life and Music,
Nightingales, the Character of Mr. Shearman, the influence of
Asparagus (Aspara*grass*? Hmm! Hmm! Brom . . .) on Truth, Norton, the
Comparative Advantages and Disadvantages of constipation – but my
mind refuses to fix upon these matters – its grip slackens . . . so sad! . . .
I swim in a trance.

But of one thing be assured, we should all be quite désolé if you
didn't arrive in the mountains *[of Wales]*. *They* obviously wanted you to
come very much; and as for me, I hardly feel as if I could bear it if you
didn't. So make up your mind to it, please Mademoiselle, and no
recoilings.

Less truthful than Maynard? How can that be? Betrayal? No, No, I
don't believe it.

Wed. morning *[2 August]*. The 'Garsington Chronicle' has come, in
green ink. Oliver was nearly sick when I showed it to him at breakfast.
Can't you contrive to stamp it out? Oh dear – after all these years! To
be so very far from the correct ton! A 'thread of eternity' – mon dieu!
The gaiety and gravity of varied lives that cross and intertwine . . . most
distressing! No, I will *not* stretch forth my skill and coloured fantasy.
No, *no*. Mais que dire, que faire? I beg you to waft it all into oblivion.

I am sitting on the lawn in front of the house, by a small square pool full of water-lilies, with the garden terracing down in front of me, and through the gaiety and gravity of varied hollyhocks that cross and intertwine I view the hills of Surrey stretching forth their coloured fantasy . . . so far it's not too hot, which is a wonder. In a minute I shall have to set to work, damn it.

Don't be too triste, ma chère bébé. Read Dr Donne (I recommend 'The Perfume'), go to Wittering, with the Seraglio en route, and float in the sea, and wash off the shady shindies of Shandygaffhall. Also, write to me again, je t'implore.

On the other side is a little poem . . . *not* for the Garsington Chronicle.

Your
Lytton

Perverse

God sends him all that earth can yield
    In richest flowers to lure his soul;
But he a daisy from the field
    Wears in his button-hole.

God sends him luscious fruits and rare
    To tempt his palate's subtlest edge;
But he rejoices in the fare
    Of the berry from the hedge.

God sends him purple wine to drink,
    And silken softness from his dress;
But he stoops to the fountain's brink
    In ragged nakedness.

God sends him ladies fair, with charms
    Brilliant and strange for his sole joy;
But he lies nightly with his arms
    About the blacksmith's boy.

1. Michael Holroyd, *Lytton Strachey*, p. 372.
2. Miranda Seymour, *Ottoline Morrell*, pp. 262–3.

‡

To Mary Hutchinson

Lytton's sister-in-law Ray, née Costelloe, was pregnant with her and Oliver's only son, Christopher. Some of the pictures in Roger Fry's collection that Monty Shearman 'gazed at' when he lunched at Durbins can be seen today in the Courtauld Gallery at Somerset House.

Durbins
August 3rd 1916

Are you still sitting in your chairs by the shed? Do you still eat in the garden, potter to the beach of an evening, and flirt (or refrain from flirting) with the sea-scouts? No doubt, no doubt. How I weep to think I am not also engaged in those occupations! It was a most heavenly interlude, ma chère, and I wish it could have lasted for seven years. I console myself as best I may with my grosse belle-soeur, the hollyhocks (thousands of them blaze in this arid garden), and Dr Arnold. The latter, I am glad to say, proceeds. Quiet, comfort, industry . . . what more could one desire? Ah! a chair by the shed!

The journey back with Mr Shearman went off fairly satisfactorily. There was hardly a word spoken, and I was able to admire the view at my ease. He gazed at the pictures with his mouth open, and went on again directly after lunch. He seems to me a most curious character, all in monochrome. So 'nice' – oh yes; and so singularly unattractive. Also, when I'm with him, I find myself perpetually wondering why he exists.

I have heard from Carrington, among other things, that she is going to you on Saturday. She seems delighted at that solution of her movements. Also, I gather that my inferences about the Mark affair were incorrect – at any rate premature; which is rather a relief. The poor creature was positively attacked by *Philip*, who led her round the pond, lectured her on the evils of virginity, and then blew her up for not lying with the Jew forthwith. Ottoline then carried her off to the asparagus bed, where she continued the attack. It all sounds most sordid, but (unless she's a horrible liar) nothing came of it. But how can any self-respecting person stay in that house?

For goodness' sake don't breathe a word to Carrington that I have revealed *anything* to you. I should be utterly ruined. And do tell Clive to be careful. As it is, she rather suspects me of having a loose tongue – which of course is not at all the case.

The only other news that occurs to me is that cette fée de province is starting what she calls 'The Garsington Chronicle' – have you had a prospectus in green ink? The whole thing is extremely lowering, and really must be stopped at all costs. I beg Clive to throw icy water on it. The prospectus (which I'll send you, if you haven't got it already) is literally à faire vomir. When I showed it to Oliver at breakfast, he very nearly brought up his bacon and eggs.

James and Noel, I hear, have gone today to Bosham; so I daresay you'll see them. Give my love to the whole $\left\{\begin{array}{c}\text{sisterhood} \\ \text{fraternity}\end{array}\right\}$ – and to the chairs by the shed.

Your
Lytton

‡

To Carrington

The holiday in North Wales was finally happening, and Lytton was pretending to be better off than he was, so that Carrington would not be ashamed to take money from him for the journey.

Durbins
Guildford
August 9th 1916

It was a relief to get your très-amiable letter in these somewhat cloistral (though to me also pregnant) surroundings. I laughed at several passages at breakfast, and the middle-aged visitors (Thena Clough and Logan Pearsall-Smith – do you know them?) raised their eyebrows. *[. . .]* I pray to God that we may all get there *[Llandudno Junction on Saturday afternoon]*. Also, I take the liberty of enclosing a pound note, to induce you to go by train, rather than bicycle, which I'm sure would be most uncomfortable, and which, I fear you may only propose to do because of the expense of railway tickets. Don't be angry, please. I apparently have a large balance at the bank, and it's only reasonable that you should not be ruined by having a holiday in my company. *[. . .]*

Will you bring Dr Donne? Or shall I?

I long to talk with some old lover's ghost.

✝

To Carrington

The holiday in Wales was idyllic, and Lytton and Carrington set off for Bath, Wells and Glastonbury on what Garnett called 'a little surreptitious tour together'. At Glastonbury they stayed at the George Hotel where, on 28 August, they shared a bed and Lytton finally relieved Carrington of her troublesome virginity[1]. The next day Carrington wrote to Maynard on hotel writing paper: 'Dear Maynard, We are staying here. A very Christian atmosphere prevails, which Lytton is enjoying incredibly [sic]. Also a miller's lad. I doubt if Lytton will ever return. He wanders day after day with a guidebook on architecture in his lean hand gazing at ancient ruins.' (It was at Glastonbury that Joseph of Arimathea is supposed to have founded the first Christian church in England, and where the staff he thrust into Wearyall Hill rooted and flowered every Christmas. The town is also the legendary burial place of King Arthur, and is rich in the ruins of Christian abbeys and churches.)

This fragment of a letter was found in Vanessa Bell's papers. The rest of the letter is missing, except for the opposite page, which has Carrington's drawing of a cat asleep on a cushion and above it these lines in Lytton's handwriting:

> *When I'm winding up the toy*
> *Of a pretty little boy,*
> *– Thank you, I can manage pretty well;*
> *But how to set about*
> *To make a pussy pout*
> *– That is more than I can tell.*

In a footnote Garnett says 'I suspect that Lytton sent these lines to Maynard to conceal that he was having physical relations with Carrington.'

The next day Carrington returned to her parents' house at Hurstbourne Tarrant, Lytton went back to Wells, and each of them wrote a letter to the other. Carrington's begins: 'Dear Uncle Lytton, I feel burdened with so much affection and gratitude towards you tonight' and ends: 'Il faut que vous boutonniez vos boutons des mouches (tous les) chacun nuit! (s) n'oubliez pas mon ami! [. . .] Quelque fois je voudrais être un garçon de moulin! votre niece CARRINGTON.'

Lytton was reading S. R. Gardiner's History of England. *From the reference to Carrington finding a cottage it appears that they were already thinking of living together.*

6, St Andrew's Street
Wells
Somerset
September 1st 1916

Oh! I am feeling so desolate! Lunch is over, tea is over, dinner is over, and here I am lying in my solitary state on the sofa among the white cushions – silent, nieceless, sad! And you, I suppose, in the family circle, relating, ever more and more ingeniously, the details of your visit to Bab . . . Indeed, indeed, it is all most melancholy. But it was delightful while it lasted, and I'm so very glad that we managed to bring it off. I only wish my innards had been less jolty – to say nothing of my elderly habit of mind. Oh, to be a smiling Hercules!

[. . .] All continues here in the most swimming fashion – cookery and politeness on the highest levels. The day has been very hot, and you must have been grilled at Templecombe *[railway station]*; but now the sky is clouded, so I daresay I shall spend tomorrow with Professor Gardiner over a fire.

I hope I shall hear from you ere long – and that I may learn that you have discovered a large cottage with an orchard in the depths of Berkshire, close to a station on the main line, to let for £15 a year.

Slumber falls upon me in solid sheets. This quill pen is too scratchy, eh? Eh? I yawn – but – where is your finger, my dear?

Your
Lytton

1. Michael Holroyd wrote to the editor on 24 March 2003 that he had been told this by Alix Strachey, in the presence of her husband, James, from whom he gathered that 'there were a *few* bed experiments of one sort or another . . . After a relatively short period, these were phased out. And yes, I was told (though Lytton had felt himself attracted by one or two girls – Katherine Mansfield, for example), Carrington was the only girl he actually took to bed. This was why August 1916 attracted so much gossip.' Barbara Bagenal also confirmed the story to Holroyd.

‡

To Carrington

Carrington had been worried by the bill she'd run up for artist's supplies, when her father told her she'd been left a legacy of £20 'by an aged doctor of 92 years who died at Bath'.

6, St Andrew's Street
Wells
Sunday, *[September 3 1916]*

Your letter, ma chère nièce, to hand this morning. What a shocking journey you must have had! I am appalled to think of it. But it's a relief to know that you were received at any rate not with denunciations – and then – the legacy! Really incredible! Was it that old doctor whose name we looked up in vain in the Bath directory? If we'd only known we might have gone and strewed flowers on his grave.

I've been having a pleasant and infinitely lazy time here. The lodgings continue all that could be desired – how clever of you it was to insist on exploring them! The weather, too, has been perfect – until today; and now it appears to have reverted in toto to the condition of our first evening. Floods of rain sweep horizontally through the whistling air. However, the changes are so abrupt from day to day that I feel fairly hopeful; and tomorrow I daresay I shall go and inspect Cheddar. Yesterday I visited the Museum and the Library – both frosts. In the afternoon, as I was drifting through the town I was . . . picked up! By an amiable old gent in the Y.M.C.A. line, who (so he said) had been born at Wells, and had to come to revisit the scenes of his childhood. I took a walk with him – but he was not exciting – in fact he was a horrid bore; so when I'd made sure that he would open out no interesting vistas, I politely took my leave. He said that by trade he was an 'Artist's colourman' in Birkenhead. I silently wondered whether Mr Hiles was one of his customers. I wish I could describe to you a more remarkable figure – a young man, wonderfully evil-looking and rather attractive, whom I suddenly came face to face with, as I was leaving the Museum, down a queer twisting alley that leads to it. The odd thing was that he immediately addressed me – on what seemed a very dim pretext – viz. 'Anything to pay to go in here?' But alas! that too was an utter frost. He had a 'companion' . . . not a niece, but – an uncle? – perhaps: a most disreputable looking middle-aged man; they were a decidedly shady pair. I should think members of the criminal classes; and they looked as if they belonged to some different species, among these soft angelic Somerset fellows. I saw them slouching about the streets all day. I wish I could give you a vision of them. One can imagine them blackmailing Ottoline in a novel by Balzac.

[. . .] Et moi aussi, ma chère, quelquefois je voudrais être un garçon de moulin. your UNCLE Write again

I'm so very glad that you really did enjoy the tour. It was very nice of you to come, and your company made all the difference to *my* enjoyment. I doubt if I shall get much further, bereft of your advancing spirit. The Caves of Cheddar – how shall I face them without my niece? N.B. I go to bed at *10 o'ck* now.

‡

To Lady Strachey

6, St. Andrew Street
Wells
September 3rd 1916

Dearest Mama,

[. . .] What a pity it is that it should now be the fashion for clergymen to believe in Christianity! I should have so enjoyed being Bishop of Bath and Wells!

your loving,
Lytton

‡

To Carrington

A map is omitted showing the 'line of Strachey's march' from Draycott to Cheddar, then around Beacon Batch and back along the cliffs to Cheddar. Next he visits the caves and walks in a circular fashion through a 'beautiful region' to Westbury. The journey from Wells to Cheddar, and presumably from Westbury back to Wells, was by rail. The Stracheys were a Somerset family at least since

the sixteenth century – Lytton's father, Sir Richard, was born in the county –
which accounts for the topographical feature called 'Strachey's Clump'. As the
food-obsessed Lytton never mentions Cheddar cheese, perhaps it was already then
rarely made in its original home.

6, St Andrew Street
Tuesday evening, *[September 5th 1916]*

Such a day! Positively something like summer. Not one of those half-
and-half, quasi-overcoat and belly-band days, but blue and warm and
rainless. I started off early, and have explored pretty thoroughly Cheddar
and its surroundings. Went up to the Beacon (the highest Mendip
point) – an agreeable spot on a high heathery expanse, with panoramic
views of England and Wales (Strachey's Clump visible in the distance),
then came down the road between those 'Cliffs' one's read so much
about – and really they're imposing objects – not made of rather soft
clay, as I'd imagined, but *immense* grey rocks, with greenery here and
there, shooting upwards quite precipitously almost higher than the eye
can reach. The road winds down to Cheddar for about two miles
between them. Unfortunately, as one approached Cheddar, the signs
of humanity become more and more persistent – motors, bicyclists,
schools picnicing, and finally the 'Caves' – mere horror, with a
showman bawling at the entrance, and ginger-beer bottles all about . . .
'lighted by electricity' say the vast placards . . . I shuddered and fled.
The village itself is rather grimy too; but I came back through what
seemed to be the best country of all – behind and above Cheddar – a
splendid table-land region of rolling grass, with grey rocks shining
through everywhere, and bracken and green paths – really very divine.
I returned via the well-beloved Westbury, where I discovered another
Inn – far more genuine and very pretty, in the L shape, with a lovely
stone doorway – *very* lovely and old *[illustrated by a diagram showing the*
position of the door] – but the landlady was even more discouraging and
repulsive than the other, so I got an excellent tea out of the kind post
office lady for 6d. . . . I hope all this doesn't bore you. I thought you
might like to hear these few details. I kept wishing all day that you
were there to enjoy them with me – and to make me enjoy them
more.

Wednesday morning. Finer than ever – blazing sun. But I am too exhausted to do anything but lie on a bench in the Cathedral green and read Venus and Adonis. Your

Lytton

‡

To Maynard Keynes

Barbara Hiles had found a house in Hemel Hempstead, unfurnished, 'with a loft for conscientious objectors', at a yearly rent of £48.[1] The scheme was to get Lytton's friends, such as Faith Bagenal (later Henderson), Saxon Sydney-Turner and his older brother, Oliver, to take 'share' in a house, paying an annual sum, which would entitle them to use the house for occasional weekends.

Garsington Manor
Oxford
September 14th 1916

Dear Maynard,

Have you heard of the scheme for a country cottage? Would you be willing to join? Barbara has already found something that sounds as if it might be suitable. Oliver and Faith are going to take shares – also perhaps Saxon. I don't know about Harold. Oh, Carrington, too.
    Perhaps you would get in touch with one of these if you approved.
    [. . .]
    I have had some slightly peculiar adventures in the West of England, which I might reveal to you, if you were more discreet.

yours with love
Lytton

1. Michael Holroyd, *Lytton Strachey*, p. 379.

‡

To Lady Ottoline Morrell

*To the post-Holocaust reader the anti-Semitic remark in this letter is offensive
and unforgivable, but to the pre-Hitler generation Jews were a group like the
Irish, Italians or Chinese, who were made the butt of jokes on the basis of
stereotypes. At least such reprehensible stereotyping was not made worse by the
use of derogatory names – these were not often heard on the lips of the upper
middle classes. Note that Lytton knew that his remark would not offend
Ottoline or anyone to whom she was likely to show the letter – which could well
have included many on the political left. In a conversation with the editor in late
2002, Frances Partridge pointed out that Lytton felt that his deep friendship with
Leonard Woolf and his affectionate relationship with Mark Gertler licensed him
to make remarks that he regarded as harmless – i.e. he thought he had sufficient
left-wing, liberal 'street cred' to get away with it.*

6, Belsize Park Gardens
N.W.
October 1st 1916

Dearest Lady,

[. . .] I left Wittering a long time ago – last Monday. It was divine there
– marvellous weather – everything divinely beautiful. I hated going, but
it had to be, and London I found quite horrible – stuffy and chilly at the
same time, and packed full and flowing over with inconceivably hideous
monstrosities. They push one off the pavement in their crowds, they
surge round every bus, they welter in the tube . . . one dashes madly for
a taxi – but there are no taxis left. In the night it's *pitch* dark; one walks
wedged in among multitudes like a soldier in an army – one peers in
vain for some vestige of beauty – all is blackness – but one can't help
hoping; then at last somebody strikes a match to light a cigarette – and a
seething mass of antique Jewish faces is revealed. No! London is
decidedly *not* a place to be in just now.

The Gower Street ménage has apparently begun. I had tea there with
K*[atherine]* M*[ansfield]* yesterday: she seemed pretty well settled in. I
haven't yet seen Carrington's apartments, but I gathered from a
telephone conversation that she was very much pleased with them. Our
country cottage still floats high in air . . . A cottage in Spain, I fear! *[. . .]*

‡

To Vanessa Bell

Following the departure of the last nurse in November 1915, Virginia Woolf had seemed as though she'd regained her sanity. But Leonard guarded her fiercely still, as they alternated living between Asheham and Hogarth House in Richmond. Lytton wanted to avoid any discussion of house-hunting in the vicinity of Asheham.

6, Belsize Park Gardens
October 25th 1916

Dearest Nessa

It was very charming of you to write. I quite realised from what Clive had said that you didn't object to our getting a house near you. I had feared that perhaps your well known love of seclusion was such that you viewed the prospect with alarm. However, I'm very glad to hear that you'ld actually *like* a little company sometimes, so do look out for a suitable residence – 5 or 6 bedrooms, and about £50 a year – not too far away. We have had rather bad luck, and I'm now not feeling very hopeful. There was a perfect house which James saw (on the other side of Lewes from you) empty – we wrote off to the village post office, and were told it was still empty – but alas! we have now heard from the owner that it is let. But I feel it's a great thing having you on the spot; in time something must turn up.

As for my joining your ménage, of course, of course – it was only a vague vision on my part.

I go to Richmond tonight with Carrington, and intend to talk very hard the whole time about politics, so as to avoid a discussion of Asheham. I gathered that his objection to *your* being in the neighbourhood was that Virginia would insist upon walking over to see you every Sunday – four miles there and four miles back – which would shatter her health. At least that's what he *said*: but I rather felt that there was some pollution theory in the background. Dear, dear, dear!

Shall I see you tomorrow afternoon at Berkeley Street? I hope so. I've just been lent an amazing book by Ottoline – a mortuary volume of two upper class youths killed at the front – quite marvellous! With letters of condolence from hundreds of people, and everything quite complete. Oh, they *are* a crew! God rot 'em.

your
Lytton

✝

To Lady Ottoline Morrell

The book Ottoline had sent Lytton was Pages from a Family Journal 1888– 1915 *(privately printed, Eton College, 1916), edited by Lady Desborough (Ethel 'Ettie' Grenfell), the society hostess. Lytton would later stay with her at Taplow Court, near Maidenhead, 'next door' to the Astors' Cliveden. She was so fashionable that a list of her weekend guests was printed in Monday's* Times. *Lord Desborough was the country's most celebrated all-round sportsman. Holroyd says he 'swam the Niagara pool, slaughtered a hundred stags in a single season, played cricket for Harrow, ran the three-mile for Cambridge, ascended the Matterhorn three times by alternative routes and fenced in the Olympics'. The 'elder youth' was his son Julian (his younger brother Billy was also killed in 1915, and the Grenfell brothers became emblematic of the loss of a whole generation of aristocratic young men), the subject of* Family Journal, *for he was born in 1888 and died of his war wounds on 26 May 1915, with his mother holding his hand. The letters are mostly by him. Julian achieved posthumous renown as a war poet on the strength of a single piece, the much-anthologized 'Into Battle'. The family belonged to 'the Souls', a group of (mostly) aristocrats known for their quick wit and amusing conversation. Margot Asquith said in her autobiography: 'Mr Balfour once told me that, before our particular group of friends – generally known as the Souls – appeared in London, prominent politicians of opposite parties seldom if ever met one another; and he added: "No history of our time will be complete unless the influence of the Souls upon society is dispassionately and accurately recorded." Lytton's scorn for the Souls reflects and emphasizes the fact that Bloomsbury was militantly middle-class – even a little anti-aristocratic – though it helps to put this into perspective to remember that his correspondent was the sister of a duke.*

Maria Nys (d.1955), the young Belgian who married Aldous Huxley in 1919, was a near-permanent guest at Garsington, and one of the few women who attracted Lytton sexually. The decorations of the house at 4 Berkeley Street, Mayfair, were a project of Roger Fry's Omega Workshop, founded in 1913. Siegfried Sassoon (1886–1967) was serving as second lieutenant in both the First and Second Battalions of the Royal Welch Fusiliers at this time, and had recently been awarded the Military Cross for exceptional bravery. In July he had been in the Battle of the Somme. Sent home from France in late July, he began to associate a bit with anti-war people such as Ottoline and Lytton, as personal losses he had suffered in the war were causing him to rethink his own position. He did not come out against the war until the next year, and Robert Graves's treacherous behaviour which resulted in Sassoon's returning to the war only began in July 1917. At least in his own social circle, Sassoon was openly homosexual at the time of writing. When Anrep's mosaics in Ethel Sands's hallway in Chelsea were finished (at a date later than this letter), one showed Lytton looking out of a cottage window at Carrington, who looked at him from the window of another cottage in a separate mosaic.

A proposition in favour of conscription in an Australian national referendum on 28 October 1916 was defeated, as was another, decisive one the next year.

6, Belsize Park Gardens
Hampstead, N.W.
October 31st 1916

Dearest Ottoline,

I sent the precious book back to Garsington. It made sumptuous reading. As usual, it struck me that letters were the only really satisfactory form of literature. They give one the facts so amazingly, don't they? I felt when I got to the end that I'd lived for years in that set. But oh dearie me I am glad that I'm *not* in it! I think it's their facility that degrades them – facility of expression, facility of sentiment, facility of thought – it's really fatal to be made like that – like taps to turn on and off: very convenient, but only water comes out: if you want wine you must go down to the cellar, and find a bottle in the dark, and bring it up, and pull out the cork with a corkscrew. I agree that the elder youth had an attractiveness about him – that of the savage. He seems to have done nothing all his life but kill animals (those extraordinary triumphant bits of Lady D! – 'this week Julian killed 237 rabbits, 38 stags, 406 weasels' etc. etc. really impayable *[priceless, a scream]*) – until he began to kill human beings, which, of course, he found even more enjoyable. But then that odd pretence at culture – reading Mr Wells, and criticising minor poets – how very odd.

I feel that volume has been my chief adventure. Otherwise nothing exciting has happened – only a good deal of mild visiting. The dinner with Anrep went off much better than I'd expected. Maria was there, also Dorelia, in a very amiable mood. Anrep I thought considerably ameliorated since the summer, much less flaunting, and even, I thought, less fat. He gave an amusing account of Maynard's vigorous proceedings with our Russian allies. Last night he took me to 'The Ring' – have you ever heard of it? A most astonishing spot in Blackfriars Road, on the other side of the river – consecrated to boxing. It was very interesting. I had never seen any before. Have you ever? I was quite close – almost touching their terrific naked bodies – imagine it! The whole thing seemed to me hardly to be distinguished from a gladiatorial show, and the attitude of the audience, roaring and gloating, frankly Roman. As I too have a Roman tincture in me I enjoyed it enormously; but how or why human beings choose to go through such things is most mysterious.

I can't think of what else I've been to look at – except the decorations at 4 Berkeley Street, by Roger and Co., which I found extremely depressing. They're in a very small room at the top of the house, and consist of colossal figures plastered on the walls like posters, but without the gaiety of posters. In the middle of the room stood Margot, very stiff and straight, in a very short black dress, and a white veil.

Today I have lunch with Mary Hutch at her new house, which I haven't yet seen, then to tea with Dorelia, and then to His Majesty's theatre with Sheppard and a party of young men. My existence isn't always so multicoloured, so don't envy me too much in your solitude. But are you still taking the waters? Perhaps you've returned to the bosom of Garsington. Do let me hear some details. Is your health any more robustious, do you think? And Siegfried, what has happened to *him*? I can't help suspecting that he has been living not so far from Valley Drive. I wonder if I shall ever see him. But if I do you may be sure that I shan't lose my heart to him. My heart is too tightly chained to my own fibres ever to be lost again.

I have had some rather nice visions of Virginia at Richmond, and hope this week to bring her and Katherine together – though what the result of that will be, heaven knows!

Otherwise I'm still working (at General Gordon), and floating, and speculating, and cursing. Oh! Ethel Sands, poor woman, I had tea with on Sunday. Very precious she was, and we agreed that the old were to be envied (the inference being, of course, that we were *both*, *almost*, if not quite, in the first flush of youth!) Anrep's mosaic is in the hall, and seemed to me very attractive, so far as I could see it.

I saw Philip's address to those Burnley people in the Manchester Guardian, and liked it very much indeed. Unfortunately, they left out bits of it – is there any way of getting it in full? I should very much like to have a complete copy. What good news it is about Australian Conscription! Really the first piece of good news there's been since the war. I believe things are just beginning to turn, don't you? Even people like my brother-in-law, a typical solid member of the upper middle classes, began to talk to me of his own accord about Peace the other day. But it will still take a horrid long time.

Well, I must be off. The great pleasure is the weather – so bright and revivifying that one can still hardly believe that winter with all its horrors is en route. I hope Harrogate has been as blue-skied as London.

your affectionate
Lytton

‡

To Lady Ottoline Morrell

6, Belsize Park Gardens
Hampstead, N.W.
November 21st 1916

Dearest Ottoline

[. . .]

Yes, I'll come
With beat of drum
And shouts of glee
Most joyfullest
With heart unvexed
And unperplexed
(But not unsexed)
On Saturday next.

[. . .]

Then it will be
A joy to see
Sitting at tea
P and thee,
And that sly Junipie,
Et la très-belle
Madamoiselle,
Also Clive
Quite alive,
And I've no doubt
That short and stout
Young gent who's enthralled us
Under the name of Aldous.

– to say nothing of Mr Massingham, who doesn't seem to rhyme with anything.

I've just returned from Cambridge, where I was almost frozen to death. I feel that the only tolerable fate in this world is that of a leg of mutton twisting in front of a kitchen fire.

So, hostess dear, I beg, unless you hate us,
Turn on, turn on, the heating apparatus.

Your
Lytton

‡

To James Strachey

Lloyd George had been running the War Office since 12 June. He had bigger plans, though. He and the Unionist leader Bonar Law planned to unseat Asquith. They forced the PM's hand with a plan for a small committee to run the war under the chairmanship of Lloyd George, and when Asquith rejected it and resigned on 5 December, so did Lloyd George. Bonar Law was asked to form a government, but declined, as Asquith refused to serve under him; the next day Lloyd George was appointed PM. Massingham's gossip about Lord Haldane and the anti-Lloyd George 'ex-Butler' seems likely to have had as its butt General William Robertson, the private soldier who rose to become the CIGS when Richard Burdon Haldane (1856–1928) was still in the Cabinet. Haldane was Minister of War from late 1905 until June 1912, when Asquith made him Lord Chancellor. He was hounded out of the government in May 1915, by a vicious campaign in which the Northcliffe newspapers falsely accused him of being pro-German. 'Ex-Butler' is probably a private joke between Lytton and James, who more than once mocked Robertson, despite sharing his dislike of Lloyd George.

Keynes was right about 'Doc W.' – President Wilson, who had been re-elected less than three weeks earlier, finally persuaded Congress and declared war on Germany only on 6 April 1917.

Lytton is comparing the Dioscuri, the brothers Castor and Pollux, who were the sons of Zeus and Leda, to Julian (b. 1888) and Billy (b. 1890) Grenfell. Both boys died in 1915 in the Ypres offensive. Julian's poem, 'Into Battle', was published in The Times *on the day his death was announced.*

Bertrand Russell's lectures mentioned here were published as Principles of Social Reconstruction.

The South Wales Borderers Territorial Army 1st Brecknockshire Battalion was formed in Brecon in September 1914. In late 1915 it was attached to 68th (2nd Welsh) Division and in November 1916, absorbed by 2/7th Royal Welch Fusiliers.

A guess at what Philip Morrell found tendentious about reprinting the piece from the New York Times: *at the time President Wilson's policy was 'peace without victory', while at the same time he favoured US participation in the war. The* Times*'s editorial policy would have dictated reprinting a piece only if it was favourable to the war effort.*

The Manor House
Garsington
Oxford
November 27th 1916

I shall return on Wednesday. It is very fine and fresh here, but damned cold. So far most of my diseases have increased, but I hope this is only the result of the first plunge, and that the reaction will shortly set in.

The Massing Bird and Maynard have been the chief figurants for the week-end. The former keeps up his usual *tout est perdu* strain, which is on the whole rather comforting. He says that the wheat supply will probably break down, that nobody in high quarters knows in the least what to do in any circumstances, and that the army is on the point of mutiny. He made a long speech (to Maynard and me in the cab from the station) on the condition of the barracks – filth, vermin, bullying, murders of sergeants, venereal disease rampant, and 'finally – sodomy'.

He seems decidedly perturbed. His only satisfaction is that L.G. is as much loathed by the War Office as by all other persons he's come in contact with. The ex-Butler had dinner with Haldane the other day, and spent the whole time in a tirade of complaints. He wound up with 'there's only one word for it, Lord 'Aldane, it's bloody piss'.

Maynard, of course, preserves his official optimism. He thinks the war will end before long – that is to say before next October. He also thinks that we shall manage the wheat supply, though he admits that sugar has altogether gone. He thinks that Doc W. will intervene in the spring, and that we shall bow to his instructions. Well, well! *I* shouldn't be surprised at all if there was some ghastly catastrophe the day after tomorrow, – and then we should find the Sibylline Books applied in a way not at all to the taste of the *Spectator*. And, by God, I shouldn't after that much care to be in the skin of a policeman.

Mr and Mrs Shove and Clive are in the cottage opposite, and seem very cheerful, so far. Besides the war, conversation has run almost entirely on the Grenfell Dioscuri – and it appeared that both her Ladyship and Pozzo were secretly in love with them. All agreed that every effort must be made to get the book published at once.

I have gone through Bertie's lectures again, and find them most exhilarating. If they come from Bickers, you'd better open the parcel.

The Times today seems to be fairly shaking in its shoes about South Wales. Mr M. thought that the article with extracts from the *New York Times* on peace was *tendancieux*.

yours
Lytton

‡

To Carrington

The sitting referred to is for the portrait Carrington painted of Lytton in the autumn and winter of 1916, in which he's shown reclining and holding a book in his exaggeratedly long fingers. The picture belonged to Frances Partridge, and is now in the National Portrait Gallery.

The Manor House
Garsington
Oxford
Tuesday *[postcard, November 28th 1916]*

I return to BPG tomorrow, and in case I don't see you, I suggest
coming to sit on Thursday morning. Will that do? All is as ever here,
except that her ladyship's hair has had a new coat of varnish.

Details to follow, by word of mouth.

Yr Lytton

✝

To Carrington

*The telephone was still a novelty in most households, and people treated it like
the telegraph, as though one were paying by the word.*

Francis Greenleaf Allinson (1856–1931) was a classicist, author of such works as
Greek Lands and Letters *and* The Greeks in Literature and Life. *In 1916
Freud published the first part of* Introductory Lectures on Psychoanalysis.
*His work on jokes and the subconscious had appeared first in 1905. Mark
Gertler, formerly hostile to Lytton, had now decided to impress Carrington by
showing that he liked Lytton as much as she did. He did not know that Lytton
and Carrington had become lovers. The coal supply had run out because money
was short and the household was economizing.*

6, Belsize Park Gardens
Hampstead, N.W.
Monday, December 18th *[1916]*

Ma Chère

As usual the telephone was too confusing. I really think I'm in too
degraded a state to allow of a Christmas jaunt. I should probably
collapse under the rigours of ambiguous country life – or at any rate be
in constant terror of it. Also there is the horror of travelling, to say
nothing of the difficulty of knowing where to go. I have accordingly
notified my acceptance of Garsington. It seems the only thing to do – I
cannot face this frightful town any more, and I shall employ every

conceivable stratagem to convince her ladyship to provide me with
enough food. I expect it will be unpleasant in various ways, but at any
rate there will be country air and an absence of responsibility.

I wonder what you will do. I hope you won't get too depressed. The
only thing to do is to consider this awful period a sort of dies non – a
mere blank in the calendar through which one must glide as best one
may with one's eyes shut.

I daren't ask you here. The house is in such a hurlyburly. I don't feel
that I've got the bodily strength to reach you. Perhaps after all you will
come to Garsington? At any rate after Christmas, let us hope for
strength, wealth and wisdom. And later on, when the conditions are less
frightful, we must have our jaunt.

I'm afraid it's a great interruption for the picture; but perhaps a rest
really will do it no harm. I'm longing to see it. When shall I?

I've done a review of Mr Allinson and am now doing one of Dr Freud.
The latest horror in this house is that the coal supply has given out. I sit
over crackling coke, trying to think of the definition of humour. [. . .]

With love
     from   Lytton

Mark came to tea, with a cold in the nose and a pair of galoshes. [. . .]

‡

To Leonard Woolf

*The never-married Sydney-Turner was at this time often in company with
Barbara Hiles (1891–1985). Virginia Woolf hoped they would marry. On
9 March 1966 Dorothy Brett told Michael Holroyd: 'I can remember an amusing
incident at Garsington, when Lytton complained that Ottoline was stingy with
the food. So the next morning, as a sort of ironical swat at him, Ottoline had a
breakfast sent up, consisting of eggs, sausages, bacon, mounds of toast, etc. To
her chagrin he ate it all! From that day he was stuffed with food.'*

*Lawrence ended his already tottering friendship with his partial portrait of Ottoline
as Hermione Roddice in* Women in Love. *'There was a terrible void, a lack,'
Lawrence wrote of his creation, 'a deficiency of being within her. And she wanted
someone to close up this deficiency. To close it up forever.' Lytton wanted Leonard to
play Trigorin. Lady Strachey was well known for the quality of her reading aloud.*

6, Belsize Park Gardens
Hampstead, N.W.
January 4th 1917

Are you back yet? If so, when can I come and see you? Sunday? Or is
that day entirely consecrated to Saxon and his bride?

It would have been delightful to have come to Asheham, but I'm
sure it was quite right to give Virginia the rest. I hope she *did* rest, and
that you had decent weather. It was horribly cold at Garsington, and the
flesh po's [sic] wore so thin that I lost my temper at breakfast: there was
a fearful scene in front of a large miscellaneous party – 'words' – it was
truly appalling. But instead of being turned out of the house, I was in
future given my breakfast in bed, with two eggs to it. The rest
continued to starve.

Your letter was brought to me opened – very odd. Her Ladyship
must have enjoyed reading it. But she must be getting used to that sort
of thing. The latest news is that D. H. Lawrence has sent her the MS of
his new novel, of which she is the heroine (Lady Hermione). The scene
is laid in Garsington, which is described with the minutest details, down
to the pugs. Debaucheries of every sort, of course. Philip pacing up and
down the passage all night to prevent her Ladyship getting into any of
the bedrooms. Young girls lured into the boudoir with fatal results. And
finally the Lady Hermione seizes a large piece of lapis lazuli with which
she hits Lawrence over the head, whereupon he sinks into a mass of
cushions on the sofa . . .

The poor woman is distracted about it, and writes to everyone by
every post, begging them to prevent its coming out. But no doubt
Lawrence (and especially Mrs Lawrence) will be relentless. It's a
charming fatality.

J'ai eu hier la visite de Saxon. It wasn't so bad as I'd feared. He was
fairly restrained, and really did seem, I thought, a good deal humanized.
However, I can imagine that it might grow wearing if repeated every
day at 1.30 on the telephone.

We think of getting up a performance of The Seagull (Tchekoff).
Do you know it? Would you take a part in it? There's an unpleasant
successful author, which would suit you. Please think of this.

your
Lytton

I wonder if you and Virginia would like to come and hear Lady S read the Duchess of Malfi on Saturday Afternoon?

‡

To Carrington

The Woolfs had lent Asheham to Carrington, Barbara Hiles and Sydney-Turner. When they arrived on 29 January, they found the house dramatically cold, and the cook/housekeeper ill. With Stracheyan irony Carrington wrote to Lytton that, if he should think of coming to join them, 'do I beg you bring only the lightest of summer clothing and some antidote for mosquitoes and gnats which infest the garden in the evenings'.

'Eagle' was 'Solomon Eagle', J.C. Squire, editor of the 'back pages' of the New Statesman. *Later in 1917, Lytton picked a terminal quarrel with him about the magazine's line on the war. But for now he continued to contribute to its pages, where all three pieces referred to here were published. Holroyd writes that Lytton often included hostile references to the Bible 'which he felt sure* must *prove too strong for the editor who, by demanding their excision, would provide him with a legitimate excuse to leave. What actually happened was less satisfactory. His contributions appeared with all their more audacious criticisms intact, but marred by many smaller changes, omissions or quite trivial words or insertions of Squire's own, almost always fractionally inferior to the original text, and, though intensely irritating, never drastic enough to provide Lytton with a high-principled reason for cutting off this small source of income.'[1] The Freud could have been the* Introductory Lectures in Psychoanalysis, *published in 1917 in the translation by A. A. Brill.*

The verse is by Victor Hugo, from Les Contemplations, *livre VI:* Les Mages.

> *Rabelais – there was nothing he did not comprehend:*
> *He rocked Adam to sleep,*
> *And his huge burst of laughter*
> *Is one of the profundities of wit.*

Lalla Vandervelde, née Hélène Frédérique Speyer (1870–1964), was the wife of the great Belgian socialist politician and statesman Emile Vandervelde. She spent the war years in England, and became an intimate of Roger Fry, whose exuberant fruit and flower design for a footboard for her bed (one of his best decorative works) has been reproduced as a popular poster. She starred with St John Hutchinson in Quashemaboo, *the comedy Lytton wrote to be performed at a charity gala the next year (1918).*

6, Belsize Park Gardens

January 31st 1917

Eh bien, ma chère – nièce? tante? petite fille?

– I was very glad to hear you were having such a grilling time among the tropics of Asheham. It must suit your delicate constitution and fragile frame. I hope you and your co-mates continue to enjoy yourselves. Do you wear muslin or alpaca?

As for me, my stalwart physique faces the snow and ice of these regions very successfully. I have not yet joined the sliders on the Hampstead ponds, but I feel that it's only a matter of time. Or perhaps a toboggan would be more suitable.

What do you think? I have positively finished Dr Freud, and despatched the horror to that wretched eagle. If you saw the New Statesman by any chance, you will have noticed Fred the Great – also perchance 'The Human Tragedy' (with two sentences added by the aforesaid eagle, damn his eyes). But probably such cultivated periodicals hardly reach your rural bowers. Or if they do you are no doubt all too busy cutting lavender and chasing butterflies to read them. – That is to say, you and Barbara. Saxon's time is I suppose fully occupied in feeling the peaches.

I positively did go to that Sale on Monday – but got nothing. The Spanish Aesop with the wood-cuts went for £3.7.6 – rather too much, I thought. Most of the other lots were very cheap, but I didn't want 'em. I found a charming little booklet called 'Merdiana' (i.e. Turdiana or Shittiana) with a very pleasant illustration of a gentleman busy in a certain posture, and a collection of anecdotes – but as it was clearly going to be expensive, *and* as it was time for lunch, I didn't stay to see what happened to it.

I also went to a performance of French plays on Sunday – quite agreeable. The whole of the rest of my time has been spent over Rabelais, and my knowledge of that subject is rapidly increasing. Who do you think wrote this? –

> Rabelais, que nul ne comprit:
> Il berce Adam pour qu'il s'endorme,
> Et son éclat de rire énorme
> Est un des gouffres de l'esprit.

And can you understand it?

I wonder if Saxon's reading of Swinburne gave you pleasure. You don't say. I once sat up a whole night with him and Woolf chaunting Dolores and the Forsaken Garden, until the sun rose, and we issued forth, and wandered through the courts of Trinity. I still think him a divine poet; but perhaps he's somehow not to the taste of my niece and her generation.

Will you write again? The illustrations were much appreciated. When are you coming back, I wonder?

Tonight I am dining with Roger, to meet . . . Madame Vandervelde, of all people in the world. I'm afraid we shan't like one another. And – have you visited your Charleston friend yet? Love to him and her (I mean S. and B.) Also to D.

your

L.

1. Michael Holroyd, *Lytton Strachey*, p. 297.

‡

To Lady Ottoline Morrell

'The Bing Girls Are There' (Ayer/Grey) opened on 24 February at the Alhambra Theatre.

6, Belsize Park Gardens

February 6th 1917

I was very glad to hear that you liked that Frederick article. I was afraid it might be rather heavy in the hand. There was another of my productions in the same number – a review of a translation from Anatole France; but unfortunately Jack Squire had taken it upon himself to add a few sentences. He is an obliging young man!

This cold weather – how long is it going to last? – For the duration of the war? – It must be really bitter on your lofty heights: but I expect very beautiful. Even the poor Heath looked wonderfully romantic this afternoon. Do you skate on the pond? I can see Gerald executing figures with his accustomed swiftness . . . And what are these mysterious occupations of yours, in the solitude of your chamber? Most intriguing! Are you writing a novel – on Lawrence and Frieda? I hope so!

Yes. Rabelais has surged over me altogether. I read very little else. I find him far the best antidote yet discovered against the revolting mesquineries *[pettinesses]* de ces jours. I read him in the Tube, and he is a veritable buckler of defence, warding off those miserable visages, with their filthy newspapers. What an adorable giant, to drop into the arms of! And then the interest of the book, from so many points of view, is so very great. I am glad I never really read it properly before: it is intoxicating to get a fresh enthusiasm when one's over eighty.

Have you heard that Saxon, accompanied by Barbara and Carrington, has established himself at Asheham? It sounds a singular party, and I fear we shall never hear a true history of its goings-on. I gather they spend much of their time tobogganing down the Downs on tea-trays. Apparently, when they arrived, late on a Saturday night, they found that the woman who was to 'do' for them had been taken ill, that in consequence no fires had been lighted, that all the water-pipes were frozen hard, and that there were no coals! Well, I hope they'll come out of it not permanently disabled – with a few fingers and toes still unfrost-bitten! –

Katherine I gather has gone, or is on the point of going to Chelsea. But this has been happening for so many months that I shan't believe it until I really see her installed. There don't seem to be many people about. I wish you would come and visit the town for a day or two. We could go and see the Bing Girls and have haggis at Simpson's.

The other day, who do you think I met at Roger's? – Lala. Do you know her? I found her (such is my well known amiability) quite amusing.

General Gordon proceeds . . . slowly.

ever your
Lytton

‡

To Virginia Woolf

Siegfried Sassoon had won the Military Cross the previous June for bringing a wounded British soldier back to British lines. He had returned to France this month, though he did not return to active combat immediately. He was wounded himself in April, and finally issued his public anti-war statement, 'A Soldier's Declaration', on 17 July. His collection of poems, many of them anti-war, was issued as The Old Huntsman and Other Poems *in May.*

6, Belsize Park Gardens
Hampstead, N.W.
February 21st 1917

That wretched woman, the Lady O. Morrell writes to me as follows –
'Do you think you could write to Virginia, and ask her if she could get
Sassoon's book of Poems, and if she would review it kindly . . . I think
if he heard that his work had "Promise" it might make him want to
Live – to do things in the Future. But it is all ghastly and he can hardly
bear it. Shall I shoot Lloyd George?'

It is indeed 'all ghastly', and probably *you* could hardly bear it. But
you see that you now have Siegfried's life, to say nothing of Lloyd
George's, on your hands. I suppose you don't as a rule review what
they call 'poetry'. Perhaps if you wrote to Richmond suggesting that
the bloody book should be noticed, it would suffice. Or what? Let
me know so that I may send some reply to that creature, who is now
I think almost at the last gasp – infinitely old, ill, depressed, and
bad tempered: she is soon to sink into a nursing-home, where she
will be fed on nuts, and allowed to receive visitors (in bed).

Shall I come to tea with you on Sunday? With or without Carrington?

your
Lytton

‡

To Carrington

*Carrington's brother Teddy – the subject of the photographs in sailor dress – was
missing in action, and, she wrote to Lytton, who was staying with the Johns at
Alderney Manor, she was beginning to despair of ever seeing him again.*

Alderney
March 8th *[1917]*

I wish you could have shared the chicken and the claret tonight, and
then drawn up your armchair by mine in front of the pine fire. The
arrangements in this world are sometimes rather tiresome. I had dimly
hoped that I might have heard from you today, but not a word has
reached me from the world – not a letter and – thank the Lord! – no

newspapers. So I haven't any idea of what may or may not have happened. I hope, at any rate, your silence has not been caused by annoyance – I don't know in the least what at; but I fear I *am* at times a trifle . . . unsatisfactory. Is it age, sex, or cynicism? But perhaps it's really only appearance – of one sort or another. The fellow, as they say, (only they don't) is good at heart. I wish I could only be of more avail. I often think that if the layer of flesh over my bones were a few inches thicker I might be. But that is another of the tiresome arrangements of this world. Ma chère, I'm sure I do sympathise with your feelings of loneliness. I know what it is so horribly well myself.

About him – it is useless to try to say anything. In some of those grand agonies of Shakespeare one may find something – at moments – that is like comfort. Directly I saw the little photographs in the sailor dress, I longed to know him. Oh ma chère! –

It has been pretty cold here – frost about – and terrific winds. In fact, really just too early for the full charm of the place. One wants to be able to sit out in the round walled garden. I have been wonderfully looked after, and have done nothing but read from morning to night, which has been most agreeable. I wonder what you've been doing. Have you finished A*[ntony]* and C*[leopatra]*?

Dorelia was extremely nice – slightly alarming, of course, also. But on the whole much easier to get on with than one thinks she's going to be. The boys appeared. Romilly has lost all his looks; but Robin is fascinating. As for Vivien, she is a most imposing personage – half the size of Poppet, and twice as dangerous. At first she completely ignored me. She then would say nothing but 'oh *no*!' whenever I addressed her. But eventually she gave me a chocolate – 'Man! Have a chockle!' – which I consider a triumph.

Well, I must go to bed. Perhaps I shall hear from you tomorrow. This letter will hardly reach you before I do. Goodnight

From your très-vieux, très-maigre, et très-fidèle
Lytton

Friday morning. The weather is so frightful that I have decided to stay on – for today at any rate. But will it ever change? – I feel I'm becoming a fixture. Your letter just came. Great hurry. The postman comes and goes . . . SNOW . . . ruin

‡

To Carrington

In her letter written the day before, Carrington reported that Augustus John had said Dorelia was returning to Alderney Manor on Monday, which would leave only Saturday and Sunday for Lytton to be alone with Carrington. In their conversation John 'gave me a complete history of his life, and parents, the mysterious sister who lives in Paris . . . You know it wasn't the Strand where he met Dorelia. I have, ever since you told me . . . thought when I was in the Strand, near Adelphi, of John looking back at Dorelia in a Black Hat, and now it was all a false vision, as he met her in Holborn.'

The Mill Carrington had been pursuing 'is only for sale, £1000 premium and £30 a year rent for 17 years!!!! So that's that . . . But . . . in the same village there are two smaller cottages to let furnished, one 30/- a week which I am making investigations about.'

The quotation from Tennyson is the famous opening of Tithonus.

Alderney Manor
Parkstone
Friday, March 9th 1917

Hum, hum! Ah, ah! Ho, ho! – The wind rages and the snow whirls madly round, the temperature sinks and ever sinks . . . Me voici in bed, having just despatched a telegram to Belsize putting off my return indefinitely, also last night's letter to you, with a hurried additional note, from which I hope you will gather the state of affairs. Lawks! And I had dreamt that winter was over. Well, here I shall remain till it is, I fancy – certainly until this blizzard ceases – in bed, or just out of it, waited on by the invaluable Mrs Gare, rummaging in books, nibbling chickens and sipping wine, snoozing off by the wood fire . . . not such a bad existence, when one comes to think of it. Why *not* come and share it with me? Couldn't you get that woman's leave? And then, if I had a telegram from you tomorrow, you should have a taxi at the station . . . Is it all a vision? – We could return on Monday, perhaps. And if you once got here, you would hardly find it colder than London, and much less confusing – also one bed is warmer than two . . . I mean . . . but I keep forgetting . . . il maestro! –

Your conversation with him sounds decidedly interesting, and I hope to have a detailed account of the biographical part of it. The Holborn news is very upsetting. I too had had such a complete and long-established vision of the Strand! – But, of course, when one comes to think of it, the Strand was too obvious. Holborn is just the sort of absurd stupid place where nothing *could* happen – and when something does – – Ouf! Ouf! The conditions are certainly severe. – A short journey in an overcoat to . . . a necessary chamber. Tiens! The window open – thick snow everywhere – the necessary seat a snow-circle, the necessary paper a snowball. Imagine ton oncle! – – But now he is back again under the blankets, thank the Lord.

How preposterous about that bloody mill! What do they mean by it? The other cottages – yes, all very well; but 30/- for one week means £75 a year. However, I suppose one might go for one week someday. But couldn't we get the furniture turned out, and take them for much less? As the summer approaches, the need for an outlet begins to simmer in my bones. Mais l'argent! l'argent!

The worst of this bed-writing system is that one's hands get so petrified that from time to time one has to give it up and germinate with only one's nose exposed to the rigours of the atmosphere. Also the sheets become covered with ink, which doesn't look well . . . though some things look worse. – Beg pardon, Missy. He always *was* a depraved fellow. At Cambridge, I remember, his conversation got so . . . well, so downright *nasty* that I was obliged to turn him out of the room . . . And now the wretch has come and got hold of my hand, and is making me write all this. But I assure you, Missy, it's not me at all – bless your pretty eyes – it's *e* as is doin it.

Schubert and Leonora – very nice, very nice indeed. Couldn't you persuade the orchestra – or at any rate a quartet – to come with you tomorrow? That would be so charming – to digest one's chicken, by the wood fire, in these dim solitudes, to some ravishing adagio of Mozart's. But no matter, in any case, there is always Shelley to sink into – the last Act of the Prometheus Unbound –

I knew it would happen. My pen has emptied itself over the bedclothes, and I am reduced to a pencil. Such is life.

When the pencil breaks, I can always use the end of a match. Such, I repeat, is life.

The woods decay, the woods decay, and fall (Tennyson).

But I can hear that amiable Mrs Gare preparing the geyser (yes! there is one – so you see –) for my bath; and I shall have to get up, or I shall be late for lunch, served in the blue saloon, by four powdered lackeys in knee-britches.

your
Grandfather

I suppose it's hardly to be hoped that you really *would* come tomorrow, but if by any chance it should be possible, it would be necessary to send me a telegram fairly early, as, in the natural course, if the weather isn't too utterly hopeless, I should begin trundling back from here about 12.30. And it would be appalling if you arrived and found desolation. If I don't hear, I shall know it's a vision.

‡

To Lady Ottoline Morrell

Ottoline's 'hegira' was her pilgrimage back to Garsington after the London rest cure.

Carrington, Barbara Hiles and Faith Henderson were busy in early March making dresses for the 'John Beauty Chorus', which formed part of the entertainment on 20 March at the Chelsea Palace Theatre. David Garnett wrote that it was 'a charity matinée in aid of the Lena Ashwell concerts for troops. There were songs and dances by Slade students: "John, John, how he's got on/ He owes it, he owes it to me/ Brass earrings I wear and I don't do my hair/ And my feet are as bare as can be." Carrington's mother was horrified at her having taken part in a performance which resulted in such vulgar publicity. Jacob Epstein scented in it a conspiracy against himself.'[1] Michael Holroyd notes that that 'everyone in the polite world' wanted to be involved in the organization of the event so that even 'a Committee of Duchesses gave birth to itself'.[2]

John Hodge (1855–1937), Labour Party member, Minister of Labour at this time, was extremely unpopular with the left because of his willingness to use the Defence of the Realm Act to charge striking trades unionists with treason.

6, Belsize Park Gardens, N.W.3
March 23rd 1917

I saw Brett this morning, and she told me of your hegira. I had gathered before that you were not visible, or I should have appeared. I hope now that you're feeling some 'benefit', as they say, from the rest – in spite of the flock pillow and the matron in black spectacles. It's a pity that the weather should have seized this moment for surpassing itself; but I daresay there's sun at Garsington as well as snow.

I should like to come very much, but I don't think that at present it would be compatible with virtue. I have been dawdling horribly lately over reviews – money was getting so short! – and now I feel that I really must set to and seriously attack the General. I'm afraid it would be fatal to leave my stool until I've captured at least his first line of trenches. But as soon as the Great Offensive is over, I'll let you know, and hope that you'll be able to have me and my good conscience.

No doubt you've heard various accounts of the Chelsea matinée and the party at John's afterwards. The former I watched crouching on the steps of the Gallery between Roger and Lala, and rarely have I suffered such a combination of physical and mental torture. Not even a flock pillow between the bare boards and my . . . ! And the boredom was excruciating. Every minute I sent up a fresh and more urgent prayer to the Almighty to drop a thunderbolt and stop it, but the Old Wretch was clearly in league with the Upper Classes, and paid no attention to my clamours. Oh, the Upper Classes! With what a singular complacency do they exhibit themselves! – The party at John's was nice, though I'm afraid Dorelia was not much pleased by its coming off there. Among others, Evan appeared – as irresponsible as ever. Do you know that he is now Private Secretary to Mr Hodge? It was agreed that the Belle of the evening was Brett.

I hope all is well at Garsington. Write to me someday.

your

Lytton

1. David Garnett, *Carrington*, p. 61, n.1.
2. Michael Holroyd, *Augustus John*, vol. 2, p. 60.

‡

To Carrington

Carrington, at home with her parents, had written that her mother was 'more erratic and insane than I expected even' and 'My father has just delivered in his best O.T. manner, with the solemnness [sic] of Isaac a great lecture on my sins.'[1]

A former Unionist Parliamentary leader, Colonel Sanderson, spoke the legendary words: 'The Home Rule Bill may pass the House of Commons, but it will never pass the Bann bridge in Portadown.'

Lord Henry Bentinck (1863–1931) was Lady Ottoline's favourite brother.

'A. Clutton-Brock's Shelley: the Man and the Poet (1910) may be recommended,' says Sydney Waterlow in Percy Bysshe Shelley.

From a contemporary newspaper report: 'Gaby Deslys is to play the lead in a new musical comedy which André Charlot is getting ready for the end of next month. Its title Saucy Suzette carries a distinct promise that Gaby Deslys will have a conspicuous rôle.'[2]

While she was in the Royal Avenue nursing home on 7 March, Philip told Ottoline that he had not one, but two mistresses, Alice Jones and Eva Merrifield (her former personal maid), and that both of them were pregnant by him. Philip, terrified of a political scandal that would compromise his allies in the anti-war movement, had a breakdown. Alice Jones was independent and supported herself, but Eva Merrifield's financial demands were dealt with by Ottoline. Ottoline herself later discovered that her lover, Bertie Russell, wanted to break with her as he was now becoming involved with Lady Constance Malleson (1895–1975).[3] This is the background to Philip's condition, though neither Clive nor Lytton seems to have known these details at the time.

6, Belsize Park Gardens
March 26th 1917

I envy your country existence, though I suspect it's infernally cold. Thick snow I imagine on the Downs – or at any rate blizzards. There have been some violent ones here today, interspersed with hot sunshine. I walked on the Heath this afternoon, and drank in the fresh air, wondering whether you were doing likewise, and whether you were getting drenched through for lack of an umbrella. Your relatives are a queer lot. *[. . .]*

Clive came to tea on Saturday, and *immediately*, before he sat down, began the story of Philip. I daresay it's already reached you from other sources by this time – that the poor man took leave of his senses, sat in his bed gibbering, moping, mowing, and babbling of green fields, until at last . . . he returned to sanity – or such sanity as he usually possesses. I never knew before that one could go mad for a week-end – like catching a cold – but so it was, and apparently he's had similar collapses before. He began by sending for Fredegond and Gerald – Clive, he said, was not sympathetic enough and would tell Mary – and assured them that, although people thought him a fool – 'Maynard Keynes thinks I'm a fool, and so does Colonel Sanderson' – he really wasn't one, no, really, – in fact he was quite intelligent, perfectly intelligent, and the truth was – only no one ever saw it – there was a touch of genius in him. As for Ottoline, she was thought very clever, but everything she knew had been taught her by him, and if it hadn't been for him she would be little better than an ignoramus. And so they could see that he couldn't be a fool really, whatever people thought. But they mustn't tell Clive; they must be sure not to tell Clive; and if they couldn't remember what he was saying they had better take it down in writing. This went on for several hours, interspersed with injunctions on farm management. Eventually they escaped, whereupon Clive was at once sent for. The same flood was poured out upon him, with constant injunctions to 'take it down – put it down on paper'. After a day or two, Gerald became so alarmed that he went up to London and told Lord Henry. Lady Henry was consulted, and Ottoline told. Then his Lordship went to Garsington, and removed Pipsey, still faintly gibbering, and assuring everybody that he had a touch of genius, to a 'nursing home'. After that telegrams began to snow down from Ott, with every kind of injunction and ejaculation; she then arrived in person; and shortly afterward, Pipsey returned – cured. It's a preposterous story, and no less preposterous was her Ladyship's notion that she could keep it dark. I suppose she must have written round to everyone, as she did to me, explaining that she'd come away from London because it was so boring. Pauvre femme! But imagine Pipsey, sitting up in bed in his pyjamas, endlessly expatiating to Clive, Gerald and Fredegond, taking notes of his observations with pencils and paper! 'I am really not a fool. Take that down, Fredegond, in case you forget it.'

Clive seemed in his usual spirits – hair rather shorter, which I thought an improvement. I was furious to hear that the wretch had mastered Italian, and was reading Ariosto. What's to be done about these languages? – In the evening I drifted to Omega, where was rather a lugubre and extremely chilly group, including Ka Cox, Norton, and the Sangers. The wind whistled down our backs as we crouched round the fire and munched those appalling biscuits.

Yesterday I had tea at Gordon Square – Clive, Maynard, Sheppard, and Norton present. It was very agreeable, especially after Clive had bustled off, and the solid Cambridge element was left talking. I lingered on to dinner, and on, and on – so delightful to be able to indulge once in a way again in a regular conversation. Every imaginable subject was discussed, from the Russian Revolution to the forgotten details of King's gossip of fifteen years ago – Love, lust, women, men, etc. etc. and oh! the bawdy! –

My state has taken a turn for the better. I've begun to feel very brisk, and have do[ne] several hours work on Gordon today. If I can only keep it up – The book question is what chiefly bothers me. But we shall see.

For relaxation I've got hold of an odious Clutton Brock concoction on Shelley. A vile fellow, a very vile fellow. Have you finished Macbeth yet? And the animal-play-picture? My only objection to the 'stallion' in an upright position is that I'm afraid that the pose will hardly show off his characteristic portion.

James and Noel (for a night) arrive shortly. The new parlour-lady is a perfect angel – a miracle – but I feel in my bones she's too good to last. Never have I been so well attended to. And if there were only a few coals in the house I should be a soul in bliss.

I must dash out to post this now. Do you really return on Thursday? The Gaby extract is somewhat mysterious – the Globe Theatre advertisements make no mention of such a thing. But I suppose it must have some foundation in fact. It would be nice to view dear Harry once again. But – economy?

Probably your people will never never go away. In June it will clearly be impossible. And I see you're weakening over Dorelia. Why not threaten to go on the stage unless they hand it over to her – or to you?

The Garsington Dame has asked me down there for Easter. Luckily, as the invitation was only through Clive, I was able to be evasive. I've almost decided not to go in any case – what with my work, and the discomforts mental and physical. But of course it's very difficult to refuse absolutely, when it comes to the point. I wonder if there's any hope of Asheham.

With love

your

Lytton

1. Quoted in Gretchen Gerzina, *Carrington*, pp. 107–8.
2. *The Weekly Dispatch*, London, Sunday, 18 February 1917, p. 6a/b; *Suzette* opened at the Globe on 29 March 1917 and ran for 256 performances.
3. Miranda Seymour, *Ottoline Morrell*, pp. 382*ff.*

✝

To Lady Ottoline Morrell

In April Russell had told Ottoline that he had taken up with another woman (Constance Malleson, though he didn't name her to Ottoline), so his presence as a house guest was actually fraught with emotional difficulties, but, says Miranda

Seymour, 'Ottoline had always put her function as a hostess before her private life.'[1]

Lytton was 'unpolitical' only in comparison to the professional politicians who were to be his fellow guests, Asquith, the now ex Prime Minister, and Augustine Birrell, who had resigned as Chief Secretary for Ireland after the Easter Rebellion. Another guest was the twenty-two-year-old poet Robert Graves, who by treating Sassoon's anti-war feelings as symptoms of shell shock, played a less than honourable role in getting him to return to the Front.

The Government was systematically reviewing the cases of those who had been exempted from military service, and on 22 May Lytton had to re-establish his status, going over all the arguments once again. This time, though, he hired legal counsel, stated his objection in three carefully drafted paragraphs, and once again asked Philip Morrell to appear as a character witness. Maynard (who was James Strachey's witness), however, thought Lytton should call St Loe Strachey, instead of the 'blundering' Philip.[2]

6, Belsize Park Gardens
Thursday, [May 23rd 1917]

Dearest Ottoline,

The party sounds a very nice one, and I should particularly enjoy seeing Bertie, who I haven't caught a glimpse of for about a hundred years. So if you can tolerate my unpoliticalness among so many lions, I shall come tomorrow, by the afternoon Wheatley train – the one that arrives at about tea time.

It will be charming to be able to rest my weary bones and spirit on your down pillows for a little. I'm so very sorry to hear that your health is still unsatisfactory. We must hold each other's hands.

The tribunal yesterday was as disgusting as usual – but the result was just what we expected. I am to be reexamined by the army doctors. My wretched barrister wouldn't even let Philip come into the room – which I'm sure was a great mistake, as if he had appeared the Chairman would have recognised him and seen that I am 'well connected' – which, as it was, he didn't grasp.

yours ever,
Lytton

1. Miranda Seymour, *Ottoline Morrell*, p. 390.
2. Michael Holroyd, *Lytton Strachey*, p. 391.

‡

To E. M. Forster

*Forster was in Alexandria, working for the International Red Cross. He was
having an affair with Muhammad al-Adl, a young tram conductor. Lytton was
unsure whether Forster's mail was subject to censorship – thus the 'sub-Sydney
Waterlow' joke.*

6, Belsize Park Gardens
N.W.3
May 24th 1917

It was très gentil of you to write again, in the face of my appalling
silence – the mere result of idleness. Your situation sounds all that could
be wished, what with one thing and another, – though I suppose you
may suppress the drawbacks . . . And perhaps you exaggerate the
Romance – for my benefit – or your own. But I don't know: Romance
can hardly ever be exaggerated.

I often pray to heaven to transport me to you. The relief of escaping
from this fraudulent country (fraudulent even down to the weather),
and of plunging into a masculine and uncreative existence, would be
extreme. Will you go on for ever where you are? – That is to say, as
long as the war lasts? Can you imagine the grimy dingy horror of life in
London? – Ouf! – Do you know that I am still struggling in the meshes
of Military Service Acts? – Still about to be examined by military
doctors, still wondering about the nature of conscience, still appearing
before 'Tribunals' (– do you know what *they* are? – in your bower of
bliss?), still going down to Faringdon for the week-end, still reading the
Evening papers in the tube, and still writing the Life of General Gordon.
However, in the intervals, the sun does occasionally warm my spine, and,
once or twice, in the streets . . . or even the tube . . . but no matter! –

Will you write to me again? Telling me to what extent one's letters
are censored? It is difficult to say much when one can't be sure whether
one isn't under the eye of some sub-Sydney Waterlow. If one wasn't, I'ld
send you reams of most interesting observations. So do let me know.

Would you come and live with me at the Hague, after our armies
have entered Berlin? I am told it is a charming place, full of canals and
fuchsias; it is also not in England which is an advantage, as the English
climate does not agree with me – nor with you either, I fancy. There

we could sit and write our perfectly futile little compositions to our hearts' content, and, in the evening, stroll out along the canals, and lazily stretch out our fingers from time to time, and pop the fuchsias . . . Don't you think it's rather a good idea? – But perhaps you'd prefer Moscow, which certainly also has its advantages.

Well, no more now! The New Statesman is a filthy rag, and I only write in it for filthy lucre. Jack Squire is now the Editor, Sharp having been removed to the trenches; the Eagle has fluttered up onto a higher perch – bought a new suit too, as I am told, and had his hair cut. One never knows what mayn't happen in these days.

Have you read the Life of our brother Alfred Lyttelton? It gives a most interesting vision of our leaders – their intelligence, good taste, etc. I should like to add him to my biographical collection, but he's too near at hand, I'm afraid.

I shall take the liberty of not signing this (why *does* one sign one's letters?) and so balking the mild curiosity of Sydney Waterlow Minor.

‡

To Carrington

George Mallory had been a master at Charterhouse, where he taught Robert Graves.

Garsington Manor
Oxford
Monday, May 28th 1917

It's really not much good writing, as we shall probably meet before this can get to you. It was impossible to put pen to paper before, and the posts are painfully scanty, so – and there are so many descriptions to be made that no one letter could hold all of them. However, I have now managed to drag a deck-chair (a minor one) into a shady patch on the lower lawn, and the empty day spreads out before me, and the opportunity for a little gibbering presents itself. I found nothing as I had expected it would be. In the first place, the beauty of the place, after London and that drab Southampton region, was really amazing. Then I found Mr Birrell at tea with her and him – out of doors, of course, and it transpired that he was staying on indefinitely. I had not met the old man before, so that was interesting. On the top of that enter the youth Graves ('poet', friend of Siegfried, Captain, teaching cadets at Oxford, etc.) who was also to stay for the week-end. These two new and remarkable figures have been the main interest. Mr Massingham was ill and couldn't come; but Mr Arnold, a Northern M.P. did – also Bertie and Sheppard; and of course there have been Clive, Gerald and Fredegond to fill up the interstices. The wear and tear have been pretty considerable – (Aldous, too, I had forgotten – and Brett.) – And more than another day of it would altogether do for me. Her Ladyship is more fevered, jumpy and neurasthenic than ever, though as usual there have been moments (especially at first) when my heart melted towards her. She seems to me to be steadily progressing down to the depths of ruin. Perhaps the whole thing is simply the result of physical causes, perhaps if she could really rest and eat and be alone for a month or two we should see wonders, but I can hardly believe that now she ever will. Philip is fearful – a ghost masquerading as a husband, and knowing that it takes nobody in – visibly worn, I think, since the lunacy. His company is in itself enough to account for any mental or physical disease.

Old man Birrell – decidedly a Victorian product. Large and tall and oddly like Thackeray to look at – with spectacles and sharp big nose and a long upper lip that moves about and curls very expressively – white hair, of course, and also rather unexpectedly sensitive and even sometimes almost agitated fingers. Altogether, a most imposing façade! And there he sits, square and solid, talking in a loud deep voice – can you imagine it? – and being very entertaining for hour after hour – telling stories and interjecting reflections and all the rest of it – and all with the greatest geniality – taking up one's remarks most good-humouredly, and proceeding and embroidering with an impression of easy strength. Underneath – there really seems to be almost nothing. The ordinary bookishness, gleaned from some rather narrow reading, and then – blank. His remarks on C[onscientious] O[bjector]s showed not so much cowardice and stupidity as the mere *absence* of good qualities – absence of courage, clear thinking, imagination, and the sense of responsibility; so that one hardly likes to blame him or get annoyed, any more than one would a child. 'Frivolous', perhaps, is the word. But the façade *is* imposing – and is a real good solid façade, finely made of choice material – quite a pleasure to look at – and why should one bother any further? – One hasn't to live in the house.

All the same, it's difficult not to bother – in these times especially. The fashion for façades has its drawbacks. For instance there is the youth Graves, with one lung shot away, keeping himself going on strychnine, and with strange concealed thoughts which only very occasionally poke up through his schoolboy jocularities. Terribly tragic, I thought. Now he has gone back to his cadets at Oxford – a slightly silly fellow, too, and, so it turns out, a pupil of dear George's, with a strong tinge of poor dear George about him – in the curiously oafish sense of humour, and in the reading-aloud voice, which, with eyes shut, I could almost imagine came from George himself. I found him (I need hardly say) attractive – tall and olive-brown complexioned, with a broken nose and broken teeth (the result of boxing) – dark hair and eyes. However, Sheppard completely cut me out with him, though for a moment I fancied he was going to make me his Father Confessor. He got on perfectly with the old man, who almost flirted with him; and it clearly never occurred to either that they were cause and effect. He called Birrell 'Sir', and even Pipsey, sometimes. But never me – no! that would have been impossible.

I wish I could give you some conception of his mysteriousness. There was one very interesting conversation about his battle experiences, rather late, when Ott and Birrell had gone to bed. Such a grim, pathetic muddle of a narrative you never heard! – All the important points lost, and a curiously futile school philosophy which left one with 'la mort dans l'âme' – oh! and the preposterous details – sandbags and 'urinating' – but I will tell you about it when we meet. *[. . .]*

Your walking adventures sound a trifle exhausting, but it must be divine among your downs just now. Why am I not at Lockeridge? I was probably a maniac to have abandoned that cottage. My health doesn't seem to me very satisfactory, damn it. But there's nothing to be done, and it might be very much worse.

Sheppard is growing very masterly, and remains very charming. His view of the general situation is distinctly optimistic – he thinks the *probability* is that there'll be peace by the autumn. Even Bertie more or less agrees, and the old Birrell fellow appeared to be hopeful. So let's pray that Maynard is once more a false prophet.

I find I've forgotten another inmate – Tony Birrell, Frankie's brother, a half-wit, but an agreeable merry one, very like a jester in an Elizabethan comedy. I daresay there are many other visitors, but I can think of no more.

Birrell père et fils have departed, also Aldous. There remain Bertie, Sheppard and myself, with more than a dash of Clive. The doorbell has just rung – is it the Asquith cortège?

Oh! What a horrid whirligig! Her Ladyship has made several efforts to detain me and to induce me to come and spend most of the summer here, but I am adamant. A three days' sample is enough.

If it goes on like this, it will be almost too hot for sight-seeing in Cambridge.

Is this a French letter? Not quite, I fancy.

With love

from

your

Lytton

‡

To Carrington

Perhaps 'Testiquienne' is a private joke deriving from testicule, *the French word for testicle.*

Charleston

Monday, June 25th 1917

Rather maniacally, I decided to stay on till tomorrow, though the poor Pozzo man has been as usual summoned back to his stool. The next 24 hours will I fear hang heavy on me – complete solitude – and now a scotch mist which hangs over the land, and makes movement intolerable. I shall sit on this cherokee-covered sofa reading Les Miserables, I fancy, till the motor comes and carries me off. Such a flat quietude as you never saw! Even Julian behaves with exemplary goodness. The three are very gentle and kind – impossible even for me to get up a crisis. Maynard spent the whole of his time weeding in the walled garden with a scarlet knitted wool cap on his head, making him look like some effete Pasha. He was a trifle tetchy, partly because of the summons back, and partly, I think because the stool is beginning to make his buttocks sore at last. Only his buttocks, though. His heart remains unaffected.

On Saturday morning, waking up in my lovely bedroom at 6.30, I leapt out of bed, looked out of window and saw divine beauty before me – so hurried on my clothes, went out, and mounted Firle Beacon before you could say Testiquienne! It was marvellous – such a freshness – and the visions of the downs and the sea; but that was about the end of it. Ever since it has been grey and coldish, and now it is positively wintry. London is obviously the only place. *[. . .]*

✝

To Carrington

Lady Strachey had had surgery, and the entire household was decamping to Roger Fry's house, Durbins, at Guildford, for her to recuperate; the plan was to shut down the Hampstead house. Two Stories was the first book published by the Hogarth Press, and consisted of 'The Mark on the Wall' by Virginia and 'Three Jews' by Leonard, with four woodcuts by Carrington. Virginia did the typesetting, binding and distributing; Leonard was responsible for the machining and the faulty inking. 'Marlow' refers to Alix Sargant-Florence's mother's house, Lord's Wood. Alix, says Michael Holroyd, had embarked upon a 'three-year campaign to win James – a campaign that had to overcome James's infatuation for Noel Olivier as well as to absorb Alix's own affairs with Bunny Garnett (inspiring him with "a longing to commit murder and rape") and Harry Norton which Virginia mockingly analysed as "Copulation every 10 days in order to free his suppressed instincts!" "[1]

6, Belsize Park Gardens
Hampstead, N.W.
Sunday, [July 15th 1917][2]

Impossible to write – oh – quite impossible. My brain is far too congested for any such thing. I hope it may some day grow less so, but I doubt it.

The flowers were, and are, glorious. Thank you immensely for them. They tower on the mantelpiece, and crouch on the writing-table under my nose. It must be perfectly divine in your regions; but London also has its divinities.

My mother is apparently at last on the mend. It is thought that the move to Guildford may occur next Saturday. James has written to a farm-house he has heard of somewhere on the N. Coast of Cornwall – nowhere near those Lawrence people, though. It seemed necessary to take some steps. [. . .] If the Cornish affair fails, there'll be nothing. Probably we shall all spend September in the verandah at Belsize.

Je suis mort (temporarily).

The Marriage of F. was really highly enjoyable. The ugliness of the decorations was not so intolerable as might have been supposed. The music was superior – even to Sir T. Beecham. The house was packed: it was a pseudo-pre-war effect, and so many Old Friends you never saw. I could fill the rest of the sheet with the list of them.

The Woolf booklet has come – but probably you've seen it. Damn them – they haven't put enough ink on your cuts. I adore the snail. Virginia I consider a genius.

James wants your advice on the Alix question. Do you think it is best for him *not* to go to Marlow next Sat? Or would it be too crushing? He thinks it might be an opportunity for getting her out of the habit of seeing him. But how can you tell?

Perhaps you'll write again, I hope so. I repeat, je suis (temporarily) mort.

yr
Lytton

1. Michael Holroyd, *Lytton Strachey*, p. 385.
2. Dated in James Strachey's writing.

‡

To Leonard Woolf

60 Frith Street, Soho, where Carrington had her studio, is currently an art gallery.

6, Belsize Park Gardens
N.W.3
July 17th 1917

I shall be charmed to come to Asheham on Aug. 17th. It's clear that I can quite depend on you for the choice of company.

The 'Two Stories' was a most cheering production. I never could have believed it possible. My only criticism is that there doesn't seem to be quite enough ink. Virginia's is, I consider, a work of genius. The liquidity of the style fills me with envy: really some of the sentences! – How on earth does she manage to make the English language float and float? And then the wonderful way in which the modern point of view is suggested. Tiens!

I go today, till Saturday, to 60 Frith Street. Then to Durbins.

your
Lytton

‡

To Carrington

Carrington had moved from 3 Gower Street to a new studio at 60 Frith Street,
in Soho, where there were still factories and workshops, with all the attendant
noises. Earlier in the year, having shed her virginity with Lytton, she finally
gave in to Mark Gertler's persistent entreaties to have sex with him. It was not a
success for her, and she had broken off the relationship, telling the painter that
she loved Lytton. By the summer, though, she was once again seeing Gertler, on
terms, she hoped, of friendship. 'Auld Reekie': the housekeeper at Frith Street
was Mrs. Reekes, and Carrington enjoyed trying to persuade her that Lytton,
who came to stay for a few days, was her uncle.[1]

Durbins
Sunday morning, July 22nd 1917

My dearest creature. I hope you are happy. Did you sleep last night, in
spite of the horse? And the petrified damozels? – I suppose you had
dinner with Mark: but how are you spending today, until it's time to go
to Richmond? Painting? Or reading? Or snoozing? Or looking out of
window? – but on Sunday there are no printers-boys to look at. I
suppose Frith Street is still standing (though perhaps it's rather rash to
suppose any such thing nowadays) – anyhow it strikes me as slightly
mythical – Italians, and horses, and damozels, and Auld Reekie – there's
an Arabian Night air about them to me now. Durbins is the only reality.
And it's after all not such a bad one (so far). It positively does seem to
be almost what you might call country. There are real weeds in the
garden, which produces real peas, which one eats for dinner. There's a
real sun, which it's too hot to sit out in, and there are real birds, which
sing on – more or less real trees. The walk from the station yesterday,
by the river, was charming; and the town swarms with real . . . soldiers,
with real khaki jackets and breeches, which conceal real bums. So after
all, you see . . . The household is less agitated than I'd expected. Roger
is very agreeable and alarmingly intelligent. I have given way, and
agreed to be painted, but it's to be done while I write. There's a
frightful arrangement of Nina Hamnett – just done by him – full length
in blue check, with carefully disposed red and yellow still life, and a still
life face.[2] Le pauvre homme!
    I am sitting under the pergola, writing this – in my white flannel

trousers! I've got an even immenser book than any of the others – a foot by a foot by a foot – on the French Revolution, which gives me much pleasure. Never have so many solid facts been compressed together into such a neat cube before. It'll be a charming relaxation from the airy nothings of Gordon. Pippa, dressed in a blue smock and leggings, busies herself in the garden. Marjorie sits pen in hand, writing either to Jos or to the Commissioners of Education. Roger is extremely active – but over what it's difficult to say. My mother stood the journey very well. She is apparently all right. Her spirits are now what's chiefly wrong. The nurse appears at every meal – a pug-faced little creature – and quite useless, I should say.

I've just remembered you were to have breakfast at Gordon Square – weren't you? – this morning: so probably you're there at this moment, chatting with those singular beings. I can visualise Sheppard in his dressing-gown, hurrying out from time to time to buy Sunday papers from little boys.

Oh! The man has begun already! – Planted himself down. With pencil and paper. Oh mon dieu! mon dieu! It's terribly constricting! Shall I ever be able to concoct my sentences? It's like shitting with someone looking on.

I hope you'd supply me with every information. And those pictures – will your severity on that subject last for ever? Ah well! – It was curious this morning waking up with no virginal bodyguard at hand. I wish this house was emptier. Later on, perhaps it would be possible for you to come. Je t'embrasse.

your antique
Fakeer

1. Carrington to Barbara Bagenal, quoted in Michael Holroyd, *Lytton Strachey*, p. 394.
2. This refers to the portrait now in the Fry Collection of the Courtauld Institute Galleries. Richard Shone (*Bloomsbury Portraits*, p. 161) thinks it 'the most successful of Fry's several portraits of Nina Hamnett (1890–1956)'.

‡

To Carrington

Samuel Solomonovitch Koteliansky (1880–1955) arrived in England in 1911
from Kiev on a three-month economics scholarship and stayed for the rest of his
life, living in St John's Wood, working as a translator from the Russian.
   Aleksandr Feodorovich Kerensky (1881–1970) joined the Socialist
Revolutionary party after the February Revolution of 1917 that overthrew the
Tsarist government, eventually becoming war minister in the provisional
government of Prince Lvov. Sheppard's news was that Kerensky had succeeded
Lvov as premier. History proved Lytton right: Kerensky's insistence on
remaining in World War I and his failure to deal with land distribution
enabled the Bolsheviks to overthrow his government later in 1917.
   Lady Strachey, now seventy-seven, had had her left eye removed, as it was
causing her pain.
   The story of the marriage of Cupid and Psyche is in books IV to VI of The
Golden Ass, *by Lucius Apuleius (second century AD).*

Durbins
July 24th 1917

I was very glad to get such a charming and long letter this morning –
with such beautiful pictures too! The damozels have won my heart. But
it's a highly compromising piece! If Marjorie discovers it –!
   You seem to have been Kotifying a great deal. If all Russians are like
him, no wonder they haven't made peace yet. I am interested to hear
Sheppard's account of Kerensky's doings. That, no doubt, is the
charitable view, but I wonder whether there's any reason for believing
it. Also, personally, it seems to me, however bad a separate peace might
be, the Russians ought to make it. Even the worst peace is peace, and I
gather from the papers that that is the opinion of the Russian soldiers.
Only of course I admit that if they could make a general peace it would
be better still.
   Life proceeds here in rather a hobbling manner. A good deal of time
has to be spent with her Ladyship, I find, so that Gordon is beginning to
get behindhand. I shall have to re-organise somehow or other – perhaps
get up at six and work for two hours before breakfast. Can you envision
that?
   This is not a letter – merely a 'merci beaucoup' for *your* letter. Why
you say it's not a 'proper' one I can't conceive. Perfectly proper, I assure

you, my dear Madam. – But it's getting late, and if I'm to be up at six
tomorrow morning – hum! hum! –

   Blessings be upon you
                    with love from your
                                        Lytton

I'd no idea the raid on Sunday morning was so near to London. How
beastly! But I gather it wasn't so alarming as the last.
   Did you realise that Cupid and Psyche occurs in the Golden Ass?

‡

To Vanessa Bell

*Vanessa was worried that Lytton had designs on the Charleston barn as housing
for himself and Carrington.*

                                        Durbins
                                August 6th 1917

Dearest Nessa,

Lawks a mussy me! How things do get about to be sure! I see that my
reputation for discretion (such as there was of it) has gone forever, and
that I shall never be allowed out by myself again. It's all too clear to me
that no one will ever believe that in this case the indiscretion was not
on my side – that it was not I who made the advances – not I who
wrote and suggested that 'showing round'. Well, it can't be helped! I
shall have to sit in silence under Maynard's sermons . . . I foresee it. And
probably also Clive's.
   Seriously, I don't think you need be alarmed. Certainly not so far as I
am concerned. Neither my passions nor my tastes are to the slightest
degree; therefore I can guarantee complete propriety of conduct. I don't
in the least want to be 'shown round' – not in the least. And, if the offer
was made, I should of course reject it. Personally, I think the 'German
spy' question more serious. It is decidedly unfortunate being so
noticeable a figure. Ought I to have my beard for the period of the war?
But would even that lull the suspicions of the yokels? It seems indeed
absurd to suggest not coming to Charleston. I had been looking forward

to it very much – to say nothing of Carrington; but if my mere presence
in the fields about involved dangers to you . . . Do you think that is so?
I don't think I *could* guarantee not to go for walks (properly
accompanied by females) – it would be too artificial. My hope is that
you don't think the case is as bad as that. But perhaps you would like
me to put off coming for the present? Please let me know your final
opinion; but don't let considerations of my loose desires enter into the
question, because (whatever they may be in other directions) they are
simply non-existent in the direction of Charleston barn.

Perhaps there's no need to decide anything just yet. I shall be at
Asheham from the 14th to the 21st, and perhaps you or Duncan will
appear there then. Please forgive me, if you can, for these imbroglios,
and don't suppose that I shall ever be offended by anything you may say
or do.

Your

Lytton

‡

To Virginia Woolf

*The original of this letter, James Strachey wrote on his 1948 copy and
reconstruction of it, 'is much damaged by damp, but completely legible'. The
reason James thought Lytton had misdated the letter is that Virginia Woolf's
reply ('The only way out is a taxi, or fly, unless you walk') is clearly dated
the 14th.*

Durbins
Guildford
Surrey
August 15th *[?13th]* 1917

I hope you won't have been put out by my wire. I find myself plunged
in a gulf of Gordon, from which it is impossible to emerge for 2 or 3
days. Then I hope the crisis will be over – though there'll be some
finishing paragraphs to be applied. Please expect me on Thursday. I shall
hope to be permitted to crouch in some corner, of a morning, with my
pen and paper and gigantic authorities. It is all extremely exhausting, but
I suppose in the end I shall drag through still breathing.

How does one get to you from Lewes? In a taxi? Are there any left?
With apologies and regrets.

your

Lytton

‡

To Carrington

*Carrington's brother, Noel, who had been commissioned into the same Wiltshire
Regiment as his two brothers, was on leave from the front, and she and he went
on a walking tour. Starting from Oxford, they walked to Wantage and stayed at
the Bear Inn, finally discovering the 'village called Ham at the foot of the big
Combe downs', where Carrington and Lytton were one day to settle.*[1]

The 'chance volume of Harper's' that gave Lytton the idea for Eminent
Victorians *was probably* Harper's Weekly, *an American publication.*

*The strange housing scheme was to take Carrington's parents' house,
Hurstbourne Tarrant. The elder Carringtons wanted to move to a town – they
had in mind Cheltenham. The low rent for their house was to have been split
between Lytton, Oliver and Harry Norton.*

*Edward Garnett (1869–1937) was a distinguished man of letters and
publishers' reader.*

A trap was a light, usually two-wheeled carriage.

I can't identify Lytton's letter-writing admirer.

Asheham

Monday, *[August 20th 1917]*

Your letters have been very interesting – what a splendid walk! I am
longing to hear the end of it – and all the details. I have stayed a night at
the Bear, Wantage. A little further along on the same side of the street,
you probably didn't observe the Temperance Hotel, where a chance
volume of Harper's gave me (fifty years ago) the idea of Gordon and
then all the other biographies. It's alarming to think that I'm still
feeling the effects of that accident! – The weather has really been rather
good, hasn't it? And of course your vigour is such that you'ld hardly
notice it, anyhow. I can hardly believe that Oliver is really going to
spend the day with you tomorrow. If this gets to you in time, add my
persuasions to yours, in the matter of the house, and assure him that I

shall be ready to go shares. But are your parents going? Are they? Oh, are they?

I am lying on the downs behind the house – not very far from where – ahem! ahem! – It's been a nice week-end. Katherine appeared on Saturday, slightly less metallic than usual, I thought. I've got some more writing done but it's not been possible to do *very* much. The wretched thing's still a good way off ending. I shall have to devote myself to it at Charleston; and I think with luck it should be done by the end of the week. (By-the-bye, how long are we going to stay there?) Otherwise, I've been attacked by violent hay-fever, which in fact I feared would develop into apoplexy, and my legs are completely covered by the bites of various bugs – but I bear up wonderfully.

Bunny and his father appeared for supper yesterday – a queer couple! Katherine of course remarked that the *père* looked like a toy sheep, and that he ought to be put on wheels. (But I don't do her justice.) I told Bunny to warn them of your arrival on Wed. They expect you. Let me know your train and I'll meet you. Shall you want a taxi? I walk this afternoon with Leonard to Firle, to order a 'trap' to take me and my library to Charleston tomorrow. Did I tell you that the other day I had another letter from *him*? Very coming-on as usual. How am I to glissade out of his embraces? – I am getting incoherent among these winds, smells, sunshines, etc., so good-bye, you darling duck. How infuriating it will be if this weather collapses just when we want to start off on our tour! If so, we shall have to get mackintoshes!

your
Lytton

1. Quoted in Gretchen Gerzina, *Carrington*, p. 118.

‡

To Carrington

There were certainly many Russian Jews in London at this time, escapees from Tsarist persecution, and then from the Revolution and there may well have been a conspicuous 'foreign' Jewish presence on the streets of London at the time of writing. (The number of Russian Jews in London during the war, of military age, not subject to British conscription because of their nationality, is put at 25,000 by one twenty-first century anti-Semitic website.) In any case, interest in

matters pertaining to Jews was acute, as the negotiations leading up to the
Balfour Declaration took place this month.
   Oliver and Lytton were both members of the Oriental Club.

Belsize Park Gardens
Monday morning, *[October 22nd 1917]*

[. . .] London is appalling. My one object is to leave it for ever. I can see
no merit in it. This room in itself is enough to undermine the stoutest
morale. It is maddening to see the blue sky over the chimney-pots, and
to guess from the squalid leaves on the pavements how wonderful the
country trees must be. As for people, after struggling for three or four
hours through dense mobs of foreign Jews, one sees somebody for
twenty minutes, and then has to dash back again though the same mob
to one's grim cellar-residence. So I shall do all I can for Tidmarsh.
   The other night Oliver, James, and I *[were]* nearer danger than we'd
supposed. We emerged from the Oriental Club (Hanover Square) at
about 11 – the streets packed with people – and we walked to the
Oxford Street tube. Just after we'd gone down, the bomb must have
dropped in Piccadilly Circus, where the scenes were apparently ghastly.
We heard nothing, as we were in the tube.
   I hope my letters have reached you. It doesn't sound like it.

your
Lytton

‡

To Clive Bell

Margot Asquith published her 'American Impressions' in the November issue of
Pearson's Magazine.

6, Belsize Park Gardens
Hampstead, N.W.
November 6th 1917

It was delightful to get such a letter from you – and I hope you'll
continue; you may be sure that my discretion (after so many painful
experiences) will be irreproachable.

I gather from Mary on the telephone that there is a possibility of our lunching together on Thursday. I hope so – on Friday I trundle to Garsington for the week-end; it's very annoying that you're not to be there. I suppose I shall be able to keep a cheerful countenance till the first trains on Monday morning; but in that place one can never be sure: nerve-storms, I find, sweep upon one, in that atmosphere, like Typhoons, or whatever the mariners call them. I sympathise with you in the article of Gertler; gracious God! he won't be there, will he, over next week-end? All the same, of course, I must confess to a certain liking for the little fellow (. . . 'certain'? you murmur . . .) and also to some admiration. But I understand only too well the unfortunate elements in his conversation. One of the curiosities seems to be the combination of him and her Ladyship. What does it mean? I should have thought, a priori, that they would have found it impossible to have anything to do with each other. It's very strange. He once told me that he liked her because she was so 'motherly'. Tiens! Perhaps they're so wildly different, that neither has any notion of what the other's like, and so they're able to mix and mingle without any difficulty – though, I suppose, after all, their interweavings don't go much further than an after-lunch pianola romp.

My plans for the future are quite devoid of mystery, I assure you. It seems now that it may be possible to put into action the project of last year – viz. to get a house, to be occupied more or less in common by Oliver, Saxon, Norton, Maynard, Barbara, Carrington, and myself – the London workers to come down for week-ends or other holidays, Carrington and I to be there more (though not altogether) permanently. I find London more and more disagreeable, and difficult to work in; and Carrington also wants to be in the country; so it appears on the whole a reasonable project. I shouldn't be able to face it alone; female companionship I think may make it more tolerable – though certainly by no means romantic. I am under no illusions. But in the present miserable, chaotic, and suspended state of affairs, it seems to me the best that can be done. A little quiet work is really almost all that one can look forward to, just now. The house is a mile from Pangbourne, so it's very easy to get at. It looked rather attractive, in a mild way. Negotiations are on foot; but it has not actually been taken yet. And in any case will hardly be habitable for months.

This rather dreary explanation will I hope satisfy you that all is above board. Please don't believe in the hidden hand. There is only one that I know of, and that can hardly be called hidden – it is too obvious, and has been too often found out. It's this wretched separation of everybody that makes one uncomfortable. But my hope is that if the house at Tidmarsh comes into being, it may be possible by the summer to have some pleasant reunions in the old style, whether the war's going on or not.

I'm very glad that you really are writing. I hope it will be more than an article. My biographies seem to be drawing to a close, and I am beginning to think of publishers. By-the-bye, talking of literature, have you seen Mrs Asquith's latest production in 'Pearson's Magazine'? Mon dieu! How can these people go about, completely lifting up their garments and displaying their squalid deformations with so triumphant a complacency? The poor woman has neither wit nor grammar, and she hurries into 'Pearson's Magazine' to tell one so! Certainly something serious has come over the governing classes. I spend most of my time reading Greville's Memoirs (do you know them?) – very dry, and as long as they are dry – just the kind of book that pleases me. He was a slow-going member of the governing classes of those days – the days of Sir Robert Peel and Lord Melbourne – and he writes with a restraint and a distinction . . . Margot's performances would have made him extremely ill. – And now the world is delivered into the hands of Margot.

Well, we shall meet so soon that I shall stop now. The only news I have is that John has been made a major. He is to go to 'the front' and paint 'the war' for 'the Canadians'. But I'm sorry to say that he will not be obliged to shave his beard.

ever your
Lytton

‡

To Carrington

Before Garsington, the Morrells had lived at Peppard Cottage, Henley. T. ('Tommy') W. Earp (d.1958) was president of the Oxford Union just before the war, and according to J. R. R. Tolkien (in a letter to his son Christopher of 6 October 1944) 'the original twerp', editor of Oxford Poetry 1915–19, *art critic and friend of the Johns. D. H. Lawrence attacked him in verse: 'I heard a little chicken chirp:/My name is Thomas, Thomas Earp,/and I can neither paint nor write,/I can only put other people right.' Tancred Borenius (1885–*

1948), the Finnish art historian, became Professor of the History of Art at University College London in 1922.

6, Belsize Park Gardens
Wednesday, November 21st 1917

I returned here yesterday, having been induced to stay on a day longer. Your letter was waiting for me, and this morning the muffetee and note arrived. Much thanks for the former – it is charming; but isn't it female? Anyhow, just now, it doesn't matter, as it's luckily turned hot, and one can walk about naked. I don't quite make out what your plans are – whether you return to London on Thursday, after Tidmarsh, or to Hurstbourne. I have a feeling that this will hardly reach you before I see you, which rather takes the heart out of letter writing. I am in a state of considerable collapse – better as to bodily health, but the mind and spirit strangely fermenting, and drifting and irresponsible. This is not the result of Garsington, which passed in a dream. I seemed to myself to be thinking of other things most of the time. Still I couldn't help observing certain facts. Virginia was in high feather, and quite dominated the assembly: very different from her demeanour about ten years ago at Peppard, when she crouched before Ottoline like a suppliant kitten. I don't think there was anyone else there – except Aldous for one night. I saw a good deal of Clive – a little of Gerald and Fredegond (who looked very ill). On Sunday Evan appeared for tea, in a taxi from Oxford, dressed in a black velvet coat, a white floppy collar, black bow tie, etc., and looking really rather pretty, though sadly effete. Then there was Earp (poor creature) and the Swiss municipal nephew of Sargent, who regaled us with Bach and Beethoven. Her Ladyship I had a great deal of, as on Monday we were left alone, even 'Brettie' absent in London. It was a sufficiently uneasy business . She is so worm-eaten with envy and malevolence one hardly knows where to tread – very unfortunate. I thought, too (after 24 hours of tête-à-tête) that I detected something like a sense of guilt, and perhaps if one got hold of her, isolated from Philip and the rest of the horrors, she might take on a new lease of life. The worst of it is that she shows no symptoms of *liking* anybody – it is all either underhand cat's-clawing or vague romantic flummery: decidedly, most unfortunate. I saw Brett's parasol picture, and liked it very much. It's not yet finished, however, and she seemed slightly vague about it. I thought it needed a little more definiteness – it is too large and the subject too important for a sketch. Borenius apparently had said that silly thing people are so fond of saying – 'Don't touch it any more. It's perfect!' – However, I've no doubt she'll have the sense to go on with it according to her own judgment. *[. . .]*

‡

To Lady Ottoline Morrell

The show at the Alpine Club was the largest Augustus John had yet had and, said The Times *(27 November), marked him as 'the most famous of living English painters'.*[1]

[6, Belsize Park Gardens]
Sunday, *[November 25th 1917]*

[. . .] Last night was the last of the operas – Figaro. It was very enjoyable, as usual, and we had the benefit of a speech from Sir T*[homas]* B*[eecham]*. What a pompous bounder! My eye!

In the afternoon there was a private view of John's productions at the Alpine Club. Such a strange well-dressed and respectable crowd! The great man appeared in the middle of it, dressed in a neat but not gaudy khaki suit, with his beard considerably trimmed, and altogether a decidedly Colonial air. On the whole, I must say I prefer him en bohémien. I was introduced to Lady Tredegar, who wasn't at all what I imagined. Also, at Figaro, studied Evan's sister – very like him, and very attractive.

If you show this to Brett, she will observe that I have received her somewhat risqué communication. But so far I've not succeeded in composing an adequate reply.

ever your
Lytton

1. Michael Holroyd, *Augustus John*, vol. 2, p. 63 and n. 461.

‡

To Clive Bell

J. M. Murry had had suspected tuberculosis the late autumn before this letter was written (in fact, it was Katherine Mansfield who actually had contracted the disease), and Ottoline had been prepared to nurse him, in the cottage he and Mansfield rented at Garsington. Katherine, however, said she couldn't manage even the tiny rent, and that they would give up the cottage. Ottoline was wounded to learn (at about the time of this letter) that Katherine was actually giving up the cottage because Murry had told her (falsely) that Ottoline had tried to seduce him when he was at Garsington in July.

Established in 1865 by a Paris wine merchant, the Café Royal, on Regent Street near Piccadilly Circus, had been a raffish Bohemian hangout since the time of Oscar Wilde. 'For more than five decades,' writes Virginia Nicholson (Clive Bell's granddaughter), 'it was as essential to London's cultural life in the twentieth century as the Café Momus had been to Paris Bohemians in the nineteenth.'[1] Mrs Nicholson mentions Sylvia Gough in a list of 'those of the artistic community brought low by alcohol'.[2]

The 'greenery, yallery' Grosvenor Gallery was founded in Mayfair in 1877 by Sir Coutts Lindsay (1839–1913). Max Beerbohm often exhibited his caricatures there.

Robert Nichols (1893–1944) was a poet and dramatist, recently returned from the Belgian-French front, now working in the Ministry of Labour and regarded as a successor to Rupert Brooke. So his opinion of Eminent Victorians *might be thought to be important.*

Lytton had written about Lady Mary Wortley Montagu as long ago as 1907. 'George Paston' was indeed a pseudonym – for Miss E. M. Symonds, who wrote the book Lytton is castigating, Lady Mary Wortley Montagu and Her Times *(1907), which contained some 'hitherto unpublished letters'. The great 1911* Encyclopaedia Britannica *says of the events Lytton refers to:*

> *At Florence in 1740 she visited Horace Walpole, who cherished a great spite against her, and exaggerated her eccentricities into a revolting slovenliness . . . She lived at Avignon, at Brescia, and at Lovere, on the Lago d'Iseo. She was disfigured by a painful skin disease, and her sufferings were so acute that she hints at the possibility of madness. She was struck with a terrible 'fit of sickness' while visiting the countess Palazzo and her son, and perhaps her mental condition made restraint necessary. As Lady Mary was then in her sixty-third year, the scandalous interpretation put on the matter by Horace Walpole may safely be discarded.*

6, Belsize Park Gardens
December 4th 1917

I should be delighted to have dinner at Gordon Square on Thursday.
I suppose you'll let me know if you're not to be up. I agree with you
as to the pleasures of London, and if one could be content to live
simply from hand to mouth, it would be absurd to leave it. But really
one must work; and for that un peu de recueillement is necessary.
My notion is not to retire altogether – but for two or three weeks at
a time; and to spend happy intervals gadding about among such
people as are left. It will be a very short journey – and then, in the
Summer, there's sure to be plenty of company for the week-ends.
Also, on the mere article of pleasure, I'm not so sure whether the
country isn't really best off – at any rate one thinks so on days like
this, with frost and a thick fog producing an icy darkness while no
doubt you're having at any rate blue skies and sunshine – though also
Ottoline. However, you apparently manage to avoid her, and now
that she has Murry to massage back to life, the Cottage must be
having quite an easy time of it. It seems an odd volte-face, but
(considering the persons concerned) not a very surprising one. Does
Katherine remain, I wonder, or is she too removed, with Pipsey,
during the week-ends? I saw Gerald and Fredegond for a moment
the other night at Omega, but it was impossible to have any talk with
them. I hope to hear details on Thursday.

I have been seeing a good deal of company – chiefly of the Café
Royal type, which you don't care for, but which I find full of interest
– and even agreeableness. The poor dears – you would hardly believe
it – are so good-natured. This, it's true, is largely the result of a
perpetual demi-drunkenness – but that's of no consequence. It
amuses me to see that debauched female, Sylvia Gough, in evening
dress and furs, wobbling, quite boozed, from table to table in that
appalling haunt, smoking cigarettes with a shaking hand, assuring
everybody that she's not drunk – that she's promised Wilfred to drink
only lemonade – giving half-crowns to casual waiters, and saying, as
she does so, with a perfect Parisian accent, 'je suis charmée de vous
voir'. But I'm afraid I can't quite give it – it will appear to you
melodramatic – and you won't sympathise. On Saturday night things
culminated in a dinner party at John's – a farewell party; he went to
France, as a Canadian Major, on Sunday. The party was a complete
frost, though full of curiosities – which I shan't describe. Poor John!

Did you by any chance go to that show of his at the Alpine Club? The impression produced by the reduplication of all that superficial and pointless facility was most painful. Naturally he has become the darling of the upper classes, and made £5000 out of this show. His appearance in khaki is unfortunate – a dwindled creature, with clipped beard, pseudo-smart, and in fact altogether deplorable. All the same, late on Saturday night, there were moments when, in spite of everything. . . . Mais assez!

But talking of pictures, there are the Maxes at the Grosvenor Gallery. Have you seen them? I thought before I went that I should be rather bored – that I'd seen enough of that business; but I was quite carried away. He certainly has a most remarkable and seductive genius – and I should say about the smallest in the world.

It was a great pleasure seeing Mary again; the melancholy thing is that I see her so rarely – the obstacles are too great. I spend the intervals of my social life in putting the final corrections into my Lives – a horrid job, but now, I'm glad to say, nearly over. Every one conspires to urge Chatto and Windus upon me – including Mr Robert Nichols, who hurried up to me the other evening, and assured me they were just the people for my book, with its delicate ironical flavour, etc. etc. as if he'd read it all, years ago. So I suppose it will have to be C. and W. – if they'll agree. I fear it may not strike them as quite sufficiently advanced.

As for Lady Mary, I admire her immensely – though the Turkish letters, which are most talked of, are I think the least interesting. Those of the last period – to Lady Bute from Italy – are in some ways the most remarkable. Are they in your edition? I have a notion that the earlier editions don't have them – or only in part. There are also some singular love-letters, which have been most unfortunately maltreated by a reptile calling himself 'George Paston', so that they're almost impossible to read. There's a savage account of her at Florence by H.W., which you doubtless remember; her Italian goings-on were decidedly dubious. It's difficult to see why she became so miserable (though more and more eminent) in the end.

ever yours
Lytton

1. Virginia Nicholson, *Among the Bohemians*, p. 269.
2. ibid., p. 274.

✦

To Carrington

The Vale and Mallord Street are in Chelsea, near the Embankment. Oswald
Eden Dickinson (c.1868–1954) was the younger of Violet Dickinson's two
brothers, and lived with her. The Dickinsons were Quakers, but with aristocratic
connections to the Edens; they were friends of the Duckworth family, and Violet
was one of Virginia's close friends. Enid (Algerine) Bagnold (Lady Jones, 1889–
1981), who became famous with the publication of National Velvet *in 1935,*
was an art student until in 1914 she joined the Voluntary Aid Detachment as a
nurse in a military hospital in Woolwich. She wrote a critical pamphlet about her
experiences, which resulted in her being sacked; she then volunteered as a driver
and was sent to France. She had an affair with Frank Harris, but married Sir
Roderick Jones in 1920 and became a writer and playwright.

Monty Shearman (Sir Montague Shearman, KC, 1857–1930), barrister,
judge, collector and in 1917, great host and party-giver, was a particular patron of
Mark Gertler. Greville, Lord Melbourne and Creevey refer to Lytton's reading.

6, Belsize Park Gardens
Sunday, December 9th 1917

Très-chère

I was very glad to get your letter, though it was rather like a serial
story, 'to be continued in our next', with the furniture question still
hanging in the balance in a most agitating manner. I hope to get the
continuation tomorrow, and that all will wend happily. If I'd been
there I think I should have insisted on staying the night at an inn in
Pangbourne, rather than face the fearful prospect of a night involved in
curtains. But I daresay really *you* would rather enjoy it. – What a mercy
that Madam Legg is so competent . . . as for her only son . . . hum,
hum! – I imagine that Barbara may be with you by now, which will be
a comfort. I am longing to come down and see it all. Is the rub-a-dub
in the library of such a nature that one can't bear it? Or is it perhaps a
discreet whirring, which might even encourage the literary flow? – We
shall see.

I've been leading a very busy life, it seems to me. All the Victorians
are now neatly bound in their red cases, ready to be taken off to the
publishers – whoever they may be. Further corrections to follow. These

manipulations took up a good deal of time. Then I went to tea with
Ethel Sands in her très-soigné Vale Avenue residence. There she was in
a black velvet tea-gown. Various other persons quickly arrived – her
brother Morty (a veritable half-wit, and ex-master of Nina Lamb).
Logan Pearsall-Smith, an upper-class young man called Ozzy Dickinson
(barmy too) – and a tiresomely elegant young female of the name of
Enid Bagnold, fresh from the Tombola Fair. It was all absurdly polite
and futile, and punctuated by milk-and-water indecencies, which made
my heart sink into my boots, and made *them* rock with laugher. Dear,
dear! I felt inclined to say 'Fuck! Bugger!' and leave the room; but
instead of that I faintly smiled, and no doubt Ozzy thought I was
shocked, while Enid cast an occasional alarmed and languishing glance
in my direction. When I'd escaped, I felt that something must be done,
so as Mallord Street was just round the corner, I went there, and found
Dorelia sola. We proceeded to the Chinese establishment, and after that
to a cinema. It was all just as usual. She was as charming and beautiful
and difficult to approach as ever. She seemed pathetic, I thought –
going back to the country tomorrow – so dim and solitary; but no
doubt she enjoys herself in her peculiar way. She sent her love to you. I
asked her to come to Tidmarsh when it was warmer, and she seemed
delighted at the idea. She got at last into a number 14 bus at Piccadilly
Circus, and I tottered to my tube at Leicester Square.

Yesterday Mark came to tea, and was very friendly. So much so, in
fact, that he asked me to go with him next Wednesday evening and
'drink wine' – and I said I would. It all rather alarms me. He is evidently
getting frightfully bored with Monty, and (in a lesser degree) with the
rest of those associates – and I suppose he found me a change. I find *him*
very attractive. I really do like him – and would like to be friends with
him; but the worst of it is that I can't feel any faith in him; I think he
plays fast and loose, and is probably too self-concentrated to care much
about anyone – except when he's in love (and that's after all hardly
more than another form of self-concentration). It's a nuisance to have to
be on one's guard, when one doesn't in the least want to be.   And it's
so silly – his way of going on – because there's no point in it. However,
I don't suppose it can be helped.

Today I go to tea and dinner at Richmond, which I am looking
forward to very much. It will be a damp journey though. Is it pouring
too at Tidmarsh? I'm afraid you must be having a lugubrious time of it.
The only relief is that that icy cold weather seems to have come to an
end. Do you go to Cheltenham tomorrow? I hope I shall hear again

from you before long. Ott comes to town, to stay with the Sands woman this week, and I shall hardly be able to escape seeing her, and I daresay I shall throw myself at her feet, and vow that I am her devoted slave. Deary, deary me.

I don't think there's any more news. Greville is nearly done, I'm sorry to say. Then hey! For Lord Melbourne and Creevey! But how am I to decide what to work at when the retirement finally comes? – ???

James says we shall have peace within the week. Hum! – We shall – oh, I beg pardon. (He's always repeating his effects. – D.C.)

Give my love to Barbara

With embraces from
                    your
                          Lytton

                          ‡

To Virginia Woolf

At the foot of his 1948 copy of this letter James has written: 'The original is much damaged by damp and in places illegible.' James's conjectured readings are in square brackets. At the head of the letter Lytton has written 'Could you someday send that General here, do you think? No particular hurry,' referring to the copy of his General Gordon chapter that he'd left after he'd visited the Woolfs at Richmond on the 9th. Prompted by this visit, Virginia made a long diary entry:

> *On Sunday Lytton came to tea. I was alone, for L. went to Margaret. I enjoyed it very much. He is one of the most supple of our friends; I don't mean passionate or masterful or original, but the person whose mind seems softest to impressions, least starched by any formality or impediment. There is his great gift of expression of course, never (to me) at its best in writing; but making him in some respects the most sympathetic and understanding friend to talk to. Moreover, he has become, or now shows it more fully, curiously gentle, sweet tempered, considerate; and if one adds his peculiar flavour of mind, his wit and infinite intelligence – not brain but intelligence – he is a figure not to be replaced by any other combination. Intimacy seems to me possible with him as scarcely with any one; for, besides tastes in common, I like and think I understand his feelings – even in their more capricious developments; for example in the matter of Carrington. He spoke of her, by the way, with a candour not flattering, though not at all malicious.*

'That woman will dog me' – he remarked. *'She won't let me write, I daresay.'*

'Ottoline was saying you would end by marrying her.'

'God! the mere notion is enough – *One thing I know* – *I'll never marry anyone.'*

'But if she's in love with you?'

'Well, then she must take her chance.'

'I believe I'm sometimes jealous – *'*

'Of her? that's inconceivable – *'*

'You like me better, don't you?'

He said he did; we laughed; remarked on our wish for an intimate correspondence; but how to overcome the difficulties? Should we attempt it? Perhaps.

He brought us his Gordon. Next day he was to take the book to Chatto & Windus.

Leonard and James's edition omits the remarks about Clive's poems. Bell's Ad Familiares *had just been published. 'The Bugger Married', Lytton's comic view of his new domestic life with Carrington, was superseded as a subject for the play he was to write for a charity gala by 'Quasheemaboo or The Noble Savage'.*

The Mill House
Tidmarsh
Pangbourne
December 21st 1917

Here I am, in considerable agony. Nature turned crusty, the 'pipes' are congealed, and it has been so cold that my nose (to say nothing of other parts) dripped in icicles. My female companion – but I must observe that it has begun to thaw, so that no doubt now the 'pipes' (what *are* they?) will [be burst] and we shall be deluged; but no matter. – My female companion keeps herself warm by unpacking, painting, pruning the creepers, knocking in nails, etc. Tomorrow [night(?) James and] Alix arrive – what *they* [will] do, I can't imagine, [illegible] etc. I try to console myself with Queen Victoria's letters – but I should prefer yours. Please write. I remain here for at least another week; after that, I gather, I'm doomed to Garsington for the New Year; after that, here again, I fancy. I still have a notion that I may be able to work in this seclusion, when all the nails have been finally knocked in. Nous verrons.

No doubt you've received 'Ad Familiares'. Good gracious me! What

– but bright comments are unnecessary, and besides, your well known indiscretion . . . I reserve my remarks. But how is one to reply to it? I should be glad of a little advice. A little advice also on a plot for a comedy would be useful. The worst of it is, it must be fit for publication. Otherwise 'Le Bougre Marié' might be a good title. But how would it end?

Will you tell Leonard that I was very sorry not to be able to go and see Philip? I had very few mornings, and they were all filled. I was very glad he liked Gordon. Have you read it yet? My fear is that it may be, in places, emphatic. [Do] you think so? The adjectives seemed to get a little thick at times, and the style altogether – if you observed anything of the sort, alterations might be made. Or in other directions. You see [there are plenty of things] to write to me about, so you really must. It [is (illegible)] having so little conversation with you; and this method's better than nothing, *I* think.

Who is staying with [you?] Are you too very dank and cold? Or will you pretend that the sun has been shining over your downs? I refuse to believe it. Nessa and Duncan I suppose you'll be seeing, with Maynard thrown in, wondrously agreeable. Ah, dearie, dearie me, I am nodding over the fire, and she's sewing an edge to the carpet, with a diligence . . . Ah, la vie! it grows more remarkable every minute.

your
Lytton

‡

To Clive Bell

The 'Christmas bouquet' was Bell's collection of poems, Ad Familiares. *Victor Duruy (1811–94) whose best-known work is his* Histoire des Romans *(7 vols, 1870–85; trans. 8 vols, 1883), also wrote popular histories of Greece and France. The historical dictionary* Biographie Universelle *seems to have run to eighty-five volumes by 1862. There are now many books with the title* Le Siècle de Louis XIV, *but Norton was almost certainly reading Voltaire.*

Lytton was well ahead of his time in seeing that Pangbourne would one day be the paragon of suburbia then (and now) represented by Surbiton in Surrey.

The 'poetaster' T. S. Eliot published in his Poems (1920):

The broad-backed hippopotamus
Rests on his belly in the mud;
Although he seems so firm to us
He is merely flesh and blood.
Flesh and blood is weak and frail,
Susceptible to nervous shock;
While the True Church can never fail
For it is based upon a rock.

Norton was browsing in Lytton's extensive library in French. Nicolas Chamfort (1741–94) was a journalist, aphorist and playwright noted for his one-act comedy 'La Jeune Indienne', 1764. Sample aphorism: 'The majority of those who put together collections of verses or epigrams resemble those who eat cherries or oysters: they begin by choosing the best and end by eating everything.'

The Mill House
Tidmarsh
Pangbourne
December 31st 1917

Dear Clive,

I hope you will forgive my long and disgraceful silence, for which there have been reasons – movements, agitations, Christmas parties, and so on, resulting in a general suspension of the epistolary faculties. I felt that it was useless to attempt to communicate until a certain degree of quiescence had appeared. Your magnificent Christmas bouquet increases my guilt. It was really charming, and I hope we shall have one every year. I think I liked the series published in the Nation best of all. My only criticism is that you seem to be rather too free with Cockney rhymes: but perhaps this is too old-fashioned an objection to count. Rupert (didn't he?) rhymed Ka and star – so I suppose that sets an unimpeachable precedent. Also, I observed the other day, to my horror, that Swinburne has dawn and morn rhyming – an extraordinary lapse, after which anything becomes justifiable.

I don't know whether answers to your literary inquiries will now be quite out of date. Probably the Walpole Memoirs were the Memoirs of George III (four vols.), and I fancy they're all right. As to Duruy – what could have put you on to him? I *have* read him – in my extreme youth;

but it's the merest schoolmasterishness – not at all recommended. I wish I was in the way of Hatchard's secondhand department – but if I did go there, I should certainly lose my head, and emerge a bankrupt, with La Fontaine's Contes illustrated by Moreau le jeune, and seventy-two volumes of the Biographie Universelle bound in purple morocco, under my arm. No, no.

Luckily the recesses of the country remove one from such temptations. I am gradually settling down (amidst a good deal of loose paint and calico) to a regular rural existence, and before long I hope really to be involved in work. We had quite a mouvementé Christmas – two very gay visits from Gerald and Fredegond – and then, on Xmas Eve, Harry arrived, carrying in a neat satchel a turkey and four bottles of claret. He has lingered on, I am glad to say, and is at the present moment sitting on the other side of the fire, reading alternately the poems of Laforgue and the Siècle de Louis XIV. On Saturday I come to Garsington – I hope to goodness you will be there. I shall stay for the bare week-end, and then return to town for a day or two – partly for the purpose of interviewing Messrs Chatto and Windus, who have accepted my book. They want to do it on the royalty system, which I think is certainly the best; but negotiations are still proceeding.

What have you been doing? I heard that you were to be at Charleston; but I suppose you can hardly be there still. What happened there? Did you see Virginia? And who else? You see I know nothing, in this curious Surbitonesque desolation; and of course I can tell you nothing. Please give my love to Mary, when next you see her. My spirit failed me over those spouting poetasters – but I wish I had been there. I went to lunch with Ethel Sands a day or two later, but of course she gave me no descriptions – except that she thought Eliot on the Hippopotamus the height of brilliance and wit. Well, perhaps after Mr Robert Nichols on everything else, one would.

Adieu. Harry has lapsed into Chamfort, and Carrington demands my assistance over the glue-pot. This life is decidedly a flux.

your
Lytton

‡

To Carrington

The left-wing 1917 Club, named for the February Revolution, was founded by Leonard Woolf and Oliver Strachey in Soho. Lady Strachey had her eye removed the previous summer, which is why she had a rota of people to read to her. Lytton meant Carrington's fellow Slade painter John Nash (1893–1977) and his wife.

Tidmarsh was found in order to rescue Lytton from Hampstead. Naturally, Lady Strachey would not have seen it in that light, so it was difficult for Lytton to break the news of it to his mother. 'Lady Strachey,' writes Holroyd, 'did not voice her disapproval – that was not her way. But her distaste was to be sensed in what she failed to say. "A curious scene at Belsize Park," Leonard Woolf reported to Lytton a few weeks after the Mill House had been taken. (January 1918). "Virginia and I at tea with her Ladyship. V. very innocently: 'Well, Lady Strachey, and what do you think of Tidmarsh?' An awkward pause and some very indistinct remarks from her Ladyship. A pause. Then across the table to me: 'What do you think of it all?' (She was referring to the general European situation, but I naturally thought she referred to Tidmarsh)".[1]

6, Belsize Park Gardens
Hampstead, N.W.3
January 18th 1918

I am very glad to hear from you this morning, ma chère, and to learn that painting operations had begun. But what an unlucky affair about the young slavey! I am very much excited at the prospect of a new withdrawing room. I find it difficult to imagine anything but the old white satinette.

London is pretty putrid – slushy and cold to a degree. Nothing happens. I find I am a good deal tied to the house by her Ladyship, as the best reading time for her is between tea and dinner – which cuts off the Club in a sad way. For which reason, I shouldn't, if I were you, be influenced by prospects of seeing me, in your views of coming to London. Why not get J. Nash et femme to go to Tidmarsh for the early days of next week? Perhaps I am jaundiced, but personally it seems to me that this town is a place to avoid, unless business summons.

Nothing heard as yet from Chatto's – I hope they got my various communications. The wretch Virginia told my mother that I was reviewing Morley. If she sees it, all will be lost, as her pet opinions are the exact contrary. But perhaps Mr Massingham will forbid it. The woman also came out with Tidmarsh, of which her Ladyship had not heard a word. But I reassured her with great skill, and it went off most naturally. This interview occurred while I was away – the Woolves came for a reading.

Nothing at all to chronicle, and so farewell.

Have you enough money?

with love, your
Lytton

1. Michael Holroyd, *Lytton Strachey*, pp.402–3.

‡

To Clive Bell

Geoffrey Whitworth was the art editor of Chatto & Windus, and had asked Roger Fry for a book on Post-Impressionism; Fry recommended Bell, and now Whitworth was publishing Lytton. The suggestion seems to be that Mary Hutchinson's broadminded husband, Jack, had banned Clive from their Valentine's Day party at their house in Ravenscourt Park in Hammersmith, West London. The pink satin shoes seem to imply that the party was fancy-dress. The Gertler fracas: the painter had only just realized that Carrington was living with Lytton at Tidmarsh, and exploded with jealousy, attacking Lytton as he and Carrington left the party. It was 'cinematographic' because the wartime blackout meant there was no street lighting. Fortunately, the other party guests named in the letter were nearby, and managed to separate Lytton and Gertler. The next day, Holroyd reports, as Lytton was dining at the Eiffel Tower restaurant with David Garnett, Gertler appeared and apologized. 'Lytton giggled and replied: "It was nothing at all. Please don't worry yourself about it."

'"I don't think," David Garnett later commented, "that it was what Gertler wanted to be told." '[1]

Sir Sidney Colvin (1845–1927) was the friend of R. L. Stevenson and was Slade Professor of Fine Arts at Cambridge and Keeper of Prints and Drawings at the British Museum. His John Keats: His Life and Poetry *was published in 1917. Keats and copulation: in 1968 my fellow postgraduate student in the Harvard English department, Robert Fichter, was able to carry out research using the papers of Keats's doctor, held by the Harvard Medical School, from which he concluded that Keats was being treated for gonorrhoea.*

The Mill House
Tidmarsh
Pangbourne
February 18th 1918

Yes, Clive, it is truly shocking – I know – I know. It has been weighing on my conscience for weeks past – And your long amusing letter – and the gratifying note of Mr Whitworth's so kindly sent me – and all met by not so much as a word. I perceive clearly that there is no excuse for such disgraceful conduct, and therefore shall attempt none, beyond the general frailty of the human race. I might also remark that I have been horribly occupied by the writing of preposterous reviews and the correcting of pestiferous proof-sheets – which is true; but hardly relevant. What is perhaps more so is that I did hope to see you at Mary's the other night, and obtain in person my forgiveness, and perhaps also retail to you by word of mouth some part of the gems which I had failed to write to you – But no! I suppose M. le Mari had issued a non possumus; and now I hardly think we can meet for six weeks or so, as I have determined to imbed myself here if I possibly can for that period, and it is still too cold and unkempt in these regions to ask you to come into them. (N.B. 'Imbed' must be taken metaphorically if you please.) I am in fact looking forward to what may be called a little solid work, after the various distractions of the last month or so. Not only have reviews, proofs and publishers' contracts been disturbing me, but the house here has been mostly full, with married couples (and occasionally triplets), and I have had two really hectic visits to London. As life proceeds, I find myself more and more in the state of a young lady at her first ball. As for growing blasé with age – mon cher, one begins by being blasé, and dies at the age of ninety in a frenzied whirl of naiveté. However perhaps you don't agree. I daresay I am exceptionally foolish, and at moments I admit that I feel profoundly ashamed of myself. For a middle-aged literary man, with beard and eye-glasses, to be gallivanting in pink satin shoes and sprigged muslin! It is ridiculous, but it has its compensations. I only wish that I could describe to you in detail some of the circumstances . . . *One* at any rate you've probably heard about – the unfortunate occurrence in the purlieus of Ravenscourt Park, after Mary's party. Anything more cinematographic can hardly be imagined, and on looking back it wears all the appearance of a bad dream. All the same, it was at the time exceedingly painful, especially as a little more presence of mind on my part might have prevented the situation; but it

all came about with a speed . . . Poor Mark! The provocation was
certainly great, and I was very sorry for him. However, as he was
obviously drunk, perhaps he was rather less conscious than one
supposed. Characteristically, Maynard came to the rescue, and
eventually led him off, and pacified him, with amazing aplomb. Monty
had already tried, and completely failed; Carrington had fled, under the
protection of Sheppard, who kept on repeating, during the height of the
crisis – 'Who *is* it? Who *is* it?' in a most pained voice; and Harry
supported my trembling form from the field. It was really an
intervention of Providence that they should all have come up at the
psychological moment, as otherwise Heaven knows what mightn't have
happened.

The party itself I enjoyed very much – especially the too-brief vision
of Mary. The bran-pie went off with great éclat, though unfortunately
my contribution to the entertainment unaccountably disappeared.
Perhaps it fell into the hands of some scandalised person, or of some ill-
intentioned one – Well, to prevent its being lost altogether to posterity,
I shall send it you with this.

Coming down here on Saturday, I saw Brett on the platform (she was
seeing Carrington off) who told me that Henry Lamb was on the point
of spending a week in London. So now I suppose you must be a good
deal more solitary than usual, with Gerald and Fredegond's departure
too. But I suppose you enjoy drawing up to the fire with a book of an
evening just as much as ever. I was much excited by the Byron scandal,
which I had not sniffed out before. I have never been able to bring
myself to read a life of him – their stupidity and general horror always
seemed so intense. What a splendid subject he would be for a really
modern and artistic biography!

I have been reading the Keats book. In spite of all Mr Colvin's
tepidity and pomposity, the tragedy of it is overwhelming – don't you
think? It seems to me one of the very most appalling stories known.
One of the worst features of it is, that one gathers that he had never
once copulated. Is it possible, though?

Maynard was here for the week-end, very prosperous, but not very
well, I thought, and full of the Lloyd George crisis. He thought it
possible that a vote of censure might be moved in the House by
infuriated back-bench Tories, that the Government might then fall, and
be succeeded by a Law-Asquith combination, including tout ce qu'il a
de plus respectable, but not pacifist, though destined to make peace. I
doubt it – and I doubt still more, if it did come off, whether it would be

any good. To be caught in the clutches of a second coalition, and a respectable one this time, seems to me a dismal fate. But it's difficult to believe that the Goat won't clamber over this fence as he has so many others.

The sun shines, I must go out into my garden and saw wood, or something of the sort. Life glides away among such occupations. Write again, if you will, and have no fear about your letters being shown to *anyone*.

your
Lytton

[Enclosure]

To The Unknown

February 14th 1918

Divine Unknown! I only bring
A rhyme – no more – no toy, no ring:
But then, today a rhyme's the thing.

A little rhyme, then, it shall be;
– A little rhyme to you from me,
– Amorous, light and fancy-free.

But who are you? And who am I?
Ah! Ah! My sweet, why peep and pry?
Love is enough, the rest's my eye.

One though alone there is to vex
Or if not vex, at least perplex,
My heart – I do not know your sex.

Too true! But then, my dear, divine,
Unknown, ambiguous Valentine,
Why bother? – *You* do not know *mine*!

1. Michael Holroyd, *Lytton Strachey*, p. 413.

‡

To Lady Ottoline Morrell

The Mill House
Tidmarsh
Pangbourne
March 3rd 1918

Dearest Ottoline,

It was most delightful to get a letter from you. Do you know, it arrived on my birthday! But how old? How old? Ah! that is too horrible to be divulged!

Unknown personages who think that I think that you think, etc. etc. etc. may surely be allowed to go gently to the Devil. We know each other well enough by this time, I should imagine, to pay no attention to such gallimaufries.

The truth is I had been intending to write to you, but had supposed that you were still in London, gadding and whirling. I'm very sorry that you should have been having colds, and I'm afraid these fearful March blasts will not be at all good for you. This wretched month seems to be up to its reputation, as usual. Perhaps, however, *you* are consoled for everything by the mysterious airmen, who sound too entertaining. How I wish such gay distractions came my way! My life passes almost entirely among proof sheets, which now flow in upon me daily. It is rather exciting; but also rather harassing. All sorts of tiresome details and minor crises – about covers, illustrations, contracts, and so on – keep turning up; but my hope is that in about six weeks or so 'Eminent Victorians' will burst upon an astonished world. In the meantime I am also struggling with a play – but it is not easy, especially as those fiends have once more summoned me to a medical re-examination, which is a disturbing prospect, in view of the tiresome possibilities that *might* ensue.

It is horrible about Gertler, I had hoped that he had quite slipped through their vulturine fingers. The thought of such a creature in the army makes one's blood boil. But I suppose, in one way or another, he will be able to bring a good deal of influence to bear. The worst of it is that the general outlook appears to be so very bad. If one could be sure that it would end in six months – but now – What a devil's cauldron we have fallen into!

One of the things I wanted to write to you about was Bertie's trial at Bow Street, which I attended, as I happened to be in London, and I thought the more friends who showed themselves the better. It was really infamous – much worse, I thought, than those other proceedings before the Lord Mayor – even more obviously unjust, and gross, and generally wicked and disgusting. The spectacle of a louse like Sir John Dickinson rating Bertie for immorality and sending him to prison . . . James and I came away with our teeth chattering with fury. It makes me abandon hope that such monstrosities should occur, openly, and be accepted by very nearly everybody as a matter of course. Ugh! –

I was interested to hear that you had come across 'my' Mr Brown (no, no, – no 'e' at the end – the plainest of plain Browns) – but I think his apparent 'inferiority' can hardly have been anything but shyness – or perhaps a certain farouche-ness. He is a *very* simple soul and, I fear, not wildly interesting. Also, in three months' time, he is to be married to a fair lady from Warrington, which sounds decidedly depressing, doesn't it?

Do let me hear of your more exciting and recondite adventures. You rouse my curiosity, madam. But I'm afraid I shan't have any to reveal to you in return. When I am here – proofsheets; and when I am in London – the 1917 Club. Voilà l'histoire de ma vie. Not very promising ingredients for the confessional! –

I wonder if there is any news of Bertie – about his next trial, and what the prospects may be. I thought his lawyer was rather a feeble creature. Would it be impossible to get a real swell?

Do you know little Ernest Winston (who came to Garsington that time with Violet Asquith) was killed last year. It happened as soon as he got out – a stray shot hit him as he was walking up to the trenches for the first time, I saw him last playing in one of those quartets that he used to ask me to. Such things are very difficult to believe,

yours ever affectionately
Lytton

Carrington spends all day in an attic, painting pictures which I am never allowed to see. When it is hot enough to sit out under the pear-tree, you must come flying over with the airmen and Brett.

‡

To Virginia Woolf

Leonard and James omitted Barbara Bagenal's name, identifying her as 'M.'
Odd, as in Virginia's reply they left the words 'Perhaps you wouldn't mind
handing this on to Barbara who seems to be staying with you.'
    Virginia had written that she was beginning to have 'faint doubts' about
reviewing Eminent Victorians, *saying that if he did, why shouldn't she review*
books by other friends, such as Clive, Desmond, Molly and Fredegond Shove.
Also, Bruce Richmond, the editor of the TLS, had 'snubbed' her the other day
when he incorrectly thought she was trying to get a friend's book reviewed, and
he'd let her know it wasn't the done thing. In the end, Virginia wrote to
Richmond asking to review it, and he refused.

6, Belsize Park Gardens
March 19th 1918

I should like very much to come to Asheham on Tuesday 28th. Will
you expect me for then, unless I write again? I have not yet consulted
Carrington, but I hope to be able to induce her to remain at Tidmarsh
with Barbara, while I gallivant. Also, I don't know definitely when
Vanessa can have me, as she was very vague and perhaps drunk when I
talked to her about it. But I'll write and find out. Perhaps, if necessary,
you would be able to keep me on at Asheham for a few days after the
Easter week-end?

    It seems to me much better not to take any steps about the
Victorians. It would never do to get into trouble with Richmond, and
so far as I'm concerned, though I should be delighted if you *did* review
it, because you would be more on the spot than anyone else, I quite
agree with you that reviews one way or the other probably make no
difference. If Richmond sends it you of his own accord, so much the
better.

    My 'medical board' yesterday pronounced me 'permanently and
totally unfit for any form of Military Service' – which is a great relief.
The whole thing was infinitely more civilised than I've ever known it
before. The doctors, and even the clerks, were positively polite.

your
Lytton

✝

To Lady Ottoline Morrell

The Mill House
Tidmarsh
Pangbourne
March 20th 1918

Dearest Ottoline,

You will be glad to hear that the result of my medical re-examination was very satisfactory, and I am declared to be 'permanently and totally unfit for any form of military service'. It's a great relief: and I can now relapse into writing and reading without that anxiety hanging over my head. The whole thing was infinitely better managed than before – far more civilised, and careful, and the doctors positively polite and even sympathetic. This comes of the military having nothing more to do with it, and could never have happened if it hadn't been for the House of Commons – which I bless daily in my prayers.

I was very glad that Gertler's affair had had the same satisfactory dénouement. Is he with you now? Garsington must be divine in this weather – though I can't help feeling it's slightly fraudulent, and that at any moment it may begin to snow.

I hope you are flourishing. Did a letter from me reach you a week or so ago?

ever your
Lytton

✝

To Carrington

Lytton had written on Thursday to ask Carrington to send him the proofs of Eminent Victorians, *which he'd left in a drawer at Tidmarsh. Commercio was an Italian restaurant in Soho. 'Barouche-Landau' – a literary joke, cf. Jane Austen,* Emma, *v.2, ch. 14.*

The reference to the steak, as to the butter and sugar below, is that owing to wartime food rationing, house guests were expected to bring those of their own foodstuffs that were on the ration. So it may be that Lytton ate his own steak while his hosts went without meat.

Lytton's copy of A Portrait of the Artist as a Young Man *would become more valuable than most of his antiquarian books, as the 1917 first edition was only 750 copies.*

Prime Minister George Canning (1770–1827) was the subject of rumours in his own day that he had been the lover of the homosexual Pitt the Younger. Lord Rosebery's 'authority' came from Lytton's presumption that the Liberal Prime Minister had had an affair with Lord Francis Douglas, another of the Marquess of Queensberry's good-looking sons. Rosebery was often thought to have been the villain in the Oscar Wilde business, blackmailed by Lord Queensberry into pressing for a trial. It was Apostolic lore that William Johnson, who wrote 'The Eton Boating Song' and later took the name Cory, had been sacked as an Eton beak [master] for a homosexual scandal involving not only Rosebery, but the future Viscount Halifax.

Le Curé de Cucugnan was by Alphonse Daudet (1840–97).

Asheham
Monday, April 1st 1918

The proofs, with your letter, just to hand. So very kind of you. I was glad to hear the Tidmarsh news, and that James had appeared all right – though I had hope that Barbara might have too – perhaps she did later – poor creature. What a time she must be having of it! So many things that I've gone through since seeing you last – I don't see how I can relate them; but about half you can no doubt easily imagine: or shall we say three-quarters? London was a frantic business – no cloak-room would take in my goods nearer than Leicester Square, so I had to traipse them there, then tottered to Commercio, after which I returned in a taxi to Victoria, neither Mudie's nor London Library visited – very wisely, as it turned out – it was already thronged – and there found Clive, who had tried to catch the previous train and failed. He was going first class, and the crush was such that it was clearly the only thing to do. When the train came in, we easily got seats, following in the tract of an octogenarian upper-class whore, who carried all before her. There we sat for ¾ of an hour before the train started. It was impossible to move – no sign of Barbara – but I supposed she must have got in somewhere. The journey was perfect, and as they didn't ask for my ticket decidedly inexpensive. At Lewes, no Barbara. Clive went to Charleston by another train. I entered the barouche-landau, and arrived here for tea. We expected

Barbara by every train that day, and the next, and the next. Yesterday morning her sad tale of woe arrived – incredibly frightful. No doubt by this time you heard it. What she ought to have done was to have got a first-class ticket and applied for assistance to the guard, who certainly would have found her a place. In our compartment there were only three on a side, and the miserable third-class were packed, standing.

The beauty of this place once more overwhelmed me – and the freshness, and the colours, and the rigour of rural life – birds, lambs, winds, woods, multiplied to 240 volts at least, and making Tidmarsh positively suburban. The human population, however, is painfully inferior. I found the comfort much greater than I'd expected – especially in the bedroom – a great fire and a mountain of blankets. My steak was admirable – tender and juicy as . . . whose shall we say? – Mr Trott's? . . . bottom, my health quite recovered apparently, Virginia enchanting, Woolf with a new book, very interesting, everything, in fact, swimming along marvellously – when – – I awoke on Saturday morning quite dished – a splitting headache and general internal ruin – oh lordy me! – followed ultimately by violent sickness, a thing I've not known for a hundred years – altogether a very acute and painful recurrence. However, it passed off in the course of the day, and yesterday I was able to get up and behave more or less as usual. I now seem all right, though rather jolted – and what can my weight be? – Imagine the miserable Count, spewing into a basin, and gasping in agony with no Mopsa to comfort him! –

I feel slightly alarmed at the thought of Charleston, which I fear may be more rigorous. I think it would certainly be a good thing if you would send some meat there. I had intended to go there yesterday, to catch a glimpse of Mr Moss, who vanishes today, but a ten-mile walk was beyond me. Mary arrives in the course of the week, so it will be a very cultivated party. I have read fifty-three books since my arrival. I have now begun 'A Portrait of the Artist as a Young Man', which considerably impresses me, But I haven't got very far with it, and I cling to the hope that it will grow very degraded as it goes on. Otherwise . . . some steps will have to be taken.

Yes, Canning was an attractive rascal; but where, oh where, to find a life of him? Also, incidentally, I have heard some shocking rumours about his tastes – via Frankie Birrell, via Mr Birrell, via Lord Rosebery, who should be an authority. – But enough of this. I must get out of bed, and toast my toes in the sunshine – such as there is of it, and discuss the European situation with Leonard, and turn over some more pages of Mr James Joyce. Oh! If I continue to be improved! – I send you my love, also a small thing composed between last night and this morning. I'll write again from Charleston. I don't think any more butter or sugar will be wanted, as they seem to be holding out.

your Lytton

Where was the Chatto & Windus announcement?
    Will I find a translation of 'Le Curé de Cucugnan' when I come back?

‡

To Clive Bell

Pierre Bayle's Dictionary *first appeared in 1697, and was the volume most often found in private libraries in France in the eighteenth century.*

The Mill House
Tidmarsh
Pangbourne
April 16th 1918

Dear Clive,

Here is what I owe you – rather late in the day I fear. Stagnation grows upon me. How are you? And what is happening to you? Are you back again amid the flesh- and stink-pots of Garsington, or once more meandering among the asphodels of Gordon Square? The gay world has grown incredibly dim to me, and that last performance of Figaro still haunts me, like the last vision of a former life. And now that the snow has come upon us again, and all that can be done is to draw up round the fire with one's volumes, existence has indeed dwindled to that of an anchoret. Even the newspapers hardly ever arrive, and when they do they raise no eyelid. Carrington busies herself with the early potatoes (what *are* they?), Alix reads Rabelais with six dictionaries. James (for he is here for the moment) plays chess with himself according to the principles of Dr Jarrasch . . . or Dr Freud. We have many projects – to build a fireplace, a bookcase, a theatre, to learn Spanish, to attach the pump to the mill-wheel by a leather band, to buy twenty-four geese, to borrow a saddle from Farmer Davis and saddle the Blacksmith's pony with it and ride into Pangbourne, to write a drawing-room comedy, a classical tragedy in the style of Euripides, and the History of England during the War. But le temps s'en va, le temps s'en va, mon cher, and we are left idling in front of the fire.

Do you know the Goncourts' Journal? Virginia put me on to it (I had had it in my mind for years) and I find it full of interest. There are many reported conversations of intelligent persons – Flaubert, Gautier, Sainte Beuve, and such. They *are* intelligent, though their Frenchness is paramount over everything. So open-minded, you know, and yet . . . Those regular clichés, which seem actually to be clichés of thought, and in fact of life itself, more than of the verbal sort. 'Ma maitresse' – 'la Femme' – 'pendant sa jeunesse' – 'la Pédérastie', etc., etc. They occur on every other page, all mixed up with the freest language and the wildest speculations. And then – 'l'immortalité de l'âme' (this comes on at dessert, apparently) – it is certainly most odd, and rather attractive too. Gautier was perhaps more sensible than the rest – I hadn't before realised his eminence. And they are all extraordinarily aesthetic.

Any news, I wonder? But I think it must be too cold for news. Or perhaps it's the other way round; perhaps, in cold weather, one's more inclined to . . . well, well – but this reminds me of a certain article in Bayle's Dictionary.

Adieu. I hope I shall have a letter from you.

your
Lytton

‡

To Clive Bell

Lytton is perhaps thinking of the Goncourt journal entry for 30 July 1861: 'How utterly futile debauchery seems once it has been accomplished, and what ashes of disgust it leaves in the soul! The pity of it is that the soul outlives the body, or in other words that impression judges sensation and that one thinks about and finds fault with the pleasure one has taken.'[1] Edmond De Goncourt lived from 1822 to 1896 and Jules De Goncourt from 1830 to 1870.

Desmond MacCarthy published a volume of his selected essays under the off-putting title Remnants. *Vernon Lee wrote to MacCarthy about the volume that 'as literature it is quite as good as Lytton Strachey (and you know that is saying a great deal) and being much more than literature it is better as literature'.[2] Big*

Chilling was a Tudor farmhouse on the Solent in Hampshire, the home of Alys
Russell and her brother, Logan Pearsall Smith. Lytton's remarks about Molly
perhaps indicate that he had been privy to her reluctant affair with Clive, which
had begun in 1912, but was long over. Clive's new book was Pot-boilers. *The*
Stage Society was a private company that specialized in staging plays thought too
recondite or narrow in appeal for a commercial production. Gilbert Cannan's
Mendel, *which was based on the affair of Carrington and Gertler, had been*
published two years earlier. South Hill Park is in Hampstead.

  Russell was serving his six months' prison sentence, during which he wrote his
Introduction to Mathematical Philosophy *(1919).*

The Mill House
Tidmarsh
Pangbourne
May 10th 1918

Dear Clive

A few words from the Desert. Comment vas-tu? Has Garsington once
more engulfed you, or do you still whisk in Piccadilly half the week?
And what have you been reading? The Goncourts seem to be in the air.
Poor wretches. I must say I don't like 'em. The Frenchification is really
too much – the bugger-bub story, for instance – too painfully Parisian –
and then they're au fond such vulgar little snobs. Jules has now died,
I'm glad to say, but Edmond remains, a most lugubrious figure in the
siege of Paris. But of course the conversations, and the general
impression of a very distinct and remarkable atmosphere, are highly
interesting, and one feels one must read it all. I suppose you've seen
Remnants – a book in the best of taste. But it's difficult not to think
that the milk has been standing a very long time, and that, though the
cream is excellent, there's not much of it. However, nowadays it
would be absurd to complain of anything that is genuinely charming.
His Asquith doings fill me with astonishment. I can still hardly
believe that he likes those people or can think it worth while to
flatter them. Perhaps really he only finds them amusing to pass the time
of day with – one can *just* imagine that – and that it *may* be rather fun
to meet the Lord Chief Justice. I saw poor Molly on the eve of
departing for Chilling: she appeared even more depressed than usual,
dreading the solitude and the children, and having to go away from
London. I can only hope that it may be good for her health. And in

the meantime he remains, I suppose, gallivanting with Lady Carter.

I wonder if your book has come out yet. The faithful Geoffrey Whitworth wrote to say that *mine* was to be published yesterday; but there has been no sign of it. I don't know whether yours was to come out on the same day, but I should be glad of any news of either. One lives in a blank mist down here, with no London correspondent, the result being that one's curiosity grows and grows, and even politics take on a tinge of excitement. I find myself positively scanning the Daily News of a morning with eagerness to see whether Asquith has turned out George, or some such nonsense. And of course one knows all the time that all the things one really wants to know are merely floating casually in gossip – so casually that when one *does* see anybody they've forgotten all about it. However, it's now at last beginning to be worth it – I mean being in the country – now that one can sit out of doors under an apple tree, take off one's waistcoat, and pretend that the birds are too noisy. So I have decided to spend next week in London. The Way of the World is to be done by the Stage Society (Gilbert Cannan as Mirabel – oh dear, oh dear!). and there's rather an attractive concert. Shall I see you at either? Or elsewhere? Write if so to 96 South Hill Park where I hope to be staying.

The latest news of Gerald sounds serious. I'm afraid he's got into an unnerved situation. And then poor Norton! – Surely he should hire an expensive and fashionable lawyer. Bertie's fate is extraordinarily satisfactory. Was it *his* lawyer that did it, or Mr Balfour? And his book – is it only to be seen in America? I've never much cared for his observations on art – he seems to think only of its creation, and to forget that all the enormous majority of mankind (poor things) can hope to do is to appreciate it. I rather suspect he fancies it's a branch of symbolic logic, but really it's not.

Do let me hear more news, and forgive my hideous silences. How is Mary? I hope to see her in London. – And Mr D! – Oh! A Middy! Oh! – After parting from you I had a very raté *[botched]* time. Existence resembled De Bry's shop, where all the nice boxes and packets on the counter turned out to be, not chocolate, but cocoa.

your

Lytton

1. In *Pages from the Goncourt Journals*, ed. Robert Baldick, London, 1962.
2. Quoted in Hugh and Mirabel Cecil, *Clever Hearts*, p.190.

‡

To Mary Hutchinson

The Mill House
Tidmarsh
Pangbourne
May 20th 1918

Ma chère

I must send you a word or two – partly to say how much I enjoyed the
Suggia party. *[. . .]* I wonder if you did get off to Wittering by nine the
next morning, but at any rate I suppose you're there now – sitting in
front of the barn, gazing at the estuary, with the sun on your toes,
dipping into a French memoir or writing a love-letter on your blue
note-paper . . . But are you really alone? Or what? I don't like to think
of your wasting your sweetness on the desert air. I wish I could talk to
you. If we were only within a walk of each other! – I should come to
lunch, and stay to tea, and linger on, and on . . . In this delicious heat,
what else is possible? The garden here has burst out into refulgence –
laburnum, lilies, buttercups, and apple blossom. I sit in the middle
of it, dressed in a Brahmin's robe, but with a mind not altogether
Brahminical. Carrington is at a table nearby, making puppets for our
forthcoming performance of the Antigone. James weeds with two
fingers, and Noel reads Havelock Ellis (Vol. IV. Sexual Inversion). So
you see it is all very idyllic. Oliver and a young female appeared last
night – a curious couple. Now they are off for a walk over the woods
and commons. I must say I don't altogether follow it, She can't be
called beautiful – spotty, decidedly – and of course too young to have
an intelligence. No doubt, when they settle down under a gorse-bush,
he will make approaches, there will be kisses, etc., but a limited etc. . . .
really I think Mr D a more reasonable excuse for such amusements.
But – . *[. . .]*

ever your affectionate cousin,
Lytton

✝

To Lady Ottoline Morrell

The Mill House
Tidmarsh
Pangbourne
May 26th 1918

Dearest Ottoline,

Thank you very much for so kindly passing on Bertie's pleasant message. I am delighted that he should have liked the book, and that he found it entertaining. If you're writing will you thank him from me, and say that I think it a great honour that my book should have made the Author of Principia Mathematica laugh out loud in Brixton Gaol?

yours ever
Lytton

✝

To Carrington

Lalla Vandervelde's maiden name was Speyer, so she perhaps really was a Jewess from Frankfurt. Ruth was Mrs John Selby-Bigge, née Humphries, a Slade friend of Carrington. Ralph Hawtrey had married the celebrated pianist Titi d'Aranyi.

The various Churchills: Lady Randolph Churchill (1854–1921), Winston Churchill's mother, the American heiress, née Jennie Jerome. Following her divorce from her second husband, Capt. George Cornwallis-West, in 1913, she reverted to calling herself Lady Randolph until her third marriage this year to Montague Phippen Porch, a colonial administrator. The 9th Duke of Marlborough (1871–1934) was also married to an American heiress, the gloriously eccentric Gladys (pronounced to rhyme with 'ladies') Deacon (1881–1977). Lord Ivor Churchill (1898–1956) was then aged about twenty. Felicity Tree, daughter of Sir Herbert Tree, married Capt. Geoffrey Cory-Wright in 1915.

96, South Hill Park
Hampstead Heath, N.W.
June 20th 1918

Ma chère,

It was shocking of me not to have written yesterday, but the pressure
was fearful – up to the last moment I hoped to be able to dash off a line
– but literally I had not a second. First with the definite news. The old
Frankfurt Jewish [sic] was stricken down with the Spanish Flu. Fell like
a sack of potatoes – and so – no play! She had risen up when I saw her –
the afternoon of my arrival (Monday), but she was still very collapsed,
and probably infectious (though she swore not) and so . . . as there were
some passages . . . no, not *quite* to bed. No doubt I too shall be stricken,
and fall like a greasy pole. However, apart from that, she declares she
still wants to do it, with Jack, for some much more chic performance
(the Madame Dorsey affair was not nearly chic enough, so it was really
a blessing in disguise that she couldn't do it) – and after that at the
Coliseum. But *when* all these events will occur remains a matter of
doubt. So after all, if you're still in London on Tuesday night, dinner
chez or with Ruth and her fair Boy would be very suitable. No doubt it
can still be arranged.

I've been having a really tiring time. Monday was colossal. After Lala
(late tea) I tore to Drury Lane for the Magic Flute. Gulped a couple of
fried eggs in a queer little Italian bouge *[dump]* in the Lane, then floated
into my seat in the Grand Circle. Mrs Hawtrey (Aranyi female) at once
surged up – Did I see that young lady in that box – Miss Saxton Noble
– she was dying to make my acquaintance. Could she come after the
first act? Etc. etc. – The music began. Then in the *[illegible]* I observed,
a little way off, an attractive young man, in evening dress, just getting
into his seat – decidedly attractive – alone, too – what could be done? –
I peered again, and recognised Duncan. Mozart was more romantic
even than usual. When the interval came, I got through the Saxton
Noble business as speedily as possible (the speed being hastened by the
painful appearance of Walter Lamb in the role of old family friend) and
found Duncan, solus, drifting in the refreshment room. Maynard had
given him the seat, but had not yet appeared. There was an empty one
beside him, which I moved into. Tiens! Reminiscent ardours almost
carried me away. In the second interval il gran Pozzo appeared,
extremely important – decisive. 'Come along to the room – Maud.

Come along at once.' We were led off like a couple of condemned
animals – into a remote region, beyond the boxes, – at last a door
opened, and we were in a curious room, rather like a first-class waiting
room in a railway station, in which were grouped various ladies and
gents. Apparently it was the room leading off the Royal Box (which of
course is Lady Cunard's) – stamped gold imitation leather on the walls –
some gold chairs – a table with a cardboard box in which was a half-
eaten bunch of grapes – at the table Margot, swathed in blue-green
crêpe-de-chine from head to foot. She sprang towards me, and we had
a heart to heart talk, at the end of which she asked me to come to
her box on the following night – for Carmen. I said 'charmed'.
Whereupon she turned casually to Maud, and said 'Which is my box for
tomorrow?' Poor Maud had no idea that Margot was having a box
tomorrow, but after a slight pause she pulled herself together, and said
'Box 7.' – So that was settled. But *what do you think*? She (Lady C) had
positively never heard of me!!!!!! – Asked Duncan who I was – 'Lytton
Strachey.' 'Oh! What does he do?' 'He writes.' 'Oh dear! – *What*
does he write. Something very rhapsodical?' – In the meantime,
Margot was saying to me 'Who is that young man next Maynard
Keynes?' – 'Duncan Grant.' 'Oh yes, of course, he writes, doesn't he?'
. . . So this is how great men get the go-by. (By-the-bye, I forgot to
mention that I discovered at Lala's that there had been a leading article
in the Times about me that morning. Rather sniffy – but still – – Oh,
Maud! Maud!)

   After these agitations, and after the opera was over – the performance
even more preposterous than usual owing to Agnes Nichols doing
Pamina in the strangest style – I returned to Gordon Square with
Maynard and Duncan, where we found a charming supper prepared –
salmon and cherries – with Harry and Sheppard also. Sheppard was very
amusing, talking most of the time about Miss Edgworth's novels. Harry
went off to bed (Oh! I should have said that, to make things complete,
Marjorie O[livier] appeared, quite mad, just after we arrived, but was
wheedled away by Pozzo.) Eventually I went off, though I didn't at all
want to. I suppose we all wanted to kiss Duncan, though Sheppard
alone did so – while I was there – after that . . . It seemed a curious
meeting: the complications of one's recollections were so great, and
nothing was said – though the others could hardly have avoided *some*
thoughts of that kind too.

   I see that if I go on on this scale, my letter will never end. Yesterday I
had an accidental lunch with Duncan and Adrian, the latter very

amusing, but eventually more emptily cynical than I could bear. Then tea with Dorelia at the 1917 Club. She was looking divine. I took her with me to Hampstead; she went to Anrep's, while I dressed; then she, Anrep and I had a delicious dinner at Commercio's. After that I tottered to Drury Lane. I was afraid I might be too early – I was only two hours late. 'Box 7, please.' – 'Yes sir' (with extraordinary subservience). I stepped into a pitch dark hole. Margot, Elizabeth, visible – Act 2 just coming to an end – a crouching gent behind Elizabeth – a khaki figure in a very dim corner. Margot shook hands, the curtain came down, 'Well, now let's go into the other room. I've had the fire lighted.' (Really one wouldn't have guessed it wasn't all hers.) The khaki figure glided out. 'Our phantasmal friend is unknown to us – quite a stranger.' Apparently the poor fellow had got in there by mistake. We passed into the strange waiting-room, where the first people I saw were Jack and Mary, and Jim Barnes. Many others surged forward – Lord Ivor Churchill, a squitter-squee of a youth in a naval uniform, with a broad white and gold stripe down his trousers, on whom Maynard mashed – but he's not *my* style at all.

Lady Randolph Churchill (as was) the Duchess of Marlborough, Lady Something else, 'straight from Ireland', a large, very tall, black-haired, red-cheeked lady, looking slightly daft, etc. etc. etc. An American admiral, too, and some dreadfully dim men. The D*[uke]* of M*[arlborough]* seemed the best of them, from first inspection – very thin, with a pointed nose. Lady R*[andolph]* C*[hurchill]* I talked to for hours, chiefly about Nigeria. 'I've just married a Nigerian . . . at least, no, not quite that – but a man who lives in Nigeria.' She was an amazing character, tremendously big and square – a regular old war-horse sniffing the battle from afar. She was dressed in a very shabby grey dress, which she from time to time rearranged, with an odd air of detachment. Maud too came up, and knew all about me. We streamed out, and streamed in. At one moment, in the corridor, I came upon the tall black and red lady, saying in a deep contralto voice, with a Lady Macbeth gesture, to nobody at all, 'My head is full of numbers' – and she swept on. Finally, in the box, during the last act, Margot seized my hand and murmured 'I want you to write Margot Asquith from Lytton Strachey in your book and give it me. Will you?' (Cadging again, I thought.) But I said that if I might I'd bring it to her. So, you see, my future is still expanding.

Margot is slightly interesting, I think. Her mauvais ton is remarkable. There she is in her box (cadged) thinking she's the very tip-top, the grande dame par excellence, and all the rest of it – and every other moment behaving like a kitchen-maid – giggling, looking round, and nudging Elizabeth. As for music, of course, it's never occurred to her that such a thing exists. Yet, as one looks at her small weather-beaten (perhaps one should say life-beaten) countenance, one wonders – there does seem a suggestion of something going on underneath.

The evening ended in an orgy at Monty's, given by the Hutches, in honour of Jim, who goes to Italy today, to control the flying corps in those regions. I enjoyed myself very much. Mark was there, the Jowetts, Felicity Tree (a dullard), and there was more salmon, and more cherries, and Asti Spumante to drink, and Mary was delightful, and I was abominably flattered, and the table was cleared away, and the pianola was played, and there was dancing (Mark holding Mary very tight, and both their bottoms sticking out – and Jim and Mrs Jowett) and at last Mark was seen in a black cloak and a top hat much too big for him, and a cane – posturing indefinitely . . . and it was time to catch the last tube home.

Well, that brings me to today. Whether all this is too dull to read I don't know; but I found it amusing while it was going on – and perhaps you like to hear of my gambolings. The upper-classes rouse my curiosity, and for the present, I think I shall proceed in my inquiries. I think I go to Cambridge on Saturday till Monday. The party here sounds rather stiff, what with one thing or another. But you'll have the opportunity of capturing B.B. (I stay here – there's room).

How abominable about the bites! I think it must be the withdrawal of my controlling genius that permits such atrocities. But you'll be all right by Friday – a perfect O. The notion of bicycling over to King's Sutton sounds a good one. I do hope it'll be agreeable, and that even your hopes will be surpassed.

Oh one peculiar piece of news from Dorelia. Little Geoffrey – imagine – guess – dismissed from the Navy (– for what? – for impudence, she *said*) – has run away, and joined the Sinn Feiners! It's really rather good, don't you think? The sweet creature! I long to write to him, but of course it's impossible. And that explains, no doubt, his not acknowledging the books.

Goodbye, my dear. I must go and get some lunch.

your

Lytton

‡

To Clive Bell

Clive had lent his room at 46 Gordon Square to a friend, for an assignation with
a young woman, but the couple used Sheppard's room in error. Clive had
neglected to warn any of the other residents, all of whom happened to be at home
at the time, of the arrangement he had made; and Sheppard did not get to bed
until the lovers left at 3.30 in the morning. Maynard remonstrated in a letter to
Clive, who, Maynard reported to Vanessa, 'took it upon himself to write me the
sort of letter an ill-bred millionaire might write to a defaulting office boy'. Clive
was furious. Though the lease was in his name, he felt he had the worst rooms in
the house, and paid too much for them. In the end, the lease was renewed in
September, but in Maynard's name, with Clive keeping his two rooms in the
attic.[1]

'Sullivan' was probably J.W.N. (1886–1937), a writer on science and music.
The book Lytton was reading was by Patrick Traherne (1885–1917). A
Schoolmaster's Diary, *edited by S. P. B. Mais, published in London in*
1918, is a teacher's diary, kept from September 1909 to April 1917. It details his
teaching at English public schools, his holiday travels, and his work as a novelist.

Clive had reported to Lytton that Virginia was jealous of the success of
Eminent Victorians.

The Mill House
Tidmarsh
Pangbourne
June 23rd 1918

Dear Clive

You do seem to have been getting into hot water lately! However, I
hope the rest of Gordon Square is by now pacified, and that you will
not really abandon it. I'm sure anything else you could get would be
horribly pokey. I haven't heard any rumours about the incident from
other quarters. Nobody writes to me from London, and the only person
I've seen from there is ce vieillard ratatiné *[withered old man]*, Saxon,
who of course is not quite in the way of such gossip. He is here at the
present moment, plus Barbara and Nick. It seems strange: one would
have thought that arrangements might have been made by which one or
the other of the two husbands would *not* have been included in the
week-end party. But no! The trio is inseparable. All are incredibly aged.

Nick and Barbara (the one without a kidney, and the other with a child) totter and potter like an old couple in an almshouse; and Saxon is wonderfully young for eighty-seven. Do you remember Barbara two years ago? A Bronzino adolescent! It is alarming: but luckily not inevitable. One *needn't* be either Nick's wife or Saxon's mistress – one really need not.

The man Sullivan interests and grieves me. The impression I got of him exactly corresponds with your account. I fear he may be a symptom of the future of civilisation, and if so the outlook is not encouraging. We should go down like the poppies in the corn . . . poor fellow! So worthy, so good at heart, so much interested in what people should be interested in, intelligent even, – and he thinks Candide amusing and Tess a great work. Ruin! Ruin! – The younger generation are on my nerves just now. Mr S. P. B. Mais – have you heard of him? Is it a real name? – I've been reading a book, apparently by him, 'A Schoolmaster's Diary', which plunged me into alarmed speculations. All the apparatus of advanced ideas – you know it? 'unconventionality', Gilbert and Rupert mentioned on every tenth page and buggery of course constantly referred to, 'open-mindedness' every everywhere – mon dieu! And behind it all, a desperately shocked Christian, tasteless, ignorant, incapable of two seconds' consecutive thought, and disgustingly egotistical. I must say, if one has to choose, I far prefer Dr Arnold. However, perhaps, after all, as another sign of general disintegration it's to be welcomed. But really the shifts, contortions, and disguises of English hypocrisy are amazing. What is to be done? I am haunted by an announcement of Isaiah's – 'I will send him against an hypocritical nation, and against the people of my wrath will I give him a charge, to take the spoil, and to take the prey, and to tread them down like the mire of the streets.' – Kaiser Wilhelm, or – ?

Lala breathes not a word – I go to London tomorrow to find out what's happening. Perhaps we shall meet in the Albert Hall – or perhaps before – I hope so.

Virginia's jealousy I can't take very seriously.

yours
Lytton

1. The story is told in Robert Skidelsky, *John Maynard Keynes*, vol. 1, p. 351.

‡

To Carrington

*Carrington and her brother Noel were on a 'pilgrimage' to Rothiemurchus.
Carrington had been worried whether the daily, Mrs Legg, would look after
Lytton adequately; so the meal for four was meant to reassure her. Lytton's visit
was to (Sir) John Amherst Selby-Bigge (1892–1973), the surrealist painter, who
studied at Oxford and at the Slade, where he met his wife, Ruth Humphries.
He was the son of Sir (Lewis) Amherst Selby-Bigge, 1st Bt (1860–1951),
Secretary, Board of Education; they were connected by marriage to the
Bowes-Lyons and thus, distantly, to the royal family. In a letter of 1921,
Carrington describes John Selby-Bigge's 'vast chicken farm' at Chiddingly,
producing '300 dozen eggs every week' from their 3,000 hens: 'John obviously
has a genius for carpentering and building.' In 1933 he joined Unit One and
produced abstract paintings and drawings based on mechanical forms. In 1936
they moved abroad, and he succeeded to the baronetcy in 1951.*
    The correct spelling is Arisaig.

The Mill House
Tidmarsh
Pangbourne
Saturday, July 6th 1918

Ariseig Hotel, Ariseig. Qu'est-ce que c'est que ça? Somewhere in Skye?
Or an unfortunate post office contortion? I can't decide, and I suppose
Time will show – and in the meantime as there's only one very dull
letter for you, and *this* will not be exciting, un peu de patience,
mademoiselle! – Patience, also, I find, is what *I* need. Everyone has
deserted me – James, Alix, the Simpson couple – all. I've wired in
despair to Mary (laid up with the flu in Gordon Square) to come down
and recover here, but she certainly won't. It is infuriating – and I might
have asked Partridge! – And I daresay, as our tastes are so different . . .
and in any case he sounds very charming . . . but I'm already becoming
incoherent – chiefly from rage. The only consolation is that the weather
is so truly revolting – such a loathsome mixture of intense heat and
violent wind – that if anyone had come down, it might have been more
gloomy than solitude.
    I returned last night, to find that Legg had prepared a dinner for at
least four. I must confess that I had not been looking forward to that
visit; but I'm very glad I went. A good deal came to light in the course

of it – about him, I mean: and his state of mind – the change from what he used to be, etc. – became explicable. He has been evidently crushed flat by the war – not its worst horrors, but the stupidity of everyone he was with, and the appalling dullness of existence. He was discontented, almost bitter, unhappy clearly – dashed, disconsolate. I thought he was really one of the most truly good people I'd ever met. Of course he's not what you might call an intellectual, and it occurred to me that his feeling for 'art' was of the nature of calf-love, but that's none of it important. His modesty, kindness, and general benevolence were almost overflowing – one wanted to throw one's arms around his neck – oh! I assure you for *no* other reason – but one would have to have known him for years before one could do that. I'm afraid I must have appeared very dull and depressing to both – too silent, I mean; but how to talk? Ruth left us together nearly the whole time, so that I saw very little of her. I asked them to come next week – they said they would, if his leave is extended, but I doubt it. Why should they come to a grim, gaunt, deserted, decayed old man? – But can you conceive it – being out there, for three years, without finding one single decent creature to talk to? And nothing but senselessness, mismanagement, and general bestiality going on all round! – It's enough to snuff out the brightest spark. But it must be relighted. Another thing was, that, so far as I could see, he had no real friends. He was black about Oxford – which was in itself enough to delight me. Such people as Maynard and Sheppard, he said, would have been impossible there. He played the flute in a perfectly charming way. Ah! If I were a little younger . . . When we parted for the night, I was distinctly émotioné. I couldn't imagine why he should be so nice to me. The house, (outside especially) I thought very beautiful. The garden less so – too mucked about – though with great possibilities. The whole thing was . . . no, would have been, a romance – fifteen years ago.

The condition of affairs here seems to be quite satisfactory. The man Justice got hold of me, of course, and told me forty-eight times about the tomatoes. While we were away, it's rumoured that a pig entered the domain, but didn't do much damage. There are peas, beans, and raspberries – such a bore! because I shall have to pick them – and eat them, I suppose, in solitary state. Among a dull batch of letters was a pamphlet from Waley on Chinese versification – quite interesting, though sad – oh so sad! Also the 'element' from Eric Rivers-Smith. Did you go and talk to him? It turns out to be a long wire snake, and what I am to do with it I've no idea. Among my other woes, I've

left my reading-spectacles at 96, so that I can only peer at print in
fear and trembling. Mr Brown's letter of refusal was slightly mysterious,
as it did not allege any reason for not coming. Was la Simpson too
shy? Or are they too poor to afford the railway-fare? Or what? – Oh,
and he says the 'rag' that I missed last Saturday was a roaring success.
Oh! . . .

The existence of Partridge is exciting. Will he come down here,
when you return, and sing Italian songs to us, and gesticulate, and let us
dress him as a brigand? I hope so; but you give no suggestion of his
appearance – except that he's 'immensely big' – which may mean
anything. And then, I have a slight fear that he may be simply a
flirt.

10 p.m. The light is lighted, the curtains are drawn, the day is over.
A large part of it has been spent on the Pangbourne road, which,
however, produced no adventures. Finally, after dinner, the solitude
growing too intense, I determined to make an assault on the Belgian
youth. I went forth, nominally to the post-box, and found him, as usual,
in the paddock, doing something to a hutch. He did not repel my
advances, and when I asked him to come and have some coffee, eagerly
accepted, poor creature! He sat with me – outside – each of us on one
of the garden chairs – for about an hour, drinking first coffee, and then
cider, two bottles of which he procured from the inn, and told me of
his adventures in the war, his present condition, and the rest of it. A sad
enough tale! The war part of it was grim, very, and the rest, if anything,
grimmer. He's not at all contented with his lot. After being frightfully –
incredibly – wounded, he's now condemned to work all night in a
munitions factory at the most grinding job, the only alternative being
apparently an internment camp, which he can't face. He's in a state of
great gloom, not unnaturally; not a cat to talk to, worked so hard that
he's too dead beat to do anything else, even forgetting French from
never speaking it, ill, too, with the results of his wound – it's dismal
enough. I don't see how I can be of much use to him – except perhaps
as an occasional person to talk to; he didn't appear to be at all interesting
– perhaps he may once have been, though I doubt it. I offered him
books, but he said he was too tired ever to read. If I had a flow of
French it would be something, but I could hardly induce him to give
up his horrid English. Well, at any rate, he's going to make us a correct
rabbit-hutch – ours, he tells me, is all wrong, so that's something. I only
hope he won't turn out an old man of the sea.

The only other news I can think of here is that Nero last night killed his first mouse. It was so minute that I think it must have been the same age as he is. What he did with it, I couldn't discover, but I think he may have eaten it, as it completely disappeared. Oh! And this afternoon I inserted the new 'element' into the cooking machine – it was a hopeless failure! A hardly perceptible degree of warmth permeated those iron bars – not enough to boil a kettle in a hundred years. So Mr Eric Rivers-Smith must be finally condemned as a traitor. That is all. Now I must read a little Cobbett, a very little, and then totter to bed. Where are you, I wonder? And *your* adventures –! No doubt I shall hear of them in good time. I hope you've been able to steer the party into a suitable direction, and that the party itself is more hopeful than you supposed. Also that you're warm. The weather here suddenly became perfect this afternoon. But I daresay it's pelting in 'Ariseig'. Well, good-night! –

Sunday. Positively today, a letter from a Duchess! Her Grace of Marlborough. She asks me for the week-end to her 'little place, near Lingfield, in Surrey'. I accept. 'Mr Asquith, Mr Astor, Lord Something or other (illegible) and one or two others' will be there. Dear me! And my white shirts? Have I any left? And will Oliver's (if *he* has any) fit me? On the whole I think I shall have to move to no. 96 on Thursday and Friday to look into these affairs. And what I really want is the Gentleman's Complete Guide to Society. If there's a copy in Ariseig, you might send it.

Also a letter from Ottoline – no particular news. She had seen Birrell, who was apparently very satirical about the attacks on my book – taking off Gosse, etc., and their complaints. Also, she says, the *whole* House of Commons are intensely anxious that I should go and visit them. This sounds a trifle excessive. I suppose I should be met at the door by the Speaker and the Black Rod. And the House of Lords. Are *they* doing nothing? And his Majesty? – Not a word from him. – Very remiss.

I've just picked some peas. The beans frighten me. As for the raspberries, I feel as if I should never worm my way under the nets. La Legg confesses herself baffled by the hens – after pretending last night that she could catch them without the slightest difficulty. I am in favour of making them tipsy – it seems to me, short of shooting them, the only plan. She, of course, thought I was mad to suggest it; but I think, with the young Belgian's help . . . we shall see.

Evening once more. The day has been spent in the writing of innumerable letters, sitting out on the pale yellow lawn, very, very hot, and mildly happy. The rambler roses are now the most marked feature of the garden – a romantic splotch of red; a few delphiniums are also visible – et voilà tout. The Belgian came after dinner, and was extremely dull. He won't appear again for some time, as he works all night and sleeps all day, so that he's only visible on Saturdays and Sundays – which is a mercy. I suggested to him that we should make the hens drunk, but he was not encouraging. To lure them into a 'run', by means of food, he thought a more practicable method. In vain I murmured that we hadn't got a 'run'. 'When the young lady comes back,' was the reply, 'we shall manage it.' – 'Yes, but my dear sir, in the meantime the blasted brutes will have picked the flower-beds to pieces, scraped up the tomatoes, and beshitted the garden generally.' (Or words to that effect.) But he was impenetrable – and Napoleon gnashes his teeth in vain.

Perhaps tomorrow morning I shall hear from you. I hope so. This letter is swelling unconscionably, and if it's not sent before long, will have to go by parcel's post. And it will take you a whole day to read it. How is Noel? And Miss Brownlow-Brownlow? And la Mopsina? By-the-bye, why didn't you take Partridge with you? Wouldn't he have made an excellent forester? And what's his address? – So that I may send him a wire and ask him down for a bathe in the 'Roman Bath'. Why not, pray? Oh, I forgot, it will take a week before I can get anything out of you, and by that time I shall be entirely absorbed by the Duchess of Marlborough, Mr Astor, and Lord X. How unfortunate! But I must go to bed. Good-night.

Monday 8th. Your letter has just come. As there's no other indication, I send this to Ariseig, hoping it exists, and doubting whether this will ever reach you. No more news. Love from

Lytton

‡

To Lady Strachey

Arnold Bennett had recommended Eminent Victorians *to Gide.*

The Mill House
Tidmarsh
Pangbourne
July 10th 1918

Dearest Mama

[. . .] André Gide I have long known by name and have read some of his works, though not as many as I could have wished. They seem full of the finesse and amenity of the great French tradition – which is a comfort nowadays. It must be amusing having him as a pupil in English. Couldn't he, as an exercise, translate E.V. into French? It would be splendid to appear under such distinguished auspices in Paris!

I hope before long to rejoin your crowded halls. It will be excellent if Elinor succeeds in getting a house near you. Tomorrow I go to Ray's, en route for a dip into 'le high-life' – a weekend at the Duchess of Marlborough's!

Ever your loving
Lytton

I suppose you know the Life of Colonel Hutchinson by his Wife! I've just got a 2nd hand copy in Reading, and find it most interesting and charming. Somehow I'd never seen it before. Cobbett's Advice to Young Men is also, in its way, a masterpiece; but its way is most singular.

‡

To Clive Bell

Sir Hugh Walpole (1884–1941), New Zealand-born popular novelist, whose family sagas were set in Cumbria (but first published in the 1930s). Sir Spencer Walpole (1830–1907), English historian and civil servant, wrote the life of the only assassinated British prime minister, Spencer Perceval, to whom he was related on his mother's side. Lindisfarne was a sixteenth-century castle on the

Northumberland coast which had been renovated by Sir Edwin Lutyens. The
cellist Guilhermina Suggia (1888–1950) was among the other guests at the house
party. James and Alix's adventures in contraception are the more remarkable
because on 10 April, 1911 James had written a letter to Rupert Brooke
explaining to him 'the whole sordid business', and saying 'pessaries are
unpleasant things'. On the other hand, he also said that 'all this information
comes from my brother Oliver, who is an adept, and who thinks that I'm on the
brink of fucking Dieu sait qui', so perhaps he had little experience himself of
using any of the devices he describes in that letter.[1]

Vittorio Alfieri (1749–1803) was considered the greatest tragic poet of eighteenth-
century Italy. He wrote his autobiography in 1790. 'Beresford': John Davys
Beresford (1873–1947), English novelist, whose first novel, The Early History of
Jacob Stahl *(1911), marked him as a writer of the Gissing-influenced realist school.*
Little Arthur's History of England *was published in 1904.*

The Mill House
Tidmarsh
Pangbourne
August 10th 1918

Dear Clive

It was really charming of you to write, in spite of my wickedness, and
your letter came as a most cheering tonic to a faded convalescent. For
all my dissipations suddenly subsided last week into a recurrent colic; I
had to take to bed, to feed upon slops, even to read Mr Hugh Walpole's
novels – so you can imagine my melancholy, and how glad I was to
hear something of real life – of Gertler, Miss Wrench, and lovely Jim.
The result is that I am now almost well again, sitting out in the sun,
looking forward to a mutton chop, and ready to substitute Spencer
Walpole for Hugh. Next week-end I hope to be in a fit condition to
reach the Wharf, where I gather I am to meet ce cher Pozzo, and
whence – who knows? – I may be wafted for Sunday tea to Garsington.
Otherwise, I'm not much looking forward to the outing: there is a
certain frigidity in those altitudes. After that I hurry to Lindisfarne –
which I suppose will be grotesque: but perhaps Suggia's cello may make
it not intolerable. You needn't be afraid of my leaving your letters
about. They only part from my person to be buried in a locked
cupboard, far from the eye of woman. And mine? – but mine are so
discreet, that perhaps it hardly matters. An enforced discretion, because

so little that is indiscreet ever comes my way, and when it does it has almost certainly come yours first. For instance, the latest – or the latest but one – James and Alix story. No doubt you've heard it – how in order to be *quite* on the safe side – *quite* – although one might have supposed that there wasn't much danger, as there was no question of entry – still, it was thought advisable that a wad of cotton-wool should be placed by the lady as a rampart to the citadel. And then, unfortunately, after the business of the evening was over, how, in making things tidy, she allowed the wad to leave its position, to become trempé, and afterwards unwisely replaced it . . . Next day, she had a queer feeling . . . doubts . . . various symptoms. The worst was feared. They consulted, and decided that a doctor had better be called in to determine *what* had happened. But who? – Of course, Noel. She was summoned, the case was explained in detail, and examination followed. The verdict was – such things have been known, but it's too early yet to be certain. 'Give me, then, some drug . . .' 'No! That is quite impossible. You must go through with it.' – but next day, the symptoms subsided – Probably you know all this too well, and the sequel, so I'll say no more.

Robertson and Alfieri sound attractive, both of them. I have often wanted to try the former, but somehow never had the energy; your account, though, is encouraging. Alfieri's autobiography I am waiting till I know Italian a little better, to attack. I've long had the highest respect for the gentleman. Certainly, we live in a barbarous age; but I fancy the mists are lifting. Have you read, for instance, 'God's Counterpoint' by somebody called Beresford? Another of these symptoms. It's about nothing but what they're pleased to call 'Sex'. And oh! so self-conscious, and tentative, and nervous, and ignorant. It's like a child's history-book, in its intellectual level, – a Little Arthur's sex-novel. But it's a great advance, all the same, and at this rate, in thirty years or so, we shall be having stories which positively take copulation naturally.

Forgive me, I am still weak and inarticulate. Oliver is here – 'in love', I'm told – good heavens! And this afternoon some Major Partridge or other arrives to carry on with Carrington. Me voilà tout seul. Not even a vision of delight to solace myself with. Your Jim, perhaps, might haunt my slumbers with his pleasant ditties; but I haven't much faith in the agreement of our tastes in that direction.

your
Lytton

Oh! Damn the editor of the Saturday Review.

1. Keith Hale (ed.), *Friends and Apostles*, pp.170–71.

‡

To Mary Hutchinson

*William Heinemann (1863–1920) was the distinguished publisher who had
known 'curiosities' such as Whistler and Ibsen. Lytton's host, Edward Hudson
(1854–1936), started* Country Life *magazine in 1897; he had dreamt it up
while playing golf at Walton Heath two years earlier. Hudson had a family
printing business, Hudson & Kearns, and his golfing partner was the publishing
magnate Sir George Newnes. The result of their eighteen holes was* Country
Life Illustrated *(incorporating* Racing Illustrated*). He bought Lindisfarne
Castle – now a National Trust property – in 1901.*

*The American couple may have seemed black to Lytton because of their
jazz-age dress or the banjo, as much as the colour of their skin. But by 1918
black people were much in evidence all over Britain (there were even race riots
in Wales), and there were plenty of black GIs in London. In Paris there was
the beginning of jazz culture. Jim Reese Europe's Society Orchestra (which
became the 369th Infantry band in France during the war) gained a general
public for early jazz and the work of black composers. George Reeves (1893–
1960) was associated as vocal coach or accompanist with many singers and
instrumentalists including Lotte Lehmann, Lauritz Melchior, Ezio Pinza,
Dame Maggie Teyte and Pablo Casals. Lady Tree (née Helen Holt) was an
actress married to Sir Herbert Beerbohm Tree. She played Ophelia to his
Hamlet in 1892.*

The Bird in Bush Inn
Elsdon
Northumberland
September 7th 1918

Eh bien, ma chère, here is a letter at last – a late, but I hope not too
late, attempt to make good my promise of writing to you about
Lindisfarne Castle. As for writing to you from it, that was out of the
question – the brouhaha made such occupations impossible. I should
like to describe *everything* (now that I have reached this completely
placid habitation) but it would take far too long, it would cover reams,

and though it would certainly be an entrancing compilation there are
limits to the capacity of mortals, both in writing and in reading too, so I
must condense. (Also, can anyone ever tell anybody *everything*, when it
comes to the point? Oh! One sets out with such excellent intentions –
but the pen eventually trembles and recoils.)

I should like, though, at any rate, to describe my arrival. – A long
drive in a tumble-down dog-cart at sunset – three miles of sand, partly
under water, with posts to show the way – rather alarming to the
nervous – then a vision of an abrupt rock with a building on it – a
village passed, and various windings – an unexpected stop. Ecco old
Hudson in evening dress – one gets out, and he conducts you in pitch
dark up various flights of stairs set in precipices, until you come to the
Castle itself, dash up and wash, and then enter the dining-room, where
are Suggia, Heinemann, Mr and Mrs Fort, etc., eating lobster and
drinking champagne. And the night before I had been having dinner
with you at Gordon Square, and the night before that, exchanging
epigrams with Elizabeth Asquith. What a kaleidoscope!

Well, Hudson you know, a pathetically dreary figure, so curiously
repulsive, too, and so, somehow, lost. He seemed a fish, gliding under
water, and star-struck, looking up with his adoring eyes through his
own dreadful element to Suggia in her inaccessible heaven. A kind of
bourgeois gentilhomme also, – but it is futile to waste more words on
him. His castle seems to me a poor affair – except for the situation,
which is magnificent, and the great foundation, and massive
battlements, whence one has amazing prospects of sea, hills, other
castles, etc. extraordinarily romantic – on every side. But the building
itself is all timid Lutyens – very dark, with nowhere to sit, and nothing
but stone under, over, and around you, which produces a distressing
effect – especially when one's hurrying downstairs late for dinner – to
slip would be instant death. No, not a comfortable plan, by any means.
Suggia was of course predominant; and let me say at once that I have
made friends with her. I think perhaps great friends, though perhaps it is
a little too early to say that yet. She is very attractive, owing I think
chiefly to (1) great simplicity – not a trace of the airs and graces of the
'Diva' with a European reputation – no bother about playing or not
playing – almost a boyishness at times; and (2) immense vitality – her
high spirits enormous and almost unceasing – which of course is a great
pleasure, particularly to a quiescent person like me. I suppose, besides
this, that she is a flirt; but it is difficult to say, and there are so many
grades of flirtation. Certainly she is full of temperament – of one kind or

another; and there was one evening when she got tipsy – tiens! Her music was of course marvellous – and I got such masses of it! I used to go with her, her mother (a pitiable old remainder biscuit) and the accompanist, to her bedroom; she would then lock the door (to prevent the ingress of Hudson I fancy) and practise – for hours – playing Bach suites one after the other, and every kind of miracle, with explanations and comments and repetitions, until one tottered down at last to lunch (for this used to happen in the morning) in a state of ecstasy. Then in the evening after dinner she gave her full dress performances. It was really all an extraordinary joy.

Next, there was Heinemann. Do you know him? I found him a fascinating figure – one that one could contemplate forever – so very very complete. A more absolute jew face couldn't be imagined – bald-headed, goggle-eyed, thick-lipped; a fat short figure, with small legs, and feet moving with the flat assured tread of the seasoned P & O traveller. A cigar, of course. And a voice hardly English – German r's; and, all the time somehow, an element of the grotesque. His talk was of considerable interest, with reminiscences of Whistler, Ibsen, in fact everybody, and his stories – old world, of course, and elaborately improper – made me laugh. But I daresay you're familiar with him, so all this is de trop. Why he was there was a little difficult to make out. Suggia, I suppose, must have been the attraction; but obviously he felt a little dépaysé, complained that he had never been in such an uncomfortable house, etc., and was grieved by the cookery. The guests fell into two groups – Hudson's and Suggia's. Mr and Mrs Fort belonged to the former. Mr F. an ex-militaire with a voice like a megaphone and an infinite heartiness – and a simplicity of behaviour – oh, strange, most strange! One evening at dinner after a good deal of champagne, carried away by exhilaration, he made a speech – a long, long speech, proposing the health of 'our host' in heartfelt sentences – one sat gasping – the unimaginable farrago seemed to last interminably; and then, if you please, ce pauvre Hudson found himself replying, at equal length, and with an even wilder inconsequence. After that it was clear that the only thing to do was to get altogether drunk.

Then there were a horrid couple of negroid Americans, inconceivably rich and amiable, and of a crudity – . He played the banjo; *she* – what did she do? – oh she, poor woman, tried to read my book, with results that were not communicated. They must have thought *me* a very peculiar product.

Finally, on my last night, Lady Lewis arrived, and seemed nice, in the cosmopolitan jew style, though she slightly distressed me by talking for hours about 'Early Victorians'. And . . . but I can see I really haven't given you much of an idea of anything – haven't described the appalling fishing expeditions organised every morning by Hudson, the inevitable village concert, my walks along the shore with the accompanist (Mr G. Reeves), Suggia's mother – a subject in itself for a Balzac novel – unable to speak a single word in every known language, perpetually neglected and perpetually good-humoured . . . and all the rest. But conversation must fill in the background – and that I hope will be soon.

Since Lindisfarne I have been perambulating over Northumberland with Carrington like a large woolly sheep trotting beside me. Our adventures were almost entirely disagreeable until a few days ago, we came to this infinitely remote and really divinely beautiful village; but in two days more we shall again be on the move – this time Southward. Durham, York, and then, I hope, Gordon Square will receive us. *[. . .]*

Adieu for the present! I hope this won't bore you horribly. I fear it may be too short – and also too long; but oh alas! the limitations of mortality!

ever your

Lytton

And so you are going to build your nest among the branches of Lady Tree.

‡

To Lady Ottoline Morrell

Violet was Old Man Asquith's daughter Violet (afterwards Bonham-Carter, Baroness Asquith of Yarnbury, 1887–1969). Cys Asquith was (Sir) Cyril (1890–1954). A son by the first marriage, he became a judge and was raised to the peerage as Baron Asquith of Bishopstone; he married Anne Pollock (1896–1964). Anthony 'Puffin' Asquith (1902–1968), a son of Margot, was the film director. Lady Tree was (Helen) Maud, née Holt (1863–1937), wife of Sir Herbert Beerbohm Tree. Joseph Texeira de Mattos (1892–1971) was an artist who moved from Amsterdam to Paris in 1938.

The occasion at the Sheldonian Theatre in Oxford was Asquith's Romanes Lecture, 'Some Aspects of the Victorian Age', delivered in June.

Siegfried Sassoon had been invalided back to England after he had been

foolhardy in attacking the German trenches at St Floris and received a wound to
his head on 13 July 1918.

The Bird in Bush Inn
Elsdon
Northumberland
September 8th 1918

Dearest Ottoline,

Ages seem to have elapsed since I was met by the welcome sight of a
letter from you on the hall table of the Wharf, and my excuse for
having been so long in answering it must be the multitude of the
vicissitudes through which I have passed in the interval. So many
people, things, places have I rubbed up against – a veritable babel! But
now for a brief breathing-space I find myself in this infinitely remote
and beautiful Northumbrian village, and have a little leisure in which to
look back, to reflect, and to remember my duties – especially as the
rains rain steadily, and there is a wonderful fire to crouch over, and an
easy chair. The Wharf was a very swift cinema-film, and really very
enjoyable. Maynard supported my tottering footsteps with great tact,
Margot was extremely kind, and the company (though not particularly
brilliant) was entertaining. There were no great nobs. The Old Man was
highly rubicund and domestic – also, I thought, a trifle sleepy. It was
chiefly a family party – Violet, Cys and his wife, Anthony, Elizabeth –
diversified by Lady Tree and one or two nonentities. Violet and I were
very friendly. She certainly has changed enormously – so much more
tolerant – at times almost humble; and even her appearance seems to
have entirely altered, the angularity having disappeared, and something
of the plenitude of the matron taken its place. She told me that she was
negotiating for Bedford Square. I wonder if that has come off: it would
be curious to me to see her among those surroundings. In a moment of
expansion, I suggested going to see her if she was there. She at once
asked me to do so at any rate at Dorset House (or whatever it's called),
and I said I would. Am I a backslider? I don't think so; and she seemed
to be almost intelligent. Even Elizabeth I got on better with (isn't it
shocking?), and Margot's goodness of heart rather won me. But what I
enjoyed best was the family side of the party – playing foolish letter-
games after dinner with the more frivolous (including the Old Man)
while the serious persons – Maynard, Margot, Elizabeth and Texeira de

Mattos (a strange figure – do you know him?) gave themselves over to Bridge. You see what I have sunk to! I even enjoyed going off to church on Sunday evening with Lady Tree – can you imagine the spectacle? And Margot gave me a volume of her diary to read, which was really very interesting, as it had a detailed account of the Cabinet-making manoeuvres of 1906, and I sat up reading it till two o'clock in the morning.

Then in one whisk I found myself at Lindisfarne (the very next day), having dinner with Suggia, in an antique castle built on a rock in the sea, and surrounded by cormorants and quicksands. It was all most singular, and much of it – especially Suggia's playing – delightful. But I don't think I'd better expatiate on my adventures any more, or you'll think that I've finally sunk into a garrulous egotism. Suffice it to say that after a week there, I departed, met Carrington, and after a few unsatisfactory peregrinations, arrived in the divine spot, where really I should love to linger on indefinitely. However, what with one thing or another, I expect we shall be back in the South again in a week or so: the weather seems to have collapsed, lodgings are difficult to procure, and prices are feverish. I wonder if you ever managed to bring off your projected excursion. But probably you were wise, and stayed at Garsington. It was really charming to get your delightful long letter – I only wish I could have seen you that Sunday; but the opportunity was not offered. Do you really think old A. has got the hump with you? If so, I wonder why – surely your expression of countenance during his lecture could hardly have been visible across the Sheldonian! From what I could see, it appeared to me almost incredible that he should ever play a big part in politics again – the poor old fellow! The worst of it is he'll hang on, and block everything. Though, to be sure, even if he did vanish, who would succeed him?

I have, of course, heard nothing of anybody, since I've been in the North. For all I know, every conceivable kind of cataclysm may have taken place – Norton may have joined the Army, Clive quarrelled with Mary, and Virginia eloped with an Irish colonel. If anything of the sort has happened, I hope you'll let me know. I shouldn't like to be *too* out of date when next I appear in civilised society.

Oh, I forgot to say that I just missed a chance of seeing Siegfried Sassoon, who was in a nursing home near Berwick, not far from Lindisfarne, but was unfortunately not well enough to come over. It was a great pity. I gathered that he was getting better: but after that –?

As my stay here is very uncertain, Tidmarsh is the safest address. Did you get a letter for me to forward on – from Lillah McCarthy? The good woman wants a play of mine to act. My heart sinks at the thought of it.

Carrington sends her love. So do I.

your
Lytton

‡

To André Gide

Gide had come to England with Marc Allegret. He had a letter from Auguste Bréal introducing him to the Strachey family. He was staying at Merton House, in Cambridge, as the guest of Harry Norton. Dorothy Bussy was in England this summer, and she was often with Gide, whose translator she would become. Later she conceived a hopeless and fruitless passion for the now confirmed homosexual Gide. Lytton was slightly hoping to persuade Gide to translate Eminent Victorians; *but Gide wrote to Dorothy that he was 'not at all sure this book may find in France many readers'.*[1]

The Mill House
Tidmarsh
Pangbourne
September 22, 1918

Dear Mr Gide,

I wonder if there is any possibility of your being able to come down here for the weekend next Saturday – the 8th. My sister Dorothy is to be here then and it would be a great pleasure if you could come too. I don't know whether Monsieur Marc . . . (surname unknown) is with you now, and whether he could also come; but if he could I should be delighted. Will you ask him? And tell him that Miss Carrington will be here?

This is not a difficult place to get at – only about an hour from London.

Yours sincerely,
Lytton Strachey

[This A.L.S. (Bibl. Doucet g 810–1) is the only letter from Strachey to Gide in the Fonds Gide.]

1. Quoted Michael Holroyd, *Lytton Strachey*, p. 427.

‡

To Mary Hutchinson

Sir (Francis) Osbert (Sacheverell) Sitwell (1892–1969), 5th Baronet, and Sir Sacheverell Sitwell (1897–1988), 6th Baronet (who was about to be demobbed), were the brothers of the poet Edith (1887–1964).

The Mill House
Tidmarsh
Pangbourne
December 4th 1918

Très-très-chère,

I arrived here safe and sound on Monday, after a pleasant, though of course extremely wet, week-end at Charleston – disappointing, also, owing to the non-appearance of Clive. But Maynard arrived, with a brace of pheasants and a kind of dwarf clothes-horse under his arm – the former to eat, the latter – so he declared – for Duncan to put his brushes on – there was a ledge apparently for the purpose – it was a curious contraption, and I think he must have had it from Margot as part payment of a bridge debt; but I don't know; its mysterious appearance suggested some complicated Freudian vice. Probably you will discover it before long, supporting one end of the dining-room table in Gordon Square – so be prepared. Nessa was immense. She immediately put on your gown, which suited her miraculously – tout ce qu'il y a de plus grotesque! She was delighted, too, by the baby-clothes, the sight of which made me long to be an infant once more to be able to dribble in such luxury. I hope you got the blankets all right, by the hand of the faithful Blanche. We talked, of course, without cessation – partly of the past, and partly of the future; and enjoyed it all very much. Do you know I believe we may still have a chance with the Captain? I put some searching questions to Vanessa, and some invidious ones to Duncan, with the result that I came to the conclusion that *so far* nothing *much* had transpired. Of course, Duncan may be playing a very dark game indeed – but I hardly think so. He was not alone with the young gent that night – Edith and Sachy were also present (whether *both* in Osbert's bed, I couldn't quite make out), and the young gent didn't go to Charleston at all . . . and so, I think, on the whole, if we took immediate steps, flew to the train, arrived panting at Scarborough, and flung our arms round his neck on the Town Hall platform, we should be very well received. But there's *no time to lose.*

Ah, ma chère, what wonderful weeks those were! If ever manna dropped from Heaven . . . I was perfectly happy, and everything passed in such a dream of contentment that it really seems to have been a dream, as I reflect on it. The varnished yellow drawing-room – are you sitting in it as you read this? I hope so – how exquisitely familiar it has become to me! – I see it all – and you on the cross-stitch sofa – the two parrots on the mantelpiece – every detail – the poker – the tongs. You were too divine to me, and I'm afraid that you may have thought me not sufficiently aware of the fact. I was so, but I found it difficult to express anything in my state of diminished vitality – a wretched invalid, engaged merely in breathing in those surrounding blessings. Please forgive me – for you see I have not yet quite recovered.

The Albertine incident –! I hope you haven't spread too many scandals about it, because in reality anything less scandalous was never known. It was a perfect example of ludicrosity. Oh, mon dieu! Those clothes! The get-up! And them – the innocents! I couldn't have imagined that a little dirt could have such an effect. Its absence seemed positively to alter shapes as well as colours. My desires sank to the lowest ebb. And then – oh, so nice! So very nice! – But all the same it was really amusing – to be so *completely* disappointed. I determined that the only thing to be done was to go through with it alla stoccata, with a rattle and a rush. And I think I succeeded. Hastings, en passant, deserves Duncan's praises; there's a faded dilapidation about it – and the ruined pier, too; it *would* be a nice place to spend the day in (or even the night) with . . . a suitable companion. As it was, after an hour, we parted – may I hope forever? – and, for all that had happened, I might have been Hubert as I got into the train.

Life here pursues its accustomed course. I've spent most of my time since my return answering letters – which have suddenly begun to stream in upon me again. I suppose they told you that poor Ted had been killed. Isn't it dreadful to think of? His mother wrote me a most pathetic letter. How hideous, how senseless is this world! It happened just a month before the armistice. – The field behind Eleanor that late September, the plough and the horses, the seagulls, the boy at the plough . . . but it's better to talk of something else.

How did you spend *your* week-end, I wonder? Alone, or with Gloriana? I hope you were not too wretched – and you might have been at Charleston! There was plenty of room. At this moment I imagine you're in London – and enjoying yourself. The new ballet? Or what? Let me hear all the news, please.

My fingers are worn to the bone with writing – but I suppose it does them good. Oh! I've just had the enclosed, which I think will amuse you. You *must* return it, as my archives would be quite incomplete without it. Do you think my little cockle-boat will ever emerge from such an overwhelming ocean?

ever your affectionate
Lytton

I ought to pay for the Doctor and his medicines. Do you think he'll send me the bill?

What do you think? On my way here, in the region of Paddington, I discovered and purchased a charming Grandison.

‡

To Clive Bell

Lytton's hand had been affected by shingles. Sir Theodore Martin's Life of the Prince Consort *came out in five volumes from 1875 to 1880;* Victoria, Queen and Ruler *by Emily Crawford was published in 1903.* The Private Life of Henry Maitland *by Morley Roberts (1912) was a thinly disguised biography of the writer's friend George Gissing.*

E. McKnight Kauffer (1890–1954), an American, came to England in 1914 and returned to the US in 1940, having created hundreds of posters for the London Underground, Shell and BP. Edward Wolfe (1897–1982), born in South Africa, was invited by Roger Fry to join the Omega Workshop in 1917. Best known as a painter, Wolfe was an early champion of Matisse.

The Bolshevik Revolution had taken place a year earlier; but Russia was on everyone's mind. Russia's war had ended in March 1918, with the Treaty of Brest-Litovsk, but having had two revolutions in 1917, by 1918 Russia was caught up in civil war.

Vanessa and Duncan's daughter, Angelica, was born on Christmas Day. Bunny's prophecy came true when he married his lover's daughter in 1942.

Tidmarsh
December 28th 1918

It was cheering to hear from you again; but I can't say I think your letters will be a good investment. My hand has recovered – but my wits? – I feel, after these solid months of retirement, incredibly rusticated – a hodge in cords grunting monosyllables by the fire. A short clay pipe and I should be complete; but, somehow or other, a short clay pipe is lacking.

Have you been having a merry Christmas? Dancing between her Ladyship and Mark to the strains of the gramophone? Tucking up with Molly? Or what? I am sure, whatever you've been doing, it's been very fatiguing; those functions in that mansion invariably are. The atmospheric strain grows even tenser than usual. I remember dreadful moments in which murder seemed not impossible. But perhaps you take these things less frenetically than me. *[. . .]*

I am engaged in a study of Queen Victoria – an interesting subject, but an obscure one. If by any chance you know of any unofficial sources of information which I could tap I hope you'll let me know. It's very difficult to penetrate the various veils of discretion. The Prince Consort is a remarkable figure; but Sir Theodore Martin's life of him in five stupendous volumes is not to be recommended to the general public. Have you ever heard of Emily Crawford? There's a book by her on the Queen which is not without merit – Irish and full of gossip about the forties – very disordered, but in parts distinctly good. I'm beginning to think that most of the good books are overlooked. For instance the Private Life of Henry Maitland is sure highly interesting – but who mentions it? I found it the other day quite by chance, and found it absorbing. Perhaps you know it – if not, I recommend it. It's not a novel, which, to my mind, is in itself a great advantage. It seems to me that all novels, except the very greatest, are impossibly futile affairs.

Harry lies beside me on the sofa, reading Marvell, in order to find out if he is the next best poet to Milton – so far, he thinks not. But Milton himself, I gather from Mr Ezra Pound, is not altogether the thing nowadays. These young men are so brilliantly paradoxical. He (Harry) gave me the Omega wood-cut book, which I like – all of it, including

Mr Wolfe, including Mr Kauffer, even including Roger. Very indiscriminate, I suppose. As for my friends in the smart set. They have abandoned me (or vice versa), I am not sorry, on the approach of Bolshevism; when that comes it will no doubt be death to be on speaking terms with an Asquith. Personally, I am rather looking forward to the régime – naturally I shall become one of the peasant members of the local soviet, which will give one all sorts of opportunities.

I suppose you're still at Garsington. I shall try to make a little stay in London during January – though I am rather afraid of the conditions of life there. It is good news that you're to become a fixture at Gordon Square. I heard yesterday of Nessa's infant, from Bunny, who apparently contemplates marriage. Other marriages I haven't heard of. They were made in Charleston, I suspect.

yours ever,
Lytton

I thought the Lopokhova poem charming.

‡

To Carrington

Lillah McCarthy, Lady Keeble (1875–1960), one of the supreme actresses of her age, worked closely with Harley Granville-Barker, to whom she was married from 1906 to 1918, and with G. B. Shaw. John Drinkwater (1882–1937) was better known as a poet, playwright and actor than as her manager. Arthur William Symons (1865–1945), poet and critic, wrote The Symbolist Movement in Literature *(1899), and was the leading authority on the French Symbolists, many of whom he knew. He believed he had gone mad in 1908, and wrote about his experiences in his* Confessions: A Study in Pathology *(1930). John painted a portrait of him. The naval cadet became Sir Caspar John (1903–84), Admiral of the Fleet and First Sea Lord; his sister Poppet (Elizabeth Ann, 1912–97), who had been married to the millionaire Derek Jackson, married as her third and final husband the Dutchman Wilhelm Pol – and became stepmother-in-law to the late Sir Paul Getty. 'Chile' was the Chilean painter Alvaro Guevara (1894–1951).*

6, Belsize Park Gardens
Friday, 24th January 1919

Oh! the cold! the cold! And a yellow fog! And nothing to eat! Oh!

I return to Tidmarsh tomorrow, hoping to get away from the Heinemann lunch in time to catch the 3.10 train. I'll notify Legg, and hope that you'll arrive for dinner.

Excitements have been decidedly mediocre. Lillah McCarthy was viewed – so handsome in the half-light; but at the last moment she rashly turned it up, and was seen to have a curiously shrunken pinkish physiognomy. She was very non-committal about the son of Heaven, but I am to see her (and her manager, Mr Drinkwater) again. Then Dorelia yesterday, plus John and Arthur Symons. Who, poor man, was incoherent with imbecility. Kasper *[Caspar]* was there, very ugly, in a cadet's get-up; and Poppet, rather flirtatious and attractive. After that I reached Gordon Square and had dinner – my dear, a *cold* dinner – with Clive and Harry – the latter in the depths of gloom. How soon will the asylum doors open to receive him, do you fancy? Today, I lunch with Osbert and Sachy (and I suppose Chile) at Swan Walk, and have tea with Marjorie. So far I haven't heard a note of music – but I'm going to the Calvé concert next week. Will George be 'at the piano'?

I forgot to mention that Oliver announced his intention of coming down tomorrow week, 'with a companion'. So be prepared! I met him, Ray, and Thena Clough at the Spanish restaurant (Dent of course in a corner). It was rather awkward about Thena, but I immediately said 'You'll shortly receive an enormous letter from me,' and it passed off.

I rather doubt whether this will get to Cheltenham by tomorrow morning. Letters seem nowadays so rarely to arrive.

your
Lytton

I said to Lillah – 'I hope *you* didn't think of acting the Empress – it wouldn't suit you – the part's too old.' She replied 'You think so? Well perhaps it is,' and was evidently delighted. Rather skilful I thought!

✝

To Virginia Woolf

Emma Calvé (1866–1942) was a French opera singer, a celebrated Carmen.

Tidmarsh
January 29th 1919

I'm afraid you will think me quite undependable. I find London impossible – James has the flu in the house, and Calvé is ill, and cannot meet me at Heinemann's – and so here I am. Will you overlook it? Later on, later on, when the snow has vanished . . . It is dreadfully dull down here, but healthy and for the moment there are fires. I foresee that I shall soon be forced to begin writing again through sheer désoeuvrement. Leonard, I fear, will hardly forgive me. But I send him my love.

your
Lytton

✝

To James Strachey

In Co-operation and the Future of Industry *(1919) Leonard Woolf developed his theory of co-operation and socialism. His concern, which impressed Lytton, was about how the consumer could influence the planning and control of what industry produces.*

Tidmarsh
February 8th 1919

I wonder how you are. I was sorry to hear (via Alix) that you had had a 'relapse', but I hope by now that you are definitely recovering. [. . .]

I've been reading Leonard's book on Co-operation, and the result is I am becoming (to a limited extent only, I hope) a 'co-operator'. It's rather interesting, though written in that dreadful style, and the format – oh Jesus! If you'd like to see it, I could send it you.

I was to have come up for a day or two this week to Oliver's, but the strikes seemed so devastating that I refrained. Perhaps it will be possible next week. My Calvé party collapsed, as the good women got the flu;

but I daresay it will come on again. Really I do think, what with one thing and another, life is just a trifle hard nowadays. *[. . .]*

‡

To Clive Bell

The ticket was probably for a performance by Dame Nellie Melba (1861–1931), who headed the Covent Garden season of 1919.

   The Creevey papers were the journals and notebooks, 1792–1838, of the politician Thomas Creevey (1768–1838). George Meredith (1828–1909) was born into a working-class family, a background he was later at pains to disguise. His education was patchy, and included some time at a Moravian school in Germany. He did not go to university, but worked as a reader for Chapman & Hall publishers, where he rejected work by Bernard Shaw. He married, first, in 1857, the daughter of Thomas Love Peacock, who left him for one of the Pre-Raphaelites, and remarried in 1861, when he began writing his masterpiece, the poetic sequence Modern Love. *By the 1890s his novels had made him regarded as one of the greatest living writers.*

   Lytton had read the first volume of memoirs by a friend of Aleister Crowley, Gerald Cumberland's Set Down in Malice: A Book of Reminiscences *(1919). Presumably the letters are those of Henrietta, Countess of Bessborough (1761–1821), sister of Georgiana, Duchess of Devonshire (1757–1806) – but these appear not to have been published on their own, and the reference is not clear.*

The Mill House
Tidmarsh
Pangbourne
February 18th 1919

Dear Clive

I wonder if you could make use of the enclosed ticket – or perhaps you could hand it over to someone else. I can't face coming up for it, and it seems a pity to waste it – though Heaven knows whether the good woman (who must by now be well on in the sixties) can sing a note.

   Is there any news, I wonder? What was the issue of the Jack affair? I hoped to have heard from you before now. But perhaps the crisis is still pending. Please give my love to Mary. I should have written to her, but hardly like to bother her just now.

The conditions of life seem hardly to be ameliorating, and so I have decided definitively to give up the gay world, to become an anchoret, to read nothing but the various lives of the Prince Consort, to gaze out of the window at the snow, and to put yet another log on the fire. Are you firmly fixed in your upper chamber? Do you do any writing? Or do you merely pass from lady to lady all day, and all night long? Also, have you any coals?

I have been reading (besides the biographies of Albert the Good) the Creevey Papers, which are highly entertaining, and that life of George Meredith, which has some slight interest – but really the man (though of course he was horribly able) was too tiresome and too reactionary. He positively wrote to his son, aged 18, to tell him always to believe in God, and always to pray. This in the 70s, if you please! And, of course, too, his affectation was, as Creevey would have said, *beyond*. How can anyone read novels when there are Creevey Papers to be had – in which there is every variety of human, political, and historical interest, sur le vif – I don't understand.

'Set Down in Malice' I have also perused, but it is the merest dish-water. Is there anything else you can recommend? I must get the Bessborough Letters. But what is their exact name? – If in your flâné-ings you should ever by chance see a cheapish copy of the Greville Memoirs, do let me know. And write before long.

your

Lytton

‡

To Carrington

Lytton seems to have appreciated that to pop the weasel was to pawn the tools of one's trade. Carrington was able to borrow from Arthur Waley because she was executing a commission for him. The ground of Lytton's prejudice against Hatchard's was probably that they held, as they still do, the Royal Warrant as booksellers. Alec Waugh's novel about public school romance, Loom of Youth, *was published in 1917. Presumably Carrington had just caught up with it.*

Tidmarsh
Sunday, March 2nd 1919

Well, I daresay you're wise, though it seems a pity – it's so warm and agreeable here, and I've ordered in such a gigantic round of beef that I shudder to think what's to become of it, unless Mr Reynolds (as I half expect) drops in – and probably by Wednesday the snow will be on the ground again. *[. . .]* I hope you'll have enough money to exist till Wednesday and bring you down here. What becomes of it?

> Up and down the City Road
> In and out the Eagle
> That's the way the money goes . . .

If necessary, I suppose you can fall back on Mr Waley.

I've had a most competent letter from Hatchard's about the G*[reville]* Memoirs – just what I wanted, and I've written off to order it at once. So *that's* done – thanks to you. I should never have thought that that snobbish establishment would have been so wonderfully on the spot. Your life sounds a trifle grim – what with the club and the attic. As for Alec, I am furious with him. What? Is this love? Admiration? Waugh! – Nero could teach him better. For, what do you think, the other evening after tea, that animal suddenly became extremely agitated – rushed to window, mewing violently – leapt up and peered out into the garden. I then heard a faint sound, as of a distant mew. I opened the window – he mewed wildly – then crouched back in great emotion – finally nerved himself and jumped out. I followed (through the door) to see what it meant. When I got round the bay tree, what should I see but Percy's grey cat with Nero beside her. Directly I appeared they looked round in a most guilty way – then made off – then once more looked round at me over their shoulders, and at last vanished into the bushes at the bottom of the garden. Did you ever hear the like? That old hag – a regular Ottoline – coming and enticing our sweet innocent young Nero to . . . I shudder to think what! Dear, dear, dear! *[. . .]*

‡

To James Strachey

James was writing a review of what Lytton called 'the utterly deplorable' Claudel for Middleton Murry's Athenaeum. *James wrote to Lytton on 19 March: 'I can hardly believe there's anything to be said for M. Claudel.'*

Tidmarsh
March 24th 1919

[. . .] I find public affairs crushing – a new war plus a revolution. We shall be lucky if the second saves us from the first. Oh dearie me! Whatever shall we do? 'Suffered under Bonar Law' will I fear be our epitaph.

Have you despatched M. Claudel yet? I hear a rumour that Eliot declines to be sub-editor. Do you accept?

your
Lytton

‡

To Carrington

Lytton was spending Easter in a lodging-house at Lyme Regis with Alix and James. Oliver seems to have kept his wife, Ray, and young child, Barbara, at South Hill Park in Hampstead, while seeing his girlfriend, Inez, at Tidmarsh. The Cobb at Lyme Regis is the curved breakwater that was the scene of Monmouth's landing in 1865.

Lyme Regis
Tuesday, April 1st 1919

I have completely lost count of time, and cannot decide whether this or you will get to Madrid first. My movements have been so multifarious that I feel as if they must at least equal yours; Lyme Regis is quite as peculiar – I assure you – as Granada. I suppose I may eventually hear from you; but in the meantime it's no good speculating as to what may have become of you, or asking questions. I shall therefore simply proceed to give a short sketch of my existence since your departure.

The Oliver-Inez week-end was in some ways distinctly trying. I found her more hopelessly repellent than ever, and her idiocy seemed unique. Oliver, too, showed no sign of realising even dimly the painful truth. However she behaved very well – did everything that Legg told her, hustled about and superintended the kitchen arrangements with the greatest conscientiousness – positively in terror sometimes. But on the whole – though we had some heart-to-heart conversations on the subject of Patsey (which drove Oliver to frenzy) – the total effect was decidedly lowering.

[. . .] Then, after communicating with James who wrote to say that he and Alix were at the Hotel at Lulworth, I set off via Reading, arrived there, and found they had vanished the day before. Some strange confusions had taken place; but I remained and they came down two days later. It was divinely beautiful – I had forgotten its full marvels – though very cold. Also very expensive, and the Hotel twelve deep on every chair. Eventually they went off to look for rooms here, and I followed a few days ago, they having discovered these excellent lodgings. It's quite different from Lulworth, and very fascinating. The town is divine – entirely late 18th Century – projecting curved and square windows of all sorts – delicate and neat – and urns in some of the houses, and Adamesque ornaments. The marine parade is charming – a sort of miniature Park Lane in effect, and at the end of it the – much to my surprise – enormous Cobb. We must really some day come here together; you would adore the place. Then the surrounding country is fine and remarkable – on a very large scale – great collapsed cliffs covered in undergrowth, through which yesterday I walked, with others – a veritable prickly-pear scrub, together with thick woods at times, and the sea sparkling underneath – most strange. The 'others' were – who do you think? – Established in the divinest of all the divine little houses on the parade we found Dickinson and E. M. Forster (the novelist) – and a rather dim friend of theirs called Barger. They've now vanished, but Dickinson may return. Yesterday's walk was organised by Forster and Barger. Alix and I joined. James stayed at home with a cold, which now apparently comes and prostrates him once a fortnight. E. M. F. has been for the last three and one-half years in Alexandria, which he recommends as a winter residence – cheaper than England, he says, also warm, also . . . there are other advantages. So perhaps that's where one will end. *[. . .]*

‡

To Carrington

The Twins of Ceylon *(1909) was written by Leonard's sister, Bella Lock (1877–1960).*

The Manor House
Garsington
Oxford
Monday, May 12th 1919

I've just seen la Crozier, who seems a very nice female – really with a touch of Legg in her looks, I thought. Perhaps she will go over to you on Wednesday, coming Pangbourne 12.19 – unless you write to put her off. I now feel distinctly in favour of her, and my main terror is that Old Ladyship will put a spoke in the wheel at the last moment out of sheer malevolence.

Such a day yesterday! A long and interesting conversation with Eliot in the morning. He's greatly improved – far more self-assured, decidedly intelligent, and, so far as I could see, nice. I hope to see more of him, but the circumstances are difficult. Madam was not at all bad, either, though with a painfully vulgar voice. Then 'Toronto' came – oafish (*why* are Old Ladyship's flames such rough sheep-dogs?) but very natural and nice – like a French youth, slightly – with slanting dark eyes, and stiff black hair. Aldous, poor creature, too . . . incredibly cultured – produced a very long and quite pointless poem for me to read (I couldn't – pretended to – ouf!). Also Mademoiselle, looking too sweet and quite rejuvenated (Ott. hates her in consequence) with her dreadful bore of a husband. Then the Bishop, who's really charming and most witty. Finally, in the middle of tea, 'Mr Asquith and Party' were announced. Inevitable, of course. Luckily, I was able to swim forward and claim acquaintance with a deplorable Princess Bibesco (cousin of Elizabeth's spouse) – but altogether it was a horrid scene. I forgot to mention a Sir Somebody Something brought by the Bishop – a Ceylon Civil Servant who asked whether Mrs Woolf hadn't written a novel . . . called 'Twins in Ceylon'.

The Eliots went off yesterday. Aldous, like a piece of seaweed, remained. Now he too is gone, and in another minute I follow him. Lunch is here. The Pipsey drives me into Oxford. Diable! I must stop. I hope all is well with you. Love

from Lytton

Please send me some stiff collars – if there are any.

‡

To Carrington

*The agitator who gave Mrs Ava Astor, the wealthy widow of Colonel J. J. Astor
(and soon to marry Lord Ribblesdale), such a fright was Robert Smillie (1857–
1940). In June 1917 he was the firebrand orator at the National Council for
Civil Liberties Convention in Leeds, which welcomed the Russian Revolution.
David Lloyd George saw Smillie as a dangerous man and offered him a post in his
government in an attempt to put him under his thumb. Smillie declined, and when
the war ended in 1918 led those who called for the Labour Party to withdraw from
Lloyd George's coalition government. In 1919 Smillie called for nationalization
and workers' control of the mines. Lloyd George responded by setting up the
Sankey Royal Commission, which failed to agree about the solutions to these
problems, though the majority of the members supported nationalization of the
mines. Smillie was livid when Lloyd George allowed the mines to go back into
private ownership. Oliver Strachey very much admired Smillie.*

*Miss Crozier was one of Lady Ottoline's servants, whom Carrington was
interviewing at Tidmarsh, with a view to employing her. She was disappointed
at the simplicity of Tidmarsh, and made a large number of demands, including
new wallpaper, so was not taken on.*

Savile Club
107, Piccadilly, W.
Wednesday morning, May 14th 1919

It sounds delicious at the Marsh, but it's very nice here too. One
positively crosses the street to get into the shade; and the evenings are
most emotional. This is purely atmospheric, though, and does not apply
to Henry, whom I met last night at Faith's – a queer party, with Oliver
and Helen A[nrep] as extras. As O. observed afterwards, he and Hubert
were the only ones in it without a Past vis-à-vis to that man. I am to
meet him again tonight at the Anreps. But to me he has little to offer.
His nerves seemed distinctly jumpy, I thought. He's returned to the
Vale Hotel, but wants to leave it, and talks of settling in the country
with the Kennedys and 'some other people'. I pity them. He also has no
money left, and says he can't paint.

Yesterday I went (at my own suggestion) to tea with Mrs Astor. For
the first time my courage began to ooze. The immense size of that vast
Grosvenor Square house – double doors flying open, a vast hall with a

butler and two female footmen permanently established in it, vistas beyond of towering pilasters and a marble staircase and galleries – it struck awe into the heart. Then a door quite close at hand was swiftly opened. And I was projected into a large square room, in a distant corner of which, on a sofa, was a lady whom in my agitation I hardly recognised – the colour of hair seemed to have quite changed – and as I advanced three small dogs rushed out at me snapping. I at last reached the sofa, and we had a long but not amorous tête-à-tête. The poor dear woman is terrified of Bolshevism – thinks Mr Smillie will lead the mob against her, and asks anxiously, 'Do you think they'll go red?' I read her a lecture on the inequality of wealth, and left her trembling, to get ready for the Opera.

To that haunt of fashion I haven't been. Maud must have forgotten to ask me. It's very remiss, but I lunch again with her on Friday and will give her a jog. In a few minutes I am due at Kent House, where lives Mrs Saxton Noble. My terror is that I shall find Walter Lamb on the hearthrug. Herbert Trench, a passé poet is to be there, damn him.

Oh! What do you think? I've just come from Mr Harris, who after a rigorous inspection, pronounced that my teeth were perfect. Isn't it magnificent? I am also due at Eliott's today, for an eye examination. Poet Eliot had dinner with me on Monday – rather ill and rather American: altogether not gay enough for my taste. But by no means to be sniffed at. I visited Clive, too, who, as there was a poor wretch called Pastor there, was very tiresome – also announced that the Picasso party was postponed,

I'm longing to hear news of the Crozier.

your
Lytton

‡

To Mary Hutchinson

Lytton was still trying to achieve a professional staging of A Son of Heaven, *and took it to Irene Vanbrugh, his (and Mary's) distant relation by marriage. The actress was born Irene Barnes in Exeter, where her father was Dean of Exeter Cathedral. When Irene and her elder sister Violet began their distinguished theatrical careers, they were the first daughters of a 'good family' to go on the stage. In her diary entry for 16 May, Virginia Woolf wrote of Lytton's*

*visit to her that week: 'We sat on the river bank, and he told us of a visit to
Irene Vanbrugh, with his comedy; how the singing of the canary birds almost
drowned his voice; and how finally she determined against it, finding a lack of
human passion. Therefore the comedy is shelved, for ever, I suspect, and he
writes, and will continue to write Eminent Victorians.' Virginia was wrong – the
play was finally produced in 1925.*

*The novelist George Moore was Maud Cunard's lover and frequent
houseguest. Her daughter Nancy published a memoir of him in 1956.*

1917 Club
4, Gerrard Street, W.1
May 15th 1919

Dearest Mary,

Irene was decidedly the Vicar's daughter – a quiet unpainted lady –
rather soothing, and reminding one of one's bourgeois youth. She was
very polite, but thought the thing wouldn't do for the Music Halls –
not enough 'simple human feeling', and too complicated for their
minds. I expect she was right – and so that's over. One thing was
curious – I had a strong prevision that there would be canaries in the
room. (Would you have guessed that?) And there were.

My smart life proceeds apace. I find it mainly simply comic, and
distinctly exhausting. No pasturage for the soul, I fear! Lady Cunard is
rather a sport, with her frankly lower-class bounce; she makes the rest
of 'em look like the withered leaves of autumn, poor things. But she
herself I fancy is really pathetic too. So lost – so utterly lost! – She takes
to me, she says, for the sake of that dear nice Bernard Keynes, who's
such an intimate friend of hers. Also, we had, at an appalling lunch at
the Saxton Nobles, a heart to heart talk about Nancy.

[. . .] I should like to tell you about my Eliot experiences – but all
that is at present in a fluctuating stage. I do like him, though. He's
changed a great deal since I last saw him – a long time ago. But the
devitalisation I'm afraid may lead to disappointments.

This is scrappy – mais que veux-tu? In this hurly-burly? I should like
to kiss you, if you wouldn't mind.

your
Lytton

Oh! I must tell you – an absurd scene at Kent House, after lunch. Lady C. suddenly said she must go and fetch Princess Bibesco (not Elizabeth – another) from the French Embassy opposite. She dashed off to do so. Reappeared very quickly, with the Princess, and – who do you think? – George Moore. He looked too preposterous – like a white rabbit suddenly produced by a conjuror out of a hat. He was furious, of course, and went away at once. Apparently he had told Maud over and over again, 'I do not want to come' – but it was useless – he was carried off – propelled into Mrs Noble's arms, and then, out of Maud's clutch for a moment, vanished. Can you imagine the scene? I thought you would have liked it.

‡

To Carrington

> 96, South Hill Park
> Hampstead Heath, N.W.
> Thursday, 22nd May 1919

[. . .] I went to the Russian Ballet last night, and found there Clive and Mary. Clive was an extreme mixture of real charmingness and pure horror. He insisted on taking me (he being in his usual raucous evening clothes, rather red in the face, and a top hat planted on the very back of his head) to the most conspicuous spot in the house, and standing there gesticulating and making a disgrace of himself. We also went behind the scenes to Lopokhova's dressing-room, where, as you may imagine, the noise was appalling. But he was very nice afterwards, pouring champagne down our throats at Gordon Square.

Tonight the evening party at the damned Asquiths,

> yours ever with love
> Lytton

‡

To Virginia Woolf

*Lytton had almost certainly met the Webbs at least five years earlier. Katherine
Asquith, née Horner (of Mells, Somerset), was the widow of the son of the
Prime Minister, Raymond Asquith, who had been killed on the Somme in
1916. Lytton was reacting to Virginia's having written to him the day before that
Ottoline had written to her (Virginia), calling Katherine Asquith 'statuesque'
and 'lamenting her lack of passion'.*

  *'Clive's luncheons': Virginia had written that Clive told her that he lunched
out every day, and when she asked him where, replied, 'Ah, with beautiful
creatures!' Murry had asked Virginia to review his poem 'Belshazzar' in the
Athenaeum, and begged Lytton, 'For God's sake, say you'll do it instead.'*

96, South Hill Park
Hampstead Heath, N.W.
May 27th 1919

June 7th will suit me very well for Webbism – lunch, of course. I again
forgot to get Kew Gardens. Could you send me a copy of it and Eliot's
poems? Or if you haven't got any with you, reserve them?

  Garsington was terribly trying. I was often on the point of screaming
from sheer despair, and the beauty of the surroundings only intensified
the agony. Ott I really think is in the last stages – infinitely antique,
racked in every joint, hobbling through the buttercups in cheap shoes
with nails that run into her feet, every stile a crisis, and of an imbecility
. . . She is rougée, too, by benevolence; every tea party in London to
which she hasn't been invited is wormwood, wormwood. The great
Picasso question plunges her into inconceivable agitations – in vain I
tell her he is only a silent Spaniard – she wires to Osbert daily, and is
convinced that Roger has intrigued to prevent them meeting.
However, at the last moment she typically recovered, appearing in a
yellow straw top hat, in which she drove me and Katherine A*[squith]* to
Oxford in the finest manner. K.A. makes the heart sink within one – a
sharp twist to the neck would be the thing for her. Bertie worked his
circular saw as usual. I've never been able to feel at ease with him, and I
can only suppose that he dislikes me – pourquoi?

  It's a mercy to be back here again, even though the Duchesses seems
to have dropped me. I *was* rung up just now, though, and by – who do
you think ? – Vanessa, who's in Gordon Square apparently. I dine there

tonight. Clive's luncheons are certainly mysterious, and I fancy apocryphal – I think when you return we'd better put on white masks and track him out.

Review Murry! Ho, ho!

your

Lytton

‡

To Carrington

York Terrace is in Regent's Park, a long walk from Hampstead, though very near Baker Street Station. The Rt Hon. Richard Burdon Haldane, OM, FRS (1856–1928), 1st Viscount, left the Liberals and became Chancellor once again in 1924 under the first, short-lived Labour government. Mrs Montgomery was the sister of Arthur Ponsonby (1871–1946), a consistently anti-war politician, who lost his seat in December 1918 when he left the Liberals to stand as an Independent Democrat. Their father had been Queen Victoria's private secretary for twenty-five years. Queen's Hall was next door to All Souls' Church (which is itself near BBC Broadcasting House); it was destroyed in the Blitz in 1941. The Hon. Geoffrey Howard (1877–1935) was the son of the 9th Earl of Carlisle. Lord Parmoor (1852–1941) was Charles Alfred Cripps.

The Wharf
Sutton Courtenay
Berks.
June 1st 1919

Good gracious me! Here I am on a stone seat by the river bank – it's after breakfast, the heat already intense, boredom pretty severe also – oh these dull dogs, what are they all up to? Yesterday was extraordinarily hectic. If only I could describe it, in detail; but it would need at least the 36 pages of that other day. It was the varieties that were so strange – the contrasts of curiosities. After leaving you, I floated to Paddington with great ease and swiftness, there took tube to Swiss Cottage, and thence walked to B*[elsize]* P*[ark]* G*[ardens]*, where I found James. He seemed in rather a crisis – about which I'll tell you when we meet; but this didn't prevent him getting very nearly all my cash out of me. I then, having collected a couple of white shirts, proceeded to 96. There I found a

note from Suggia with a ticket for her concert. Things now looked
pretty crammed. Lunch with Lady K*[itty]*, Suggia concert, train to
Wharf – and all the packing up etc. What I want is a man – there's no
doubt of that – when shall I have one? I reached York Terrace with
some difficulty just in time, and found there Haldane and Mrs
Montgomery (Arthur Ponsonby's sister – rather old and extremely
nebulous). That was the party, and it was the queerest affair you ever
saw. Old Haldane holding forth with infinite imperturbability, while
those two women chattered, one on each side of him, like a couple of
magpies. The conversation was at times quite delirious – his Lordship
unwinding his narratives about Lord French and April 1915, while they
wildly interjected remarks of frantic irrelevance. 'I was standing on an
island in the middle of the street, when my chiffon was blown out by
the wind, a motor bus was passing, and didn't quite catch it' –
'Somebody said Mr Strachey looked like Our Lord, but I said he looks
like *[the]* Devil trying to look like Our Lord' – can you imagine it –
dimly? No imagination could come up to the intensity of the mania. At
one point old Haldane said 'My dear Miss Ponsonby' to Mrs M,
whereupon she remarked 'I'm afraid you've forgotten, but I *have* been
married for the last thirty years,' with complete sangfroid, and the
conversation proceeded. At last I saw that the only thing to do was to
ignore the two chatterboxes (at one moment I feared that Lady Kitty
was tight – her nose turned red; no, she's *not* even pretty) – and to get
as much out of his Lordship as possible. He hitched on to this, and
when it broke up walked along with me to Baker Street unwinding and
unwinding his histories. He's certainly full of attractions – a fascinating
face to look at – very shrewd and humorous, with a most elaborate
mouth – perhaps rather too much like the obvious idea of a cunning
kindly old statesman, but his eyes are charming – very blue and very far
apart, his skin old ivory colour – his mind strangely woolly, and yet one
saw the ghost of a competence.

It was fun walking along with him. 'Where are you going, Mr
Strachey?' 'To Piccadilly.' 'Ah! To Piccadilly! Then you go by train.'
I hadn't known it, but I said 'Yes,' and he conveyed me along to
Baker Street Station and left me there with infinite suavity. By this
time I was slightly alarmed about the money question. I had 1/6
with which to get to the Wharf and back. So I tore to the 1917
Club, where by the mercy of heaven they cashed a cheque for me,
then rested in a taxi to the Queen's Hall. Suggia was in the middle
of her Schumann Concerto. When it was over, I got to my seat,

which was next to George! His sister was beside him – quite
presentable, in spite of the telephone, but little George brushed her
aside, and went off into fits upon fits of the giggles directly I opened
my mouth. The preposterous creature was wonderfully up to sample;
but I couldn't stay long – had to fly to Paddington and mount into
the gloomy train to Didcot. It was horribly hot and slow, and I was too
poor to go first. At Didcot there was a car, and two other guests of the
young male species. One sat beside the driver, the other beside me
inside – dullness incarnate, and oh! the correctness – a slightly fat,
projecting-eyed young man. My heart sank and sank – and sank still
further on reaching the house, which is really a worse house than
Charleston to arrive at. No sign of Margot – only a faded group of
completely unknown people. I lost my head – opened a door, and
found myself projected into a twilight chamber, with four bridge-
players in the middle of it. Complete silence. Margot was one of them.
At last, after a long time, in which nobody even looked in my direction,
she said 'Oh, how d'you do?' – I fled – fled to the other house, where
my bedroom is – opened another door, and there, at the other end of
the room, alone and dim, was the Old Man. He was as usual most
cordial, and conducted me with incredible speed all round the garden,
and then back again to the other house.

He's a queer nervous old fellow, really. My woes were slightly
alleviated by Geoffrey Howard, who seemed nice and with whom I had
a rather interesting tête-à-tête – then dressing for dinner – then dinner,
which was most unexpected. There's a vast party – none of whom I
knew – except that dreary Baker man – to none of whom I have been
introduced – Generals, Americans, females of all sizes. I imagined a huge
dinner – but no! Margot, Baker, myself and the young man of the taxi
had it together apart from the rest, waited upon by an attractive young
footman called Cecil. The young man of the taxi turned out to be a
Colonel – Cripps by name – I fancy a son of Lord Parmoor. His
demeanour to me quite changed, having been told who I am. He
declared my book had had a great circulation in his regiment! By this
time, having drunk a good deal of cider-cup, I viewed the Colonel
more favourably. Margot too was apparently in love with him, and
put on her most alluring airs – not without success. There's no doubt
she has an odd eminence – the Lady Kittys fade in comparison. If only
she'd stop for a single second to think! As for after dinner, it was
inconceivably tedious, and now here I am, having just survived a
breakfast the ghastliness of which was beyond description – so I'd better

stop describing – at any rate for the present – hoping that I shall not expire with boredom before the happy release tomorrow morning – ouf! –

with love your
Lytton

Excitement reigns – Mrs Astor married Lord Ribblesdale on Friday! –

‡

To Carrington

Lady d'Abernon was one of Lytton's posse of society hostesses. Her husband, Viscount d'Abernon (1857–1941), financier and diplomat, was better known as Sir Edgar Vincent. Either 1) Noel Olivier had made an appointment with Robert Henry Scanes Spicer (1857–1926), surgeon-in-charge of the throat department at London's St Mary's Hospital, known for his developments in the surgical treatment of sinus disease, or 2) in Cambridge Lytton was going to meet his son of the same name, who was an embryo at King's, and elected to the Apostles in March 1920. Tantalizing though the postscript about Derain and Picasso is, there is nothing more in the correspondence about this meeting.

96, South Hill Park
Hampstead Heath, N.W.
June 6th 1919

[. . .] My avocations have been of the usual kind, except for a slightly painful misadventure, about which I'll tell you when we meet. Lunch chez Colefax (many curiosities). Dinner chez Osbert (many more curiosities, including Arnold Bennett and W. H. Davies, gnome and poet). Today lunch chez Bibescos. Tomorrow lunch chez Woolves, and Cambridge. Virginia has had a great success with Kew Gardens. There was a good review in the Times Lit. Sup. with the result that they have been flooded with orders, and will have to reprint it. I think she's now beginning to boom.

I should return on Tuesday, I think, if it weren't for his wretched Lordship d'Abernon, who keeps me hanging in the air. I feel slightly elegiac. (What does *that* mean?) But perhaps Cambridge and Mr Spicer will set me up. Noel has written fixing Monday as the date for that horror. Dear me! Dear me! Dear me! Am I a maniac?

I hope Alix is enjoying country life.

with love, your
Lytton

I ordered the Athenaeum to be sent to me here.

Derain Ballet last night – Alix will have told you about it. Most enjoyable.

Also – the other day at G*[ordon]* Square – lunch with Derain and Picasso. Not so enjoyable.

‡

To Carrington

Lytton did not go with Lady Cunard to Kedleston Hall, much though he would have profited from conversation with 'that very superior person', George Nathaniel Curzon (1859–1925), who had become Viceroy of India when he was only thirty-nine. The story of HH Princess Marie Louise (1872–1956) is striking. A granddaughter of Queen Victoria, though she had a German title, she was very English. In 1891 she was married to Prince Aribert, son of the Duke of Anhalt, who used his royal prerogative to annul the childless marriage in 1900. Rumour had it that Prince Aribert was homosexual. But Princess Marie Louise's uncle, Edward VII, summed up the situation, saying, 'Ach, poor Louise, she has returned as she went – a virgin.' The Prince of Wales (from 1901 to 1936) was the future Edward VIII and later Duke of Windsor.

La Fille de Madame Angot: Au temps des Incroyables et des Merveilleuses *is a three-act operetta by Charles Lecocq.*

1917 Club
4, Gerrard Street, W.1
July 2nd 1919

There's some danger of my being engulfed for the week-end – but it's not yet certain. Maud yesterday asked me if I would go with her to Lord Curzon's! But whether there's a room for me remains doubtful. I shall no doubt hear before long. I don't much look forward to it, though I suppose it would be curious. – but I'll let you know.

Walter Raleigh was also at the Colefax's – very superb – talking the whole time, and pulverising everyone else, including Desmond, who was reduced to complete silence – except Maud: the scene between them was perfectly hectic, and lasted till nearly four. The Princess M*[arie]* L*[ouise]* is according to Maud 'off her head' – 'a person to be avoided'. I asked when I was to meet the P*[rince]* of W*[ales]*. She said 'Oh, we must bring off that – at lunch, perhaps – but the poor boy's kept so hard at it with public functions, he never has any time.' I must confess I'm a good deal taken with this utterly crazed scullery maid.

I also paid a call on the Webbs yesterday. There they were, sitting one on each side of the fire on low chairs. They were very affable, and their mentality after the smart set, amazing. Tonight a family party at La Fille de Madame Angot – Drury Lane. The Cunard asked me to her box. I said no, I was going with someone else. 'Who?' – 'My brother.' 'Your brother! Are you so much attached to your brother? – Loyalty, I suppose! English loyalty!'

Your bicycle shop sounded a regular cave of mystery. I hope you made a bargain, but including so far, to and from Reading, and the nervous strain of Reading platform you didn't gain much, it seems to me! I'm afraid it must be horribly cold on the marsh – it is frightful at 96 of a morning.

I had tea with Katherine on Monday. She was very amusing, and read me some extracts from a letter from Virginia describing Garsington – superb.

yr

Lytton

✞

To Carrington

The third person with Ralph and Carrington was her brother Noel. Lytton's list of the Asquiths' hypothetical second-rate guests begins with Sir John Lavery (1856–1941), an Irish-born society portraitist of the Glasgow School and RA. Frederick Herbert Trench (1865–1923) was also Irish. He was a poet, dramatist and theatrical producer. Lindsay is the family name of the 27th Earl of Crawford, who had a large number of daughters. Charles Latham, 1st Baron Latham (1888–1970), public servant.

The Mill House
Tidmarsh
Pangbourne
Berks.
July 11th 1919

Your letter and postcard and the little book arrived this morning. How I
wish I was in your shoes! Bath! Wells! Glastonbury! The hay cart! Oh
luxury! And here am I disconsolate, solitary, idle – with worse before
me. But never mind. I thought the little mask book charming; evidently
the highly improving words had been written round the woodcuts –
how nice and vague people were in 1776! I suppose by now you are
feeling quite an old inhabitant of your valley. By-the-bye, I don't know
what your address is – Marshland Cottage, perhaps? – so I daresay this
will never reach you. The weather, you see, is perfect – just as I
prophesied, so that you are probably at this moment splashing – all three
– in the stream. Lord! Why am I not a rowing blue, with eyes to match,
and 24? It's really dreadful not to be, I assure you. And what do you
think I *am*? – A maniac! Yes, a complete one. The proof of it is – I am
going tomorrow to spend the week-end at the Wharf. Too shocking! –
and after all my determinations! But yesterday a vast wire came from
Oliver to say that Margot had rung up to ask me – that the party was to
be most interesting – artists, writers, men of intellect – and my presence
was specially requested. (Query – had the stories reached her of my last
week-end?) In a moment of frenzy I accepted. I hardly knew why; and
now I see how much happiness I would have been [sic] here, alone with
the tiger lilies (just coming out). Probably the artist will be Lavery, the
writer Herbert Trench, and the man of intellect Jack Hutchinson. My
only hope is that I may be able to reach La Lindsay's, and discover there
Lord Latham; but I see that that's infinitely improbable. A visit to
Garsington, perhaps . . . I fear you don't pity me, for the absurd reason
that I've brought it all on myself; but don't you see that only makes it
worse? Well! Unless everything turns out the exact opposite of what I
expect, this really *will* be the last time.

My laziness has been horrible. Instead of writing Victoria, I have been
dawdling over plans of plays. I can only hope the Wharf may spirit me
up, and I shall return on Monday bursting with vigour. It is
extraordinary how idle one can be, sitting out of doors, and turning
over bits of paper. Among other absurd occupations, I read most of my
poems: as usual they conveyed very little to me – too familiar I suppose.

There's no domestic news, except that the hens have stopped laying and that Nero has become too disgusting to be borne. Luckily he only appears at very rare intervals. It was so hot last night that I sat out till nearly ten, reading what do you think?

How kind it was of the Major to think of providing me with that final basket of raspberries! They were indeed heavenly. I suppose he would be shocked if I suggested that you should give him a kiss from me. The world is rather tiresome, I must say – everything at sixes and at sevens – ladies in love with buggers, and buggers in love with womanisers, and the price of coal going up too. Where will it all end?

Not that *I* am in love with anybody – oh, no! no! a thousand times no! Even the vision of George in a white surplus (as you say) playing on the organ does not move me. Even the hay cart leaves me (comparatively) cold.

This is a ridiculous letter, I quite realise that, but I am in a ridiculous mood. – Discontented, slightly – isn't it preposterous? What on earth have I to be discontented about? 'Oh Mr Strachey! So successful! So brilliant! Such a future! Such a past!' – And a week-end at the Wharf, besides. – All the same, to be a rowing blue, with eyes to match, and 24 years old! – Ah! *That* would be something! But I perceive you're all splashing about in the stream so that I'm getting very little attention.

your
Lytton

‡

To Carrington

Lytton's snobbery was even-handed. William Bruce Ellis Ranken (1881–1941) was an old Etonian. The ex-Slade painter of royal portraits was a fellow guest with Sir Alfred Munnings (1878–1959), son not of an ostler, but, like Constable, of a miller. Lady Drogheda, a patron of the arts, had commissioned a Vorticist frieze and mantel in the dining-room of her house at 40 Wilton Crescent, London.

Aubrey Nigel Henry Molyneux Herbert (1880–1923), though nearly blind, was an intrepid traveller, diplomat and secret agent. He was the model for John Buchan's Greenmantle, *an ally of T. E. Lawrence, and in 1913 was twice offered the throne of Albania, which he refused on the advice of his host, Asquith. His wife Mary Gertrude was an heiress, the only child of the 4th*

Viscount de Vesci and his rich wife, Lady Evelyn Charteris. Margot was one of
eleven children of Sir Charles Tennant, and had five sisters. 'Viola' is Margot's
stepdaughter, Lady Helena Violet Bonham-Carter (1887–1969) and her
husband was Sir Maurice (1880–1960). The sole topic of conversation was the
journey of the airship R.34 from East Fortune, Scotland to Mineola, Long
Island, USA and back to Pulham, Norfolk.

    'Anrepina' was the Anreps' (expensive) maid whom they were hiring to work
at Tidmarsh that summer.

    Lytton's reading was actually Far Away and Long Ago, *a memoir by*
W.H. Hudson.

The Wharf
Sutton Courtenay, Berks.
Sunday morning, July 13th 1919

Good lord! This is pretty bad. – Just as I feared, in fact. The
incoherence is terrible – and the second-rateness. However it's perhaps
slightly better than last time. There's a middle-aged Scotch woman who
plays chess with me while the others play bridge, and there are not quite
so many absolute imbeciles. The 'painters' are that creature Rankin (the
white-haired pseudo Eddy) and a little sporting fellow – an ostler –
called Mullings, I gather, who also paints race-horses for his living –
each in their way a frightful bore. But positively – what do you think? –
John is expected today! – Or so Margot declares; personally I don't
believe it; I can hardly imagine him coming to such a grim entertainment. There's also Lady Drogheda – appalling – large-featured, highly
coloured, highly fashionable – au fond a dingy whore. A big man called
Erskine. Aubrey Herbert, more sympathetic, with some brains in fact,
but oh! such incredibly good manners, and his wife – tall, hook-nosed,
short-haired and half-witted. Mrs. Graham-Smith, Margot's sister,
almost completely paralysed in every limb, paints water-colours (or did)
of an incredible ineptitude. Henry not here – in Germany. Margot
herself much the best of the bunch, but the least possible to talk to. And
Viola and her husband to come this afternoon – dearie, dearie me. I am
well punished for my folly. The boredom nearly the whole time is so
frantic that it's all I can do to prevent myself screaming. If one could just
sit quite still and observe, without speaking and above all without
listening, it would be tolerable. But to discuss for hours the arrival of
R.34 and – but I can really think of no other subject of conversation –
it's desperate work. I long to go into the servants' hall – though I

daresay they're also infected – or to La Lindsay – but she's probably even worse.

Tomorrow I return by the first train. The silly Anrepina had not written to say when she was coming. I only hope she'll arrive after me. Legg's beatitude continues at its normal height. We must use all our arts and keep her. Are you happy? Are you warm? The weather seems to have taken rather a dubious turn – that's what comes of prophecies. By a miracle I observed a postcard from you to Legg in the kitchen with your address on it. So I hope you will have got my last letter by this time.

I've got 'Long Ago and Far Away' at last, and find it delightful – but too short – it'll be finished in a twinkling. Do you admire that writer? – A letter from Mr Trott, asking for the loan of Eminent Victorians, to read in Harrogate! Rather peculiar. A letter from Mary at Wittering, saying she's perfectly happy. Also rather peculiar. And that I think is all the news. The pot of Devonshire cream arrived as I was leaving. I thought it wouldn't keep, and left it at Ray's during my flash through London – better, I thought, than bringing it here for those idiots – though, to be sure, I might have given it to Cecil. Who is Cecil? The footman.

This letter seems to be as incoherent as its surroundings, so I'd better stop, and go look for the middle-aged Scotch woman. Oh, I've forgotten one of the guests – an American Colonel, hideously handsome, with whom Lady D. is in lust all over the table – ugh! And perhaps Rankin too – but more discreetly.

your

Lytton

⸸

To Mary Hutchinson

T. S. Eliot's 'grim' letter, which threatened their infant friendship, is quoted by Holroyd.[1] In reply to Lytton's reflections on having read 'Prufrock' Eliot says:

> *Whether one writes a piece of work well or not seems to me a matter of crystallisation – the good sentence, the good word, is the only final stage in the process. One can groan enough over the choice of a word, but there is something much more important to groan over first. It seems to me just the*

*same in poetry – the words come easily enough, in comparison to the core of it
– the* tone *– and nobody can help one in the least with that. Anything I
have picked up about writing is due to having spent (as I once thought,
wasted) a year absorbing the style of F. H. Bradley – the finest philosopher in
English – 'App[earance] and Reality is the Education Sentimentale of
abstract thought.'*

Then, reacting to the content of Lytton's letter, the employee of Lloyds Bank
writes the passage Lytton found grim:

*You are very – ingenuous – if you can conceive me conversing with rural
deans in the cathedral close. I do not go to cathedral towns but to centres of
industry. My thoughts are absorbed in questions more important than ever
enter the heads of deans – as* why *it is cheaper to* buy *steel bars from
America than from Middlesbrough, and the probable effect – the exchange
difficulties with Poland – and the appreciation of the rupee. My evenings in
Bridge. The effect is to make me regard London with disdain, and divide
mankind into supermen, termites and wireworms. I am sojourning among the
termites. At any rate that coheres. I feel sufficiently specialised, at present, to
inspect or hear any ideas with impunity.*

Dorothy Bussy translated Gide's La Porte Etroite *(1909) as* Strait is the Gate.

The Mill House
Tidmarsh
Pangbourne
July 17th 1919

Remiss – very remiss – I know! Mais que veux-tu? In such hurly-
burlies of various sorts as I live. But now at last I am a little calmer.
About ten days ago, I think, I retreated down here – to face Victoria;
for faced she has to be, I'm sorry to say. There's so far been only one
interruption – one of those deplorable Wharf week-ends, after which
one comes away, murmuring 'never again, never again', and now I am
fairly in it, or should I say Her, immersed, pegging away daily, and
quite, so far, enjoying myself. I daresay horrors enough will crop up
later. Carrington is in Cornwall with one of her young men and a
brother, so I'm entirely solitary here, except for Anrep's cook, who has
come down to save us, and keeps up a curious rattle whenever she gets
a chance, which, poor creature, isn't often. It's horrid being alone, *I*
think. But *you* are never really quite that. You have children, and

heaven knows what other gay companions – Sitwells for the week-ends – Mrs Eliot in a boat – Gordon Square, too, at intervals: so you can't judge. Wittering must be divine just now – no wonder you enjoy it. The barn! The barn! – Shall I ever come down and see you? In August, perhaps? – I shouldn't venture to suggest such a thing – but Jack said something of it one night at the ballet, and the vision of the estuary rose up before me, quite obliterating Cleopatra.

No, it's quite true, not a word have I written to Eliot, since that grim letter of his. I do intend to spur myself up, though, as I don't want to drop him. Only I rather fear it will take him a long time to become a letter-writer. It is curious how much easier it is to write letters (I don't mean good ones particularly, but any at all) when one's writing other things all day. The writing habit gets hold of one. So now I have many wonderful intentions – all sorts of correspondences – Virginia prodded up, etc. etc. The worst of it is, though, the more one wants to write, the less there is to write about. Nothing but the Anrep cook and the rambler roses. Never mind, Forster is coming down for the week-end, and he should provide material for several letters. Do you know him? A curious triangular face, and a mind, somehow, exactly fitting. But I mustn't use him up beforehand.

How is Clive? London? Good heavens! . . . I can hardly bear to think of it, I love it so much – to distraction. To call up Shaftesbury Avenue before the mind's eye – the Soho streets – Soho Square – the little passage into the Charing Cross Road – Tottenham Court Road along and along – a dive sideways – the trees of Gordon Square . . . and so on endlessly. Every shop window, every paving stone is visible. And at this moment – 9 o'clock – the cool of the evening – the lights coming out, but still weaker than the daylight, and the lovely creatures (for surely there *are* lovely creatures? – surely, surely!) flitting along the streets! – Are you there? Or where? – Wittering again, perhaps? – Then you'll sympathise most acutely, I hope.

I hardly dare to beg for another letter. But all the same I do.

your
Lytton

Have you read 'La Porte Etroite' by Gide? Decidedly remarkable.

1. Michael Holroyd, *Lytton Strachey*, p. 456.

✝

To Carrington

Carrington's £100 was worth £2,750 in 2002.

Tidmarsh
July 22nd 1919

[. . .] Rather an unexpectedly large cheque arrived from the Athenaeum this morning. It was wanted. The 'books' have been terrifying. We must institute financial reforms. The outlook is dark. Don't you think the time has come to think seriously of beginning to show your pictures? Unless you do, I don't see how you can hope to sell them – and that will really be essential, if you ever want to stand on your own legs.

Also I forgot to say that I think you'd better ask Noel about that £100 and your bankers. It would be a great nuisance if it became involved in your trustee capital, and there's no reason at all why it should. *[. . .]*

✝

To Carrington

Mary Berenson (1864–1945), née Pearsall Smith, was the sister of Logan and of Alys Russell, and the wife of the connoisseur Bernard Berenson. They lived at Villa I Tatti, in Florence. Violet Keppel Trefusis (1894–1972) was the daughter of Alice Keppel, the mistress of Edward VII, who was often thought to have been Violet's father. Violet was the lover of Vita Sackville-West, a fact widely known to Society, when later this year she married Denys Robert Trefusis, an officer in the Royal Horse Guards.

André Morellet (1727–1819), economist and writer, was one of the last of the philosophes. *Voltaire called him* 'L'Abbé Mords-les' *because of his biting wit. Lytton was probably reading his posthumous* Mémoires sur le XVIIIème siècle et la Revolution *(2 vols, 1821). The Major is Partridge.*

Eleanor
West Wittering
Chichester
Thursday, August 28th 1919

[. . .] La Colefax was frightful. Not a creature, imagine it, except La
Berenson and two quite insignificant men (and one of *them* an
American) – all the lions had wired at the last moment to say they were
ill and couldn't come! The house was horribly, desolatingly perfect, a
restored antique, without a hair awry, and tasted of such a chicness
reigning everywhere that, after one had gone about, upstairs and
downstairs, peering distractedly into every corner in the hope of finding
something wrong, one sank back at last, positively vomiting. I was just
beginning to do so on Sunday after lunch – basin actually in hand –
when a motor was heard outside. I rushed to the window, and lo and
behold Violet Keppel accompanied by three youths was advancing up
the garden path. I tore down to welcome them – threw my arms round
their necks – flirted with them behind the lavender hedges – when,
suddenly another motor – Mr and Mrs Stoop! It was almost, for a
moment, Garsington; but in the twinkling of an eye that had all
vanished, and I was alone once more with La B. and my hosts. La B.
was a slight relief in the circumstances – begged me to go to Florence,
etc. – and was rather amusing with her massive form sweeping along
supported by a very wrinkled pair of high buttoned boots. I reached
here on Monday, via Brighton, meeting Mary and then Jack at
Chichester – all unchanged. The weather has been pretty good though
windy, and the country beautiful, up till today, when the tornado
(equinoctial?) has finally burst. It is melancholy to look out and see the
field where Ted used to plough all day with the sea-gulls swooping
round him. Yesterday I discovered his 'mate' (so he described himself)
a pleasant-spoken young man, by trade a carpenter, with grey eyes and
eyelashes which (if one were of the other sex) I should imagine one
would find wonderfully attractive. Query: shall I ask him to make a
book case for us? Perhaps, for one reason or another, he would do it
cheap.

There are two new pictures in the house – a Derain, not at all
characteristic – nudes in blue, pink, and green outline, also a tree and a
blue swan – a large water-colour sketch – and not admired by me; and
a head in oils by Modigliani, I think most attractive – less strident than
the oils at Heal's, more like the drawings, and decidedly Duncanesque.

I've been very lazy, so far; but I suppose soon I shall attack L'Abbé Morellet. I wonder if you finished the Major's picture, and if he is still sitting to you, in all his beauty, instead of going to Spain.

your
Lytton

‡

To Ralph Partridge

Lytton had not yet renamed Partridge 'Ralph'.

The Mill House
Tidmarsh
Pangbourne
September 6th 1919

Dear Rex

It was wicked of you not to have stayed and had some lunch this morning. I had hoped to hear about your Spanish adventures, and had even imagined you might have been induced to spend the night – which I am now doomed to pass in solitude. You will have to be punished – probably by being put in the village stocks when next you appear; the pillory is remitted in view of the charming miracle proclamation, which I found on my table and have enjoyed immensely. How it would have delighted Voltaire! The variety of the objects is truly wonderful, and surely there never was authenticity so unim-peachable. I like very much 'une bonne partie de la peau du bien-heureux St Barthelemi' and 'un des trente deniers pour lesquels le fils de Dieu fut vendu par Judas' is an excellent idea; and the lists of Saints at the end is stupendous. By-the-bye, why is it that the relics of the holy are never of the more intimate regions of the body? Surely Christ's prick would be highly edifying, and the buttocks of St John the Divine would attract many worshippers. I can see no sign of a date – is it early 19th century, do you think? And why is it in French?

I've been having a most strenuous time in London, divided between grubbing in the British Museum MSS and helping my family mansion to pack itself up. I'm now quite exhausted, but hope to recover after a few days' complete idleness here, after which I'm afraid I shall have to return to another bout of London. DC seems to be enjoying herself in Brittany – but no doubt you've heard from her. I fancy she'll hardly return till *early* in October.

I doubt whether this will reach you – but ça ne fait rien.

Yours ever
Lytton Strachey

‡

To Virginia Woolf

At the beginning of the month the Woolfs moved from Asheham to Monk's House and on the 14th Virginia wrote a long letter to Lytton whose sole purpose, she said, was to get him to write back to her. The Woolfs owned five properties altogether, including three cottages in Cornwall.

Gordon Square did become a sort of College, though not the one Lytton had in mind, as house by house became part of University College London.

James and Leonard removed the words 'A vision of wedded bliss' from their edition. Virginia had not merely singled out Wilfrid Blunt's diaries, she went on to say she disliked 'aristocratic writing', the Souls and George Wyndham.

The Mill House
Tidmarsh
Pangbourne
September 28th 1919

It was charming of you to write to me. Please do so again, in spite of my backwardness in answering. Also inability. I, who once filled reams a day, now sit gnawing my pen after the first sentence. Old age? Middle age? Or what? In any case, something deplorable.

It makes me weep to think that I've seen the last of Asheham, and even the chaste beauties of your Monk's residence will never really console me. How can you bear it? And what has happened to the cottages in Cornwall? I rather fancy that they're mythical.

I have been having a grim time of it, presiding (or rather assisting) in the move which is shortly to take place of my family from Belsize Park to Gordon Square – for *that* is where pure Chance has decided that they're to dwell in the future. No. 51. Yes, a few doors along. Very soon I foresee that the whole square will become a sort of College. And the rencontres in the garden I shudder to think of. The business of packing, deciding what is to be sold, what sent to Tidmarsh, what given to the deserving poor, etc. has been fearful, and is still proceeding, the brunt of it of course falling on the unfortunate Pippa. *I* am fit for little more than wringing my hands. In the intervals I go to the British Museum, and try to dig up scandals about Queen Victoria. Altogether a distracting life, and the comble was reached in the small hours of Friday morning, when the policeman's wife who acts as caretaker gave birth to a baby just outside my bedroom door. After that I retreated down here, and now the railway strike . . . what, oh what! is going to happen? I am alone, with a strange servant lent by the Anreps, no newspapers reach me, I know nothing, and I daresay the next thing I shall hear will be the proclamation of the Soviet Government. Have you decided what steps to take in that eventuality? Leonard, at any rate, will hardly escape the guillotine.

Your appearances in the Athenaeum alone keep me in good temper with existence. You should have seen Mrs Berenson heaving with laughter over the Royal Academy article, in the train, en route for . . . well, never mind. When is your novel coming out?

I had lunch with Nessa and Duncan the other day in the Regent Square domicile. A vision of wedded bliss.

Adieu

your

Lytton

I'm very glad you dislike Wilfrid Blunt, and I hope you'll write about him.

‡

To Katherine Mansfield

The Mill House
Tidmarsh
Pangbourne
October 3rd 1919

Dear Katherine

The government tells one only to write letters that are necessary – so be it! This is the letter of a loyal subject, because I can think of nothing more necessary than to tell you how much I admire your Athenaeum reviews, and how grateful I am to you for such charming weekly titillations. 'Sensitiveness' today is really perfect. I have read it twice with greatest joy. I don't know where you are – I hope possibly in more Southern climes, as the autumn here is decidedly beginning to be nippy. I should be very glad to hear any news of you – but I don't want to give trouble – only let me have word or two some day – either from yourself or Murry. I think the Athenaeum is keeping up magnificently. This number is particularly good, it seems to me. (Personally I can't bear Santayana, I confess – but that must be considered as a mere personal idiosyncrasy.) I feel rather guilty at not having done a biographical article for so long, but I have been horribly hampered by various impediments – among them a family house-moving, which has taken up a great deal of time. However, in the enforced seclusion produced by the strike, I hope to get to work again. I luckily escaped from London just before it occurred. The world grows odder and odder. I perceive that we must resign ourselves to a life in a lunatic asylum. A little sanity nowadays is a blessed thing – hence this letter

from your affectionate
Lytton

‡

To Carrington

Ottokar, Count Czernin von und zu Chudenitz (1872–1932), served as Austro-Hungarian Foreign Minister from 1916 to 1918. Lytton was reading his reaction, in April 1918, to news of the peace settlements at Brest-Litovsk. People who contributed to the running of the household would expect their Christmas 'boxes' (tips, or a bonus for the year) on 26 December; Lytton is saying that he couldn't find the right opportunity to tip the workmen.

The Carfax Gallery was started in 1898 in Ryder Street, St James's, by Arthur Bellamy Clifton (1862–1932) with John Fothergill. They were associates of Oscar Wilde's friend Robert Ross.

The Mill House
Tidmarsh
Pangbourne
Tuesday, December 9th 1919

A delicious dinner is over – the fire burns bright (racked together from every quarter), the chair is drawn up. Count Czernin is finished. So a few words to the Mopsa. Not that there's anything to say. The cold has been, and still is, extreme – but the sun shone, and there was no wind, so the walking was enjoyable. I had a chat with Percy in the morning. He was most gracious – said that the repairs were necessary for us – that the wall should be pointed, etc. He looked very fine with a layer of flour all over him – in his long cream-coloured coat. The workmen have apparently been very busy – including the nice little plumber. But unfortunately I failed to provide them with their boxes, as I didn't see how to manage it.

I observed in the course of my walk that two large trees have been felled in the avenue that leads to the Grange from Farmer Davis. So some wood ought to be obtainable from that quarter. The ground is covered with masses of branches, among which two emissaries were hacking and sawing when I passed.

Queen Victoria, poor lady, totters on, step by step – as she's still in her youth, what will she be like in age, at this rate? I can only hope that she may proceed in inverse fashion – growing speedier and speedier as she gets older, and finally fairly bundling into the grave. Then hey! for merry Italy! hey! for merry Italy, hey! for merry Italy and Spain!

I wonder what you have been doing – whether you went to Carfax's and found a good show – or what? And now? Do you sit en tête-à-tête with your mama? I hope you won't find it too crushing, and that you'll manage to get a good many outings. And are you really going to re-attack that shocking trunk? A postcard came for you tonight from (I think) the owner of it. I hurriedly redirected it, and hope you will get it tomorrow morning. I feel terribly uncertain, though, about your address.

I was very much touched by the young man's affection, and I am very glad that I know him so much better now. I think it was chiefly owing to you that this good result came about. The only thing is that between you you make me feel scandalously pampered – a regular old egotistical humbug, and my immortal soul is in grave danger, I'm sure.

With a great deal of love and a great many hugs,

your
Lytton

‡

To T. S. Eliot

This is Lytton's first letter to Eliot. While the '(Strachey)' of the signature is not in Lytton's hand, the rest is.

The Mill House
Tidmarsh
Pangbourne
February 13th 1920

How good, Eliot, your Blake article! It makes me feel the splendour of Poetry. Thank you so very much.

I'm here all alone – a little distressed and distracted – heaven knows why. I wish you were here, and I could talk to you. I send you my love. Will you write to me, I wonder!

How terribly complicated is life!

yours
Lytton *(Strachey)*
i.e.
('Eminent Victorians')

‡

To Ralph Partridge

The Mill House
Tidmarsh
Pangbourne
February 20th 1920

[. . .] I looked into Principia Ethica, and found a brief paragraph dealing with your objections – too brief perhaps. I wish you could meet Moore. He's the only man I know who seems to me really great.

Lots of love
from
your
Lytton

‡

To Carrington and Ralph Partridge

To D.C. & R.P. March 1st 1920

Suppose the kind gods said 'Today
You're forty. True: but still, rejoice!
Gifts we have got will smooth away
The ills of age. Come, take your choice!'

What should I answer? Well, you know
I'm modest – very. So, no shower
Of endless gold I'ld beg, no show
Of proud-faced pomp, or regal power.

No; ordinary things and good
I'ld choose: friends, wise and kind and few;
A country house; a pretty wood
To walk in; books both old and new

To read; a life retired, apart,
Where leisure and repose might dwell,
With industry; a little art;
Perhaps a little fame as well.

‡

To Virginia Woolf

The photograph on the postcard has the legend 'Granada – Alhambra. Peinador de la Reina'. The black pigs are the famous Iberian breed, of which those called pata negra produce the world's best ham.

[postmarked Granada]
April 3rd 1920

Well, how are you? We arrived yesterday – very chirpy. But so far I have not bought a herd of black pigs.

Lytton

‡

To Mary Hutchinson

The sometimes trying 'emotional situation' was the triangular nature of the relationship among the travellers, with Lytton loving Ralph, who loved Carrington (and was pressing her to marry him), while Carrington loved Lytton.

Yegen
April 11th 1920

Ma chère

Look at the map of Spain, and find Granada. Thence draw a line of 40 miles in a southwesterly direction, across the Sierra Nevada, and you will arrive – here. Yegen is a village among the mountains high up with a view of the Mediterranean in the distance, and all round the most extraordinary Greco-esque formations of rocks and hills. Never have I seen a country on so vast a scale – wild, violent, spectacular – enormous mountains, desperate chasms, endless distances – colours everywhere of deep orange and brilliant green – a wonderful place, but easier to get to with a finger on the map than in reality! Such a journey from Granada as you never saw, taking three days. And beginning with a frantic motor-bus (the roads, ma chère, the roads!) and ending with a complete day on mule back (Carrington on a donkey) winding up and up by the bed of a river, crossing and re-crossing the water up to our beasts' bellies – oh it *was* a scene! – the sun scorching, the wind whistling, the rain drenching, at last the night coming on – Lady Hester wasn't in it: emotional crises, too, of the strangest sort – until finally arrived in pitch darkness and almost dead at our singular destination – the abode of an amiable lunatic by name Brenan, who has come to live here in pursuit of some Dostoievsky will o' the wisp or other, and whom Partridge had engaged himself to come and visit with solemn vows. Well, I hardly guessed that I should ever live to be led to such a spot by the beaux yeux of a major! I am treated with the utmost consideration, of course, and I am enjoying myself greatly, but I shan't be sorry when this section of our trip is over, and we return to comparative civilisation. At the best of times travelling in this country is hard: all train journeys last for 12 hours at a minimum, and the slowness of one's advances is heart-breaking.

We had a fearful night coming out of Portugal – the first-class carriage blocked with sucking babies and drunken commercial travellers – poor Ralph reduced to sleeping on the portmanteau in the corridor, etc. etc. But still, one does progress, and the sights one sees are worth the horrors. From Lisbon we went to Seville, thence to Cordova, thence to Granada and Toledo and Madrid are in front of us. All these places have been much more remarkable – more extreme – than I'd expected. Granada is astounding – very high up, with immense snow mountains directly over it, and the Alhambra is sheer Earl's Court, but the general grandeur of situation and outline remain. Cordova is much more oriental – a network of narrow narrow streets, and a very big and beautiful mosque, in the middle of which the astonishing Christians have stuck a huge rococo church – the effect is dizzying. One evening we went in after sunset, and found a mass in progress. A full orchestra was at work in the baroque building, a tenor was singing an aria by Mozart, and all round, dimly lighted by a lamp here and there, were the pillars and arches of the antique mosque, stretching away in every direction into far distant darkness. It was incredibly theatrical and romantic, and I felt like Uncle John, very very nearly a Roman Catholic.

I wish I could write about *all* the details! The emotional situation is at times trying – decidedly; but at other times not at all so; and I think with luck we shall weather through. Tomorrow, I fancy we shall set out again, and before long reach some pictures which will be cheering. And not so very long after that we shall be back in England. I seem to have been away for years; but you, I suppose, have hardly noticed more than a few strikings of the clock since last I saw you. London! I try to imagine it, but it's difficult. I'm sitting, 5,000 feet above the sea on a steep mountain side, by a brook, with bright green poplars, and leafless chestnuts round me, the sun blazing, the wind nipping, a vast view in front of me – ridge upon ridge, range upon range, – and then such queer rocks and flowers all about – quelle vie! We have just had lunch. Brenan has gone off to pumpship, Carrington and Ralph to bathe; I remain among the débris – quelle vie! quelle vie! I wish I could write poetry: but somehow that vein seems to have become intolerably constipated.

Brenan is most peculiar, and deserves several chapters to himself – but it would be endless – and they are coming back, and it is time to do the things up, and wander down again to the curious house for tea.

Farewell, I send you my love, and am longing to see you.

your

Lytton

‡

To Ralph Partridge

Lytton had been in Paris with Ralph and Carrington, staying in a hotel on rue Jacob, where they ran into Barbara and Nick Bagenal. All five went to Versailles together. But on the Saturday, Ralph heard his mother was ill and left immediately for England.

Paris

Sunday, April 22nd 1920

[. . .] Today has been 'gris clair' and rather chilly – very arduous too – every picture in the Louvre and the Luxembourg examined. We had lunch at Foyot's, which was splendidly discreet, but I thought the cooking was *not* perfect, and altogether it was a slight pest, as Carrington suddenly found herself deprived of the desire to eat, which condition lasted exactly as long as we remained within those famous walls. At the Luxembourg we observed many pictures that would have pleased you – a lady being operated upon (surgically, surgically) etc. There was also a recumbent statue, whose buttocks were thought to be in your taste; but

then, in circumnavigating this chef d'oeuvre, it was observed to be after all more suitable to *mine* . . . Tonight we go to a concert of classical quartets, the existence of which we miraculously discovered quite close at hand. But I rather distrust the frogs at music. Tomorrow is to be devoted to the minor picture shows, and possibly, if it's fine, to a re-visit to Versailles in the evening. Existence has been considerably ameliorated by the capture of the Bagenal Baedecker. Can you bear to think of me walking in it – monsieur le Prince?

I dread the thought of the journey sans courier – and the expenses – the expenses! – At more than one moment today his Highness would have shuddered!

A great many kisses and hugs, and a great deal of love from

your own
Lytton

‡

To Carrington

The Manor House
Garsington
Oxford
Sunday, May 23rd 1920

Ma chère

I've hardly time for more than a word – the pressure here is so tremendous. It's all very nice (so far!) – chiefly owing to the miraculous weather, I think, which makes the surroundings even more than usually beautiful, and puts one in good temper with the humans and pugs. *[. . .]*

I profoundly sympathise with you, my unfortunate creature, cooped up in that abominable hospital ward – this blaze of glory. It's too sickening. But it'll go on being hot now, it *must*. I can only hope you enjoy your marmalade. As for Forster's novels, I agree with all you say of them. Attack him certainly; but however loud you yell he won't hear.

with love
your
Lytton

✝

To John Middleton Murry

Tidmarsh
May 28th 1920

Dear Murry

[. . .] After examining the H*[enry]* J*[ames]* volumes *[of letters]* I reread your article, and was more impressed than ever by it. It seems to me really profound. What's puzzling is that, quite apart from art, one does somehow feel, in spite of everything, that there was something distinguished about him – something big; but one doesn't quite see what. On the artistic side, one of the strangest things, I think, is that re-writing of his early novels in his later style. What did he mean by it? In one of his letters he positively says that he's not making any substantial changes – merely writing every other sentence over again! Is it possible that he supposed that substance and style were separable? It's very odd indeed. – I'm afraid, so far as your noble effort goes of screwing round poor old O*[ttoline]* M.'s head into proper position the task is hopeless. No spanner will ever move that particular nut.

yours ever
Lytton Strachey

✝

To Carrington

The Rt Hon Lord Chalmers, PC, GCB, KCB, CB (1858–1938) had just left the Treasury; he became Master of Peterhouse from 1924 to 1931. He was an Oriental specialist, and published Further Dialogues of the Buddha *in 1926. Frank Laurence ('Peter') Lucas (1894–1967), critic and poet, was elected to the Apostles in January 1914, and got a first in classics in 1920.*

   Spicer had been elected to the Apostles on 6 March. Walter John Herbert Sebastian Sprott, of Clare, was an embryo – finally elected on 23 October.

   Patrick Shaw-Stewart (b.1888), killed in action in 1917, was the intellectual star of his circle at both Eton and Balliol, which included his future biographer, Ronald Arbuthnot Knox (1888–1957), who was to convert to Catholicism in 1917, and wrote six thrillers among his dozens of books.

King's College
Cambridge
Monday morning, May 30th 1920

Here I am in Pozzo's large apartment – (*he* is in the adjoining small one, writing an article for America, for which he's to get £250). All is well so far – comfortable and not too cold. Mine host is extremely gracious, and expects me to stay till Wednesday, which I suppose I shall do. Lord Chalmers is a pussy-cat of an old buffer with white hair and great urbanity – a plum on a wall, very far gone – squashy, decidedly. He makes long elaborate speeches, likes dragging in the eminent dead, and when he does so usually turns to me with a slight bow and says '– a friend of Mr Strachey's' – how Pozzo can take such an obvious absurdity at all seriously quite beats me. We had a most pompous dinner yesterday in Hall, with the 'Combination Room' afterwards – the wine-bibbing dons assemble round a long mahogany table, and drink port, slowly, glass after glass (not very good port, I thought). Then I went to Trinity, and talked for some hours with Lucas, who appeared to me decidedly fascinating – though exactly why I'm blessed if I know. The young, otherwise, seem to be rather in retirement, though Maynard promises me a luncheon tomorrow with Spicer and Sebastian Sprott (he tells me a real person). The Sheppard-Doggart affair has completely fizzled out, they say, with the result that Sheppard's spirits have risen and he's no longer a bore, spending his days in flitting from flower to flower. Mr Pickering Phipps (also a real person) is his latest. I hope to see him tonight. I am now off to Merton House, where I intend to get some lunch – then I daresay tea at Newnham. Cambridge is certainly a cosy sympathetic spot after the grim grandeurs of Oxford – quite middle-class, which is always such a relief – at any rate for a day or two.

I hope you continue to emerge, and are behaving with unremitting virtue. A regular Rubens Mopsa is what I hope to behold. I wonder what happened with Forster – any love-passages (of one sort or another)? Give the normal things to Ralph. I am longing to hear about Goldie's paper, etc. etc.

Ronnie Knox's book on Patrick Shaw-Stewart is here – good lord, how dreadful, how very dreadful! A clever creature, too, but in the horridest way – only I rather guess, towards the end, a little battered into decency. Dilly Knox, by the bye, is to be married to an undeniable female – poor helpless vanished thing.

One of the great comforts here is that nobody has read Henry James's letters.

adieu – with love from

your

Lytton

‡

To Ralph Partridge

Woolf's book was Empire and Commerce in Africa *(1920).*

The Mill House
Tidmarsh
Pangbourne
June 20th 1920

What a villainous wretch! Am I never to see you again? And so much to talk about – Steele, the Exam papers (which I've never seen), your Labour party past, etc – but you vanish in a mist of dances, Garsington, portraits, motors, and next, I'm told, there's Henley . . . so the Lord alone knows when I shall be able to pull your wicked orejas. However, I console myself with Dizzy and her Majesty, sitting out in the ambiguous air among chickens and roses, while you gad in Leander mufflers and make splendid speeches before drunken Dons and Deans.

Have you read Woolf's book? Don't you think it's terrific? I saw him the other evening, and he said that besides an insignificant (I gathered) man, you have a female rival – Miss Catherine Marshall – for that position. She is all that is most unpleasant – pale, enthusiastic, with a projecting tooth; was a devotee of Bertie's till they quarrelled; also secretary of the No-Conscription Fellowship. The Secretary of the Labour Party favours her, but Cole is dead against, and Leonard said he would threaten resignation if she got it. So you have supporters – but I'm afraid she's a dangerous candidate. Her revoltingness alone will recommend her to those gloomy persons who'll decide.

When's the speech? Shall I have an account of it? And will you send me the papers, if they're not destroyed? It would amuse me to see them – and how ignorant I am.

Carrington's account of Alan and the portrait sounded very interesting. Give her my love. Also him – 'if he'd like to have it'!

How I should like to be with you for a little, and – hmm! – the sentence must be finished by the Fancy and the Imagination.

With a very great deal of the very nicest love to my dear one
from his
Lytton

‡

To T. S. Eliot

The Mill House
Tidmarsh
Pangbourne
July 13th 1920

Dear Eliot,

I wonder if by any chance you would be able to come down and spend a night with me on Saturday next (17th). I should enjoy it so very much – please do. My sister Dorothy and her husband Simon Bussy (painter) will be here – and I think you would like them.

A train leaves Paddington at 3.10 and arrives Pangbourne in time for tea. I believe you have to return on Sunday nights always – there's quite a good train back then – and of course excellent ones early on Monday mornings if you could stay till then.

The garden is rather nice now. You never saw anything so délabré, and my theory is that by that time it will be hot, and we could sit out in the grass.

I do hope you will say yes; not having seen you for so long.

yours ever
Lytton Stratchey.

Of course no evening clothes!

[Houghton Library, Harvard]

‡

To Carrington

The painting in question is Carrington's best-known work, the view of the Mill House at Tidmarsh, with the black swans reflected in the pond. Jean Marchand (1883–1941) had a single painting included in the Manet and Post-Impressionism show organized by Fry and Bell in 1910, and his work was collected by, for example, the St John Hutchinsons. But he is more often remembered as in the context of this letter, as an example of what was wrong with French art post-Cézanne.

Winander Mere is in the Lake District, the setting of Wordsworth's Winander Boy: 'There was a Boy. There was a Boy, ye knew him well, ye Cliffs/ And islands of Winander!' The 'new Conrad' novel was The Rescue.

Tidmarsh
Monday, July 19th 1920

Just a word or two before the post goes. Dorothy and Simon have departed after, I think, quite a successful week-end. Jack and Mary appeared punctually for tea – très chic: the weather has been singularly favourable. But I must at once tell you – guess what! – Simon on your picture! (The Mill.) He was . . . enthusiastic is not the word. – Looked and gazed, talked, praised, extolled – on and on he went. 'Better than anything at the London group' – but that was by no means all. 'Better than most French things – better than Marchand "et tous ces gens" – *much*!' Finally the Douanier Rousseau was brought out. 'Yes, it reminds me of the Douanier Rousseau – not that it's in the least an imitation – oh no! – but it has some of the same kind of charm' – I only wish you could have heard him – concealed in Brett's baronial chest. There was no doubt about the genuineness of it all. 'I am not a French complimenter,' he said in his curious English, and it's quite true. At last, after he had been going on about it for about half an hour, I really began to feel rather bored! Dorothy also liked it very much. Jack too . . . So there's no doubt that you'll very soon have to have a one woman show! But I was sorry there were not more things to show Simon. He liked the tulips too, but not so much as the Mill. Of course he was very sorry at not seeing you; but you really must before he goes back to France.

I wonder what has been happening to you. A 'slight breakdown' at

Oxford sounded rather ominous, but I imagine you by now installed on Winander's shores. It really looks as if the weather *had* taken a turn for the better – how splendid if it's fine for you! Here it's perfect – a great deal of sun, but a lot of wind too – large clouds pacing across the sky. Percy is very busy getting in his hay – but not too busy to be very seductive also. All is well. Masses of food. Victoria proceeding.

I hope to hear very soon all your adventures. Give my love to Ralph – and ask him whether he'd like me to send the two first volumes of Gibbon – it would be quite easy.

Love from
your
Lytton

I hope I've got your address right – McIver, Maciver, or MacIver? The new Conrad is very romantic and exciting.

‡

To T. S. Eliot

The Mill House
Tidmarsh
Pangbourne
July 20th 1920

Dear Eliot,

I was very sorry you couldn't come last Saturday. I think you would have liked the Bussys, and then the Hutchinsons paid a flying visit too. And it was hot enough to spend the whole of Sunday out of doors.

If by any chance you could reconcile it with your conscience to come next Saturday, I wish you would. I shall be alone then, and it would be indeed delightful to see you. I am working, but would like a *little* interruption wouldn't *you*?

Books are indeed awful things. But, somehow or other they do get done.

yours ever
Lytton Strachey.

‡

To Ralph Partridge

The Mill House
Tidmarsh
Pangbourne
September 1st 1920

My dear one

It was good of you to write.

I am feeling much better, and the depression has passed off. After a little more idleness I think I shall be fit for finally slaying (or exorcising) the succuba.

The Secretarial appointment sounds excellent and full of interest. I hope there will be enough to do; but if you are going to be a publisher and a printer as well, I think there ought to be. What a pity it is there seem to be so very few masterpieces handy, to bring out!

My week-end was fairly quiet, though diversified by the appearance of Oliver and the fair Inez, whom both the boys found entrancing. I envy yours – for one thing it sounded so much warmer. Virginia is I believe a more simple character than appears on the surface. Her cleverness is so great that one doesn't at first see a kind of ingenuousness of feeling underneath.

I am looking forward so very much to seeing my dearest one again before long.

With all my love,
your
Lytton

‡

To Carrington

The occasion for the letter was Carrington's continued nervousness about whether she should try to live with Ralph at 41 Gordon Square.

Charleston
Saturday, September 4th 1920

Très-chère

I was very glad to get your letter. All is well here, and just as may be
imagined. Maynard, Mary, Clive, Duncan, and Vanessa are the
company, plus the three children. Life seems to roll along rather
vaguely, with pretty substantial meals at slightly odd intervals and a great
deal of talk and laughter. Typically, Maynard has insisted on . . . you'ld
never guess what: – altering the time! So that the clocks are one hour in
advance even of summer-time, with curious consequences. For one
thing, Jessie disapproves, won't have it, and has let her kitchen clock
run down, so that the servants have *no* time. Then Clive is fretful on
the subject, and insists upon always referring to the normal time; and
altogether the confusion is extraordinary. How mad they all are!
Maynard, though he sees what a rumpus it causes, persists. Vanessa is
too feeble to put him down, and Clive too tetchy to grin and bear it.
The result is extremely Tchekhoffesque. But luckily the atmosphere is
entirely comic, instead of being fundamentally tragic as in Tchekhoff.
Everyone laughs and screams, and passes on.

The weather yesterday was perfect. I thought it was the locality – but
no! They told me it was icy the day before, and your letter tells me it
was equally fine at Tidmarsh. And now today, the frigidity has come on
again. Lord ha'mercy upon us!

My dearest, I am sure that all is really well between us, which is the
great thing. Some devil of embarrassment chokes me sometimes, and
prevents my expressing what I feel. You have made me so happy during
the last three years, and you have created Tidmarsh, as no one else could
have – and I seem hardly to have said thank you. But you must believe
that I value you and your love more than I can ever say. It seems to me
that your trying the Gordon Square experiment is probably right. But
whatever happens you must rely on my affection.

Let me hear from you again. I am writing this on my bed in an attic.
I send you a great deal of love – and won't leave your letters about!

your
Lytton

‡

To Carrington

*Lytton has put a question mark for the day when dating this letter, but it is
dated on the top in James's writing as 'Sept. 9th'.*

   *The pictures in question at Monk's House were three oil on wood nineteenth-
century portraits of the Glazebrook family, the former owners of the house, for all
three of which the Woolfs paid four shillings. Virginia's description of them
makes it clear that the style was primitive: the artist 'began the heads very large,
and hadn't got room for the hands and legs, so those dwindle off till they're
about the size of sparrows claws – but the effect is superb – the character
overwhelming'.*[1]

Charleston
Firle
Sussex
September ? 1920

Très chère,

I find this a difficult place to write letters in, or indeed to do anything
but chatter. Though the painters and Maynard work, Clive and Mary
are forever beside one, book in hand, but not reading, so that the stream
of gossip and generalisations flows on perpetually. It has been delightful
to get your letter. I was very glad to hear that the week-end had gone
off so successfully. I had too an affectionate letter from Ralph, saying
how much happiness he felt. I only hope that things will continue
satisfactorily. I was rather perturbed by the Woolves' conception of his
job – so far as I made it out in a brief conversation – that he was to be a
setter-up of type – which doesn't strike me as a suitable employment for
him. However, perhaps this was a distorted view, and probably when it
comes to the point, it will be the secretarial and business part of the job
that will actually occupy him. I think the printing should be an
amusement – or not much more. But I go there tomorrow, and will
talk further about it. They both evidently like him very much.
   Monk's House seemed to me charming – somehow, in spite of its
incredible ramshackleness, beautiful and even comfortable. The sitting-
room quite perfect with its fireplace, pictures, and books. I loved the
pictures; they're much better than I'd supposed they would be – really,
in the Rousseau class – such elegance of detail, and in the portraits such

power. I wanted to cut that wretch Clive's head off: he hadn't seen
the long family piece before – and he looked at it with supercilious
inattention, jabbering about something else all the time. He might at
any rate have *pretended* to care. Oh dearie me! No kiss for him. No!

The household continues in its singular course. There have been
great crises over the potatoes – at every meal they were asked for – at
every meal there were none. Jessie was in revolt, as, in addition to
the time system, her nerves were wrecked by absence of coal. So,
though there was masses of coke and wood, she refused to cook, and
nobody could, or would, make her. Maynard is a most queer fish –
inveterately middle-class – and wildly obstinate. Then with a brain . . .
he gave a lecture on economics of thrilling interest, which converted
me (at any rate for the time being) from Socialism. Yet his feelings
(about the coal strike) at moments really seemed to be those of a
pompous Colonel in a club. He is now visiting Barbara, but returns
here tomorrow, He was very benign, and will I think help me a good
deal over Victoria.

I read them the latter, and they seemed to like it very much.
However, I'm not sure that their critical faculties are of the highest;
nevertheless it was a relief to find that they weren't bored – which
was my chief terror. My health and spirits have recovered, and I shall
be able to fall upon Her Majesty with renewed zeal. My plan is to stay
at Rodmell till next Tuesday – then to proceed to Mary's, where I
thought of staying till Saturday (I think 18th) when I should shoot
back to Tidders. Or I suppose I might stay with her till the Monday;
but I think I'd rather not. If you go to Barbara's next week, perhaps
you would like to come on here for a night also. I'm sure they'ld be
charmed to see you. But I don't know how easy it would be for you.

Winchester sounds enchanting. Your weather has been better than
mine – there hasn't so far been a single hot day. I quite agree that it's
most mysterious that the Norman style should have gone out – the
natural degradation of mankind, no doubt, accounts for it. Did I tell you
that I too read Pride and Prejudice again – while you were at the Lakes?
My feelings towards Darcy were precisely yours. And Bingham is
obviously Alan. Perhaps Mr Collins is too much of a caricature – what
do you think? I hope you're bearing up among your terrible
surroundings. A Forster novelette I insist upon – also a Tchekoff play.

It has really been a very pleasant week here. The general ease and
unbuttoned-ness of everything is most alluring. If only Clive were a
little different it would come near to perfection. The country is

beautiful – but I suspect the Rodmell country's better still. Is Ruth still at Kingston, do you think? And how am I to get hold of her? We had a divine motor drive back from Monk's House, through Lewes – a perfect evening, and all the Downs most grand. I tried to spot the Selby-Bigges' house, but couldn't. Virginia says there's a large farm house, very fine, to be had in the neighbourhood, with 'a good deal of land, which one could let out'. Shall we set up as Farmer Giles and Milkmaid Mopsa in Sussex? With Ralph at the plough, whistling all day long.

Only yesterday did I discover the little box with the toffee in it. Most delicious! Everybody munched and scrunched a bit with intense joy.

A shocking event occurred in London. My preposterous barber cut off very nearly the whole of my beard! It has been reduced to Jamesian proportions. But, God willing, it will grow.

A letter from little Spicer – very stilted and touching, with a highly complimentary sentence about you. He also says that the Dog has fallen a complete victim to the fair Inez. Mais je le doute.

I believe today *is* going to be hot, at last. I wish you were here; we would walk up to the top of Firle Beacon together – then on and on – to Asheham – to Lewes – and heaven knows where. The present company doesn't much like moving. A great deal of love to you

from your
Lytton

The little jug is exciting. Write again to Monk's House.

1. Quoted in Hermione Lee, *Virginia Woolf*, p. 424.

‡

To James Strachey

Charleston
September 10th 1920

[. . .] The Carrington-Major question came to some sort of a crisis about a week ago. She has now agreed to go and live with him in Gordon Square at any rate till Christmas – on a more or less

experimental basis. This means week-ends at Tidmarsh, where I shall be for probably about the two first months. What it precisely involves it's difficult to say. But all parties are I gather satisfied so far as can be seen for the present. The emotional complexities are considerable. At the same time Woolf has engaged the Major as his secretary, assistant in the publishing business, and compositor. The prospects of this arrangement, too, are vague. But at any rate it gives RP an excuse for not plunging into some unpleasant position or profession, until it turns out to be definitely hopeless. And of course there's always a chance that it may turn out a financial success. They've made about £200 out of the Gorky-Tolstoy booklet – will publish stories of Virginia, which ought to pay, etc. But I don't see the Partridge setting up type.

[. . .] The company in this house is its sempiternal self. Duncan and Vanessa painting all days in each other's arms. Pozzo writing on Probability, on the History of Currency, controlling the business of King's, and editing the Economic Journal. Clive pretending to read Stendhal, Mary writing letters on blue note-paper, the children screaming and falling into the pond. I went over for a day to Leonard and Virginia in their new Rodmell establishment, which is a most peculiar structure – small, higgledy-piggledy, with rooms like cupboards and cupboards like lavatories, gardens projecting among various wells, a plaster bust of Jesus on a cistern, an orchard with hens and onions, but altogether quite attractive, and I fancied even comfortable – but I shall discover this more fully tomorrow. They strike one as being absolutely happy; he looks more gaunt and eminent than ever, and she a schoolgirl, almost, in cheap red beads. While I was there, a parcel arrived for Leonard: it was Mr Wells's History of the World, from the Author. I've been looking into it but it's very dull and detailed and wordy and won't do. Clive is writing his great work on civilisation; but he tells me that it will not clash with Mr Wells.

I hope to hear from you more fully before long. Do you want papers or things sent? Let me know what. My love to Alix.

your
Lytton

‡

To Carrington

Monk's House
Rodmell
Saturday, September 11th 1920

[. . .] I took a walk with Virginia yesterday after tea, and was completely
bowled over by the country. I wish we'd known about it before, as I
really think it might have been worth while looking about for a new
residence. However, in time many things may be possible.

So far I've only been able to detect two slight drawbacks to this
residence, – viz. (1) the cat, and (2) the E*[arth]* C*[loset]*. But they're
fortunately neither of them always before one. You didn't tell me
that there was *another* picture here – by a certain female artist! I like it
very much. But I think it isn't finished. Don't you think it ought to
be? *[. . .]*

‡

To Mary Hutchinson

*Arthur John Bigge, Lord Stamfordham (1849–1931), private secretary to King
George V, had learned his trade in the service of the aged Queen Victoria,
starting in 1880.*

51, Gordon Square
[dated Friday 1st but postmarked October 5, 1920]

I was very sorry to miss you last night. I hope you're expecting me to
lunch on Wednesday. Just back from Buckingham Palace and an hour's
interview with Lord Stamfordham. His Majesty did not come up
through a trap–door in the middle of it – as I'd rather expected he
would. The poor old thing (a respectable maiden lady) was very
amicable, though at moments pettish. The point of his remarks was very
difficult to catch, but I rather gathered that the elder Princesses had
insisted on 'something being done'; and that this was all they could
think of. The world grows steadily more and more fantastic, I find. Is
it its nature? Or do we, perhaps, make it so? And oh, it's horribly
exhausting. I totter back to Tidmarsh tomorrow for the week-end, only

to return to this scene of hectic bizarrerie on Monday morning. My feeble frame faints and quavers – but God's will be done.

your
Lytton

‡

To James Strachey

Now in Vienna, James had begun his analysis with Freud. The musicologist Edward Joseph Dent (1876–1957), portrayed as Philip Herriton in Forster's Where Angels Fear to Tread, *left King's in 1918 to go to London and work as a critic.*

The Mill House
Tidmarsh
Pangbourne
Wednesday, November 24th 1920

Your account of things appears to me a trifle highly-coloured, and I think there must be a flaw somewhere. Alix's postcard indicated a crumpled roseleaf of a highly unpleasant kind; but I fancy others. For instance, can it be really warm? Perhaps you haven't had really real cold yet. It has arrived here, and is pretty bad: some effective central heating would be welcomed; but it seems to me too paradoxical to suppose that one would really be warmer in Vienna. The music sounds amazing. I should like to come and hear it, but Victoria hangs back horribly, and I doubt whether I shall be free for months. *[. . .]* A more interesting book, which has just been sent to me by an admirer, is Frank Harris's Life of Oscar Wilde. It has a fair amount of rather new information, though of course it's not nearly detailed enough, and isn't really *very* well done. However, the story is a most remarkable one. The admirer is called Mr Hesketh Pearson, and is apparently some sort of agent for Frank Harris in England. He sent me the book in order, as he said, to find out what the greatest English biographer thought of the greatest American one – a slightly double-edged compliment, I fear. But *is* FH American? Or what?

Your account of the Doctor sounds odd – personally I have never been able to believe that *I* should suffer from *any* 'resistance' – but one never knows. Does he ever make jokes? Or only German ones? And in what language does it all go on? I wish to God he could have analysed Queen Victoria. It's quite clear, of course, that she was a martyr to analeroticism: but what else? What else?

In the old days I always adored Leonora No. 3. Then I heard it lately in the Albert Hall, and could detect no merit in it. And now you tell me . . . And Oliver, whom I questioned on the subject, assures me that it *is very* good. So I suppose it must be. Altogether, I've detected in various quarters a tendency to a rise in the Master of Bonn. Dent, too, continues to attack him. But oh! To hear a good Seraglio!

I'll try to write again, when I'm more au courant with affairs.

your
Lytton

Is there a censorship? I can't see any trace of one in your letter.

‡

To Virginia Woolf

Virginia replied to this letter the next day from Hogarth House, Richmond:

> *Ah − but this is what I may have dreamed of, but never hoped for. What could I like better? Only my inordinate vanity whispers might it not be Virginia Woolf in full? Some Victoria Worms or Vincent Woodlouse is certain to say it's them, and I want all the glory to be mine for ever. But it's better than a glory and comes on my birthday too.*
> *We look forward to Saturday, and shall we have Vic?*
> *Dearest Lytton.*

The published dedication was to 'Virginia Woolf'.

The Mill House
Tidmarsh
Pangbourne
January 24th 1921

A slightly pointless book, I'm afraid, on a distinctly depressing subject. However, such as it is, may I dedicate it to you? I feel that the mystic initials V.W. would cast a halo – and besides that as you're more unlike Old Vic than anyone else in the world, it's only proper that she should be inscribed to you.

I go to 51 Gordon Square tomorrow. Are you coming to Tidmarsh next Saturday? I hope so.

With love

from

Lytton

‡

To James Strachey

The £4,000 to £5,000 Lytton expected to net from Queen Victoria *was the equivalent of £121,000 to £151,000 at 2001 values, and the 15-shilling cover price of the book equates to £22.70.*

The wealthy London draper Sir Ernest Debenham, chairman of Debenham & Freebody department store, was a public benefactor who built a model village in Dorset, erected a memorial to the Tolpuddle Martyrs and commissioned a house in Kensington by Halsey Ricardo.

Juana Gandarillas was Spanish: in a letter of 3 May 1921 to Sydney Waterlow, Virginia Woolf says she is 'very stupid, but so incredibly beautiful that one forgives it all', and says that Gandarillas gives dinner parties for three where she provides food for ten, 'and loads of plovers' eggs, ices, and salmon are wheeled off to the servants' hall'.[1]

James became an authority on Mozart (which he pronounced – as did Sir Thomas Beecham – in the French manner as two equal syllables with a silent T), and his programme notes on the Mozart operas continued to be used at Glyndebourne until the 1990s. Lytton's criticism of Beecham's recordings goes against the common opinion that the early recordings were better than the later ones.

William Russell-Cooke was a solicitor with offices in Lincoln's Inn and many aristocratic clients. Lord Northcliffe was the proprietor of The Times.

51, Gordon Square
W.C.1
January 27th 1921

I've been a long time without writing – but I believe as a matter of fact
I wrote last, though at Christmas I got the Mozart Calendar, which is
charming – in spite of a few German lapses – and I want if possible
to have it bound, as otherwise it will become dissipated. My state has
been appalling – given over to Victoria for weeks and weeks without
cessation – a fearful struggle, its horrors being increased by the 'relaxing'
conditions at Tidmarsh – however, it's now done – typed and actually
handed over to Chatto's. The relief is enormous. But the worst of it is
that various crises are still pending. The American question is acute and
complicated. Maynard has been acting as an intermediary with
Harcourt, his American publisher, who, after some havering, offered
$10,000 for all the American rights complete. At that time this was
worth nearly £3000 – and I thought it would do, and accepted. But
since then the wretched dollar has sunk, so that it's now worth only
about £2660. But still the contract has not been fixed. There are also
various difficulties about the serialisations – in England and America –
and their dates. The Times (also via Pozzo) is being negotiated with,
but nothing has been settled yet. In the meantime, Chatto has paid
me £750, as advance royalties, payable on receipt of the MS. The
arrangement is that I get 20% on the first 5000 copies, and 25% after that
– viz. on the swelling price of the book, which will probably be 15/-.
So that the advanced royalties covers the first 5000 copies. If I get £700
for the serial rights – which is conceivable – I may net something
between 4 and 5,000 – which doesn't seem so bad – though I still shiver
in my shoes over the American question which continues to hang in the
wind. I suppose I shall have to invest it – which seems rather dull – and
I daresay really the best thing would be to buzz it all straight off. I wish
to goodness you had been here to assist me in these terrific transactions.
And as for the proof-correcting, I shudder to think of it. Chatto and
Windus say they'll have it out on April 7th. As for the work itself,
I hope it's readable, and that it steers the correct course between
discretion and indiscretion. I feel rather doubtful as to whether the
presentment of Her Majesty forms a consistent whole: the tone seems to
shift so wildly – from tragedy to farce, from sentiment to cynicism; but
let's hope it all forms up. It's almost impossible for me at the present
moment to get an impartial view of it. The strain of such a long

continuity has been extreme. I don't feel as if I should ever be able to face such a bulky affair again.

Private life has been conditioned by this preoccupation. I've been at Tidmarsh (except for about a fortnight before Christmas), while Carrington has been at 41 with R*[alph]* P*[artridge]*, they both coming down for week-ends. I'm not sure that she really would have done this by nature – but I daresay being in London had a good many advantages for her. Now I am established here for the present, so that we are all more or less reunited again. RP continues to be very charming, and I don't think he obsesses her with maritalism too much. The ménage here is very much as usual, but a good deal more comfortable and convenient than Belsize. Mama's vitality is greater than ever. I believe her becoming definitely blind has increased her energies, by removing the effort to see. She has moments of depression and exhaustion – otherwise she rushes about with the greatest vigour. Pippa seems less accablée by the office, and quite cheerful. MCS *[Marjorie]* is away all day at her school – but – horror of horrors! – she, together with the whole institution has been given a term's notice by that fiend Ernest Debenham – into whose blasted firm, at the same moment, Vincent has at last plunged. Probably in a day or two he'll get a month's notice too. The only excuse is that 'business is bad'. This makes up the household.

The chief piece of gossip (which perhaps you've already heard) is that Clive has given up Mary and fallen madly in love with Madame Gandarillas, a female dago of the dark and passionate type – immensely rich and with the finest underclothes in Europe. Whether this will last is considered doubtful. In the meanwhile he dines nightly at the Ritz. And it is supposed that Mary is au désespoir – but I've not yet seen her, and nothing is definitely known.

I hope your condition continues to be tolerable. Do you find it rather grinding to be away for such a long time at a stretch? It's a great mercy that the Freudian part of it is so successful. I long to hear about the details. The accounts of Mozart operas fill me with frenzy. Hélas! Hélas! One only hears him here on the gramophone – though that's better than Tommy *[Beecham]*.

Your letter to Mama arrived yesterday. The heat sounds extraordinary. It's been just the same here – really better than in August, with flowers sprouting, trees bursting into leaf, and birds twittering in the early mornings. But one hardly expects such phenomena in Central Europe.

I must now cease – and hurry off to interview . . . that little rat

Russell Cooke of all people, who, for some mysterious reason, is the agent of The Times in the serial affair. Lord Northcliffe has given his personal approval to the scheme in principle – whatever that may mean.

No doubt I shall be charmed. Quelle vie!

With love to Alix

your

Lytton

1. Nigel Nicolson and Joanne Trautmann (eds.), *The Letters of Virginia Woolf*, vol. 2, *1912–22*, p. 467.

‡

To Boris Anrep

51, Gordon Square

W.C.1

February 2nd 1921

My dear Boris

I found your note, but I have only just discovered the mosaic itself modestly hiding in brown paper. You really are too noble, and I am overwhelmed. It is a most beautiful object – the sun shines on it as I opened it – a glorious sight! I only wish I had some suitable and permanent niche for it to go in, but for the present it will have to stand on a mantelpiece – between a Japanese bronze and a picture by Burne Jones – rather a strange combination. Would that I were Queen Victoria so that I could thank you with a truly *royal* emphasis! But I can only send you speechless gratitude.

your

Lytton

I hope you're expecting me tomorrow to dinner
Is it a mouth or a tongue?

‡

To Carrington

*The Independent Gallery was at 7a Grafton Street. Percy Moore Turner, who
had spent some time in Paris, and had a serious interest in contemporary art,
owned it. He was for a long time Duncan's principal outlet, and gave Vanessa
her first one-woman show. Leonard Borwick (1868–1925) was a former pupil of
Clara Schumann.*

*Ye Olde Cock Tavern, with its carvings by Grinling Gibbons, had been at
22 Fleet Street since it moved across the road in 1887. A fire in 1990 destroyed
much of the Cock, and more recent refurbishment has ruined what remained.*

51, Gordon Square
Thursday, February 10th 1921

Très-chère, your long letter has just come. Here I sit, having finished
my breakfast, over the gas fire in the little dining-room. Marjorie has
departed for Debenham's, Pippa is not yet down. What are you doing at
the present moment, I wonder (10 o'clock)? Inspecting the garden,
flirting with Percy, painting pots and pans? It looks, as far as I can judge
from a small triangle of so-called sky visible from the window, as if it
must be delightful at Tidmarsh. I'm very glad you're enjoying being
there, and not feeling too lonely. As for me – and my 'drifting away' –
I don't see any reason to suppose that I shall do so! But of course one never
knows – perhaps *you* will drift away! – and probably the only thing to do is
to grapple with the present, and bother as little as one can about the
future. At any rate, don't think that because I'm sometimes vague or
peevish or inexpressive that therefore I'm a whited sepulchre. But I don't
suppose you do. Only I *am* rather a gad-about . . . it can't be helped!

I went to the Independent Show yesterday, and was considerably
depressed by it. Even poor old Dora, hobbling about in her drab
garments, was a cheering phenomenon compared to those boring works
of art. I quite agree with you that Duncan and Boris stand out from the
rest. I think I liked the 'snow-scene' the best; but still the depression
remained. I rather feel that Duncan may be getting into a rut – as if
things were getting too easy for him – but of course one doesn't like to
dogmatise. That seems to me so cheering about your productions in
their liveliness – no depression there!

The concert yesterday was interesting – Borwick at the piano – quite
a ghost of my youth – once red-haired and sprightly, now aged with a

silver lock. He played a remarkable affair which I'd always longed to
hear – 33 Variations on a Waltz of Diabelli's by Beethoven. An absurd tune
– but the variations marvellous – in the master's very latest manner. Some
of them tremendously obscure, and all, I thought, beautiful. One of them
was a tune out of Don Giovanni – very amusing! – you suddenly saw that
it *was* a variation of the Diabelli Waltz. Then he played some Chopin,
and then some most modern Ravel – but by that time I was pretty well
done up. We tottered out, leapt onto a bus and arrived at the Cock, to
find there Leonard, Virginia, and Oliver; Eliot followed. It was rather
queer – the meal strangely heterogeneous – the rooms in Clifford's Inn
oddly bleak. But I enjoyed it all very much. *[. . .]*

⁂

To James Strachey

*Sir Edmund William Gosse (1849–1928) was the most powerful critic of his
time. Ray Marshall's (d.1940) elder sister was married to Lytton's nephew, Dick
Rendel, and her younger sister was Frances (1900–2004), who was soon to figure
importantly in Lytton's life. Lytton, Duncan and Francis Birrell's 'howl of
execration' surely had as much to do with their dismay at Bunny's sudden
conversion to heterosexuality as to their dislike of his wife-to-be.*

51, Gordon Square
April 14th 1921

I'm afraid I have been very remiss in the writing department, but
business and pleasure have sadly occupied my time. Q.V. came out last
Thursday (April 7th) accompanied by enormous boostings in the press –
an article on the leading article page of the Times, as well as a long
review in the Lit. Supp. – posters whirling on carts – reviews in all the
other papers, etc. etc. The result was that of the first edition of 5000
copies, 4000 were sold (to the booksellers) by the following day, and it
is being hurriedly reprinted. After the first 5000, I shall begin to make
money on the royalties, at the rate of about £200 a thousand copies, but
it remains to be seen whether the sales will really continue, especially if
the Strike which hangs over our heads comes off. All the reviews take
the line that it is far more discreet, and 'mature' than E.V. – which may
be only another way of saying that's more tedious and flat. At any rate I
feel that I ought to do something particularly outrageous for my next

book, in order to revive my reputation, It's alarming to be welcomed with open arms by Gosse and Jack Squire, and the Times – though I suppose it's paying also. The American edition comes out on June 7th, and in the meantime selections (which I beg you not to read) are appearing in the New Republic. I sent off a copy (of the book) to you a day or two ago, and I hope it will reach you all right, though I suppose it's always rather a lottery. It's a great bore being separated for such a long time, but I now see that I shan't reach Vienna. In any case the horrors of the journey, and the grimness (even if not visible) of the state of affairs there would have deterred me; but now I have had an invitation from Mr Berenson to go and stay with them in Florence, and I have decided to accept, my plan being to stop there about a fortnight at the beginning of May, and then move to Venice, where Pippa swears she will join me. Possibly Carrington and Partridge may go out later too. But of course everything is only arranged subject to the Eternal strike. I gather that Oliver and Inez are going to Vienna in the middle of May – this will probably be a pleasant diversification for you, especially if you don't see too much of Inez (who after all isn't so bad) – and no doubt they'll go about a good deal together independent of you. As for summer plans, a farm house in a secluded spot in the Lakes is adumbrated for August, but nothing definite has been done yet. I hope before long it will be possible to report progress, and that it will turn out to be possible, as it sounds an agreeable place. Tidmarsh is at the present moment divinely beautiful, with the tulips and wallflowers, so it seems shocking to be going away from it. But London also has its points.

The proof-reading of Victoria was very arduous, and I'm convinced that owing to your absence there are multitudes of fearful errors; but I don't know, as I haven't yet brought myself to read it through again, and even if I did they'ld no doubt escape me. The crisis of the American negotiations were also febrile, but they all smoothed themselves out in the end quite satisfactorily. The payments from that region only come in gradually, while the wretched dollar continues to sink. However Maynard, by a mysterious operation, has I think checked some of the worst effects of this. Another horror is the income-tax question. So far as I can see my income will reach a supertax level this year. But as the authorities are apparently unaware of my existence all is well so far.

Private life continues to flow on very smoothly. The curious ménage or ménages work, I think, quite well. Ralph is really a charming creature, and seems quite content, and Carrington appears to be happy. When you return, and they have to leave 41 Gordon Square there may be a slight crisis – but it's no good forestalling things. I lead a very desultory existence. I've got the Grands Ecrivains edition of Racine (nine volumes) which gives me great pleasure, and occupies most of my week-ends, and I have also, at last, embarked upon Swann, which I am enjoying very much – in spite of the terrifying demands upon the attention. I dip now and then into social life, but that seems rather duller than before, and some regions of it have also been damaged by the appearance of Clive, bursting with fat and lust, shouting, shrieking, and pulling his trousers up ever higher and higher – until I am amazed that the fair ladies don't turn him neck and crop out of their drawing-rooms. His love affairs grow ever more successful as he grows more undesirable. Mary and La Gandarilla both . . . but enough of him. As for another favourite of the sex, I gather that you've heard of Bunny's marriage. It has raised a universal howl of execration – in which my voice has loudly joined. It seems quite maniacal. The female (do you know her?) is hideously ugly and as mute as a fish. They are going to live in lodgings off the Gray's Inn Road, overlooking a cemetery, and intend (I'm told) to have a very large family. A charming outlook! Why they couldn't have gone on as they were in Taviton Street, Heaven knows. But there's a rumour that she was adamant – would not grant the last favour unless the bars were put up – and so he, like an idiot, gave way. But this seems almost too scandalous. Francis is in despair, Duncan callous. I, personally, am a little put out. The shop is a queer business: but somehow it subsists, though how, one hardly knows, considering the extreme dreaminess of the shopmen.

I hope you continue to progress satisfactorily. The story of the Prof's treachery to Alix over her translation was very shocking, but if yours holds good, I suppose she can now devote herself to that. I do *not* like the accounts of the environs of Wien. Ah! Mon dieu! But the thought of the music desolates me – my only hope is that there's not much Mozart, and a great deal of Wagner. It will be fun if after all we have a revolution here before you. The situation is 'very critical'. The Triple alliance has give notice that it will strike tomorrow at 10 p.m. Oh dear, oh dear! I pin my faith, rather waveringly, on the solid good sense of my countrymen. The streets are filling up with khaki personages – iron helmets – able-bodied seamen. Tents fill Kensington Gardens. Posters implore the passer-by to join the Citizen's Defence League. *I* want to start a Citizen's Fence League – i.e., a league for those who sit on the fence. But . . . The root of the evil is that Mr Lloyd George will persist in being Prime Minister. It seems a strange taste. Pourquoi? Pourquoi?

Max has arrived in London, and taken up his residence at the Charing Cross Hotel. He rang me up, to ask me to go and see him, explaining that he drew a caricature of me, and wished to 'verify his impressions'. I went yesterday, and found him, plump and white haired, drawn up to receive me. 'Let us come out onto the balcony, where we shall have a view of the doomed city.' He begged me to turn my profile towards him, and for a minute or two made some notes on the back of an envelope. He was infinitely polite and elaborate, and quite remote, so far as I could see, from humanity in all its forms. His caricatures are to be exhibited in three weeks – 'if England still exists'.

Well, I'm feeling rather worn out, and must totter to bed. I wish I could write more often, My laziness is frightful. But after all there's nothing to say. Perhaps tomorrow, though, after 10 p.m., there may be too much. The worst of it is that at that moment I shall be having dinner with Lady Curzon in Carlton House Terrace – probably it will be the first house that the mob will attack. I shall take a red handkerchief in case of accidents.

your
Lytton

Mama is much better. Practically all right again I think. Though I don't think her general health is very good. She pants a great deal after walking, which isn't a good symptom. But her vigour is terrific, and she looks perfectly well. Trevor, too, is extraordinarily active – coming by tube in grey tweed knickerbockers.

‡

To Carrington

51, Gordon Square
W.C.1
Monday, May 2nd 1921

Important

Could you bring me when you come a small red book with addresses in it (of the Apostles)? It is in one of the two right-hand drawers in the little yellow writing-table (I think the bottom). I have to deal with it before I go.

Could you also bring the circular air-cushion (emblem of mortality) which should be in the wall-cupboard in my bedroom? It would be very kind.

I hope you've had a happy and peaceful day. In the mob in Bond Street this afternoon I suddenly thought of the ducklings on the lawn, and very nearly shrieked like Jeremiah 'Woe! Woe! Woe to all ye who tap pavements and look upon whoredom . . .' etc. etc. But I suppose I should have myself come under the curse. I had lunch with a cousin of the King of Spain and a granddaughter of Victoria and the Czar of Russia.

with love

from

your

Lytton

‡

To Carrington

Lytton was a bit confused about the Scotts. The 'two mistresses' were Geoffrey Scott, who was responsible for the decoration and furniture in some of the new rooms at I Tatti, and Nicky Mariano, Berenson's secretary and later companion. Mary Berenson hoped Scott and Mariano would marry and live nearby, and look after her husband. But during the war Scott married Lady Sybil Cutting.[1]

I Tatti

Settignano

Florence

Monday, May 8th 1921 *[misdated: Monday was May 9th]*

Just to say that I arrived here safely last night. The journey from Paris was very comfortable and quick, and I had time at Pisa to take a turn in the town and look at the Campo Santo and Byron's Palazzo, not to mention the Leaning Tower – a curious dead town, but full of charm. Florence seems thoroughly alive, on the other hand, though as yet I hardly had more than a glimpse of it, having been whisked up here in the motor yesterday evening. The house is just what I imagined – large – full of beautiful objects one can hardly look at, and comfort that somehow is far less comfortable than Tidmarsh. A sister of Berenson's and her husband (poor American creatures), Lord and Lady Berwick, and some female secretaries (I gather) make up the party so far. His Lordship looks like an imbecile butler, and I should think was one. Lady B is a sad pseudo-beauty. This afternoon BB is to take me to tea with the Scotts – the two ex-mistresses who married one another and live nearby. There is a distant air of civil war about, which is slightly unpleasant. Otherwise everything seems perfect. It is quite hot.

What a confused good-bye we had! I hope the anonymous show played up properly. Were you at Tidmarsh for the week-end? I suppose so. And the ducklings? And the chickens? Oh dear! oh dear! When I see them again, it will be on the dining table! Let me hear the news. My best love to you and to Ralph

your
Lytton

1. See Michael Holroyd, *Lytton Strachey*, p. 736, n. 73.

‡

To Carrington

Bernard Berenson (1865–1969) was a Lithuanian Jewish immigrant to America who studied at Harvard (to whom he left I Tatti), and became the leading authority on Italian Renaissance art. His connoisseurship, which was very great, was put at the service of the dealer Joseph Duveen. The result was that some of their collector-clients, such as Isabella Stewart Gardner, were occasionally misled, and many of Berenson's attributions have now been questioned. BB was married to Mary, Alys Russell's and Logan Pearsall Smith's sister. As her daughters Karin and Ray married, respectively, Adrian Stephen and Oliver Strachey, the family was strongly connected to Bloomsbury.

I Tatti
Settignano
Florence
Sunday, May 15th 1921

My dearest creature, I was very glad to get your letter, though I was sorry that you should have been depressed. However, I hope by now that you are happy again, that all jars have disappeared, and that you're busy getting ready for Italy. This ought, I think, with luck, to reach you before you start. I wish that these disturbances did not arise. Why can't my love for you both abolish them altogether?

The last week has been rather a dismal one for me. I have had an attack of the gripes – exactly the same as the Granada one, though rather less acute, and evidently the result of the change of temperature, cooking, etc. It's now gone off, and I seem to be all right again, though slightly faded – perhaps owing partly to the heavy heat which has descended and doesn't seem inclined to go off – a thunderous grey-skied, oppressive heat, caused, they say, by a south wind from Africa (the Sirocco).

This establishment, also, can hardly be described as a gay one. Never have I felt so acutely the charms of Tidmarsh, and the infinite supremacy of that way of life. I think at moments that one ought to become an evangelist and preach the Tidmarsh gospel to all the world; but no doubt really it would be useless, and the people who live in the Tatti would be just as wretched when they had become converted and wherever they lived – I daresay even more wretched still. B.B. is a very interesting phenomenon. The mere fact that he has accumulated this wealth from having been a New York gutter-snipe is sufficiently astonishing; but besides that he has a most curious complicated temperament, very sensitive, very clever – even, I believe, with a strain of niceness somewhere or other, but desperately wrong – perhaps suffering from some dreadful complexes – and without a speck of naturalness or ordinary human enjoyment. And this has spread itself all over the house, which is really remarkably depressing, and (as Clive said of Henry Strachey's mother) 'as dead as a nit'. Garsington is greatly to be preferred to it; for Garsington, with all its horrors, is alive – very much so; while here one is struck chill with the atmosphere of a crypt. Oooh! – And so much of it, too – such a large corpse – so many long dead corridors, so many dead primitives, so many dead pieces of furniture, and flowers, and servants, such multitudes of dead books; and then, outside, a dead garden, with a dead view of a dead Tuscan landscape . . . a dead Florence, one almost thinks – but that's an illusion, I'm sure if one were here, in other circumstances, one would find Florence alive enough. But as for the country round, though it's full of wonderful beauty, I can't say that it seems to me the sort of place to live in. For one thing, it's horribly crowded, villas of every shape and size peppered over it thickly – and then there is an outlandishness about it . . . how English it makes me feel! Of course, though, I may be jaundiced by the fearful way in which I usually see it – viz. tearing in a deadish, a quite dead! – motor, up and down the zig-zaggy narrow lanes, till one's eyes almost jump out of their sockets, and one's soul screams out for Alan and the flats of Berkshire. I see that this letter would be endless if I went on to describe all there is to describe. Mother B. for instance – a pathetic figure – half-conscious of the horrors of the situation, but quite unable to get rid of them – a lost soul. And then, mon dieu! B.B.'s sister and her husband – caricatures of Americans – she with a voice like a steam saw, screaming out an endless stream of platitudes, and he, poor man, a literature professor in a female College near Boston. So that the result is boredom more than anything else. You can imagine how glad I shall be when Pippa arrives, and when you appear. Where shall we meet? I suppose you have consulted with her. How exciting it will be!

You don't say whether your picture was hung by Roger, but I imagine so. What a pity it is that Barbara and Nick can't manage to stay and look after Tidmarsh in your absence. I hope you succeed in getting someone to. It would be very dangerous to leave so many wild animals together on the lawn! Gerald's letter was most charming – full of interest, and very appreciative of the right things. He is really a noble figure. I only hope that some day he'll return to England.

I've only been to Florence twice so far. Now the elections are taking place, and everybody seems to think that for the next few days there may be more or less of a revolution – so the outlook for sight-seeing is a trifle hazy! I spend most of my time dozing in my sitting-room, and turning over the pages of B.B.'s books. Today I lunch with Lady Sybil and Geoffrey Scott. On Tuesday I go to see the Sitwells in their Castle, which ought to be amusing.

I forgot to mention Goldie and Norton – the latter certainly very much better. He returns to England on Tuesday, when Dickinson I'm glad to say, comes here.

I gave Ralph £30 in a cheque, which I hope may cover a good deal of your journey expenses, But I think the expenses of Tidmarsh may have been rather great while I've been away, and of course I must share that.

with love and blessings
from
your Lytton

‡

To Carrington

Though this letter bears the same date as the previous lengthy one, the omitted portion seems to imply a later date for this.

I Tatti
Settignano
Florence
Sunday, May 15th 1921

[. . .] I do so hope you will enjoy Italy. During the last week, I have been feeling, if possible more acutely than ever, the wonderful delights of our Tidmarsh life. My dear, don't let us do anything which will make that other than it is! – I want to ask you to tell me all you can, if you are ever in difficulties or distress. Though of course it depresses me to think you're not happy, it depresses me still more not to know. But I hope that you are perfectly happy – or as near to that as humanity allows. Do you know how much I love you?

your own
Lytton

A letter has come from Conan Doyle, asking whether Queen Vic was a spiritualist!

‡

To Carrington

Sir Robert Walpole was created Earl of Orford on his resignation as Britain's first prime minister in 1742, and his youngest son, Horace Walpole (1717–97), the writer and creator of Strawberry Hill, was the 4th Earl. The Lady Orford in question was therefore Horace's sister-in-law.

I Tatti
Settignano
Florence
Monday, May 16th 1921

I must add a less gloomy postscript to my letter of yesterday. The lunch
with the Scotts was decidedly cheering. They live in a most superb villa
called the Villa Medici, some way off, and a little higher in the hills. It
was built by Lorenzo de Medici in the Renaissance, and in the 18th
century was occupied by Lady Orford, a highly disreputable personage
and a connection of Horace Walpole's, whose letters are full of accounts
of her scandalous doings in Florence. It is not a palace, but a house, and
you never saw such a grand one – high and magnificent, with rows of
huge cypresses leading to it, and a garden on different levels, with a
wonderful view from the terrace of the surrounding country, and
Florence with its dome and campanile in the middle of it. The rooms
are splendid – very high, and the walls are covered with the most
wonderful Chinese wall-paper, dating from the time of Lady Orford. In
one room, every piece is different – a lovely vast pattern of branches
and astounding Chinese birds of different sizes and shapes all over it. It
is really an exciting work of art. Then on a lower level, by itself, with a
massive terrace of its own, is another room, not 18th century but early
Renaissance – superb and simple – which Geoffrey Scott uses as his
study. Dear me! It was a relief to find oneself in such surroundings after
the cut and dried specimen atmosphere of this establishment The
company, too, seemed very sympathetic – for one thing, it was
positively English – oh, what foreigners Americans are!

Scott himself is even Oxford, and there was an agreeable young man
from the Embassy at Rome, who was also Oxford, and we three went
down to Scott's study and talked about books and people, and laughed,
and made bawdy jokes, and then Dickinson came in with his curious air
of other-worldliness, and everything seemed as delightful as it could be.
Lady Sybil is apparently the daughter of an Irish peer, rather faded and
nervy, and talks away sixteen to the dozen; but I thought her not so
bad. And she has a daughter (by her other husband) aged 17, who made
me feel randy; there was also an Italian footman of the same age.

Then we whisked in the motor to a very different ménage – to old
Mrs Ross, a Victorian relic, 80 years old, who lives by herself in the
grimmest solitude, surrounded by innumerable mementoes of her past
existence – an interior very like my mother's room at Gordon Square,

only on the vast Italian scale – hideous room after hideous room, with drawings by Watts and photographs of Tennyson plastered thick all over them. You would give anything to paint the old hag herself – a stern, aristocratic visage, with dark staring eyes, and such black thick eyebrows! – And a deep inhuman voice.

The odious Sirocco still continues. 'Exceptional weather', everyone says. Last night I was woken up by what sounded very like a rifle shot, so perhaps the revolution has begun – or perhaps it is over, as there were no more. I lie in bed, writing this. Did I tell you that a thin wire gauze covers every window so that only half the right amount of air penetrates, and one sees the outside world through a haze? – To keep out the flies, if you please. You see, flies are alive, and therefore their presence in this abode of bliss would be most unsuitable.

Good-bye. I hope to hear before long something definite about your plans. Only another week in this sarcophagus! Hurrah!

with love from
Lytton

‡

To Carrington

Carrington and Ralph Partridge married the next day, May 21st. They had their honeymoon first in Paris, then in San Gimignano, Siena and Perugia where, Carrington noted in a diary, 'We got rather drunk and had one of our brawls, I suspect in loud voices.' They went from Tuscany to the Romagna, and met Lytton in Venice on 6 June.

I Tatti
Settignano
Florence
Friday night, May 20th 1921

My dearest and best, Pippa came this evening with your letter of last Saturday. She was rather a long time on the journey, so it took more time to come than it need have, and now I'm afraid that this may not be able to reach England before you start – in which case you might not get it till you reached Venice, and in the interval be uncertain as to what I was thinking. So I am sending you a wire tomorrow morning to ask you to let me have your Paris address, in order that I may send this there. I hope by this time you will have had my other letters – though I am afraid they may have seemed a little inadequate – I was writing more or less in the dark. But I hope that in any case you never doubted of my love for you. Do you know how difficult I find it to express my feelings either in letters or talk? It is sometimes terrible – and I don't understand why it should be so; and sometimes it seems to me that you underrate what I feel. You realise that I have varying moods, but my fundamental feelings you perhaps don't realise so well. Probably it's my fault. It is perhaps much easier to show one's peevishness than one's affection and admiration! Oh my dear, do you really want me to tell you that I love you as a friend! – But of course that is absurd, and you *do* know very well that I love you as something more than a friend, you angelic creature, whose goodness to me has made me happy for years, and whose presence in my life has been, and always will be, one of the most important things in it. Your letter made me cry, I feel a poor old miserable creature, and I may have brought more unhappiness to you than anything else. I only pray that it is not so, and that my love for you, even though it is not what you desire, may make our relationship a blessing to you – as it has been to me.

Remember that I too have never had my moon! We are all helpless in these things – dreadfully helpless. I am lonely and I am all too truly growing old, and if there was a chance that your decision meant that I should somehow or other lose you, I don't think I could bear it. You and Ralph and our life at Tidmarsh are what I care for most in the world – almost (apart from my work and some few people) the *only* things I care for. It would be horrible if that were to vanish. You must not believe, too readily, repeated conversations. I think that possibly some bitterness or disappointment makes you tend to exaggerate the black side of what you're told. I cannot be certain – but I think you exaggerate. Certainly, I thought it was generally agreed that one didn't quite believe everything that came through Virginia! As for the physical part, I really think you exaggerate that too. I find that in those things I differ curiously at different times, and what I said to Ralph on that occasion I can't remember, and I think it may have been a passing phase.

Perhaps all this isn't very important; but you seemed in your letter to suggest that my love for you has diminished as time has gone on; that is not so. I am sure it has increased. It is true that the first excitement, which I always (and I suppose most people) have at the beginning of an affair, has gone off; but something much deeper has grown up instead.

So far as I can judge, I believe you are right, and that if Ralph wants marriage it is best for you and for him that it should be so. But I hope that (apart from his happiness) it *won't* make much difference to anybody! I do so long to see you and talk to you both. I don't quite understand how you propose to get married so quickly – I thought that sort of abrupt business was hideously expensive. But perhaps the father Partridge will stump up! It is infuriating to hear no details. Well, at any rate, I hope you will get off to Paris, and have an enchanting holiday. That wretch Ralph has not written me a word! What is to be done with him?

It continues to be pretty dreary here, but on Monday Pippa and I depart for Siena, which will be a great relief – especially if by that time the weather takes it into its head to clear up. Thunder and oppression continue day after day. The visit to the Sitwell Castle of Montegufoni was most entertaining – a truly astounding place – but too much for me to describe now – it is fearfully late and I am dropping.

Oh! My dearest dear, I send you so very much love! I feel happier now that I have written, and hope what I have written will seem as it should be to you. There is much more to say, but that must be for talking.

Give my love and kisses to the wretch.

from your own
Lytton

Sunday morning

Your wire has just come, and I am sending this to Pippa, as I calculate that it will get there before you. Go and look at Byron's palazzo there on the Arno – where he wrote some of Don Juan – and I think you will like the Campo Santo etc. and the whole dead town. Pippa and I leave here tomorrow, probably for Bologna – then, via Ravenna, to Venice.

much love from
Lytton

PS If you wrote to Poste Restante, Ravenna, we should probably be there in about a week.

‡

To Virginia Woolf

William Beckford of Fonthill, Wiltshire (1760–1844) was best known as the
author of Vathek. *Mary Creighton ('Dobbin') was the daughter of Mandell*
Creighton, Bishop of London, whom Lytton had considered as a candidate for
Eminent Victorians *and about whom he wrote in* Portraits in Miniature.
Jacques Auguste de Thou (Thuanus) (1553–1617) was a French historian.
Lytton could not have failed to notice that Lord Esher, a War Office colleague,
wrote soon after Kitchener's death that the absence of biographical comment on
Kitchener's relations with women 'leaves incomplete the story of his life or betrays
a flaw in his nature'. The word omitted in the version published by James and
Leonard was 'cretinous'.

Charles Repington, the celebrated military correspondent of The Times,
published a book entitled The First World War 1914–1918 *in 1920. The*
Italian philosopher Benedetto Croce's Ariosto, Shakespeare and Corneille
was published in English in 1920.

James was reading J. Varendonck's The Psychology of Day-Dreams
(1921).

Virginia's reply to this letter includes the lines that, even at Lewes Free
Library, 'Lytton Strachey predominates. I want to turn an honest penny; and
behold, when I come to write about old Mrs Gilbert [unidentified by VW's
editors], *it runs of its own accord into two semi-colons, dash, note of*
exclamation, full stop. Do you recognise your style?'

c/o Mrs Wilson
Watendlath Farm
Keswick
Cumberland
August 23rd 1921

Have you read 'Biographical Memoirs of Extraordinary Painters'?
I think it may amuse you – by Beckford, and in the pseudo-romantic
style. But it only lasts for half-an-hour, which is annoying, as, in the
scarcity of books, I feel myself driven ever nearer and nearer to the
abyss of Swann – I shudder and draw back – interpose Maynard on
Probability, 'The Group Mind' by Mary Creighton's cretinous husband,
Lord Esher on Lord Kitchener, and the insipid memoirs of
De Thou.

All is in vain, and Swann continues to loom. There is only now the first half of Colonel Repington between me and it, for I cannot read Signor Croce on Corneille and Ariosto, which seems to be the only alternative, except a study of Strindberg in American, proving that he was probably homosexual and certainly in love with his mother – the conclusion is too obvious, one passes on, though one sentence is attractive – 'In the Belvedere he stood for an hour before the Venus of Guido Reni, resembling his adored wife in every respect, and all of a sudden he felt an irresistible longing for her person, packed his grip and returned suddenly.' This is what the language of Milton has come to.

I am sitting, as you may guess, rather comatose, in a small cottage apartment, green mountains out of window, the stuffed head of a very old female sheep over the window, etc. etc. Alix, James, Mr and Mrs P. and l'ami Brenan wander in and out with fish-hooks and hard-boiled eggs done up in newspaper. Some of them declare that they are going out to squat among the heather and the damp ferns, in order to have lunch and tea. Needless to say, James and I remain at home – James on an enormous air-cushion balanced upon a horsehair sofa, reading the psychopathology of day-dreams by Dr. Varendonck . . . One wonders whether one has been quite wise in coming North. The rain and cold have been fairly continuous, though for three or four days it was extremely hot, and we walked over the stony hills until our feet were covered with blisters – they still are – at least mine are, and I can only wear silk socks and slippers, in which I totter occasionally into the air. But the air is unfortunately relaxing, as they say – very different from yours, which I wish I was breathing – are you enjoying it and growing robust? If you can't write, perhaps Leonard will, with all the news. I wonder whether Monk's house is doomed – or what. Have you been having visitors? And how are the inhabitants of Charleston? In about a fortnight I shall be floating towards your smooth downs and redbrick houses – or so I hope – and what a relief it will be! Oh, to see an outline, instead of *[zigzag line]* on the horizon! But I must turn away from such visions, and face the inevitable Swann.

your
Lytton

‡

To Carrington

In late August, the Partridges, Gerald Brenan, Marjorie, Lytton, James and Alix Strachey had made up a party at Watendlath Farm, near Keswick in Cumberland, where Brenan had played out his drama of lusting after his best friend's wife.

The Fat Boy of Peckham was an obese child who eventually weighed over forty stone and joined a freak show when his mother could no longer afford to feed him. Quentin Bell was then eleven and, as a watercolour portrait of him by his mother shows, a plump boy.

Charleston

Monday, September 5th 1921

I wish you were here. I am out of doors in the grass at the foot of the Downs, in the sun, happy but somehow rather lonely. Les gens ici sont très aimable, mais . . . I should like to be back with my family and all the comforts of Tidmarsh. The sordidness of this establishment is a trifle trying. Everything is allowed to rot from year to year, including the rats killed by poison, whose smell is now wafted through the house. 'It will be gone in a day or two,' says Vanessa drearily. Well, *I* shall be gone tomorrow – when I drag myself to the Wolves [*sic*]. On Friday I go to London, where I shall stay the night, and on Saturday to Tidmarsh. Hurray!

I hope you have been having a not too dreary time at Waley Castle. And I wonder how the journey from Watendlath went off. It seemed to me like arriving in Italy, when I reached London, such was the difference in the temperature. But here once more the mornings and evenings are distinctly chill. Horror of horrors! The belly-bands will soon be in full swing again – to be followed by the furs, the mittens, and all the muffetees [*mufflers (obs.)*] of winter. Why don't we follow the swallow? Why, oh why?

The two young men, Sebastian and Douglas, went off to Germany together some days ago.

Douglas had regained his looks, but brains, I fear, were never his. His hours pass in a gentle trance. Sebastian was looking very robust and ugly. I must cultivate him further, but I'm afraid he may be really too young for me to be able to have any natural conversation with him. Maynard, who went off to Margot's this morning, has arranged all my money affairs with the greatest detail. It now only remains for me to carry out his instructions, and then to abide the dreadful consequences. It is 'a curious nerve', as my father used to say, and, with all his extreme cleverness and unexpected benevolence, remains exasperating. Also – am I mistaken? – or is it true that his eyes have strangely diminished in size and light? They now appear to me pale, small, pathetic bird's eyes, instead of those large lustrous orbs that fascinated me so – once! Very odd – but it may have been only an 'effet de lumière' as he sat before the window, bending over his calculations, and advising me to sell out of Cunard Debentures and buy Bolchow Vaughan Reference Deferred.

The boys behave better than I'd expected. Julian is exquisite though icy, and t'other simply the Fat Boy of Peckham, whose portrait one sees from time to time in the Daily Mirror. Angelica is a sylph.

Clive's tummy has now burst all bounds: it has pushed its way through waistcoat and trousers into public view clothed in nothing but an ancient shirt. His example terrifies me, and I think I shall have to take to gymnastics in self-protection.

I read for the first time the (almost) complete account of Oscar's trials, which they have here. It's very interesting and depressing. One of the surprising features is that he very nearly got off. If he had, what would have happened, I wonder? I fancy the history of English culture might have been quite different, if a juryman's stupidity had chanced to take another turn.

Farewell! My love to Ralph. I'll see you I hope in less than a week.

your

Lytton

‡

To Mary Hutchinson

Elizabeth Asquith (1897–1945) married Prince Antoine Bibesco (1878–1951), a Romanian diplomat in London, in 1919. She was in Washington with her husband from 1920 to 1926, though they normally lived in Paris, in the Bibesco townhouse on the Seine with huge murals by Vuillard, where she was taken up by her husband's friend, Proust. At the time of this letter she was having an affair with Katherine Mansfield's husband, John Middleton Murry.

Virginia Woolf came to share Lytton's view of Princess Bibesco, but when she first met her, she wrote in her diary for Sunday, 6 December 1919: 'Elizabeth was nicer, and less brilliant than I expected. She has the composed manners of a matron, and did not strain to say clever things.'

The young lady on the toboggan is in Chekhov's 1886 story 'A Joke'. It is the narrator who plays the joke on Nadenka by whispering 'I love you, Nadya' every time the toboggan carrying the two of them takes off into the air. She doesn't know who has said it, but relishes hearing this so much that she insists on repeating the toboggan-run over and over despite her terror at the descent. As Lytton says, she was quite right about what she heard – the question Chekhov raises is what was the narrator's motive in saying it?

Tidmarsh
Wednesday, October 26th 1921

Ma chère

[. . .] My epistolary conduct has been, I quite realise it, even more shocking than usual. But just lately I have had something of an excuse. I was to spend the last week-end at Garsington. This had the now inevitable result – a terrific cold fell upon me. I was crushed into bed, where I remained stunned, and have only just begun to emerge, feeling still like an old man who has been clubbed to earth. However, I rise, I rise. The worst is that the prospect of a Garsington week-end still confronts me.

It was particularly disgraceful not to have written after that divine few days at Eleanor. Have you recovered completely from that fearful crick in the back? The Princess's conduct has been causing me some disturbances. An appalling lunch at the Savoy, my dear, tête-à-tête – it was impossible to escape it, and oh, I really detest the woman. Her suffisance *[self-importance]* and utter idiocy are only fit for a Restoration Comedy. She insisted on stuffing herself and unfortunately also me with pâté de foie gras and some very thick and sugary white wine, which, she declared, was Maynard's favourite, until I reeled away on the brink of vomiting. She told me of Murry, Katherine et patati et patata *[and so on]* – poor twaddle. But Middleton I cannot understand. She had the audacity to threaten a descent on Tidmarsh and at any moment I positively believe she may arrive, in spite of my violent injunction to the contrary. Luckily she returns to the pastures of Washington at the end of the month.

I enjoy the country – tottering out into the sun and fields for half-an-hour at a time and then coming back to my new pullman car chair and an infinitude of books. But there are moments when I regret London. You must tell me all about that impossible region when you come. I am longing for the moment. The young lady on the toboggan was quite right about what she heard as she flew through the air – and of course she couldn't have had any doubts really.

My love –
your
Lytton

‡

To Virginia Woolf

Princess Bibesco's book was Fir and Plane. The Four Ages of Poetry *is by Thomas Love Peacock. Maynard's 'affair' is his courtship of Lydia. Lytton's father had belonged to the Oriental Club. Clive is the person for whom Leonard and James substituted 'N' in their published version of this letter and Princess Bibesco was 'Q'. Though it doesn't explain the need for such discretion, Virginia wrote on the same day to Lady Robert Cecil that 'the lily livered journalists are afraid to praise the work of a Princess – even a sham Princess. My brother in law Clive, who drives about in motors with her and drinks cocktails and all the rest, says she is just as clever as any gutter snipe; and a very good hard-working woman.'*[1]

The Mill House
Tidmarsh
Pangbourne
February 6th 1922

It is sad to think of you ill, and sadder still to think that your recovery depends upon your friends' letters. Good heavens! Your case is hopeless! How can anyone write to you, I should like to know? Certainly I can't. Perhaps Clive can. I envision his elegant elaborations. Only, if they cause your recovery, I shall never speak to you again, and in that case will recovery be worth while? Better to languish and languish into an at least honourable grave. But I expect everyone (except Clive) is more or less languishing at the present moment. *My* state has long been quite deplorable. I put it down to the winter – the agony of thick underclothes, etc. etc; but of course it may be sheer deliquescence of the brain. Anyhow, from whatever cause, I am sans eyes, sans teeth, sans prick, sans . . . but after that there can be no more senses – and on the whole I feel more like a fish gasping on a bank than anything else. It is terrible. I hope wildly that a change will come with the swallows (whenever that may be), and in the meantime I pretend to read. Books arrive from the Times Book Club (I am a *guaranteed subscriber*). But I hardly look at them. I spend hours turning over the leaves of the Dictionary of National Biography. When that gets too exhausting, I take to Who's Who. I sometimes dip into the Old Masters. I find Swift very good, though a dreadfully unpleasant character; Dante ditto; Milton ditto. Does one have to be dreadfully unpleasant to be in the first division of the first class, do you think? But then there is Rabelais, who is reassuring. To descend abruptly, I wonder if you will be able to get through Madame La Princesse's little volume. I suppose there is some kind of cleverness in it, but, how I hate the woman, with her dried pea of a soul! 'The Four Ages of Poetry' is brilliant. That man knew how to write prose – vide the last enormous sentence – which is more than Shelley or Browning did. Yet, besides Clive, who has heard of him?

The Maynard affair is most peculiar. So far I have only heard Vanessa's account, but I hope before very long to get a first-hand one. What are we all coming to, pray? The Universe totters.

Do you know that I have joined the Oriental Club? You must come and have lunch with me there when the swallows are with us. – A vast hideous building – have you been there? Filled with vast hideous Anglo-Indians, very old and very rich. One becomes 65, with an income of 5000 a year, directly one enters it. One is so stout one can hardly walk, and one's brain works with an extraordinary slowness. Just the place for me, you see, in my present condition. I pass almost unnoticed with my glazed eye and white hair, as I sink into a leather chair heavily with a copy of the Field in hand. Excellent claret too, one of the best cellars in London, by Jove. You *must* come! I'll write again soon, if you can bear it.

your
Lytton

1. Nigel Nicolson and Joanne Trautmann (eds.), *The Letters of Virginia Woolf*, vol. 2, *1912–1922*, pp. 501–2.

‡

To Virginia Woolf

Virginia had been seriously ill, first with influenza, then high fevers and a heart murmur. In her reply to this letter (11 February), she says that 'Princess B[ibesco] exactly suits my tank. Poinsettias, arum lilies, copulation in tepid water, spume, sperm, semen − that's my atmosphere.' Again, in the earlier version, Princess Bibesco was disguised as 'Q'.

The Mill House
Tidmarsh
Pangbourne
February 10th 1922

The accounts of you lately have not been very good, but I hope that you are now beginning to mend, and that letters load your plate every morning. If one has to be in bed, this is certainly a good time to choose for it. The horror of getting up is unparalleled, and I am filled with amazement every morning when I find I have done it. To my mind there is clearly only one test of wealth, and that is − a fire in one's bedroom. Till one can have that at any and every moment, one is poor. Oh, for a housemaid at dawn!

Have you looked at the Bibesco's piddlings? And don't you think them vile? The horrid atmosphere of 'luxe' over them! − Poinsettias − what on earth are they? − and chandeliers. But the reviews, such as I have seen, have been pretty crushing. Mr Masefield has produced a very strange little book − an 'adaptation' of Racine's Esther − the most deplorable give-away you ever saw. And the Lit. Sup. treats it quite seriously, and implies that Mr. M. is a better poet than Racine. We are a nation of barbarians, I fear. The wretched man clearly hadn't the faintest idea what he was up to. Oh oh! Style, words, common decency, mean nothing to him − or to the Lit. Sup − nothing. He converts Racine's exquisite silk, length after length of it, into odd patches of rough canvas with perfect complacency − and the Lit. Sup. is charmed. However, he's sent me back to my old love, and I spent last night in a rapture over Athalie, which I had rather forgotten − good gracious me! Reading it, I almost felt like a Frenchman, and that there really was nothing like *that* in the world. It took quite an effort to remember King Lear and in fact I'm still rather doubtful whether . . . Well, I'm coming up to London next week, and hope you'll be well enough to see me a little then. I'll ring up Leonard.

May Sinclair's book 'The Life and Death of Harriet Frean' has some merit, though nasty. Have you seen it?

I wish you *would* read my proof-sheets. I don't know yet when they'll begin.

your

Lytton

‡

To Carrington

Then living with the Sitwells, (Sir) William Turner Walton (1902–83) ended his life laden with honours, including the OM; but the fledgling composer had left Oxford without a degree. Goupil's was the international art firm to whose London branch at 17 Southampton Street Vincent van Gogh was sent to work in 1873. Simon Bussy showed at the Goupil, as Duncan Grant did later.

There was a general election on 15 November, marking the final destruction of coalition government and a return to party politics, with a large majority of Bonar Law's Conservatives.

51, Gordon Square
W.C.1
February 13th 1922

I went to Osbert's, and immediately found that our most adventurous guess was true: there was Sibbie C*[olefax]* in the hall! Also Clive, as well as a poor old General Sitwell, his young wife (*'charming!'*), to say nothing of Sachy and Walton. The latter is really too much – I sat next him, and might as well (or better) have sat next the black kitten. I tried subject after subject, thing after thing, – they fell like stones into a stagnant pool – not a ripple, not a gurgle. As for la Colefax, she was in fine form – it was a reconciliation lunch, and went off admirably. Clive, in spats and extraordinary black worsted socks, or possibly stockings, as they apparently reached his knees, bellowed and grimaced without once stopping. His vulgarity is most complicated and remarkable.

Osbert was as usual very sympathetic – and declared that he was going to make a raid on Tidmarsh. I said 'Wait till the warm weather.'

I hope he will. Of course Sibby booked me up for a tea party. Tra-la-la! Tra-la-la! I struggled off at last, arm in arm with Clive in spite of my efforts, and reached Goupil's, where luckily Clive is not allowed to enter (a useful thing to know!) I liked the still lives [*sic*], but they seemed rather expensive. The horseman between two curtains, which was the one you liked best, costs £40. The long-shaped one is also £40, but sold. I don't feel *enthusiastic* about any of them, so I shall wait. If you are still very much in favour of any, let me know.

Tea at the good old Oriental, in the greatest luxury.

Oh! I forgot to say – what do you think? – Clive was completely taken in by the Bernard Shaw letter! 'He wrote me a perfectly preposterous and furious letter – too absurd! – Poor old man – quite gaga. I replied that he was the last person in the world whom I wanted to hurt the feelings of. He wrote again, pretending he hadn't written before – quite gaga, poor old fellow!' – etc. etc. So you see the signature must have been forged very brilliantly. I couldn't have believed that he wouldn't have had a single doubt!

You will shortly receive the first instalment of a 'birthday present', or perhaps I should say a present to the Tidmarsh Club, which I feel is not complete without it.

Tuesday morning. Very cold and grim by the gas-fire. No breakfast-in-bedding here – oh no, oh no. What a lovely valentine, though! Quite cheering up – but the vision of a heart in a beard has its drawbacks!

I have approached Pippa on the holiday question. She was vague, but less impossibilist than I'd expected. She would evidently like to come, but fears a General Election, which might require her presence. Perhaps with a little judicious pressure she will agree.

I hope the population flourish. Does the broody brooder still brood? How strange to think that Tidmarsh and London exist at the same time! Oh, I wonder if the Rector has called yet. What *will* you say to him, when he does?

Oliver has phoned to say he thought they were to come next Saturday – and that they will do so. Hilda T. has phoned asking me to lunch. Leonard has 'phoned asking me to Richmond this afternoon. So you see things are filling up already.

With much love to both
your Lytton

‡

To James Strachey

There were hunger riots in Vienna, as Austria was cut off from wheat supplies in the Ukraine by the Bolshevik Revolution. 'Missie Freud' was Anna (1895–1982), the sixth and last child, already on the way to becoming an analyst herself.

Keynes's 1922 publication was A Revision of the Treaty: Being a Sequel to The Economic Consequences of the Peace. *He had first met Lydia Lopokova in October 1918.*

London was still experiencing the tail-end of the Spanish flu pandemic of 1918–19, which is believed to have killed more people than died in the war – perhaps more than 40 million world-wide. It is not surprising that someone so tender about his own health would be so worried about catching it.

51, Gordon Square
W.C.1
February 14th 1922

Your letter to Pippa with a grim account of Vienna arrived this morning, and I only hope that by this time, things will have improved, and that another letter will shortly arrive with more cheering news. The frigidity alone sounds fearful. But it's a great mercy that you're not quite deserted, and that Missie Freud comes round with milk. It occurred to both Pippa and I *[sic]* that the temperature might be the result of the serum – at any rate if it's at all comparable to the typhoid one.

I wrote to you sometime ago, but the letter was posted a day or two before the riots in Vienna, and so I think it may not have reached you. I also sent a week or so ago a copy of Maynard's new book; and I gather Pippa also did. The world here is pretty much as usual, I think. And Pozzo's Lopokova extravaganza is the only novelty. For a moment Vanessa feared the worst – viz. marriage; but I am told that is now considered hardly probable. *To what extent* the affair has gone cannot be discovered. I therefore suppose that it hasn't gone very far.

As to future plans, I expect Alix's illness may possibly alter your views. The Partridges, as you may have heard, think of going to Spain at Easter, and I thought of accompanying them – for at any rate part of the way – and perhaps with Pippa. This practically means April, so that we should be back in May. But I hardly think we could again leave for the country so soon. However, everything must remain vague for the present.

The influenza has been pretty bad here, and has by no means vanished. I have been lurking in terror at Tidmarsh, but have at last come up for the inside of a week, shaking in my shoes. My latest affaire is Lady Astor – hum! – but it progresses damned slowly. My collected essays – 'Books and Characters' come out early in April. A dreary business! I was delighted to hear of the doctor's approval of Eminent Victorians, and I agree with his preference of it to Q.V. With love to Alix.

your
Lytton

‡

To Carrington

Oriental Club
Hanover Square, W.1
Wednesday, February 15th 1922

Good-morning, good-morning! How are you bearing up? I hope you are well and all the creatures are well. I am well.

I went to Richmond yesterday, but there was no Secretary. Virginia seemed very cheerful and talked a great deal, but she looked decidedly ill. However, she is pronounced to be improving.

Rather grim news arrived today in a letter from James to Pippa. Alix was ill, with tonsillitis, and unpleasantly high temperature, keeping on and on. James had been ill, the cold was terrific, so that he couldn't go out. He sounded wretched and rather nervous. But the doctor declared it was simply tonsillitis – no complications – so it is hoped things are improving, though when he wrote (Saturday) she was still bad. A great thing is that they have several friends who visit them daily, and are very kind. Two doctors (English and American) students of Freud – and especially Miss Freud, who lives quite close, and brings a pint of milk (a great luxury) daily. It sounds pretty appalling. Tomorrow I hope there'll be another letter, with better news.

I lunched today with the Astors. Their house is one of the finest in St James's Square. The inside is very magnificent, but difficult to judge at the first go off. Mr Thomas was there (with a stiff neck), and two others. Her Ladyship continues attractive, but she lives in an impossible whirlwind.

I went to Birrell and Garnett's, and have got a nice Peacock first edition – that is to say nice internally, for the binding is poor. They seemed just the same as usual. The partner crouched and smiled, and Bob Trevy gibbered on every conceivable subject.

My intention, which I hardly think will change, is to return for dinner on Friday and probably by the 6.15. This place still seems to me alarmingly influenzic. People are still dropping on every side. Vincent, etc. So I don't think I shall return yet awhile. The grimness of the streets, too, is considerable. All the same, it's attractive, and I _adore_ the dear old Oriental.

If there's more news of James and Alix, I'll send word.

yours with love,
Lytton

The Astors' house is in the corner opposite the London Library – the one with an immense cornice – do you remember?

‡

To Carrington

Carrington had volunteered to go to Vienna to help James nurse Alix. They had for a moment thought of sending for her mother, 'old Madam'. Leslie Chaundy & Co. were booksellers in Oxford from 1910 to 1936. Taviton Street is in Bloomsbury, and was home to many booksellers. Carrington had played the practical joke on Clive. She thought a review of Clive's in the New Republic *had been unfair to Shaw; so Ralph typed a letter and she forged GBS's signature: 'Dear Clive Bell, Thank you for the numerous compliments you have paid me in this week's New Republic. I am sorry I cannot return the compliment that I think you or your prose, "Perfectly respectable" . . . You do not, it would appear, lead a very enviable aesthetic life; to me it seems dull. Yours, Bernard Shaw.' Clive was taken in, and replied to Shaw.*

The Mill House
Tidmarsh
Pangbourne
Friday evening, February 24th 1922

My dear, here I am back again, very glad to be installed among these comforts and quietudes once more, but rather sad at being so solitary! Pippa hopes to come down tomorrow, which will be pleasant if it occurs. All seems quite satisfactory here. Annie beaming and really very pretty – no animals dead (or so she declares), enormous fires burning, quantities of food, etc. etc. It is fearful to think of you whizzing through Central Europe at this moment. I hope the journey goes off all right. A 'smooth channel' I saw announced at the Oriental – so far so good!

A letter arrived from James (dated Tuesday) this morning. It was rather depressed, but had no definitely bad news. The 'Mrs Florence' enigma is now elucidated. It seems that for a moment they thought of sending for old Madam, and then refrained. She appeared at 51 this morning en route for Cambridge – just as usual. Her 'demonstration-lecture' had gone off brilliantly at Oxford. She gave an exhibition of how to do frescoes before the audience's eyes, and when she applied some green ('the fashionable colour' she said) there was a round of applause.

I am feeling anxious and tired, but I am sure it was best for you to go, and that your arrival will be of the greatest comfort to James. I only hope the horrors of the journey won't have been too great. A slightly alarming detail is that James says the trains are only to go every other day – so that you may get held up somewhere for a whole day; but I hope this hasn't come into force yet, or that if it has, you will have hit on the right day.

I wonder what's happened to the champagne!

I looked in on Leslie Chaundy's shop today, and found them in a state of excitement, having just bought an old gent's library, which contained all sorts of treasures. They will evidently make thousands out of it – Newtons, Plutarchs, and Folio Shakespeares strewed the ground. An amusing existence, I think. That is to say, if one *does* buy old gent's libraries, instead of going into a Taviton trance.

I shall run out and post this now, so that it may catch the morning post. It is wonderfully warm here, and James says the weather has begun to improve in Vienna, which is fortunate. Very much love to you and to him and Alix

your own
Lytton

Virginia writes to say 'I think you *must* now tell Clive the truth. It is evidently making him the laughing-stock of London, and his accounts get wilder and wilder. I'm not sure (ahem! ahem!) he didn't say he was going to write to Shaw again. He says he's shown the letter to several good judges, who all agree that Shaw has been driven mad by Clive,' etc. Doosid awkward!

‡

To Carrington

'Rothensteins': Sir Willam (1872–1945) was a Slade painter, and at the time of writing principal of the Royal College of Art; his son (Sir) John (1901–92) became director of the Tate Gallery and married into a family from Lexington, Kentucky. Lewis Vernon Harcourt (1863–1922) held the Cabinet office of Secretary of State for the Colonies during 1910–15. Educated at Eton, 'Lulu' Harcourt never knew his mother, Thérèse Lister, who died in 1863, and was the first wife of his distinguished father. Sir William Harcourt, an Apostle, was Home Secretary 1880–85, at which time Lewis acted as his Private Secretary. He was Liberal MP for Rossendale, Lancashire, 1904–16, Baron Nuneham of Nuneham Courtenay, Oxon, and was created the first Viscount Harcourt, of Stanton Harcourt, Oxon, on 3 January 1917. He had married in 1899 Mary Ethel Burns, daughter of Walter Hayes Burns, of New York and North Mymms Park, Hertfordshire. They had one son, William, and three daughters. His diaries record being told in a deathbed confession by a chaplain to Queen Victoria that the clergyman had married the Queen and her servant John Brown. The circumstances of his death on February 24th were suspicious, and the coroner recorded a verdict of 'death by misadventure'.

Augustine Birrell (1850–1933), Frankie's father, was Chief Secretary for Ireland, 1907–16. (Beatrice) Venetia Stanley (1887–1948) was the youngest child of Lord Sheffield, confidante of H. H. Asquith (he wrote to her very intimately, as though to a mistress).

A 'raree-show' was a street show, a public exhibition.

By the next year Carrington had developed a passion for Henrietta Bingham, the bisexual beauty from the Louisville, Kentucky family who owned the Courier-Journal *newspaper. Her father, Judge Robert Bingham, became US Ambassador in London. To Gerald Brenan, Carrington wrote that she had 'the face of a Giotto Madonna' and that her accomplishments included singing 'exquisite songs with a mandoline' and mixing 'such wonderful cocktails'.*

Oriental Club
Hanover Square, W.1
March 1st 1922

Your postcard from Nuremberg has arrived, also your wire from Vienna. Various letters and wires from James are reassuring, but clearly it will be a long business. I'm afraid your journey must have been rather tiresome, with that hard unexpected wait. What wretches not to give warning in England! Also, James says that the weather has now become 'tropical', so perhaps you will go about groaning in your furs. I long to hear what happened about the champagne. Perhaps a letter will come tomorrow. Another of the disadvantages of the train stoppage is the infrequency of your posts.

Life here has been proceeding in its usual style of utter dullness punctuated by hectic frenzies. One of the latter occurred last night – a very absurd party at Lady Astor's 'to meet Mr Balfour' – a huge rout – 800 extremely mixed guests – Duchesses, Rothensteins, Prime Ministers, Stracheys (male and female) – never did you see such a sight! As it was pouring cats and dogs, the scene of jostling taxis and motors in St James's Square was terrific – it was practically full up – no one would get out it was so wet – for hours we sat ticking and cursing – occasionally edging an inch or two nearer the portals of bliss. To add to the confusion, various streams entered the Square by the side streets, and mingled with the queues. However the police and the good nature of the English lower classes saved the situation. If such a thing had happened in Paris it would have been simply Pandemonium. As it was it was merely a great bore. The P.M. was leaving as we entered. Horror of horrors! The Rt. Hon Gentleman did *not recognise* Lytton Strachey! – though he bowed very politely – as also did Mrs Lloyd George – an unparalleled frump. Mr Balfour was very complimentary behind large demi-ghostly spectacles. And we meet again on the Friday. For the faithful Maud has asked me to dinner then 'to meet Mr Balfour'. The poor man must be getting rather tired, I should say.

I've seen Maynard and Clive – the latter said nothing about Mr Shaw, nor about an anonymous communication which I have reason to believe he received yesterday. A very odd communication indeed – in verse, and in a feigned handwriting, and apparently indicating that some mistake had been made, about Mr Shaw too, and then the first letters of the lines read downwards spelt – 'Sidney Turner'! *Very* odd! Perhaps some more about this will transpire later on. Maynard, wrapped in towels, discovered the demise of Lulu Harcourt – the darkest rumours are afloat on that subject. A harridan whose lovely son he leapt into bed with at Eton has been going about denouncing the poor old creature. So they say he took poison. But I say (and Maynard agrees) that it's absurd. Why such a drastic step, when a déménagement and a Venetian Palazzo would easily have met the case? But certain it is that the scandals have been unbridled. One day a good gentleman called on him, when he was at the Colonial Office, and threatened to denounce him for having . . . leapt into bed, etc. etc. Lulu asked if it would make any difference if a Colonial Governorship was offered him? The good gentleman replied 'Hum! I'll take two days to think it over.' And in two days returned and said 'Yes, I'll accept the Governorship on one condition – that all my official correspondence is completely through the *Under*secretary.' Thus his conscience was salved! This story comes via Frankie, via old Birrell, via Venetia, so I should think was entirely false. But you see what delightful topics absorb the conversation. I forgot to ask Mr Balfour what *he* thought of it. But perhaps on Friday . . .

I had lunch with Bunny, and do you know they *are* moving their shop – to a street off Conduit Street. I don't see how they can possibly survive such a thing. They seem to me, partner and all, to live in a complete mist. A twelve years lease! I've forgotten how many hundred pounds. A faint effort was made to make me subscribe 150 – but I was not rising, oddly enough.

Margot, you'll be glad to hear (this reaches me from Maynard, via the Old Man) is having, far from a failure, a roaring success in America. She shrieks, whistles, dances, and is in fact a regular raree show, which delights vast audiences, and brings her in an average of £550 a night. It is supposed, however, that she will return no richer than when she went. There are apparently so many things to buy in America.

I can't think of any other London news at this moment – except that Lytton Strachey is 42 today. Hoots, toots!

I must go to bed now. I wonder how you are getting on. I hope it is not too dismal. I think of you both a great deal. How I wish we were all at Tidmarsh again, saying goodnight!

Tuesday. Your postcard from Vienna arrived this morning, also a letter from James. It is a great mercy to hear that Alix's condition continues slightly to improve. How extraordinary about the champagne-jelly confusion! And how wonderful that the grapes were such a success. I'm afraid James must be a good deal worn out, but he is delighted that you've arrived. What are you going to do about the future? Perhaps, you, madam, will stay a little longer, and you, sir, come back in a short time. But I shall no doubt hear the arrangements before long.

I've been an idiot, and delayed the posting of this till too late. It ought to have gone off last night, and now it will have to wait till Saturday morning. What a bother! Well, I shall send it off tonight. It may catch some unknown train, and whirl along somehow.

I am going down to Tidmarsh for the week-end (i.e. on Saturday) returning here on Monday.

Lunch today with La Bingham, and tea with Hilda. Oh, *thrilling*!

I send you both my fondest love.   your

Lytton

‡

To James Strachey

Lytton's prejudice against Joyce's novel is hard to understand. Virginia, though she and Leonard had wanted to publish it four years earlier, was now repelled by it, as she was to indicate to Lytton in her letter of 24 August, where she writes that she will contribute to the Eliot fund on condition that Eliot (who had brought the book to her attention) 'puts publicly to their proper use the first 200 pages of Ulysses. Never did I read such tosh. As for the first two chapters we will let them pass, but the 3rd 4th 5th 6th — merely the scratching of pimples on the body of the bootboy at Claridges. Of course genius may blaze out on page 652 but I have my doubts.' It is difficult to believe that Lytton was put off reading the book because Virginia found it vulgar and common.

The Mill House
Tidmarsh
Pangbourne
Monday, May 7th 1922

It was a great relief to get the news that the operation had been indefinitely postponed, because of unexpected improvement. I hope this continues and that by now the corner has been turned, and real convalescence is beginning. If this is so, you will perhaps find it possible to think of future plans. Pippa said you still thought of Italy – and I don't see why it should be too hot then in some high region. *[. . .]* I thought of going to Venice about the middle of June. Sebastian says he will meet me there about June 22nd *[. . .]*

All is well here. A little warmth has at last crept into the world, but so far only a little. It is possible to sit out in the garden, but sneezing and in furs. We have been cheated of our motor which was ordered for May 1st and hasn't yet appeared. Whether it will prove a curse or a blessing remains dubious. Wealth continues to flow in, in enormous cheques, but as I feel bound to invest practically everything, one doesn't see much of the colour of one's money, though, to be sure, a feeling of precarious opulence does float about. 'Books and Characters' is now advertised to appear on the 18th – why this delay I don't know. My idleness continues to be devastating – but it seems to be sheer inability as much as anything else. I hope some day it will end. My only serious occupation is the reading of Proust, and that I do find a pretty strenuous business. As for Ulysses, I *will not* look at it – *no, no*. Did the witch book reach you? I thought it rather interesting. Pippa gave me some very mouth-watering accounts of Viennese musik.

your
Lytton

‡

To Carrington

Evelyn John Strachey (1901–63), the future Labour politician and minister for food, had gone to Vienna in late March with John Rothenstein and Eddy Sackville-West.

51, Gordon Square
Thursday evening, May 16th 1922

[. . .] Wandering afterwards *[in Oxford]*, I met John Strachey on a
bicycle. He said he'd been to Vienna and seen James. Vienna, he said,
was 'entirely homosexual', no women in the streets – only painted
young men – 'Oh, entirely homosexual?' – 'Did that suit *you*?' I
couldn't help asking . . . 'No – no – as a matter of fact, that sort of thing
doesn't.' 'Ah! Goodbye, then, my dear fellow' – ! *[. . .]*

‡

To Sebastian Sprott

*W. J. H. 'Sebastian' Sprott was reading moral sciences at Clare College, and
was now sitting the tripos. He had had an affair with Maynard in 1920 and
1921.*

*Molly MacCarthy started the Memoir Club in 1920 (based loosely on the
Novel Club she had founded during the war, which was designed to force
Desmond to write his ever-anticipated book), in Desmond's study at Wellington
Square. It lasted until the mid-1950s. The original members were Desmond,
Molly, Roger Fry, Vanessa, Duncan, Leonard and Virginia Woolf, Mary
Hutchinson, Clive Bell, Sydney Waterlow and Maynard.[1] E. M. Forster and
Lytton joined later. 'Janus diagnosis': Robert Skidelsky suggests this reading –
i.e. facing both ways; a reference to Keynes being bisexual.*

Lady Hester Stanhope and Mr Creevey were the final two essays in Books
and Characters, *published the month before.*

*He signs himself 'your J.C.' because he has to be absent from Sebastian's
Last Supper in college.*

The Mill House
Tidmarsh
Pangbourne
June 6th 1922

It was charming to get your letter, and I am very glad your torments are
over. But you must have a mind of iron – to be able to read Proust
during an examination! Worse than a tripos it seems to me in itself. I
mean as far as required concentration goes, for I do admire it greatly.
I'm afraid I shan't after all be able to come to Cambridge for the week-

end, and I am writing to Maynard to that effect. It seems absurd, but I am hag-ridden by a dreadful thing I promised to write for an affair called the Memoir Club (very private), and I don't see how I can do it in time unless I sit solidly with pen and paper. Oh dear, how I loathe the process of writing! So you see the central figure will be absent from the Last Supper. But I imagine you will be at the next Dinner instead, and that in that case we might talk a little then – about the Venice arrangements, etc. My notion was to go there as swiftly as possible in a train with beds and all complete. Would you perhaps be able to start at 8 o'clock in the evening of the 20th? This I think would make a cooler journey. Otherwise the following morning. I too am looking forward to it very much, and I hope fortune will accompany us. Our fate *in* Venice is rather dubious. There's a chance of rooms on the Giudecca (d'you know what that is?) – or if that's impossible, we shall have to sink into a hotel. The best of it is that we shall have a gondola (with a grand though not romantic gondolier) at our disposal all day and night. The chief drawbacks will be mosquitoes (to some extent) and Fascisti (heaven knows to what extent). It will also be decidedly hot, but I hope you won't dislike that. Bed in the middle of the day circumvents the disagreeable part of it. I might have to go a little before the 12th July to meet James and Alix somewhere – but that is all rather vague at present.

Maynard is rather mysterious. I've only talked to him vaguely (and not very lately) about his states of mind, but I didn't at all gather that he liked you less. I think that your Janus diagnosis is the right one, and that his field of consciousness *is* rétréci *[shrunken]* – one of the main horrors, it seems to me, of l'amour, or whatever you like to call it. The Lord deliver us from all dispensations!

I think I agree with you that those essays on Lady Hester and Mr Creevey are better than the others – for one thing, they're short, which is the great merit to my mind. Also, the point of view is more definite. The result of age, I presume! As for youth, it has other advantages . . .
[. . .]

With love

from

your

J.C.

1. See the account in Hugh and Mirabel Cecil, *Clever Hearts*, p. 201ff.

‡

To Ralph Partridge

Ralph was having an affair with Valentine Dobrée. Carrington accepted this, which made her feel free to write again to Gerald Brenan – who then spent the last two weeks of May at Tidmarsh with her. But Valentine told Ralph about Carrington and Gerald, and he had a drink-fuelled scene with Carrington.

Tidmarsh

4 o'clock, Monday, *[June 19th 1922]*

My dear one, I think it *is* all cleared up now. I conveyed to her what you had gathered from Gerald. She denied nothing. It seemed useless as well as painful to probe into details, or ask questions, but it was clear that in everything important the facts were as you told me this morning. I think I was able to make her realise your feelings and point of view. Of course she was, and is, terribly upset. She said that you were essential to her – that Gerald was not at all – that this crisis had made her realise more than ever before the strength of her love for you. I explained your dread of a scene, reconciliations, etc., and said you wanted to sleep in the yellow room. She quite understood. I am sure that she does love you deeply. Be as gentle with her as you can when you come.

We must try now to forget all those horrid details and trust to the force of our fundamental affections to carry us through. At any rate, we know where we are now, which is a great thing.

Poor Gerald goes off in a few minutes. I must say he seemed to me very charming! I am very *sorry* for him. He has injured himself very badly, and his life at the best of times was not a particularly pleasant one.

As for me, my dear, I can't say how happy your decision to try going on here has made me. I suppose I *could* face life without you, just as I *could* face life with one of my hands cut off, but it would have been a dreadful blow. What you said to me this morning made me so proud – but really it is futile and quite unnecessary for us to expatiate on these things in letters!

I'm afraid *this* letter is jerky one. We'll fill up the details when we meet. My nerves are rather on the jump, and I am longing for your presence – the best restorative I know of!

I sympathise with you so absolutely, so completely, my dear, dear love. Sometimes I feel as if I *was* inside you! Why can't I make you perfectly happy by waving some magic wand?

Keep this letter to yourself.

I didn't mention to Carrington that Valentine was at Hogarth last night. It seemed a slight deception, but I thought Valentine would prefer it.

> Always your own
> Lytton.

I wanted to say, dear – of course you know the little car belongs to you

‡

To Ralph Partridge

> Casa Frollo
> Juidecca
> Venezia
> Saturday, June 24th 1922

My very dear one

Just a word or two with my best love and a little news. This seems a tolerable spot, with only one drawback – the typical Venetian one – i.e. Noise. An ice factory, if you please, is next door, and naturally chooses the hour of 3 am for its most agitating operations – sounds of terrific collapses and crashes shake the earth, and I wake in terror of my life. Otherwise there's very little to complain of. The rooms are large and bare – and as for the petit déjeuner, with new laid eggs and honey complete, it is a dream. Francesco carries one to the Piazzetta in about 10 minutes, according to wind and obstacles. He is exactly the same as ever. It was luck being able to have him. According to Mrs Blaydon, a few weeks after we went away last summer a new rule was made by which no one was allowed to hire a gondolier for more than a day at a time – except old clients – under which heading I mercifully come! Apparently Berenson last July tried to take Francesco as I did, with the result that a mob of enraged gondoliers collected, booing and shouting, and he was nearly torn limb from limb. But *I* was at once recognised, and no mob assailed me. She says the rule was made by the degraded gondoliers, who found they were losing all their custom. It seems to me next year they'll do away with the blessed privileges of 'old clients' as well. The pigs.

The weather has been rather queer – several thunderstorms – but now a strong East wind blows, which I should think was a good sign. Sebastian enjoys everything very much, and keeps up a constant chatter of a mild kind, which just suits me at the present moment. I can't say he looks ultra respectable, with a collarless shirt, very décolleté, and the number of glad eyes he receives is alarming. However so far his behaviour has been all that could be desired.

This afternoon I am going to tea with the Johnstons – the American friends of la Colefax. I should think it would be a bore. On Monday we go to a performance at the Fenice. We usually spend our mornings inspecting objects of art, our afternoons in siestas, and our evenings adrift.

I constantly think of you. I am now (unless something fresh comes from James) in favour of returning to England direct. I should really like that best. I hope your courage is carrying you along. All my love to you both

your own
Lytton

‡

To James Strachey

Casa Frollo
July 2nd 1922

A hurried note to ask whether you could write a short letter of introduction to Prof. Freud for Sebastian (Sprott) who is going to Vienna to ask him to come and lecture in Cambridge. If you could just say that he was a friend of mine and a student of psychology at Cambridge, it would be enough. Sebastian does not know his address – so you might add that, and send it to him at the Wien poste restante. *[. . .]*

your
Lytton

☩

To Sebastian Sprott

'The sinister sister' must refer to Minna Bernays, the sister of Freud's wife Martha. Minna never married and lived with Martha and Freud for more than thirty years. Carl Jung claimed in an interview after Freud's death in 1939 that Freud and Minna had had a long-term affair. It is evident from this letter that rumours about their relationship had been current for a long time before Jung made his still unsubstantiated allegation.

Near Hereford
August 16th 1922

Dearest Sebastian, it was a great pleasure to get your letter. I had almost begun to doubt the existence of the exterior world. Since the beginning of the month I have been submerged – in a 'motor tour' – too terrible! It has consistently poured and poured, and the temperature has never risen above zero. We have passed (the Partridges and self) through most of Southern and Western England, dripping and shivering, putting up at ruinous and horrible hotels, hoping – hoping – despairing – and then at last, yesterday, a perfectly beautiful day – blazing sun, etc., etc. Off we went beaming like Cheshire cats, when – the car broke down. It is now in a garage in Hereford (a wretched town) being mended – it may take a day or two days or a week, and here we are, and of course today the weather has collapsed again – so . . . it is really too desolating, and the worst of it is that Tidmarsh is let till September, so that we are forced to wander, shivering and dripping, over the face of the earth till then. Hélas!

In September (happy month!) will you come and see us? I hope so. Your account of Freud was very interesting. I had not heard of the sinister sister before. I suppose the condition of affairs in Austria may account for *some* of his bitterness, though no doubt not all. His compliments were gratefully received.

Your adventures in Berlin sound most alarming. How you could have ventured –! – Well, well!

[. . .] I feel old and shattered; and when I die 'the weather' will be found written on my heart. *[. . .]*

Je t'aime beaucoup. Your
Lytton

‡

To Virginia Woolf

The earlier published version of this letter contains a misreading in the
antepenultimate sentence, where it gives 'may' for 'wag'.

c/o Mrs. Edwards
Solva
Pembrokeshire
August 22nd 1922

I think of moving through Sussex early in September. Would it be
possible for you to house me from (approx.) the 8th (Friday) to the
11th? I suggest going to Charleston from (approx.) the 5th to the 8th,
and have written to Clive to that effect, adding that if it was more
convenient I might invert the order – or come later, if necessary, but
that would not be so easy.

    I am almost completely shattered – simply by the weather. Otherwise
(apart from fiendish expense and the vileness of hotels) all goes well.
This place is in the region of Manorbier – near St Davids, if you know
where that is, and I believe very pretty, but the snow and sleet have
prevented my seeing much of it. The ice carnival takes place this
afternoon, and we shall all look charming in our furs, cutting figures of
eight. Did you know that the Atlantic is often quite frozen over up
here? The seals look so funny, sprawling about among the glaciers, poor
things – and then you should see the cormorants breaking the ice with
their long thin bills and pulling out the jelly-fish – so cleverly!

    Have you any news? The prospectus of the 'Criterion' reached me in
these fastnesses the other day, and I was glad to see that the world was
still wagging. But *I* wag no longer. I am stiff – frozen stiff – a rigid
icicle. I hang at this address for another week, and then slowly melt
southwards and eastwards – a weeping relic of what was once your old
friend

[Not signed]

‡

To Virginia Woolf

The previously published version omits the whole of the second paragraph, as it does all the rude remarks about Ottoline in the next paragraph, and the name of Shanks, 'X' in Leonard and James's editing.

Walter James Turner (1884–1946), critic and poet, was born and educated in Australia and moved to London in 1907. Included in Eddie Marsh's Georgian Poetry *for 1916–17, he refused to be included in the 1922 sequel He was at the same time theatre critic of the* London Mercury, *literary editor of the* Daily Herald *and music critic of the* New Statesman. *Writing about him to Sebastian Sprott two days earlier, Lytton remarked that Turner's wife was Jewish – a fact he omits in this letter. Edward Shanks (1892–1953), poet, novelist and critic, was assistant editor of the* London Mercury *from 1919 to 1922.*

Tidmarsh
September 19th 1922

I totally forgot to leave a pourboire for the admirable Lottie. Will you therefore kindly press the enclosed piece of paper into her palm for me, with appropriate speeches? She really *is* very obliging.

There have been various conversations on the Hogarth question – with rather indeterminate results. I think the poor creature is really anxious to continue, but foresees difficulties. He is already brushing up his energies! On the whole I gather that he thinks less printing and more business might be a solution. Perhaps if some department of the business could be handed over in toto to him he would fling himself into it with more zest. But this is only a vague suggestion, so please don't draw conclusions from it. I suppose he will write himself before long. The distance-from-London question is a very trying one.

My week-end at Garsington was not very stimulating. Mr. and Mrs. W. J. Turner were the only other guests. He said he had met you – admires you very much, etc. etc. – a very small bird-like man with a desolating accent, a good deal to say for himself – but punctuated by strange hesitations – impediments – rather distressing; but really a nice little fellow, when one has got over the way in which he says 'count'. Ott. was dreadfully dégringolée – her bladder has now gone the way of her wits – a melancholy dribble; and then, as she sits after dinner in the lamplight, her cheek-pouches drooping with peppermints, a cigarette between her false teeth, and vast spectacles on her painted nose, the effect produced is extremely agitating. I found I wanted to howl like an Irish wolf – but perhaps the result produced in you was different.

Your visit, I gather, had been the greatest success, and you were the only person mentioned without some virulent acidity.

The Turner man told me that Shanks was completely changed by a little alcohol, which makes him 'a different being' – he flows, beams, etc. A pity we didn't know this – we might have had an uproarious evening.

I wish I saw you both more often.

ever your
Lytton

‡

To T. S. Eliot

The Mill House
Tidmarsh
Pangbourne
October 6th 1922

Dear Eliot,

I hope my non-answering has not annoyed you. I have been away in Berlin, and only found your letter on my return the day before yesterday.

It was nice of you to ask me – and I shall like very much to write for the Criterion; but I am afraid really I am hopeless. I have other things to do, and until they are done it will be impossible for me to stray about – and I foresee very clearly that they won't be done for ages. Also, even when they are done (if ever) I don't feel that I could guarantee the production of 5000 or fewer brilliant words. So it seems to me that you must not announce me as a contributor. I am sorry. If only my make-up were of a different sort you would be inundated by contributions.

I am looking forward with great excitement to the Criterion's appearance, and send my very best wishes for its success.

Yours ever
Lytton Strachey

[Houghton Library, Harvard]

✝

To Virginia Woolf

The Mill House
Tidmarsh
Pangbourne
October 9th 1922

I finished Jacob last night. A most wonderful achievement – more like poetry, it seems to me, than anything else, and as such I prophesy immortal. The technique of the narrative is astonishing – how you manage to leave out everything that's dreary, and yet retain enough string for your pearls I can hardly understand. I occasionally almost screamed with joy at the writing. Of course you're very romantic – which alarms me slightly – I am such a Bonamy. Once or twice I thought you were in danger of becoming George-Meredithian in style – or was that a delusion? Something of the sort certainly seems to me *the* danger for your genre. But so far you're safe. You're a romantic in Sirius, I fancy – which after all is a good way off from Box Hill. The impression left on one as a whole is glorious. And then as one remembers detail after detail – the pier at Scarborough, the rooks and the dinner-bell, the clergyman's wife on the moors, St Paul's, the British Museum at night, the Parthenon – one's head whirls round and round. Jacob himself I think is very successful – in a most remarkable and original way. Of course I see something of Thoby in him, as I suppose was intended.

It's not much good writing – we must talk soon. By a sickening mischance I went and engaged myself for Wednesday – will you tell Leonard? – to some old cats here. If Thursday or Friday would suit him they'ld do for me perfectly – he can tell Ralph. If Wednesday is for him the only day, I'll come then and cut the cats.

your loving
Lytton

A horrid misprint page 190 – Dick for Nick. Then also Dick Graves, as well as Dick Bonamy – rather a plethora perhaps.

✝

To Sebastian Sprott

In a letter written on 22 September, Lytton had told 'dearest Seb' that he was 'going to rush off to Berlin on Tuesday next for the inside of a week. James will be there for a psycho-analytic "Congress" – and the opportunity of having his guidance and company seems too good to be missed. If you can think of anything particular that you recommend . . . night-clubs or what not.' 'One's astounding wealth' was owing to the weakness of the German currency. There were several 'dancing palaces' in Berlin, though the most famous, in Delphi Terraces, wasn't constructed until the late 1920s.

The Mill House
Tidmarsh
Pangbourne
October 29th 1922

Très-cher,

I have been lazy, I fear about writing – but that has now become my melancholy habit. I enjoyed Berlin very much indeed, partly because of one's astounding wealth – but it also seemed to me by nature a simpatico place. Never have I been treated so politely by the Prussians! Unfortunately it was impossible, at the last minute, to go to the Dancing Palace, but we did go to tea in the Nurnbergstrasse, with much amusement – I'll tell you the details when we meet. *[. . .]*

I met Mr Walter De La Mare t'other day for the first time, and he mentioned you with affection. I thought him a nice man, and even intelligent, but only talked to him for three minutes and a half. Do you know him well? Or what? *[. . .]*

As to Proust, I am told that the girls at Balbec are merely boys – in rather short petticoats; which, on reflection, appears to be true. I thought at the time that they were very queer girls indeed – so I suppose that's the explanation. But it rather mixes things up.

I can hardly believe in any Americans.

your affectionate
Lytton

‡

To Carrington

Lady Wemyss (née the Hon. Grace Blackburn, d.1946) married the 10th Earl of Wemyss in 1900. She was one of the 'Souls'. Men Like Gods (1923) is by H.G. Wells. Churchill's book was the first volume (of six) of The World Crisis.

Oriental Club
Hanover Square, W.1
January 15th 1923

I was very glad to get your letter yesterday. The exhaustion is becoming very great, and I doubt whether I shall live through the next 12 hours. Last night was pretty hectic. First dinner chez La Wemyss – Rudyard K*[ipling]* the chief guest – also Evan Charteris, Maurice Baring, and Lady Desborough. Then such a party at Sassoon's. You never saw the like. Winston was there, and I talked to him a great deal. Do you know, in spite of everything, I couldn't help liking him? H.G. says very much the same thing in 'Men Like Gods' – one somehow *can't* dislike the poor creature. He was delighted when I said that I thought his book very well done, and hardly seemed to mind when I added that I also thought it very wicked. There were moments when the violent vulgarity of the party reached such a pitch that I very nearly rushed shrieking from the house. It appeared to be extremely distinguished, but Melba (in spite of promises) did *not* perform. Tonight is the dinner, and the preparations for speech weight me down to the ground. Now I go off to lunch at the Colefax's. I was interested by your account of Ramsey.

yours with much love
Lytton

Till tomorrow morning!

‡

To Mary Hutchinson

Andrew Marvell (1621–78): 'Had we but world enough, and time, This coyness, lady, were no crime' and from 'Thoughts in a Garden' – 'Meanwhile the mind from pleasure less / Withdraws into its happiness; / The mind, that ocean where each kind / Does straight its own resemblance find; / Yet it creates, transcending these, / Far other worlds, and other seas; / Annihilating all that 's made / To a green thought in a green shade.' 'My Garden' is by Thomas Edward Brown (1830–97).

The Duchess of Marlborough was formerly Gladys Deacon, of Boston. She married the 9th Duke in 1920, and later became a reclusive eccentric.

The Mill House
Tidmarsh
Pangbourne
July 11th 1923

Ma chère

[. . .] Your letter was charming and amusing. I'm very glad you liked the Marvell. I sometimes wonder whether there's a better poet. Is the Coy Mistress or the 'green thought in a green shade' his best? A propos of the latter, have you ever read a shocking thing by J. E. Brown, beginning 'A garden is a lovesome thing, God wot'? Do, if you want to plumb the depths between the 19th and 17th centuries.

I've been spending the week-end at Blenheim – a large and variegated party. But nobody was particularly interesting (except, perhaps, the Duchess) – it was the house which was entrancing, and life-enhancing. I wish it were mine. It is enormous, but one would not feel it too big. The grounds are beautiful too, and there is a bridge over a lake which positively gives an erection. Most of the guests played tennis all day and bridge all night, so that (apart from the eating and drinking) they might just as well have been at Putney. *[. . .]*

‡

To Virginia Woolf

This was omitted from James and Leonard's edition, presumably because it is trivial – though other letters dealing merely with practical arrangements were included.

The Mill House
Tidmarsh
Pangbourne
July 20th 1923

I wonder if you could by any chance come down on Monday next, and stay the night? G. Rylands will be here. If Leonard could come too, so much the better, but I fear he may not be able to leave the Nation. I gather that you are dining with Clive on Tuesday.

Do come if you can. It will be the last chance before Winter comes upon us. You will find a charming kitten – one might say two.

your
Lytton

‡

To Carrington

Gide himself had invited Lytton to the annual Entretiens d'été at the Abbey of Pontigny, with its associations with Thomas à Becket. This ten-day international talking-shop consisted of 'eminent thinkers from several countries' and Lytton was assured by Gide of meeting 'several friends who have a lively desire to make your acquaintance'.

Abbaye de Pontigny
Yonne
Sunday morning, August 26th 1923

[. . .] I'm getting on fairly well here. My health has practically re-established itself. The food is very suitable – light and good, though the absence of an egg at breakfast is slightly crushing. Also, in my beautiful monk's bedroom there is no looking-glass and no chamber-pot. And the sanitary arrangements altogether are *not* all that could be desired. I fear I don't make much headway with the actual frogs. Except perhaps with one – a young author, thought very highly of – I think rich and upper-class – but unfortunately a frog in face and figure as well as otherwise. He seems to have some glimmering of what I mean, and positively laughs when I make a little joke. A pathetic intellectual young man. There is also a Swiss, rather like a brisk Dog, if you can imagine such a thing, who is also trying to be a doctor – rather pretty. And young Mr. Blaise Dejardins – largish, pale, unhealthy, who sings very well – but apparently particularly dislikes me, hélas! Then I have made friends with the black-haired American young lady, who turns out to be an artist, and who has already forced me to sit to her. Gide is hopelessly unapproachable. He gave a reading last night of one of his own works – in a most extraordinary style – like a clergyman intoning in a pulpit. It was enormously admired. Jane is a great standby; and I am becoming gradually converted to the Hope woman, who is undoubtedly intelligent. The worst feature of the whole thing are the 'entretiens' which go on, if you please, from 2.30 to 4.30 – two solid hours, during the siesta periods, of gibberation on the subject of translation – and for ten days in succession. It is surely mania, and I can't see how it is to continue till next Sunday. Of course, in spite of all their assurances, they make constant efforts to force one to speak – hitherto unsuccessfully. How *can* I speak in French before 40 people about nothing at all? Fearful, fearful! However, I suppose it will pass off somehow, and if only Blaise were a little less severe I should be reconciled to my fate. As it is, I foresee that I shall drearily have to fall back upon the Frog Prince.

Your letters are the greatest comfort and joy to me. Please go on with them. I send you all my love. Don't be depressed. Now that the weather has taken this good turn, I think you ought to have plenty of painting, which ought to set you up. Give my love to Barbara.

your own
Lytton

To Virginia Woolf

Virginia had sent Lytton a postcard asking whether she ought to buy the new Nonesuch edition of Congreve, which was expensive at three guineas. All

William Congreve's (1670–1729) plays were written when he was a young man; his last was Squire Trelooby, *a collaboration with Vanbrugh (adapted from Molière's* Monsieur de Pourceaugnac). *The Congreve piece duly appeared in the* Nation, *and was collected, along with the piece he did finally write on Harington, in* Portraits in Miniature. *Sir John Harington (1560–1612) appealed to Lytton especially for his sudden inspiration that led him to invent the flushing water-closet, which he discussed in his book* The Metamorphosis of Ajax, *'a crowningly deplorable pun' – viz., 'of a jakes'. 'Queen Elizabeth was amused,' Lytton wrote, but then, she was Sir John's godmother.*

The Mill House
Tidmarsh
Pangbourne
October 6th 1923

I think for ordinary purposes there's no point in getting the new Congreve. The new material is really quite unimportant. Squire Trelooby is nothing – otherwise there were three or four jokes, which were cut out of the comedies afer the first editions. Also, Mr Montague Summers is extremely trying and much too much in evidence. The Mermaid Edition, though, has one rather annoying blemish – it divides up the acts – heaven knows why – into tiresome scenes, which detract (unless one realises that they're really non-existent) from the sense of unity and continuity. An early 18th century edition would be all right; and I think Mr George Street's two volume edition of the Comedies is quite satisfactory – though to be sure it seems a pity not to have that clever piece the Mourning Bride.

I hope to send Leonard my Nation lucubrations on the subject in two days. They cannot by any stretch come under the heading of 'a study of past characters', I'm afraid; so I shall do one of those – perhaps to some extent on Bentley – for October 28th. I had got one all ready on Sir John Harington – a very amusing person – but the appearance of Raleigh's collected essays with one on him has ruined me. If it had only come out a fortnight later I should have been saved.

Won't you come and examine the Nonesuch Congreve for several days?

your
Lytton

‡

To Carrington

Lytton's confidence that no other potential buyers would discover Ham Spray in midwinter was because then, as now, it can only be reached by an unpromising dirt road that runs past farm buildings.

The Mill House
Tidmarsh
Pangbourne
Friday, December 21st 1923

You escaped in time. The cold has come – the snow falls – 'seasonable weather', in fact. According to the Times the channel boats yesterday were completely covered in snow. I hope by now you're at Granada, and that the sun shines. I was very glad to get your Paris letters. No news here. A letter from Thake and P. to say that 'we have seen our client in regard to Capt. (!) Partridge's offer and beg to inform you that it has not been declined. On the other hand the owner has not yet given an acceptance, but has promised to let us have his definite decision before the end of the month.' Slightly alarming, but there don't seem anything to be done. I can't believe any explorer will reach Ham Spray in this weather. Also, all the stocks and shares have crashed – appalling! But it will affect other buyers as well as us. I suppose I shall hear in a week.

Alec Penrose spent two nights. It's a great pity that with his rat-bitten face, green hair and blue lips he's almost indistinguishable from one of the bathers in Henry's picture. Apart from that he has his points – a very definite character – a complete womaniser – adventurer, etc. etc. But egoism reigns. However, I like him, though it may be an odd taste.

O*[liver]* and I*[nez]* are expected this evening for dinner, and they will *both* stay till Thursday next. Dear, dear! – I suppose by the time this reaches you (heaven knows when it will be) you will hardly be able to believe in the existence of Tidmarsh. But still, there it is – books, cats, and lamps complete. I am longing to hear of your post-Parisian adventures. What a mercy that you were forced to take supplements! But I shudder at the thought of Madrid.

A letter came from Alix – about jugs, which I don't forward. Nothing else.

How is Gerald? Give him my love.

Two pretty books arrived from Italy yesterday. No other events that I can think of. Oh, the snow! the snow! Darkness falls. And the handle of the front door has completely collapsed, so that we have to take to the bolts, till they make a new one. Just like it. My fondest love to you both.

your own
Lytton

One of Alec's good traits is his gourmandising. He loved the ham, and adored the sherry!

‡

To Carrington

Lytton's next bid was to be one farthing short of £2200. Topsy Lucas was born Emily Jones. In Norman Douglas's travel book, Together, *published in 1923, his companion, referred to in the book as 'R', was a fifteen-year-old named René.*

The Mill House
Tidmarsh
Pangbourne
January 1st 1924

I've been waiting to hear something definite about Ham Spray before writing – nothing came till this morning, when a letter from Thakes appeared saying 'We regret that although we have done our utmost in this matter we have been unable to secure our client's acceptance. Unless Capt. Partridge is prepared to make an increased bid we are afraid nothing further can be done.' Not very encouraging! After some wobbling I have replied, offering £2100 – I enclose my letter. I hardly felt that I could sit doing nothing till your return, I think I shall rise up to £2199.19.11 3/4, and if they refuse that, let them wait. It has been very wearing – so little sleep at nights, in expectation of posts which brought nothing! However, so far the house is not sold to anyone else, which is something.

Oliver and the hag departed on Friday, Sebastian having arrived on

Thursday evening. I really think she is an unpleasant fishy (in every sense of the word) creature, and was glad to be rid of her, though of course she left the most revolting black semi-transparent object – possibly a dress – behind her. Sebastian was a great relief. He went off this morning – to Garsington, where he stays a night, and then goes on to stay with Braithwaite in Banbury. I sent Ott. a small book at Christmas, and received from her a most revolting little match box, together with a letter fairly falling on my neck. Really rather pathetic. But I cannot and will not go there – oh no, no! Sebastian told me all the latest developments of his various love-affairs. In the evenings, I read Racine to him out loud – most exhausting. Topsy and Peter came to tea – and yesterday Peter again, by himself, very dim and donnish. Sebastian's clothes have improved. He now wears a jersey (grey) and a collar open at the neck, which produces quite a romantic appearance. But the rings remain.

The letter describing the perfections of Yegen was very pleasant. Somehow or other, in spite of all the beauties and comforts, I do not wish to be there, except to be with you, and so I am not in the least envious, and can consider your enjoyment of it all with unmixed satisfaction! Old age, I suppose, but, for whatever reason, the solid calmness of Tidmarsh exactly suits me. The weather is curiously muggy, and of course it is nearly always dark as dark can be, Annie continues (so far as I can see) quite cheerful, and my only regret is the unfortunate penchant of Tabitha to piss in the exact middle of the beds, one after another. My beautiful counterpane has been sadly damaged in this way; and now every bedroom door has to be kept shut.

[. . .] As to getting things in Spain, I should think Almeria might be quite as good as Madrid in many ways, and no doubt cheaper – if they really will send things to England by sea. If you don't know about Ham Spray in time, it might be possible in Madrid to note articles of furniture (if any seemed suitable) to be sent, if you wrote for them from England. How maddening about the Moroccan skins! Shall we have to make a pilgrimage there after all?

I wish I had some entertaining gossip for you, but, except for Sebastian's fifth form adventures, there is nothing to tell. I hope your brilliant sunshine continues and that all goes well. Give Gerald my love. I should like to hear what he has to say about Norman Douglas. My convictions on that question (as on all contemporary writers) are not *very* strong.

An article for the Nation has to be written in a minute or two. Then, I think, another. Then . . . Paris? Hotel Lutétia is where I shall go to, in case of accidents. I notice that a letter takes just under a week to get here from Yegen.

All my love to both my darlings
from
Lytton

I don't enclose my letter to Thake after all – it's not very interesting.

‡

To James Strachey

Lytton sent James the enclosed draft letter to the editor of The Times, *which James altered considerably. Lytton paid the 2002 equivalent of £82,000 for Ham Spray House.*

The 'genius' conductor of the Vienna State Opera was probably Clemens Krauss (1893–1954), though Lytton might have meant Richard Strauss, who resigned as co-director of the Opera later this year and often conducted himself.

The Mill House
Tidmarsh
Pangbourne
January 4th 1924

I don't know whether this is the slightest use. Alter, of course, as much as you like. The difficulty of writing for other people is very great – besides all the rest. I think if A*[rthur]* B*[alfour]*, G.B.S*[haw]* and I signed it would do – no need for Vaughan W*[illiams]*. But somehow I think they'll jib.

your
Lytton

I believe I've bought Hamspray for £2,300 – but it still totters.

To the Editor of 'The Times'
Sir

All lovers of music in England must view with grave concern the attempt which is being made to put a stop to the proposed visit of the

Vienna State Opera Company to Covent Garden in the ensuing season. Whatever may be the motives for the attempt, they can have little to do either with art or common sense *[crossed out by James, and replaced with* public spirit; *James has also excised the following passage: How is it possible to draw a line between the Vienna Opera Company and any other foreign artists? What reasons can there be to justify the exclusion of the former which would not apply with equal force to the hundreds of other distinguished foreign musicians to whom we habitually extend our hospitality? And if Viennese flautists and trombones are to be kept out, why not Spanish dancers, French comedians, and American authors? On the other hand]* it is a delusion to suppose that such exclusions can do any good to British music. The opposite is the truth. The whole history of our cultural development as a nation is one of foreign influences successively welcomed, assimilated and reproduced in new and native forms. Music can be no exception to this rule. No art will flourish in a ring-fence.

In the present case, perhaps the public does not fully realize what it is in danger of losing. The Vienna State Opera is one of the great institutions of Europe. *[Excised by James: Its traditions go back uninterruptedly, through Mozart, through Pergolesi, to the days of Metastasio, in the]* consummate perfection of its technical accomplishment the very voice of civilization itself seems to be audible; and it happens at the present moment to be conducted by a man of genius. That English audiences should be deprived, owing to foolish sectional hostility, of this unique experience, would be certainly a very melancholy thing. In our opinion, it would not only be very melancholy but also very disgraceful.

We are, Sir, yours etc.
Lytton Strachey

‡

To Virginia Woolf

The Mill House
Tidmarsh
Pangbourne
May 1st 1924

Could you come for the week-end on Saturday week – viz. May 11th, je pense? You and he – I hope Sebastian may be here, and that the sun

by that time may be shining. Please make the effort – and perhaps we
might go over and look at the new house. I wish we could have panels
in it à la yours – but . . .

I am overwhelmed with horrible letters to publishers and monsters of
all sorts, so

good-bye

your

Lytton

‡

To Ralph Partridge

Hôtel de Dauphin

Vannes

July 21st 1924

My darling, we arrived here on Monday evening. Yesterday I sent you
a telegram with this address, which I hope you have got. Vannes is a
very pleasant town, largely old, with charming old houses, half-timbered,
the wood painted in pale colours – grey, brown, a pink – which has a very
pretty effect. Unfortunately the modern frogs have built various atrocities
all over it; but not enough to ruin the place. Our hotel looks over the
chief square, in which the Breton boys tumble over each other in
endless pleasure all day long. In the evening we sit outside the café,
listening to the strains of a cultured trio as darkness falls. Yesterday we
went in a steamer on an expedition to a village on the Atlantic sea,
treading our way through the 'Morbihan' – an enormous sort of inland
sea or harbour, which you will see on the map, and which you reach
from Vannes down a river of about three miles. Unfortunately the
weather is not as good as it might be. It invariably rains in the course of
the day, which is annoying, as if it was really fine it would be delightful
to glide about on steamers to the various little places on the harbour.
My health seems to be very good, though an unfortunate circumstance
for the time being shattered me. At Le Mans, as we were going to our
train, there were no porters at the station, so I took up my two green
suitcases and proceeded to walk down the platform. Suddenly, without
a word of warning, my back literally went crack – it was a fearful
sensation – more terrifying than painful – as if something had broken

inside. I tottered to a bench, and Pippa managed luckily to find a man who put the things into the train. When there I felt so shattered that I thought I was going to faint. However, some food and brandy improved matters, and I was much better by the time we reached Rennes. But the result was that I've missed Les Roches, Madame de Sévigné's house, as the following day was the only possible one for it, and I was too tired and my back was too stiff for me to move. By dint of lying down a good deal, it gradually got better and better, and now I am completely all right again – but we now send the suitcases in the van! In the train between Le Mans and Rennes, as I lay pale and dim, a country youth with red hair, and as they say, 'the very picture of health', got in. I longed to be him, with a body which would do its work properly, and well, an adequate mind. However, in the evening, at Rennes, feeling rather better, and sipping my coffee to the strains of the band, I perceived that the change, after all, would not have been a wise one.

I hope the stuff that I got at Rennes for the curtains for my sitting-room will turn out all right. I didn't feel at all sure that the colour would suit the walls; but the pattern seemed to me so attractive that I thought I'll risk it – and in any case it can always be used for something else. It wasn't very expensive – 216 francs – about £2.10.0 for the 12 metres.

At Caen, there was a most upsetting moment. I found a bookshop on the morning of our departure – there seemed to be nothing particular in it – I bought a small book after a long delay, and was going away, when the man flung open a door and revealed an inner room, filled with fascinating volumes. I had no time to do more than cast a hurried glance round – the train had to be caught – I saw volume 2 of a priceless Racine, but it was useless without volume 1 – heaven knows what besides – I had to fly – the tears streaming down my face as I did so.

Do you remember the museum at Le Mans? I had quite forgotten it, but when we went there this time it all came back to me – the stuffed ducks in row upon row on the walls – the incredible pictures 'presented by the state' – endless little stones in glass cases, carefully tabulated – the full size statue of an adolescent cupid, with 'On ne touche pas' written underneath – and the guardian, as old and abject as everything else. It was perfect.

I enjoyed seeing the cathedral there again very much. Also the tapestries in the other church. But the food at the hotel *was* a disappointment, and on the second night the band didn't play at the café, so I never re-discovered the little violinist.

I am hoping to have a letter tomorrow or the next day. It is indeed dreary having to exist for ages without your news. I don't know in the least whether we shall leave here, or what, on Friday. I think we must come to these regions some day in the car and see Les Roches – and go to the bookshop at Caen, etc. etc.

Pippa seems to be distinctly more lively. I must go out with her now to the patisserie and get some tea.

I send you all my love. How I agree with Madame de Sévigné's friend that no separation should last longer than two hours!

your

Lytton

‡

To Carrington and Ralph Partridge

Hôtel du Dauphin, Vannes

Saturday, August 2nd 1924

My darlings *[. . .]*

The day before yesterday we went for an expedition by rail and motor to inspect various Druidical remains. They were very interesting, and those at Carnac were in particular extraordinary – hundreds and hundreds of stones set up on end and arranged in parallel lines – covering field after field, and getting bigger as you went west, till the ones at the end were almost of Stonehenge size. Then there were various other curiosities – dolmen and tumuli – tombs in underground chambers, etc. etc. Luckily it was a fine day, and we had some very pretty views over the flat country out to sea.

Otherwise we have been rather idle. Today is market day in this town, and the streets have been filled with countrywomen in their lace headdresses and grand aprons, and vieillards in smocks and black velvet hats and streamers, mostly engaged in selling pigs with the utmost vigour. Finally the King and Queen of the Pigs drove by – the fattest creatures you ever saw, lying at full length, side by side, in an immense cart.

I wish I knew what your adventures have been and are. I seem to have been away for such ages! – I was very glad that you liked the butterfly book. I had only a most fleeting glance at it in the shop. Then the carpets. I hope they came all right, and that you liked them. I hardly venture to imagine what Ham Spray may be like by this time. A dream of beauty? Or demolished by order of the Sanitary Engineers and Huth? Well, no doubt these mysteries will be revealed eventually. Farewell. I send you all my love.

your

Lytton

‡

To Mary Hutchinson

The Hon. Philip Ritchie was then an Oxford undergraduate. The eldest son of Lord Ritchie of Dundee, he became a barrister in the chambers of C. P. Sanger.

Ham Spray House

Hungerford

Berks.

September 17th 1924

How charming of you to write me such a long, amusing, and delightful letter! I have been wanting to write to you for a long time, and have only been prevented by what appears to be some merely mechanical difficulty in the brain. Some cog-wheel refuses to catch – I can't think why – and so day after day passes, and all the remarks I am longing to make remain in a painful obscurity. And now am I too late? *[. . .]* I mean to come to town in October. Won't you be there then? I shall be able to more than whisper then – perhaps after that won't you and Clive come down here and take a look at this really rather fascinating place? – Such books, plates, curtains, downs and blizzards as never were seen before. The truth is, I hardly dare to consider the pleasures of my existence. There is a romantic beauty about everything here which ravishes my heart. Don't mock at me. The weather is quite enough to keep me from losing my head – the weather and – ah well! –

Your rumours are of course absurd. P*[hilip]* R*[itchie]* has been here twice since my return from France – once for the day (accompanied by a friend) and for a Tuesday to Friday visit. Voilà tout. The history of my feelings would be more extended. The chief point to observe is that I still perfectly well know where I am. To say this is, I realise, itself rather a serious indication – but nothing more. I am, though not cool, collected. Another important point is that I am more and more attracted by the mentality – a dangerous symptom also, do you think? – Well, dangerous or not, there it is. He *is* very intelligent, amusing, originating – and in a way that I find fits in very deliciously with my particular taste. I can talk to him with great pleasure for hours. Another point – of paramount importance – is that his Heart is . . . engaged. Yes! I'll tell you the details when I see you, unless rumour has already informed you of this too. I have passed through some agitations – I hope no more will follow. I think all is well; but nothing has happened (to speak of) – yet. These details also remain for our meeting. In the meantime I beg you to be discreet – to damp down rumours or waft them aside. I don't want him to have an impression – which would really be quite false – that I am in any kind of state which would be a nuisance for him. I should be désolé if he were to think that. Our relations now seem happy and simple – let them remain so!

I'm afraid this is all rather boring – it will be more amusing after lunch at River House. For one thing, it won't be a monologue. It's a blessing to have you to talk to. I believe in your discretion. As for mine, I can't think why it should be so suspect – and what secrets I am unjustly accused of revealing.

Dear me! – In this connection a remark by La Rochefoucauld occurs to me – 'Comment prétendons nous qu'un autre garde notre secret, si nous ne pouvons le garder nous mêmes?' But I see that it is not a very opportune quotation.

I've been rather absorbed by that writer lately – otherwise I can't think what I've read. Oh! La Princesse de Montpensier – do you know it? – by Madame de La Fayette. So wonderfully short! And abstract! Oh, remarkable! – Your wet weeks in France sound enjoyable. I travelled extremely mildly in Brittany with Pippa, where it wasn't too wet to sit most of the day and night in some ridiculous café sipping vermouth and soda. *[. . .]*

‡

To Carrington

Ciro's Club was a night-club on Orange Street, off Haymarket.

51, Gordon Square
Friday, October 17th 1924

I ought to have written before, ma très-chère, but I have been so much occupied – with doing nothing! London is enthralling – but also wrecking; and while I sometimes long to stay in it for months, I really see that I should become an absurdity if I did. The young men are all that is most kind; but there is only one perfect young man in the world, and he lives at Ham Spray.

Please, however, both of you, try to like – or at any rate not dislike – my Philip. I assure you he's a great rarity. It's true that he's not immediately attractive to look at, and that he probably has no taste in pictures; but he's intellectual (a good point); and he's sensual (also good); and he gives not the slightest value to anything but what is really valuable (very good indeed). Also, when he gets tipsy . . . There was an orgy last night of a most remarkable kind – and I fear no description will even do justice to it. A floating party that began in the Café Royal and ended in a flat in Pall Mall – then there was another flat (near Buckingham Palace) – flights of crammed taxis – colloquies in Piccadilly Circus – a debauched youth in a black cloak – supper at Ciro's – magnum upon magnum of champagne. Oliver in the middle of it all – and how it ended I don't know. Perhaps I shall find out tonight when I dine with Dadie. In the meantime I am feeling, as you may imagine, a little exhausted. I am sitting by the fire in this pitch-dark drawing room, and I can do nothing but read Maynard's most brilliant biography of Prof. Marshall.

With luck I shall arrive for lunch tomorrow, and go to sleep for three days.

All my love
Lytton

‡

To Carrington

The 'Roger' encountered at Cambridge was probably Fry, as Roger Senhouse was an Oxford friend of Philip Ritchie, though they probably did first meet at about this time. Lytton usually wrote the theatrical farces performed at Ham Spray, but this letter sounds as though they were planning to act one of Beaumarchais's plays. Stephen Tomlin had taken Henrietta Bingham to Scotland in July, so Carrington had known of the affair for quite a time.

Oriental Club
Hanover Square, W.1
Monday, December 8th 1924

My dearest,

I've just returned from Cambridge, and was very glad to get your letter
at no. 51. It was très agréable there – very typical, in every way –
including a bedroom of incredible bleakness, multitudes of young men,
Newnham, etc. etc. Topsy rather boomed and boomed, which (for me)
was a novelty. Roger and Duncan were also guests. And I travelled back
this morning with Hewie Anderson (do you know him?) – an Oxford
ex-tart, I presume. Perhaps you may have heard about Dadie – a
temperature, apparently indicating the flu, then a rash, *possibly* indicating
measles. Altogether rather a gloomy business, and I tremble for the play.
If he can't act, what shall we do for a Cherubino?

I realise how distressing the H*[enrietta]* B*[ingham]* affair must be to
you. All one can say is that it's better to know these things than to go
on without knowing; but that doesn't make the discovery any less
horrid. And then, poor Tommy! The one hope for him, it seems to me,
is her return to America.

I am longing to see the glass pictures, and the panels, which sound
most exciting. I haven't done anything about the curtains yet. Topsy
told me that Kelim rugs wear out very soon, unless they are lined with
felt – so I think we'd better do that. I thought there must be *some* snag
about them. She produced, poor creature, a peculiarly hideous carpet
which she's just got for her new house. Her taste is *not* impeccable. But
she has a marvellous black cat, whose grandfather came from East
Africa. All my love to you both

Lytton

‡

To Carrington

*The trial of nineteen-year-old University of Chicago law student Nathan
Leopold Jnr and eighteen-year-old Richard Loeb for the kidnapping and murder
of their Chicago neighbour Bobby Franks began on 21 July 1924, with Clarence
Darrow acting for the defence. His eloquent plea against invoking the death*

*penalty was accepted, and on 10 September they were sentenced to 'life plus
ninety-nine years' in prison. The press was coy about reporting that they were
lovers; though, as the State's case turned partly on sexual deviance, and as they
were kept apart in prison, Lytton had no trouble in reading between the lines.
Lytton was reading one of the transcripts of the trial that had been published as
early as the winter of 1924. The case was a legal milestone because it established
that the judge could exercise some discretion about capital punishment; the
defendants' homosexuality was not relevant to its legal importance.*

  *'The Prince' = Ralph (Rex); the lawns at Ham Spray were extensive, and
an efficient lawnmower was important. Ralph was in love with Frances Marshall
and it was about now that Carrington and Ralph stopped having sexual
relations; the conspiratorial matchmaking with Mary Hutchinson came at a time
when Frances was seeing Gerald Brenan, and also becoming interested in another
man she called Hamish, with whom she went dancing.*

c/o Mrs Boswell
Sherborne Lane
Lyme Regis
Monday, March 30th 1925

Très-chère

I was very glad to get your letter about the painted goose, etc., this
morning. How preposterous of Sebastian to try and get up a secret
correspondence with Roger! I have said nothing about it – but will
keep my eyes open.

  There's not much to say. My health seems to be improving.
Yesterday was a nice day – positively hot in the sun. Arthur W[aley]
appeared after dinner, Sebastian knew that this was impending, but
hadn't dared to tell me! However, I bore the shock fairly well, and
today we had lunch with him at his hotel. Owl Enfield is also on view
every day: we take off our hats and pass on rapidly. Tomorrow A.W.
comes to dinner. S[ebastian] is extremely charming, gay and talkative.
I only hope he doesn't find this an almost dreary spot. At the present
moment he is out walking with the amiable Mandarin, whom he
declares he adores. My feelings are not quite so intense. We play piquet
nearly the whole time, and at intervals read the Trial of Leopold and
Loeb. (Have you heard of them? – The two American-German-Jew-
boys who murdered a dear little schoolmate aged 14. Unfortunately the
really interesting details are suppressed.)

Will you try and take the Prince to look at the mowing machine at 5 Victoria Street? Tea with Mary Hutch sounds hopeful for the bookbinding department and also for the bedding department. Give my love to him. My present notion is to stay on here over the week-end after S. goes – viz till about April 6th or 7th. I've written to Pippa to ask her to come. All my love.

your Lytton

PS. Give my love to Philip!

‡

To Carrington

Philip's gambling partner was C.H.B. Kitchin, the novelist. Roger is Senhouse (1899–1970), Lytton's last lover. Lytton had met Raymond (Bell) Mortimer (1895–1980) two years earlier.

Lytton has misquoted from Andrew Marvell's 'The Garden':

> *What wond'rous Life is this I lead!*
> *Ripe Apples drop about my head; . . .*
> *The Nectaren, and curious Peach,*
> *Into my hands themselves do reach.*

51, Gordon Square
Thursday, April 16th 1925

My darlings, I wonder where you are by this time. Somewhere very far off! Surrounded by blossom, sunshine, Roman ruins, and every beauty! Well, I hope this will be found by you at Nîmes.

I seem to have seen a great many people – but really it's rather an illusion – the result of so many weeks of seclusion. Philip appeared yesterday, full of his Paris adventures. He went off almost at once to Winchelsea, but returns to work next week. I saw his mother (rather a melancholy, drawn woman) and his younger brother, Colin, on the station platform – a frailer Philip, aged 17. Too much of a rosebud for me, but pronounced by Roger to be the most beautiful creature extant. There were a fair number of unrepeatable Paris stories. Among the repeatable is this following. Philip was taken by Kitchin to gamble somewhere, so left nearly all his money with Roger, in order not to lose everything. However he soon lost all he'd taken – returned to Roger, and found that Roger had rushed out, directly his back was turned, and bought La Jeune Parque – a rare and valuable poem by Valéry – with the money, so that they were left penniless. They had to beg their way back to London . . . more or less! After seeing Philip off I went to tea with Raymond whose rooms I thought in very bad taste. But he was amusing and intelligent I thought, and I managed hardly to look at all at the newspapers or the pierrot or the other monstrosities. He goes to Paris almost at once. A young man, who has almost everything to make him happy – and yet doesn't seem to be completely so. Why?

Then – what do you think! I had dinner with Roger! At his Club – the Travellers', next to the Athenaeum – rather a sympathetic place, in spite of its size – a good dining-room, long, with white and gold panelling and three superb chandeliers. Altogether très-chic. The gilt, however, was slightly rubbed off the gingerbread by the presence of Victor Butler, one of the co-mates of Roger – a harmless dull young man. After dinner we went to Warwick Square. The other co-mate was away. We sat and looked at books and things, when – imagine my surprise, agitation and emotion – Roger suddenly produced La Jeune Parque, and said he'd got it as a present for me! I very nearly flung my arms round his neck, in spite of Mr Victor Butler. It really is too charming – a most beautiful book, which I've longed for ages to possess. Of course his method of presentation was exquisiteness itself. I came away with a fluttering heart. Everyone is really wonderfully kind.

> 'What kind of life is this I lead?
> Ripe apples drop about my head.
> The nectarine and curious peach
> Themselves into my hands do reach'

as the poet says, though perhaps he didn't quite apply the same meaning to 'curious peach' as some of his modern commentators!

Alec comes to Ham Spray for the week-end. I shall try and get Tommy too – but doubt it. Philip will come the week-end after, and Roger (and presumably also Philip) the week-end after that. Next week I shall crouch at Oliver's, as Ray will be away, and I shall be able to use the sitting-room. Bad news of my eldest brother, who is returning, worse, from Spain.

Everyone says it must be perfect now in Provence. I hope it is, and that you're not getting too exhausted. With all my love,

your

Lytton

‡

To Carrington and Ralph Partridge

Hotel Lago di Dobbiaco
Thursday, July 23rd 1925

My dearest ones, We arrived here yesterday, after various adventures, including a night at Alleghe (a lake in the Italian style) which we reached in a one-horse shay, and a night at Cortina – a rather smart gay place, full of hotels – which I see only I have a degraded taste for. *[. . .]*

Our Dolomitic tour has been rather briefer than I'd expected, but it's impossible (unless one walks enormous distances with packs on backs) to get anywhere except on the motor-bus, which we got thoroughly sick of by the time we reached Cortina. It's a most wearing method of travelling – there are crises at every turn – one never knows whether one will get a seat – then one's packed in with countless Germans got up like escaped convicts – and finally the machine breaks down on the top of a mountain 10,000 feet high and 18 miles from anywhere. This is what happened to us. There we sat, as night fell, among the convicts, the rain thundering down on the canvas roof – horror on horror! However, we got in safe at last. The weather is not quite all that it should be – it's very thundery, with about one incredibly violent downpour a day. *[. . .]* Sebastian is charming, and makes existence possible by his command of the German tongue. I hope all goes well at Ham Spray. All my love.

your Lytton

‡

To Ralph Partridge

The Alte Pinakothek's famous El Greco was a 1583–4 copy of the Toledo picture The Spoliation *or* The Disrobing of Christ, *though Lytton's objections are a mystery. The 'Tate'-like museum with the Cézannes is the Neue Pinakothek.*

The Chauve-Souris was a celebrated cabaret/nightclub in Munich – Oskar Kokoschka (1886–1980) did some of the decorations, and participated in some 'performance art' productions there; Katinka *was a musical by Rudolf Friml. Lytton meant that he would have to make money from the cinema to pay his income tax – but only the future* Elizabeth and Essex *was made into a film. The £7,000 must have been hyperbole: it amounts to more than £250,000 in today's money.*

Pension Abbazia
Munich
July 31st 1925

I found four letters waiting for me yesterday at the Poste Restante. I hadn't gone there before, because I thought there wouldn't be anything so soon. It's shocking to think of the mass of material at Bolzano; but I fear it will have to stay there till the day of judgement. Those wretched Italians would never dream of forwarding anything. It must have got there just after me – unless they were lying – which is highly probable. I can now hardly remember when I was anywhere, or what any place in particular was like. A kind of cinematograph haze of a hundred utterly discordant visions flashes through my mind when I try to recall the last fortnight. However, since being in Munich things have become more definite. It's a sympathetic town – large but leisurely, with wide empty streets, plenty of trees, and a fair number of good-looking inhabitants. We spend most of our time sight-seeing. The picture gallery has much that is very good – but *not* that particular snake Greco; there is also an antique sculpture gallery, and a modern kind of Tate, with some very good Cézannes and other French in one room. The ex-royal palace is rather amusing – one wanders for hours through endless miles of preposterous rooms. Unfortunately, after some very nice days, the weather has taken a bad turn, and today it has never stopped raining. If it improves, we shall go to Nymphenburg (the Versailles of München) and perhaps to Augsburg, which is only an hour off. In the evenings, we usually go to some entertainment or other. Last night we went to the Chauve Souris – and there was Katinka, just as ever! But the rest of it seemed dreary stuff. One night we went to a dancing café, which was amusing; but so far nothing at all in our special line has been discovered. Propriety reigns. Except of course for an occasional adventure on the part of Sebastian. Today at lunch we fell in with two young gentlemen from Kings – *not* very exciting – but the first English we've come across the whole time. On Sunday is the Magic Flute and on Tuesday Figaro *[. . .]*

Never did I hear anything so shocking as the story of the sting. I hope to goodness you're all right again. It must have been most appalling. As you don't mention it in your letter this morning, I hope it's quite gone off. The Income tax now looks pretty grim. Yes – I must certainly make at least £7000 from cinemas. I get the Times here – two days old and have just seen the portraits of Lydia and Maynard – (the latter slightly rejuvenated). It was delightful to get all the Ham Spray news yesterday. I enclose a postcard – most of the photographs of the pictures are worse than useless. This Botticelli is magnificent.

With all my love
Lytton

‡

To Virginia Woolf

Sir Almeric Fitzroy (1851–1935) was clerk of the Privy Council. His memoirs (1925) covered his political work, the Boer War and World War I.

Virginia had become ill at an evening party for Quentin's birthday and Maynard and Lydia's marriage at Charleston on 19 August, when she suddenly, said Quentin Bell, 'turned exactly the colour of a duck's egg', and had to be put to bed.[1] 'When I was at my worst,' Virginia wrote to Lytton on 8 September, 'Leonard made me eat an entire cold duck' and, she says, she was sick for the first time in her life – though she seems to have heard that Lytton is sick every Monday – and it's 'a hideous and awful experience'. Leonard and James omitted from their edition the baffling phrase 'the Russian carpenter's bed'. Perhaps it simply refers to Lydia. There were certainly carpenters involved that summer in constructing the studio in the courtyard of Charleston, but they would not have slept at the house; and it is too early in 1925 to be a teasing reference to Vita Sackville-West.

Ham Spray House
Hungerford
Berks.
September 11th 1925

My conduct is certainly shocking – but there! – I cannot stay with you.
I am booked for Charleston and Mr. and Mrs. K; but shan't I see you?
I arrive at Iford about Sept. 24th – in tears, I expect. I feel, too, as if
I should not be able to write anything for the Nation for many a long
day. It is all most disgraceful. And the comble is that I cannot recall the
misprint in the Common Reader. All this is I believe the result of Sir
Almeric Fitzroy, whose 'memoirs' I have been reading, and who has
reduced me to state of sawdust equal to his own.

Your letter is obscure in parts – *Where* were you sick after the
complete duck? In a Russian carpenter's bed, I seem to gather; but
it is mysterious. Unfortunately, I am never sick now – only sterile –
every Monday, and all the other days of the week.

your
Lytton

1. Quentin Bell, *Virginia Woolf*, vol. 2, p.114.

⸸

To Carrington

*Mr and Mrs D'Arcy Japp, neighbours at Ham Spray, are mentioned by
Carrington as her dinner guests in her reply to this letter, dated 26 September:
'The Japp world arrived at half past seven. The dinner was indescribably grand.
Epoch-making; grapefruit, then a chicken covered with fennel and tomato sauce,
a risotto with almonds, onions and pimentos, followed by sack cream, supported
by Café Royal red wine, perfectly warmed. (The cradle took Mrs Japp's breath
away.) [. . .] You would hardly have recognized old Japp. He became so
flirtatious and talkative. Helen [Anrep] was a great support and was very polite
to the Japps. [. . .] Helen and I go to Japp's tonight to a return dinner.
Apparently Mrs Japp is renowned for exquisite cuisine and was very agitated by
our gorgeous display. So this is a rival supper party.'[1]*

The Japps also gave Carrington a kitten she named Biddie. Henry Lamb

turned up the next day, stayed the night and gave Carrington one of his sleeping
pills. He was worried that Lytton was feeling hostile to him.

Charleston
Thursday, September 24th 1925

My dearest creature, I was delighted to get your letter with the elegant
silver swan yesterday. I hope I may find another at Maynard's, whither
I progress this afternoon. The first day here was as appalling as it was with
you: but yesterday was divine. And now this morning I am positively
sitting out of doors in the sun. All has gone well here – except for the
piercing cold of Tuesday. The boys have luckily returned to school.
Angus was here till yesterday – very pretty and squashy. Judith (daughter
of Barbara) is in the house. Hardly had I entered it when she ran down
a passage, through a door, flung herself upon a bed, and broke her
collar-bone. However, the doctor pronounces it to be nothing – she
goes about in a bandage, and is an extremely exemplary child. All the
horror of a year or two ago seems to have departed. Angelica remains as
much of an affected minx as ever. But I avoid the petit peuple to the
best of my ability. The new studio is a great success – a very nice light
room, opening on to the garden, with a superb wood-block floor; it
must improve life immensely for the painters. Clive, whose clothes are
really too shabby even for me – sprouting bits of cloth at the shoulder-
blade – buttons hanging on threads down from the trousers – is an
indefatigable walker – out we go for hours over the downs. In the
evenings we sit up till half past one chatting. The Maynard-Loppy
exacerbation grows more and more violent – it's difficult to make out
exactly why. A kind of unofficial war rages. On leaving 46, Vanessa
claimed a picture of Duncan's, which Maynard maintained belonged to
him. Duncan was appealed to – he supported Vanessa – strange to say.
Maynard thereupon had the picture screwed on the wall in his
bathroom. Yesterday Vanessa went up to London, armed with a
screwdriver, entered 46, unscrewed the picture, and transported it to 37.
She now confesses she is terrified. What Maynard will do to her when
he returns and discovers the loss, heaven alone knows. As for Lydia,
she's a half-witted canary. Ottoline, as we supposed, has been in the
offing. She wrote to Virginia, proposing to take lodgings, with Pipsey
and Julian, at Rodmell. And that they should all have meals at Monk's
House. Imagine the horror of the Woolves! Virginia replied that they

never ate anything but gooseberries and water, so that she imagined Ott would find the fare too monotonous. This put a stop to the project, and Ott wrote V a despairing letter, ending 'your saddened friend'. I'm sorry to say Virginia's health has been rather bad lately – headaches, etc. – and it's thought she overdid it in London in the summer. She can't work, and it's a little doubtful whether I shall be able to see her.

The Japp world sounds too sordid for words. How can anyone as intelligent as Henry pass his life among such abjectivities. I hope Helen is all right, and that she is enjoying herself. I wonder what you did in the fine weather yesterday – an expedition? – or gossip in the garden? This house is a regular Shandy Hall compared with Ham Spray. Doors that, once shut, can only be opened with a gimlet – draughts whistling over linoleum, etc., but of course it's only intended to be a summer residence, and as such does very well. The surrounding country is more like Scotland than anything else – the mountains are so enormous and the wastes so desolate.

I must stop now, and take this to the post. By-the-bye – no discretion was needed in re Faith and Ellie – as the whole story was known here. I wish I could talk to you.

all my love – your
Lytton

1. David Garnett, *Carrington*, pp. 328–9.

‡

To Roger Senhouse

'*Adieu, mon bel ange. Je baise le bout de vos ailes, comme disait Voltaire à des gens qui ne vous valaient pas.*' From a letter by Pushkin, 11 October 1830.

Ham Spray House
Hungerford
Berks.
January 20th 1926

Dear Roger

Your letter has just come. It was stupid of me, but I was under the
impression that we had rather airily said we wanted a cheese, so when
one appeared I hardly imagined it could be a gift. As it is, I'm afraid you
must have thought us very remiss in saying not a word about it. Really
you are too noble in your gifts! It was perfectly charming of you to
think of it, and Ham Spray raises a triune chorus of gratitude. At every
meal we all three lick our chops and declare the glories of Stilton in
general and the supreme glories of this Stilton in particular. Mr and
Mrs P. are away at the moment, having gone to some dreadful party, so
that I am alone here, and can only give tongue for them by proxy. For
myself, I speak from a full belly.

Your water troubles sound appalling. But those things generally do
look rather worse than they are. Oddly enough we've been going
through very much the same vicissitudes here, owing to the snow
blocking up the drains on the roof. The water poured onto the landing
in a perfect shower-bath, hundreds of basins had to be ranged
underneath, and Carrington had to get up at 3 o'clock in the morning
to empty them, or they would have overflowed and the whole house
been deluged. However, we're all right again now, and I hope you are
also.

I've made the acquaintance of a new young man, who appears to me
to be intelligent, nice, and good-looking. Est-il possible? Naturally, I am
slightly excited – but I dare say it'll turn out all too soon that I'm quite
wrong, and have merely been taken in by youth (which is undeniable).
I'm expecting him for the week-end – also Philip, who will judge him,
no doubt, with sufficient severity . Well, we shall see!

Adieu, mon très-cher Roger. Je baise le bout de vos aîles, as M. de
Voltaire says.

your
Lytton

‡

To Sebastian Sprott

This letter responds to Sebastian's commiserations about the upset to the alteration in living arrangements at Ham Spray caused by the decision of Ralph and Frances to live together in London.

Ham Spray House
Hungerford
Berks.
May 7th 1926

Thank you very much, my dearest creature, for your charming letter. The situation here is slightly dubious, but not, so far, quite as serious as you adumbrate. Some sort of arrangement has been come to, by which Ralph is to divide his time (more or less) between this and London. How far this will take effect remains to be seen; but if he really does come down here about every other week, I think it ought to be possible to carry on an existence without too much horror. The circumstances have been unpleasant – shattering for Carrington and also for me – but everyone has behaved with great magnanimity, and I don't see that blame attaches anywhere – but it's unfortunate.

In any case, you must come in June, and be useful or not, as you like.

I hope there will be a June for you to come in. At the present moment, I rather suspect it will be on strike. C and I live here in a vacuum. I hope Nottingham has not become too appalling, and that you are supported by your various friends, old and new. I long to hear about the latest developments.

I hope this will reach you.

Carrington sends her love, and so do I.

your
Lytton

‡

To Carrington

The Trades Union Congress called a General Strike on 3 May 1926. The miners did not return to work until August. The painter Robert Medley

(1905–94) and Rupert Doone (1903–33) were a life-long couple. Doone had been an occasional lover of Duncan's and modelled for Glyn Philpott RA (1884–1937). Georges Duthuit, married to Matisse's daughter, Marguerite, gave Lytton a copy of his Byzance et l'art du XIIème siècle *(1926). Jean Cocteau (1889–1963) published his first major work of criticism,* Le Rappel à l'Ordre, *in 1926.*

Hotel du Navigateur
49, Quai des Grands Augustins
Paris
June 3rd 1926

Très-chère, Dadie's card, saying that the 12th would be better than the 5th made me decide to stay on here till Tuesday – whether wisely or not, heaven knows. The exhaustion is of course appalling, and the weather vile. Otherwise one occasionally has amusing moments. Our rooms (side by side) front the quay – the noise is terrific. The rain pelts, the wind blows. I suppose it is equally bitter at Ham Spray; and from the dim remarks in the French papers, I gather the coal crisis is getting worse, so that I fear even a hundredweight a week may be now out of the question, and the steamers to Southampton – will they be going on Tuesday? If they do, I shall ring you up on Wednesday morning. And petrol – will there be any left by then?

What was curious was to discover Medley up three flights of stairs, Rue Bonaparte, in the arms of Rupert Doone, ballet dancer. Who would have guessed at such a consummation? However, in spite of it the poor young man remains as nice and as dull as ever. As for the ballet dancer . . . oh, a most curious type. Impossible to explain just now. Ran away from home at the age of 14 – became a model (to Glyn Philpott), then a dancer – is now 21. I went to see a dancing class in an enormous room at the top of a theatre. It was very amusing – not at all like Degas. Dear Rupert was much the best of them, and in fact his legs . . . He hopes to get an engagement before long, and a tour in Germany. In the meantime we have become boon companions, I believe. Fair hair, with a wave in it. You can imagine the rest.

Then there is Monsieur Georges Duthuit, who is married to the daughter of Matisse. He is incredibly witty and an incredibly handsome young man, in the complete French style – a kind of bronze medal – admires me enormously. Clive and Mary gave a party in our honour at Montmartre – a mad affair, Mary having asked as well a deplorable kind of male tart, with no pretensions to gentility – imagine the pained surprise of la fille de Matisse at finding herself in such company! But Georges kept up such brilliant sallies that all was well. I am to see him again tomorrow. He has presented me with his latest book – on Byzantine art, and unfortunately written in so complicated a style as to be unreadable.

The result of it all is that I feel alternately wildly elated and profoundly miserable. It is a dream really – omnia somnia – and damned noisy at that. There are no books, of course. I have brought two sets of stuff, for my room and the dining-room. I *hope* the colours will do, but in any case it doesn't much matter, as the whole lot cost less than £2. Pippa spends most of her time with Suffragettes at the Sorbonne – with some punctuations of Rouchard, whom up to the present I have avoided. Miss Ward (a suffrage emissary) in a Café is a fearful sight.

Give Tommy my love. Is there any chance of his still being at Ham Spray when I return? I hope so. If I could press a button and find myself there I would immediately do so. But no! Off I must go to dine with some dreadful French woman. The great – the shattering – news is that Cocteau has become a Catholic! The world is staggered. But I must say *I* am not very much surprised.

All my love.

your
Lytton

‡

To Carrington

At the time of this letter Rosamond Lehmann was married to Walter Leslie Runciman (1900–1989), later 2nd Viscount Runciman of Doxford, Eton and Trinity, who once remarked that he learned his good manners from a gamekeeper. They were divorced the next year, and she married Wogan (later the Communist Lord Milford) in 1928.

[. . .] Mr and Mrs R[unciman] share the establishment with a young man
called Wogan Philipps – quite nice – and then there was Dadie – and
that was the party. Leslie Runciman is to me extremely attractive – in
character, even, as well as appearance. But I don't suppose many would
agree with this. He is pompous, moody, flies into tempers, and is not
mentally entertaining by any means. Perhaps you would be bored by
the poor fellow. But oh! he's so strong, and his difficulties are so curious
– and his eyelashes . . . there's a childishness about him that – I daresay
all grown-up people are childish in some way or another – I find
endearing. Rosamond is a much brighter character . . . though not as
good-looking – gay, enthusiastic, and full of fun. She and Dadie get on
like a house on fire. Wogan lies vaguely and sympathetically at their
feet. And then Leslie makes a pompous remark, to which no attention
is paid, looks divine, scowls, until I long to fling my arms around his
neck. [. . .]

‡

To Carrington

*'Pokey' Knole in Kent is supposed to have 365 rooms. Vita Sackville-West felt
cheated, as, being female, she could not inherit the largely untouched medieval
house with its Jacobean embellishments. Instead it went to her cousin, Eddy
(Edward Charles Sackville-West, 1901–65, 5th Baron Sackville, who succeeded
his father in 1962). Educated at Eton and Christ Church, Oxford, he was a
writer and music critic.*

Oriental Club
Hanover Square, W.1
Monday, August 30th 1926

Dearest Creature

Perhaps I could meet you and Ralph tomorrow at Paddington, if you
would let me know the train. Will you ring me up in the morning?
    Would you have lunch with me?

I have just returned from Knole, which I found sadly pokey. There was a great deal of music, which helped to pass the time – but I couldn't listen very much. Barbara and Nick to lunch were a distinct relief. Eddie is oh! so pleased with his surroundings, and, even more, with himself. I could see no sign of taste anywhere, and have become a communist.

my love,
your
Lytton

‡

To Roger Senhouse

Richard Barnfield's The Affectionate Shepherd *(1594) also contains the stanza 'If it be sinne to loue a louely Lad:/Oh then sinne I, for whom my soule is sad.'*

Ham Spray House
Hungerford
Berks.
September 9th 1926

Dearest Roger

[. . .] Bunny comes for the week-end on Saturday; otherwise C and I remain alone – a good thing, as 'delightful Slater' has been seized with lumbago, and taken to her bed – and the washing-up problem is serious. I have rather scandalously dropped Elizabeth for the moment, and am writing something on Racine. You might suppose that I had exhausted that subject – but no! This is a new theme – not *very* serious and one might say esoteric – I will show it you when it's done.

I have also been looking into Barnfield again. He is a comic fellow. In his 'Lamentation of the Affectionate Shepheard' (addressed to 'Ganymede') he says –

> 'I have a pleasant-noted Nightingale' etc . . .
> 'Her shalt thou have, and all I have beside,
>   If thou wilt be my Boy – or else my Bride' !!

Really, the fatuity of the Elizabethans reached astonishing heights; and yet they always (even Barnfield) manage to be beautiful.

[. . .] I hope your weather continues to be propitious, and that purple peacefulness still surrounds you. How heavenly – those smells, Roger! Strange that when all is said and done one comes back for one's subtlest delights to that archaic contraption – the nose!

There's not much in this letter, I'm afraid, but it's pleasant to talk, if only on paper. Yours was such a good one, dear.

my love
Lytton

‡

To Carrington

Lytton was staying with Sebastian Sprott in Nottingham. The newly founded (by Bunny Garnett) Cranium Club (named after the phrenological Mr Cranium in Thomas Love Peacock's Headlong Hall*) of course met in London. Thomas Humphrey Marshall (1893–1981) was Frances Marshall's brother. Educated at Rugby and Trinity, Cambridge, he was a fellow of Trinity until 1925, when he went to the LSE. He had been a civilian prisoner in Germany throughout the war. Originally an economic historian, he went, via social work, to sociology, and did original and important work on social class. C. P. Sanger wrote a celebrated essay on* Wuthering Heights. *Lytton was disappointed by Professor Weekley, Frieda Lawrence's former husband. He said he was 'a pompous old ape, [who said things like], "You keep a manservant, Sprott?" and so on'.*[1]

29a, Clumber Street
Nottingham
Saturday, [October 9th 1926]

Très-chère, I was delighted to get your letter this morning. I am so very glad that you have both been happy. I send you all my love.

The flowers were admired, and my visit here approved of; so all was well. R[oger] was having some rather dull characters to dinner, so I went off to the Cranium – for the first time in my life, and sat down to table between Tom Marshall and Mr Wright. However, it wasn't so bad – the food quite good, and the wine excellent. Kennedy was interesting about architecture, Sanger chatted about the Brontës, which was all that

Nottingham could desire. Today the Professor of English comes to tea. On Monday, Professor Weekley. *[. . .]*

1. Quoted in Michael Holroyd, *Lytton Strachey*, p. 567.

‡

To Carrington

Oriental Club
Hanover Square, W.1
Friday, October 29th 1926

My dearest, I am afraid I was rather dim as I went off – what with the rain and the pelican! – but I didn't mean to be – far from it. You are an angel – and perhaps I am a trifle absurd and tiresome. I love you very much.

your
Lytton

‡

To Roger Senhouse

Ham Spray House
Hungerford
Berks.
November 6th 1926

Dearest Snake *[the 'S' is a drawing of a snake]*

Please tell me – Are you going to have a family party on your birthday? I rather imagine so – but if not, will you come for a little outing with me that night – supper at the new Boulestin's, perhaps? I ask this early because the Colefax has asked me for dinner that date (18th) and I should be delighted to have such a good reason for regretting my inability to accept as a previous engagement with a serpent – will you tell me, as I ought to answer the woman?

I hope I shall also some day have an account of your dances, and learn whether as a green and white harlequin you had any developments of previous circumstances – and how many young ladies fell in love with you, etc., etc. I suppose you are now at Wogan's. What can one do at Newmarket, if one's not a jockey? Rush hither and hither in a large car, perhaps. Drink brandy. Discuss Van Gogh. Such I imagine to be your preoccupations – am I quite wrong?

There is still a certain beauty here, in spite of cold and rain. The beech tree on the lawn has put on a divinely brilliant russet hue – will it last till you come? I think it may, if no gales blow. The aspen is already almost completely naked. Tommy's statue stands up white against the black bay. Indoors, there will be a surprise for you. Ha, ha!

Philip came last night, bringing the Schubert Trio with him. We played it after dinner – it is the most glorious work. Roger, I thought of you as I listened, especially in the scherzo with that lovely trio, which you played to me one night. Est-ce que tout va bien, mon cher? Is your tummy behaving itself? By-the-bye, I've got a belt for you – but heaven alone knows whether it's the right kind.

I went to the Cranium dinner on Thursday, and rather enjoyed it, sitting between Sanger and Arthur Waley. The food was good, and so was the wine – I drank a good deal of it – and the consequence was . . . a totally unexpected, decidedly ridiculous, and I fear distinctly discreditable adventure. I dare not tell you more.

You know how happy I was at Brighton, don't you? It seems impossible to expatiate with pen and ink, but I want to tell you how much I enjoyed our talks by the fire – almost as much as anything else. This looks silly – please imagine it whispered into your indulgent – yes, indulgent! that is the right word! – ears.

My love
Lytton

‡

To Roger Senhouse

Antony and Cleopatra, II,2: 'The city cast/ Her people out upon her,/ and Antony, Enthroned i' the market-place,/did sit alone, Whistling to the air.'

Ham Spray House
Hungerford
Berks.
February 11th 1927

Dearest old creature, what a villain you are! It was certainly settled that you were to keep Monday for me, and now I gather you've arranged to do something else. Tut, tut! What is to be done with you? What fearful punishment? – To stand with the right ear nailed in the pillory, I think, at Piccadilly Circus, from midday to sunset on that very Monday! – Well, I suppose it can't be helped. But I think I shall come up in any case. I want to consult with James about the possibility of my taking rooms in his house, also to see Mary, and if possible repay some of Raymond's hospitality. That is the one night when I can be away, as Ralph will be here then to look after Carrington. If by any chance you would be free after dinner – and I presume dinner is hopeless, though you don't actually say so – perhaps I could come in about 11.30 or so. A light in your bedroom to say when you're free? Let me know – though I shall hardly hear now till Monday.

Carrington goes on as ever – still almost immovable, but I suppose that's to be expected. The cold continues to be intense. Yesterday was a divine day of sunshine and poetical beauty; but today the mist has come upon us, and all is drear. I do a certain amount of writing daily – it's sometimes exciting – not always, I'm sorry to say – and very tiring, which is a bore. However, it does go on. *[. . .]*

Quite an adventure here yesterday. As I was returning from my walk in the afternoon, an aeroplane was seen to be gyrating round the house. Three times it circled about us, getting lower and lower every time. Intense excitement! The farm hands, various females, Olive and her mother, all the cats, and myself, rushed towards it; and Carrington was left solitary on her bed, like Antony 'whistling to the air'. Finally the machine came down in a field exactly opposite the lodge gates at the end of the avenue. There I found it – a group of rustics lined up at a respectful distance. I took it upon myself to approach – but in a moment perceived that the adventure would end in a fizzle. No divine Icarus met my view. Only a too red and stolid officer together with a too pale and stolid mechanic. They had lost their way. I told them where they were, asked them to tea, which they luckily refused, and off they went! – It might have been so marvellous! – What surprised me was the singular smallness and compactness of the contraption – not nearly as big as a motor bus.

I agree with you about the Aldine capitals – they're certainly a mistake – and italic capitals can be so particularly beautiful – e.g. the Baskerville ones. I can't imagine why they didn't have them.

As for my cheeks, the curious thing is that they've become smoother than ever before. So it's obviously the proper treatment. My love

Lytton

✝

To Mary Hutchinson

Ham Spray House
Hungerford
Berks.
March 30th 1927

Ma chère, I am sorry about tomorrow – but my outing will now probably be on Friday, so it's doubtful whether I shall be in town till then. All is well in that direction, though of course I am not so optimistic as you are.

I meant to tell you about the case of Annette Tonge, which is a most peculiar one. She was the first cousin of my grandmother and of your great-grandmother – so you see it goes rather far back. As she died without children and intestate, and as her brothers and sisters and their children are dead without issue, her property goes to the collateral descendants of her father and mother – but on her father's side nearly all the Plowdens and their descendants come in. Truly appalling! The old hag lived to be 97 – and always refused to make a will. The result will be that her lawyer will be the only person to score, apart from the death duties office – and her wretched maid, who was with her for 30 years, gets not a penny. I went to see the objects, which filled three or four gigantic rooms: they looked to me perfectly ghastly, but I suppose there may be some good things among the mass of utter frippery. Several ghouls were peering round – of the Plowden denomination – a horrid set, to my mind. Heavy lugubrious females in pitch black. I didn't venture to ask how much she'd left; but unless it's a million, what's the good?

This is a sketch of the situation: but Amelia and Henrietta had several brothers and sisters, from whom descendants pullulate: Amelia herself

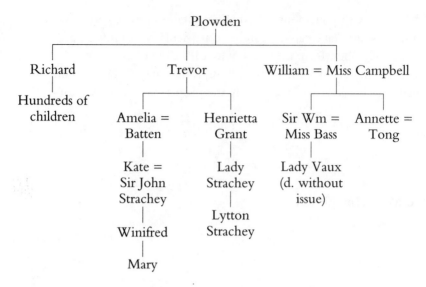

had about ten children (by her three husbands); you have five uncles and aunts – so you see the divisions are sufficiently minute. One curiosity (apparently not known to the lawyers) is that one of Amelia's children (Charlie Foster) was illegitimate, having been born before she married General Pa. But who was General Pa? – Enough! Enough!

Perhaps you'll ring me up on *Saturday* morning? Do if you feel inclined. Chez James. Mus*[eum]* 3976.

My love,
Lytton

‡

To Roger Senhouse

The Hon. Garrow Tomlin was Stephen's brother (their father was Lord Justice Tomlin). He was killed in a flying accident in 1932.

Cosi fan tutte was performed at the Kingsway Theatre, London in April.

The original 1927 American print of Fritz Lang's Metropolis *no longer exists. In this first science fiction film, a class of enslaved workers who live entirely underground maintains a magnificent, boldly imagined futuristic city.*

Ham Spray House
Hungerford
Berks.
April 3rd 1927

Dearest Roger

Why did you tell me to tear up your letter? I was half afraid there might
be a horrid potion in it, but on the contrary I found nothing but what
was pleasant.

Was it, Roger, perhaps *slightly* wicked to get engaged for next week-
end, considering that you were going home for Easter? [. . .] And don't
make me go down on my knees about engagements too much! [. . .]

The party is in full progress. I have had breakfast in bed for once in a
way, and am scribbling this among the sheets. Morgan is very charming.
James merry, Alix argumentative, and Garrow . . . not such a bore as
might have been expected. — Oh! What do you think almost the first
thing he said to me was? A propos of pain and pleasure making a
difference to one's sense of time — 'The intervals between the strokes
when one's being beaten — I don't know whether you've ever been
beaten . . .' I vaguely smiled, and the conversation passed on. Wasn't it
ridiculous?

I am very happy. Are you? Mozart and the divine B flat are still
wandering about in my head. How astonishing that one world should
contain them both! — I had a letter from Molly, with a diatribe against
the vulgarity and hideousness of the production of Cosi. All true,
I expect. But I can't help being grateful to those creatures for giving
me the chance of hearing such music. James agreed with you that the
baritone (Johnson) was the best.

[. . .] I liked the critique of Metropolis. Tell me what is to happen
to it.

Some piercing darts of love
    from
        your
            faithful
                Zebra

‡

To Roger Senhouse

Sylvia Townsend Warner (1893–1978) published her first novel, Lolly Willowes, *in 1926, and* Mr Fortune's Maggot *in 1927. Emil Ludwig's* Napoleon and His Generals *appeared in 1926. Dadie Rylands got Rosamond Lehmann to send her first novel to Chatto, who accepted it straight away, but did not at first realize that they had a best-seller. Lehmann was always a little rueful that she never again achieved such a success.*

Ham Spray House
Hungerford
Berks.
May 11th 1927

[. . .] I have only just looked into Sylvia W's book – it seemed to me rather better than might be supposed – though the facetiousness is very distressing at moments. I shall read it through, when I've finished Ludwig on Napoleon, which is interesting, though really second-rate. As to Dusty Answer, it seemed to me to have decided merit, and for a first novel remarkable. The disadvantage, to my mind is that it is too romantic and charged with sunset sentiment. A youthful fault, I suppose. Not sufficiently 'life-enhancing'. But very well and carefully done – without horrors in taste (a rare thing nowadays!) and really at moments moving. But you will see.

Personally I enjoyed the Lighthouse more than Dalloway. But it really is a most extraordinary form of literature. It is the lack of copulation – either actual or implied – that worries me. A marvellous and exquisite arabesque seems the result. I suppose there is some symbolism – about the lighthouse, etc. – but I can't guess what it is. With anyone else, the suggestion would be fairly obvious, but it won't fit into that sexless pattern by any manner of means.

Yes, do write again. L.

‡

To Roger Senhouse

'La Chatte' was made for Diaghilev's Ballets Russes. The story Lytton found unclear came from Aesop – a young man falls in love with a cat and prays to

Aphrodite to transform her into a woman; but on seeing a mouse, the woman abandons her lover to chase it. Henri Sauguet wrote the music; Balanchine choreographed the piece for Serge Lifar as the male lead. The Constructivist sets and costumes were by Naum Gabo and his brother Antoine Pevsner, who used the new translucent but shiny material talc – mica.[1]

Xavier Marcel Boulestin (1878–1943), who had been 'secretary' to Colette's Willy, wrote his first cookery book in 1923, and opened his Southampton Street, Covent Garden restaurant in 1927. He became Britain's (and thus the world's) first TV cook.

William Somerset Maugham (1874–1965), serving with the Red Cross in France in 1914, fell in love with Gerald Haxton (1892–1944), a twenty-two-year-old from San Francisco in the same ambulance unit in Flanders. Tony Paxton in Our Betters *(1917) is supposed to be Gerald Haxton, as is Rowley Flint in* Up at the Villa *(1941). Maugham married Syrie Wellcome, daughter of Dr Barnardo, and they had a daughter; but, even while the marriage lasted, Maugham spent most of his time travelling abroad with Haxton. Haxton was deported from Britain in 1919 as an undesirable alien. Maugham divorced his wife in 1928. The next year he bought a villa on the Côte d'Azur and called it Villa Mauresque. Gerald Haxton died in an alcoholics' ward in a hospital in New York in 1944.*

Ham House
Hungerford
Berks.
June 20th 1927

Yes, I should like to go to the ballet on the 28th or 29th very much. Do you think it might be a good plan to try the Pit? Ralph told me he got into the 2nd row without having to wait, and that that is really in the stalls, as they have been so much reduced owing to their absurd expensiveness. With luck, too, we might worm ourselves into gangway seats!

[. . .] As to the Cat, I gathered from Raymond's ecstatic account of it (in which I thought I detected some traces of unconscious guilt among the raptures) that it couldn't really be very good. But it is always quite pleasant to look at Lifar. And then – the talc scenery – *that* of course hit off Raymond exactly – and perhaps it might be rather entertaining for once in away. I agree with what you say about the story in these affairs – its being so rarely made clear. – A typically modern disease, I fancy.

I flew from pillar to post in London without cessation. Dinner with

Dadie at Boulestin's (I'd never been there before, and didn't much like the atmosphere). An odd and unexpected adventure, which would interest you, I think, but it is too complicated to narrate in a letter – And then a rather amusing lunch at Christabel's. Osbert was there (distinctly charming) and also Somerset Maugham – a hang-dog personage, I thought – do you know him – with a wife. Perhaps it was because I eschewed such things for so long that I was amused – the odd mixture of restraint and laisser-aller struck me freshly, but eventually it's just that that becomes such a bore.

After an icy week-end, the sun shines again and I am out in it.

My love
Lytton.

1. I am indebted to Richard Morphet for these details. See *The Tate Gallery Illustrated Catalogue of Acquisitions 1984–86*, p.148ff.

‡

To Mary Hutchinson

Lytton's 'young man' was Roger Senhouse.

Ham Spray
July 15th 1927

Dearest Mary,

I had tea with Clive on Wednesday and found him more cheerful than I had expected. It seems to me that it *is* probably best that he should not see you at present, so long as he feels as he does, and I believe you would both gain in the long run, in spite of the dismalness of the separation. I tried to convey to him what you asked me to, and I think more or less succeeded. He was very charming. I do hope all will be well eventually.

As for my young man, whom I went to on leaving you – he was unexpectedly delightful – really most coming on – the villain! I had a most enjoyable dinner with him and Dadie; but maintained my sangfroid throughout! Afterwards D and I went to the nautical party where I saw Christabel as Britannia, who told me you couldn't come –

very disappointing. It was really a very amusing party – several creatures I'd not seen before – a few flirtations – drink and comfort – a sensation of being quite at home as an Admiral – perfect contentment, in fact! – It was sad leaving London yesterday. But I have no money and must work. In October I shall have a bounce, I hope.

Topsy and Peter are here. We discuss Freud, Sainte Beuve, Love, and Cambridge, with great gusto, while the rain pours down in sheets.

Adieu, adieu,
my love,
Lytton

‡

To Mary Hutchinson

Michael Holroyd says the sculptor Stephen ('Tommy') Tomlin, 'being bisexual, for a time occupied a virtuoso position in the Ham Spray régime'.[1] *In fact at the end of July he married Lytton's niece, Julia Strachey. The 'darling' who has 'abandoned' him was Roger.*

Ham Spray House
Hungerford
Berks.
July 19th 1927

Dearest Mary, I hope my letter wasn't tiresome. I wrote it in rather a distracted moment, and feel that it may have been, in some way or other, abrupt. However, I daresay it wasn't really! – I am leading a decidedly queer life. Both T[ommy] and D[adie] are devoted to me – and I to them; they please me in every way – though, to be sure, the ways are different! As for R[oger], the dinner with him and D was evidently a success – he has written me quite an amiable letter, and positively sends his love! So *that* is on the upward move at the moment at any rate. My relation with T is exciting – there is strength there – and a mind – a remarkable character, – but there is a lull in the proceedings, for he is to be married on Thursday (I believe). There is also a lull with D, who has gone to Cambridge – a delightful, gay affair that one. So you see altogether I have plenty to think about in my seclusion. But I must tell you a little more about the end of the nautical party – perhaps you heard of the scene with the fearful Jew host – poor Dadie, having broken some wretched vase, taken out on to the landing, talked to loudly by the beast, abused, and finally told to 'get out'. The poor creature was in a miserable state, though, to be sure, slightly cheered to feel, as he got into the taxi, the footman caressing his bottom. But at last his feelings became too much for him, and he quite broke down. I put him to bed – about 4.30 – a dim dawn beginning – he was weeping bitterly, and cried himself to sleep, while I crept away in my Admiral's uniform, to meet, as I went downstairs in the twilight, Douglas returning – but that was nothing. The child was quite cheerful again next day, and that evening I had dinner with the other one, and we came back to my rooms afterwards, and I was extremely happy. Then returned here for Topsy and Peter – and, on their departure, – complete prostration! The week-end has been spent in bed. Sometimes in tears, from utter exhaustion and the grief and pain of being abandoned by my darling, at other times dipping into Swift's filthy poems – or dreaming over my strange lot. Was there ever such a world? Such lives? Such peculiarities? I constantly reflect on you and the roses – and on other singular events. Don't, please, imitate Topsy in your treatment of letters; and put them somewhere out of sight. Shall I write to you again? A sort of diary? – But I must not be too egotistical, you know.

I am feeling stronger now, and intend to go to London tomorrow, for a night – I don't think I shall have any time to see you in – but you come on Saturday. A party at Philip Sassoon's is what (apparently) takes me up.

my love
Lytton

1. Michael Holroyd, *Lytton Strachey*, p. 585.

‡

To Mary Hutchinson

Lady Pansy Lamb's 'attractive' brother was Frank Pakenham, later Lord Longford. 'Paul' may have been Paul Odo Cross.

Ham Spray House
Hungerford
Berks.
July 27th 1927

Dearest Mary,

I hope you enjoyed your visit as much as I did! – But of course it was
far too short – and the bad weather somehow made it shorter – no
spacious maunderings on lawns – no moonlight seat-sittings: really
someday you must come and stay tête-à-tête for at least a week – then
we should have time for a little conversation. But a reversion to the
18th Century would be the only satisfactory plan – a two months' visit.

My adventures took rather an odd turn yesterday. I had brought from
London a suit-case crammed with old letters and papers of all sorts – for
Sebastian to arrange, and I couldn't resist peering into them. Oh, such a
'plunge into the past!' – and so many pasts! Hectic undergraduate days –
absurdly melodramatic. George Mallory later – rather sweet. A bundle
from Rupert Brooke – nice, decidedly. Some vague Duncan letters –
very amusing. The Bunny budget. And so on – until the present seemed
to fade into the same kind of mirage, and unreality reigned. I'm afraid
my biography will present a slightly shocking spectacle! In the middle of
it all, as I was dreaming over a snapshot of George I'd forgotten all
about – so alluring! – the door opened, and who should come in but
. . . Henry! Yes – that ghost! But accompanied, this time, by a far from
spectral entity – his Pansy – a gay, sturdy, light-haired, dark-eyed young
lady – positively attractive! (her brother, so Henry says, is no less so –
oh! oh!) He seems set up – perhaps that will end happily – perhaps she'll
be able to quell his evil spirit. Though I fear she'll never make him a
good painter. But that hardly matters, I suppose.

D[adie]'s letter from Venice was charmingly affectionate; but they had
both been ill, and there was not a word to say he was enjoying it. But
I hope for the best; it would be too fearful for that poor Peter if, after
such a romantic whirl, there was another failure. I have asked Paul to
come down for the week-end when Carrington's away. Will he be able
to? Oh, such a fascinating voice on the telephone!

I think of R[oger] still – no doubt too much. I wish I didn't. Things must
take their course, and it seems unlikely that I shall see him again before the
autumn. There must be something tiresome about me, when seen very
near at hand; but his reactions have I think been a trifle extreme.

Any news of Clive? Perhaps you have already started for St . . .
I don't know what – so I send this to Albert Road, presuming that the
police inspector will forward it. I hardly saw T*[ommy]* at all when he
was here – an embrace and a two minute conversation. And he never
writes – that's all right, though. I feel quite firm in that direction. He's
a treasure – and D*[adie]*'s a darling.

my love
Lytton

‡

To James Strachey

*Sebastian Sprott, having filed the mass of letters to Lytton, was now evidently
doing the same service for James. 'Walter' was Walter Lamb, who had an affair
with the undergraduate James.*

Ham Spray House
Hungerford
Berks.
August 2nd 1927

I enclose cheque – though heaven knows what you'll do with it.

An extraordinary revelation has just occurred – or whatever a
revelation does: A letter from Clive to you, dated September 1914,
and asking for information as to how he is to get into the Army Service
Corps or some other non-fighting unit, as his health forbids his going
into the active army. Did you remember this? Did you suppress it? It
really seems extremely strange. What *could* have been occurring in his
noddle? A most useful letter for a blackmailer.

Who was A.L. Johnston (Alec, I think)? To my mind, a distinctly
attractive boy. A letter from Mr Towsey, which was amusing. Did you tell
me he was dead? I should be sorry. Walter's letters to you make curious sad
reading. On the whole, the past strikes one as exceedingly passé.

your
Lytton

Sebastian sends his love to you both.

☩

To Mary Hutchinson

Paul Odo Cross wrote The Snail That Climbed The Eiffel Tower, *published by John Lehmann and illustrated by John Minton. Sir Cedric Morris painted a townscape from a window of his house at 45 Brook Street, Mayfair. He died c.1963, when a painting by Vuillard was sold from his estate. Sir Thomas Urquhart's version of the first two books of Rabelais appeared in 1653.*
    Margot Asquith published her Lay Sermons *in 1927. The Proust was* Le Temps Retrouvé.

Ham Spray House
Hungerford
Berks.
August 9th 1927

Dearest Mary,

I should have written before, but I have again been ill – for no apparent reason – reduced to bed, with Sebastian looking after me. I am now better again, but still rather wobbly – a great nuisance.
    My emotional life has been less extreme than usual, naturally, though still rather accidenté *[bumpy]*. S has not played any part in it, however. He tends to be remote. Very busy, too, with my correspondence, and I believe quite happy, sorting endless letters and tearing up innumerable envelopes. Of course he is most sweet. I had a curious spasm about a week ago, on looking into a collection of love letters from Ralph P. The whole situation – so intensely romantic and moving – rushed back upon me, and I felt strangely upset. There he was, downstairs – the same person, really, I couldn't help feeling; but six years or seven had gone – and where were we now? – I longed to say something – but it was impossible to do more than murmur some vague word or two, and he returned to London.
    You will smile to hear who was my week-end visitor. I had asked Odo Cross – he couldn't come. The coast was clear. What should I do? – I suddenly sent a telegram to R*[oger]* saying that I should be alone here with Sebastian, and asking him to come. Rather to my surprise he accepted, and came on Saturday. By a curious chance *exactly* a year had elapsed since the visit on which I had first had him, and he kept the

anniversary by sleeping, for the first time, by himself! However, such coincidences are ridiculous. I put him next door to S, hoping that something might occur in that direction, but nothing did. I am hardly jealous at all, you know, and had few qualms. He looked far from well – pale and puffy – no beauty that I could see – really almost someone different. So dreadfully fat! – All went well, he was most amiable. I behaved with the highest propriety, he seemed to enjoy himself, and positively on going away gave me an entirely unsolicited kiss. A queer creature, certainly. Decidedly charming, very pleasant indeed to be with. Not clever, oh no! But likes books and their minutiae, which is pleasing to me. We spend a happy hour comparing Rabelais in the original with Urquhart's translation. He picked wild flowers and branches from shrubs on our morning walk – more flowers in the garden – and went back with a huge armful – to my mind a sympathetic thing to do, and what no one else I know (except Carrington) would dream of doing. Aren't things strangely – exasperatingly – mixed? What does one want? What does anyone want? – Really? Ah! so little – and so much! –

A letter from D[adie] this morning, full of spirits and sympathy – in Cambridge. On the subject of Cross he says – 'Did you hear that at the sailor party he seduced two members of the band *and* a gentleman in a neighbouring house?' No – I confess this was news to me. But nowadays one is hardly surprised.

I was delighted by your letter – there were many charming things in it. Please write again, if you have time among all your distractions. The N[ouvelle] R[evue] F[rançaise] arrived yesterday, but the Proust is too much for me. I can't get there in a jump. Sebastian also declines. But I'll convey it back to R[aymond] M[ortimer].

From some faint indications, I guess that the Nation review of Margot was by Virginia – but I've no knowledge.

your
Lytton

‡

To Mary Hutchinson

Leigh Ashton was an expert on Chinese art. Malcolm Davidson, Douglas's brother, was the London-born composer (1891–1949), who had been at

*Cambridge. Wogan Philipps, 2nd Lord Milford (1902–93), married first
Rosamond Lehmann; he later married an Italian aristocrat, and then the
Russian widow of an eminent Communist. He joined the Communist Party
himself, and spoke for it in the House of Lords. Robert Medley and Rupert
Doone founded the Group Theatre, which in the 1930s produced plays by
W. H. Auden and Christopher Isherwood, among others. Lytton was reading
Louis Madelin,* The French Revolution. *Following Katherine Mansfield's
death in 1923, her husband edited and published her* Journal *in 1927.*

Ham Spray
August 26th 1927

Dearest Mary,

I should have written before now, but I have *again* been ill, and in
consequence everything came to a standstill. The outlook is rather
gloomy. I don't know what is to happen – how am I to get well – how
am I to finish Elizabeth – when shall I ever be able to frisk again. I am
taking tonics. One of them is called 'Elixir No. 145' – but I don't feel
much faith in it. I have given up all thought of going abroad – the
discomfort would be far too great. Perhaps later on I shall struggle to
the seaside with Carrington. The annoying thing is that I have no
symptoms, except this eternal decrepitude, which makes me feel a
hopeless imbecile – et voilà tout. I was just able to struggle up to
London for a night last Monday – to meet Dadie, who was on his way
through from Cambridge. During one of my relapses, I had suspected
him (from something in a letter) of perfidy – at the same time one of
R*[oger]*'s desolating epistles arrived. Despair on every hand! – However,
D turned out, poor child, to be perfectly innocent, and even old R not
so bad as I'd thought. There has been trouble at no. 37 in the upper
floors, which were let to Leigh Ashton, D's male servant remaining. A
burglary – various objects missing – the servant suspected – etc. etc.
The two boys (Dadie and Douglas) were in a great taking. The servant
was dismissed, but not before it was discovered that he had been
carrying on in the most shocking manner with Malcolm Davidson,
who had been lent Douglas's room for a night or two. Quite a
bombshell for the two boys, who don't at all approve of that sort of
thing, as you may imagine. This is of course highly private: what is even
more so is that that wretch Sebastian had also been having a finger in
the pie – but this neither of the boys is in the least aware of; and it is

thought that 'Albert', as his more intimate friends call him *[the servant]*, has disappeared for ever.

D was charming. I gave him dinner at the Ivy, and so on. I also had lunch with R at Boulestin's – he looked far from well, but is going off for a holiday in Germany with his ex-love – the blue-eyed gazelle, Wogan Philipps. The blue-eyed gazelle (as might be expected) is not very bright in the head – ah, no! – but, after all, why should he be? We went to a picture-gallery in Bond Street, and there was Robert Medley – do you know him? – a most attractive young person, in my opinion. But he is inextricably involved with the deplorable little dancer Rupert Doone. In vain I tried to undo some of the strings – no go! – and so here I am down here again, pale and wan, and expecting the visit of Morgan for the week-end, with doubts as to what I shall find to say to him.

Your life sounds all that it should be – something of a phantasm, perhaps, though. I am reading M. Madelin on the French Revolution – very interesting in a straightforward way. Is there anything else to read? Have you seen K. Mansfield's diary? Send me a word or two, if you ever have the leisure, between snipe-shooting and education.

my love,
Lytton

‡

To Virginia Woolf

Virginia had written a long, cheering letter to Lytton on 3 September, because she had heard that he was ill. Philip Ritchie died on the 13th.

Ham Spray House
Hungerford
Berks.
September 16th 1927

My dearest Virginia,

I was on the point of answering your charming letter, when the news of Philip's death came – and now it seems impossible to say very much. Only it was really divine of you to write to me so entrancingly – as I

read I felt my health positively mounting upwards and my spirits, etc.
I am now decidedly better. I hope to see you ere long.

My love to you both.

Lytton

‡

To Carrington

*Philip Ritchie had had tonsillitis on and off during the summer and, following a
relapse, he died suddenly.*

Caledonian Club
St James's Square
S.W.1
Tuesday, September 20th 1927

Dearest creature, I have only a moment as I am just off to Victoria. I was
very glad to get your letter this morning. You have indeed been a comfort
to me in this horrid time. Nobody could have been more charming and
affectionate than Roger last night. As we thought, he has moments of
terrible self-reproach – and I don't altogether like leaving him. But he said
he didn't want me to stay, and I didn't want to force myself upon him, and
he has a few other friends in London whom he will see. One great relief is
that that wretched estrangement of the last few months has disappeared – it
is a mercy as it *[is thus]* possible for me to do all I can to comfort and
console him. It seems to me most unfair to think harshly of him. No one
who saw him last night could do so. An unfortunate thing is that Ken and
Jennings have apparently gone off without making an effort to see him –
so that all he has heard was in a hurried telephone conversation with
[illegible], who has also gone abroad. My dear, he got the first news in
the most dreadful way in Paris. That silly servant sent him in an
envelope a cutting of Philip's portrait from the Daily Mirror with the
announcement of his death – and this was the first thing he opened.
Luckily Wogan was with him. His sister has returned from Scotland,
and is not far off – in Hertfordshire. He spoke most affectionately of
you, and liked your letter very much. Poor Roger, poor Roger.

‡

To Roger Senhouse

Charleston
Firle
Lewes
Sussex
September 22nd 1927

[. . .] Virginia and Leonard came over to tea yesterday, which was a great pleasure. V looking very young and beautiful. She says we must all write our memoirs – on an enormous scale – and have them all published ten years hence.

Life here is pleasant – if only it wouldn't pour with rain it would be pleasanter still. It is infuriating to have the most heavenly country two inches off, and be unable to put one's nose into it. Inside the house is rather ramshackle – a regular farm-house, not done up in any way – but very beautiful in parts, owing to the taste and skill of Duncan and Vanessa's decorations. They paint most of the day in a studio they have built out at the back, but I haven't yet been allowed inside. Clive spends the morning writing his Great Work on Civilisation. After dinner we gossip and play the gramophone. *[. . .]*

All my love, my dear Roger.
Lytton

‡

To Roger Senhouse

'Miminy piminy' is from W. S. Gilbert, Patience, *Act II: A 'Francesca di Rimini, miminy, piminy, / "Je-ne-sais-quoi" young man!' which might well describe the heavily made-up Stephen Tennant.*

Ham Spray House
Hungerford
Berks.
October 17th 1927

Dearest Roger

[. . .] Oliver and Inez came down for the week-end. I had asked Oliver,
but owing to the ambiguity of the English 'you' he apparently presumed
that I*[nez]* was included, and she came without any announcement. It
was all right, of course – she's not so bad – and proceedings were
enlivened by the arrival yesterday for tea of Osbert, Christabel,
Siegfried, and Stephen Tennant – a most strange irruption! – from the
Glenconner-Grey establishment near Salisbury. S.T. was more than any
of us could brook – a miminy piminy little chit, entirely occupied with
dressing-up. The night before they had all dressed up as nuns, that
morning they had all dressed up as shepherds and shepherdesses, in the
evening they were all going to dress up as – God knows what – but
they begged and implored me to return with them and share their
raptures. When dressed up, they are filmed – and the next week-end, I
suppose, the film is exhibited. Can you imagine anything more
'perfectly *divine*'? One would have imagined them to come in a vast
Daimler, but not at all – a small two-seater (open) with a dicky behind
was their vehicle. They came very late, having lost their way on the
Downs, and I shudder to think of the horrors of their return journey.
Strange creatures – with just a few feathers where brains should be.
Though no doubt Siegfried is rather different. *[. . .]*

All my love, my dear Roger
　　　　Lytton

‡

To Roger Senhouse

Ham Spray House
Hungerford
Berks.
December 13th 1927

[. . .] I haven't been able to do much in the way of cheering up Dadie,
I fear. He has discovered, much sooner than I'd expected, the horrors of
Cambridge, and as they are very real, to my mind, it's difficult to know
what to do about it. He feels lonely – the dons are hopeless – and he's
out of it with the undergraduates. It certainly is wretched to be there
without a single intimate friend.

   In the meantime, his affairs go on very much as usual. As for Noel
Coward, he has quite given him up – because, if you please, Sirocco
was such a failure! – this seems to me quite a new view of Love!

> I love you not for your fair face,
> Much less for any inward grace,
> Not for your wit, nor for your art,
> Nor for your gentleness of heart,
> Nor even for your amorous feats;
> But for your Box Office Receipts.
> And as those go from high to higher
> So mounts up too my hot desire;
> But when they show a downward curve,
> My constancy begins to swerve;
> And should they fall away to zero
> – Pooh! – I must find another hero.

My fondest love
   to the best of monkeys
      Lytton

‡

To Mary Hutchinson

*In 1903 Norman Douglas (1868–1952) was divorced from his cousin, Elizabeth
FitzGibbon. In late 1916 he was arrested for sexual misconduct with a boy and*

the following year fled England to escape trial. In 1928 he published his wonderful Some Limericks. *Douglas was a famous proto-foodie, author of the most famous book of purportedly aphrodisiac recipes, and a friend of Elizabeth David. His 'marked accent' probably reflected his birth and upbringing in Germany as much as his Scottish parentage. He really could not afford to pay for Lytton and Roger's meals, but Lytton returned the favour immediately by introducing Douglas to his own publishers, Chatto & Windus. The Hotel Foyot was on rue de Tournon.*

Nancy Cunard's cousin, Victor (1898–1960), was Paris correspondent for The Times. *Clifford Sharp, the editor of the* New Statesman, *lost an expensive libel action in 1928, compounded by remarking injudiciously that no one could 'hope for a fair hearing in a court presided over by Justice Avory'. Frederick William Jowett (1864–1944) was a Labour MP and a socialist.*

Ham Spray House
Hungerford
Berks.
February 22nd 1928

My dearest Mary, I hope your letter indicates only a passing mood of depression – one of those sinking feelings that one does sometimes have – and that you are now on the crest of the wave again. But I do wish I could see you and talk to you. I would come, but I feel that I must stick to this wretched grindstone, or all will be lost. Its serpentine prolongation is getting past a joke. I think I shall be up on Thursday 1st for the night. Could I have tea with you then? It would be very nice. Rather far off! Almost a Peter Lucas assignation! Here I sit in the verandah, positively grilling in the sun. It is really astonishing – a heat haze envelops the downs – the cows group themselves in a regular trance. It must be beginning to be lovely with you, I fancy. Dear me! You must not feel shattered. All that you say to me is most charming. I have always felt our friendship to be one of the most excellent of things. An extraordinary sympathy . . . does it come from Edward Strachey (Carlyle's friend) do you suppose – our common ancestor? – Perhaps from his wife, the enchanting Julia Kirkpatrick. I suppose they did exist once – though it hardly seems conceivable – in Fitzroy Square, too! What on earth could have been their experiences, and what could they think of us?

I have been longing to tell you all about Paris. It was well worth it, though terribly exhausting. The gale on that Friday night was so violent that we neither of us slept a wink as we crossed, and I arrived a mere ghost. However, N[orman] D[ouglas] was extremely sympathetic, and soothing – seemed to understand at once my dread of those trailing café parties, and brushed it all aside, declaring that he too didn't at all care for them. So I was able to rest and recover. We went to the Foyot hotel, which was very good though appallingly noisy – unpretentious and comfortable and not at all expensive. ND was rather older than I expected – not flamboyant (as I had rather feared) – in fact rather the opposite – very neat – something (as Roger said) of a schoolmasterish effect in *appearance* – one of those old benevolent unexpectedly broad-minded schoolmasters one sometimes comes across. Superb in restaurants, adoring food and so on. A curious, very marked accent – partly Scotch, perhaps partly – I don't know what – distinctly fascinating. The talk was mainly on a certain subject. Roger played up admirably, quite admirably, and made everything go much more easily than would otherwise have been the case. He seemed to be not particularly literary – which was slightly disturbing; and I think just a trifle too old – I mean belonging to a generation almost too distant for really intimate approach – a touch of Sickert – but perhaps I'm wrong. He's obviously a most charming person, and perhaps with time one might really get to know him well. He said he thought he was coming to England this summer, and if so would certainly come to Ham Spray. Rather exciting! We must have a party for him at Boulestin's, I think. A slight effect, you know, of having been not very well treated by life. He's been very unlucky with publishers, and has made hardly anything out of his books. One would like to surround him with every kind of comfort and admiration and innumerable boys of 14½.

Nancy went off all right too. We had a lunch party on Sunday – with Victor Cunard as well. (Do you know him? – A white cat – on the Times.) Their relations were not very easy to disentangle. Christian names reigned – and they were all three living in the same hotel. ND insisted on coming to the station to see us off – insisted on paying for every meal – and eventually tried to tip the porter! Roger was as perfect as possible throughout, and the return journey was quite smooth, so that it was possible to sleep . . . etc. But what a nuisance the Channel is! How one would rush to Paris for lunch and dinner, if it was only a question of a few hours in a train. I found the place more sympathetic than usual – and oh, the food and drink!

With all my fondest love,
Lytton

‡

To Roger Senhouse

Roger consulted Who's Who *to learn the date of Lytton's birthday – it was 1 March, three days after this letter was written (1928 being a leap year); birthdays are indeed given in* Who's Who.

Douglas published Some Limericks: Collected for the Use of Students & Ensplendourd'd with Introduction, Geographical Index, and with Notes Explanatory and Critical *(Boston, privately printed, 1928). This edition was recently offered by a bookseller as a 'Superb collection of very obscene limericks with commentary by Norman Douglas'.*

Molly MacCarthy and Cyril Connolly had got into a fight. He had spent part of the summer of 1927 with the MacCarthys at Shulbrede Priory. Molly soon disliked him, and warned her sister Cecilia against him for sponging off women, with the result that her daughter 'Racy' was forbidden to speak to him. He was convinced that the Cornish sisters disliked him because he was poor. Molly actually told a friend 'that the only person I have ever met in the large and varied community to which we belong whom I consider crude enough to be described as Bogus is Cyril Connolly'.[1] But what probably interested Lytton was that Molly was sceptical about Connolly's interest in Racy, and told her sister 'that he was really still a "bugger", which Connolly, when he heard about it, violently resented'.

Ham Spray House
Hungerford
Berks.
February 27th 1928

Dearest Monster

You may well sue for forgiveness! Not a word for more than a week, and I left to imagine you ill, enraged, or in despair . . . but I rather gather from your letter that the word 'woolgathering' is a better summary of the case. And even now you say nothing of what you've been doing, where you've been, or all sorts of things I should have liked to hear of. 'I am here' – are you indeed? A postmark indicated Herts – I expected to see the Moon! Well! I'm glad that you got seats for Thursday in the '3rd row' (?of the Gallery). As for Who's Who I fear you have wasted your time over it, as I cannot believe it reveals the birthdays of the great and famous. Your notions about my wanting to be alone at Cambridge are quite imaginary, sir! Archevangelicalism will probably not occur, and anyhow it won't affect matters. So you'd better confirm Dadie. We now come to the worst delinquency. You really are a perfect little PIG to pay no attention whatever to my repeated invitations. I had been hoping daily to hear whether you could or could not come to meet Rosamond on the 3rd and I am now left to infer that you can't – late in the day for asking anyone else! – Villain! – The Queen must say that she considers Mr S's conduct *most reprehensible*, and doubts very *much* whether she will speak to him in *future*! (So far Queen V. – Queen E. follows –) By God's Death! The Knave must be taught his mannyrs! He shall be whipt, shall stand in ye pillorye, and loose his eares – yea, marry! After they have been nailed thereunto for the space of an howre! – Finally Lady Colefax adds, in letters she hopes will catch your eye – CAN YOU COME ON THE 17TH ?

If you can, it will literally be four months since you were here last! I fear this dreamlike weather will have departed by that time. 'I am here' – i.e. on the verandah, surrounded by 10,000 books, which have just arrived from 10,000 booksellers – of every variety of price and attractiveness. Have you any bookshelves for sale?

A letter has come from N[orman] D[ouglas] – *slightly* remote, I cannot but think! – *You* have become Senhouse. I'm afraid I must have made a hash of my tone. But still of course he's very charming – regrets not having asked you for a single Limerick – and thinks he might someday 'sum up courage' to do so.

I've been in rather a stew over Elizabeth – découragé, etc. – but now am feeling better – reckless, I suppose. But it really is a horribly difficult job.

Have you heard the story of Molly and Connolly? Are you going to gamble with Oliver on Friday? Well! A larger letter than you deserve, sirrah: all the same, hugs and love from Lytton.

1. Quoted in Hugh and Mirabel Cecil, *Clever Hearts*, p. 230, where the entire story is delectably told.

‡

To Roger Senhouse

Ham Spray House
Hungerford
Berks.
March 6th 1928

Dearest Creature

I hope you are quite well. I am quite well. It is hot here. Is it hot in your Square? Have you been a good boy? I hope so. I have been a good boy. If you have been a bad boy you must have the rod. Bad boys have the rod. And so do good boys too. For the world is not what you might think it. (End of exercise in words of one syllable.)

And now please listen to this. If you think we needn't reach Dadie till tea-time and if it's fine on Saturday, do you think we might have lunch at Saffron Walden – almost in the direct line between London and Cambridge? It is the original home of the Strachey family, and I have always wanted to see it. *[. . .]*

Here I am all alone – it is undoubtedly warm and peaceful – a faint mist hangs about – but so far I have managed to keep it out of my head. The Bess crisis is pretty serious – a regular death-grapple! But I hope the worst will be over by the end of the week.

I tried my hand yesterday at a Housman poem, but the result didn't seem very satisfactory, so I shan't send it you just yet. Mr Allardyce Nicoll on Shakespeare (Hogarth Lectures No. 4) has arrived, containing examples of la sottise humaine which would have delighted Flaubert. Goneril and Regan, it turns out, were *quite in the right!* Oh, may the Lord reward according to their deserts all professors who write on Shakespeare!

All my love, you blue-nosed baboon,
Lytton

‡

To Carrington

Hotel Phoenix
Copenhagen
August 8th 1928

Dearest Creature

We are enjoying ourselves very much in this agreeable dim town. The sea voyage went off smoothly, then we mounted into 2nd class sleepers, which were perfect – much better than wagon-lits – broad and spacious, and side by side, instead of one on top of the other. In the morning of Monday we steamed into Copenhagen – knew not the name of a single hotel, so Roger, as we were leaving the station, asked a Cook's emissary who was standing by if he could recommend one. He told us of this, which is exactly our style – middle-class, comfortable, and in the prettiest part of the town. Really at moments I am reminded of Aix! So many 18th Century houses in the rococo style – most charming – though no caryatids at the doorways. There is a lovely square, with four small palaces on each side and a statue of a King on horseback in green bronze in the middle. You would love it. I never saw any of this when I was here before with that dolt Daisy McNeil. Unluckily the sun has departed and rain falls, so that I can't take any photographs. I omitted to do so on Sunday, when I might have – I pray for fine weather tomorrow. We have had all sorts of meals in all sorts of restaurants – have spent hours in second-hand bookshops, with no result – have walked through endless streets and gardens – and so far seen no 'sights', except a small collection of pictures in a private house near here, of which the Rembrandt I am sending from a dim postcard of is the only object worth looking at. Some of the older houses and streets are very attractive – 17th Century – flat and coloured with different pale twists. The inhabitants are pleasant, but oh! so lacking in temperament! Duty seems to guide their steps, and duty alone. I hope all goes well with you, and that all the works are proceeding as they might. I send everything to Ham Spray, as it seems safest. The Lord knows where you may be when you get this. Roger sends his love. I send my fondest love too.

Lytton.

☩

To E. M. Forster

The subject of this letter is the prosecution for obscenity of Radclyffe Hall's lesbian novel The Well of Loneliness. *The author made considerable difficulties for her supporters, by insisting that they defend it on the grounds of its being a literary masterpiece, a judgement from which Lytton and Forster demurred.*

Ham Spray House
Hungerford
Berks.
August 28th, 1928

Dear Morgan

I wired, but as I thought time might be an object I thought I'd risk ringing up too. I hope it was worth the horrors involved!

The letter seems to me excellent. My only criticism is that one doesn't quite see to whom it's addressed. Mr. Cape seems to me to be the chief villain. However, I should think it could only do good, if you can get a sufficient number of fairly respectable names – Galsworthy for instance?

I suppose the book itself is pretty frightful. Did you, by the bye, read that traitor and pig Cyril Connolly in the New Statesman?

I returned last week from Scandinavia which I enjoyed very much. Won't you come down here soon? Any week-end or non-week-end.

Yours
Lytton

‡

To Roger Senhouse

There was a mysterious fire at Rushbrook Hall, at Bury St Edmund's, and Suffolk's largest and finest moated Tudor mansion was demolished without permission in 1961. Pevsner called it 'a capital loss'. Lytton was there in a very small party consisting of himself, Evan Charteris and Lord Hugh Cecil. Lord Hugh (who remarked in his will that he hoped nothing said about him by Mrs

Asquith would be believed), though a natural ally of Lytton's in many ways, was not pigeon-holeable, and his strong Christianity distressed Lytton.

Rushbrook Hall
Bury St Edmund's
Suffolk
Saturday evening, *[October 6th 1928]*

[. . .] I don't see how I can possibly shine! My fears are increased by the view, as I passed through a vast sitting room en route for my bedroom, of a bridge table laid out. Hopelessly inadequate, I'm afraid! I am scribbling this half dressed for dinner in my pompous bedroom. The house is distinctly fascinating – a large red-brick Tudor building (with a moat), converted in Queen Anne to a renaissance style, most success-fully. If only one could chuck out the present inhabitants, what a nice party one could have! It's getting late, and I must finish my dressing. A little more before I go to bed. By a miracle I realised in the train that I hadn't brought any evening collars – bought some in Bury! – Otherwise I should have appeared with a naked neck.

Midnight. Oh dear, oh dear, *not* a very entrancing evening. However, there are always moments of amusement; but when it comes to discussing (a) Margot's manners, and (b) capital punishment, my spirit sinks. *[. . .]*

‡

To Roger Senhouse

William Allen Jowitt (Earl Jowitt 1885–1957) became Lord Chancellor at the end of a varied and complicated career in the law and politics, leaving the Liberals to join Labour, being expelled from the Labour Party in 1931 and so on, rising through the peerage from baron to viscount to earl. The DNB says he was 'outstandingly handsome and his carriage was gravely dignified'. It would have done him no good if the contents of this letter had been generally known.

Maples was a large furnishings store in London.

Ham Spray House
Hungerford
Berks.
November 5th 1928

Dearest creature, *[. . .]* Everyone has departed not without some
difficulty, as there was a puncture and Billy *[Winkworth]* and Saxon had
to come back and wait for a later train. The former was very sweet,
though I'm afraid rather ill – Carrington liked him very much. Boris
bubbled along in a perpetual fountain of amusement. An absurd story
of William Jowitt in Paris – do you know the solemn handsome
personage? He confessed to Boris that his one pleasure was whipping
women, but he didn't know how to manage it – could Boris tell him
what to do, and where to go? Boris handed him over to one of his
numerous friends, who had every renseignement at his finger tips.
William Jowitt announced that he had only four hours – had to leave
Paris after that. They sat in a café discussing every possibility. William
Jowitt could not quite make up his mind what he would like best. The
friend described a certain lieu, where the naked ladies entered the room
on all fours, pecking grain from the floor like chickens, while the
customers lashed their behinds. William Jowitt was struck by this . . .
and yet . . . did not after all feel *quite* sure that it was exactly what he
wanted . . . And so it went on, until at last the four hours were up, and
he went back to England. The poor fellow's debauches are always of
this nature.

Boris was very funny about Orlando, which he admired immensely,
but could *not* get over the fact that no Russian princess could have
come to England in a ship in the reign of Elizabeth. He thought he
would have to write to Virginia to point this out.

An old walrus arrived this morning from Maples, and put down a
couple of carpets – such a change! – One treads on padded swansdown.
My new bedroom is nearly done. You'll be lost in this house.

It has been another divine day. A dreamlike stillness – and one sits
basking in the verandah. Nevertheless the leaves continue to fall faintly,
and the ash is almost bare now, and the bowling-green is a thick red-
brown underfoot. It must have been perfect on the River. Roger, my
angel, good-night.

Lytton

‡

To Ralph Partridge

Ham Spray House
Hungerford
Berks.
November 6th 1928

My dearest, I am writing this without telling Carrington, and perhaps
you may think it best not to show it to Frances, but of course you must
do just as you like. I have felt for some time rather uneasy about F., but
have been unable to bring myself to say anything. What worries me is
her coming down here with you so much, and staying for so much of
the time you are here, so that we see so little of you alone. It is not
quite what I had expected would happen – and I think not exactly what
you intended either. I am afraid you may suppose that this indicates
some hostility on my part towards F., but this is far from being the case.
Can you believe this? I hope so. I hope you will trust that I am telling
the truth, and believe in my affection for you, which is something I
cannot describe or express. I feel it too deeply for that. I know that this
must be painful to you, but it seems better that I should tell you what
is in my mind than that I should continue indefinitely with a slight
consciousness of a difficulty not cleared up between us. Perhaps it
can't be cleared up – but at any rate I think it's better open than secret.
I don't want to force you into anything unwillingly. If you feel that you
can do nothing – then it can't be helped. If you feel that you cannot
answer this either by writing or in talk, do not do so, I will say nothing
more about it, and all will be well between us. But conceivably it might
be possible for you to suggest to F. that it would be better if she came
down rather less often – and that if that could be managed the situation
would be very greatly eased. It is for you to judge what you can do.
I trust your judgement. I only feel that you may perhaps have allowed
things to drift from an unwillingness to take an unpleasant step. I don't
know. And please do not do anything under a sense of 'pressure' from
me. I press for nothing. I only ask whether perhaps it may not be
possible, without too much pain, to make me happier.

I say nothing about C – she does not say very much to me about
these things, and does not guess that I am writing now. I am coming up
(with her) on Thursday, to arrange my move. I shall sleep that night at

37, I think. Come and see me there on Friday morning, if you like! –
The ping-pong room has been metamorphosed completely by its new
windows; it is now to my mind perhaps the nicest room in the house.

>With all my love, my dearest,
>>your devoted
>>>Lytton

☩

To Roger Senhouse

Henry Lamb had recently married his second wife, Lady Pansy Pakenham.
   James Stephens (1882–1950), poet, playwright and author of novels such as
The Crock of Gold *(1912). Racine,* Britannicus *(1689), Neron to Narcisse:*
'Mon génie étonné tremble devant le sien.'
   Sickert: Lytton saw the drawings for 'Rear Admiral Lumsden' (1927–28),
which portrays the subject in full uniform, holding a sword and standing in front
of a tall window but with his back to the viewer and his body turned so that his
left side and full face are visible.

>>>>Ham Spray House
>>>>>Hungerford
>>>>>>Berks.
>>>>November 10th 1928

My dearest creature, I have a short breathing space before my week-end
party begins, which consists this time of Henry Lamb and his bride, and
my sister Pippa (whom you met twice when I was ill at 41). I should
look forward to it with more gaiety if Henry Lamb were a little less
egotistical in conversation – impossible ever to talk about anything
unless *he* starts it – in the end this becomes a grinding bore. But he
means well, presumably.
   I went to Ottoline's on the spur of the moment on Thursday, and
found a literary tea party quite in the old style – not only Aldous but
James Stephens (did you spot that from those initials?) whom I hadn't
met before. I have little doubt but that you are a fervent votary of his
works – as for me, without having read a word of them I'm convinced
they're no good ('just like his narrow-minded presumption!') – and I
saw nothing in the man himself to lead me to change my opinion. A

little gnome-like Irishman, with a touch of the nautical, quite nice of course, but gassing away thirteen to the dozen with endless theories and generalisations. One of those essentially frivolous minds that mask themselves under a grand apparatus of earnestness and high-mindedness. On and on he went – inveighing against 'destructive criticism' (that tedious old story), pointing out that no one now could write about love, but only about sex, lamenting that there were no epics, etc. etc. Aldous didn't say much – he was very agreeable, as usual. I enjoy his company, partly because (I can't help it) I somehow feel so definitely his superior! – A question of astral bodies, or auras, I think. – 'Son génie étonné tremble devant le mien' – or something of that sort. Do you believe in those magnetic effluences? I almost do – how otherwise to account for the mysterious aversions, engouements *[infatuations]*, dominations, etc. that seem to have no reasonable explanation? – Ethel Sands filled up gaps with her appreciative shining teeth, and Pipsey interrupted and floundered as usual. I couldn't give very much attention to Mr J. S. – partly because I was seized with a desire to fart – many times – and could think of little else. I did so as silently as possible, but wondered whether Ottoline heard me, or if not, whether she smelt them, and, if she did, whether she traced them to me. The result was that when I was suddenly asked by her to give my opinion upon some long-winded dictum of Mr J.S.'s on medieval clothes – the difference between the sexes – beauty of women – love – and all the rest of it, I was rather at a loss, and could only say with a shriek 'Armour, I'm in favour of armour!' (mentally adding, 'it's such a good fart-protector'). Mr J.S. condemned me, of course, as destructive.

After leaving you, I had dinner at the Ivy with a young man, whom I'd happened to meet in the street that afternoon, and for whom, during the war, I had had a violent, short, and quite fruitless passion. Hadn't seen him for ten years – young no longer! – dried up, 31 years old, occupied with scraping together enough money to live on, and taking his 'art' immensely seriously – at which, it's all too clear, he'll never be any real good. For he's a painter by profession – name Geoffrey Nelson. – Oh, the boredom! He came back to 37, and droned on and on till half past twelve – which is the explanation of my being up then, and looking out of the window into the Square, with the vague notion that I might see somebody pass! . . .

I'm just going to bed. The Lambs arrived half dead in a motor. He is in an extremely amiable mood, and all goes well. I have moved into my new bedroom – am sitting on my new bed. I can hardly bear having to wait another fortnight before I display its beauties to you. However, by that time it will be more beautiful still. Goodnight, my angel. I hope you're enjoying yourself very much at this moment (11.40 p.m.) – A party at Maynard's, I daresay, is just beginning.

Sunday morning. All this, I fear, will seem very remote to you when you get it, after the distractions of Cambridge. Rather like an account of doings in the 18th century.

Before coming down here on Friday I just had time to go and look at the Sickert drawings, which impressed me a good deal. I thought the Admiral magnificent, and Mr H. Preston very amusing. Surely he is standing on that large balcony where you saw the amorous boots. I seemed to see that clock-face in the background, and the diminishing perspective of the front. I must stop now. Very best love to the mouse's ears and the rat's snout

> from
> > the
> > > old
> > > > bearded
> > > > > Jerboa

‡

To Roger Senhouse

This letter invites Roger to celebrate his birthday and that of Elizabeth and Essex *by dining at Boulestin's.*

Lady Pansy's good-looking brother was the crusading nemesis of pornography, Francis Aungier Pakenham KG (1905–2001), who succeeded their elder brother as 7th Earl of Longford.

*Valid syllogisms were assigned mnemonics. 'Barbara' is of the first figure, and where all three parts are type 'A' (from affirmo), or universal affirmations. There were verses to help budding logicians memorize the rules that would generate every valid syllogism. The first begins, 'Barbara celarent darii ferio baralipton'; in another version 'Barbara, Celarent, Darii, Ferio*que*, prioris'.*

Ham Spray House
Hungerford
Berks.
November 12th 1928

[. . .] The baa-lambs are just going off, in their car that won't start. She is, I must say, very pretty – extremely fair, but with dark eyelashes. Delightful, no doubt, for those that way inclined, to go to bed with. Henry is a decrepit wreck, looking about 60, a brain like a fret-saw, but one quite sees why she is devoted to him. – Her younger brother, they say (not Longford) is equal to her in attractiveness. – Ah! –

My new bed is all that I hoped for – fifty times as comfortable as the old one. The Duncan watercolour hangs over my bedroom fireplace. You never saw such calves! – The two young men are playing musical instruments – one a fiddle and t'other a pipe; but they might at any moment, one feels, drop them, and . . .

Oh, the beech, the beech! It dwindles away before my very eyes. And only about sixteen pale green leaves hang on the aspen. The ash is quite bare. Oddly enough the last leaves seemed to linger on the top rather than lower down, as one might have expected. It's really shocking, I am becoming a nature-lover and observer – fatal! – The intellect fades in proportion. Ruinous to know the difference between a blackbird and a thrush; one is never quite at home with a syllogism afterwards. Barbara grows dim as one notices the crocuses.

Adieu, Roger. All my love,
Lytton

✝

To Virginia Woolf

The subject of this letter is Virginia's obituary sketch for the Nation *(22 December) of Lady Strachey, who had died in her sleep on the afternoon of 14 December.*

Ham Spray
December 21st 1928

Nobody in the world but you could have produced such a perfect piece. It is absolutely right – most beautiful, most ingenious – moving, too, for me – but you will understand all that. Yes, the bulk! – How on earth did they manage it? By some eliminations, presumably – a sort of pruning – not going very deep, consciously at any rate, in certain directions. Anyhow, the result was superb.

Dearest creature, we shall all be most grateful to you. But that is not the word for what *I* feel.

your devoted
Lytton

‡

To Roger Senhouse

Ham Spray House
Hungerford
Berks.
January 16th 1929

My very dear Roger,

I was so glad to get your letter this morning – it was most good of you to explain so much about the Wharf. But it was rather wicked to say that such things 'ought not to trouble me in the least'! In fact, it would have been *very* wicked, except that you know well enough that it's all nonsense. What am I for, I should like to know? It suddenly flashes upon me that our little game in the half finished library that afternoon was highly symbolical – typifying the fact that I am here to listen to everything you like to say to me, always and for ever! It's difficult to advise, but it seems to me that if you think – as I gather you do – that a stand should be made, it's better to get it over; though I know well enough how wretchedly difficult it is to do such things. Two considerations may make it easier – (1) Even if the worst came to the worst and you had to leave, and thereby lose the prospect of a large income in the future, – it's quite possible that this would turn out an advantage in disguise and that comparative poverty with greater freedom would suit you better. And (2) will you allow me, Roger dear, to say seriously that you must consider a part of this sudden fortune of mine as yours as well – in the form of a loan, if you would prefer it so – towards a bookshop, perhaps – or any other business, according as things may turn out? Anyhow, please remember this as an extra support in your struggle with these damned directors.

You say that 1929 is to be very different to 1928. Excelsior! But surely 1928 hasn't been so very unsatisfactory? I must say if I had been your housemaster during that period you would have had quite a good report! You know there really is something divine in some forms of depression and discontent – for one thing they are often signs of youth – and that I believe is your case. All decent people remain young for an incredible length of time and suffer accordingly. It is the penalty for being decent. It would certainly show that there was something very wrong if you were satisfied at the age of 29!

I sympathise with you on the laziness question. But I think we are alike – both capable of great laziness and great industry – which makes things complicated, but is not without its advantages. I am luckier than you in one way, though – 'un des fortunés de la terre', as Henry Lamb used to say – because I have a decided bent in one direction (i.e. writing) and am a dunderhead at pretty well everything else, whereas you are equally good in about a hundred occupations. I believe you would make an excellent trapezist, or instructor in discobolos-throwing, or Russian Emperor, or whipped guardsman!

By-the-bye, that film sounds most exciting, and just what I would like. The Sunday Greek one is also alluring, but I have an instinctive suspicion that the beautiful young men always had, by some odd coincidence, towels flapping over a very important part of their anatomy.

I have been meaning to expatiate a little about myself and my aims and objects – but perhaps there is not very much to say. Do you know how ambitious I am? Don't breathe a word of this to anyone, but I long to do some good to the world – to make people happier – to help to dissipate this atrocious fog of superstition that hangs over us and compresses our breathing and poisons our lives. – But it can't be done in a minute!

I must stop now. Masses of love to you, Roger, and kisses to the angelic lolls

from

your

Lytton

‡

To Roger Senhouse

Mark Lane is in London EC3, off Fenchurch Street. Lytton found the location unlikely because there was a Mark Lane Underground station until 1946, when it was renamed Tower Hill. There are still wine bars and restaurants in Mark Lane. Julius Kayser & Co. were not exclusively wine merchants, but there is a Julius Kayser Zeller Schwarze Katz 1995 mentioned in some current internet tasting notes. Tom Mosley (1896–1980) was soon to become the Fascist Sir Oswald Ernald Mosley and, after Lytton's and Carrington's deaths, the husband of their friend Diana Mitford Guinness. This was unlikely to be Lytton's first meeting with him. Count Johann Heinrich von Bernstorff (1862–1939) was, until recalled in 1917, German Ambassador to the United States. He had an American wife and strongly pro-British views, and had retired from the diplomatic service. The Beerenauslese, whatever it was, cost the 2002 equivalent of £820 a case.

Lytton was flirting with Louis Bromfield (1896–1956), a now-forgotten agrarian reformer, popular novelist and essayist, who was then living with his wife and three daughters in Senlis, north of Paris. Lytton could have read either of his first two novels, The Green Bay Tree *(1924), set in a small town in Ohio, or* A Good Woman *(1927). Either would have nipped his infatuation in the bud.*

The Old Rectory Farm
Kidlington
Oxon
March 20th 1929

Dearest old creature [. . .]

I arrived here with Dadie on Monday – enjoying myself very much. Such a luncheon on Monday, before coming down! – At 59 Mark Lane, of all places! Chez Julius Kayser and Co. A wine-tasting affair. Jack Hutch was there – also Tom Mosley, Bernstorff and others. We drank *eleven* different kinds of Moselle and Hock – working gradually up from good to better, from better to best, from best to <u>supreme</u> (Mussbacher Hundert 'morgen Beerenauslese – £20 a dozen). You can imagine the state I was in when I went off at quarter to four to catch my train at Paddington. [. . .]

How amusing about Brom! Unfortunately one of his novels is here.

I have dipped into it – don't much like it . . . but then of course I *am* very difficile! Oddly enough, he appeared again the day after the Colefax lunch, at tea at Virginia's. Somehow too healthy, I fear. Really, I should say, in spite of all appearances, fitter for family bathing than anything else. *[. . .]*

‡

To Ralph Partridge

In 2002 purchasing power, the amount brought in by Elizabeth and Essex *to 31 March 1929 was £223,847.29.*

Ham Spray House
Hungerford
Berks.
April 6th 1929

My dearest

The Chatto accounts have just arrived, but luckily no cheque. Luckily, because the total, *after* £2000 (already paid) has been subtracted, is £4052.15.5. The total brought in by Elizabeth (up to March 31st) is £5457.7.6. Just under 30,000 copies sold. Oddments reach between 5 and 600 £s. Do you think I had better ask Prentice to hold over something till next year? £250, perhaps? But I can't remember whether we calculate the dividends from investments as part of the grand yearly total £4000. If we do, a good deal more should be kept back. I don't think there's any hurry about this. I've told P. that I shall write again, and that he's not to send a cheque till then. *[. . .]*

‡

To Roger Senhouse

The envelope enclosing this letter reads:

Deliver this to SENHOUSE (Roger)
  I prithee, postman debonair!

He is the handsome upstairs lodger
  At number
        14 BRUNSWICK SQUARE.
        London,
            W.C.1.

The first sheet has a drawing of Senhouse's face and a pair of round, black-rimmed spectacles of the sort we associate with Le Corbusier, and which Lytton is depicted wearing in some pictures. I think the drawings are by Lytton, rather than Carrington.
   Kyrle P. Leng (d.1958) photographer and printer, lived with Robert Gathorne-Hardy (1902–73, Lady Ottoline's editor and defender), at the Mill House, Stanford Dingley, in Berkshire.

Ham Spray House
Hungerford
Berks
April 23rd 1929

Dearest Angel,

There is a private view of John's things at Tooth's tomorrow. Is it conceivable that you could lunch with me at the Oriental at 1.15, and go on there afterwards? [. . .]
   The Stanford-Dingley visitors came with a camera as well as pigeons – but wouldn't take any of ours in return, for fear of spoiling 'their' tumbling breed. Toujours des symboles? Kyrle was particularly charming – especially after three glasses of sherry. The conversation was amusing, though rather too technical for my taste – i.e. too much bugger shop. I was a good deal impressed by Eddie's knowledge *and* feeling about books – not a very common combination. [. . .]
   I dreamt last night that I read a poem by Browning (a thing I haven't really done for ages) – fairly long, about a boy he had known at school. When I woke I could only remember this –

> 'How he boxed, with a cunning satanic
> Of false, luring-on fears
> – Mixed with actual panic.'

Rather brilliant, don't you think? Both the rhyme and the psychology seem very characteristic. [. . .]

‡

To Roger Senhouse

Molly MacCarthy was growing increasingly deaf.
  The general election was held on 30 May.

Ham Spray House
Hungerford
Berks.
April 30th 1929

[. . .] Molly was here, also Raymond, who stays till tomorrow. He was
perfectly wonderful with her, keeping the conversation alive most
successfully, in spite of every impediment. She is very amusing at
moments – and at others quite mad.

I saw Mary before leaving London. She wasn't very well, but
otherwise cheerful, and gave a very amusing account of her
electioneering experience in the Isle of Wight.

The John party was entertaining, but sadly lacking in beauty. I was
forced to talk for hours to that deplorable creature, Willie King. Ugh!
His wife seemed even worse, but luckily I hadn't got to talk to her,
though at one moment it seemed as if I should have to kiss her. 'Will
you join our kissing club?' was her method of attack. Ugh! Ugh! Nina
Hamnett, out of jealousy, fell upon another woman, and tore her hair
till she screamed with agony – but her cries were drowned by a frightful
band, which played a feeble jig the whole time, one semi-tone sharp.
What was nice was the largeness of the studio, and a certain atmosphere
of vagueness that prevailed. [. . .]

‡

To Roger Senhouse

The climber is clematis.
  *Lytton's frequent rival as a book collector, Edward Charles (Eddy) Sackville-
West (1901–65), 5th Baron Sackville, writer and music critic, suffered a good
deal of ridicule both from his cousin Vita Sackville-West and from Virginia
Woolf; he was the model for Nancy Mitford's comic invention 'Uncle Davey' in*
The Pursuit of Love. *'Harold' is probably Nicolson.*

Ham Spray House
Hungerford
Berks.
June 16th 1929

Dearest, I came down here yesterday by the morning train, with Ralph,
Carrington, Frances, and Julia. Such energy! But I felt extremely strong
when I leapt out of bed at 9.30. Tommy came from Swallowcliffe in the
afternoon, and seems to be in a very benign humour. Now (Sunday
morning) I'm not quite so energetic, though I slept like a log last night
– some of the vagueness of that curious long-drawn-out party still
lingers in my cerebellum. It is delightful to be here again, in spite of the
moody weather, but one has such a sense of freedom and ease and the
dolce far niente, among these green expanses and climbing columbines
(only really they're not columbines – I can't think of their name). It was
delightful returning in my taxi to Gordon Square – then mounting the
just faintly lighted staircase – going into my bedroom, and leaning out
of my window, and sniffing in the dawn, and looking at the morning
star, still shining through a high tree, while you by that time were
already fast asleep . . . and in three minutes I was too . . . very, very
delightful!

This afternoon the last barrel of the new wine is to be bottled, but
I'm not sure that I shall take part in it; I think I shall sit arguing with
Tommy about the nature of portraiture and artificiality – or something
of the sort – he positively sometimes agrees with what one says, I find,
which is stimulating; but perhaps you don't think so.

You are talking to Eddy now – I have a complete vision of it – a
good deal of music too – and Harold? But I have other visions – more
alluring – Que tu es charmant, beau, dans tes rythmes superbes, mon ange
divine, unfitted, however, for a description in a letter. Impossible, quite
impossible, to translate into writing the romance of a June sunrise, so why
attempt it? Julia appeared just now, dressed in a pale salmon pink dress
with a hyacinth blue toque (is that how you spell it?) – she looks distinctly
fascinating, with a fringe, and Carrington is painting her picture.

I hope you'll be amused by Knole – I daresay you'll like its rather
stuffy and over-decorated interior better than I did. The Elizabethanism
lowered my spirits, and as for King James's hairbrushes, they gave me
the creeps. Did you dream a little in the page's room, next door? Et moi
aussi. One can call up all sorts of scenes, of a delicious bizarrerie, but
after all there's no need to go back three centuries for that . . . [. . .]

‡

To Roger Senhouse

The flaxen-haired friend is Dadie; Brian Howard had jet-black hair.

Ham Spray House
Hungerford
Berks.
June 24th 1929

Dearest Roger,

[. . .] We have had a distinctly mouvementé week-end. Yesterday was a
most curious day, with the unexpected appearance, in Dadie's suite, of
Brian H[oward] and Sandy B. They came to lunch – stayed till after
dinner. It was most amusing and interesting to me. A curious,
disorganised party – poor Janey in the dumps, Carrington cynical, the
sudden appearance of James and Alix – luckily only for tea – Brian's
most strange character – the lovers' decidedly outré behaviour –
haircutting of Sandy in my bedroom, etc. etc. I enjoyed it all. The three
boys and myself went off to the bathing place after tea, and had all the
fun imaginable, I can tell you, sir! Sandy's looks seemed unaccountably
to have disappeared: but no – accountably: the gentle lights and the
romantic effervescence of Peter's party explained sufficiently. But I
thought him quite a nice child – I fear he's in for a rough time with our
flaxen-haired friend, whom he adores, and who is, of course, already
cooling. Brian is a curio – one of those rococo objects one suddenly sees
in the recesses of an antique shop – the sort of thing, one feels, that
some people would buy at once, but that most people would think in
bad taste. He has an extraordinary energy, with all his looks of collapsed
decadence – energy both lingual and corporal – a flow of talk and such
wild whirlings in the lawn – such races through the fields – such
wrestlings and embracements . . . Well! Well! Now Dadie is left, Janey
is just off, and Mr and Mrs Ph[ilipps – *Wogan and Rosamond]* arrive this
evening. So the kaleidoscope changes. [. . .]

‡

To Roger Senhouse

Lytton was reading Ethel Colburn Mayne, The Life and Letters of Anne Isabella, Lady Noel Byron *(London, Constable, 1929) and Jean-Jacques Brousson,* Itinéraire de Paris à Buenos-Ayres: Anatole France en Bateau *(1928).*

Hotel de l'Europe
Amsterdam
July 4th 1929

Dearest old creature, though I haven't been away a week, I feel as if ages had passed since I last saw you at Sotheby's *[. . .]* There wasn't anything particular at Rotterdam where we spent the first night; but the Hague was fascinating – such an atmosphere of aristocratic eminence and repose! Such lovely houses in the Lange Voorhout! Such good bookshops, to say nothing of the pictures. After that we went to Leyden (on the recommendation of Nancy Cunard) and found it charming – a small, out-of-date place, where we wandered along canal after canal with their trees and perfect house-fronts – each more entrancing than the last. C and I are in perpetual ecstasy over the solid grandeur of these Dutch houses, all looking very much the same at first, but in reality so full of individual invention within the limits of the admira*[ble]* 17th century convention to which they all conform. And now in Amsterdam all is life and movement. It is exciting to be in the very middle of such a whirl of traffic of every sort. Delightful huge barges glide past the hotel windows and disappear under flat bridges. This afternoon we went for a 'rondvaart' in a motor-boat, among the canals and out into the harbour, for about one and a half hours. Tomorrow we shall visit the fishing villages if the weather holds up. In various ways I've been pleasantly surprised – (a) the inhabitants seem to me (though I gather to nobody else) to be far from unattractive; (b) they are most obliging and (c) they all without exception speak English. So what is there to complain of? – Only, slightly, of the weather, which is occasionally wet and cold; but at critical moments the sun has not played us false. We are at present in a large comfortable hotel, whose hideousness horrifies Carrington, but *I* find it a great relief after the comparative squalor of the previous ones. The chief extravagance has been in meals, so far: we had a gay feast at the Restaurant Royale at the Hague, the pièce de résistance of which was (so the waiter informed us) 'wild pork'! And last night a *most* recherché dinner – everything done with perfect skill and quietude down to the smallest detail. Will you come and have dinner with me some day at the 'Bagatelle'?

All seems to be going well so far as the party is concerned. Ralph of course is a rock of confidence. Sebastian is as charming as ever. But oh! his taste! He has this moment appeared, bearing in his hand a glass of the most frightful description – pink ornaments, etc. etc. – and has presented it to me! I hardly know what to say! –

Did you visit the prison at the Hague? Where Cornelius de Witte was imprisoned, and thrown out of *[the]* window to the mob? An interesting place, full of instruments of torture – far more than at the Tower, and of considerable variety. I will describe them to you, if you didn't see them. – At a little bookshop in Leyden I got an Aristophanes that had belonged to Cardinal Mazarin – but so far no other finds.

Haarlem and Utrecht are still before us. *[. . .]*

The new book on Lady Byron is full of interest, though there's rather too much of Miss Mayne in it. In lighter moments I've been reading the Brousson book about Anatole France's voyage to Buenos Aires. Do you know it? Most amusing in spite of the author's being such a little beast. Then I've read Gide's latest – l'École des Femmes – a thin affair. By-the-bye, it suddenly occurred to me the other day – couldn't we look in at Pontigny when in Burgundy? Gide is to be there this year. Wouldn't it be rather fun? *[. . .]*

‡

To Mary Hutchinson

Lytton's travelling companions were Carrington, Ralph and Sebastian. 'Delicious dinners at a pound a head' in 1929 actually were the equivalent of spending just over £41 in 2002.

Hotel d l'Europe
Amsterdam
July 4th 1929

Dearest Mary,

There was no photograph to be had of the Venus and Adonis at The
Hague. And incidentally it was described on the frame as '*after* Rubens'.
A pretty picture, though – with two swans interlacing rather improperly
in the background. Have you seen it? Have you ever been to this
hydrotrophic country? My days pass pleasantly enough, though amid
the discomfort of travelling and the dubious recollections of love.
I have *three* companions! – Rather a multitude; but they are very
charming, and I have no right to feel lonely – none at all – and yet – it
is idiotic – I keep imagining what it might be with . . . almost saying to
myself, if only . . . were here! Almost, because I'm not really quite so
silly as all that, and enjoy everything – pictures, houses, canals, even
barges, just as they come. It makes an odd mixture of impressions. The
few days before I left England were curiously filled with experiences,
and these are as much present with me as the beautiful seventeenth
century doors and windows – so solid, so rich – that line the waterways,
and the Rembrandts and De Hoochs in the picture galleries, and the
delicious dinners at a pound a head that one stumbles into quite
accidentally, having intended simply to have a snack at an A.B.C.
When we meet, I'll try and tell you of a few things – mostly
unimportant, to be sure; but it is true that I am troubled about
Roger – in an unexpected way. It is not easy to know one's own
mind – not easy to balance instinct and reason – not easy to be sensible
and in love. Do not mistake, though – I am *not* unhappy – only
speculative, a little dubitative, faintly uneasy, perhaps. I wake up
at three o'clock in the morning and lie awake for an hour, trying
drowsily to disentangle the puzzle of my mind and heart – and then
sink to sleep again, having accomplished nothing and not in the least
put out. I wish I could write poetry; but the mould seems to be lacking
into which to pour the curious fluid – melted silver? porridge? gilded
sealing-wax? – of my emotions. I have found no solution in these
antique masterpieces – another world! another world! With them
everything is fixed and definite and remote; but with me there is
nothing but hazard, interiority, and interrogation. I hope it was not
some misfortune that parted us that evening. I return early next week.

Will you write to me at Ham Spray? And I will let you know when
I am in London.

With all my love – your devoted
Lytton

‡

To Roger Senhouse

*The principals of the Warren Gallery were Dorothy and Philip Trotter. John
Robert Clynes (1869–1949) was Home Secretary in the second Ramsay
MacDonald government of 1929–31. The British refused to have Trotsky after
20 January, when the Soviet OGPU (General Political Administration)
deported him to the Turkish island of Prinkipo, once used by the Byzantine
emperors to exile their opponents. Stalin took away his Russian citizenship, and
he lived in Turkey (1929–33), France (1933–5), Norway (1935–6), and Mexico
(1936–40). Following the Hague conference on the Young Plan, 6–13 August,
the German acceptance finally led to the evacuation of the Rhineland by French
troops.*

Ham Spray House
Hungerford
Berks.
July 15th 1929

[. . .] I suppose you heard about the police raid on Lawrence's pictures
at the Warren Gallery? I saw Dorothy and her spouse at Boulestin's one
evening, and heard her account of it. The police appear to have been
singularly idiotic, but D. herself, it seems to me, was almost equally so.
They were on the point of seizing a drawing by Blake of Adam and Eve
as obscene, and she was silly enough to tell them it was by him, and so
make a cheap score; but if she had only let them do it, there couldn't
have been a better exposé of their methods. Next day I had lunch with
Mary and she showed me the book of reproductions from the pictures.
They are wretched things – no drawing or composition, so far as I
could see – and in fact no point – not even that of indecency; there
are some pricks visible, but not a single erection, which one naturally
supposed would have caused the rumpus. What a hopeless set our
governors are! The Labour people are quite as bad as the last – Clynes

simply in the hands of the permanent officials at the Home Office – and reaction reigning everywhere. Trotsky has been forbidden to come – a perfect disgrace! I doubt if we shall really leave the Rhineland; and I fully expect that the next announcement will be that fourteen new Dreadnoughts are being built, in case of accidents. Well, well! Nothing could have been more delightful – cursing those apes and monkeys, as one sat having lunch with Mary on her lawn, plied with lobsters' claws by her fascinating footman who, however, doesn't altogether approve of me, as he is convinced I'm the lover of his mistress with whom he himself is in love. *[. . .]*

[. . .] A charming duodecimo has arrived from Paris (Noury). Containing some first editions of things by Diderot. There is a superb 'Entretien avec la Maréchale –' in his best atheistical manner. It is *very* strange that the Victorians found it necessary to take up the fight against Christianity all over again, after what one would have supposed was the thorough demolition of the 18th century.

[. . .] I want to consult your Catullus when you come back. There is a not altogether clear allusion to a passage in him, on the part of Anatole France (in Brousson's book) à propos to some abuse by a Parisian workman. Catullus compares his enemy's tool (so I gather) to a salt cellar! Decidedly mysterious! But perhaps that sugary translation will have funked it – so I shall depend on your Public School Education to take you straight to the passage in question, and translate it idiomatically!

> How odd the fate of pretty boys!
> Who, if they dare to taste the joys
> That so enchanted Classic minds,
> Get whipped upon their neat behinds;
> Yet, should they fail to construe well
> The lines that of those raptures tell
> – It's very odd, you must confess –
> Their neat behinds get whipped no less!

[. . .]

‡

To Carrington

Mells Manor is what remains of an H-shaped Tudor mansion, restored at the turn
of the century by Sir John and Lady Horner, employing Lutyens and Gertrude
Jekyll. Lady Horner's daughter Katherine was married to Raymond Asquith, son
of the former Prime Minister. Their son Edward Julian George (b.1916) inherited
from his grandfather and became the 2nd Earl of Oxford. Mells had been a
centre of cultural and political life in the Victorian and Edwardian periods.
   John Banting (1902–72) learned to paint in evening classes with Bernard
Meninsky; his first exhibition was this year, 1929. He exhibited in the
International Surrealist show in London in 1936, which led to his becoming art
director of Strand Films in 1939. At Ham Spray he painted a surrealist mural
showing a pregnant Ralph bearing his own twin. Brian Howard (1905–58) was
born in England to an American family (his mother was from Kentucky), and
educated at Eton and Oxford. He wrote poetry and was a central figure in the
bohemian social scene between the wars; but alcohol and drugs played a large role
in his life, and he killed himself in 1958. He had jet-black hair. Carrington's
reaction to the John Banting–Brian Howard gossip was 'Isn't it rather a good
mark for Brian taking to John Banting?' (21 August).[1]

The Manor House
Mells
Frome
Monday evening, August 18th 1929

Dearest Creature, I had rather hoped to have heard from you by now,
but I daresay I shall tomorrow. Though nothing much happens here
there seems to be little spare time – the hours pass in vague movements
and vapid conversations. Besides old Birrell, who is charming and
amusing, but of course 80, the other guests are Sir Herbert and Lady
Jekyll (she is Lady Horner's sister) and the eternal Bogey Harris.
Dimness reigns. Sir Herbert is a complete nonentity. Lady J. a fat old
thing, with an endless stream of placid talk. Katherine and her brood
have gone and left this morning for Scotland. The Earl of Oxford, her
son, aged 13, was the most sympathetic member of the party. The only
distraction has been the Park, where the McKennas live. (Mrs McKenna
is Lady Jekyll's daughter.) There are two boys there – Eton boys – aged
18 and 19, who were something of a discovery. But oh no, no, I fear
vanity of vanities is all that's to be gathered in that direction. I have had

two rather long talks with Michael, the elder, a nice, simple, slim lad with a gay laugh, nothing much to look at or indeed in any way. David is less developed even than his brother – a schoolboy pure and simple. This afternoon we motored to Bath – exhausting and dreary it turned out, wandering with Bogey and the aged crones from antique shop to antique shop. I nearly dropped dead from fatigue and general desolation. I shall make off tomorrow morning – back to London, where Dadie and his two boys await me. Rosamond and Wogan were most charming at lunch on Saturday. They both seemed very well and happy. They rather converted me about the Philipps house plan – that is to say I saw that there might be something to be said for it. They were perfectly reasonable on the subject. Wogan has discovered cubism and begun to paint in that manner – not, I thought, very successfully, but I suppose one has to go through that phase. Mrs H's house was très-chic by daylight, with a small garden where we sat sipping coffee.

At 37, John Banting appeared – yet another inmate. And what do you think is the latest liaison? He and black Howard! Off they go to the South of France together, where they intend to take a cottage and live for months and months. So presumably poor pale Paul is to be left on his poor pale shelf.

I hope your week-end has been not too bleak. Perhaps Dermot was pleasant. And Saxon? Such a story of the Treasury! – I'll tell it you when we meet – but when will that be? – the details are too complicated. I must stop now and dress for dinner – good Lord! good Lord! Will add a little tomorrow. Goodnight, beloved creature.

Tuesday, after lunch. Returned to London this morning. Found your letter with the shirt. Thank you very much. It's very silly – my train stopped at Hungerford – in fact, it was the 11.30 – so that if I'd only known I might have got out and had lunch with you, and come here in the evening. I hope your cheerfulness has returned and that Alix has appeared. I cannot try to say all you are to me, I feel that I am often as bad in my way as Roger! But I hope not always!' – I go to Cambridge on Thursday.

All my fondest love
Lytton

1. David Garnett, *Carrington*, p. 416.

‡

To Roger Senhouse

During the first two weeks of September Lytton was obsessed by the treatment of
'crabs' – pubic lice – which he either caught from or gave to Roger, though there
is no reason to believe that Lytton had any other sexual partner. Another
constant topic was his concern that his edition of Augustine's 'Confessions'
lacked important details about his childhood, 'but still of course he was the first
person to attempt any plain speaking at all'.
   Sir Steven Runciman (1903–2000) wrote The Emperor Lecapanus and
His Reign: A Study of Tenth Century Byzantium.

Ham Spray House
Hungerford
Berks.
Monday, September 9th 1929

Dearest Angel *[. . .]* Thank you very much for the bottles – but I
haven't used their contents, as a painful circumstance has arisen. The
previous applications had a terribly violent effect on my unfortunate
skin, which has been excoriated and inflamed over rather a large area.
The irritation is worse than that caused by the crustaceans themselves,
and so I have been occupied in trying to soothe things down with
calming lotions. I'm better now; but the worst is that I still can't be
absolutely sure that the original monsters have been eradicated. It's
terribly difficult for me to see, but after peering many times with the aid
of that small mirror I could detect nothing – so hope for the best. *[. . .]*
   I've made a sad discovery about the edition of the Confessions
(I expect yours will be the same) – it omits some vital passages of great
interest, on the score of indecency, which are given in a later edition
I've got, printed from the MS. Very tiresome! *[. . .]*
   I've just finished Steven Runciman's book on the Emperor
Lecapenus or possibly Lackapenis – incredible learning and industry is
displayed, but one doesn't really in the least gather what those odd
beings were like. I've now relapsed into my beautiful new Gibbon to
see how *he* treats the subject. By-the-bye, I must copy out a list of
crimes which Pollard says a Fellow of Magdalen (temp. Henry VIII)
was charged with (he afterwards became Bishop of London) – 'heresy,
theft, perjury, adultery, witchcraft, neglect of duties, spending the night
at Sandford without leave, and christening a cat'! *[. . .]*

‡

To Roger Senhouse

*The R101 airship resulted from a competition between Vickers and the British
Air Ministry (with Vickers producing the rival R100). The lifting gas was
hydrogen, which caused the completion of the project to be put back from 1927
to 1929; the final design had two decks and a dining room for sixty people. It
departed for its first flight to India on 4 October 1930, but crashed in France
the next day with forty-eight casualties.*

[Oriental Club]
October 14th 1929

[. . .] I caught the 12.5 and arrived here for lunch, during which there
was a mouvement générale towards the windows – the wine-waiter and
I rushed together to one, and, leaning out as far as we could, beheld,
just over the trees at the bottom of the Square (or so it appeared) the
enormous improbable form of R101! It was a truly charming vision, and
I hope you also enjoyed it – I think you must have, as I see it also went
over the City. How much more attractive than those wretched funny
little aeroplanes! But what would it do in a storm?
[. . .]

‡

To Roger Senhouse

Richard Aldington had just published his first novel, Death of a Hero.
Esher is in north Surrey, just beyond the borders of Greater London.

Ham Spray House
Hungerford, Berks.
October 19th 1929

[. . .] Since my last note I thoroughly turned against Mr Aldington.
Weak Wells most of his book seemed to be – and, as you said,
incredibly vulgar. Really no good at all – except, I suppose, for the
hatred of the war, which seemed genuine, though not very elegantly
expressed. As for the actual war-descriptions I could hardly read them,

the dullness (as always to my mind) being so intense. Some other method will have to be evolved, instead of this impressionistic no-verb-in-the-sentence one, before that subject can be dealt with effectively.

My attempt at seeing the world was a fiasco, I fear! Joe Ackerley arrived one evening at six and took me in his two-seater to Esher (where is Esher?) where General Charlton and his friend Tom reside. A small villa residence in a row met my gaze in the moonlight. The general appeared, tall and polite, and then Tom – oh, mon dieu, so sadly unattractive! Tom was once in the lower classes – still does the housework and the cooking, but otherwise is above stairs, sits at the dinner table, etc. and is mildly arch with Leo (the general) to whom he has been married now for ten years. Leo is a consequence of the war – so I understand from Joe – was converted during it from the condition of hearty womanising in which he went into it – and is now what one sees – a depressed, earnest, sentimental man, devoted to Tom. They were all very nice indeed, but . . . No! It was certainly not the world! A curious little backwater. Homosexuality reigned – impossible ever to escape from it; back and ever back came the conversation to that enthralling topic. They considered it in every light, and à propos of everything, in positively bouche beauté absorption. They did not think the Russian Novelists any good because they don't mention it. They went through the list of the English Bugger Kings. They . . . but it is cruel to be harsh about them, as really nothing could be more admirable than their general state of mind. But something was lacking, sadly lacking. I reflected upon what it could be, as I whizzed back in the tube from Hammersmith where Joe deposited me at midnight, and came to the conclusion that it was a touch of the eighteenth century. Not a particle, in their pudding, of that attic salt! Or perhaps, really, it was simply that Tom was so plain . . . ah well!

The evening before, James produced some music for us on his wireless gramophone – the G Minor Symphony and that wonderful song of Susannah's in Figaro, sung by Elizabeth Schumann in the most perfect way. I've always thought that music was the solution of life – but I'm not sure that you agree with me. Perhaps you do. But it's difficult to speak about such things.

[. . .]   Oh! Could you bear to have dinner with me at the Oriental on Wednesday? The truth is that I want to try some Port which can only be obtained in half bottles – I mean nothing less – and I should like your advice, as there is some for sale, and it's said to be particularly good. One can generally get quite a good meal at that place. [. . .]

✝

To Roger Senhouse

The 1929 biography of Henry Petty-Fitzmaurice, 5th Marquess of Lansdowne (1845–1927), was written by Lord Newton; in 1917 Lord Lansdowne had advocated peace by negotiation. Lord Shelburne (1737–1805) was the statesman who became the 1st Marquess of Lansdowne and made the great collections of pictures and books at Lansdowne House and Bowood, Wilts.
   Virginia Water *is by Elizabeth Jenkins (b.1907) and was published in London by Victor Gollancz.*

Ham Spray House
Hungerford
Berks.
October 30th 1929

[. . .] Your rummagings in the Foreign Office sound perfectly fascinating. Did you discover any skeletons in the cupboards? I've just read the life of Lord Lansdowne – not so badly done. He was an admirable dull man – though descended from Lord Shelburne (now, Senhouse, who was Lord Shelburne?) *and* Talleyrand. But the curious thing was that at the very end of his life the old Whig blood asserted itself, and he alone in England (except the professed pacifists) tried to stop the War. It's no less curious that his biographer now ventures to say that he was right.

   I know there are various other things to tell you – but I have such a 'heavy mail' that I dare not expand. One item is a new novel, called Virginia Water – have you seen or heard of it? There seems to have been a mistake in the title – an 'and' omitted – or possibly an apostrophe s. It is all about . . . me! And the authoress very tactfully gives me the name of . . . Roger! A schoolgirl's dream, as the real Virginia said. Most of the Strachey family come in – couleur de rose isn't the word. Unfortunately, in spite of myself, I couldn't finish the blessed thing, which, after being rather bright at first in a Virginia-cum-Proust manner, resolved itself into the merest maunder. *[. . .]*

✝

To Roger Senhouse

Ham Spray House
Hungerford
Berks.
November 4th 1929

[. . .] The rush was chiefly caused by my having to go over to Stephen
Tennant's instead of his coming here. It was rather amusing – I took
Morgan and Carrington – a lovely drive. When we got there, we found
. . . no Siegfried, but Arthur Waley, Willie Walton, and Rex Whistler.
We had lunch on the lawn, in such blazing sun that our host was given
an excuse for sending for a yellow parasol for himself and a series of
gigantic plaited straw hats for his guests. We were filmed almost the
whole time by the footman (a dark young man in spectacles). We
inspected the aviary – very charming, with the most wonderful parrots
floating from perch to perch and eventually from shoulder to shoulder.
Finally we went indoors, and in a darkened chamber were shown
various films of the past. Worked by the footman, who also turned on
a gramophone with suitable sounds. Stephen was extremely amiable,
though his lips were rather too magenta for my taste; Arthur was
positively gay; Morgan shone as required; W.W. said absolutely
nothing; and I, sitting next Rex Whistler, couldn't make up my mind
whether I was attracted or repelled by his ugly but lust-provoking face.
   Morgan was charming at the week-end – full of accounts of Africa
from bottom to top. He read two stories to Carrington and me –
improper – quite amusing – but there always seems to be a trace of
Weybridge in his style, whatever the subject may be. *[. . .]*

‡

To Roger Senhouse

*Whatever Lytton and the doctor thought was the cause of his symptoms, we
know with hindsight that he had cancer of the stomach, and that the growth was
blocking the intestine. The niece-doctor was Elinor Rendel. The letter ends
abruptly.*

Ham Spray
Saturday, January 17th 1930

[. . .] The crisis I spoke of was of a physical nature. The curious pain
which I had begun to feel before I left you continued rather dimly in
the night – next morning it was worse – unpleasant to move, to bend,
or to sit – not exactly pain but discomfort of a tiresome kind – slightly
internal, and not at all like the piles I've been accustomed to. So at last,
on Thursday evening, considering that my niece-doctor could really *not*
be consulted on such a point, I had the brilliant idea of ringing up
Pierre and asking him to pay me a professional visit. He came, was very
tactful – understood everything at once – hardly a detail, and of course
not a name mentioned. He said it was certainly an internal pile – made
out a prescription for some 'suppositories'. Three arrived from the
chemists late at night. I used two in the course of the night – and woke
up in the morning miraculously cured! It was really astonishing. I rang
up P. to tell him of his success – said I had used two of the sups. He
replied 'Keep the third for next time!' which was nice of him . . . but
. . . hum!

In spite of some difficulty in moving I had lunch with Mary at
Boulestin's on Thursday and successfully concealed from her that I was
in rather a parlous condition. She was in the highest spirits – and fashion
– a white turban – black kid gloves, etc. etc. – with the result that 25%
was taken off the bill! A peculiar compliment! Previous to that I had
been obliged to give an interview to two of my great-nieces if you
please, who had begged for the privilege of meeting me. Ah! If they had
only been great-nephews their looks would have charmed me more
intimately and I would have told them of their father Andrew (the
name tangs a string in *your* heart too!) whom I was much attached to, a
beautiful small subaltern, who was of course killed in the War. How
well I remember seizing a sudden kiss from him in the drawing-room
at Lancaster Gate – and his half furious . . . *[letter ends here]*

‡

To Carrington

*Lettice (née Baker) was the widow of the philosopher Frank Plumpton Ramsey
(b.1903), who had died a few days earlier. She was an old Bedalian, and close
friend of Frances, while Frank had known Lytton through the Apostles.*

Gerald Heard (1889–1971) had several careers – as a writer, as a historian of costume and architecture, as a writer of detective stories and as a writer on religion. The Russian historian Igor Vinogradoff married Lady Ottoline's daughter Julian.

51, Gordon Square
W.C.1
Monday, January 21st 1930

My dearest,

You will have heard from Ralph about his proposal that Lettice should come down to H[am] S[pray] next week – with Frances. I don't know what you think, but so far as I am concerned I should be very glad, if that unfortunate creature would like it. This I said, and that I was going to be here from Monday 27th until the following week-end.

A yellow fog bestrides this town – ugh! – I imagine blazing sun in the champaign of Wiltshire. I hope you're enjoying it, and that the car trundles merrily. Last night there was quite a party in Bernard Street – Gerald Heard and Miss Matheson of the B.B.C., to say nothing of Igor. Miss M. seemed quite nice, and less hideous than most competent females. Roger insists on a new Bloomsbury Weekly to take the place of the dead or dying Nation. I proposed that it should be called the W.C. 1 – which Miss M. found almost *too* risky a joke. Tonight Vanessa – and Duncan, I hope.

All my love,
Lytton

‡

To Roger Senhouse

51, Gordon Square
W.C.1
January 29th 1930

[. . .] Probably you saw about Frank Ramsey's death, but I expect it didn't mean very much to you. It was really a dreadful tragedy, he was a real genius, and a most charming person – infinitely simple and modest, and at the same time obviously a great intellect. I have been feeling wretched about it, and I'm afraid Dadie has been a good deal upset. The loss to Cambridge is incalculable. He was very young – only 26. Some mysterious failure of the liver was the cause of his death – there was an operation, but it was useless. *[. . .]*

‡

To Roger Senhouse

Ham Spray House
Hungerford
Berks.
February 11th 1930

[. . .] There has been another sad piece of news – probably you saw it in the Times – Charlie Sanger's death. I had known for some days that it was inevitable. A nervous breakdown was the apparent cause. I fear it was the result of a long process of overwork, underfeeding, and general discomfort – a wretched business. He had an astonishing intellect; but accompanied by such modesty that the world in general hadn't any idea of his very great distinction. And he was so absolutely unworldly that the world's inattention was nothing to him. I knew him since Cambridge days, when he constantly came down for week-ends for the Apostles' meetings – and then in London, when, at first, they lived in a little set of rooms at Charing Cross – and afterwards, by a curious chance, Philip became an added link between us. How he loved Philip, and how often he used to talk to me about him, with mild expostulations over his idleness! – And so all that is over now, and I shall never go to New Square again.

It is rather bitter down here, though when one can escape the northeast wind and crouch in the sun one can almost imagine the spring is approaching, and luckily inside the house it's warm. Nobody but Ralph and Frances for the week-end, and now Carrington and I are left together. I think I shall try reading some Pater out loud in the evenings. I haven't looked at him for such ages that I've no idea what he'll be like. I daresay intolerable. *[. . .]*

‡

To Roger Senhouse

In My Father and Myself, *Lytton's friend Joe Ackerley explained: 'His Majesty's Brigade of Guards had a long history in homosexual prostitution. Perpetually short of cash, beer, and leisure occupations, they were easily to be found of an evening in their red tunics standing about in the various pubs they frequented, over the only half-pint they could afford or some "quids-in" mate had stood them.'*

Ham Spray House
Hungerford
Berks.
February 28th 1930

[. . .] I must write to you for the last time before I'm a century! *[. . .]*

I want to tell you why it was that Dadie didn't appear last night. Somehow I hadn't thought of it – but he paid a visit to the American millionaire friend of Beverly *[Nichols]*'s who was 'cordial and even looking forward' – I told you about him I think – in his rooms at Claridge's. He turned out (so Dadie said) to be quite nice – much nicer than could have been expected – and at last *extremely* nice, though there were several interruptions from the telephone. That was why he arrived late at the Ivy, where Roger, Helen and I were waiting for him. After our very enjoyable dinner, he insisted on our all accompanying him to the BBC to sit with him while he was broadcasting. It went off very well – after some preliminary agitation – he had left his paper with them – there was an ominous pause – and I was convinced that the Harold N*[icolson]* story was about to be repeated. But no, it was discovered in time. I thought it very good – distinctly literary, but not too much so, and I should think the delivery was good, but we heard his actual voice, so couldn't really judge of that. On leaving Roger and Helen went off to bed, and Dadie then said that we must go to a pub near Oxford Circus. I agreed, but found some difficulty in getting him into a taxi, as at that moment two very large and very hideous guardsmen passed by. I had to be quite firm, and assure him that it was out of the question, so reluctantly he got into the taxi, and off we went to the pub. I suppose you know it – a most louche place full of big young men with disreputable expressions – and among them (though not big) was Freddy the trumpeter. Though standing exactly three feet off, Dadie failed to recognise him, and it was only after I had insisted that it was so, that, after several squinnies, he admitted I was right. The little wretch, however, steadily refrained from giving a single glance in our direction. After a little, someone else was selected, possibly a bugleman, and was given a drink, at which point my departure seemed to be indicated; and I went home to bed *[. . .]*

‡

To Carrington

Lytton was in Rome with Dadie from 4 to 21 April, but he felt homesick and wrote often to Carrington. They found the traffic noise at night around the Hassler (where Lytton had previously taken Roger Senhouse) disrupted their sleep; though nothing could be done about that, they became more comfortable when they 'moved into a larger room, with a bath attached'. Bernard ('Beacus') Penrose had a cine-camera, with which he made home movies produced by Carrington and Stephen Tomlin. The eccentric aesthete Lord Berners (Sir Gerald Hugh Tyrwhitt-Wilson, 1883–1950) lived most of the year at Faringdon House, Berkshire, but had a house in Rome overlooking the Forum. 'Gone agley' – like the best laid schemes of mice and men.

The notably good-looking (John) Beverley Nichols (1898–1983) made a good deal of money from writing thrillers, plays, novels and books on cats and gardening. He was relatively open about his homosexuality, at least for the times; but he wrote to Michael Holroyd: 'It is true that I knew a young American called Warren Curry who came over to England to study for a short while and stay with me. But we certainly never wandered "in despair over Europe and Africa". We never went near Africa, and our only excursion abroad was a brief trip to Rome where, far from quarrelling, we had a very enjoyable week-end.'[1]

The Labour Chancellor, Philip Snowden, had presented his Budget on Monday, 14 April.

Hotel Hassler and New York
Rome (6)
April 19th 1930

My dearest creature – your letter from Swallowcliffe arrived yesterday. You seem to have been moving about rather – and in singular company.

For who – or what is 'La Marquisa'? I was glad to hear of a new cinema plot, and should think the mooncalf would be only too delighted to take the part of a curate. Strange to think of you gossiping with Tommy through a morning! So the old life goes on in the Old Country. Here, everything goes from bad to worse, as far as weather is concerned. Thunder, lightning, hail, horror, all day and every day. So we plunge more and more into social life. Yesterday there was a particularly mad lunch party at Lord Berners'. A desperate antique American hag (by marriage an Italian Princess), dressed in flowing widow's weeds, and giving vent to a flowing stream of very dimly veiled indecencies, kept the table in a twitter. The idiot Berners had asked Lady Sybil, the Ambassadress, too, and the effect was frightful. Poor Dadie was almost out of his mind with agitation – so distressed on poor Lady Sybil's account, and at the same time pinching the thigh of Warren Curry, Beverley Nichols' young man, under the table.

Beverley is écrasé as his affair with W.C. has gone agley. They've been wandering in despair over Europe and Africa, and now openly quarrel standing in the street outside hotels.

Lunch today with old Lady D'Abernon – and dinner with . . . I really don't know who. Tea yesterday with an American Contessa – very different from the Widowed Princess – an infinitely cultured Henry James lady, friend of Whistler, etc. She lives in a flat in an enormous affair called the Palazzo Borghese, where Pauline, Napoleon's sister, once was. Lovely Empire decorations on the walls, left by Pauline, presumably. But could one live in this mad back-water? Impossible, I think.

The budget seemed to me rather less fearful than it might have been – but no doubt quite bad enough. The Slater crisis sounds agitating. I hope all is really well at last.

We went to St Peters for a service, but didn't see much, except the enormous crowd, walking up and down, as the church grew gradually darker and darker – a remarkable sight.

> My fondest love.
> Back in London on Thursday night.
> Lytton

1. Michael Holroyd, *Lytton Strachey*, p. 748, n.32.

‡

To Carrington

The Hon. Diana Mitford (1910–2003) had married Bryan Guinness the year before. (Sir) Harold Mario Mitchell Acton (1904–94) was the complete dilettante – the son of Arthur Mario Acton, who was English, and the American heiress Hortense Mitchell, whose fortune allowed them to live in flamboyant style at the Villa La Pietra in Florence. At Eton he fell in with Brian Howard, and at Oxford had an affair with Evelyn Waugh. In 1932 he went to China, learned the language and cultivated his considerable aesthetic sensibility; he also met the love of his life, Desmond Parson. On his death he left La Pietra, with its fifty-seven acres and a $500m endowment, to New York University. Presuming on the small acquaintance hinted at in this letter, Sir Harold incautiously wrote a negative review in 1972 of the Strachey pieces collected in The Really Interesting Question *by the present editor.*

The 2nd Baron Redesdale, David Bertram Ogilvy Freeman-Mitford, was the father of all the Mitfords, Tom, Nancy, Jessica, Diana, Unity, Pamela and Deborah, Duchess of Devonshire. He was seriously unhinged and, when a series of bad investments in the 1920s crippled him financially, he joined a number of anti-Semitic and right-wing organizations. Part of his eccentricity was to believe in the Jewish dietary laws – he and Lady Redesdale (née Sydney Bowles) effectively kept a kosher household at their peculiar house at Swinbrook, in Oxfordshire, for the isolation of which he compensated by buying at the same time a large London house at 26 Rutland Gate. Tom was killed in Burma in 1944.

Of the potential guests at Ham Spray, the first Roger is Senhouse, the second is Fry, who was now living with Helen Anrep. Clement Attlee was Postmaster General in 1930, in Ramsay MacDonald's government.

51, Gordon Square
W.C.1
May 28th 1930

Très-chère,

It was delightful to get your charming letter this morning. I had quite an interesting time last night, though I started off in a fit of depression to no. 10 Buckingham Street. On the way I fell in with the endless stream of motors going to the 'Court', each filled with its said bevy of débutantes – and an occasional redcoat. A considerable crowd lined the

Mall, gaping at this very dull spectacle. I found again a large party –
about 18 – with Eddie Marsh, but not Lady Cunard – again sat next to
Diana. Once more Harold Acton figured – I feel myself falling under his
sway little by little. At last, after rather a dreary dinner, we reached
Rutland Gate, where, as I'd feared, Pa and Ma Redesdale were in
evidence. However it really was a pleasant and very gay party –
everyone looked very nice and behaved very well, it seemed to me –
such good, gentle, natural manners – no stiffness – no blatancy – more
like a large family party than anything else. The effect was rather like a
choice flower bed – each tulip standing separately, elegant and gay – but
a ghostly notice glimmered – 'Please do not pick!' Tom Mit*[ford]* was
undoubtedly the beau, the fine fleur, of the ball – and I was considerably shattered by his charm and beauty. Harold A told me a great
deal about him, as we stood on a landing together while the couples
floated up and down. One of the standbys – for my situation among
these thrushes and blackbirds was slightly conspicuous – was la vieille
Hamersley, who flapped her owlish wings rather less disconsolately than
usual. Eventually, with some difficulty and embarrassment, I managed to
have a talk with the Tom Tit, and he promised to have lunch with me
some day . . . but the Eagle, as he stepped and hopped into his taxi, felt
a trifle rusty and Bohemian, and doubted whether his claws hadn't
perhaps lost their cunning – hélas! hélas! – but it was amusing and even
a little exciting – and perhaps H.A.'s lunch to which I promised to go
next week may lead to developments.

Roger can come for Whitsuntide, which is nice. And I hear from
Ralph this morning that the Sea Trip is probably off. So that's all right.
But – Roger and Helen can't come for this week-end – have to go to
Suffolk and depart for France immediately afterwards. Duncan and
Vanessa, whom I asked, also can't come. So the outlook's rather black.
I shall try Virginia and L*[eonard]*. I hope to meet V at Old Queen Cole's
this afternoon – she cleverly caught me – so I have tea there and then
go on to the Mooncalf. I'll let you know what V says.

I hope that you're enjoying the warmth, which seems really to have
set in now – and that the tiles have arrived at last.

I've just written a tedious letter to the Times – not about the
Postmaster General but Greville. All my love. L.

✚

To Carrington

Carrington's proposed £100 salary was the 2002 equivalent of £4,863. Donald Beves was a lecturer at King's.
 George Derwent Thomson (1903–87) was an Apostle and classicist at King's.

King's College
Cambridge
Wednesday, June 11th 1930

Dearest Creature, I feared that you were rather sad at my departure. Perhaps it was a dream, and anyhow I hope it was only temporary. Have you been slaving at the tiles? I wonder if you feel an absence of money. If so, would you like a sort of salary or pension of £100 a year? – I could very easily manage it, if it would in any way be a comfort to you. Why not?

Dadie seems quite cheerful, but the whole place is feeling rather shattered by W's death. They hardly know who to get to replace him. For a moment Gerald seemed a possibility, but he said he couldn't face it; and now I gather that the dull fellow Beves is to have the job. Social life has been rather extreme, so far, but nobody very exciting has appeared. Such an argument with George Thomson about Ireland last night! The man's a fanatic – but oddly enough, a nice one.

I had a curious adventure at the National Gallery where I went yesterday afternoon to see the Duveen room – a decidedly twilight effect. There was a black-haired tart mooching round in india-rubber boots, and longing to be picked up. We both lingered in the strangest manner in front of various masterpieces – wandering from room to room. Then looking round I perceived a more attractive tart – fair-haired this time – bright yellow and thick hair – a pink face – and plenty of vitality. So I transferred my attentions, and began to move in his direction, when on looking more closely I observed that it was the Prince of Wales – no doubt at all – a Custodian bowing and scraping, and Philip Sassoon also in attendance. I then became terrified that the latter would see me, and insist on performing an introduction – so I fled, perhaps foolishly – perhaps it might have been the beginning of a really entertaining affair. And by that time the poor black-haired tart had entirely disappeared. Perhaps he was the ex-King of Portugal. *[. . .]*

‡

To Carrington

The Cambridge spy and Keeper of the Queen's Pictures, Anthony Blunt
(1907–83), was Apostle number 273, elected on 5 May 1928, immediately
preceding Julian Bell (17 November). (The other Apostolic spy, Guy Burgess,
was not elected until 12 November 1932.) (Sir) Edward Wilder Playfair (b.1909)
was Bell's closest friend at Cambridge. He was an important civil servant, and
Chairman of the Trustees of the National Gallery. The 'reprobate' was A. J.
Champernowne of Trinity, not D. G. Champernowne of King's, the discoverer
of the Champernowne number. Both were Apostles.

(Rudolph) John (Frederick) Lehmann (1907–87), Rosamond's brother, was
a Trinity friend of Bell, and went to work the next year for the Woolfs at the
Hogarth Press. Romilly John, the aspiring poet, was aged twenty-five.

51, Gordon Square
W.C.1
Friday, June 13th 1930

Back again here! I arrived for lunch, having had a really delightful time
at the Old Varsity. I saw a good deal of the dear boys, and they are
certainly a most charming collection. Our river party on the Ouse on
Wednesday evening was a great success. We went in two cars – Harry
Ellis in his two-seater with Dick Steele, and the rest – i.e. Dadie, Francis
Cornish, Anthony Blunt, Eddie Playfair (perhaps you don't know him –
a small black-eyed birdlike and eager creature) and self in a taxi. After
about three-quarters hour's driving we reached the Pike and Eel – a
small pub on the banks of the Ouse – far, far away – or so it seemed –
from anywhere. There a certain number bathed in the small charming
river winding dimly among willows and meadows, while others floated
in a boat and took photographs. After that we had dinner of fried eggs,
bacon, cheese and beer, sitting outside the inn, as twilight gradually
descended. Romantic and delightful – especially as I managed to get a
seat next Harry Ellis – whom you don't know either – a regular
charmer – a country gentleman – more or less of the Rogerian type.
But of course the dimness was oh! infinite. Rather to my surprise, A.
Blunt was the life and soul of the party – by-the-bye, do you know *him?*
– I think you must, so I won't describe him. We got back again, rather
faint, at about 11.

Next day in the afternoon, there was the Pageant, which I was amazed to find I positively found enjoyable. An amateurish affair, of course, but the music was very pleasant, and the rest not at all bad – except for the reprobate Champernowne – the bell in the fog, who tinkled even more remotely than usual. Why he's always chosen to be a leading actor, when he can neither speak, move, or stand, I can't imagine.

In the evening, Dadie and I had dinner with Dick Steele at Magdalene – the college with Pepys's library – where I'd never had a meal before. It was all very quiet and agreeable – and then we moved on to a singular gathering in a pub (the Maypole) in a little back street (Portugal Lane) where we found in a darkened upper chamber a whole crowd of shirt-sleeved youths – mostly poets one was told – who smoked and drank and chattered and roared with laughter like anything, while somebody played the piano in a dreamy way. I talked a good deal to the larger Wilkinson, whom you liked, and found him sympathetic. In the middle A. Blunt and another youth climbed in by the window, etc. etc. There were a few beauties, etc. etc. And I enjoyed it all very much – the naturalness and the merriment were so attractive.

Various other incidents I won't detail – a visit to Peter – lunch with Braithwaite – a *faint* flirtation with John Lehmann – a curious party, lasting from noon to midnight at an out-lying college, with nothing but flagons of ale to drink. Probably you can imagine most of it. Dadie was very sweet throughout – correcting examination-papers at every spare moment.

I go with him tonight to some wretched play or other that he's to review for the Nation. I start for Islington Grange tomorrow afternoon.

It has been perfectly charming to have so many letters from you. One from me ought to have reached you by now. How fearful about the Pansy muddle. I hope when she did come it went off all right. The tiles sound hectic – how can you achieve such things? The weather is miraculous, and seems to buoy one up in an unaccountable manner: probably the mere absence of druggets makes all the difference. Nothing from Morgan so far – rather a nuisance. Who is to meet him? I've quite lost count. But if he don't come it don't matter.

Well, I must stop. Perhaps at this moment you're at Fryern. Chi lo sa?

My fondest to you, dearest creature.
        Lytton

I really thought Romilly's poems quite good – except for one rhyme – calm and farm, which put my teeth on edge.

‡

To Carrington

Lytton was hoping to meet Tom Mitford at his sister Diana Guinness's cocktail party. Toulouse-Lautrec made his best-known image of Yvette Guibert in 1894. She delivered her scandalous lyrics standing almost still, gesturing sparingly with her thin, black-gloved arms. Marjorie Strachey's party trick was to sing shockingly filthy songs with a completely straight face and lady-like demeanour.

51, Gordon Square
W.C.1
Monday, June 19th 1930

[. . .] It must be perfect now at Ham Spray after the storm and frenzy of yesterday. It is lovely here – cleared air – warm sun, etc. I am going off to a cocktail party at the Guinea-hen Guinnesses, where I hope to meet Tom Tit. Yesterday I went with Roger to Yvette Guibert's remarkable performance – a super Marjorie, if such a thing is conceivable. A vast strange old woman, with a power of expression and a French exacti-tude, which are positively alarming. The flowers have been a great embellishment, but now they are dropping into ruin.

I thought I would stay at H.S. for the whole of next week – so I hope you will too. All my love,

Lytton

What! *More* tiles!

‡

To Roger Senhouse

Many of Lytton's earlier letters to Roger Senhouse include a touch of whimsical sado-masochistic fantasy, though it is never clear, until this letter, unique in the correspondence, whether Lytton is interested in inflicting pain or suffering it. Lytton seems to have been 'crucified' by Senhouse, and the cut referred to was, I think, one made – à la Longinus and with conscious blasphemy – in his side. Senhouse himself preserved this letter, and sold it to the Berg Collection. Unlike many of the other letters to him, he has not annotated this one. The next day, 31 July, Lytton wrote a chatty letter, wishing Roger the best possible weather for

*his coming holiday, and adding: 'I'm feeling unusually vigorous – set up, it
seems to me, by that surprising trinity. – The violent colour still remains, but
hardly a tingle.'*

51, Gordon Square
W.C.1
Wednesday, July 30th 1930

My own dearest creature. Such a very extraordinary night! The physical
symptoms quite outweighed the mental and spiritual ones – partly
because they persisted in my consciousness through a rather unsettled
but none the less very satisfactory sleep. First there was the clearly
defined pain of the cut – (a ticklish business applying the lanoline – but
your orders had to be carried out) – and then the much vaguer after-
pangs of crucifixion – curious stiffnesses moving about over my arms
and torso – very odd – and at the same time so warm and comfortable –
the circulation, I must presume, fairly humming – and vitality bulking
large . . . where it usually does – all through the night, so it seemed. But
now these excitements have calmed down – the cut has quite healed up
and only hurts when touched, and some faint numbnesses occasionally
flit through my hands – voilà tout, just bringing to the memory some
supreme high-lights of sensation – and there are other things I want to
talk to you about. First of all, my dearest creature, it was such a relief
and comfort – more than I can say – to be able to talk to you so easily.
What blessedness! The wretched thing was that the certitude of your
affection, which had been quite solid in me for years, began (about
three or four months ago) to weaken and waver – with sad results. The
anchor had lost hold, and I was drifting.

Now that is entirely right again, and at the same time from what you
said to me I am able to see the situation more clearly, I think. My hope
is that I shall now be able to grasp the facts firmly. I had failed before to
imagine with proper sympathy your states of mind, and my own had
become out of tune in consequence. I hope things may improve . . . at
any rate it's cheering to think how much worse they might be! With
love on both sides all must be well really. To me, our relations have
always been among the greatest blessings of my life – that I have never
doubted. The truth is I'm gorged with good fortune, and really if I can't
be extremely happy with what I've got it's a scandal.

You were a perfect angel last night. The sweetness of your temper is a
perpetual astonishment to me – and the wonderful indulgence and

comprehension with which you embrace my moods makes my
happiness when I am with you something positively magical. I should
like to say a great deal – yes, a great deal, more – but you would snap
my nose off. So instead I'll just add –

A footnote on D[adie].

I suppose you realise that he's (unconsciously) jealous of both of us –
that he wants (unconsciously) to supplant each of us with the other –
and all to no purpose, because he couldn't possibly make anything out
of it if he did; and yet, of course, he's so charming, so truly affectionate,
and enhances life so immensely that those underground vagaries can be
discounted – so long as one realises their existence, and keeps a good
look out (which I'm sorry to say I haven't always done).

I'll write a little more tomorrow. My fondest love and 100 k[isse]s to
the l[oll]s. Lytton

‡

To Carrington

*The Viceregal Lodge in Phoenix Park was home to James McNeill, the Irish
Governor-General. Henry Yorke was Henry Greene (1905–73), then the author
of the novels* Blindness *and* Living. *He told Michael Holroyd that he
remembered Lytton being well-dressed and 'a real charmer'. He remembered
Lytton as a very good listener, though he could, with a few words, deflate the
person he had just encouraged to speak. However, said Green, those to whom he
had applied this technique seldom felt aggrieved, for his humour was absurd
rather than malicious.[1] Lytton's hostesses' sister, Nancy Mitford (1904–73),
published her first novel,* Highland Fling, *the next year, and married Peter
Rodd in 1932.*

*Strachey had been on a disastrous holiday in Scotland and Ireland with
Henry Lamb in 1912. Though in love with Lamb (but claiming only to be his
best friend), he cheered the painter on in his affair with Ottoline, for whom his
rival was the halitosis-afflicted Bertrand Russell. Lytton was then so devastated
by his time with Henry that he had to go to Ottoline to recuperate.*

Knockmaroon
Castleknock
Co. Dublin
Saturday, August 9th 1930

My dearest, I got here all right last night – a very good journey – trains extremely comfortable – sea smooth – *but* of course owing to the incompetence of the idle rich was not met at Kingstown – had to take the train to Dublin – thence a taxi – which wandered for hours in the purlieus of the various Maroons and Knocks – the rain all the time pouring cats and dogs . . . however, I arrived at last – to be informed that after dinner we were all to go to a ball at the Viceregal Lodge. So you see it was lucky that I had my white waistcoat. As for my tweeds, alas! alas! they were *far* too loud, and I was received with looks of faint horror by Lady de Vesci, an ex-beauty of mature years, who has fortunately now gone, taking with her, though, her son (I *think*) Lord Rosse who was foolish and attractive. Henry will obviously be my great support in this gathering of the young and semi-imbecile. No hope, I already see, of any special excitements! The company winnows down to Henry Yorke and his wife, a non-descript Peregrine Willoughby, and Nancy Mitford (sister of Diana). I don't think anyone else.

Hamish Erskine (a tart) leaves this evening. (Pansy has already gone.) Henry is a great success. They all adore him, and he is evidently quite happy. A strange unlooked-for transformation. Great play was made of his having an evening rig-out for the ball – 7/6 the night. I'm not quite sure how I shall manage to survive for a week – but if the weather improves it will be easier. The Wicklow mountains are within a motor-drive, and are said to be delightful. Then I suppose there's Dublin to be looked at. The Viceregal ball was very tedious. Rather a beautiful house, though, in the middle of the enormous Phoenix Park. Not a soul that I knew – even Hazel, whom I'd relied on falling into the arms of, had just departed. But I met Mr Lennox Robinson, the controller of the Abbey Theatre, and Lord Thompson (silly man). How curious to be thrown together with Henry after all these years, and in Ireland, too, where such a fearful crisis was once enacted between us.

I hope all is well with you. How delightful to have come into the possession of a gull! As for me, I shall be very glad of a little rest in this

place, where there is at any rate comfort and good cooking. A kind of
Irish Richmond, was we supposed.

>All my best love,
>Lytton

Will write again soon.

1. Michael Holroyd, *Lytton Strachey*, p. 749, n.37.

‡

To Carrington

*The neighbouring Guinness house was Glenmaroon, which is now a convent.
At the top of side four of this letter Carrington has written*

>*'Huge winds blow on Leigh Hills*
>*The gull comes against the rain'*

*and at the bottom of the page, under Lytton's signature, 'The Blind eat many
a fly.'*

>Knockmaroon
>August 12th 1930

[. . .] It will be pleasant to get back. All goes well here – but one begins
to pine for one's familiarities. The party grows less and less; now the
only other guests are Henry and the nondescript Peregrine, who turns
out to be a cousin of Bryan's. Both these two have developed violent
colds in the head, so that, as at the best of times they are dimsies of the
dimsiest, you can imagine the brightness of their conversation. Diana
remains very dashing and superb. She adores monkey puzzles! – So
I suppose you adore her! –

Henry and I went yesterday to the National Gallery at Dublin, and
inspected all the pictures – there is nothing really colossal, but many
are excellent – and comparatively unknown – a most lovely Poussin, in
pale colours and full of complicated architecture. The weather is
piggish, so that no real expeditions have been made so far. Tea with
some neighbouring Guinnesses afforded some amusement – enormous
wealth, two indescribably hideous houses on each side of a road and
joined by a bridge-passage, a ghastly garden crammed with incoherent

flowers, an indoors running bath artificially heated, etc. etc. Oh the rich! the rich!

So long as I don't catch one or both of the dimsy colds I shall be happy!

My fondest love,
Lytton

‡

To Roger Senhouse

Knockmaroon
Castleknock
Co. Dublin
August 12th 1930

[. . .] Dublin itself is attractive – chiefly in brick, which I hadn't imagined – 18th century houses – very large squares – some nice public buildings – altogether a sympathetic place. We went one night to the Abbey Theatre, when Diana Guinness grew so restive over the brogue and the boredom that she swept out in the middle of the performance, with the whole party at her heels. The weather continues rather bestial, but we are promised a mountain expedition tomorrow (my last day) coûte que coûte. *[. . .]*

‡

To Roger Senhouse

This letter reveals that Roger suspects another infestation of pubic lice, and has warned Lytton to be on the lookout for them – he seems to have suggested that Lytton is the responsible party this time. But Lytton replies, 'in a rally at badminton, who's to say which player the shuttlecock started with?'

Alix was staying in Corfe with, Lytton wrote on 20 August, 'that strange and rather dingy group of satellites, who all seem to crouch in bungalows or inns in that region'.

Lytton had been worried for some time about the reception of Rosamond Lehmann's second novel, A Note in Music. *He had himself expressed reservations to Roger about the story of two unhappy marriages in a glum northern setting – and he asked him not to let on to Ros before publication, as there was nothing she could do to alter the book. She was suffering second-novel syndrome, exacerbated greatly by the huge success of the first,* Dusty Answer *(1927).*

A worry about Brittany was (he wrote to Roger on 29 August) that though 'my hand has healed wonderfully', the marks of their sado-masochistic 'tigerism' might be revealed 'if I have to bathe'.

Ham Spray
Sunday, August 24th 1930

[. . .] James departed yesterday with Alix who arrived again from Corfe to carry him off. She was looking magnificent, occasionally draped in a long military cloak, which showed off her stern beauty very well. She had a story about one of the male members of her coterie (name forgotten) and Mary Butts (I suppose you know that blowsy red-haired antiquity). They entered into a financial arrangement, by which she was to receive a 20% commission of all gains she procured him. She discovered a Polish Count, who only wanted to beat, nothing more, and was willing to pay heavily. The youth decided that he must make a nett profit of £100, so he charged £125, and this was agreed upon. Really rather expensive! (Especially if you'd seen the young man in question, as I once did at a party.) However, all went off well, and 'the curious thing was', said the recipient afterwards, 'I really rather liked it.' The result was that he and M*[ary]* B*[utts]* were so pleased with it all and each other that from finance they went on to passion, and cut crosses on each other's arms with a penknife, so that they had to be sewn up by a surgeon, and now – typical conclusion of this tale of modern moeurs – they are 'engaged to be married'!

Other visitors were Wogan and Rosamond, who came for the night on Thursday. Her book had come out that day, but we didn't get any presentation copies. Modesty? There was rather a damning-with-faint-praise review of it in yesterday's New Statesman. I am beginning to feel decidedly nervous about the Brittany expedition. Between Wogan's harumscarumness and Dadie's passion for chic, the Lord knows where I'll get landed – but of course everything really depends on the colour of the sky. The worst of it is that we've let this place to Alec Penrose, so that my retreat will be cut off – tra-la-la! *[. . .]*

‡

To Roger Senhouse

Les Mouettes
near Douarnenez
September 9th 1930

Dearest Creature, we have reached this spot but are off again today – to Quimper. Our movements have been peculiar and almost continuous since I sent off that postcard to you from St Malo. Fortunately the car holds food and is quite comfortable, in spite of its having nearly all the luggage *inside* (one of Wogan's little oddities). From Trébeurden (the first stopping-place) we went to Brest. It was in vain that I assured Dadie that it fully deserved its name of 'le pot de chambre de la France' – his passion for the Marine would have its way. So we journeyed there, only to find, at once, that it was an utterly hopelessly squalid place, to be left without a moment's delay. So we came on here – a minute seaside village, to the south of Brest. It would be perfect if the weather were so. A nice sea-shore – where we could have lain out reading, or bathed, or strolled, and quite near the fascinating fishing town of Douarnenez, with its perfect little port, filled with fishing-boats, and sailors mostly dressed in russet coloured clothes – a place to while away the hours in, sipping Cointreau, quite indefinitely – *if* it was fine! But oh, the weather has completely collapsed – floods of rain, icy wind, – quite hopeless! And here we are perched in the tiny 'annexe' of a tiny inn, which is a good walk away, and which has to be reached for every meal – so departure has been decided on. Quimper is at any rate a town, with presumably some resources or others for the rained-on traveller. After that, all is utter vagueness. The moral-mental-spiritual situation is a little obscure. Dadie and I seem to be leagued (so far) in favour of movement – if possible inland and southward – Wogan is completely vague – and Rosamond as far as I can judge, chiefly occupied with anxiety for little Hugo's welfare (little Hugo being safely tucked away in the Isle of Wight with his nurse and grandmother) and an obsessional craving for sea-bathing (which alas! has obviously become an impossibility). She is rather depressed, I expect, about her novel, but has not yet seen the really crushing review in the Times. Lit. Sup. which I have suppressed all knowledge of – no point in anticipating this bit of unpleasantness. Dadie seems a little more temperamental than usual – perhaps he finds the contrast to his positively paradoxical time in

Corsica, where everything combined to flatter and enthral, a little trying. Wogan now seems to be aged about ten. However, we are really all enjoying ourselves immensely, and they are all perfectly sweet to me, If only, if only, the sun would shine!

I fear it may be equally wet and windswept in your Isle of Arran – though sometimes I've known the north of Scotland weather to be the exact opposite of the state of things further south. I hope this may be the case now. I've been imagining your existence as being the converse of ours in every way – such comfort, such solidity, such respectability – port, cigars, dinner-jackets, boredom – but lovely walks, too, I hope, and perhaps some exciting fishing and shooting. I do hope you're not finding it all too unrelievedly dull, and that you're making some headway with F[rank] C[urzon] in the direction you wanted. It's wretched having no hope at all of a letter, but without an address, one can do nothing. Rather a strange existence, this, so altogether cut off from the world – life on a raft, in fact, in mid-ocean, with three companions – a drifting, vague, and yet concentrated life. [. . .]

I think of you a hundred times a day, and want you to be here to listen to a thousand comments on things that pass and things in general. Which, without your lolls to be poured into, fade away into nothingness. As for my lolls, they say that they're badly in want of a little tormenting, so will you, please sir, send them some by post! Otherwise, I may remark that if my head were cut off you would still be able to recognise the body among a whole field of the slain: though whether this will still be true a fortnight hence is doubtful. I find that France is not a good country for cigars – is Scotland any better? I somehow suppose that those provided by F.C. are not altogether satisfactory! But I've known it happen in country-houses that some stray guest, or even – who knows? – a footman may produce an excellent brand.

Dadie sends his love – he has read all his books, and all everyone else's. So now he is thrown back upon making a cross-word puzzle, as there are none to solve. We lie in our different beds in an odd little kind of watch-tower, looking over the sea, and the pretty houses of Douarnenez. Soon we shall have to get up and face the elements and get some lunch (of a sort) among a herd of squalling children. Oh la! la! R and W are out walking – or bathing – for all I know! – in the frigid ocean.

All my love, dearest angel, and many blessings
    from your own Lytton

‡

To Roger Senhouse

Chartres
Monday, September 15th 1930

[. . .] Dadie and I elected to linger here for a day more, as the sun has
come out – the first time, really, since I landed in this blessed country! –
and the cooking is *at last* excellent in this hotel – and we have had an
admirable lunch, and an estimable bottle of Vouvray between us
[. . .] The cathedral here is *[a]* hundred times better than the rather
pretentious object at Bourges. It was wonderful coming into it yesterday
in the dusk, only able at first to discern dim shapes of pillars and those
astonishing blazes of stained glass – gradually, as our pupils expanded,
we saw more and more – all the glorious proportions at last, and the full
sublimity. Oh, my dearest creature, I wished so much for you to be
with me as I stood at that most impassioned point – the junction of the
transept and the nave, where the pillars suddenly soar and rush upwards
to an unbelievable height, and one is aware of the whole structure in its
power and its splendour. The christian *[sic]* religion itself positively
almost justified! And I made wishes *for* you, too – but what they were,
ah! I cannot tell you. *[. . .]*

‡

To Roger Senhouse

*Eliot Hodgkin (1905–87), artist and writer, became known for his splendid
botanical pictures. He was a member of the distinguished Quaker family, and
thus related to the Frys.*

The Italian novelist Alberto Moravia (1908–90) published his first novel,
Gli Indifferenti, *in 1929, at his own expense. Both Mussolini and the
Vatican banned his work. He was working as a foreign correspondent for two
Italian newspapers at the time of this meeting. Beryl de Zoete (1896–1962),
orientalist and critic, did the classic English translation of Italo Svevo's* As a
Man Grows Older. *She was ten years older than Arthur Waley, who lived
with her in the top-storey flat in Gordon Square for twenty-six years until her
death.*

Philip Dennis Proctor (b. 1905) edited The Autobiography of G. Lowes

Dickinson and other unpublished writings *(Duckworth, London, 1973), in which he revealed Lowes Dickinson's shoe fetish, suppressed by Forster in his biography of Lowes Dickinson. Proctor had been elected to the Apostles in 1927, preceding Anthony Blunt and Julian Bell.*

Since summer 1929 Lytton had been working on a new edition of the Greville diaries. In Thomas Morton's 1798 play, Speed the Plough, *Dame Ashfield continually asks what her neighbour, Mrs. Grundy, will think.*

Ham Spray
November 15th 1930

Dearest of divine creatures, *[. . .]* I have been thinking of you constantly and yesterday did have time to give instructions for fifty birthday presents to be sent to you. I hope they'll reach you safely and that you'll find them to your taste.

I sent out a whole heap of invitations for the sherry party on Monday – among others, to Mr Eliot Hodgkin, Mr and Mrs B. Guinness, and the Blue Stag; so I hope you'll appear, not too late, to entertain them. *[. . .]*

Rather a solid week-end begins this afternoon, as, most unexpectedly, Vanessa (who has come back from Cassis without Duncan) is coming as well as Clive – also Oliver and Inez. What shall we talk about? Love, lust and the Musical Glasses, I imagine.

I had lunch on Thursday with Morgan at that palace of faded grimness, the Reform Club, to meet a young Italian novelist, Moravia by name. E.M.F. had assured me that he really was good-looking – however (knowing the peculiarity of his taste) I wasn't surprised to find a human weasel awaiting me under the yellow-ochre Ionic columns of the central hall. Otherwise he wasn't so bad, as foreigners go. He's apparently written a novel that is so shocking that even Beryl de Zoete refuses to translate it. 'I deescra-eeb nékeed weemin' was his explanation. (Rather a disappointing one!) I can't remember what else I've done, or who I've seen – except Topsy, at lunch at the Ivy – an occasion chiefly remarkable for the interlude of M. Abel absolutely losing his temper, gesticulating frantically, and shouting abuse at a waiter – a sight I've never seen before. (This all passed quite unnoticed by Topsy, who was busy at the time explaining how Goldie's passion for the White Rabbit, Denis Proctor, combined with the White Rabbit's 'fixation' on her had resulted in her becoming the object of a 'mother-complex' on the part of Goldie.)

[. . .] Which reminds me that I've discovered (quite accidentally during my Greville grubbings) the origin of Mrs Grundy. Very curious.

Lord D'Abernon is the man for me. Did you see his speech on depressions and currencies in the Times this morning? When I last saw him I thought he was entering on the gaga stage, but this disproves it.

I hope your lolls didn't suffer too much. But if they're the colour of my left shoulder it *would* be fun.

All my fondest love,
Lytton

‡

To Roger Senhouse

Ham Spray House
Hungerford
Berks.
November 25th 1930.

[. . .] I gather (from a quotation in a detective novel) that minor criminals in Japan still have their ears cut off as a punishment. Is this really possible? Mightn't we go there at once and find out?

I think of you a great deal, dearest angel, with wonderful happiness and more love than can possibly be got into this (or indeed any) envelope. My love is old-fashioned – Newtonian and Euclidean – it doesn't curve round in a twist à la Einstein, but goes on in a straight line for ever. Many kisses for the enchanting lolls and all my devotion to their owner –

Lytton

‡

To Roger Senhouse

Lytton changed his view of Lord David Cecil (1902–86) and came to think this distinguished academic and man of letters very clever; this year Lord David had met and fallen in love with Rachel MacCarthy, the daughter of Desmond and Molly, which drew him into the Bloomsbury orbit.

Trevelyan shuddered at the vulgarism 'went pop' to describe the death in
Spain of Prof. E. A. Freeman in Lytton's essay on Froude in Life and Letters.

Ham Spray
Friday, December 19th 1930

[. . .] I found little David Cecil at the Woolves the other night – quite
nice, but rather pointless, to my mind. – What do you think? Virginia
had just met Lord Esher who had told her that *he* had just met George
Trevelyan, who was foaming at the mouth with rage. 'Really! I should
never have believed that a writer of L.S.'s standing would use an
expression liked that – "went pop"!' So *some* effect has been produced,
which is something.

Mr Guy Chapman's idiocies were more than I could explain on the
telephone. Do you remember somebody called Hodgkin, with whom
he feverously quarrelled in the Lit. Supp.? Well, Hodgkin is convinced
(so Mr Guy Chapman says) that the young gent (Lord Courtenay) with
whom Beckford was accused of going to be with, was really a girl in
disguise! Beckford's own explanation of the story, i.e. that he went
into Lord C's bedroom and locked the door, in order to . . . give him
a whipping! – Very likely . . . but yet Mr G.C. 'is convinced' that
Beckford was 'innocent'. Almost stupider than Hodgkin, it seems
to me.

[. . .] Looking forward very much to Tuesday, when perhaps I shall
be punished (or rewarded) according to my deserts. Fondest love – and
to the lolls too – Lytton

‡

To Roger Senhouse

Ham Spray
Saturday, December 20th 1930

[. . .] Rather an intriguing letter came before I left London – a proposal
that I should co-operate with Mr Aycliffe (the producer of the Barretts
of Wimpole Street) on a play on Elizabeth and Essex. What is to be
done? What would such a thing involve? Might one make one's
fortune? Would one be eternally disgraced? Would the fortune
counterbalance the disgrace? Or vice versa? Such are the questions that

arise in my agitated brain. I have said that I will see Mr Aycliffe, which will perhaps enable me to get some idea of the possibilities. Carrington wants me to write a Racinesque drama on the subject, brushing history aside – but . . . but . . . If it did come off, it might be rather fun – I mean the view of life behind the curtain, etc.; but I suppose the frenzy and worry would also be colossal. I am to meet the man on Tuesday, if all goes well. Rather awkward not having seen the B's of W. St.!

[. . .] Sebastian has got a new young friend called George – an ex-guardsman, I think. It was rumoured in Nottingham that George had knocked someone down. Sebastian accused him of this, and George admitted it. – Why? 'Well, a bloke came up to me in a urinal – wanted some of it – all right, I didn't mind – but what do you think? – he wanted it for fuckin' pleasure – for *fuckin' pleasure*! – bloody cheek! – so I knocked him down.' On the other hand, when somebody else offered Black Sambo money, Black Sambo knocked *him* down. So altogether life seems difficult in Nottingham. [. . .]

‡

To Roger Senhouse

Lytton and Carrington had lunched with Wogan and Rosamond Philipps and met Stephen Spender (1909–95) there, 'whom I liked very much'.

Ham Spray
December 27th 1930

[. . .] A gay, lively creature, youthful and full of talk. Has written a homosexual novel, which he fears will not be published. Thinks of living in Germany with a German boy, but hasn't yet found a German boy to live with. Writes poems after lunch, and reads them aloud to Rosamond. In spite of red cheeks, blue eyes, and a very charming expression, doesn't move the cab particularly. The three of them were to have come over to dine and dance tonight, but Ros has got a cold, has taken to her bed, and apparently poor old Wogan feels he can't leave her. Clive and Vanessa arrive in the baby Austin this evening, but the party is ruined, and Carrington, who has been preparing pâté and artichoke brandy is almost in tears. [. . .]

‡

To Roger Senhouse

Lytton took his sister Pippa here for a week to recover from a cold. The letter begins with some banter about failing to write to Roger on 'a previous Christmas', and being 'condemned to the pillory' as punishment, which segues into anecdotes about people having their ears cut off for boring Scheherazade 'by their stories' and Mardouk, who also had his ears cut off.

Gloucester Hotel
Weymouth
December 31st 1930

[. . .] The latest scandal is that the Woolves (aided and abetted by Dadie, of all people) are trying to lure John Lehmann to join the Hogarth Press, and to put in all his capital as well as to devote his working hours to doing up parcels in the basement. And the large ape is seriously tempted. *[. . .]* Is it conceivable that I shall get another letter before I return? Is it, oh is it, divine Scheherazade? But what mean these flashing eyes? This flashing blade? . . . Mercy, mercy! But not too much mercy

to

your trembling and
adoring
Mardouk

‡

To Mary Hutchinson

In old age, Somerset Maugham returned to the Villa Mauresque where he lived with Alan Searle, whom Lytton called 'my Bronzino boy', and who introduced Lytton to Maugham. 'D.Wilde' is, I think, a camp fiction, composed of the cant phrase for a homosexual, 'friend of Dorothy', plus 'Oscar Wilde', and refers to Alan Searle, who is also 'she'.

'G.B.' is George Bergen (b.1903), a handsome Russian-American Jewish painter of talent, who shed his Yiddish-speaking past, won a Prix de Rome at eighteen, was taken up by a clutch of British aristocrats, returned to the US to paint portraits of Hollywood celebrities, including a famously stolen one of Charlie Chaplin, and had an affair with Duncan and, much later, with

Duncan's daughter Angelica. This extraordinary character, even by Bloomsbury standards, is surely the only person who slept both with Lytton and with Lillian Hellman.

Ham Spray House
near Marlborough
Wilts.
March 15th 1931

Dearest Mary,

[. . .] It's brilliant down here at the moment, though the air is still slightly acidulated. The usual horror of spring. Whether it's this, or something physical I don't know, but I can't help feeling a little drear about my future. So difficult! So difficult! I rather think that I shall have to retire from London a little, in order to write . . . but heaven knows what. I had lunch with R*[oger]* yesterday before coming down here. He was perfectly charming. To have him about me all day and every day would be a dream of bliss. If only one were Mr Somerset Maugham! I see that he is entiché *[besotted]* with D. Wilde – why not? – and that she (in a curious way) makes his relations with H*[axton]* easier. Perhaps he will find happiness in that direction – why not? Why not? – It would be shattering for me at first, no doubt, but if it was really a solution of his difficulties one couldn't complain.

I think constantly of Master G.B. – the only person I've met for ages who has really impressed me. For goodness' sake don't let him slip out of sight . . . but in two years, in three years, where and what shall we all be.

Carrington, it turns out, is unhappy with her Figure-head. She finds him boring. Good God! I'm not surprised. But he is a Figure-head – and that is almost enough to make up for everything.

Till Saturday, I hope.

My best love,
Lytton

'Victoriana' (ed. by Osbert) is quite amusing.

‡

To Roger Senhouse

Ham Spray House
near Marlborough
Wilts.
April 9th 1931

My own dearest creature

[. . .] As for me, my fears proved groundless and I am feeling distinctly
stronger since the week-end. And your sweetness was so overflowing
that I've been able to garner up a store of it, for solace during this
wintry absence. Wintry in every way, though I gather, to my rage, that
in London spring reigns, while here the old grey desolation continues.
All the same, I had a charming walk yesterday – over almost the same
ground as our Terrace one – such beautiful pale faint colours – such
friendly unemphatic shapes! I continue with Keats, who is perfect. He
would have been exciting to know – impossible not to try at any rate to
raise some spark of excitement in him – but his womanising tendency
seems to be very strongly marked – though, to be sure, with modern
views (supposing he were to come to life now) . . . enfin . . .

A long letter arrived from Ottoline yesterday, all about old times –
the result of reading old letters – rather difficult to answer. A certain
amount of sentiment was clearly required – but how to provide it? You
can't get milk when the udder is dry. She was a splendid figure, but
disaster seemed to fall on all her relationships. The result, I think, of an
utter lack of self-knowledge combined with violent contradictory
instincts which could not be controlled. Poor thing, she realises
something of this, and speaks in her letter of 'ashes and poisonous
vapours scattered on what might be too good'; but the ashes and the
vapours, alas! were of her own making. *[. . .]*

‡

To Roger Senhouse

*Rule 2 of the Athenaeum Club provides for the annual election of 'a certain
number of persons of distinguished eminence in science, literature, or the arts, or
for public services'.*

Admiral of the Fleet and First Sea Lord Sir Caspar John (1903–84) was instrumental in setting up the Fleet Air Arm.

Ham Spray House
near Marlborough
Wilts.
April 17th 1931

[. . .] I wonder if you saw in the Times that I had been elected to the Athenaeum under rule 2? Very glorious, but the only result so far has been that I have had to stump up £47.5.0. However, it's rather fun, and I'm longing to explore that pompous edifice. *[. . .]*

Life trundles along here in the quietest style – the question of the next book to read is the only pebble that ruffles the surface of the pond. Yesterday there was an event, though – two visitors by aeroplane – viz. Dorelia and Kaspar *[Caspar]* John. The latter took Carrington up for a turn – she adored it; but *I* refrained – the attraction, somehow or other, was not sufficient. *[. . .]* Julian Bell arrived for lunch with his young woman. He seemed thoroughly on the spot about Pope (on whom he's writing a Fellowship dissertation); but Miss X seemed only on the spot about Julian. *[. . .]*

‡

To Roger Senhouse

On 20 March Lytton wrote to Roger, 'How splendid for Dadie to dash off with Raymond through France and Spain!' Parts of Morocco were Spanish territory (Ceuta still is), and travellers in the 1920s and 30s often crossed from Spain to Morocco.

Forster began his affair with Bob Buckingham, a police constable, in 1930. The relationship carried on even after Buckingham's marriage to May the next year. 'The Creator as Critic' was the title of Forster's English Faculty lectures, given in the Lent Term of 1931.

The young John Gielgud (1904–2000) played Lear in 1931.

Omphalos (meaning navel – from the conundrum as to whether Adam and Eve had navels, as they had no mothers and thus no umbilical cords) was the work in which the senior and fundamentalist Gosse attempted to account for the fossil record (and thus for Darwinian evolution) by saying that God made it in order to test our faith.

Ham Spray House
near Marlborough
Wilts.
April 21st 1931

Dearest, dearest creature

I am so glad that Monday will do. These ages of absence are very
desolating – will you recognise me when you see me? My retroussé
nose and sky-blue eyes have probably by now quite faded from your
memory, and I daresay if an impostor arrives on Monday, obviously
disguised in a beard and spectacles, you'll be completely taken in. Ah
well! You'll be able to recognise me by my extreme thinness – quite
equal to that of Raymond in his bath – caused by this starvation diet.
Not a loll will have passed my lips for – how many weeks? – by the
time I see you again. Kindest monster, in these circumstances, do you
think we might also spend Thursday evening (30th) together? Perhaps
this is against the rules – but perhaps you won't have any very enticing
invitation for that night . . . apart from the present one. [. . .]
    [. . .] A letter from Dadie at Tocklington contained the following –
'The Spaniards do not quite see eye to eye with us in affairs of the
body, but there was a guide at Marrakech – and R[aymond] bargained
(in vain) for a child of five summers. I was much distressed.' –
Presumably owing to the bargain being attempted, rather than its
failure.
    So it's been cold in London too! Here we hardly ventured our nose
out-of-doors during this week-end, but sadly inspected the pale green
buds being lashed by the sleet, as we crouched and clambered round the
hot water pipes. Morgan was delightful. More fayish than ever, having
achieved a complete success with a member of the lower classes, aged
24, who lives in London – these were the only particulars I could elicit
– never has he been so happy, and he is 53. 'And have *you* an affair,
Lytton?' I murmured an affirmative. 'Hm! – I suppose *yours* is with a
gentleman.' I murmured another affirmative. He was not very
enthusiastic about Cambridge – had suffered from its provinciality, said
that the acting was a perfect pest, and complained of the expense of
giving lunches to the undergraduates. But his lectures (which I gather
weren't very successful) sound extremely interesting – he says he won't
print them, but I hope he may be persuaded to.
    I am longing to hear about King Lear. All the reviews I've seen have

been very favourable but one can't judge much from them. From what
they said it sounded as if he'd got the hang of the part – for one thing
not making Lear a decrepit and already half-cracked vieillard, as the
actors generally do, thereby making nonsense of the whole thing; but
I doubt whether his physique would have been equal to it – though
I suppose with sufficient eminence one might get round this.

My reading grows more and more miscellaneous. The Gosse father
and son are absorbing – there is an excellent biography (as well as *Father
and Son*) and now I've got 'Omphalos', the work in which it is
explained how God put the fossils into the earth to give the scientists
something to scratch their heads over. *[. . .]*

‡

To E. M. Forster

Ham Spray House
near Marlborough
Wilts.
April 24th 1931

Dear Morgan

I've read the lectures with the greatest interest and pleasure. I see that
they are not to be published as they stand; but I do wish you would do
something about it – the questions are so fascinating, and (as you say)
have never been treated before. Tasso is enthralling. And what you say
on Dryden and Coleridge is excellent. It seems sad that all this should
only see the light of day in a King's lecture room.

Of course I don't agree about Matthew Arnold – A good poet – but
qua critic his high nobility drives me mad. No doubt Dante is a greater
poet than Chaucer; but surely it's rather tiresome to say so – and if your
object's to 'help' people I should have thought you'ld do so more
effectively by pointing out the supreme merits of Chaucer. Then in his
particular judgements he seems to me to be very nearly always wrong.
How hopeless to prefer Byron to Keats, to think that Racine is
valueless, and to rave about Joubert and St. Paul! And then his method
of proving that (a) is better than (b) by little snippets from their works
juxtaposed – most extraordinary! – His snippet from Pope, for instance.

I wanted more about Henry James, and missed not having his Letters to look up the references. I'm sorry to say I agree with him in re Tess. I've just re-read The Awkward Age. It's all very strange. His cleverness is positively diabolical – and the artistry, and so on . . . What's so odd is the vulgarity of mind in combination with this. He's most distressing both about sex and money: but perhaps The Awkward Age is not the best example. It seemed dreadfully boring, too – one really had to force oneself to go on, which can hardly be right.

Sebastian has just arrived, looking very elegant. Bunny and that woman who writes those stories arrive tomorrow, for some strange reason. They'll none of them be helpful about Henry James, I'm afraid – so we shall have to revert to aeroplanes.

Yours

Lytton.

I shall return the lectures tomorrow.

‡

To Sebastian Sprott

L. ('Lizzie') Susan Stebbing (1885–1943), A Modern Introduction to Logic *(1930). Professor Stebbing was at Girton from 1905 to 1908.*
   St Simon comme historien (1865) is by Pierre Adolphe Chéruel (1809–91).

Ham Spray House
near Marlborough
Wilts.
May 11th 1931

Dearest Sebastian

[. . .] I've been reading Miss Stebbing on Modern Logic – found it absorbing at first, but later on it seems rather to wander into generalisations about the nature of Science and so on – even History – which are stodgy. I should have liked more about logic pure and simple – but perhaps I'm wrong – and have missed some vital parts.

I've also at last after all these years got from the London library that book on St Simon 'comme historien'. It is full – almost too full – of

interest – such masses of information – and His Grace comes out
pretty badly – no, not at all to be relied on (as indeed one imagines).
Vendôme, for instance, *in spite* of his shocking debaucheries, was
(M. Chéruel shows) an admirable general. One rather wishes one had
known him – in his retirement – at the Temple.

Life here plods along among a perfect ploughed field of books.
Solomon was an ass, to say there were too many of them. The bother is
that one can't read quickly enough; remembering doesn't seem to me so
important. How are you? No more burglaries, I hope. Does the market
place still buzz? and are caps still worn?

Carrington has gone sailing, sailing, so I am alone at the moment.
That toad Colefax suddenly announced that she was coming to lunch
the other day. We laid in several salmon, a mountain of ice, and 24
pineapples. In vain! A Duke intervened, and she wired that she couldn't
come after all.

> All my love
> Lytton

‡

To E. M. Forster

Forster had written to Lytton on 16 May saying that the New York Herald
Tribune *had asked him to do four more articles on the same terms as before,
which would allow him to help Sebastian financially as much as he had the
previous year. He said he was telling Lytton 'also in case you can tell me what
to write about. They leave me free, as long as it's literary.' He said he'd already
got one suitable subject, 'Coleridge as a Dragoon', and needed three other similar
ones – and wondered whether Gibbon had had such an experience.*

> Ham Spray House
> near Marlborough
> Wilts.
> May 31st 1931

Dear Morgan

I failed, you see, to answer promptly, so presumably you're now at
Ab*[inger]* Ham*[mer]*. It's excellent news about the Herald Tribune; but

my mind is rather a blank about subjects such as you ask for. Of course Racine and Boileau did go to the wars as historiographers, and got a good deal laughed at by the courtiers, but how to make an article of this? Even dimmer is the information about Gibbon at the Devizes. Then – more remotely parallel – there was Verlaine as a schoolmaster at Bournemouth – But the vistas that open there wouldn't quite suit the Herald Tribune, I fear. I wish I could think of something more.

Are you in London ever? I shall be at 51 most of this coming week – and next – Couldn't we meet? Ring me up – MUS*[eum]* 2755 – if you're there.

Yours
                    Lytton

                              ‡

To Carrington

The Week-End Observer held a competition this summer for the best profile parodying Lytton's own style. It was won by 'Mopsa' – Carrington, who described, prophetically, Lytton's own death. In her spoof Lytton sees, lying on the grass, 'a loose button, a peculiarly revolting specimen; it was an intolerable, an unspeakable catastrophe. He stooped from his chaise longue to pick it up, murmuring to his cat "Mais quelle horreur!" for once stooped too far – and passed away for ever.'

Hilton Hall, Huntingdon, Bunny Garnett's country house, is twelve miles from Cambridge.

King's
Tuesday, July 21st 1931

Très-chère

I was delighted to get your letter yesterday. But how, oh how, am I to write an answer? I exist on a semi-dream – and, though I seem always to be doing something or other, there appears to be no news at all. What a triumph that you should have won the prize in the Week-End review! There's no doubt that you must take to your pen, and write a novel or a series of portraits through the microscope or the Life of Queen Mary the Vast. Well! Well! – I hope the week-end went off successfully, but by the time you get this you will almost have forgotten all about it. Of course give copies of P*[ortraits]* in M*[iniature]* to whomever you like. As to the Candide, I feel some doubts. If it's a true first I shouldn't really want it, as I have one already. And its expense would be vast. If it isn't it might be interesting; but in that case wouldn't be worth very much. Perhaps I could have a look at it when I return.

[. . .] How curious about Bunny and Philip Sassoon. Perhaps I shall hear about it from him, as we may go over to Hilton one evening. If it ever stops raining or freezing here. The boys here are all aged 7½, and as for the buildings their beauty remains (I believe) as virginal as ever. But I can't see them through the Scotch mist.

Farewell! Farewell! I'll write again before long. No adventures – oh no! all my fondest love, Lytton

‡

To Roger Senhouse

Ham Spray House
near Marlborough
Wilts.
August 18th 1931

Dearest Creature

Forgive me for not writing. The truth is I have felt unable to do so – rather dim and hopeless – and still hardly know what to say. My mood lately has been a new one for me. I've had the feeling that our relationship was coming to a dead end – or perhaps just fading away. Is this more or less what you mean in your letter by stagnating and existing in the past rather than the future? There is some truth in what you say, I think. I'm afraid it may be some kind of impossible mixture of the occasional and the profound – or at least impossible for me who am neither a saint nor an acrobat. It makes me wretched to think that I am a cause of bother and perplexity to you; and when I consider how infinitely sweet you have been to me for the last ten months I feel that I have no business even to dream of anything more or different . . . and yet I cannot help doing so.

Believe me when I say that I try to trust in your love, though it still remains half strange to me. Perhaps the fault lies in my love – that if it was stronger and deeper all would be well.

This is rather incoherent, I'm afraid, but I hope you won't misunderstand it. I also hope you won't mind if I don't come up on Friday. Enjoy your holiday, my beloved angel – I'm sure you will – and come back brown and vigorous. I had a notion of going by myself early in September for a little perambulation in France – if the weather suits and my health etc. seem in good working order. It would be Eastward of Paris, and our paths would not intersect. I have a craving to drink champagne in Reims!

Let me have a card from the South.

> All my love,
> Lytton

‡

To Carrington

Lytton set out on his last, solitary journey on 3 September. Portraits in Miniature, his final book, had been published in May. He was still confused about his relationship with Roger Senhouse, and, contrary to the feelings and habits of a lifetime, wanted to be by himself. He pampered himself by staying in more expensive hotels and eating good meals. He was, of course, already suffering from the undiagnosed cancer of the stomach that was to kill him in only a few months.

> Grand Hotel du Lion d'Or
> Reims
> Sunday, September 6th 1931

Dearest creature

I arrived here on Friday, after a very pleasant evening in Paris. The 'flood lighting' of the Place de la Concorde is really magical. The next morning, the sun came out for a minute or two, and I tottered along the Rue St Honoré. Oh, the chairs and sofas I saw! Each more perfect than the last – but also, I fear, more expensive. After that of course the rain began again. I went in slight despair to the Louvre – pitch dark – nearly all the pictures pitch black – so I departed and went in a cab to lunch at Foyot's. The scene there was exactly the same as ever. Those curious discreet waiters, acting some High Drama – all about . . . Nothing! Not even *very* good food. However, it was amusing.

I decided to abandon Meaux owing to the rain and came straight here. The town, as well as the cathedral, was almost completely destroyed in the war, so the effect is rather miserable. But one advantage is this new, modern, and efficient hotel, where I have a comfortable bedroom and bathroom on the sixth floor – not cheap, certainly, but decidedly soothing. The weather has been absolutely piggish, up to the afternoon, when it took a turn for the better. But I cannot believe that this will last. Nevertheless I've been enjoying myself thoroughly – drifting about from café to café, from restaurant to restaurant, and even – positively! – every evening (so far) filling up my diary. As usual the food in the minor places is usually better than what you get in the expensive rather obvious resorts. At a small lower middle class eating house yesterday I had a divine sole, done with some sort of mayonnaise sauce in which floated shrimps and mushrooms. Gracious me! Then I've been to see the champagne cellars of Messrs Mumm. A gloomy proceeding – despair owing to the depression, the dryness of America, and finally the wetness of the weather. Personally I see little reason to believe that any champagne is ever made in this icy country, swept over with deluges of rain. The million old bottles in the deep deep cellars of Messrs Mumm were I suspect mere dummies, and my theory was supported by the fact that in the middle of the endless underground avenues, exactly six sweet creatures were sitting, bottling some wine, *by hand* – et voilà tout. As to what I said to the sweet creatures, the word is – mumm!

I'm feeling rather excited about Nancy, whither I go tomorrow. From the description in the book it sounds divine. And if only the sun continues to favour me! – Well, I hope all goes well with you, and that when you get this you'll be safely established at Fryern. I'll write again from Nancy, and also probably telegraph.

My fondest love,
Lytton

Extraordinary and alarming circumstances! The death's head of Adrian suddenly appeared half an hour ago – peering out from a motor-car. Don't think he recognised me – and they seem to have vanished.

‡

To Carrington

*The 'Mooncalf' was Alistair MacDonald: 'in the meantime I've written to
AM. It was inevitable. Absurd to have come here without doing so, and yet,
curiously enough, the two things are quite disconnected. Nobody I suppose, will
believe this – R[oger] least of all. As for A himself – will he really suppose that
I've come all this way for the sake of his beaux yeux? Probably he won't think
much about it anyway; and then there's always a considerable chance that he
won't be able to see me – that he'll be completely engrossed with women – has
gone away[. . .]'*[1] *'He came last night. He went this evening – to Paris; a
shorter visit than I'd expected. Also, more successful . . . What will happen to
the poor child I can't imagine. Thank goodness he's got the diploma he went to
Strasbourg for two months ago – a good deal to my surprise.'*[2]

Grand Hotel
Nancy
Wednesday, September 9th 1931

Très-chère

My weather-luck has turned at the critical moment, and my days here
have been perfect. A good thing, because I can't imagine anything more
wretched than Nancy in the rain – a bedraggled butterfly! As it is, the
bright sunshine is exactly what's wanted – especially for the lovely
gilded iron-work in the central square (Place Stanislas) where this hotel
is. The square and its surroundings are laid out in the most perfect way
– all sorts of vistas – a triumphal arch or two, and a delightful little park,
called the Pépinière, completely in the French style – regular alleys of
charming trees, amateurish lawns, neat flowerbeds, a fountain, some
statues, etc. Here one sits from time to time on a metal chair, smoking a
cigarette, watching babies and lovers, and generally dreaming away the
hours. You must certainly come here some day, and when you do you
must have lunch at the café Stanislas, of which I've become a habitué.
In vain I decide every day to go to some really cheap little eating-house
– somehow when it comes to the point I never do! –

My present plan is to stay here over tomorrow, and go on Friday to
Strasbourg for the week-end. I've written to the Mooncalf, but have
had no answer yet. I daresay he's too lazy to put pen to paper; but it
don't much matter – if he's not available, no doubt Strasbourg will

provide various distractions for the week-end. I might return to Paris on
Monday or Tuesday, and get back to London on Wednesday or
Thursday (16th or 17th) – but I'll let you know as things develop. It's
slightly grim not having any letters, but on the whole I'm sure the fuss
would have been too great. So far, one copy of the Daily Mail has been
my only news of England. I hope the weather has changed with you
too, and that you're basking at Fryern. It seems literally years since I've
been away, and in reality it's less than a week! I've had one fearful
adventure – four or five of my best shirts have completely vanished!
I may have left them at the Reims hotel – I've written to them – but
my hopes of ever seeing them again are faint indeed. Perhaps I left
them in the Paris hotel. Oh dear! All my new ones, so elaborately
made the other day at Cambridge. As it is, it's doubtful whether I
shall get through without buying some horrors ready-made. The
shops aren't up to much – in the way of books and antiquités. Two
silly little volumes are all I've discovered so far. This is rather a
moribund hotel – purely 18th Century, with a splendid front. But the
lift only goes up – never down – very lucky it's not vice versa! My diary
continues – so you'll have more to read – but I fear it's not exactly
thrilling. All my love,

Lytton

1. Michael Holroyd, *Lytton Strachey by Himself*, p. 172.
2. ibid., p.181.

‡

To Mary Hutchinson

*Before Lytton left England, he had asked Mary for the name of the hotel she
recommended.*

*'Tom' and 'Cimmie' Mosley (Sir Oswald and Lady Cynthia Mosley) spent
the summer of 1931, as they usually did, in the South of France. 'No doubt he
[Roger]'s engulfed by Bill Burton in that grotesque villa we know of with the
imitation cobwebs and El Grecos.'*[1] *Later he writes of Roger and 'the original
Burton affair two years ago'.*[2] *Bryan and Diana Guinness's enormous but not
pretentious house was Biddesden.*

*In his journal for 10 September Lytton wrote: 'I am happy – amused –
energetic. It may all hang by a thread, I feel, but the thread holds. I must write*

*to Mary and try to give her some notion of my condition – how admirably well
she would appreciate it.*[3]

Grand–Hotel
Place Stanislas
Nancy
Friday, September 11th 1931

Dearest Mary,

I've been floating about now for more than a week – very happily and
vaguely – the only curse being the weather, which has been devilish
almost the whole time. However, it was fine for two days in this
charming place – a heavenly two days – but now it pours once more and
I peer from the dim hotel window upon utter desolation. But really you
must come here – you would adore it – a kind of miniature and rococo
Bath – laid out neatly with squares, vistas, gardens, triumphal arches,
and the most lovely gilded iron-work by a resident with the propitious
name of Lamour. That is to say he did the ironwork; the architect was
Héré, and the grand deviser and author of it all was the good King
Stanislas, late of Poland, and father-in-law of Louis XV. The Place
Stanislas – upon which I peer – is on a fine day a divine spectacle –
fountains, cupids, and gilding everywhere – if only, instead of motors,
there were a few elaborate and enormous coaches floundering about! –
I stayed a few days at Reims, which is really hopeless – wiped out by
the war; and yesterday I went for the night to Strasbourg – a most
attractive German medieval city. Paris was rather inspiring – especially
the new lighting of the Place de la Concorde. Your hotel seemed very
nice and cheap – but hardly, I thought, a place to stay for long at. I have
committed my reflections nightly to an exercise book – or at least a
selection of them – rather small beer, I cannot but suppose! However,
you shall see them if you like on my return. At the present moment I
am waiting for the Mooncalf, who announced himself for this week-
end – heaven knows whether he'll really come, or if he does and the
weather continues thus, how the long hours will pass in this singular
meeting-place. The food and drink have been on the whole admirable,
but I've had to mitigate the latter a little – very tiresome, as I should
love to drink at least two bottles of wine every day. I am feeling (for
me) curiously composed in the region of the heart – an agreeable
change – but I suppose it may not survive the re-crossing of the

Channel. At present I feel as if I couldn't be much worried by anything of *that* sort – the india-rubber ball having bounced up against a brick wall for seven million times, at last quietly sinks onto the floor. R*[oger]* would not go away with me, but went to the Riviera instead – the Mosley's *[sic]*, Burton, etc. I've heard nothing from him for many weeks. I wouldn't go and say good-bye to him – don't know whether he's in a rage, lazy, or merely sensible. I shall get no news of any sort or kind till my return to England, which will I think be on Wednesday next (16th). Is it possible that you may be back in London again by then? I have a notion that your summer normally ends rather soon. I hope you're enjoying your castle, and that by now you're quite strong again – but I fear this damned weather must have been a sad drawback for you. The Greek voyage came to nothing, owing to various crises, a sad blow for Carrington; but really I was glad, as it seemed to me such a hopelessly wild-cat expedition. P appeared for a moment at Ham Spray – en route for somewhere – and very charming, of course. Wogan and Rosamund also stayed for a night – their stock rather sank – W after having been 14 for so long, is now eight, and Ros is not a very competent governess. We saw a good deal of the little Guinnesses in their enormous house – an odd ménage – no chairs – no visitors – but also no pretensions. I think seriously of leaving England for the winter, and setting up somewhere (Africa or S. Spain, perhaps) for several months. The torture of this climate is getting past a joke – and I could hardly be idler or more extravagant than I am when oscillating between Ham Spray and London. The Bronzino spent a week-end with me before I left – a failure. But perhaps you hardly remember who the Bronzino is – I'm not sure that I do either. The rain is ghastly, but the merry French dance lavoltas under the statue of good King Stanislas in the square. I see them doing so at this moment. I think I must take my umbrella and join them, thus putting a stop to this extremely décousu *[disjointed]* letter, which otherwise might go on until the rain stops – i.e., 100 years. I shall spend the evening in a café, listening to a trio playing selections from Gounod – a dreamy occupation! My best love,

Lytton

1. Michael Holroyd, *Lytton Strachey by Himself*, p. 164.
2. ibid., p. 168.
3. ibid., p. 178.

‡

To Carrington

The MacCarthy house was in Wellington Square, off the King's Road in Chelsea.

Number 41 Gordon Square belonged to James and Alix, who let the L-shaped flat on the first floor to Frances and Ralph. They were all Labour supporters. The general election had been held the day before (the last to take place on a day other than Thursday), and the party was being held to hear the announcement of the results. The dispute over spending and wage cuts as a solution to the world-wide economic depression had split the Labour government fatally. The political deadlock that resulted caused investors to panic, and a flight of capital and gold further destabilized the economy. In response Ramsay MacDonald, urged by the King, decided to form a National Government with the Conservatives and the Liberals.

On 24 August MacDonald submitted the resignation of his ministers and led his senior colleagues in forming the National Government with the other parties. As a result MacDonald and his supporters were expelled from the Labour Party and adopted the name 'National Labour'. The remaining Labour Party, and some Liberals, led by Lloyd George, went into opposition and denounced MacDonald as a 'traitor' and a 'rat' for what they saw as his betrayal.

Soon after this, the General Election was called, resulting in a Conservative landslide victory, with the now leaderless Labour Party winning only forty-six seats in Parliament. Although MacDonald continued as Prime Minister until 1935, after the 1931 election the national government was Conservative-dominated.

Maud Cunard changed her name to Emerald in 1926. Phyllis de Janzé was an old friend of Carrington from Slade days.

The 'window picture' is a trompe-l'oeil window, in which a cook in eighteenth-century costume peels an apple, while a cat on the kitchen table stares at a caged canary. It was intended as a surprise for Diana Guinness when she returned to Biddesden, near Andover, from London, following the birth of her second son.

51, Gordon Square
W.C.1
Wednesday, October 28th 1931

Très-chère

[. . .] My train was an hour late at Pad*[dington]*! And a horrid throaty fog
infested London. The result was I only just reached Argyll House in
time. Found there the Huxleys, Noel Coward, Desmond, Lady Cunard,
and one or two others. It was rather amusing – consisting chiefly of a
game of badminton between Noel and Maud. Desmond in a light grey
suit and bright green tie was amusing. We walked away together, and
he confessed he was in despair at having to review the Waves. I left him
wringing his hands in Wellington Square.

The worst of it is that the 41 party was quite a good one! I feel sure
you would have enjoyed it – or almost sure – one never really knows.
But there weren't very many horreoddities – and somehow, in a vague
distracted way, everything glided along in a pleasant haze. Oddly
enough I seemed to spend many hours in a tête-à-tête with . . . Mrs
Enfield! – I can't remember much else. Ralph looked very fine in a
velvet coat and dark blue shirt. Eddie was in a bright mustard check
suit. Tony Bruce was a perfect duck. Some handsome dark juives
floated about. The wireless announced the ruin of labour and in the
intervals played dance music on the gramophone. At a quarter to three
I was to be seen seated, in hat and coat, in the kitchen, sipping white
wine from a teacup – oh so vague! By three I was safe in bed. Ralph
said he *might* come – of course didn't – And I didn't mind in the very
least. – However, to put on the other side of the balance, there was the
divine weather you describe at Ham Spray. Not a particle of sun have
I seen since I left.

Today lunch with Maud. Phyllis was there. Sent her love to you –
says she is still in her little house, with only a kitchen-maid – living on
her capital. A slightly worn appearance, I thought – but she was very
charming. The others were the beautiful Mrs Norton, Oswald Balfour,
and . . . the last guest was late. 'Well, we won't wait for Ivor,' said Lady
C*[unard]*, 'I'm not sure whether he's coming.' I thought – good
heavens! Can she really have asked Lord W. to such a very small party?
– too mad! Phyllis I thought looked rather ashy. We sat down. The
door opened – and . . . Ivor Churchill entered. The truth is one's always

amused when that preposterous piece of gallimaufry Maud (or Emerald) is present.

Tonight poker. How shall I survive my social life I don't know. Tomorrow there's tea with Ethel Sands, the evening with the Mooncalf, and Friday, lunch *again* with Sibby, and dinner chez Maugham. Well, so far I enjoy it all!

I hope you've finished the window picture and been happy in the sunlight. Don't worry too much about the servant question. These things settle themselves somehow or other. And there's always Malaga if the worst comes to the worst!

Very best love,
Lytton

Maud couldn't bear Aldous – 'I hate the sight of him. He looks like a wilted asparagus.' All too true! But I tried in vain to make her believe that looks aren't everything.

‡

To Carrington

Lytton, now feeling ill and exhausted, went to stay the weekend in Brighton with Roger. Though he was still making plans, his undiagnosed cancer was in fact in its final stages. This is the last letter Lytton wrote to Carrington.

Bedford Hotel
Brighton
Saturday morning, November 14th 1931

Très chère

I arrived last night before dinner, and already feel much better. It seems quite a comfortable place – on the old-fashioned side. R arrives at two. The party has been abolished – and a small supper had been substituted. I've asked Geoffrey Toome for Sunday – but don't know whether he can come. Shall we ask Billy too? I saw Eddie, who said he was going down to H[am] S[pray]. I hope you'll have an amusing week-end. Shall I see you on Wednesday? I'm writing to Old Queen Cole to refuse Wednesday week.

Peter Lucas appeared at lunch at the Ivy.

The sun shines, the wind blows – and I suppose it's my duty to join the plodding constitutionalists on the front. So farewell.

> All my love
> Lytton

‡

To Ralph Partridge

> Ham Spray House
> near Marlborough
> Wilts.
> December 2nd 1931

My dearest

I was so glad to get your letter this morning, with all its reassuring information. I am now longing to be off! If the road is good from Gib. to Malaga I think it might be well worth while taking the car. La Caleta sounds a positive paradise – but I suppose there must be a serpent in it – Mr Young?

My health seems to be on the mend. The morning adventure was distinctly less pénible – so I hope for the best.

The sun shines through the fog quite brightly, but a violent gale has sprung up from the South.

> All my love,
> Lytton
> Morris's Havana Cigarettes
> If I don't have them, what regrets!

‡

To Roger Senhouse

This appears to be the last letter Lytton wrote. The undiagnosed cancerous tumour grew; the post-mortem showed that it had completely blocked the intestine and perforated the colon. He died on 21 January 1932, having said the

day before, 'Darling Carrington. I love her. I always wanted to marry
Carrington, and I never did,' and later, 'If this is dying, then I don't think
much of it.' Carrington made her first suicide attempt on 20 January. Then,
on 11 March, having decided she could not live without Lytton, she shot herself.

Ham Spray House
near Marlborough
Wilts.
December 4th 1931

Dearest Creature

[. . .] I'm sorry to say I'm still sadly pulverised – have been for some
days in bed – now creep about, but in an enfeebled semi-miserable
condition. I cannot feel that I'm really on the mend yet. A sudden
reversion to a state of affairs that I thought had gone for ever about
15 years ago! I don't feel strong enough yet to go to London to see my
medical woman. Perhaps I shall be able to induce her to come here.

This is a gloomy recital, I fear! – In a way particularly annoying
because there doesn't seem to be anything serious the matter. Only an
eternal lack of equilibrium inside. Hélas!

Luckily there are a lot of books to read.

I've been planning a hegira to S. Spain – but can a deflated frog stand
the journey?

It would certainly be pleasant to have a few stories when you write
next.

all my love
Lytton

Index

GLS = Giles Lytton Strachey

Hamnett, Nina (Mrs Edgar de Bergen, 1890–1956), 598
  Roger Fry portrait, 359, 360
Harcourt, Lewis Vernon, 'Lulu' (1863–1922), 302
  death by misadventure, 509
Harcourt, Sir William George Granville Venables Vernon (Apostle), 509
Hardie, (James) Keir (1856–1915), and Independent Labour Party 265
Hardman, Freddie (d. 1914), killed in war, 241–2
Hardy, Godfrey Harold (1877–1947)
  and Apostles, 30, 214
  and Russell Gaye suicide, 180–81
Hardy, Thomas (1840–1928), 172
Harington, Sir John (1560–1612), 529
Harold (not identified), 261, 284
Harper's Weekly, and idea for biographies, 364
Harris, Bogey, 606–7
Harris, Frank (1856–1931)
  Enid Bagnold and, 374
  Life of Oscar Wilde, 475
Harrison, Jane Ellen (1850–1928), 35, 37, 199
Hatchard's, GLS and, 427, 428
Hawtrey, Mrs Ralph (Titi [Hortense Emilia Sophie] d'Aranyi), 397, 398
Hawtrey, Sir Ralph George (1879–1975)
  and Apostles, 18
  and irrelevance, 50
  at G.M. Trevelyan's wedding, 23
  on secondary qualities, 88–9
Haxton, Gerald (1892–1944), and W. Somerset Maugham, 565
Heard, Gerald (1889–1971), 614
Heinemann, William (1863–1920), 412, 413, 414
Hellman, Lillian (1905–84), and George Bergen, 639
Henderson, Lady (née Faith Marion Jane Bagenal, b. 1889), 254, 255

and house share, 325
and 'John beauty chorus', 346, 347
Henderson, Sir Hubert Douglas (1890–1952), 254
Henderson, Sir Nicholas, 'Nicko' (b. 1919), 254
Herbert, Aubrey Nigel Henry Molyneux (1880–1923), 444, 445
Hereford, GLS in, 519
Hexham, GLS at, 552–4, 554–5
Hiles, Barbara, *see* Bagenal, Barbara
Hobhouse, Sir Arthur Lee, 'Hobby' (1886–1965)
  and Apostles, 40, 43, 48, 51, 186
  and Science Tripos, 126, 129–30
  as 'Edgar Duckworth', 34–5, 36
  GLS and, 42–3, 56–7
  J.M. Keynes and, 74–5, 116
Hobhouse, Henry (1854–1937, Hobby's father) 34
Hobhouse, Margaret Heyworth (née Potter, d. 1921, Hobby's mother) 34
  finds compromising letters, 137
Hobson, John Atkinson (economist, 1858–1924), 260–61
Hodge, John (1855–1937), and Defence of the Realm Act, 346
Hodgkin, Eliot (1905–87), 633
  row with Guy Chapman, 636
Hogarth Press, *Two Stories*, 357, 358
Holland, Bernard Henry (d. 1926, Apostle), 33
Holman Hunt, Gladys, *see* Pollock, Jack
Homere sisters, 9–10
Horner, Lady (née Frances Jane Graham, 1854/5–1940), 606
Horner, Sir John Francis Fortescue (1842–1927), 606
Hotel de l'Europe, Amsterdam, 1929, 601–4
Hôtel du Dauphin, Vannes, 1924, 535–8
Hotel Hassler, Rome, 1930, 617–18
Hotel Phoenix, Copenhagen, 1928, 584